ROBERT HOLMES
A LIFE IN WORDS

ROBERT HOLMES

A LIFE IN WORDS

Richard Molesworth

First published in the UK in 2013 by
Telos Publishing Ltd
www.telos.co.uk

Telos Publishing Ltd values feedback. Please e-mail us with any comments you may have about this book to: feedback@telos.co.uk

ISBN: 978-1-84583-091-5 (paperback)

Internal design, typesetting and layout by Arnold T Blumberg
www.atbpublishing.com

Printed in the UK by Berforts Group Ltd

British Library Cataloguing in Publication Data.
A catalogue record for this book is available from the British Library.

'The Doctor switched the machine off and sank back into the control chair with his mind racing. Although he would instantly recognise the Brigadier or Leela or any of his past companions, he had scarcely any recollection of how he himself had appeared in past forms. Nonetheless, he thought, it was all Lombard Street to a China orange that the chap in the tailcoat was himself. In which case, not only had his sartorial taste improved, but at last it was all beginning to make sense.'[1]

With thanks to:
Bob Baker, J Jeremy Bentham, Richard Bignell, Chris Boucher, Colin Brockhurst, Steve Broster, Sue Cowley, Russell T Davies, Terrance Dicks, Robert Fairclough, Philip Hinchcliffe, William Hood, Barry Letts, Simon M Lydiard, Andrew Martin, Richard Marson, Russell Parker, Andrew Pixley, Anthony Read, James Richards, Laurian Richards, Steve Roberts, Gary Russell, Eric Saward, Matthew K Sharp, Cliff Shelton, Tom Spilsbury and *Doctor Who Magazine*, Robert Banks Stewart, Jon Thurley, Paul Vanezis, Oliver Wake, Ian Watson, Ian Williams, the BBC Written Archive Centre at Caversham, and the fishpeople of Atlantis.

And, of course, the biggest thanks of all go to Robert Holmes.

---

1 Excerpt from 'Doctor Who – The Two Doctors' by Robert Holmes (Target Books, 1985). Chapter Five, 'Creature of the Darkness', p66-67

CONTENTS

Foreword by Robert Banks Stewart.. 8

Introduction 10

Chapter One: Army, Police, Magazines: 1926-1959...................................... 16

Chapter Two: A Knight's Work: 1959-1964 24

Interlude I: *Family Solicitor*: 'Man of Straw': 1961 35

Chapter Three: A Case to Play With: 1964... 39

Interlude II: *The Wednesday Play*: 'Plunkett-Bream
    Was Six Foot Four': June 1964 46

Chapter Four: From One Doctor, To Another: 1965....................................... 51

Chapter Five: Hiding in Public: 1965-1968 60

Interlude III: *Public Eye*: 'You've Only Got To Sneeze': 1968 83

Chapter Six: A Doctor Calls: 1968-1969 90

Interlude IV: *Doctor Who*: 'The Trap': June 1968 101

Chapter Seven: Fraudulent Honey: 1968-1969.. 104

Chapter Eight: New Faces: 1969-1970 111

Interlude V: *Doctor Who*: 'Facsimile': March 1969 119

Chapter Nine: Plastic Fantastic!: 1970-1971 137

Interlude VI: *Doctor Who*: 'Spray of Death': June 1970 143

Chapter Ten: Making a Name with Aunty: 1970-1972 157

Chapter Eleven: Dish Rags: 1971-1972.. 173

Interlude VII: *Doctor Who*: 'Out of the Labyrinth': June 1971 180

Chapter Twelve: Field Marshall Hol Mes: 1973 196

Interlude VIII: *Doctor Who*: 'The Time Fugitive': March 1973 203

Chapter Thirteen: Traps and Hospitals: 1973-1974 213

Chapter Fourteen: Editing Scripts, and other Pastimes: 1973-1974 218

Chapter Fifteen: Baker's Dozen: 1974 224

Chapter Sixteen: Pyramid Power: 1974 242

Chapter Seventeen: When the Going gets Tough: 1975 250

Chapter Eighteen: Assassins on Every Corner: 1976 269

Chapter Nineteen: Bloody Aliens!: 1975-1977 297

Interlude IX: *Aliens in the Mind*: 'The Web' and 'Counter Attack': 1976..... 307

Chapter Twenty: Killing Time: 1977 316

Chapter Twenty-One: Papers, Pilots, and Pandemics: 1977-1978 335

Chapter Twenty-Two: Briefly Back on Familiar Ground: 1977-1978 346

Chapter Twenty-Three: Freelance Nightmare: 1979-1985 352

Chapter Twenty-Four: Time, Gentlemen!: 1982 376

Interlude X: *Doctor Who*: 'The Six Doctors': September 1982 386

Chapter Twenty-Five: Caving In ...: 1983-1984 391

Chapter Twenty-Six: The Final Act: 1985-1986 403

Chapter Twenty-Seven: Goodnight Sweet Prince 418

Chapter Twenty-Eight: Target Cutaway 428

Appendix: Robert Holmes: Television Writing Credits................ 433

About the Author 443

FOREWORD

These days one of the most irksome practices of television is to run the end credits of practically all drama series brutally squashed, whilst the other half of the screen promotes new programmes visually and vocally.

If that affront had happened in past years, you might have missed the name of Robert Holmes, an outstandingly talented story editor and successful writer of series and individual plays, who deserves a place of honour in the history of British television.

But first, let me introduce you to a small group of journalists in the mid-'50s, who would have a monthly lunch together at Lyons Corner House in London's Oxford Street. I was a newly-arrived feature writer on the staff of the magazine *Illustrated*, published by Odhams. Another magazine in their stable was *John Bull*, where Robert Holmes was one of their sub-editors. I got to know him, and he invited me to join this lunchtime get-together. Shall I name a few names? Among our colleagues were: a fiction editor, subsequently best-selling novelist, Lionel Davidson, his books often adapted for the small screen; Wilfred Greatorex, Assistant Editor, later creator/producer of ATV's *The Plane Makers*, *The Power Game* and eventually screenwriter of the legendary *Battle of Britain* movie; Robert Holles, who would become a novelist and television playwright; and John Sandilands, distinguished television documentary writer and co-originator of the popular series *Tenko*.

Maybe some of our ambitions rubbed off on each other, but certainly none of us knew then that the lunch 'club' would somehow in the future make a quite hefty contribution, one way and another, to the world of television and film.

None more so than Bob Holmes who, after military service as a young subaltern, began his professional life as a copper on the beat. Knowing of this background, I could easily imagine him as an old-style bobby, helmet, big boots and all. His tall, slightly stooped figure and gait fitted the picture, along with the occasional lugubrious expression.

That, however, belied the fact that he was a most jovial and witty character, reflected of course in his boundless creativity as a writer.

Our careers would overlap for over 30 years. He would write for projects of mine, and *vice versa*, and worked as my script editor on *Shoestring*. But it wasn't just an old pal's act. We always aimed to be among the best 'foot soldiers' as writers on this television series or that, and I gained a lot personally from our colleagueship.

One of his great talents was for structure and a non-linear approach to building a story, as well as his unique ability to come up with hordes of weirdly convincing names for aliens in *Doctor Who*, that would have put J K Rowling – in a different context – in the shade.

I won't dwell on Bob's admired worklist – that's what this book sets out to do, a celebration of the career of an enormously clever and likeable guy, who shocked and dismayed us all by his rather premature death.

Robert Banks Stewart
Creator, producer and writer: *Shoestring, Bergerac*
Creator and writer: *Undermind, Jukes of Piccadilly*
Producer: *Intrigue*
Writer: *Knight Errant Ltd, Danger Man, Ghost Squad, Dr Finlay's Casebook, Public Eye, Fraud Squad, Doctor Who*
Story editor: *Harriet's Back in Town, Armchair Thriller*

INTRODUCTION

Shortly after *Doctor Who* triumphantly returned to BBC1's screens in 2005, lead writer and series showrunner Russell T Davies was interviewed by Richard Johnson for the *Telegraph* newspaper. Instead of spending all of his time discussing the new incarnation of the series, for which he was largely responsible, Davies instead encouraged Johnson to look back to *Doctor Who's* past for examples of television at its very best. 'Take "The Talons of Weng-Chiang", for example,' Davies told Johnson. 'Watch Episode One. It's the best dialogue ever written. It's up there with Dennis Potter. By a man called Robert Holmes. When the history of television drama comes to be written, Robert Holmes won't be remembered at all because he only wrote genre stuff. And that, I reckon, is a real tragedy.'[2]

Davies's replacement as showrunner on the series, Steven Moffat, was recently asked about his favourite *Doctor Who* writers. And who did he single out? 'Robert Holmes wrote all the best ones. Go find a list of favourite *Doctor Who* stories and look for the writer with the most entries! That's our Robert! He took *Doctor Who* down from space and planets, and slipped all that horror and scariness under your bed and at the back of your hall cupboard. Then he went back to space and planets and put real people there, speaking real dialogue. And gags! So many gags and so many scares – proper *Doctor Who*, that is! On a good day, when I'm writing this show, I'm Robert Holmes. The other one hundred percent of the time, I'm just trying to be.'[3]

Gareth Roberts is also a writer that grew up with *Doctor Who* as a child, and now writes scripts for the new incarnation of the television series. 'Robert Holmes was one of the most talented writers of his generation,' noted Roberts back in 2003. 'Better than Dennis Potter. He knocks Alan Bleasdale into a cocked hat. He towers over the Rosenthals and Platers of the TV world.'[4]

It may seem like hyperbole and bluster, but Davies and Moffat and Roberts are all being deadly serious. Robert Holmes is quite possibly the most unregarded and unsung great television scriptwriter of his generation. The plaudits that the likes of Dennis Potter, Tony Garnett and Alan Bleasdale have quite rightly received for their scripts and programmes were never given to Holmes for his work during his life. He was never nominated for a BAFTA, or even pictured at an awards ceremony in a smart tuxedo, standing next to his leading man or woman.

---

2 *Master of the Universe* by Richard Johnson, the *Telegraph*, 11 March 2007.
3 'Ask Steven Moffat', *Doctor Who Magazine*: Issue 458, April 2013.
4 *Doctor Who Magazine* Special: *We Love Doctor Who*, November 2003.

And the reason for this, as Davies notes, is probably down to the type of television programme for which he wrote. Not for Holmes the intense single play or the moody working-class drama series.

Like many of the noted television playwrights of his generation, he forged his craft in the 1960s, working on whatever series and serials that he could sell his scripts to, adapting his writing style to fit the general structure of each series as he went. But unlike most of the big-hitting, feted television dramatists, Holmes was happy to stay in the world of television series and serials, content to adapt his stories around the confines of the characters and situations that others had previously devised.

This was one of Holmes's key strengths as a professional, jobbing writer; his ability to adapt his work to whatever requirements were imposed on him. He could sculpt dialogue and situations for characters that had been forged and scripted by countless other writers before him, and still usually managed to produce something that was head and shoulders above the standard runaround scripts that these series often churned out.

In the early 1970s, Holmes found himself increasingly drawn to the strange and quirky fictional world of television's time-travelling Doctor. Although he first wrote for *Doctor Who* during Patrick Troughton's final year at the helm of the TARDIS, these initial scripts, although always solid and workmanlike, offered no real indication of the passion that Holmes would soon develop for the programme.

During the years that Jon Pertwee spent in the lead role, Holmes would write four stories that not only helped define the third Doctor's era, but would also shape the future of the series forever. In terms of characters, Holmes wrote the scripts that saw the first adventures of the third Doctor, Liz Shaw, Jo Grant, the Master, Mike Yates and Sarah Jane Smith. He set up the template for the third Doctor's Earthbound adventures, re-introducing the character of the Brigadier as a series regular and the organisation of UNIT (devised the previous year by Derrick Sherwin) as the Doctor's temporary home-cum-employers. He created two major new adversaries for the Doctor in the shape of the Autons and the Sontarans; two foes that still pop up to menace the Doctor on screen today. It was Holmes who decided that Time Lords should have two hearts, and named their planet of origin as Gallifrey.

When writing for and script editing the series during Tom Baker's tenure in the TARDIS, he would further decide that Time Lords would be limited to 12 regenerations, giving them a possible maximum total of 13 incarnations. This arbitrary figure was easy enough to impose when the series had only had four Doctors, but this is perhaps now something of a limiting factor when we are up to Doctor number 12!

Basically, just about everything that we think we know about the Doctor today seems to have been bequeathed upon the series by Robert Holmes.

To define Holmes's career just in terms of *Doctor Who* would, of course, be quite palpably unfair. His scripts for series such as *Public Eye*, *Mr Rose*, *No Hiding Place*, *Blake's 7*, *Bergerac*, *Juliet Bravo* and *Jukes of Piccadilly* – to name but a few of those to have benefitted from his involvement – are very often the high-water marks of quality that those particular series have to offer. But his association with *Doctor Who* is so strong, and his resulting stories are quite often so dazzlingly superb, that it's hard not draw the conclusion that Holmes and *Who* were just made to go together.

Quite *what* it is that sets Holmes's scripts above and apart from those of his contemporaries is sometimes quite hard to define, and I've deliberately shied away from over-analysis in this book. But one important facet is that Holmes was undoubtedly one of the best writers of dialogue in the business, as earlier mentioned by Davies, Roberts and Moffat. He is often noted for creating excellent 'double-acts' in his scripts, but this is more of a function of creating a good bit of conversation in order to drive the plot forward, than necessarily developing a creditable pair of characters. That memorable characters are formed isn't up for debate; it's just that one person cannot hold a conversation with just themselves. Holmes's skill was to create characters that could hold our attention just by talking to each other.

Holmes was also extremely talented in the art of forming the 'backstory'. Not for him the clumsy info-dumps of some of his less-skilled contemporaries. Consider his much-feted *Doctor Who* story 'The Talons of Weng-Chiang'. He effortlessly and efficiently paints in the past histories of Magnus Greel and Mr Sin with the barest of lines of dialogue that allude to greater things. We are given just the briefest of glimpses of notions such as Time Agents, the Peking Homunculus, the Butcher of Brisbane, and the battle of Reykjavik, which help to fill in whatever background the audience needs to make the story work.

But despite the sublime and exquisite lengths Holmes went to in order to invest his stories and scripts with energy and vigour, he would, when pressed, vehemently renounce any suggestion that his programmes were worthy of any deep intellectual or artistic praise. He was once asked if he thought his *Doctor Who* scripts should be considered a modern form of art. 'You're joking,' Holmes replied. 'If anyone decides that *Doctor Who* is an art form – writers, producers, directors – its death knell will be sounded. It is good, clean, escapist hokum, which is no small thing to be. When it's done well, it is the best thing of its kind around.'[5]

How you perceive Robert Holmes as a writer perhaps depends on how you first came to know of him and his work. I, being born in the late 1960s, came to know of him initially through *Doctor Who* in the 1970s. As the decade progressed, and as I grew more attentive to the production credits of other television programmes, I noticed that the name Robert Holmes was one that often seemed to crop up; certainly more so than most other *Doctor Who*-related names that I'd also watch out for. By this point of his career, Holmes had carved a niche for himself as a genre writer of some considerable repute. His four scripts for the BBC's other seminal science fiction series, *Blake's 7*, are remarkable not simply for their quality – and they are all excellent – but for their sheer diversity of style; not one story resembles any of the other three in terms of their structure, characters, tone or format. His dramatisation of David Wiltshire's 1978 novel *Child of Vodyanoi*, which the BBC screened under the rather more lurid title *The Nightmare Man*, is one of the most compelling, gripping and frightening dramas of its time.

Perhaps coming so late to the party, as it were, now meant that I was subconsciously pigeonholing Robert Holmes as a one-trick pony, a writer of mere fantasy and whimsy. It was only when his name then cropped up on the credits of programmes such as *Juliet Bravo, Shoestring* and *Bergerac* that I realised that he was capable of more. So very, very much more.

Studying Robert Holmes's earlier 'back catalogue' of scripts and programmes from the 1960s demonstrates at once the fallacy of the notion of him being a science fiction specialist. Here was a master craftsman at work; someone who could sculpt with words whatever was required of him. Any limitations as to his eventual canvas (if I can mix metaphors here) were seemingly of his own choosing.

If I may be allowed, I'd like to get a touch personal at this point. Please, indulge me. After all, this will, in part, detail one of the reasons why I wrote this book.

In 2003, I was commissioned by the BBC to make a DVD documentary about the *Doctor Who* work of Robert Holmes. While I was making the programme, I had hoped to be able to talk to Holmes's widow, Patricia, about her late husband's life and work. I was given Patricia's address, and so I wrote a short letter to her to explain about the project that I was making, and asked her if she would consider appearing in the programme. I heard nothing back for quite a few weeks. Then, out of the blue, I had a phone call from Robert and Patricia's daughter, Laurian. She told me that her mother was seriously ill in hospital, and so wouldn't be in a position to get involved in my project in any way. But Laurian then invited me to visit her – she was then living in the modest thatched cottage that Robert and Patricia had moved into in the late 1970s – to talk about her father. And so a couple of weekends later, I found myself driving down to Robert's old house to meet his daughter. When I got there, Laurian met me at the front door, and told me that Patricia was still desperately ill. And with sad eyes, she added that they were now expecting the worst. Sadly, she was proved correct just a few weeks later.

But in the meantime, Laurian had dug out a few old photos of her father, which she then lent to me for use in the documentary – not many, as she ruefully confessed that they weren't the sort of family to take many photographs. She then showed me into her father's old study, in which a large wooden ottoman in the corner contained all of his old files, scripts and paperwork. Left alone, with a welcome cup of coffee for company, I began to carefully sift through Robert's files. Then I stopped for a moment, and looked around. The room, like the cottage itself, was small and homely. There were no real concessions to modern-day life. No computers, no CDs, no videotapes. Instead, there were books, and reams of paper, and a small typewriter stood on the well-worn desk. The wooden ottoman, once opened, proceeded to fill the room with the musty, heady odour of old pipe smoke. It was not an unpleasant smell at all. All of a sudden I realised that, nearly 20 years after his death, I was suddenly in a little echo of Robert Holmes's life. Sitting at his desk, smelling his tobacco, reading his own manuscripts next to what was probably the very typewriter he'd written most of them on … I think that was the moment when I finally realised how hugely important Robert Holmes's contribution to the sphere of television writing had been, how big a loss to the industry his untimely death was, and yet how little recognition he had ever received for his work.

The life and writing career of Robert Holmes has been one of the television industry's best-kept secrets for far too long. His work is long overdue the wider scrutiny and appreciation it so richly deserves. I hope that this book is but the first step along this path.

If I may, I'd just also at this point like to explain and inform you, my dear readers of this tome, of my *modus operandi* in compiling the text of this book.

As I previously mentioned, in 2003 I made a DVD documentary, *Behind the Sofa*, about the *Doctor Who* work of Robert Holmes, which subsequently appeared on the BBC's DVD release of his *Doctor Who* story 'The Two Doctors'. For this, I interviewed Terrance Dicks, Barry Letts, Philip Hinchcliffe, Chris Boucher and Eric Saward about their recollections of working with Holmes.

Not everything that these friends and colleagues told me at the time made it into my final documentary, and I am indebted to Messrs Dicks, Hinchcliffe, Boucher and Saward for agreeing to let me draw from their full interviews for this book. Alas, Barry Letts sadly passed away in 2009, and so his words from 2003 now stand as single legacy to his heartfelt respect for Holmes.

Later, in 2006, I produced another DVD documentary, *Built for War*, which specifically looked at Robert Holmes's potato-headed creations the Sontarans, and which subsequently appeared on the DVD release of 'The Sontaran Experiment'. For this, I interviewed both Eric Saward and Terrance Dicks again, as well as Bob Baker and Anthony Read. I subsequently interviewed Anthony Read a second time for another documentary I produced, *AfterImage*, which looked at the making of the *Doctor Who* story 'Image of the Fendahl', and which featured on the DVD release of that adventure. The subject of Robert Holmes naturally came up as part of these interviews.

All of the unattributed quotes from these gentlemen in this book come from those three interview sessions, with their kind permission. And in the cases of Bob Baker, Chris Boucher, Terrance Dicks, Philip Hinchcliffe and Eric Saward, these fine gents kindly allowed me to quiz them afresh about their memories of Robert Holmes while I was preparing this book, as did Robert Banks Stewart (who crossed career paths with Holmes many, many times), Jon Thurley (Holmes's agent of many years' standing) and Ian Watson (Holmes's brother-in-law).

All the other interview quotes used in this book are fully attributed to their various sources.[6] These include several published interviews with Robert Holmes himself, many of which come from fanzines that Holmes kept in his own files, having been sent his 'contributor's copy' by the various (no-doubt deeply appreciative) fanzine editors in question. Fanzine editors Simon M Lydiard and Colin Brockhurst both kindly let me have access to letters from their own files for use in this book.

The only exception to this rule is an unpublished interview with Robert Holmes that was conducted by Richard Marson in August 1985. Richard very kindly supplied me with an audio recording of the interview, which I was able to transcribe myself for this book. As the interview was never published, no attribution can be given for these quotes.

Richard Molesworth
April 2013

---

6 ... in footnotes similar to this!

CHAPTER ONE
ARMY, POLICE, MAGAZINES
1926-1959

Robert Colin Holmes was born on Friday 2 April 1926, in Hitchin, in the county of Hertfordshire. To put this date into some sort of context, Queen Elizabeth II was also born that same month, as were the Northern Irish politician Ian Paisley, *Playboy* founder Hugh Hefner, BBC sports commentator David Coleman, and the novelists Harper Lee and Anne McCaffrey. In Britain in 1926, King George V sat on the throne, and Stanley Baldwin occupied 10 Downing Street.

1926 was an odd period in British history, sandwiched as it was midway between the two World Wars, and many years later, when Bob's writing career was in full swing, he would often state a degree of affinity for this inter-war period, along with the three or four decades that preceded it. It was almost as though he was looking back, in some envious way, to the years prior to his birth, perhaps yearning for an idyll that his parents or their peers may once have enjoyed. And perhaps for Bob, growing up in a decade of post-war austerity, only to then plunge headlong into World War II and its associated horrors in his late teens, it was not difficult to yearn for something better.

Ah, yes – Bob! Throughout my researches and investigations into Robert Holmes's life and career, one thing has been abundantly clear. Although the Christian name on his birth certificate was Robert, to his family, friends and colleagues he was known simply as Bob. Every reminiscence that has been reported to me by colleagues, every conversation that has been recalled by friends, have all been prefixed with the words, 'Bob said …', or 'Bob told me …' This, seemingly, was the informal form of address that Mr Robert Holmes preferred, so to call him by any other name on the principle of formality seems rather churlish. So for the remainder of this book, if I may be so bold, I'll be addressing him as Bob as well.

Not much is known about Bob's youth. His father, Colin, was a school headmaster, and he surely must have been a strong influence on Bob's early life and academic career. Bob also had a brother, Clive, who tried to get out of his National Service by pretending to be slightly unbalanced, building a full-size mock-rocket out of silver foil on his parade ground (ostensibly in order to help him fly away from the army!)

It is said that Bob began writing at an early age, and that by the time he was 11, he was already submitting short stories on spec to the editors of his favourite comics and magazines, but with little or no success. The large number of rejection letters he received did not deter him, however, and he kept submitting his ideas.

'English was one of the few subjects that I actually liked or was any good at during my schooldays,' Bob once recalled. 'At the age of 13 I decided to try to turn this to account by trying to become a writer. But it was a good ten years – with a bit of World War II intervening – before I had anything published.'[7] Beyond this small insight, Bob's early life and education are veiled in the mists of time.

What we do know is that he signed-up to join the British Army while still in his mid-teens, and while World War II was still in full swing. His future friend and colleague, Terrance Dicks, recalls how Bob once recounted to him the story of his sign-up. 'Bob was quite a character,' says Dicks. 'I only learned these things a bit later on, but he'd been the youngest commissioned officer in World War II. He'd joined the army early, and lied about his age. He told me they caught him out at the Commission Board, but he said, "Some old General on the Board said, 'Well done, my boy – did the same thing myself in 1914!'" So they sort-of passed him through!'

When war was declared in September 1939, Bob would have been 13½ years old. The British government had brought in a conscription law in April of that year, but at that point it was only for men aged between 18 and 41. Bob, therefore, wouldn't have been due to be called-up until April 1944. His family recalls that Bob actually managed to get himself signed-up to serve in the Army when he was only 16½, which would have been some time in late 1942. It was by no means unusual for boys under the age of 18 to apply to, and be accepted for, the armed forces; a blind eye was usually turned, so long as the Army was satisfied that the individual involved knew full well what he was signing up for. Bob's enrolment at the age of 16½ was pushing things a little, but it would seem that his claim to have been the youngest officer of his time does have some degree of merit.

Bob's army career began with him serving in the Black Watch, 3rd Battalion of Scotland (known as '3 SCOTS'), which saw him stationed in such exotic places as Burma and India at various times during and after World War II, leading to him developing something of a passion for the culture and cuisine of the Far East.[8] One of Bob's prized possessions at this time was a bulky, finely-sculptured statue of some minor Chinese deity, which he had 'acquired' during his travels, and which then accompanied him through thick and thin during a lengthy period of service overseas. He also 'acquired' two samurai swords, which he also brought home to England. Bob left the Black Watch after three

7 Robert Holmes Interview, *Renegade*: Issue 1, 1984 – Interview by Matthew Wicks.
8 Bob's lifelong friend, Robert Banks Stewart recalled: 'I remember Bob telling me how he served in the Black Watch, which was one of the famous Scottish regiments. I remember he told me once that he used to laugh whenever he had to wear a kilt. Can you imagine Bob in a kilt!'

years' service, joining the Queens' Own Cameron Highlanders regiment.

At the end of the War, Bob stayed with the Army for a short period of time, presumably because he had no other career to consider, like many of his other post-war contemporaries. Then, after leaving the Army, he opted to continue with another career in uniform. He joined the London Metropolitan Police on Tuesday 3 August 1948, at the age of 22, where he was designated Constable 9090. After training at Hendon Police College, Bob was stationed at the historic Bow Street police station; this was the first police station to have been opened in the country in 1829. At the time, one of Bob's best friends in the force was a fellow police officer by the name of Ken Newman. Newman would stay in the police force for the rest of his career, and was knighted for his service. Sir Kenneth Newman, GBE, QPM, was Chief Constable of the Royal Ulster Constabulary between 1976 and 1980, and eventually became the Commissioner of the Metropolitan Police between 1982 and 1987.

One day, while on duty, Bob pulled over a young lady driver for a minor motoring offence. Her name was Patricia Watson. 'My sister Patricia drove for the Ministry of Supplies, and she used to drive these VIPs around London,' recalled Bob's brother-in-law Ian Watson. 'She wore this rather fetching bottle-green uniform, with matching cap. She had just dropped off one of these VIPs in London, and Bob – being a policeman – pulled her up for a minor traffic offence, which he then let her off. Looking at my sister in uniform – wow! You would have let her off too!' When Bob learned that the surname of the young woman he'd stopped was Watson, he smiled at her, and said, 'Hello Watson, I'm Holmes.' This ice-breaker worked a treat, and Bob and Patricia began dating, despite her being six years older than him. They soon realised that this was no brief fling, and they got engaged. Bob and Patricia were married in 1950 in Hammersmith, London. Two years later, Patricia gave birth to their son, Nicholas. A few years after that, in August 1954, they had a daughter, Laurian.

Looking back from a modern perspective, it's easy to imagine that Bob must have drawn on his time and experience working in the police force to inform his later writing career. But although Bob occasionally contributed scripts to crime drama series such as *Public Eye*, *No Hiding Place*, *Fraud Squad* and odd episodes of *Dixon of Dock Green* and *Juliet Bravo*, it was not a genre that he particularly sought out as a writer. The degree to which his own experiences as a beat copper were later recycled into his own scripts is therefore difficult to ascertain, or even to speculate on. However, in later years, Bob was a generous sounding board to other writers who were also gainfully employed in the writing of police dramas.

Bob Baker, who along with his writing partner Dave Martin would encounter Bob Holmes during their time writing for *Doctor Who* in the early 1970s, recalls using Bob as a handy resource at this time. Baker and Martin were commissioned to write two episodes of the long-running BBC police drama *Z Cars* in 1974[9], and went to Bob looking for his insights of what life was really like on the beat. 'I remember Dave and I went out with him once,' recalls Baker. 'We were "off duty" from *Doctor Who* and were about to do an episode of *Z Cars*. Being an ex-policeman, Bob told us so much about what it was like to once be a policeman. We put a lot of it into our *Z Cars* scripts. I think what we were tempted to do was not make our episodes too cop-y; not just plot-plot-plot-plot. We said to him we wanted to get off the plot a little, you know? And Bob understood immediately, and talked to us about things like "boot money", for instance. As a policeman, you would get so much allowance for your boots each week, which you were supposed to use to save up for a new pair of boots every so often. And Bob also told us a story about a policeman he knew who'd discovered a dead body. I forget how he opened the conversation, but he said that somebody he knew found this body, and all the fleas that were in the dead man's clothes got on him, and so this policeman had to strip off his uniform and burn it using copies of the *Police Gazette* … He had to burn his own clothes – incredible! It was all so fascinating, and it was such important detail. I was really thankful to him for giving us that sort of information.'

However, Bob soon realised that the life of a serving police officer was not really for him. 'I don't think the police were right for Bob,' recalls Ian Watson. 'I think he was far too intelligent to be a police constable on the beat.' Another factor may have been that the shifts he was required to work didn't sit too well alongside his new relationship with Patricia. Whatever the reasons were, Bob stayed in the Met for only a little over a year, eventually resigning on Sunday 21 August 1949. He was duly issued with a discharge form from the Assistant Commissioner of the Met, Arthur Young, which certified that Bob's conduct as a policeman was 'Good'. That was it – just one word! It's hard not to think that a year's service pounding the beat should have warranted more of an insightful review from his bosses than that, but Bob left the police safe in the knowledge that he'd been a 'Good' copper! Bob's discharge form also goes on to state that, at the time, Bob was 23, was six feet tall, was of medium build, with a dark complexion, brown hair, brown eyes, a straight nose and an oval face. One final box on the form was given over to list any 'Peculiarities'.

Disappointingly, perhaps, it notes that Bob had 'Nil'.

The most telling fact amongst all the above was Bob's recorded height.

---

9 Baker and Martin wrote the *Z Cars* episodes 'Quiet as the Grave', screened on BBC1 on 4 November 1974, and 'House to House', screened on 16 December 1974. Both these episodes still survive at the BBC.

Anyone who ever met Bob during his life would instantly notice one thing about him – how tall he was. Noted as being exactly six feet tall on his Police discharge form, Bob towered over most of his contemporaries. He had been blessed with quite a thin, angular face; the most defining feature of which was his striking Bruce Forsyth-esque chin. 'Physically, he was sort of tall, and bony, and rather severe-looking,' recalls Terrance Dicks. 'He was gaunt, with a long, rather-melancholy face. He was rather intimidating, Bob, he used to frighten people quite a bit. But he didn't frighten me, we got on very well! And he was quite abrasive, you know, he would say something challenging or tough, and what he'd want you to do was bounce back at him and say something equally aggressive. He would push a bit, to try and test you out, to see how far he could go.'

Bob had also picked up a passion for smoking a pipe from an early age. Photos and what little film footage exists of him usually have him either puffing at or clutching a pipe. And these usually weren't small, discrete smoking implements, but big, chunky, ornate, menacing pipes, of the type Sherlock Holmes would have been proud to be seen smoking while considering his latest piece of detective work.

So in late 1949, Bob left the world of regular, salaried employment with the Police and decided to follow his earlier passion for writing. In 1950 he initially found work as a freelance writer on small newspapers in the Home Counties, working mainly as either a sports writer or a court reporter – his time with the Police giving him a little insight into the workings of the legal system. Bob and Patricia then moved to Walsall in the West Midlands, where he worked for a couple of years as a staff reporter on a local newspaper. At the time, they lodged in house with a rather puritanical landlady. 'The house they went to was haunted!' recalls Ian Watson, with a cheeky grin. 'The landlady they had rooms with, she was not amused to find that they both used the bath together! Being a young, married couple, they thought it was really funny, but apparently the landlady was a bit straight-laced. They couldn't have been married very long at that point.' Eventually, Bob and Patricia returned to the Home Counties once again, where Bob went to work for the press agency PQ, who were based in Fleet Street in London. He also began submitting short stories to the various magazines that flourished in Britain in the post-war years, and found early success working on one called *John Bull*.

John Bull himself was a fictitious caricature of an English gentleman who had first appeared in the tabloids in the 18th Century. He was usually depicted in cartoons and art as a tubby, Union Jack-waistcoat-wearing elderly gent in breeches, with a top hat perched at a jaunty angle atop his greying hair. He was a figure synonymous with stories and ideas that evoked patriotism, and *John*

Bull magazine strongly embodied this patriotic theme.

By the mid-1950s, Bob had begun working as a sub-editor on *John Bull*, which was published by Odhams, one of the largest publishing firms of its day, which at the time had a large portfolio of newsstand titles. Working in the office next door on *Illustrated* magazine was writer Robert Banks Stewart[10], who quickly became good friends with Bob. 'The offices were in High Holborn,' recalls Stewart. 'It was the magazine headquarters of Odhams, the publishers. They published a lot of magazines, including *Woman*, *John Bull* and *Illustrated*. At the time, *John Bull* had many well-known writers such as Lionel Davidson, who wrote *A Long Way to Shiloh*[11], Robert Holles who did that movie with Richard Attenborough[12], and Wilfred Greatorex, who wrote *The Plane Makers*[13]. They were all there at *John Bull* when I arrived to work on *Illustrated* in 1956. We all used to meet up and go to the Lyons Corner House, and various pubs, and we all used to have these great conversations …

'*John Bull* was an odd kind of magazine,' continues Stewart. 'Articles were pieces of fiction, or exclusive chapters from an upcoming book, or were profiles of a well-known public figure. Bob Holmes, he would be editing, cleaning up each article as it came in, checking on the facts, trying to cut out any unnecessary verbiage, editing fiction that was too long and getting it ready to go into the magazine. So he would be sub-editing the magazine.

'Now, to give you some idea of Bob, and his general personality around about the time that I first met him, and leaving aside his natural wit, he had the gait and the facial gravitas associated with an old-style copper. He was from the days when coppers had helmets; he would have had a helmet, not a cap. He'd be a copper of the old style, almost out of an Ealing/early British film. I wouldn't have thought he was ever *Dixon of Dock Green*! When I knew that he'd been a cop, you know, I thought he just looked perfect for the role. As a person, he was tall and slightly bowed, and he had this odd gait, you know. And here he was, an absolutely brilliant story editor and writer'.

Bob spent the next couple of years working on *John Bull*, eventually becoming its editor for its final issues. As well as working on the editorial side, he also

---

10 Robert Banks Stewart wrote his first television scripts under the name Robert Stewart. He was persuaded to add his middle name to his credits by his agent, Beryl Vertue, in the mid-1960s, in order to make his on-screen credit that bit more noticeable. For the sake of consistency, I'll be referring to him by his more established full name throughout the book.

11 Lionel Davidson (1922-2009) had a long career as a spy novelist. *A Long Way to Shiloh* was published in 1966, and tells the story of a hunt for a long-lost holy relic by opposing secret services.

12 The film *Guns at Batsi*, starring Richard Attenborough, was based on Robert Holles's book *The Siege of Battersea*. Holles is also credited as the writer of the film.

13 *The Plane Makers* (1963-65) was an ATV series that revolved around a fictitious aircraft manufacturer. The MD of the company, John Wilder, was played by Patrick Wymark, and the character would go on to appear in the spin-off series *The Power Game* (1965-69). Wilfred Greatorex (1922-2002) would also write for *Danger Man*, *Oil Strike North* and *Airline*, and created the cult telefantasy series *1990*.

occasionally contributed stories for the magazine. He wrote 'Champagne for Miss Walsh' in the edition dated 13 October 1956, 'That Special Magic' in the edition dated 8 December 1956, and 'Tansy's Bluebells' in the edition dated 13 April 1957.[14]

Bob also contributed short stories to other magazines during this time, most notably *London Mystery Magazine*. This title had originally been published by Hulton Press, but had closed after 15 issues in 1952. The magazine was then purchased by the enterprising South African publisher Major Norman Kark, who had moved to England in the 1930s, and operated (with the permission of the Abbey National Bank, who actually owned the premises) from 221b Baker Street, the address of the fictitious detective Sherlock Holmes. Under Major Kark, *London Mystery Magazine* flourished, and provided writers such as the brothers Peter and Anthony Shaffer[15] and Philip Youngman Carter[16] a platform for their short stories, revolving around murder mysteries, the occult and the supernatural.

Bob wrote two short stories – 'The Massingham Experiment' and 'The Girl in Soho' – which were both published in issue 43 of *London Mystery Magazine* (December 1959). The former revolved around a group of scientists experimenting with synthesized insect hormones in a quest for a new type of insecticide. The final experiment ends with the mass spawning of thousands of giant, carnivorous flies, which then devour the head scientist, Massingham, as he sleeps. The latter story was something of a *police noir* bit of detective fiction, about a rookie policeman on the trail of a gang flooding London with fake banknotes. He tracks the gang down to a seedy private club in Soho, where he is helped by a pretty Welsh singer he meets there. This story was published under the pseudonym William Hood (of which, more later …), and earned Bob the princely sum of 10 guineas (21 shillings in old money, equivalent to £10.05 in decimalised currency). Bob was something of a science fiction buff, even in these early days of his career, and the chance to write short stories that had strong science fiction overtones obviously appealed to him greatly. It's telling that he was happy for his name to be associated with the story that bore these hallmarks, while he left the romantic fiction to his *nom-de-plume*.

Bob was once asked in the 1970s about his earlier magazine writing career. He estimated that, over the years, he had written '… about a hundred short stories and serials for magazines'.[17]

---

14 One – presumably unused – short story of Bob's, which he kept on file, tells the story of two warring neighbours, William Litefoot and Harold Cobbing, whose estates are separated by a large hedge, which is the initial source of contention between the two of them. As the neighbours' dispute gets more ugly, they descend to hurling dog poo at each other, and Bob lovingly describes each slung turd with a kind of fetishistic glee.

15 Peter Shaffer went on to write plays such as *Equus, Amadeus* and *The Private Ear and the Public Eye*. Anthony Shaffer went on to script the movies *The Wicker Man, Sleuth, Death on the Nile* and *Murder on the Orient Express*.

16 The husband of noted crime writer Margery Allingham, creator of the detective Albert Campion.

17 Robert Holmes Interview, *Type 40*: Issue 1, 1978.

The success of magazines such as *Illustrated*, *Picture Post*, *John Bull* and *London Mystery Magazine*, which had dominated the fields of creative writing, journalism, and news in the 1940s and early 1950s, was soon to be challenged by the rise of the new medium of television. As news and current affairs began to be covered in depth by television, with a degree of immediacy that totally undercut the magazine market, the circulation of many of the big-name weekly and monthly magazines began to decline. 'Lots of people whom I worked with on *Illustrated* moved into television to become documentary makers,' recalls Robert Banks Stewart. 'It could well be that the people that Robert Holmes worked with on *John Bull* moved from writing magazine fiction to writing television scripts – Bob was a very clever writer.'

Bob started looking to television for his work. At around this time, he became a client of Robin Lowe, one of the agents working at Christopher Mann Ltd, with offices at 140 Park Lane, London. Lowe would represent Bob for the next few years, guiding him though his early television career. The firm of Christopher Mann Ltd also represented Robert Banks Stewart at this time. 'Christopher Mann Ltd were the leading agents in London,' Stewart later recalled, 'and Robin Lowe was one of the agents at Christopher Mann Ltd, I remember. At that time I was a something of a name, because I'd written a couple of films, and Christopher Mann himself was my agent.'

For Bob, the writing was on the wall as far as contributing to magazines was concerned when *John Bull* declined to print a 4,000 word story he had penned for them in late 1959, entitled 'The Christmas Party'. He decided it was time to move full-time into television scriptwriting. The typed-up but unpublished short story was returned from *John Bull* to him via Robin Lowe in January 1960.

Later in 1960, Bob met up with television writer and producer Peter Wildeblood. Wildeblood was an ex-Fleet Street journalist who in 1953 had caused something of a stir when he was involved in a homosexual 'entanglement' that also included two RAF airmen and Lord Montagu of Beaulieu. This was at a time when homosexuality was still illegal in Britain, and Wildeblood, along with Montagu, was sent to prison for that 'crime'. Upon his release 12 months later, Wildeblood began working in the television industry, and it seems that Bob may have had ideas about collaborating with Wildeblood on a particular project. Nothing appears to have come of that early meeting, however.[18]

---

18 It's often been reported that Bob's first work in the television industry was on the medical soap drama *Emergency Ward 10* for ATV (Associated Television), which had the franchise for the ITV region in the Midlands, and also London at the weekends. This was the first-ever British soap opera, and had begun airing twice-weekly in 1957. Various sources credit Bob with writing as many as four episodes in the years between 1958 and 1960, although this has not been verified. When preparing Bob's resume in 1960, his agent at Christopher Mann Ltd made no mention of *Emergency Ward 10*, which would suggest that these claims hold no substance.

CHAPTER TWO
A KNIGHT'S WORK
1959-1964

Robert Holmes's first big break in the world of television came in late 1959, when he got a job as story editor on the television series *Knight Errant* for Granada Television, alongside producer Warren Jenkins.

The premise of the series was that the titular hero, Adam Knight (played by John Turner), was a sort of private eye-cum-hero for hire. Knight advertised his services in newspapers as follows: 'Knight Errant. Quests undertaken, dragons defeated, damsels rescued. Anything, anywhere, for anyone, so long as it helps. Fees according to means.'

Knight was aided and abetted in his weekly adventures by ex-journalist Liz Parrish (Kay Callard) and a young writer by the name of Peter Parker (Richard Carpenter[19]). John Turner would eventually leave the show at the end of the first series, and a new lead character, Stephen Drummond (played by Hugh David[20]), was brought in for series two. Perhaps because of these cast changes, the programme regularly also changed titles, beginning as *Knight Errant '59* for its 1959/60 series, then becoming *Knight Errant '60* for the remainder of the first series episodes screened in the New Year, and then finally returning as *Knight Errant Ltd* for its 1960/1961 run.

Bob was working as story editor on *Knight Errant* when he first came into contact with future *Doctor Who* producer Barry Letts, who at the time was just establishing himself as a writer. 'Well, funnily enough, Bob Holmes was the story editor of the show I wrote for when I first started to write,' Letts later recalled. 'I was an actor, but the very first script I wrote that appeared on the screen was for *Knight Errant,* and he was the story editor.[21] I didn't have an awful lot to do with him; it was commissioned through the producer, Warren Jenkins. I met Robert, obviously, but curiously enough I think he did end up doing quite substantial re-writes on my episode. Because the script was initially accepted – the producer accepted it – I went off on holiday, to the Lake District, with my father. I didn't leave a number anywhere, because we were travelling around, and when I got back there were loads of messages. "Where have you been? Where have you been? We wanted you to rewrite the opening scenes ..." Because the director had

---

19 Carpenter would go on to create the television series *Catweazle* and *Robin of Sherwood*.
20 Hugh David would also move away from acting, becoming a director who would go on to work on *Doctor Who, Z Cars* and *The Pallisers.*
21 Barry Letts' episode was entitled 'Wines and Spirits', and was broadcast on 20 October 1960, part of *Knight Errant Ltd.*

got hold of the script, and said he didn't think the opening scenes worked. So that was my first contact with Bob, but it was at arm's length, I didn't have much to do with him personally.' Bob ended up rewriting the opening scenes of Barry Letts' first ever television script.

Roger Marshall was another writer working on the series. 'Bob and I first met at Granada in the last couple of months of 1960. Bob was working as a story editor for a producer named Kitty Black on a show called *Knight Errant*. The lady's claim to fame was that she translated Jean Anouilh plays. Television was more amateur in those days! I think that was Bob's first TV job. His background was magazines and short stories. Before that he'd been a cop and a soldier. We always hit it off. I stayed with the programme – it was the first one-hour thing I'd ever done.'[22]

Another writer who worked on *Knight Errant* at this time was Robert Banks Stewart, although he doesn't recall having anything directly to do with Bob on the series. Like Barry Letts', his script was commissioned by someone else.

As well as script editing, Bob wrote four episodes of *Knight Errant*, all of which were screened in 1960. The first of these was 'The Creditor', shown on ATV on Tuesday 16 February 1960[23]. The *TV Times* described the episode thusly: 'One of Adam's friends is driven by bankruptcy to the verge of suicide. A creditor suggests a way out of his difficulty, but Adam suspects the man's motives, fears that murder is afoot, and decides to investigate.' The second was 'The Wall of Death', shown Tuesday 26 April 1960, of which the *TV Times* blurb stated: 'Liz Parrish is sent by her newspaper to report the crash of an aeroplane in which the pilot is missing, presumed dead. But when an Irish sovereign medallion with a broken clasp comes to light it sends the Knight Errant team into action.' The next of Bob's episodes was 'Brother Cain', shown on Tuesday 10 May 1960: 'The Knight Errant team go to Majorca to search for an American whom they suspect of trying to obtain money by false pretences from a wealthy young widow. But Peter's hopes for a lazy holiday in the sun are dashed when events take a more sinister turn.' The final episode written by Bob was 'The King of Kandoga', shown on Friday 1 July 1960[24], the script for which was the only one Bob kept from the whole series.

---

22 Private correspondence with Colin Brockhurst, dated 23 June 1992. The article about Robert Holmes that Brockhurst wrote as a result of his various correspondences with figures from Bob's life was published in Issue 1 of *Circus*.

23 All ITV transmission dates quoted in this book are for the Midlands region. Some programmes weren't networked, and others may have aired on different dates in other regions.

24 *Knight Errant* was transmitted live, and none of the episodes that Bob wrote for it survives in the Granada archives. In fact, of the whole series, only one complete episode, 'The Golden Opportunity', still survives, along with some incomplete sequences of another, 'The Joker'.

'The King of Kandoga'[25] finds Adam Knight learning that an old school friend of his, 'Corky' Nerin – who happens to have since become King of a small country called Kandoga – has returned to England for a minor operation at a private hospital in London. Nerin has previously seen off a coup for his throne, spearheaded by his cousin, Mohan, who is now living in exile in Tunbridge Wells. During the course of the episode, Knight discovers that the patient surrounded by high security and police protection at the hospital is a decoy, while the real King has been booked in under a pseudonym in another ward at the same hospital for his surgery. Mohan's daughter just happens to work at the hospital and recognises Nerin, and assists her father in an attempt on his life while Nerin is in the operating theatre. Knight and his cohorts manage to foil the plan at the last minute.

It's a very typical slice of '60s television derring-do, but it's also a very tightly-plotted, well-written script. One of the minor characters is a streetwise old porter at the King's hospital. At one point in the script, Holmes has him dismiss a couple of rag week students collecting for charity in a fairly risqué manner:

PORTER: (INDICATING RAG ANNOUNCEMENT ON WALL BY HIS DESK) Well, sir, they say it's in aid of the hospital but if you ask me it's just an excuse for Mafeking about (CLEAR ENUNCIATION HERE PLEASE).

As story editor, Bob would occasionally be called on to undertake some fairly dramatic surgery on scripts that had probably already been revised numerous times by the original writer. Television deadlines being what they were, it was sometimes necessary to ask the original writer to walk away from a commissioned script that just wasn't working out, and for the story editor instead to try to knock it into shape in time for it to go before the cameras. If the original writer was happy with the finished result, the episode would still go out under their own name. But if they weren't too keen on the final script, they would sometimes ask that it be put out under a pseudonym. In either instance, the original writer would receive the full royalties. Whenever a writer requested his name be taken off the finished script on *Knight Errant*, Bob would use the pseudonym William Hood for the on-screen credit, and this happened in three instances.

The first was an episode of *Knight Errant '60* entitled 'Something in the City',

---

25 The script gives the title as 'The King of Kandogar', whereas other reference sources such as *TV Times* give it as 'The King of Kandoga' – perhaps it was changed for transmission? And although the series was by this point known as *Knight Errant '60*, the rehearsal script calls it just *Knight Errant*.

screened on Tuesday 14 June 1960. 'Scientist John Stranger makes a valuable discovery in plastics and Horatio Noble, an unscrupulous businessman, tries to blackmail him into revealing the secret. Knight Errant Ltd use business methods to beat Noble at his own game.'

The next instance happened at the start of the second season (the one titled *Knight Errant Ltd*), with the episode 'The Jazzman', which was shown on ATV on Thursday 22 September 1960. 'Bandleader "Buddy" O'Brien meets his young daughter for the first time in seven years and tries to win her away from his ex-wife. With the child's future at stake, Stephen Drummond must find a way to end the conflict.' A review of this episode in *The Stage and Television Today*, which appeared a few days after the episode was screened, was decidedly unenthusiastic. Under the headline *Knight Errant Rides Shakily Again*, reviewer Guy Taylor wrote: 'The firm of Knight Errant is back again. But Adam Knight has gone abroad leaving colleague Stephen Drummond (Hugh David) to look after things in his absence, with the assistance of his enthusiastic secretary (Wendy Williams). Hugh David as Drummond is potentially a better choice for the hero of this series than John Turner, but he does not have much chance in "The Jazzman" by William Hood. A little girl is to go to Rome to study the piano but her divorced mother and stepfather must get the written agreement of her real father, a successful jazz pianist who has not see his daughter since she was a baby. It is feared the father may interfere with the child's career when he knows that she plays the piano. Knight Errant is hired to act as go-between. The story was quite promising as a character study of the irresponsible father, but developed too slowly. As a plot for *Knight Errant* it was weak. In fact, he seemed largely superfluous to the action, although Liz Parrish (Kay Callard) from the original team makes a welcome return and pulled him through as she did his predecessor.'[26]

A further William Hood episode, 'The Elopement', was shown on Thursday 22 June 1961, towards the end of the series' run. 'The newly-engaged Stephen and Frances have their first quarrel. Stephen undertakes to find a runaway society couple who have eloped to Scotland. Frances unwittingly takes on the same assignment ... but for a very different client.'

As previously mentioned, all the episodes of both series of *Knight Errant* were broadcast live on ITV. Bob later recalled how this led to writers having to write their scripts in a particular manner. 'Well they used to say, about that time, that tape was so expensive, they had to wipe it and re-use it, and they couldn't edit it. We used to write scenes when I started in television that were called "buffer" scenes. A camera would close in on you and you would go on talking as

26 *The Stage and Television Today*, 22 September 1960.

if I were still there, and you would go on talking for quite a little while, while the other chap would be changing into his pyjamas and hopping into bed. And we used to have to write them like that because the action was continuous.'

At around the time Bob was working on *Knight Errant*, he and Patricia moved to live in York Road, New Barnet in Hertfordshire. This was just a few miles away from Borehamwood, which housed a small number of film and television studios, including ATV Elstree and the now-demolished MGM British Studios. Elstree was home to the studio where most of ATV's live television programmes were recorded, including such mainstays as *Emergency Ward 10*. Bob was perhaps hoping that his proximity to such establishments would stand him in good stead for future writing work.

On Monday 26 September 1960, Bob's agent, Robin Lowe, wrote to the BBC, looking to interest them in employing his client. His letter was addressed to Vincent Tilsley, writer and script editor on the programme *R.C.M.P.* (which stood for Royal Canadian Mounted Police, the subject of the series). Tilsley was also an occasional writer and producer of the BBC's *Sunday Night Play* (alongside producer John Elliot) and would later go on to be the first story editor of *Dr Finlay's Casebook*. Lowe wanted to know if the BBC were interested in a six-part science fiction story idea that Bob had come up with, and submitted a story breakdown of that idea along with his letter[27]. Lowe also gave a potted breakdown of Bob's television career to date: 'The author, Robert Holmes, entered television through the short story market and, having been assigned by Granada to write a number of scripts for *Knight Errant*, he has since been acting as script editor for them, but becomes available again at the end of this month.'

At the time, Tilsley was on annual leave from the BBC, and so Lowe's letter, along with Bob's storyline, made their way instead to the BBC's Central Scripts Library. Receipt of them was acknowledged to Lowe on Thursday 13 October 1960. Bob's storyline was then passed on Tuesday 25 October 1960 to the Head of the Script Department at the BBC, Donald Wilson, who immediately noted that this six-part science fiction serial would probably clash with another idea the BBC were actively pursuing at the time. This was a serial idea by the cosmologist Fred Hoyle, who was working alongside producer John Elliot, and called *A for Andromeda*. Wilson didn't give Lowe any details about this, but instead wrote to him on Wednesday 2 November 1960, expressing an interest in Bob's story idea, but regrettably rejecting it due to a clash with other, unnamed, similar BBC projects. Thus Bob's first brush with the BBC came to nothing.

---

27 No known copy of the actual storyline is known to survive, but it may well have been an early form of the 'The Space Trap' idea that he would take to the *Doctor Who* production office in 1965.

So in 1961, with *Knight Errant* coming to an end after two series, Bob threw himself headlong into the world of freelance television scriptwriting. Luckily for him, there were a couple of newly-created ATV series with which he quickly found favour. His close proximity to Borehamwood had perhaps proved to be useful after all!

Harpers West One was a soap opera set in a large department store in London's West End. The series ran for 32 hour-long episodes, starred a young Wendy Richard (before she found fame working behind the counter of another department store, Grace Brothers, in *Are You Being Served?*) and also gave early leading roles to actors Graham Crowden and Bernard Horsfall.

Deadline Midnight was a drama that revolved around the lives of the characters who worked for the fictitious newspaper the *Daily Globe*. Writers such as Louis Marks, Allan Prior, Ken Taylor and Hazel Adair all worked on this series.

And then there was *Family Solicitor*, a rather staid legal soap made by Granada, which starred Robert Flemyng and A J Brown as senior partners in the legal practice Naylor, Freeman and Wigg. The series is perhaps best remembered for giving an early platform for the acting talents of Geoffrey Palmer, who appeared in many of the episodes as the junior solicitor Hugh Cowley. Bernard Horsfall also featured, in the regular role of Francis Naylor.

In 1961, Bob wrote one script for *Harpers West One*: the second episode of the first series, shown on ATV on Monday 3 July 1961. He then wrote three episodes of *Family Solicitor*. 'Man of Straw'[28] was the first of these, shown on Wednesday 26 July 1961. *TV Times* noted of this episode: 'Gordon Hawkins and his bride have nowhere to live while their new house is being finished, so he buys the last few months' lease of an old house. After signing the deed – without properly understanding it – they find they have to restore the house to the landlord's satisfaction. Francis Naylor takes the matter up.' The second of Bob's episodes was 'Strike Action', shown on Wednesday 9 August 1961. 'A workman at Jim Buxton's glassworks is hurt in an accident. He brings a claim for damages against the firm. Jim Buxton consults Anthony Freeman – and faces a strike threat,' said *TV Times* of this one, which also starred *Knight Errant* writer Barry Letts in one of his last acting roles.[29] The final *Family Solicitor* script Bob wrote was the episode 'Statement of Affairs', shown on Thursday 9

---

28 This episode's convoluted plot involved a newly married couple being duped into taking over the last few months of a lease on a dilapidated property on exceptionally reasonable terms, only to learn it was a 'repairing lease' which made them liable for all repairs on the house at the end of the lease's term. Although Bob Holmes never kept a script for this – or any of his other episodes of *Family Solicitor* – he did keep his four-page story outline. See Interlude I below.
29 He was credited as 'Barrie Letts' for this appearance.

November 1961.[30] *TV Times* noted: 'An irresponsible artist declares himself bankrupt to avoid paying his wife maintenance under a deed of separation. He soon finds it is cheaper to stay married!'

Bob also wrote a single episode for the second series of *Deadline Midnight*. His episode, 'Man in a Frame', was shown on ATV on Saturday 30 September 1961.[31] 'Len Bryan, financial editor of the *Daily Globe*, has stumbled on a story which will expose financier André Gudenian as a swindler. But Gudenian knows that if he can delay publication of the story for 24 hours he will be safe – and he lays a trap for Bryan,' noted *TV Times* that week. None of Bob's three episodes of *Family Solicitor* survives in the archives, but his single 1961 episode of *Harper's West One* as well as the *Deadline Midnight* episode are both known to exist, and as such are the earliest surviving examples of Robert Holmes television scriptwriting.

Also during 1961, Bob worked alongside his former *Knight Errant* producer Warren Jenkins in developing an idea for a series set in a holiday camp, which he tried to interest both Granada Television and the BBC in making. The series proposal, written by Holmes and Jenkins and entitled simply *Holiday Camp*, reads like a contemporary version of *Hi-Di-Hi*[32] without the humour or sitcom trappings, mixed in with a dollop of *Bergerac* for good measure. The holiday camp in question was set on a fictitious small island – Pendragon or Treganna Island were mooted as possible names for it – just off the coast of Cornwall, which had previously been a nudist colony and also a prisoner-of-war camp. Every week, it was planned, the regular cast of workers at the camp would become embroiled in events that surrounded the visiting guests; from accidents at sea while scuba diving to mysterious guests masquerading as seal-watchers, from jewellery thieves and lovestruck Spanish football stars to nudists and escaped convicts. Despite their obvious enthusiasm for their pitch, Jenkins and Holmes were disappointed to find that they had no takers for it, and the series idea was left to gather dust.

Bob also tried his hand with other projects in 1961. Another series idea was simply titled *The Long Thumbs*[33], which he peddled around the BBC and various ITV franchises, all to no avail. He also pitched a story idea entitled 'Counterfeit Club' to the Rank/ATV crime drama series *Ghost Squad*, but this also wasn't taken up.[34]

---

30 *Family Solicitor* wasn't fully networked on ITV – the early episodes weren't shown in Scotland until much later. The transmission dates quoted here are, as usual, for the ATV region.

31 Again, this series wasn't networked on ITV – Scotland once more missed out.

32 *Hi-Di-Hi* was a sitcom set in the late 1950s and early 1960s, written by Jimmy Perry and David Croft for the BBC, which ran between 1980 and 1988.

33 There is a note in Holmes's files about this pitch, but no details of the story idea are recorded.

34 Again, there is a note in Holmes's files about this story pitch, but no detail of the story itself.

1962 saw Bob joining the writing team of ATV's *Emergency Ward 10*. It would appear that he wrote or contributed to the scripts of a staggeringly impressive number of episodes – 49 were credited to him – all screened between 19 June 1962 and 20 December 1963[35]. That's about a third of all the episodes of *Emergency Ward 10* that were made in this 18 month period! Bob was joined on the series by Roger Marshall, with whom he had worked at Granada on *Knight Errant*. 'The programme where we met up again was *Emergency Ward 10* in 1962,' recalls Marshall. 'There were always three writers on the show. Him, a lady named Diane Morgan and me. I only stayed for a few months, then got a contract to work on *The Avengers* which, as you can imagine, was much more fun. The medical advisor on the show was a doctor named Phyllis Gibbons, now Phyllis Mortimer. She and Bob were both sci-fi buffs and always concocting story fragments, ideas, etc.'[36]

Bob never retained any of his scripts for *Emergency Ward 10*, but he did keep the medical reports and case studies that were drawn up for the episode runs to which he contributed. Each record would include the backstory details of the character that was to be afflicted with a particular medical condition, details of the condition and the various treatment options the character would be given, the number of episodes that character was to appear in, information on how well or how badly the character was going to respond to the treatments, and a short breakdown of the 'story-arc' each character was to go through before they either recovered and were discharged, or they succumbed to their illness.[37]

During this time, Bob also contributed another two episodes – the tenth and the fourteenth – for the second series of *Harpers West One* for ATV. The first of these was shown on ATV on Monday 19 November 1962, and the *TV Times* noted for the episode: 'There are three supervisory positions to be filled at Harpers, but there are four applicants for promotion. Who will fail?' The second of Bob's second season episodes was shown by ATV on Monday 24 December 1962, and *TV Times* reported: 'On Christmas Eve Harpers holds the annual party for former members of staff. For one of them, John Ramsey, it is an evening that changes his future.' Neither of these episodes survives at

---

35 Unfortunately, all of the episodes that Bob wrote for *Emergency Ward 10* between 1962 and 1963 are missing from the ATV television archives. However, full transmission details of these episodes can be found in the appendix at the back of this book.
36 Private correspondence with Colin Brockhurst, dated 23 June 1992.
37 The case notes that Bob kept included: *Notes of Multiple Myelomatosis* (episodes 502-513), *Notes on Idiopathic Stearrhoea* (episodes 510-519), *Mike Scott's Story* (episodes 523-539), *Notes on Cerebral Abscesses* (episodes 540-547), *Medical Story of Lucy Jones* (episodes 549-556), *Mrs Lena Horsey's Story* (episodes 553-562), *Dr Griffiths' Story* (episodes 563-573), *Elizabeth Trench's Story* (episodes 571-588), *Notes on Leprosy* (episodes 595-601), *Notes on Cysticercosis, Notes on Pancreas Tumours* (episodes 600-608), *Notes on E Coli Septicaemia* (episodes 607-619), *Harry Decker's Story* (episodes 625-629), *Notes on the effects of Alcohol on the Body, Medical and character notes of Mrs O'Brien*, and *George Ryder's Story* (episodes 631-638). These all relate to episodes Bob either wrote or worked on in some capacity.

the ATV archive.[38]

Bob also wrote an episode of the ATV series *24 Hour Call* (a spin-off from *Call Oxbridge 2000,* which in itself was a spin-off from *Emergency Ward 10*), entitled 'Never Leave Me'. Bob wrote this under his William Hood pseudonym, perhaps to disguise the fact that he was moonlighting away from *Emergency Ward 10.* 'Never Leave Me' was shown by ATV on Sunday 3 March 1963 (although it was originally meant to be screened the following week, on Sunday 10 March 1963, which suggests that it was pre-recorded and not live).[39] *TV Times* said of this episode: 'A selfless act, in an emergency, leads Dr Hamilton into trouble with the police. Trouble which can have far reaching consequences for him – and others.'

After his failed pitch the previous year, Bob finally got to write an episode of *Ghost Squad,* the ITC-distributed series based on the bestselling book of the same name by John Gosling, for the 1962 run of the series. The premise of *Ghost Squad* was based around a fictitious, elite, division of Scotland Yard's police force whose job it was to infiltrate themselves into situations that were either too sensitive or too hazardous for normal government operatives to investigate.

Bob's episode, 'The Green Shoes', concerned the theft of a small bar of experimental radioactive material, which could potentially be used to make a neutron bomb. It is smuggled out of the country to Warsaw inside a green ballet shoe, but not before the man who unwittingly planted it in the shoe dies from radioactive poisoning. Craig, a member of the Squad, rushes to Warsaw on the trail of the green shoes, fearing that the ballerina who is meant to wear the shoes will suffer the same fate, but he is too late to stop her performance. However, the ballerina has switched her shoes on a whim, and the culprit behind the scheme is apprehended.

While the production of 'The Green Shoes' is very slick for its time – the episode is made entirely on film, as opposed to videotape – many of the cast deliver their lines in a very stilted manner, which makes it somewhat difficult to view from a modern perspective. It can be argued that the central plot McGuffin of the green shoes being switched in the final act would have been harder to pull-off had the programme been made in colour, and not in black and white. Nevertheless, 'The Green Shoes' is an important milestone in Bob's career, being his first contribution to a really prestigious television series.

The line-up of writers on *Ghost Squad* reads like an impressive *Who's Who* of British scriptwriters of that era. Holmes was in the company of others such as Dick Sharples, John Lucarotti, Philip Levene, Lewis Griefer, Louis Marks,

---

38 Again, the earlier episodes (at least) of this second series weren't networked on ITV.
39 This episode – like most of the series – is missing from the ATV archive.

Reed De Rouen and Malcolm Hulke, as well as his old friend Robert Banks Stewart. 'There were about two dozen writers who all came into television at about the same time from the magazines,' recalls Stewart. 'There was a lot of work around. You'd sometimes share the same agent, and so when a series was commissioning, if one person got in, the agent would push his other clients.'

In late 1962, Bob and Patricia moved to Lyonsdown Road in New Barnett, which was just around the corner from their old house in York Road, and still close to the Borehamwood studios. Bob then spent nearly all of 1963 working on *Emergency Ward 10* for ATV. However, he had by now set his sights on a possible escape route. On Tuesday 25 June 1963, Bob's agent, Robin Lowe, wrote to the BBC again.

This time, the recipient of his letter was John Hopkins, who at the time was a prolific writer and script editor on the BBC's new police series *Z Cars*. In the letter, Lowe wrote, 'I would appreciate it if you would give thought to Robert Holmes as a contributor to *Z Cars*. Apart from being a most experienced and talented television writer, he has the added qualification of having served in the Police Force. He is currently doing time on *Ward 10* from which he is anxious to escape! Credits include *Knight Errant, Ghost Squad, Harpers West One, Deadline Midnight, Oxbridge 2000*[40]; and he has recently written for an as-yet unscheduled Associated Rediffusion series *The Search*[41].'

Hopkins passed Lowe's letter on to the new acting script editor of *Z Cars*, John Gould, who had taken over from Hopkins on the series. Gould replied the very next day, offering to meet up with Bob to discuss any ideas he might have had for the police series. Lowe then sent Gould a copy of Bob's script for the 'Man in a Frame' episode of *Deadline Midnight* in advance of the suggested meeting. Gould received and read the script, which he found competent, if not entirely convincing in terms of plot (at least, in terms of what *Z Cars* were looking for).

Gould invited Bob to submit a storyline to the *Z Cars* production office, indicating that if it was deemed suitable he would then be asked to write a first draft script of the episode. However, Bob would be formally commissioned – and paid – only if this first draft script was assessed to be suitable; and even then, he would also be expected to do at least one rewrite to reach a final script. Presumably, Bob wasn't too impressed by this request to write a whole script 'on spec' and unpaid. Or perhaps he just didn't have

---

40 *Call Oxbridge 2000* was a medical soap-drama made by ATV, which ran from 1961-62. There is no record of Bob writing any of the transmitted episodes, so any work he did on the show may have never made it to production for whatever reason. Or this could be a mistaken reference to Bob's script under the William Hood pseudonym for the spin-off series *24 Hour Call*.
41 There doesn't seem to have been an Associated Rediffusion series called *The Search* in 1963, so it – and therefore Bob's script – may have been abandoned before production.

any story ideas for the series. Whatever the reason, no storyline or script was forthcoming from Bob. *Z Cars* was thus deprived of a writer who – given his police background – would surely have ultimately been able to contribute a great deal to this popular police drama series.

Undeterred, Bob tried once more to get his foot in the door at the BBC. This time he wrote directly to Elwyn Jones, the BBC's Head of Drama, on Tuesday 31 December 1963. Jones had been one of the original co-creators of *Z Cars*, which is perhaps why Bob thought he might be sympathetic to his new pitch. In his letter to Jones, Bob wrote:

'It seems to me that there is now little chance of providing any freshness or variation within the framework of a dossier-type series. The other basic type is the one where the heroes just happen to be in a particular place at a particular time. But the M1 is hardly long enough to substitute for Route 66.[42] The answer, I suggest, is to set up a series using the British canal system as a background. Because canals are not greatly used today it would be necessary, I think, to backdate the thing about 30 years. Canal folk – by which I mean the thousands of people whose lives were in some way connected with the canals – were very much a closed community with their own customs, folklore, superstitions and slang. This setting and the slight period flavour – which the success of *Dr Finlay's Casebook*[43] shows to be no disadvantage – ought to provide interesting story material. At the moment I am working on a presentation of the idea – two partners, their motorised barge, plus a girl – together with some brief story outlines. If you would care to see this when it is finished, or if you would like to discuss it before I go further, perhaps you would let me know.'

Once again, Bob was to fall victim to having a similar idea to one that was already on the table at the BBC. This time it was a series idea from writer Cyril Abrahams, which he was developing with producer Vivian Daniels.[44] Bob's letter of rejection for his 'canal' series was sent from the BBC on Tuesday 7 January 1964.

Bob's luck with the BBC was just about to change, however …

---

42 The M1 was Britain's first ever motorway, which ran for 74 miles, and was opened in 1959.
43 *Dr Finlay's Casebook* was a television series that was first broadcast on the BBC from 1962 and ran until 1971. Based on a series of A J Cronin-penned books beginning with the 1935 novella *Country Doctor*, *Dr Finlay's Casebook* centred on a general medical practice in the fictional Scottish town of Tannochbrae during the late 1920s.
44 The series was probably an early incarnation of *King of the River*, which revolved around the King family and their sail-driven barge transport business, and which ran on the BBC for 17 episodes from 1966-67.

INTERLUDE I
FAMILY SOLICITOR:
'MAN OF STRAW'
1961

Robert Holmes' full original storyline proposal for the 'Man of Straw' episode of *Family Solicitor*, a Granada TV series that ran for 24 hour-long episodes in 1961, is reprinted here as originally submitted, complete with Bob's original spellings and punctuation:

FAMILY SOLICITIOR - STORY OUTLINE BY ROBERT HOLMES
'A MAN OF STRAW'

Gordon Hawkins is twenty-six and works in the accounts department of a multiple store in Brampton-on-Mersey*; his wife, Phoebe, is three years younger and is a secretary in a shipping firm. They have been married nearly a year and having a £3,200 house built in a suburb of Brampton. Francis Naylor is handling this house purchase for them.

(* Or whatever name is finally settled on.)

Phoebe and Gordon are eagerly awaiting the time when they can move into their new house because, at the moment, they are living apart. They are saving hard to furnish their house and cannot afford the high rents that are asked in Brampton for furnished flats. Phoebe lives at home, Gordon has his dreary lodgings, and on winter evenings they walk together in Brampton Arboretum.

Quite naturally, therefore, they are delighted to get the chance of cheap, temporary accommodation. They are offered the lease of a biggish house in the centre of town. The lease has only a few months to run and will expire about the completion date of their own house.

ROBERT HOLMES: A LIFE IN WORDS

Gordon is a little dubious about this piece of luck; he wonders what the catch is. However, they have only a few hours to decide whether or not to accept and, at Phoebe's urging, he takes over the lease without consulting Francis Naylor. And Mr Cullen, the kindly gentleman who has offered them the lease, is able to dispel some of his doubts.

Mr Cullen frankly agrees that the house is a bit worse for wear. His firm has used it as a store for many years. But now they have moved into new premises, with plenty of storage room, they don't need this house any longer – it is really just a liability. That is why he is practically giving the remainder of the lease away …

A more sophisticated couple – or a couple less in love – might have been more suspicious of the generous Mr Cullen. But Gordon happily buys the remainder of the lease and moves in with his wife. Phoebe is delighted. With a bit of tidying up, and with their new furniture installed, she reckons they will have quite a cosy home. And in any case, now that the fine weather has arrived, it won't be long before their beautiful new house is ready for them.

The builders reach joist level and Gordon again goes to see Francis Naylor. Francis has arranged for him to have a 90% mortgage and the money is being advanced by Brampton Building Society in stage-payments. In conversation with Francis, Gordon reveals that he and Phoebe now have their own home. He tells Francis how he acquired the lease. Francis asks one or two questions and his face clouds. He asks Gordon to let him see the lease.

Gordon has been uneasy about the lease for some weeks – ever since in a conversation at the office, he realised that he might have been duped. He has kept this worry to himself.

(LEGAL BREAK: The lease, of course, is a repairing lease and requires the leaseholder, at the expiry of the term, to make good all dilapidations. In the case of Gordon's house, this would come to a great deal of money – far more than he has or is ever likely to have. I understand that it is not unknown for leasehold premises to be passed in this way to a poor man – a man of straw, as the legal phrase has it – in the knowledge that the lessor will be unable to recover damages.)

Francis has to tell Gordon that he has made himself responsible for repairs that may cost thousands of pounds. Gordon tells Phoebe. There are reproaches and recriminations. Phoebe, guiltily feeling that she pushed Gordon into this position, threatens to leave him. Not only are they faced with financial ruin but it appears that their marriage is going to end before it has properly started.

Up to this point the story (which, I feel, is somewhere towards the end of the second act) we have been into the offices of Naylor, Freeman & Wigg two or three times to follow the sub-plot. This deals with the Northern Star Disaster (1893) Fund.

The Northern Star was a merchant vessel that went down in sight of Brampton one wild night in 1893. She sank with all hands and many local men perished. A public subscription fund was set up to aid the dependents of those who died.

John Naylor is secretary to the Trustees of this fund. They meet four times each year to attend to its administration. Gradually, of course, over the years, the sailors' dependents have died, disappeared, or stopped submitting claims, and a few years ago the Trustees agreed that the fund had outlived its usefulness. In any case, very little capital was left.

However, no sooner had they reached a decision to wind up the fund when – bingo! – the Indian Government agreed to repay former stockholders whose railway it had nationalised. The Trustees of the Northern Star Disaster (1893) Fund

ROBERT HOLMES: A LIFE IN WORDS

found themselves embarrassedly holding £30.000 and having nobody to give it to.

(LEGAL BREAK: Public Trusts are very difficult to wind up. Whatever money is left in the till has to be utilised in a way that is in line with the trust's original purpose. This invariably leads to a lot of legal discussion and interminable meetings with the Commissioner of Trusts.)

At the time of the story, John Naylor is at last in a position to report to the Trustee that the Commissioner has accepted their latest recommendation in regard to winding up the Northern Star fund. John is naturally gratified at this achievement.

Meanwhile his son, Francis, is troubled by the mess that his client has got himself into; as for Phoebe and Gordon, they are just sick with despair and on the verge of parting for good.

As Francis handles most of the property work (now that Christopher Little has been stuck off the briefing!), it is natural enough for John to ask him to keep his eyes open for a property near the town centre which might be obtained at a reasonable price. John describes his requirements; Francis then tells his father about the house that Gordon is leasing …

Things move fairly swiftly from this point. The Trustees look over the house and agree it is just what they want in order to establish their 'Northern Star Home for Seamen'. They approach the lessor and he agrees to sell the house and freehold title.

The end result is that the Trustees are pleased; the Naylors, father and son, are happy; and Gordon and Phoebe, saved from their folly, walk away hand-in-hand to their new house.

CHAPTER THREE
A CASE TO PLAY WITH
1964

Bob's citing of *Dr Finlay's Casebook* in his letter and 'canal' pitch to Elwyn Jones could very well have been the catalyst for what happened to Bob next. The BBC had launched the series *Dr Finlay's Casebook* in 1962. Based on the medical novels of A J Cronin, which followed the gentle exploits of a small doctor's practice in Scotland, its lead character was Dr Finlay (Bill Simpson), the practice's junior partner, who was ably accompanied by his senior partner, Dr Cameron (Andrew Cruickshank), and their receptionist-cum-housekeeper, Janet (Barbara Mullen). The series had quickly become extremely popular with viewers, and although many of the earlier episodes borrowed plotlines from Cronin's novels, it also required an influx of new writers and story ideas, including some early scripts from Bob's old chum, Robert Banks Stewart. Sometime toward the end of January 1964, Elwyn Jones put Bob in touch with Donald Bull, who was at the time the script editor of *Dr Finlay's Casebook*, and as a result Bob was invited to pitch a storyline for a prospective episode of the second series. What's more, Bob didn't need to jump through as many hoops on *Dr Finlay's Casebook* as the production team of *Z Cars* had wanted him to.

On Friday 31 January 1964, Bob sent Donald Bull an outline for an episode entitled 'The Hallelujah Chorus', which was quickly re-titled 'The Hallelujah Favourite' before becoming 'The Hallelujah Stakes'. Bull liked the story, made a few small structural alterations to the storyline, and then commissioned Bob to write the script. The resultant episode of *Dr Finlay's Casebook* – which was Bob's first paid work for the BBC to make it onto screen – was shown on BBC1 on Sunday 10 May 1964.

'In Tannochbrae, as elsewhere in the Scotland of the 1920s, the war between the "wets" and the "drys" was a hard-fought affair with no verbal quarter asked or given. A particularly sharp engagement in that war is the subject of tonight's *Dr Finlay's Casebook* episode, called "The Hallelujah Stakes"', declared the *Radio Times* in the week the episode was due to be screened on BBC1.[45] The article continued: 'The principal local champion of the "wets" cause is Dougie Mumford, a tough veteran of the Black Watch and landlord of the Buchanan

---

Arms. Opposed to him is Annie Feenan, the doughty little widow who is the most zealous member of the Tannochbrae Salvation Army corps. Every time she enters Dougie's bar to sell copies of *War Cry* the accusations fly, but one night she brings with her her son Patrick. And since Patrick is known to be rather simple-minded, the customers decide to have a few laughs at his expense – but the joke turns out to be a very bad one indeed.' The article ends by noting: '… the script-writer of "The Hallelujah Stakes" is Robert Holmes, a former journalist who himself served … in the Black Watch. Tonight's play will be his first contribution to BBC TV.'

Just weeks later, in February 1964, Bob was again contacted by Bull, who asked him to help out with a rewrite on another episode of the series that Bull was unhappy with. It seems that the expertise in medical matters that Bob had picked up from working on *Emergency Ward 10* was a key factor in Bull's decision here. The script that Bull asked Bob to assist on was one entitled 'The True Lochiel', written by Rachel Grieve, and revolved around the subject of haemophilia. It would appear that Grieve had so far written at least two versions of the script, and Bull wasn't happy with either version.

Having looked over Grieve's original scripts, Bob got to work on rewriting the episode. He contacted Bull in late March 1964 with his observations on the task so far. The detail of his written memo to Bull gives a good indication of how seriously Bob took this opportunity to do more work for the BBC, having now got his foot in the door, as it were:

'The deeper I get into this rewrite the more roadblocks I come across. First, the complicated business of haemophilia. We agreed Angus was Morag's grandfather and that his son – killed in the war – was in the army and therefore not a haemophiliac. This seemed okay at first and I have a scene where the doctors, learning that Morag's father was a soldier, deduce he could not have had the disease.

'The point is that in Rachel's second script we get the statement: "The females carry the disease to the males". This seems to imply that a son would not inherit the disease from his father – only from his mother. And if this is so, then it makes nonsense of the scene between the two doctors. They would not have expected Morag's father to be a bleeder. However, in Rachel's first script – and she sent an accompanying letter certifying the accuracy of the medical details – Morag tells Bruce she has a brother who died of the disease. (As in this version Angus was her father, not her grandfather, the inference is that he passed the illness down.) I am confused.

'A minor detail: Cameron tells Morag that if she has a daughter there will be no way of knowing if the illness is still extant until the daughter makes

Morag a grandmother. This seems to rule out the business of Finlay running a blood-test on Morag. It wouldn't tell him anything.

'Angus's rather fey reaction to Cameron as "Lochiel" has also been worrying me. Lochiel – Sir Ewen Cameron – was knighted by Charles II for his services to the Royalist cause. He died in 1719 – 26 years before the Young Pretender raised his standard at Glenfinnan. So either there was another Lochiel – a grandson of the only one mentioned in my *Concise Universal Biography* – or Rachel has mixed up her Charlies.[46]

'I think the character of Angus is developing quite well now. I have been boning up on Scottish history and the House of Stewart in the hope that, in his final scene with Cameron, I could plant just some slight suspicion that there was something behind his claim to a royal lineage! Unfortunately, I can't see a way of doing it. As things stand, he walks out of the story exactly the same as he entered it – a potty peasant with delusions of grandeur. When I agreed to have the script back with you by Thursday I had forgotten the Easter holiday intervened. Unless the second half goes unexpectedly smoothly I shan't finish before Friday. I hope this is all right?'

Bob delivered his revised script, and 'The True Lochiel' was shown on the BBC on Sunday 24 May 1964. The episode was credited to Robin Baker and Rachel Grieve – Robin Baker was a pseudonym employed by Bob in this instance. Hence his contribution to this script was essentially uncredited.

'Tannochbrae, lying well south of the Highland Line, does not bother its hard head too much with the high-romantic notions of the clansmen,' read the preview in the *Radio Times* in the edition published the week the episode was shown.[47] 'So when a stately old Highlander from Western Ross comes to live with relatives in the town, and proclaims his descent from the royal Stuarts, his pretensions earn small respect either from the locals or from the doctors at Arden House. But among old Angus Macleod's kingly attribution is the bleeding disease of haemophilia – the "royal disease" which touched most of the ruling houses of Europe – and this does call for the serious notice of Drs Cameron and Finlay. Particularly when his grand-daughter Morag, wife of a local barber, is expecting a child and is mortally afraid that it too will be a haemophiliac. Tonight's story is called "The True Lochiel" because the old gentleman naturally identifies Dr Cameron with his eminent Jacobite namesake, Cameron of Lochiel ...'

At about the same time that Bob was re-writing this particular episode of

---

46 There was indeed another Lochiel – Donald Cameron (1700-1748), grandson of Sir Ewen Cameron. He was known as the 'Gentle Lochiel', was a fervent supporter of Bonnie Prince Charlie, and was instrumental in the Jacobite uprising of 1745.

47 *Radio Times*, w/c 23 May 1964.

Dr Finlay's Casebook in March 1964, Donald Bull proposed to his BBC bosses that Bob be formally appointed as his assistant script editor on the series. The appointment was to be for only three months, which would take Bob through to the end of production on the programme's second series. Bob's duties would include attending all the rehearsals and doing any on-the-spot rewriting that was required. Producer Elwyn Jones was happy to grant Bull's request, and so Bob became a member of BBC staff for the first time, albeit a temporary one.

As assistant script editor on *Dr Finlay's Casebook*, Bob in April 1964 rewrote the episode 'The Old Indomitable' by William Woods, which was shown on Sunday 31 May 1964 and jointly credited to the two writers. He also rewrote the final episode of the series, 'The Doctor Cried' by Alan Gosling, which was shown on Sunday 28 June 1964 and credited to both Gosling and Holmes.[48] The *Radio Times* gave minimal coverage to 'The Old Indomitable', but said of the final episode: 'Alan Finlay remains the same impulsive character, who in "The Doctor Cried" is sorely troubled by a situation which runs out of control. Two boys inquisitively exploring his car while he visits a patient; the disappearance of an ophthalmoscope; a police investigation – and Finlay, whose sole intention was to recover a valuable instrument, finds himself powerless to stop an apparently cruel legal process.'[49]

During this time, Bob also re-wrote an episode of the BBC series *Catch Hand* during April and May 1964, at the request of John Gould (with whom he had previously been in contact when Gould was script editing *Z Cars*). *Catch Hand* was a ten-part BBC series focusing on the exploits of two casual labourers (played by Mark Eden and Anthony Booth), and the script Bob worked on was called 'The Man Upstairs' by John Finch. The reworked script was delivered by Bob in early June 1964, but when the series began its ten-week run on the BBC (from Wednesday 1 July to Wednesday 2 September 1964), the episode wasn't one of those that was screened. Presumably either the script proved to be unsalvageable or was abandoned not long after Bob handed in his rewrite.

After his three-month spell as assistant script editor on *Dr Finlay's Casebook* had finished, Bob tried once again to find favour for his own projects within the BBC. On Tuesday 30 June 1964, he wrote directly (i.e. not through his agent) to Roger Smith, story editor on the prestigious BBC drama strand

---

48 None of the four second series *Dr Finlay's Casebook* episodes that Bob had a hand in exists in the BBC's Film and Television Library. However, BBC Enterprises did once hold 16mm film copies of the episodes for overseas sale, as all four were sold to both Zambia and Kenya in February 1967. Three of them (not 'The Doctor Cried') were also sold to Uganda in March 1966, to Nigeria in June 1966, to Barbados in October 1969, and to Jamaica in July 1971. Two of them – 'The True Lochiel' and 'The Old Indomitable' – were further sold to Eire in September 1968. 'The Old Indomitable' was the only episode of the four that was sold to Sweden in April 1966.

49 *Radio Times*, w/c 27 June 1964.

Teletale, which was about to be re-launched under the new title *The Wednesday Play*. Bob and Smith had obviously had a conversation prior to this about a potential story idea, and now Bob wanted to try to follow this up with a more detailed pitch. His letter to Smith read as follows:

'This is an idea that I once mentioned briefly to you and which I have now developed. I'm submitting it because the other day you were looking for a *Rififi*[50] style story. Although this is not as grim as the film I think the situation could generate a lot of tension. In the outline I have stuck to the action but there are other aspects that would bulk more largely in the script – there would be a fairly strong budding love element, for instance. The title indicates the approach I should like to adopt with this story.'

The storyline Bob proposed, under the fairly surreal title 'Plunkett-Bream Was Six Foot Four', was a potential 75-minute play for *The Wednesday Play* slot. (See Interlude II for Bob's story breakdown for the play.)

For whatever reason, Roger Smith didn't take matters any further, so Bob's first attempt to write for *The Wednesday Play* came to nothing.[51]

By the end of 1964, Bob Holmes was 38 years old and had been writing for television for the best part of five years. He'd honed his craft as a storyteller in his own right, as well as serving lengthy stints script editing for *Knight Errant*, *Emergency Ward 10* and *Dr Finlay's Casebook*. In short, he had amassed quite a large amount of experience in a very small period of time. What is more, he was now well on the road to earning himself a reputation as someone who could deliver well-honed, well-crafted scripts to very tight deadlines.

More importantly, he had at last got his foot in the door of the BBC.

Bob's philosophy toward his chosen craft as a television writer was ably illustrated some years later, when he wrote a short, self-deprecating essay for the book *The Doctor Who File* (edited by Peter Haining). This piece also demonstrates in no small part his talents for writing in a conversational and dryly whimsical manner, which is why it's perhaps appropriate to quote the opening section at this juncture:

'You are known,' wrote Peter Haining, the editor of this volume, 'for your feeble humour. So if you want to try to be funny about your

---

50 *Rififi* was a 1955 French crime film adapted from the novel of the same name by Auguste le Breton. It was notable at the time for the detailed depiction of a burglary at a jeweller's shop; the scene lasted for about 30 minutes, and was shot in near silence without dialogue or music.

51 One other unused idea of Bob's from sometime in the early 1960s was an untitled play proposal for a heist/whodunit type of story, the components of which include a safe on a timelock, a consignment of diamonds, a couple of are-they-real-or-are-they-fake policemen, and a missing diamond broker. The last-minute twist in the tale is an elegant piece of plotting by Bob, and would have made an entertaining 60-minute drama. The plot outline is undated, and there is no clue as to whom Bob might have pitched the idea to.

experiences on *Doctor Who* we won't object. But do keep it down to fifteen hundred words.

Fifteen hundred funny words! Does the man realise that four words an hour is my top limit? And that is on a good day. On a bad day, in this matter of word mileage, ancient friars illuminating religious texts in gold leaf disappear into the distance. Arthritic stonemasons chipping pious warnings on headstones – *As I am, so shall Ye be* – leave me goggling with admiration.

During one of the economic ice ages that regularly grip my household I bought a Citroen 2cv. The salesman assured me that this machine was the last word in frugality with an engine that ran on gnat's water. 'Ran', in this context, is probably the wrong word. It sort of ambled. But it was a fine car and gave one plenty of time to admire the scenery. There was also the excitement of burn-ups with passing tractors and invalid carriages.

I mention this only because it fills up some of my fifteen hundred words and also to make my point that I am the 2cv of scriptwriters.

Furthermore, not much funny happens to you when most of your life is spent in solitary confinement staring at a typewriter, not funny-funny things, anyway. Statistically, I suppose writers must cop their fair share of ordinary funny things like train accidents and boilers going bang in the night.

I once dropped a coal-hod containing half a hundredweight of Phurnacite on my foot. As the steel rim splintered into the metatarsal that controls my big toe I remember screaming, 'Good gracious! That's funny.'

Later that day I was talking to Louis Marks, a valued though infrequent writer for *Doctor Who*. I mentioned the appalling agony I was suffering and Louis, who is a doctor, took immediate clinical control.

'Take a needle in a pair of pliers,' he advised, 'and heat it until it's incandescent. Then drive it in through the toe-nail.'

Louis is one of the funniest chaps I know, as well as being a doctor of philosophy.[52]

Although it may be tempting to imagine that Bob had dreamt up his ownership of a 2cv just for the purposes of this whimsical passage, his brother-in-law Ian Watson recalls him owning this very car – along with a catalogue of other

---

52 From 'A Life of Hammer and Tongs' by Robert Holmes, published in *The Doctor Who File* by Peter Haining (W H Allen, 1986).

weird vehicles. 'He was absolutely mad on old cars, like me,' says Watson. 'He had some weird and wonderful machines. He owned a car called a Panhard, which he took me out in one day, and tried to see how fast it went round a bend. The car nearly turned over and it frightened us to bloody death! He had another car, a DKW, it was a two-stroke thing, and it would never work or run properly. He was totally mad on cars. I used to meet him in Barnett when he lived there, and we used to go up to the local garages to look at all these cars. He was keen on funny cars that were quite oddball. He was never into new Bentleys or Mercs, it was always oddball cars. I'd often ask him, "What have you bought that heap of shit for?" I remember the 2cv, he told me, "It doesn't start well, I must admit." I pointed out to him that two-stroke cars are never very reliable cars.'

Nevertheless, the 2cv of scriptwriters was just getting revved up …

INTERLUDE II
THE WEDNESDAY PLAY:
'PLUNKETT-BREAM
WAS SIX FOOT FOUR'
JUNE 1964

Robert Holmes's full original storyline proposal for a play in *The Wednesday Play* strand, 'Plunkett-Bream Was Six Foot Four', is reprinted here as originally submitted, complete with Bob's original spellings and punctuation:

'PLUNKETT-BREAM WAS SIX FOOT FOUR'
– A 75-MINUTE PLAY OUTLINE BY ROBERT HOLMES

Pier 26, New York. Three men board a big passenger liner on the transatlantic run. Two of them - Plunkett-Bream and Malleson - are travelling to England. The third, Dicquet, has come to see them off.

In the pre-sailing bustle the surprising amount of cabin luggage they ferry aboard goes unremarked. If Chief Master-as-Arms Howard notices them at all it is only because they are not quite the usual collection of tired businessmen.

Plunkett-Bream is immensely tall, thin, and well-groomed. The blue-jowled Malleson looks as though he has narrowly survived several nasty accidents and Dicquet, a swarthy French Algerian, gives the impression that he would be more at ease in the crew's quarters than in Plunkett-Bream's first- class cabin.

Together they go over their plan for the last time. All three are keyed up, betraying their tension in different ways. Plunkett-Bream is a professional cracksman. He intends to rob the ship's bank on the homeward trip.

46

They have planned this robbery with tremendous care. Every detail has been thought out ahead – even down to a puncture-repair outfit for the inflatable dinghy. Plunkett-Bream has a complete set of navigation charts and has taught himself to use a sextant. Dicquet knows the time of his flight from Idlewild and even the precise train he must catch from Waterloo.

The stakes are high. There will be over £50,000 in the safe on the night before the ship docks in Southampton. It is months now since Plunkett-Bream reconnoitered the ship and booked three cabins for this particular trip – one for himself, one for Malleson and the third for Hargreaves. But Hargreaves' cabin is next to the bank and as Hargreaves never existed he will not be travelling.

Once they have been over the plan they separate. Dicquet goes ashore and Malleson and Plunkett-Bream will not meet again in public.

The ship sails. The purser crosses Hargreaves off his passenger list.

At dinner that night Plunkett-Bream finds he has been seated at the doctor's table – an amiable young man called Morgan. An attractive Philadelphian, Carol Rhodes, is also at the same table. She and her mother are vacationing in Europe.

Each night, after dinner, Plunkett-Bream slips into the empty Hargreaves cabin and works on the bulkhead between the cabin and the bank. He chose the cabin with care – he is able to work through the back of a built-in wardrobe, thus concealing from a casual eye the marks left by his oxy-acetylene equipment.

As he is working directly behind the safe there is no chance of detection from the other side of the bulkhead.

ROBERT HOLMES: A LIFE IN WORDS

The work goes ahead smoothly – though he has one hair-raising moment when Master-at-Arms Howard and the First Officer, on their nightly tour of inspection, are brought to the cabin by the smell of his oxy-acetylene burner – and two days after leaving New York he is working on the back of the safe itself.

Normally, a safe-breaker does not have the time to tackle the back or side of a safe and concentrates on cutting through or blowing out the lock. Plunkett-Bream, with two nights in hand, intends to cut almost through the back with the burner. The final assault will be made with a 'wheel' – a device like a giant can-opener which demands the strength of two men to work it.

During the days Plunkett-Bream flirts with Carol Rhodes. This is a development that the misogynist Malleson (with his face he has to be a misogynist) views with misgivings.

But though normally no slouch with women, Plunkett-Bream is too fatigued in daytime, and too busy at night, to make as much progress as he would wish. Regretfully, he sees Doctor Morgan pulling ahead. And anyhow, pretty as Carol is, £50,000 is even prettier.

On the last night before the ship docks in Southampton there is the usual fancy dress ball. Under the cover of their costumes Plunkett-Bream and Malleson can at least make overt contact.

Plunkett-Bream slips away to collect his 'wheel'. But when he arrives at the Hargreaves cabin he finds Carol there, just about to go to bed. Her mother has had an asthma attack and the doctor has arranged for Carol to be moved into the unoccupied cabin. (I would think more for carnal than medical reasons, though one would not want to probe his motives.)

At first, naturally, Carol misinterprets Plunkett-Bream's

intentions. But he scares her into keeping quiet and sits back to wait for Malleson.

There is a knock at the door. Plunkett-Bream thinks it is Malleson. Instead, it is the doctor. The safe-breaker, with an automatic concealed against the girl's spine, convinces Morgan this is one scene where he is not wanted. Morgan leaves with a very low opinion of American girls. This is hard on Carol because her feelings for Morgan have gone a bit deeper than she has yet revealed.

Malleson arrives. By now time is pressing. Plunkett-Bream selected this particular voyage after a great deal of hard study of tide-tables. He has kept a careful record of the ship's progress across the Atlantic. She is now entering the narrow straits between the Isle of Wight and Southampton. Dicquet, the French-Algerian sailor, will already be puttering out from Fishbourne in a motor-launch. The money has to be over the side by four a.m.

Working fast, the two men cut the back of the safe away and scoop out the contents. There is even more money than they expected. They pack it into plastic floats and attach these to an ex-R.A.F. dinghy of the type that is self-inflating.

There is a small radio-transmitter in the dinghy that will automatically send out a short-range signal on to which Dicquet will home. (This is another bit of standard life-saving equipment available in surplus stores.)

Now, of course, Carol is their big problem. They will not be able to walk off the ship with their false passports and innocent baggage in the way they had planned. Malleson wants to put her over the side as well. Plunkett-Bream, a cracksman and a gentleman, won't stand for murder.

In any case, if Carol is missed he knows suspicion will fall on him because Morgan had seen them together. Malleson, a direct-action tough, privately decides in that case that both Plunkett-Bream and the girl can go over the side. He and Dicquet will have a larger share of the loot. Plunkett-Bream knows the way Malleson's thoughts are moving.

Meanwhile, back in the surgery, Morgan is having second thoughts about the scene in the cabin and deciding that all was not quite as it looked. He goes back to the cabin and finds it empty – and a hole through the bulkhead to the bank.

On the after-deck, Plunkett-Bream and Carol are doing exactly as Malleson tells them. Malleson has a very big gun in his hand.

Morgan arrives, distracting Malleson. Plunkett-Bream makes a dive at him and is shot. Morgan and Malleson struggle for possession of the gun and Plunkett-Bream pulls himself off the deck to clobber Malleson with a handy marlin spike or something. Then he collapses and Morgan is left with the girl.

CHAPTER FOUR
FROM ONE DOCTOR,
TO ANOTHER
1965

By 1965, Bob and Patricia had moved house again, and were now living in the small village of Pitstone, near Leighton Buzzard in Bedfordshire. It was slightly further out of London than their previous abode, but the commute was fairly easy for Bob, and the tranquillity of the rural location made a perfect backdrop for him to be able to concentrate on his writing.

1965 started with his final script for *Dr Finlay's Casebook*. This came about after a pointed letter from Bob's agent, Robin Lowe, was sent to Donald Bull on Friday 1 January 1965, asking that Bull keep his client in mind when commissioning new scripts for the show's third series, due to begin on BBC1 later that year. By this time, Bull had moved on and been replaced by Pat Dunlop as story editor. Lowe's letter to Bull was passed on to Dunlop, who was sympathetic to Lowe's request, and duly invited Bob to submit some ideas. However, if Bob did send in any original ideas at this point, then they weren't acted upon. Instead, Bob was asked to play script doctor one more time.

A script entitled 'The Widow's Mite' by Arthur Swinson had been submitted to the *Dr Finlay's Casebook* team in August the previous year. Swinson had written a number of other episodes for the series, had worked extensively in the television industry in the previous decade and, like Bob, had served in Burma during World War II. But the new producer of the series, Gerard Glaister, had a huge list of problems with Swinson's latest script, and decided that someone else needed to give it an overhaul before it was handed it over to the director.

Bob was given Swinson's script and re-wrote it under the new title 'Charity, Dr Finlay'. The episode, credited to Robert Holmes, from a story by Arthur Swinson, was shown on BBC1 on Sunday 14 February 1965; and unlike Bob's previous forays with the series, it is an episode that is still retained in the archives of the Corporation.

The episode revolved around the eponymous doctor befriending a young girl, Jeannie, who is accused of shoplifting from the village greengrocer. Being a kindly soul, he gets the charges against her dropped, and also gets her a job at a local old folk's care home, St Bride's, at which he has also just taken responsibility for the residents' welfare. Finlay is alarmed at the state of care the residents are receiving under the penny-pinching auspices of Matron Meiklejohn, the 'old bissum' in charge of the home. Meiklejohn resents Finlay's intrusion into her affairs, and when she suspects that Jeannie has stolen a pie from the kitchen's larder, dismisses her without pay. Jeannie runs off after stealing a small amount of money from Meiklejohn's desk, along with her bank account savings book. Finlay tracks Jeannie down and retrieves both the money and the savings book. Finlay's colleague, Dr Cameron, notices that there is quite a tidy sum sitting in Meiklejohn's account, and realises that she's been siphoning off funds from the committee running the home, headed by one Lady Fitzwilliam, with the help of the local greengrocer, who's been submitting falsified invoices and then getting backhanders from Meiklejohn in return. Dr Cameron forces Meiklejohn to quietly return the money to the kitty, and also to drop the charges of theft against Jeannie, in return for him not getting the authorities involved in investigating her scam.

Bob's script is full of the old-world charm that was key to the success of *Dr Finlay's Casebook*, but also has some deft dialogue written for the established characters of Drs Cameron and Finlay. 'Matron, you are a hypocrite and you are also a thief. And I dislike the first the more,' Dr Cameron sternly tells Meiklejohn at the episode's conclusion.

Unfortunately for the BBC, they didn't do their usual negative checks on the characters in the script, to ensure that there were no real-life individuals with the same names. So they were rather caught out a few weeks after the episode was screened when the solicitor for the real-life Earl and Countess Fitzwilliam contacted the BBC's legal department and complained in the strongest possible terms about the use of his client's name in the script. Threatened with a charge of libel, the BBC's solicitors asked the acting Head of Drama, Andrew Osborn, to investigate why the standard production process had seemingly not been followed during the production of this episode. In the meantime, the BBC slapped an immediate ban on the sale of the episode overseas by BBC Enterprises, and issued a full apology to the Earl and Countess Fitzwilliam. The master transmission videotape of the episode was subsequently altered to remove any mention of 'Lady Fitzwilliam', the name 'Mrs Jean Smithers' being clumsily overdubbed. New 16mm film prints were then made for overseas sale.[53]

Bob then briefly returned to ATV's *Emergency Ward 10* in early 1965. He wrote four episodes, all under his William Hood *nom-de-plume*, which were screened in March and April 1965. *TV Weekly* had a cryptic plot description for only the second of these four: 'Edwin Firbank pulls the long bow beyond

53 The episode was subsequently repeated – with the required re-dubbed dialogue – by the BBC on Friday 30 July 1965, and was then sold overseas to Zambia and Kenya in February 1967, and to Singapore in October 1975.

breaking point, aided and abetted by Doctor Large and Doctor Murad.'[54] No other details are known.

It's unclear why Bob used his pen name for these episodes – perhaps he didn't want people in the television industry to associate him with this series any longer?[55]

The British television landscape had dramatically shifted in the previous 12 months or so. The BBC's second television channel, BBC2, had gone on air in April 1964, giving viewers in the UK three channels to choose to watch. The increase in airtime that the second BBC channel afforded meant that the Corporation were on the lookout for new ideas and new programmes to fill this void. *Doctor Who* had begun on BBC1 in November 1963. It followed in a long tradition of BBC science fiction serials that had started in the late 1950s with *Quatermass* and followed through with programmes such as *A for Andromeda* (1961) and its sequel *The Andromeda Breakthrough* (1962). The BBC had also occasionally been known to put on short, self-contained serials of a similar genre, from Nigel Kneale's *The Creature* (1955) to the four-part offering *The Monsters* (1962). BBC2 was also looking to begin a science fiction anthology drama series, under the title *Out of the Unknown*.

This was the backdrop that led Bob to decide that he wanted to try his hand at writing something a lot more fantastical.

In early 1965, Bob had an idea for a science fiction story which he thought he'd try his luck with at the BBC. As he later recalled in a 1985 interview with *Doctor Who Magazine*, this storyline led to his first involvement with the series he would later become inexorably linked with over the next 20 years – *Doctor Who*. 'I sent the idea in, not as a *Doctor Who*, but I sent it to the Drama Department as a story called "The Space Trap", for inclusion in a series they were doing of four-part science fiction thrillers, because I thought it was a suitable idea. Then I got a letter back from Shaun Sutton, the Head of Serials at that time, saying that they had decided to discontinue this series, and he'd passed the idea on to *Doctor Who*.'[56]

There are no known copies of this standalone submission, but the anecdotal recollections of those who remember it indicate that it involved a stranded space ship that analysed the various life forms it encountered in the hope that one of them would be of sufficient intelligence to aid its crew, who were kept

54 For Episode 1973, transmitted on 16 March 1965; *TV Weekly*, w/c 13 March.1965.
55 The four William Hood episodes of *Emergency Ward 10* were screened by ATV on 12 March, 16 March, 2 April and 6 April 1965.
56 Interview – Robert Holmes, *Doctor Who Magazine* Issue 100, May 1985. This does, however, seem very similar to what happened in 1960, when Donald Wilson turned down Bob's idea for a six-part science fiction story, so it is perhaps possible that Bob was misremembering the sequence of events here. Alternatively, it could be that the idea Bob submitted in 1965 was a reworking of his 1960 proposal.

alive in a state of suspended animation. This would certainly tie in with the later, *Doctor Who*-ised version of the storyline.

Bob wasn't initially thrilled to be dealing with the makers of *Doctor Who*. 'I was not a keen watcher of *Doctor Who* before I began writing for it,' he noted in a separate interview, 'but I watched it occasionally. As a bit of a science fiction buff I always found it something of a disappointment in its early days.'[57]

Nevertheless, Bob duly got in contact with *Doctor Who*'s story editor, Donald Tosh, who had only just joined the programme himself, and the two of them met up for a chat on Friday 23 April 1965. Tosh seemed interested in Bob's idea, so Bob spent that weekend revising his storyline to incorporate the Doctor (as played by William Hartnell) and his companions.[58] Bob sent his revised storyline back to Tosh a couple of days later, on Sunday 25 April 1965, as a potential four-part story. It was actually untitled at this point, but would become known as 'The Space Trap' when it took on a new incarnation in later years. It read as follows:[59]

Following our meeting on Friday I thought about the new image of Dr Who and eventually came up with an idea that I hope might be an acceptable blasting-off point.

On an uninhabited planet the travellers find a great space craft. They approach it cautiously but can detect no sign of life within. Vegetation has grown up around it in a way that indicates it may have lain there for centuries.

Growing bolder, they move still nearer, start searching for the entrance hatch. Inside the space ship a dynamo purrs into life. A robot-figure in the control room moves a switch and Dr Who and his companions flicker into vision on the television scanners, etc ...

Anyway, after a bit of this sort of thing, the travellers find themselves briefly surrounded by a thin, clammy mist which seems to come from

---

57 Robert Holmes Interview, *Type 40*: Issue 1, 1978.
58 This was about the time that the story 'The Chase' was in production, and the final stories for *Doctor Who*'s second season were all by now fully commissioned. Holmes's outline makes specific mention of the fact that there were to be three companions, as it probably wasn't fully known what the ongoing companion characters were going to be at this point. Vicki (Maureen O'Brien) would have certainly been one of the companions Bob was given to work with, possibly alongside Ian (William Russell) and Barbara (Jacqueline Hill). A new male companion, Michael Taylor (later renamed Steven Taylor and played by Peter Purves) was being developed at this point in time to replace Ian, who was due to leave at the end of 'The Chase'. Quite late in the day, it was decided to write out Barbara at the same time. *If* the story had gone ahead, it would have probably taken up one of the slots in *Doctor Who*'s third season that was eventually occupied by either 'Galaxy 4' or 'The Myth Makers', where the TARDIS crew would have been the Doctor, Steven and Vicki. Bob already knew a little of this change of line-up, because he noted (by hand) on his typed manuscript that the TARDIS crew no longer numbered four. Presumably, had the story gone ahead at this time, it would have been tweaked so that the humanoids would now require only two new recruits, rather than three.
59 All spellings and punctuation are as per Robert Holmes's original manuscript.

nowhere and disperses as mysteriously as it appears. At first, they feel no ill effects and press on in their search for the entrance.

Actually, they have been enveloped in an amnesia gas which progressively anaesthetises their memory cells. They forget their most recently acquired skills and knowledge first, then their purpose, what they are supposed to be doing, who they are, where they come from – gradually it all goes until they are reduced to a state of almost infantile helplessness.

Then they are collected by two Robots and taken into the ship.

In the next episode they find themselves being weighed and measured and scientifically examined in a number of ways. The temporary effects of the gas are now wearing off. The Robots offer no explanation of what is happening. They make two or three attempts to escape but their actions always seem to be anticipated. When they need food and drink they have to 'win' it through intelligence and manual dexterity; they realise they are being treated like chimpanzees in London Zoo.

In the third episode the humanoid controllers of the space ship wake from their state of suspended animation and we get an explanation of the set up.

Thousands of years earlier the ship had been cruising through space when it had run into a galactic ionization belt – or whatever. The brutal deceleration involved had split the ship's thermal shield, killing five of the eight man (woman or mixed) crew. They had to make an emergency landing on this deserted planet to carry out the necessary repairs.

When these had been completed however, they faced the problem of handling a fresh blast-off with only three crew members – a complicated operation physically possible only for a crew twice their number. The Robots, pre-tracked to perform only a certain number of functions, could not be utilised; in any case, they had built-in governors precluding them from being adapted to carry out humanoid tasks.

The solution had been that the humanoids had put themselves into suspended animation, prepared to wait for thousands or millions of years, while the Robots maintained a lonely sentinel duty – pre-tracked to catch any sentient creature that might stray near the space craft during the rest of time.

The Robots were charged to obtain three such captives, possessing a certain minimum level of manual and mental ability, enough to fit them for training in crew duties, before re-animating their humanoid masters.

In a word, Dr Who and his companions have been press-ganged and now find themselves facing the prospect of a long trip to a distant planet and with no hope of ever returning to the Tardis.

Before the ship can take-off, however, they have first to be trained in their flight duties. And as there are four of them (and the humanoids only require the services of three) they discover that at the end of the training period the least proficient of them will be bumped off. The humanoids are quite without sentiment.

In the end, of course, they manage to sabotage the ship and make their escape. There are two or three ways that occur to me in which this might be done, but I don't want to go into great detail at this preliminary stage.

The best point of the idea, to my mind, is that it gets away from the usually pattern up to now – in part, at any rate – so that Dr Who & Co. have only themselves to worry about. If you think there is anything worth discussing here, please drop me a line and I will come in and elaborate madly.

Donald Tosh liked Bob's story, but both he and producer John Wiles feared that the role of the robots in it was perhaps too similar to that of the Mechonoids in Terry Nation's 'The Chase'. Nevertheless, Tosh asked Bob to keep working on ideas for the series, and sent some updated notes on new characters that were due to be introduced. Bob never did follow up with any more ideas at this time – he was presumably sidetracked by other projects (probably writing scripts for *Public Eye*) – but his storyline was kept on file by Tosh at the *Doctor Who* production office.

This was almost Bob's last dealing with the BBC for some years. He unsuccessfully pitched some story ideas to the producers of a BBC drama series called *The Flying Swan* at the same time as he was talking to the *Doctor Who* team. This was set in a hotel in the Midlands and starred the real-life mother and daughter duo of Margaret and Julia Lockwood. The programme's script editor, John Barber, asked Bob on Monday 26 April 1965 to come up with a submission. Bob sent something to Barber, but no copy exists. Whatever it contained, it was deemed unsuitable, and was formally rejected in August 1965.

However, Bob's script-doctoring skills were briefly required once more by the BBC in the summer of 1965. The Corporation was getting ready to launch a new upmarket 30-minute twice-weekly soap opera set in a swish London apartment block in Kensington. It was to go by the title of *199 Park Lane* (the address of the fictional apartment block in question). In August 1965, the programme's script editor, Richard Beynon, asked Bob to rewrite some of the scripts for the early episodes.

During June and July 1965, Bob got to work rewriting the scripts for the tenth, eleventh and twelfth episodes (which were subsequently shown on BBC1 on Friday 3, Tuesday 7 and Friday 10 September 1965 respectively). Beynon was more than happy with Bob's work, and commissioned him on Friday 4 June 1965 to write four episodes of *199 Park Lane* in his own right. The four scripts were to be for episodes 27 and 28 (due to be shown on Tuesday 2 and Friday 5 November 1965) and episodes 41 and 42 (due to be shown on Tuesday 21 and Friday 24 December 1965). However, *199 Park Lane* proved to be something of a flop, and only 18 episodes were ever made and shown by the BBC before it was cancelled and disappeared from the screens without much fanfare. Bob was apologetically paid off for the work he'd done.[60]

Bob had various other television play or series ideas during the mid-1960s, none of which seems to have been given any degree of consideration by either the BBC or the independent television network. None of them is dated in Bob's files.

Crabtree's Kingdom was an idea for a comedy series of 30-minute episodes set in the fictional village of Oxetter. It revolves around the character of Maurice Crabtree, the newly-arrived village policeman, who has moved to Oxetter dreaming of an easy, idyllic, country village life, with nothing more to concern himself with than clipping the ear of scallywags who scrump apples from the orchard. When he arrives in his new job, he takes the local ne'er-do-well, Percy, under his wing. The pair of them would then get involved in some kind of comedic derring-do or scheme during each weekly episode. A small cast of local village characters was also drawn up by Bob, with two or three of them scheduled to appear in each episode.

Also from this period, Bob began work on a script entitled *My Neighbours Whispered Behind My Back*. It begins with a character by the name of Wilfred Strongwater being acquitted of an unspecified crime at a magistrates' court, then being smuggled out of the building by a hack newspaper reporter, Rollo Faraday. Faraday gets Strongwater back home without being seen, and tells him his newspaper want his story as an exclusive – the headline will be 'My Neighbours Whispered Behind My Back'[61]. The script, however, stops at page five – where Bob was going with this story will never be revealed.

Similarly curtailed is a five-page untitled script that tells of the first meeting

---

60 Not one of the 18 transmitted episodes of this series survives at the BBC.
61 *My Neighbours Whispered Behind My Back* sounds just like the sort of title that *Public Eye* would use for an episode – was this what Bob was writing here?

of two men who are looking to share a flat together. Stanley Hutchinson is aged 20 and rather naive, while Gavin Flowerdew is written as being slightly older and is given some slyly camp dialogue by Bob. The script mainly concerns itself with the two men getting acquainted for the first time – whether or not they would have eventually ended up sharing the flat is uncertain.

Another untitled series proposal of Bob's, which looks to be from the mid-1960s, focuses on an ex-policeman who's just finished serving a prison sentence for a crime he did not commit. 'Money changed hands when Harry Foy went to prison. The two screws who stood beside him in the dock had to have some interest to keep them awake. "Shameful betrayal of the high and honourable traditions of the Metropolitan Police," said the Judge. "Conspiring with criminals to pervert the course of justice ... corrupt and despicable ... show no leniency ... five years." The screw on Foy's left gave a faint grunt of satisfaction. Another half-dollar. He reckoned five years all along. Harry Foy earned his full remission. He served four years of that sentence. Our series begins on the day he gets back to London. The day he stops being a victim and becomes a hunter. At this time he is 32 years old. His mind has curdled with bitterness. His dreams, hopes and ambitions have crumbled into dust. He lives now with just one fixed purpose – to find out who it was that framed him. This is the obsession that drives Harry Foy, dominating every conscious moment of his life. On the day that he finds the person responsible, if he ever does, it is quite probable that he will become a murderer.'

On Thursday 9 December 1965, Bob had another go at interesting the BBC in one of his ideas for *The Wednesday Play*, writing in a letter to script editor Tony Garnett: 'Although we haven't met, I am taking the liberty of submitting this play outline, *The Perfect Murderer*, in the hope that it might appeal to you and that there is still room in your programme schedules. The basic idea is a bit horrific, as you will see, but I think a very stylised treatment would counterbalance this and turn it into a slightly macabre comedy.'

The Perfect Murderer begins with two business partners, Daniel Chinnor and Edward Polkington, at loggerheads with each other over the multi-million pound business they own equal shares in. Each has tried, unsuccessfully, to buy the other out in the past, leading to a bitter feud between them. One day, Polkington discovers the dead body of a tramp on his estate, and arranges for Chinnor to be kidnapped by his housekeeper. The dead tramp is given Chinnor's clothes, and his body is dumped in Polkington's car and then set alight. Chinnor is then kept captive in a small cage by Polkington's housekeeper, while Polkington is arrested and charged with Chinnor's murder. His plan is to stand trial for the murder, and if acquitted, he will then be free to kill off his business partner and take full control of his company. Even if Chinnor's body is subsequently found, Polkington knows he cannot stand trial for the same crime twice. If, however, he is found guilty of killing Chinnor, then all he has to do is get his housekeeper to release Chinnor, which will prove that no crime was committed in the first place, and he will again be acquitted. At the end of the trial, Polkington is found guilty, and so Chinnor is released by the housekeeper … only to fail to return to his own house. Chinnor's daughter takes full control of the company after Polkington's trial. Polkington's housekeeper visits her some weeks later and asks her where her father is. She just about keeps a straight face when she points out that he should know, as his employer is behind bars for her father's murder. But on the wall behind her is a postcard from Chinnor, who is now living luxuriously – but anonymously – in the French Riviera.

It's a good, witty, well-plotted storyline, but it didn't get very far. Garnett had a full contingent of scripts to take him up to the end of the current run of *The Wednesday Play*, which was set to conclude later that month, after which a new production team were due to take over. Garnett did pass the storyline on to David Benedictus at the BBC's Script Unit, but Benedictus adjudged it too similar to another that was currently under commission by the BBC. It was left to Robin Wade, a script supervisor at the BBC, to write to Bob on Wednesday 29 December 1965 and inform him that the BBC were rejecting his idea.

CHAPTER FIVE
HIDING IN PUBLIC
1965-1968

Back in the 1960s, Independent Television (ITV) was a vastly different beast from the national network it is today. It began life as a group of regional broadcasters that shared programmes between them, but each controlled their own regional broadcasts. These regions had all started broadcasting separately at different times, beginning in 1955 and going through to 1962, when the last went on air. Alongside these, Incorporated Television Company (ITC), helmed by Lew Grade, had tried and failed to acquire one of the original regional television broadcast licences, and so had instead started making its own programmes, which it then sold to other ITV regional broadcasters. However, it very quickly formed links with Associated Television (ATV) in the early 1960s, when ATV ran into funding trouble.[62]

All of which meant that, in terms of ITV companies, the big players were Rediffusion, ABC, ATV, and Granada. Bob had already worked for the latter two, and was about to work for the remaining two.

Public Eye was an Associated British Corporation (ABC) Television series created by writers Roger Marshall and Anthony Marriott, who wanted to get away from the traditional square-jawed heroes who seemed to populate most films and television programmes of the time. The series starred Alfred Burke as Frank Marker, a middle aged, down-on-his-heels private detective. The early promotional trailer for the series explained: 'Marker isn't a glamorous detective and he doesn't get glamorous cases – he doesn't even get glamorous girls! What he does get is people who are in trouble – the sort of trouble you can't go to the police about, even if you *are* innocent.'

Bob wrote scripts for two episodes of the programme's first season. The first was 'And A Very Fine Fiddle Has He', which was shown on ABC on Saturday 13 March 1965.[63] The episode was described in the ABC publicity blurb of the time: 'Robert Spanier hopes to become an MP. He is sorting out his divorce but his sponsor Mrs Sutton-Piper assures him of support provided he avoids further problems. Then he receives a blackmail letter alleging perjury ...' *TV World*, the television listings magazine that replaced *TV Times* in the

---

62 This is a *huge* simplification of what actually happened with ATV/ITC, but you get the idea.
63 This episode was also shown by STV and UTV on this date; other regions screened it later, going right into October 1965 in some cases.

Midlands for a number of years in the 1960s, had a rather more surreal take on the episode: 'Wed; Light Lunch. Halston, solicitor, at 2.30 pm. Wealthy client being blackmailed: nasty world – nasty business.'[64]

The second of Bob's episodes, 'You Think It'll Be Marvellous – But It's Always A Rabbit', was shown on Saturday 27 March 1965: 'Footballer Jimmy Sale is injured by a hit-and-run driver and resorts to Frank after becoming dissatisfied with the police investigation. It is not just the driver who hopes to avoid the truth being uncovered.'[65] Or, as *TV World* had it: 'Tuesday 2.15; James Sale, Ward C, County Hospital. "Hit and run – says the law's shelved the case. 18,000 cops can't work it, will I – he's joking!"'

By contrast to the newly-launched *Public Eye*, *No Hiding Place* was a long-running Rediffusion crime drama series. The series had begun in 1957, and followed the many cases of Detective Chief Superintendent Tom Lockhart, played by Raymond Francis. Each self-contained 60-minute episode featured a new case for the police sleuth and his team. In 1965, the script editor of the series was Louis Marks, whom Bob would almost certainly have got to know when writing for both *Deadline Midnight* and *Ghost Squad* a few years earlier – Marks had also written for both series.

Bob was asked by Marks to write two scripts for the seventh series of *No Hiding Place*. The first, 'Blood and Water', was shown on ATV on Monday 15 March 1965, while the second, 'A Cry for Help', was shown on Monday 21 June 1965. Neither of these episodes survives, although Bob did keep a copy of his script for 'A Cry for Help'.[66]

'A Cry for Help' revolves around Cochrane, a jilted husband who phones up a Samaritans-style helpline and threatens to kill himself unless his wife, Margot is persuaded to return to him. He tells them where they can reach Margot, and then rings off. Margot is contacted by the helpline, and returns home, only to find her husband lying dead. She tells the police that she doesn't think he killed himself, insisting that he has been murdered. Lockhart discovers that Margot was about to leave Cochrane, who was a crime journalist on a Fleet Street tabloid. Margot's story doesn't convince the police, and she confesses to her boss, Lacey, that she found and destroyed a suicide note from Cochrane before the police arrived on the scene. Lockhart discovers that the

64 *TV World*, w/c 13 March 1965.
65 Neither of these episodes of *Public Eye* survives in the archive of Lumiere, the company that acquired the remains of the ABC archive in the 1990s. In fact only five episodes out of 41 in total from the first three ABC seasons of *Public Eye* survive at Lumiere; and none of them was written by Bob.
66 When Associated Rediffusion ceased trading in 1968, the vast majority of its archive of films and videotapes was destroyed. What little remains of its television output now resides at the BFI National Archive. Only around 20 episodes from the entire run of *No Hiding Place* survive. Over 200 episodes of the series, including all of those written by Bob, are now missing.

insurance policy Cochrane had taken out on himself will now pay Margot very handsomely, and he gets suspicious of her account of the events of the night of her husband's death. Lockhart discovers that Margot had been having an affair with Lacey, and was at his house, alone, the night Cochrane died. He also discovers that Lacey was involved in a dodgy property business, which Cochrane was going to expose in his newspaper column. One of Cochrane's newspaper colleagues, Beale, discovers the details of the property story, and attempts to blackmail Lacey, who agrees to pay him off. But Beale passes all the details to Lockhart, and Lacey is arrested for Cochrane's murder.

Bob's old colleague from his magazine days, Robert Banks Stewart, was by now also making his name in the television industry. Stewart had found some success at ABC writing scripts for *The Avengers*, and had managed to persuade them to make a science fiction series he had devised: *Undermind*.

Undermind followed the exploits of brother-in-law and sister-in-law Drew and Anne Heriot (Jeremy Wilkin and Rosemary Nichols), who unearth a plot by a mysterious alien force that seems to be mentally influencing those under its control to undermine Earth's politics and economy (hence the title of the show). The series followed their attempts to alert the authorities of this threat. Stewart asked Bob to write for the series, and this gave him his first opportunity to write science fiction for the small screen.

'I started on it in 1964,' recalls Robert Banks Stewart. 'It's one of the earliest sci-fi television series, but I didn't really think of it like that. People were taken over by some kind of strange manifestation … I mean I'm not even sure I can give you an explanation of it myself! I took it to ABC Television, where George Kerr was Head of Drama, and I put the idea up before him, and he said, "Oh, we love it!" And all of a sudden I found myself not only being the creator of a television series, but also story editor, with Michael Chapman as the producer. So anyway, at that point I knew Bob Holmes well, and we'd obviously become friends and colleagues, so I would have said, "Hey, come on Bob, I've got this commission to do this series, why don't you write one or two episodes."'

Bob wrote what proved to be the final two episodes of the programme's 11-week run. These were 'Waves of Sound', which was shown on ABC on Saturday 10 July 1965, and 'End Signal', which was shown the following week, on Saturday 17 July 1965.

'Waves of Sound' follows Anne and Drew as they investigate the link between an old vaudevillian performer-turned-cornflake-salesman to a clinic in Tunbridge Wells, where they uncover a plot to unleash a new strain of 'flu virus upon the world, which will make the population of the planet more susceptible to the aliens' brainwashing signal. The episode ends with the aliens' plan to infect the population thwarted, while Anne and Drew also manage to get hold of a list of names and addresses of everyone currently under the aliens' control. Bill Edmund, writing a few weeks later in *The Stage and Television Today*, said of this episode: 'The only thing I don't like about ABC's *Undermind* is the way Anne and Drew Heriot seem to choose the most wooden-headed officials to tell their suspicions to. It seems a pity that they can't meet one with a little more of the old common. I was glad to see George Moon as James and Ruth Denning as Dr Whittaker who gave good performances as two of the latest baddies in "Waves of Sound" by Robert Holmes. They died the death at the end of the play but they made their presence felt first.'[67]

The final episode, 'End Signal', follows the efforts of the authorities to block the aliens' signal and round up those already under its influence, using the list found by Anne and Drew in the previous instalment. However, Anne and Drew are targeted for assassination by those who are already under the signal's control. They discover that the names and addresses on the list have all been switched for those of innocent people, meaning that the people controlled by the alien signal are all still at liberty. Anne and Drew think they've tracked them down to a resort on the Isle of Skye, but realise they are on a wild goose chase. They head back to London, where a final confrontation between the pair and an unmasked agent of the Undermind aliens ends with the next scheduled signal from space being successfully blocked, ending the menace for good.

Bob kept his rehearsal script for this episode, and the differences between it and the transmitted episode are interesting to note. The episode begins with one of the controlled suspects being arrested and taken away by the authorities; in the televised version, it's a Mrs Smith, but in Bob's script, it's a Mr Wyatt. A scene where Drew and Anne are attacked by a man brandishing a spear gun was scripted as ending with a spear being shot from the gun, narrowly missing the pair and shattering a nearby fish tank. As seen on screen, though, the spear whizzes harmlessly over their heads and the nearby tank fails to shatter. However, the final scene of the episode-as-screened, where Drew and Anne realise that the threat is over and they go their separate ways, is not present at all in Bob's script.[68]

Robert Banks Stewart explains why it was left to Bob to write the final episodes of the series: 'I was offered the producership of another project by ABC Television. It was originally called *The Spy Next Door*, and then we called it *Intrigue*, or something like that. So what happened was that I was offered the producership of that series, and so I didn't have time to write the final two

67 *The Stage and Television Today*, 25 September 1965.
68 The whole series of *Undermind* survives in the archives of Lumiere and has been released on DVD by Network – Lumiere acquired what remained of the ABC television archive in the 1990s.

scripts of *Undermind*. I wouldn't know at that point what Bob was doing, I would have just rung him and discussed with him how to wrap it up. I seem to remember he liked *Undermind* …'

It was during 1965 that Bob had his one and only brush with feature films.[69] Roger Marshall, who had worked with Bob on *Knight Errant* and *Emergency Ward 10*, was now involved with Merton Park Studios, who were at the time based in Wimbledon, South London, and were going through a last-gasp attempt to keep in business.

'Bob and I both worked on *Emergency Ward 10* for a spell in 1963,' recalls Marshall. 'While doing this, we both got to know the medical advisor, Dr Phyllis Gibbons. She and Bob were always doodling sci-fi ideas. This was never my scene, so I left 'em to it. Then they produced the *Invasion* idea, which was very medical in context. Bob took it to Jack Greenwood at Merton Park, where I'd been working off and on for some years, doing an Edgar Wallace-type of one hour movies. For some reason, Jack was wary of using Bob as the writer because he'd never worked "on film". I was out there for some reason and he asked me if I'd do the screenplay. I told him Bob was a good mate and that would not be easy. He seemed determined that Bob wouldn't do it, and if I said no, then he'd find someone who'd say yes. I called Bob straight away. Predictably he was very sweet, saying he was glad it was me, rather than somebody else. I think I would have been a lot less philosophical. To know Bob you have to appreciate that in his laid back, pipe-smoking way he was never terribly ambitious. I always felt he should have pushed himself harder and done better things. Bob and I talked it through and he said, "Do it, but involve Phyllis." Knowing of Phyllis's contribution to the original story, and it's a very medical sci-fi subject, I went straight back to her and we did the script virtually together. In its way it was a great success: it cost very little and still pops up on BBC TV occasionally. (I made precisely £990 out of it!) I have absolutely no recollection of whether we'd kept to the storyline or changed it. Similarly I have no idea how much was me and how much was Bob. I didn't watch any shooting. Merton Park wasn't that sort of outfit. It was all very "get on and get it done."'[70]

The film, titled *Invasion*, was given a U certificate by the British Board of Film Classification in October 1965.[71] Made in black and white, and running to 77 minutes, it tells the story of a mysterious flying object that crashes into

---

69 A Robert Holmes received a 'Thanks to …' credit at the end of the truly dire 1982 Cannon and Ball film *The Boys in Blue*, for reasons unknown, but it is not entirely clear if this is 'our' Robert Holmes. Perhaps Bob supplied the producers or writers with some of his own tales of life on the beat?

70 Private correspondence with Colin Brockhurst dated 23 June 1992.

71 The film's credits read: 'Screenplay by Roger Marshall, from an original story by Robert Holmes'.

woods near a rural hospital. A couple out in their car at night hit a man in strange clothing and take him, unconscious, to the hospital. The doctor treating the man realises that his patient isn't human. The hospital is then surrounded by a force field that prevents anyone from leaving, as the alien patient reveals he was a prisoner on the downed spaceship. He took advantage of the crash to escape his captors, who are portrayed as oriental-looking female aliens.

The mainly British cast were all solid performers with good television and film experience behind them, but there were no real star names to pull in the audiences. Standout names in the cast (albeit with the benefit of hindsight) include Edward Judd, Barrie Ingham (fresh from his role as Alydon in the big-screen adaptation *Dr Who and the Daleks*), Glyn Houston and the fine comedy-character actor Norman Mitchell. To say that *Invasion* was something of an underwhelming film is perhaps damning it too much, as it boasts reasonable production values for its day, and workable performances from its cast. But it failed to make much of an impact, mainly due to being made in black and white, and it remains something of half-forgotten curiosity today.[72]

Bob briefly returned to magazine writing in late 1965, although in a wholly television-related way. During the 1960s, the regional ITV franchises were initially covered by regional editions of *TV Times*, the television listings magazine that gave upcoming details about the next seven days of ITV programming. But in 1965, the Midlands edition of *TV Times* was scrapped, and a new title, *TV World*, was launched to take its place. Published by Odhams, the firm that used to employ Bob on *John Bull* magazine, *TV World* was shamelessly pro-ATV, giving over most of its page-count to coverage of the weekly schedule from the weekday Midlands broadcaster. The weekend output for that region, provided by ABC at the time, was given the bare minimum of coverage. Given its strong ATV links, the magazine was an occasional haven for a television scriptwriter such as Bob. One of its back-up features was a weekly short story, usually in two, three, or four parts, that related a new off-screen adventure featuring a popular television character of the day.

Danger Man was a hugely successful ITC/Pimlico Films spy thriller that starred Patrick McGoohan as the titular hero (prior to him appearing in *The Prisoner* a couple of years later). Despite not having written for the series, Bob wrote a short three-part *Danger Man* story for *TV World*, titled 'Shark Bait: Nightmare on the Bend of Death'. The introduction to the second instalment of the story explained: 'A British agent named Miles disappears

---

72 I'm contractually obliged to observe at this point – as everyone who has seen *Invasion* invariably does – that sections of this film's plot were reused wholesale by Bob when writing his script for the *Doctor Who* story that would eventually become 'Spearhead from Space' in 1969.

ROBERT HOLMES: A LIFE IN WORDS

in Yugoslavia. John Drake is recalled from holiday and sent to find him – or to take his place. Harris – who briefs Drake on his mission – says that Miles had been waiting for a Russian bio-chemist called Vorov. The Russian was in Albania, working against his will for the Chinese and Albanian governments. Vorov now plans to defect, says Harris, and is bringing over a sample of some new gas or virus the Chinese have developed. Before leaving England, Drake goes to the Midlands factory of a hardware company. Miles was ostensibly the company's representative in the Balkans, and Drake will purport to work for the same firm. Once he reaches Belgrade, Harris says, Drake will find a local agent named Shastrif waiting …'[73]

The Plane Makers was a popular ITV series made by ATV, which ran from 1963 to 1965, and told the story of the struggles between the shop-floor unions and the management of a fictional aircraft manufacturing factory. The standout character of the series was John Wilder, played by Patrick Wymark, who was later spun-off into his own series *The Power Game* (1965-69). Bob never wrote for either *The Plane Makers* or *The Power Game*, but he did write a three-part short story for *TV World* featuring John Wilder.[74] The story-so-far blurb for the final instalment ran: 'John Wilder had returned to Drayton Barr where his father had been a doctor. He was there as a Director of Elbertson's – a London merchant bank – to put through a take-over deal which the bank was underwriting. Finlayson's, a small family firm, was vitally important to the expansion plans of the bank's clients, Merrimen Limited. But they had already rejected a million pound offer made by Merrimen's representative, O'Gorman, and Sir Gerald Merle, one of Wilder's fellow Directors. Wilder could not increase the offer. But he could try to make it seem more attractive. He knew these people – Keith Finlayson, the Chairman, was an old enemy. And his wife, Adele Finlayson … Adele was someone to dine alone with in a private room at his hotel …'

Bob rounded off 1965 by penning another episode of *No Hiding Place*, 'Run Johnny, Run', which was shown by ATV on Wednesday 15 December 1965. This episode no longer survives in the ATV television archives, but Bob kept a copy of his script.

'Run Johnny, Run' sees Detective Chief Superintendent Lockhart investigating the fatal shooting of a casino owner called Silver, just as the casino was closing for business in the small hours of the morning. Silver was shot by a local gangster called Goldie Padgett, who had discovered that Silver was having an affair with his girlfriend, Marilyn, a croupier at the casino.

73 'Shark Bait: Nightmare on the Bend of Death' ran in the editions of *TV World* that covered the weeks 7 August 1965-13 August 1965, 14 August.1965-20 August 1965 and 21 August.1965-27 August 1965.
74 '*TV World's* John Wilder Serial' ran in the editions of *TV World* that covered the weeks 27 November 1965-3 December 1965, 4 December.1965-10 December 1965 and 11 December 1965-17 December 1965.

66

Initially, it appears there were no witnesses to the crime, but a gambler at the casino named Johnny Crown saw everything before fleeing through the casino toilet window. Lockhart gets an anonymous tip that Padgett was behind the shooting, and brings him in for questioning. Marilyn warns Johnny that Padgett now suspects him of grassing to the police, and Johnny goes looking for somewhere to lie low, while Padgett's gang begin looking for him in his usual old haunts. Lockhart manoeuvres the barman at the casino into admitting he saw the shooting, and Marilyn is forced to confess the identity of the killer. She admits that Johnny Crown was also at the club, and Lockhart realises that Padgett's gang will be looking for him, thinking he's the informant. Marilyn tells him that Jacko Caulfield, one of Padgett's men, was the real grass behind the anonymous tip. Lockhart and his men find Padgett's gang just as they are about to ambush Johnny Crown, and arrest them all.

The episode's script is littered with numerous examples of risqué cockney rhyming slang, and Bob also smuggles in a few near-the-knuckle phrases. At one point, a character refers to glamour-girl Marilyn as 'Goldie's bit of Khyber', while Johnny insults an immigrant café owner by saying, 'Your nosh gives me the apple fritters.' All-in-all, 'Run Johnny, Run' is a piece of writing that seems very ahead of its time.

During December 1965, Bob worked to formulate his own idea for a television series, which he tried to interest Rediffusion Television in making. His title for the series was *Time Over Again*, and the basic premise was contained in a two-page format document that he prepared for their consideration.

The basic idea of *Time Over Again* is a very simple one: it is to trace the course of a man's professional career and private life through a television series.

The man could be a politician, a journalist, an industrialist – anyone who treads an adventurous or precarious path. William Jago, however, is a policeman.

I believe that in terms of audience-appeal, policemen still top the ratings. Everyone is interested in a policeman's business life. And in terms of our format, Jago's occupation has these other advantages:

1) It is reasonable to assume that in 25 years he would play a dramatic part in several exciting cases; therefore, stories and scripts can be contributed by other writers.

2) Policemen are able to retire after 25 years' service. A man's appearance need not necessarily alter greatly during that span of time.

3) During their service, police officers – particularly successful

ones – are moved around a good deal; therefore it will not be necessary for Jago's colleagues to be running characters.

The series will cover the years between 1935 and 1960 when Jago retired as a Detective Chief Inspector. This means, assuming it is planned to produce 13 episodes, that there will be a fictional time-lapse of roughly two years between each episode.

Obviously, crime will form a large part of the content of the episodes but it will not be a conventional thriller series. There will be scope to portray Jago's human problems, his marriage, his divorce, his financial difficulties or whatever, set against the pressures of his work. It will also show something of the internal rivalries and politics in Jago's chosen profession.

I believe that by developing in depth in this way, the series will become more entertaining and exciting than it would if restricted to a straightforward crime format. During its course there will be changes in moral values, social standards, and the central character. It will not be static.

As a simple instance, the ingenious youngster of 1937 might trust a crook and suffer disastrous consequences. By 1957 he is a hard-bitten cynic who refuses to let a prisoner visit his dying wife. We know how he got that way. We have watched his prejudices hardening to match his arteries.

The series will require fairly close editorial control. As a first step, a detailed biography of William Jago will have to be prepared. Contributing writers will use this material mainly as background against which to set their own stories.

It may be that this idea will be considered over-ambitious. But something similar has been attempted in films such as *Giant* and *Goodbye, Mr Chips*. Inevitably, running only two to three hours, these films suffered from the effects of over-compression. It seems to me that television is the ideal medium for this sort of project. The once-weekly slot provides its own illusion of the passage of time.[75]

Bob's agent, Robin Lowe, sent a copy of this proposal to Gervis Frere-Cook at Rediffusion Television, but it would appear his initial reaction was not favourable. Bob then elected to send a copy of the proposal also to Stella

---

75 For those interested in such matters, Bob has by now (1965) written a short story that features a character called Litefoot, and a series proposal that features a character called Jago. His 1977 *Doctor Who* story 'The Talons of Weng-Chiang' would feature two characters with the same names.

Richman at Rediffusion on Friday 3 December 1965. Richman had become Head of Series at Rediffusion in 1964, having previously worked at ATV, where she was in charge of commissioning single plays. Richman's and Bob's paths had probably crossed a few times in the past, so he obviously hoped that this might buy him some favour with her.

> I hope you are now looking for a series to follow *Blackmail*.[76] Anyway, I am enclosing a very brief outline of an idea which I now feel might interest you.
>
> My agent, Robin Lowe, sent a copy of this, hot from the typewriter, to a man at Rediffusion called Fred or Frere (Cook?) earlier this week. But I'd rather have my ideas rejected by someone I know.
>
> I think it has exciting possibilities but I have eschewed any suggestions of a sales pitch in the outline and so I won't start one now.

Richman quite liked Bob's ideas in principle, especially the notion of trying to cover such a long period of time across a 13-episode series. However, she had a problem with the central character being a policeman, thinking that too many drama series at the time relied upon the protagonist being a copper. She encouraged Bob to rethink the career of the central character, and rework his idea. He took her encouragement to heart, and on Saturday 29 January 1966, he wrote back to her:

> I'm glad you like the basic idea of *Time Over Again*. Your objection to a policeman, I imagine, is that the character is a hackneyed one. Presumably, therefore, one can eliminate doctors and lawyers too.
>
> Thinking about the overall shape of the series (in terms of dramatic progression and the development of the character) I am beginning to doubt whether any occupation can legitimately meet all our requirements.
>
> Few people follow a straight path from A to Z. Their lives contain unexpected twists and turns – they're like cyclists zig-zagging up a steep hill, always climbing but not always going straight up. I think it is these twists and turns that produce the surprises and the excitement.
>
> I knew a man who started life as a schoolteacher. Later he became a clergyman and subsequently a prison chaplain. He is now the

---

76 *Blackmail* was a series of plays made by Rediffusion, all revolving around the concept of blackmail or being blackmailed, which Stella Richman had produced during the latter half of 1965. It was considered a success, and a second series was made in 1966. However, it seems that Bob wasn't aware that a second series was on the horizon when he pitched his own series idea to Richman.

governor of a borstal. It's not hard to see a pattern here, a unifying theme that directed the course of his career, but it was not the result of a conscious plan.

What I have tried to do, therefore, is to select prototypes whose careers can develop logically, over 13 episodes, within this sort of overall, unifying theme. I have also tried to find careers that are interesting in themselves, that contain an element of hazard, and that bring the subject into contact and conflict with a wide range of people.

The Hustler: I know that journalists are cliché-characters but, despite this, my first suggestion is that William Jago (or whatever he's called) starts out as a journalist. But then, as so many journalists do, he moves into advertising and the high-pressure life of the big agencies. His first wife might be an artist who's hocked her palette for an air-brush.

Jago then moves to public relations (a world we've not seen on television) and finally sets up his own firm of PR consultants. He becomes an expert apple-polisher, a manipulator of opinion, lending a well-paid hand to all manner of dubious promotions.

There is something ironic in the idea of a man who starts his career trying to tell the world the truth and ends trying to conceal it. Dramatically, it makes a very satisfying shape.

The Politician: Through the OUDS[77] or through the trade union movement – depending on which side of the political fence he sits – Jago develops an interest in politics, an ambition to serve in public life. He gets into Parliament after a time and we trace his progress from backbencher to (Shadow?) Cabinet Minister.

There is a lot of scope here (*No Love For Johnny*[78] type development, backroom deals at Westminster, problems of constituents, etc.) but I imagine the subject might hold problems, ITA-wise[79]. It could, of course, end about 1955. One needn't touch on any current political controversies.

I think it would be a fascinating series to develop. One could show the compromises that a man makes as the years pass, the pressures to do what is expedient rather than what he knows to be right, the gradual fading of his convictions. No-one believes anything as fervently as when they were 20 – I'm sure this goes double for politicians.

The Academic: The cloistered world of a university may not seem

---

77 The OUDS is *probably* the Oxford University Dramatic Society.
78 *No Love For Johnny* was a 1961 film that followed the political fortunes of Labour MP Johnnie Byrne, played by Peter Finch.
79 ITA – The Independent Television Authority – was the supervisory body created in 1954 to look after the ITV network.

immediately attractive. But it does provide all the dramatic unities in a nice, tight framework. It is a microcosm where all the struggles of the wider world are fought out in miniature – and consequently with greater intensity.

Settling for an academic life, Jago would progress from undergraduate to senior tutor. There are too many possible lines of development to go into at this stage, but his private life would obviously be of central importance in such a setting.

The Industrialist (or speculator or budding tycoon): The triumphs, intrigues and double-deals of the business world have been sufficiently well charted, particularly by American novelists, for this to need no elaboration. Certainly there would seem to be ample scope here.

The Gambler: Perhaps this is a wild one but I have just read the biography of a professional gambler named Arthur Rothstein[80]. This is full of riveting material and I'd say that a driving compulsion like his, an obsession that soured all his relationships and brought him time and again to the brink of ruin, would also make gripping television. Provided the character was sympathetic, it would be difficult not to become personally involved in the saga of his changing fortunes.

These five suggestions are my personal short-list. There are many other possible prototypes for a biography series but I believe these offer the greatest promise from the point of view of character development and entertainment potential. However, if I had to make a final choice I would probably settle for either the Hustler or the Gambler. I think this is because – although the action would span a couple of decades or more – both of these seem somehow to be very modern and contemporary characters.

Anyway, I hope one of these suggestions appeals to you enough for me to come and discuss the idea in detail.

Although Rediffusion never commissioned Bob to write or develop this series, Richman was intrigued by the ideas put forward; intrigued enough for her to keep the proposal on file for the next few years. She finally wrote to Bob on 10 May 1968, to return his proposal and paperwork, as she was clearing out her files in preparation for the closure of Rediffusion prior to its merger with ABC.

Sometime during late 1965 or early 1966, it would *appear* that Bob *might*

---

80 It seems that Bob got the gambler's name wrong! He's almost certainly referring to the book *The Big Bankroll: The Life and Times of Arnold Rothstein* by Leo Katcher, which was published in 1959. In fact the book had, by this point in time, already been adapted into a film, entitled *King of the Roaring Twenties*, which was released in 1961.

have been commissioned to write an episode of the ITC series *Danger Man*. At this point, as has been noted, he had already written a three-part John Drake short story for *TV World* magazine in the summer of 1965. Bob retained in his files a script for an episode of *Danger Man*; an episode that was never filmed – or never entered into production – during the programme's run on television. However, the script is missing its first page, which means that the episode title and writer's credit are absent. It would *appear* to be Holmes's work, and there would be very little reason for Bob to retain a script in his files if it wasn't one that he'd actually written. The script is fairly consistent in appearance and layout with other *Danger Man* scripts of this era (1965/6), so it can only be assumed that this is the production period the script hails from. It also features elements very similar to the *TV World* short story that Bob wrote in the summer of 1965, which would again strongly suggest that Bob was the author.

The episode revolves around John Drake's attempts to locate a missing field agent, Hemmings, who may or may not have got hold of a sample of a potentially deadly new virus being developed as a weapon in a secret research facility in Bosnia. Drake locates Hemmings, but discovers that the agent has smuggled the virus out of the laboratory by injecting himself with it. Drake thinks the virus might be fake, nothing more than a propaganda tool, but has to race against time to keep one step ahead of the enemy agents that are pursuing them, and to get Hemmings to medical help.

Bob's writing of an episode of *Danger Man* that didn't eventually make it onto television would neatly explain his apparent lack of activity during the early months of 1966.

On 26 April 1966, Bob celebrated his fortieth birthday.

The first on-screen work of Bob's to be transmitted in 1966 consisted of two more episodes of the Rediffusion series *No Hiding Place*. The first of these, 'The Night Walker', was shown on ATV on Wednesday 15 June 1966, while the next, 'Golden Boy', was shown on ATV on Wednesday 6 July 1966. Neither of these episodes survives in the television archives, but Bob did retain a copy of his script for 'The Night Walker'.

'The Night Walker' begins with Detective Chief Superintendent Lockhart giving evidence at the inquest into the death of a vagrant who was found hanged. Suicide is ruled out, and Lockhart admits that the police are still trying to identify the man. A number of tramps have been found dead in recent weeks in the same manner, and the story begins to make headline news in the papers. One magazine despatches a junior reporter, Dilke, to pose as a tramp for the night to try and get a story about the murders. Dilke in turn hires a freelance photographer, Dennis, to keep tabs on him in order to get pictures for the article.

Meanwhile Lockhart finds another tramp, Bowlder, who claims to have seen the last victim go off in the company of an Indian gentleman from Southampton a few nights earlier. The police see that Bowlder is given a place at a local hostel, where he runs into the Indian man, Ghomboos, whom he had earlier described to the police. The police then arrest Ghomboos. Dilke, dressed as a tramp, goes out on the streets that night, and meets up with a drunken dosser, Mahoney, who steals his cigarette lighter. Mahoney then tries to attack Dilke, but Dilke fends him off. Mahoney falls backwards down some stairs, and breaks his neck. Dennis arrives on the scene, and persuades Dilke to let him take photos for the magazine article. They string up Mahoney to make it look like he was hanged in the same manner as the other victims, photograph the dead tramp, and then flee the scene. But as soon as Dilke's editor sees the photos the next day, she calls the police. Dilke and Dennis are both arrested, and Ghomboos is released. Lockhart questions Dilke and Dennis, and soon learns the truth. He goes in search of Ghomboos, who is soon found dead, killed in the same manner as the other vagrants. Lockhart and his assistant, Det. Sgt. Perryman, then run into Bowlder, who is now wearing Ghomboos's shoes. Bowlder runs away, but is killed when he tries to flee across a train track, being hit by a train when his shoes become stuck in the track.

'Golden Boy' was previewed in the issue of *TV World* published in the week before the episode was screened: '"He liked himself, didn't he? I mean not just a passing infatuation. It was the real thing with Hutch." So when Hutch – part-owner of a man's fashion shop – is found dead, it means that Lockhart can rule out suicide and must look for his killer.'[81]

Bob followed up these two episodes of *No Hiding Place* by writing two more episodes of ABC's *Public Eye*. The first of these, 'It Had to Be a Mouse', was shown on ABC on Saturday 20 August 1966.[82] The ABC publicity blurb says of this episode: 'Puritanical newspaper owner Minster refuses to take an ad for Frank's agency. However his own marital life is in difficulties and he has to recruit Frank to trace his missing wife. Mrs Minster though is not the only person who is being investigated'. *TV World* meanwhile had this surreal preview for the episode: 'Monday. "South Staffs Record." How am I to get business if they don't run an advertisement? I'll take my 25 bob elsewhere.'

The same issue of *TV World* also contained a minor feature to publicise the episode, which included a small quote from Bob: 'Robert Holmes, author of the episode, knows well the ways of local journalism, as he used to work on weeklies in the West Midlands. "I wouldn't say the newspaper pictured here is

---

81 *TV World*, w/c 2 July 1966.
82 Most other ITV regions saw the episode a day earlier, on Friday 19 August 1966.

typical, with its domineering owner and unscrupulous editor, but people like that do exist," he said.'[83]

The second *Public Eye* episode, 'Twenty Pounds of Heart and Muscle', was shown on ABC on Saturday 17 September.[84] 'Frank is employed by Pauline Garrity to search for her father's very valuable racing whippet, which has gone missing. He has his own suspect and may take the law into his own hands unless Frank is successful and soon.'[85] Or, as *TV World* would have it: 'Friday – 9.30. Pauline Garrity – wants me to look for "our Jackie." Haven't read of anyone missing – hope he's not a budgerigar!'[86]

At about this time, Bob switched agents for the first time, moving from Christopher Mann Ltd to Lom Associates in Maddox Street, London, where he was initially looked after by Rae Ellison.

This change of agents coincided with Bob meeting up with producer William 'Bill' Slater to discuss the possibility of him writing for the BBC drama series *Vendetta*, which concerned the anti-Mafia league and was quite a notorious programme at the time. Some confusion arose following this meeting. Bob came away with the impression that although he'd proposed some storylines that were potentially interesting, including one about a lorry driver, nothing further had been agreed or even hinted at. Then, however, he was formally commissioned by Slater on Wednesday 22 June 1966 to write a storyline for a *Vendetta* episode entitled 'The Moonstone Man'. The commissioning letter and paperwork were sent directly to Bob's home address, and as soon as he received them, he rang the BBC, trying to contact Slater. He left a message saying that he didn't know anything about this commission, and asked Slater to contact him. It seems that the message never got through. Bob did, however, pass all the paperwork he'd been sent to his new agents, Lom Associates, who promptly contacted the BBC and haggled a higher fee for him to write the episode!

Weeks passed, and Slater eventually started to panic at the non-arrival of Bob's storyline. He got John Henderson, the BBC's Assistant Head of Copyright, to write to Lom Associates in early September, asking why nothing had been forthcoming. Henderson went on to insist that he had to have the storyline by Sunday 25 September, or else Bob would be found in breach of his contract. Rae Ellison contacted Bob, and it was only then that it was realised

---

83 *TV World*, w/c 20 August 1966.
84 Again, most other ITV regions screened this episode a day earlier, on Thursday 15 September.
85 Neither of these two *Public Eye* episodes survives in the television archives. However, an off-air audio recording of 'Twenty Pounds of Heart and Muscle' was made at the time of transmission. This was included as an extra on the Network DVD release *Public Eye: The Complete 1971 Series*.
86 *TV World*, w/c 17 September 1966.

that there had been a mix-up. Ellison wrote back to the BBC, saying, 'I am afraid that the storyline which he discussed with the editors of this series did not in his opinion work out. In fact, he did discuss several ideas but in the final analysis he was not happy with any of them.' This evidently resolved the matter to everyone's satisfaction.

Bob's final television work in 1966 was writing for another ABC series, *Intrigue*. *Intrigue* was created by writer Tony Williamson, produced by Robert Banks Stewart and starred Edward Judd as investigator Gavin Grant, with Caroline Mortimer as his sidekick, Val. The premise revolved around industrial espionage, but the series never really gripped the public's imagination and was cancelled after just 12 episodes. Bob's episode was the eighth, entitled 'Fifty Million Taste Buds Can't Be Wrong', and was shown on ABC on Saturday 19 November 1966.[87] The edition of *TV World* for that week had this rather enigmatic insight into the episode: '*Trading was bound to be affected by this new form of freezer.* "Don't misunderstand me. He's a splendid chap. Works 19 hours a day making a fortune for us both. He'll be dead in another five years, unfortunately. Treat this as confidential, won't you Grant?"'[88]

1967 began with Bob writing for a Granada series called *Mr Rose*. This was something of a television oddball, as it was the final part of an unplanned trilogy of series that Granada had started in 1960 with *The Odd Man*, a police drama that starred Edwin Richfield but also featured William Mervyn as an occasional character, Chief Inspector Rose, who soon became an established regular. After three years, Rose was given his own series, *It's Dark Outside*. Rose then retired from the police force, and a new series, *Mr Rose*, followed his adventures as he lived in retirement in Eastbourne, writing his memoirs.

Bob wrote two episodes for the first series of *Mr Rose*. The first of these, 'The Jolly Swagman', was shown by Granada on Friday 17 March 1967, and this was followed a week later by the second, 'The Unquiet Ghost', on Friday 24 March 1967.

'The Jolly Swagman' reuses certain elements from Bob's pitch for *The Wednesday Play*, 'Plunkett-Bream Was Six Foot Four', in that it's a witty heist caper set on board a cruise ship. Mr Rose, along with a retired New York Police Captain, Ed Quinn, and a retired French Inspector, Pichot, are all sent complimentary tickets for a cruise to South Africa; when they try to contact the person who sent them the tickets, an Arnold Beal, they find that he doesn't actually exist. On board the ship, they discover that one of the passengers, Kuyper, has deposited a collection of diamonds worth over a million pounds

87 'Fifty Million Taste Buds Can't Be Wrong' no longer survives in the ABC television archives.
88 *TV World*, w/c 19 November 1966.

with the ship's purser. They also discover that a notorious jewel thief, Hugo Varney, is on board. Varney has slipped through the clutches of all three retired policemen at some point over the past few years. Rose, Quinn, and Pichot are convinced that Varney is scheming to steal the diamonds, but as they investigate him, he seems to be too obvious a suspect. Kuyper reveals that he was the one who sent the cruise tickets to the three ex-policemen, as extra insurance against the diamonds being stolen, but when they think that Varney might have breached the ship's security, Kuyper begins to panic. It seems his suspicions are borne out, when the diamonds indeed appear to have been stolen. However, Rose deduces that Kuyper himself was behind the theft, and the missing diamonds are found on him when he's searched. It turns out that Kuyper had substantial debts and hoped to sell the diamonds on the black market in order to pay them off, while also recouping the insurance on the gems. The script from Bob is a lovely little tale, with plenty of ingenious twists and turns along the way, and the episode has some lovely performances throughout – not least that of *Dad's Army* star John Le Mesurier in the minor role of the ship's purser.

'The Unquiet Ghost' sees Rose contacted by an Australian he's never met, Oscar Malleson[89], who unsubtly tries to blackmail him into letting him ghost-write his memoirs. Malleson claims to have evidence that Rose took a £20,000 backhander while serving in Scotland Yard, in return for letting a foreign merchant flee the country after shooting the husband of an exotic dancer that he had booked for a 'private dance' in his hotel room some years previously. Malleson contacts the dancer in question, Phoebe Partridge, and tries to persuade her to help him in his pursuit of Rose, telling her that he had met the foreign merchant in Hong Kong, and had recorded a conversation between them in which he was told the whole story of the murder and the bribe. Malleson is later found dead in Rose's house, and Rose is arrested on suspicion of murder. Rose's right-hand man, Halifax, gets hold of Malleson's tape, and then also proves that Phoebe and her 'new' husband murdered Malleson. Furthermore, he deduces that her first husband was never in fact murdered at all; they had stage-managed the whole thing by using a gun containing blanks, and were both part of the scheme to extort the money from the merchant. Rose is released without charge, while the Inspector who arrested him is fooled into confessing that he impersonated Rose all those years ago, and was part of the scam with Phoebe and her husband.

Bob's script for this episode, while full of the sort of twists, turns and

---

89 Bob's re-use of the character name 'Malleson' from his *The Wednesday Play* pitch 'Plunkett-Bream Was Six Foot Four' would seem to confirm that he had recently re-read this storyline while writing these two *Mr Rose* episodes.

red herrings that such a story needs, ultimately relies a little too much on a number of unlikely coincidences to seem believable. Nevertheless, the episode is still a jolly little romp.

It was about this time that the BBC had a massive success with *The Forsyte Saga*, a 26-part series that chronicled the fortunes of the Forsyte family between 1879 and 1926. This led to Bob re-drafting his ideas for *Time Over Again* into a new series proposal document, which specifically made reference to the success of *The Forsyte Saga*. On Saturday 20 May 1967 he sent his reformatted idea to Andrew Osborn, who was now Head of Series, Drama at the BBC. Osborn had previously handled the fallout from the *Dr Finlay's Casebook* episode that Bob had inadvertently name-checked the Fitzwilliams in.

Bob's new pitch for *Time Over Again* began as follows:

The undoubted success of *The Forsyte Saga* encouraged me to review a series idea that I have had in mind for several years. The idea, very simply, is to trace the course of a man's professional career and private life over a quarter of a century. *Time Over Again* seems an apt – if uninspired – title for the series. For obvious reasons the protagonist should be an adventurer by temperament and should be in some profession where success is precarious and short-lived.[90]

Osborn replied back to Bob a few days later, explaining that he was in the midst of developing a spookily similar series idea with the writer Bob Compton Bennett and his agent Derek Glynne[91], and as such, had to reject Bob's proposal.

Bob's final script for the Rediffusion series *No Hiding Place*, entitled 'Who Is This Mortimer?', was shown on ATV on Thursday 8 June 1967.[92] *TV World* says this about the episode: 'Why do the Galloway brothers claim that nobody gives away good information for nothing? What does Lockhart discover about the mysterious Mr Mortimer?'[93]

During the final few months of 1967, Bob began working on another outline for a potential new series. He gave this the title *Schizo*, and finalised his pitch document in December 1967.

The incidence of schizophrenia is increasing throughout the world: This

---

90 Bob might have got a better response from Osborn had he not misspelled his name as 'Osbourne' on his letter to him. Twice!

91 Bob Compton Bennett and Derek Glynne were the co-creators of the 1971 BBC series *Brett*, which might have grown out of these initial 1967 discussions.

92 'Who Is This Mortimer?' no longer exists in the television archives.

93 *TV World*, w/c 3 June 1967.

increase is, proportionally, sharpest in the most developed countries.

In an attempt to explain these facts, two research graduates of McGill University postulated the theory that many cases of schizophrenia were the result of evolutionary forces.

The pressure of a highly organised, technological environment was causing the animal that lived in it to adapt genetically to a form more capable of coping with the new way of life.

Many schizophrenics, they suggested, were nature's sports, 'boss-shots' as it were, on the path to *supra homo sapiens.*

This theory was rejected with the usual contumely that scientists display for ideas that are unsupported by measurable evidence. Man, it was declared, is a developmentally flexible creature and therefore genetic adaption was not on the cards.

However, I wonder … 'You can't change human nature' is a phrase one is always hearing. It's a truism good enough for day-to-day application. But it can't be true permanently. It is not an eternal truth; man is *not* an immutable species. He has changed in the past, though not since the Neolithic revolution, and he will change in the future.

It seem a logical assumption, too, that the next genetic transmutation will not affect man's physiology (unless there is a drastic change in the climate of the planet) or basic anatomy. He is a thinking animal and the change is likely to be in the genetically determined quality of his mind.

Now suppose, for the sake of a series, those two young Canadians just happened to be on the right track. And suppose John Baxter, a London neurologist, stumbles across confirmation of their theory?

In fact, Baxter gets several stages further. He detects a pattern in the ramblings of his schizophrenic patients. They are like badly-tuned radios receiving signals from several different stations. And pretty soon Baxter becomes aware that while his patients might be evolutionary failures, an unknown number of successful mutants are already at large in society.

I use the phrase 'at large' because it is quickly made clear that the Mk II Human feels no more kinship for his ancestors than we feel for the apes. The mutants, by general standards, are all mental prodigies – though they may take care to hide this fact – and they possess faculties of ESP that in a less permissive society would have led to their being burnt at the stake.

Counterbalancing these great gifts, however, the mutants have lost their less 'useful' qualities. They are incapable of feeling compassion, love, pity, tenderness – though, of course, they may counterfeit these emotions where it seems politic to do so.

The mutants are aliens in the blood. They form a small, hostile elite working separately and together in the centres of power. Their aim is to manipulate society to create conditions favourable for their own development at the expense of their unwitting hosts.

Highly advanced and 'inhuman' biological techniques might be developed for increasing their number. They would certainly seek to identify and isolate the particular gene that had done the trick for them – and then to spread it widely through the host community. But it is by the manipulation of society that the mutants seek to achieve the vital breakthrough.

Mutation and natural selection are complementary. Most mutations are disasters that fail to survive in a world where survival belongs to the fittest. But occasionally, perhaps once in a thousand years, a mutation turns up and proves to fit better. And then it survives and flourishes.

The Mk II Human is better fitted for the conditions of life in the 20th Century. Therefore, any intensification of those conditions must be to the benefit of the mutants. Ultimately, they may so degrade, depress, and fragmentise society that there can be no organised opposition.

Until then, they rely on stealth. Until then, anything that spreads alarm and dissention, anything that increases tension at international, national or community level, anything that causes disruption or confusion, anything – in short – that reduces the quality of life, is to their advantage.

Baxter is the one man who recognises the danger. The series covers his battle with the mutants. His attempts to alert his fellow-men. The mutants' counter-ploys to discredit and disgrace him. His fight to frustrate their plots and extirpate individual mutants from the corridors of power. One dogged man's battle against SMERSH[94], the Magic Circle and the TUC.[95]

This is only a brief outline. But I think it gives an idea of the scope of the series. The stories would be unusual, offering engaging possibilities for exploiting contemporary problems. It should be a

94 SMERSH was the real-life counter-intelligence unit of Russia's Red Army, which operated between 1942 and 1946. The name (which was derived from the Russian phrase 'Smĕrt Špionam', meaning 'Death to Spies') was also borrowed by Ian Fleming for the fictional Russian crime organisation that was James Bond's nemesis in the early 007 novels.
95 The TUC is the Trade Union Congress, the federation that encompasses all of the trade unions in Britain.

cinch, on this basis, to produce a subtle and exciting series capable of generating interest beyond the level of the immediate action.

To a mutant super species man might seem little more than an inquisitive monkey playing about in a powder magazine. But he has established dominion over the other beasts of the Earth – and not merely by virtue of his unique ability to commit rape or to contract syphilis. He is also unique in his desire to compose symphonies or to construct radio-telescopes.

What I am trying to say – perhaps rather badly – is that any challenge to man's central position must necessarily contain philosophical implications of deep importance. Therefore a series based on the premise of such a challenge should release those 'volatile essences' that inform the best writing in any field from poetry to television scripts.

This series outline would crop up in many different forms in Bob's career over the next ten years. Unfortunately, there are no clues in his remaining files as to where and to whom he pitched it initially (either in late 1967 or early in 1968).

Bob then wrote what would be his final two episodes of ABC's *Public Eye*, which was now being produced by Michael Chapman, whom he had first worked with on *Undermind*. The first of these, 'It Must Be the Architecture – Can't be the Climate', was shown on ABC on Sunday 23 March 1968. *TV World* simply states: 'The death of a girl; malicious gossip; prejudice. A man's whole career in doubt. If he's innocent he's being victimised and if he's guilty he's getting away with it.'[96]

This was followed a week later, on Sunday 30 March 1968, by Bob's second episode of this season. This script started life under the title 'You've Only Got To Sneeze', but was retitled 'It's Learning About the Lies That Hurts' for broadcast. Bob's scene breakdown of the episode (See Interlude III) tells of Frank Marker's investigation of the mysterious sudden death of an influential businessman, Cecil Gathercole, whose body was found in a local park.

The *TV World* promotional blurb for this episode reads: 'The Morning after the Night before – and what a "night before" it must have been to die of it. Moreover this particular dead man certainly has a tale to tell.'[97]

Bob then returned to the Granada series *Mr Rose*, which had been re-

---

96 *TV World*, w/c 23 March 1968.
97 *TV World*, w/c 30 March 1968. Neither of these 1968 episodes of *Public Eye* survives in the television archives. A five minute fragment from 'It Must Be the Architecture – Can't be the Climate' was included in a 1969 ABC promotional showreel of its programmes, and still survives on 16mm film. The surviving sequence has Frank Marker looking to help a young doctor whose career is at risk after a young female patient, Paulette Hinckmann, died under his treatment. What complicates things is that the doctor had a previous relationship with the woman, and therefore his conduct is under question. His future at the hospital is under threat, and the medical grapevine could make matters worse for him elsewhere. Can Frank clear his name?

commissioned for a second season, and penned the opening episode of this second run, 'The Frozen Swede', which was shown on ITV on Friday 31 May 1968. The episode opens with Mr Rose moving into a new flat in London, assisted by his new secretary, Miss Dalton, and his trusted legman, Halifax. However, they soon discover the body of the flat's Swedish architect dead inside the walk-in freezer in the kitchen. Rose tries his best not to get involved, and leaves the police to arrest the architect's bride-to-be and business partner, Letitia Jolly, when the gun used to kill the Swede is found in her car. But when the forensic report insists that the man shot himself, Rose becomes drawn into the case, and uncovers a bizarre set of circumstances that implicate his new secretary and even Halifax in the events that led up to the architect's suicide.

Again, Bob delivers a script that dodges and weaves in various different directions, and rarely allows the audience the time or the space to second-guess each plot development. On top of this, he comes up with some exceptionally strong and witty dialogue along the way. Marjorie Bilbow, writing in *The Stage and Television Today*, was full of praise for this episode: 'If you should happen to be searching around for an example of the inequality of awards among the various media, you need look no further than the opening episode of *Mr Rose*, "The Frozen Swede", written by Robert Holmes. Apart from the restriction set by length, it was an amusing whodunit such as one could readily imagine having a comfortable run in the West End before producing a regular repeat income for its author from repeated revivals by the repertories and the amateur companies. Polished, escapist entertainment; a conversation piece rather than a story of action – and, in its context, none the worse for that. Mr Rose and his associates are given to acid repartee and although the star always gets the last word he takes many a sharp thrust *en route*. Devotees of the principle that television is a medium for deeds rather than words may see the verbosity of the script as a failing, but I found it stimulating to see it demonstrated that the art of writing lively amusing dialogue is not being allowed to die for want of a market. It is even more satisfying to observe that wit can have its place in a popular series.'[98]

Bob developed another ultimately unused series idea at around this time. *Phobia* was the prospective name of an anthology series that Bob pitched to Louis Marks at some point in the late 1960s. 'There is a case for a short anthology of plays under the generic title *Phobia*. Agoraphobia, claustrophobia, androphobia, hydrophobia and hypnophobia and xenophobia are common parlance among us what is educated,' wrote Bob, with his tongue firmly planted in his cheek.

He continued: 'How many more types of morbid fear must have been studied and categorised by psychologists. Arachnophobia, photophobia ... I mentioned the other day the lady who blanched at the sight of an unloaded airgun. Anybody is likely to be afraid of a gun in the hands of a maniac (except, perhaps, another maniac) but why should a gun by itself, loaded or unloaded, ancient or modern, cause such a reaction? Penalphobia? The plays will be about fear. About stress. About the disgusting or irrational or quixotic behaviour of people who are frightened ... In a general way I think the series might resemble *Seven Deadly Sins*[99], insofar as the plays should not make it too obvious, from the beginning, exactly who is afraid of precisely what.'

Presumably, Louis Marks was not convinced by Bob's earnest proposal, and the series never happened.

---

99 *Seven Deadly Sins* was an Associated Rediffusion drama anthology series that ran for seven hour-long episodes in 1966. A follow-up, *Seven Deadly Virtues*, also in seven hour-long episodes, came the following year.

INTERLUDE III
PUBLIC EYE:
'YOU'VE ONLY GOT TO SNEEZE'
1968

Robert Holmes's full original storyline proposal for the *Public Eye* episode 'You've Only Got To Sneeze', which was eventually retitled 'It's Learning About the Lies That Hurts', is reprinted here as originally submitted, complete with Bob's original spellings and punctuation:

'YOU'VE ONLY GOT TO SNEEZE' - BY ROBERT HOLMES

1. (LOCATION[100]) Park attendant George Picton (54) finds body of City Alderman Cecil Gathercole.

2. (BLACK DRAPES) Tributes to the dead man's distinguished record of public service, etc., in press obituaries and at a meeting of the City Council.

We intercut between snippets of these testimonials to Gathercole's character and a similar eulogising address from Lawrence Friend (48), the company secretary in Gathercole's business, Rotax Switches Ltd.

3. (BOARDROOM) Finally, having clearly established Gathercole's life and times, we stay with Lawrence Friend. He is speaking to a Board Meeting. Spinster Louisa Gathercole, 33, is present

Apart from Friend and Louisa (who, it appears, is unfamiliar with the daily business of the company) there are two other board members.

Gathercole, who was the managing director, built up the

---

100 Although Bob's manuscript is typed, he had gone through it at a later date and annotated by hand with his suggestions for locations for some of the scenes he had outlined. These are included here in brackets.

83

business from scratch over thirty years. It is a small concern but quite profitable.

Louisa, now the majority stockholder, is elected managing director in her father's stead. Friend suggests she might want to leave as there is no other important business. Louisa, showing an obdurate streak, insists that from now on she will keep office hours.

4. It is now evident that something is going on which Friend and his associates wish to keep from Louisa. (They must find an excuse to confer hurriedly elsewhere. The washroom?)

5. (BOARDROOM OR LOUSIA'S HOUSE) Walter Dunlop, the chairman of Dunlop Plastics, brings Louisa her father's document case which has been missing. Dunlop apologises, claiming he took it by mistake after dining with Gathercole the other night. He has only just discovered it is not his. (Note: it is one of those flat, expensive metal-framed jobs with a Chubb lock.)

6. Dunlop leaves. Louisa finds her father's keys and opens the case. The contents are innocuous but something strikes her. She rings Friend and asks him to call round.

7. Louisa points out why she knows this is not her father's document case.. (maybe she had bought him the original for a birthday present and has his monogram embossed on an inner flap.) Friend is taken aback but asks what she suspects.

Louisa hardly knows herself. It is just that there are too many oddities surrounding her father's death. She lists them (or, maybe, Marker should list some of them)…

a) Dunlop taking the case in error.
b) Not discovering the error for five days.
c) Her father's apparent decision to take a three-mile

walk the night of his death.
d) Falling asleep in the park.
e) His heart pills untouched.
and now
f) The substitution of his document case.

Friend tries to pooh-pooh her fears. Dunlop and her father were not business rivals, he points out, but close associates. They have put in a joint tender for a Government contract and were discussing it on the night they met.

And obviously Gathercole had tried to climb out over the park railings and had collapsed. That is why his heart pills were not touched.

However, he says, to allay all Louisa's qualms he will get an investigator to make a full report on the affair.

8. (MARKER'S OFFICE) Friend, apart from his seat on the board of Rotax Switches, has his own law firm. He talks with his managing clerk about a suitable man, saying the detective they usually employ is perhaps a bit too high-powered for this case. The clerk gets the message and in due course Marker presents himself to be briefed.

9. (LOCATION) Marker starts with Picton, who found the body, and gets his first hint that Gathercole's death might not be as simple as it seems.

10. (LOUISA'S HOUSE) Just to make the first act curtain – Marker meets Louisa, questions her about Gathercole's business and his private idiosyncrasies. Louisa becomes incensed when he asks about women friends. She goes along with the public image of Gathercole as a latter-day saint. To justify himself Marker then reveals her father was probably buttoned into his jacket when unconscious or dead and, presumably, the button-fastener was a woman.

11. (RESTRUANT) Inquiries at the restaurant. Now, for the first time, it is discovered that a third man was present at the dinner.

12. (DUNLOP'S OFFICE OR FACTORY LOCATION) Marker goes to see Dunlop. He asks Dunlop who the mystery man was. Dunlop is reluctant to answer. There are business reasons, he says, for keeping the name of the third man out of the affair.

Marker asks to see Dunlop's document case because it might have an embossed 'CG' inside it. But Dunlop doesn't have one. So how come Dunlop picked up a case at the restaurant thinking it was his? Dunlop, being pushed further into a corner every moment, suggest it was because he was a bit tight. But Marker has seen the restaurant bill. Tight on a third of a bottle of hock?

Dunlop, shaken and harassed, flies into a rage and tells Marker to get out.

13. Dunlop tells Friend that Marker is going to cause trouble. He blames Friend for putting him onto the case. Friend says he had to in order to appease Louisa.

14. (LOCATION) Marker is still trying to discover the identity of the third man. And he is trudging round the cab ranks. Where did the three men go after leaving the restraint? The trial peters out when they were dropped from a taxi on the corner of a pleasant residential avenue out at Bromsgrove.

15. Marker asks Louisa if she has any idea who the third man might have been? No. Had her father any friends in this part of Bromsgrove? None that she knew of.

16. (LOUSIA'S HOUSE) Friend expresses dissatisfaction at the inconclusive nature of Marker's inquiries and wants to drop the matter. Louisa won't hear of it. She thinks

Marker is making progress. Friend now comes the heavy father bit and tries to warn Louisa that no good will come from investigating further. He speaks with real concern but Louisa – who is becoming a stronger and more independent character as the play progresses – pays no attention. End of act.

17. Marker is trying to trace a taxi driver who is known to have picked up two men and a drunk out in Bromsgrove around midnight. But he finds that the taxi driver, together with his wife and three children, has left abruptly for a holiday in Majorca. How he has suddenly afforded such a splurge is a source of amazement to his neighbours. It's always been a week at Weston-Super-Mare before.

18. Marker discovers the taxi-driver's benefactor is Mrs Mayne-Butler of – surprise, surprise – Bromsgrove. (There are many ways he can do this but most probably he has to pressure the boss of Midi Tours, a slightly tatty travel agency.) He sees Mrs Mayne-Butler and her unsavoury role is revealed. Dunlop, trying to stay in the background, had asked her to square the taxi-driver.

18. Alternatively – (as it may not be necessary or desirable to bring in the travel agency / Mrs Mayne-Butler characters) Marker may have got enough circumstantial evidence by this stage to go back to Dunlop and force him to come clean.

19. Board meeting of Rotax Switches to which Marker brings his report. The Board has just heard that the Rotax-Dunlop Plastics joint tender for the Government contract has been accepted.

Marker – with Friend filling in the blanks – is now able to reveal how the contract was won:

The sealed tender, signed by Dunlop and Gathercole, was submitted by the due date. A Ministry official, Gilmore, told them their tender was too high and it was arranged that they would put in another tender at the appropriate figure. (It is, of course, past the closing date for the submission of tenders but Gilmore is in a position to fix that little difficulty.)

This is what the three of them were discussing on the night of Gathercole's death – Gilmore, of course, being the mystery man Marker was puzzled about.

Gilmore's reason for being so obliging is partly because of the usual financial kickback and partly because Gathercole understands and caters for his (perhaps slightly peculiar) sexual pleasures.

However, when Gathercole passed out there was panic. Mrs Mayne-Butler buttoned him into his jacket and Dunlop and Gilmore took him off in a taxi. Their first intention is to get him off the premises to somewhere more respectable. But before they had got very far they found he was dead. Gilmore was terrified at the prospect of involvement; therefore they left the dead man in the park.

Dunlop kept Gathercole's document case (because it had the returned tender in it) but forgot to take the key from his pocket. As a result he had to force the case open and then shop around for a case with an identical lock.

(Note: he needed the tender because it was signed by Gathercole, anyway, and also because its discovery in the document case would have been disastrous.)

Since Gathercole's death the figures in the tender have been adjusted and the document returned to Gilmore.

Louisa Gathercole is shattered by the revelation that her father had a Hyde to his public Jekyll; that he was a pimp and pander and ready for any shady practice that would advance his business.

Friend and his fellow-directors try to persuade her that Gathercole's tactics were legitimate business practice. Louisa rallies and declares that if the company can't win business honestly then it will fail honestly. They will start by repudiating the Rotax-Dunlop tender. And she is ready to accept the resignations of her fellow directors, beginning with Friend.

* * *

In this breakdown I have not touched on the central theme of the story - (because it isn't plot) which concerns Marker's problem on how far he should go in destroying the reputation of a dead man in the eyes of a loving relative.

In the matter of the document case, on second thoughts I don't believe it should be identifiable by anything as definite as a monogram. Perhaps Louisa knows, however, that her father's case had an ink-stain or something in a particular place. The object of this is to leave a certain element of doubt about whether or not it is the same case.

CHAPTER SIX
A DOCTOR CALLS
1968-1969

The BBC's science fiction series *Doctor Who* had started life in November 1963 with William Hartnell playing the mysterious time traveller. Its first story editor, David Whitaker, had trawled a number of writers' agencies on the lookout for potential scriptwriters. And while the likes of Terry Nation, John Lucarotti and Dennis Spooner had enjoyed repeated success penning scripts, most writers for the series tended to be of the one-hit-wonder variety. Spooner replaced Whitaker as story editor for the second year, and was then succeeded by Donald Tosh in 1965.

Many of the writers Bob had rubbed shoulders with in the mid 1960s would have had some involvement in the series. His old friend Robert Banks Stewart – who had been asked to write for *Doctor Who*, and had declined – was by now a client of Associated London Scripts, who also represented Terry Nation; Nation and Stewart were quite good friends at the time. Other early *Doctor Who* writers had been around and about in Bob's professional life over the years; William Emms had written for *Public Eye*, John Lucarotti had written for *Ghost Squad* and *Dr Finlay's Casebook*, while Louis Marks was script editor on *No Hiding Place*.

So by the time that Bob had pitched his *Doctor Who* story idea to Donald Tosh in early 1965 (see Chapter Four), he would have known and met several writers who had contributed to the series. Whether Bob actively followed-up his 1965 pitch or just got sidetracked with other work isn't totally clear. Regardless, Donald Tosh's stint as story editor lasted only six months, most of which was spent getting the epic 12-part story 'The Daleks' Master Plan' onto the screen. Tosh then departed, and Bob's involvement and story outline were soon forgotten.

How Robert Holmes came back onto the radar of the *Doctor Who* production office as a potential writer for the series in 1968 is not entirely clear, although it would appear that he initiated the contact. Speaking on stage at the *Doctor Who* Appreciation Society's Panopticon IV convention in August 1981, he said, 'I had put in a storyline in the very early days of *Doctor Who*, and they turned it down. Then I was moving house and I discovered this storyline about five years later, and I re-submitted it. Terrance Dicks was then the junior script editor, and he thought, "There's some promise in this storyline." So the producer said, "Right, commission it if you think something's there." And so he did, and together we put together this four-part story. We didn't think we were going to get it in that season, but one of the other scripts fell down – as they frequently do – and Terrance said, "I happen to have about my person a four-part story." And that was "The Krotons".[101]

In 1985, when Bob was interviewed by *Doctor Who Magazine*, he recalled the events in a slightly different manner: 'What happened with "The Krotons" was that I sent the idea in, not as a *Doctor Who*, but I sent it to the Drama Department as a story called "The Space Trap", for inclusion in a series they were doing of four-part science fiction thrillers, because I thought it was a suitable idea. Then I got a letter back from Shaun Sutton, the Head of Serials at that time, saying that they had decided to discontinue this series, and he'd passed the idea on to *Doctor Who*. And I never heard any more about it. Three years passed and we were moving house and then I came across the thing and thought "Well that's not *too* bad", so I rehashed it specifically for *Doctor Who* and sent it in again. Terrance Dicks was script editor by then and he commissioned it.'[102]

In this *Doctor Who Magazine* interview, it sounds like Bob could be mixing together his recollection of submitting a six-part science fiction storyline to the BBC in 1960 together with events in 1968, while ignoring his 1965 pitch to Donald Tosh. Assuming, that is, that all of these weren't essentially one and the same basic storyline. As no copy of Bob's 1960 submission exists, or for that matter a copy of the Doctor-less version of 'The Space Trap', then it's hard to know for sure. Certainly, the existing correspondence between Bob and Tosh from 1965 suggests that, at the time, Bob's story idea was instigated specifically for *Doctor Who*, and wasn't a re-worked version of a Doctor-less story that had been forward to Tosh from elsewhere in the BBC.

What's also odd is that in both accounts, Bob mentions that he found the storyline again while moving house, but he and Patricia had been living at the same address in Pitstone, Leighton Buzzard since 1965, and would still be living there well into the 1970s. So we may well have to take Bob's own recollections of events here with a small pinch of salt.

By 1968, the post of story editor on *Doctor Who* had been renamed as script editor[103], and at this point in time Terrance Dicks and Derrick Sherwin were sharing the role, alternating between scripts, but with Dicks very much as the junior partner. Most of the scripts planned for the programme's sixth season, due to run from autumn 1968 though to spring 1969, had already been decided on at this point, mainly by Sherwin, so the task of dealing with Bob's

---

101 Panopticon IV Convention, Queen Mary College, 1-2 August 1981.
102 Interview – Robert Holmes, *Doctor Who Magazine*: Issue 100, May 1985.
103 The roles of story editor and script editor were identical; the two terms were used interchangeably on end credits and programme documentation over the years.

story submission fell to Dicks.

'I first came into contact with Robert Holmes when he sent in a story idea which was one I think he'd sent in before,' recalled Dicks. 'He'd heard there was a new script editor, and so he thought he might try again with somebody who hadn't seen it. I'm not sure if that was what became "The Krotons", or whether it was another idea, but whatever it was he sent in, I liked enough to ask him to come in and see me, and so we talked things through, and got on well. And eventually I commissioned him to write the scripts that became "The Krotons"[104]

'We worked out this idea, which I quite liked, and I was sort-of junior assistant script editor at the time; I hadn't fully taken over. I went to Peter Bryant (producer) and Derrick Sherwin (script editor), who were running the show. The idea at the time was that Derrick was going to go off to another job, and I would take over from him. But he didn't get the other job, and so I was stuck for quite a long time as his understudy. And at one point, Bryant and Sherwin said, "We're full up – everything's commissioned for this season." I said, "This story idea from Bob Holmes, it's a good idea. Can't I develop it as a spare, in case something goes wrong, or maybe for next season, so at least we will be a script in hand?" Because we were in constant script trouble in those days, with scripts coming in late … and I wanted to get ahead a little bit. So they said, "Oh, all right, if you like", and I was left alone on that as a sort of hobby project, as something that would keep me quiet and keep me out of trouble. Bob and I worked on it together, and I eventually got in from him a set of four-part scripts, called "The Krotons" – after the name of the monster.

'What then happened was that the story that Bryant and Sherwin were working on, which was a comedy, fell to pieces. They suddenly went off it in a big way, and didn't like the scripts as they came in. They sent them back [to be rewritten], and they came back worse as far as they were concerned, so there was a big crisis meeting. David Maloney, who was the director, was very upset, and said, "I can't cope with this – what are we going to do?" I then modestly said that I did happen to have this alternative four-part serial, and said to David, "Would you like to see it?" And he said, "Yes, okay, it's got to be better than this." I gave him the four scripts, and he took them away. We had another meeting later on, and he came back saying, "Yes please – please let me do this." So the ill-fated comedy was abandoned, and we did "The Krotons". And that was my first meeting with Bob, and my first experience of working with him.'

At the time, Dicks didn't know much about Bob's writing pedigree. 'I knew

---

104 Even Dicks isn't sure what Bob initially submitted, it seems!

he was a reasonably established writer, but that was the first time we'd actually met,' he recalls. 'I think I would have probably looked up some of his other television scripts, and got some kind of idea of his background; at the BBC, you could always get things sent to you from the script library. I knew he was a reasonably established, well-known, professional scriptwriter. There were lots of scriptwriters about at that time. And he hadn't sold to *Doctor Who* before, but he'd certainly tried to sell an idea to Gerry Davis or whoever, and so he certainly knew about the programme, he was working in that kind of area. There were more detective and drama series about in those days, and Bob had done quite a lot of work for them.'

A little detail about the background to all this might help clarify the sequence of events here. The *Doctor Who* production team already had the stories 'The Dominators' and 'The Mind Robber' in the can for the programme's sixth season, as these two tales had been made at the end of the fifth production block and held back for transmission. The sixth production block began with the Derrick Sherwin-scripted Cyberman story 'The Invasion'. This story was the first to be officially script edited by Terrance Dicks, newly appointed as Sherwin's heir-apparent. Sherwin, meanwhile, was being groomed to take over as producer of the series from Peter Bryant, who had been at the helm since late 1967, and was looking to move on. This arrangement saw Sherwin and Dicks alternate script editing duties over the next few months, but with Sherwin still very much the senior script editor on the show. 'The Invasion' was initially meant to be only a four part story, but was expanded to run for eight episodes when another four-part story, 'The Dreamspinner' by Paul Wheeler, was deemed not suitable for the series and abandoned before it went into production. 'The Invasion' was then due to be followed by another four-part story called 'The Prison in Space', something of a comedy science fiction romp, commissioned by Sherwin and Bryant from veteran comedy scriptwriter Dick Sharples in April 1968, with the scripts due to be delivered in August and September 1968.

Then on Monday 20 May 1968, Bob wrote to Bryant, completely out of the blue:

Clearing out some old files this weekend, I came across the enclosed letter setting out the basis of a *DR WHO* adventure. I've no trace of a reply or any memory of discussing the idea further. Which is strange because it's a lot better than most of my old ideas! I imagine that either Donald moved on or I became involved in something else around that time. Anyway, as it still seems to me to be a valid idea for the programme, I'm resubmitting the thing. But if you don't like it, please chuck it away – I don't want it back in the files!

Enclosed with this letter was Bob's copy of the letter he sent to Donald Tosh in 1965, with his story idea laid out over two pages.

The idea seemed good enough still, so Bob was contacted and asked to work it up for the current TARDIS crew of the second Doctor, Jamie, and Zoe.

According to the commissioning paperwork retained by the BBC, it was Sherwin who on Friday 31 May 1968 formally commissioned Bob to put together a revised storyline, under the title 'The Space Trap', and not Dicks. However, as Sherwin was still technically the senior script editor on the show, then perhaps it was just normal production protocol for him to sign off the paperwork. It seems that Sherwin had very little involvement in the story beyond issuing these forms. There is little doubt that Dicks took on all matters relating to this story from here on in.

Bob's revised basic storyline, now titled simply 'The Trap', was delivered to Dicks on Friday 14 June 1968 (see Interlude IV). Basic it might have been, but the storyline met with Dicks's approval, and he formally commissioned the scripts for the four-part story from Bob on Tuesday 25 June 1968. The story was commissioned under the title 'Dr Who and the Space Trap', and all four scripts were due to be delivered on Thursday 1 August 1968.

However, this was not a commission for a 'just-in-case' story. At this point, 'The Space Trap' was scheduled to go into production in April 1969, as the planned last-but-one story of the sixth season. Bob began writing the story, and delivered his scripts for the first two episodes to Dicks on Thursday 18 July 1968, with the final two following on Monday 12 August 1968.

Things now start to get complicated. At around this point, series regular Frazer Hines decided he was going to leave, and initially the departure of his character, Jamie, was going to happen quite early on in the sixth series' run. Dick Sharples was accordingly asked to rewrite 'The Prison in Space' to incorporate the new male companion, Jamie's replacement, a character by the name of Nik.

Only Hines then changed his mind. He was persuaded to stay for the rest of the series by Patrick Troughton, in order that they could both then leave at the same time. Sharples was asked to rewrite 'The Prison in Space' again in order to reinstate the character of Jamie. This seems to have been the straw that broke the camel's back for Sharples, and he announced he was withdrawing from the project. However, it's also fair to say that both Sherwin and Bryant by now had serious reservations about the story as a whole, and so weren't unduly concerned about its loss.

What it did do, however, was leave a gap in the production schedule once work on 'The Invasion' had been completed, and the only scripts that the production team now had in hand and in a workable state were Bob's for 'The Space Trap'. Director David Maloney had already been assigned to make 'The Prison in Space', and was then given the option of making 'The Space Trap' instead. After reading the scripts, he readily agreed to helm its production. 'The Space Trap' was later re-named 'The Krotons' during rehearsals.

The quick decision to push 'The Krotons' into production earlier than intended had other consequences. The pressing problem of having a story to follow 'The Invasion' into production was now solved. However, there was now a gap in the schedule where 'The Space Trap' was originally meant to have sat. More stories were now needed for later in the series. Terrance Dicks must have mentioned this to Bob, because on Tuesday 22 October 1968, Bob wrote to him: 'Here is the idea that I spoke to you about on the telephone last week. I don't think the title has enough zing for *Doctor Who* but I had to stick something on it for the time being. I hope you like it. If you want to talk about it I can come in any time this week except Thursday morning and I'm pretty free most of the next week as well. How is "The Trap" coming along?'

Attached was a new three-page *Doctor Who* story outline, entitled 'The Aliens in the Blood', which borrowed a great deal of its premise from Bob's series proposal for *Schizo*, written the previous year (see Chapter Five):

Mutation and natural selection are complementary. Most mutations are disasters that fail to survive in a world where survival belongs to the fittest. But occasionally, perhaps once in ten thousand years, a mutation turns up that is better suited to conditions than its parent species. And then it survives and flourishes.

The premise of this story is that a mutant human species has sprung into being in an isolated, inbred community of scientists and technologists – the sort of community one might postulate as a probability in the 22nd Century AD.

The community is OSCOC (Outer Space Commission Of Control) and is a supra-national development of Cape Kennedy. From its remote island in the Indian Ocean, OSCOC controls and guides the movement of every ship on the interstellar spaceways.

Most of the traffic at this time consists of freighters. The pioneers and settlers, the explorers and colonists have gone out among the stars and now the treasures of the universe are being ferried back to Earth for the benefit of the soft-living terrestrials. The whole structure of civilisation depends on the constant flow of the new materials that space exploration has released.

Not everyone, of course, has adapted to the new ways. In various remote corners of the world there are still pockets of primitives who cling to the old life. OSCOC itself shares the island with natives, mainly fishermen and farmers, a sullen and hostile bunch in the main. But a few of them are employed in menial tasks around OSCOC campus.

(OSCOC is organised like an American university, with its various faculties. Its Dean is a man named Thawne. Almost as important in the hierarchy is a psychologist called Khotajhi.)

The story opens with the captain of a spaceship getting his course and speed from OSCOC. He follows it, realises that something is wrong, that the ship is on disaster course, and tries again to contact OSCOC.

But down in the OSCOC plot room his frantic SOS is switched off (we don't see by whom) and the doomed ship plunges into an asteroid belt.

At about the time the TARDIS is materialising on the north end of the island, Dean Thawne is visited by an agent from the WIB (World Intelligence Bureau); too many freighters are vanishing mysteriously; in the past few years the hazards of space travel appear to have increased beyond all belief to the point where the fabric of Earth life, as it is now constituted, is seriously endangered; the agent clearly suspects there may be a saboteur operating inside OSCOC.

The native islanders think the TARDIS is something to do with OSCOC and show every intention of forming a lynching party for the Doctor and his friends. However, they escape and reach the safety of the campus. The welcome they receive here is far from warm, of course; outsiders are never welcome in the rarefied OSCOC atmosphere and when they turn up with the preposterous claim to being time travellers … It's a case of the sanatorium and Dr Khotajhi.

Shortly after this the WIB agent is found dead. He has been murdered and the principal suspect is one of the native menials named Rafe. The Doctor has already had some contact with Rafe and he is quite sure the boy is innocent. Proving it to Thawne is a different matter, but it is in his attempts to do this that he first begins to worry the mutants.

I haven't developed the story in detail beyond this point. The mutants are Mark II Humans and, to the casual eye, indistinguishable from the old-fashioned kind seen in any edition of *Spotlight*. But they may, when the Doctor gets to know them better, have some visible physical feature like an extra-long thumb that can be shown to the audience at the appropriate critical moment – as for instance when Zoe is about to confide all to the kindly, grey-haired grandmother who has befriended her. (Because the mutants, of course, can be of either sex and any age.)

The mutants are all mental prodigies and possess powers of ESP that in earlier times would have had them burnt at the stake.

Counterbalancing their gifts, however, they have lost less 'useful' qualities. They are incapable of compassion, love, pity, tenderness – though they may counterfeit these emotions where it seems politic to do so.

They regard Mark I Humans rather as we ourselves regard the apes. Their aim is world domination. And because, at the moment, they are few in number it is necessary for them to work secretly towards the destruction of mankind while concealing their existence.

The Doctor's task is made more difficult than usual because he can never be sure of anybody – at any moment an apparent friend can turn into a vicious and ruthless enemy.

Hunted by mutants and duped Mark I Humans, helped by Rafe and the other islanders, the Doctor and his friends have some bad times before eventually they win out. The climax, as I see it at the moment, is signposted at an early scene in the first episode.

While in the sanatorium under Khotajhi's observation, the Doctor became intrigued by the apparently high incidence of patients from OSCOC showing schizophrenic tendencies. (This, as we learn later, is due to the fact that the mutants first become aware of their 'group consciousness' at about the time an ordinary lad's voice starts to break. Until they learn to understand and control their extra faculty, many of them tend to talk and act irrationally; they are like radios picking up too many signals at one time.)

The Doctor makes use of this finally by constructing a very advanced and powerful machine similar to those used in electric shock therapy. With a captured mutant acting as control, the Doctor is able to broadcast shock treatment on the right mental wavelength and burn out the ESP centre in the brains of all the mutants. This point is reached – naturally – only at the very last moment when it seems nothing can stop the mutants' final masterstroke.

Terrance Dicks read through Bob's proposal in full, and then went back over

ROBERT HOLMES: A LIFE IN WORDS

the storyline and made a number of notes and observations at the side of the pages. He thought the initial set-up of OSCOC, comprising a multi-national cast of characters, was too similar to that in the recent story 'The Wheel in Space', which featured a multi-national space station crew. He also couldn't really see the benefit of setting the story so far in the future and suggested instead moving to a near-contemporary setting. He liked the sequence of the doomed ship crashing into the asteroid belt, and suggested that it could perhaps be some sort of 'robot airliner'. The notion that the Mark II humans could be distinguished by a physical feature such as an extra-large thumb was one he found to be very similar to the aliens portrayed in the American science fiction series *The Invaders*[105], and suggested that something more subtle should be used, such as the Mark II humans having a different blood, or the ability to heal rapidly. Dicks wasn't happy with Holmes's assertion that the Mark II Humans' aim should be given simply as 'world domination' ('Why?' he noted at the side of the page at this point), and goes on to comment about the resolution of the story: 'Bit tough on the mutants this – maybe we shouldn't lose the superior powers for humanity. Some good mutants.' His final assessment of the storyline was: 'V Derivative but promising ...'

It would seem that these reservations were enough to scupper the idea, because the story was not taken any further by the *Doctor Who* production office. However, further workable scripts were still needed for the sixth season. Writer Brian Hayes had a six-part Ice Warrior story in development, which became 'The Seeds of Death', and would follow 'The Krotons' into production. Sherwin then asked Dicks' old writing colleague Malcolm Hulke to come up with the final story of the season; a story that would see the departure of Patrick Troughton's Doctor. The episode count of this final story would ultimately increase to ten, gaining Dicks as a co-writer, as other storylines fell through.

While Dicks was busy both re-writing the final episodes of Hayles's story, and writing the final story with Hulke, Sherwin got in contact with Bob and asked him to come up with another *Doctor Who* idea. On Saturday 9 November 1968, a little over two weeks after Bob had submitted his proposal for 'The Aliens in the Blood', Sherwin commissioned him to write another storyline for a six-part adventure, under the title 'Dr Who and the Space Pirates'. This was to be delivered by Bob on or before Friday 15 November 1968. Bob then submitted his more detailed scene breakdowns for Episodes One and Two on Friday 29 November, and those for Episodes Three and Four on Tuesday 3 December.[106]

---

105 *The Invaders* was a Quinn Martin production that was being screened by ITV at the time. In this, the aliens impersonated humans; the only difference being their little fingers, which couldn't bend.
106 Unlike most of Bob's other *Doctor Who* storyline submissions of this time, the one for 'The Space Pirates' doesn't appear to have survived at the BBC, or in Bob's own files.

Based on these four scene breakdowns, the scripts for all six episodes of 'Dr Who and the Space Pirates' were commissioned from Bob by Sherwin on Tuesday 3 December 1968, with a target delivery date of Monday 16 December – less than two weeks later. Bob then delivered his scene breakdowns of Episodes Five and Six on Friday 6 December.

Working at an impressive speed (and one that surely gives the lie to his later '2cv' comments), Bob submitted his script for 'The Space Pirates' Episode One on Thursday 12 December, and that for Episode Two on Tuesday 17 December. Episode Three's script arrived on Thursday 19 December, Episode Four's on Thursday 2 January 1969, Episode Five's on Monday 6 January, and Episode Six's on Friday 10 January.[107]

'"The Space Pirates" was commissioned and I don't remember any difficulties in writing it,' said Bob about this story. 'The key to the script for me was the cargo skipper played by, I think, Milo O'Shea. I wanted the space equivalent of Masefield's "dirty British coaster with salt-caked smoke-stack …", a rocket ship held together by bits of wire and faith.'[108]

'It was originally intended as a four-part story,' Bob later recalled, 'but at the last minute became a six-parter when one of their other six-parters fell through, so I went back and reworked some of it. I remember that the germ that got me going on it was this odd captain-type chap in his battered space vessel who, every time it went wrong, kicked it or hit it with a beer bottle and got a result. I can't remember too much about it myself, but my wife insists it is better than any of the others I've done!'[109]

Terrance Dicks has only hazy memories of this story. '"The Space Pirates" was Derrick Sherwin's project,' he later recalled. 'I'm not quite sure why – we tended to work on things separately rather than together. I think I might have been busy on some other scripts, and so I had very little to do with "The Space Pirates".'

At the time of transmission, 'The Space Pirates' was generally well received by the popular press. Writing for *The Spectator*, columnist Stuart Hood observed: 'Having, at the end of the last adventure, survived engulfment in what looked suspiciously like a well-known brand of detergent, Doctor Who is off again. This time in a space beacon and under attack from space pirates. As usual, these are threatening figures which contrive to behave like ultra-modern robots and yet look like a nightmare version of Homeric warriors. The archaising element in

---

107 'The Space Pirates' is the only *Doctor Who* story of Bob's that the BBC doesn't hold complete in its archives. Only the second episode survives in full, although some film inserts from the first episode, alongside off-air audio recordings of all six episodes, also survive.

108 Robert Holmes Interview, *The Time Meddler*: Issue 3, October 1981 – Interview by John M Kahane. Bob is quoting from the poem 'Cargoes' by John Masefield (1902). Oh, and the character Milo Clancey was played by Gordon Gostelow, not Milo O'Shea!

109 Interview – Robert Holmes, *Doctor Who Magazine*: Issue 100, May 1985.

science fiction is curious and ought some day to be examined more closely. Why should visions of the future be peopled with bits and pieces from the myths of Greece and Rome ...? What is the Doctor himself, after all, but a wily Odysseus, prepared to lie, to simulate, to feign death, matching his human cunning against giants and monsters or the machines which are their modern equivalent.' Hood went on to say, of the serial's space-walking sequences, that they were, '... so excellently simulated that for a moment or two I was undecided whether what I saw was not perhaps a piece of documentary film fed into the programme. It is one of the great strengths of *Doctor Who* that, while it refers back to archetypal situations involving extreme danger and survival from it, it also aims at credibility in detail.'[110]

However, to most observers of the series, 'The Space Pirates' suffers from being made by a production team and cast that have almost-but-not-quite run out of steam. *Doctor Who* was treading water at this point, and 'The Space Pirates' seems less of a good story that needed to be told, and more of a reasonable way of filling six episodes' worth of airtime. Bob comes good with his characters and dialogue, but the series really needed something to perk itself up once again.

Officially, producer Peter Bryant left *Doctor Who* after the last episode of 'The Space Pirates' was recorded, and Derrick Sherwin finally made the step up to producer and replaced him.[111] In turn, Terrance Dicks now became the sole script editor on the series, and would remember Bob's work in years to come.

---

110 *The Spectator*, 14 February 1969.
111 I say 'officially', but Peter Bryant was still in charge of *Doctor Who* until July 1969, by which point planning for the seventh season was well underway.

INTERLUDE IV
DOCTOR WHO: 'THE TRAP'
JUNE 1968

Robert Holmes's full (if rather brief) storyline proposal for the *Doctor Who* story that eventually became 'The Krotons' is reprinted here as originally submitted, complete with his original spellings and punctuation:

THE TRAP

EPISODE ONE

In the hall of learning we see the Gonds prepare to sacrifice their students to the "machine".

The Tardis arrives. Doc. and co. see shattered student, exit from machine and sprayed by acid. They go on to Learning Hall where they see Vana going into machine. Doc nips back to tumulus – saves her on exit and takes her home. Thara attacks the machine – and is watched on scanner. The machine makes identikit picture of Doc and a metal hose comes out of the machine to get him …

EPISODE TWO

The Doc escapes from the hose by shielding his face. The hose sprays a Gond instead and retreats. Avrik, Selris's deputy, urges tough line with machine.

The Doc and Zoe submit to learning machine tests, make top score, and voluntarily enter machine. In the control room they are further treated – and their success brings the machine to life – a man like form begins to emerge from the tank. The Gonds, lead by Avrik, plan to attack the machine. Jamie looks for a way in …

Inside a passage of the machine Doc and Zoe try to escape.

101

ROBERT HOLMES: A LIFE IN WORDS

In the control room the Krotons now fully formed, cut off the acid spray as they don't want to kill them. Zoe and Doc escape but Jamie is lured into the machine. He is tested and blacks out.

EPISODE THREE

Jamie collapses and Krotons stop testing. They question him and learn of the Tardis. Doc and Zoe are seen on the scanner about to enter the Tardis – and a Kroton leaves the ship. When Doc and Zoe leave the ship, one Kroton guides the other towards them. In the ship, Jamie sabotages the guiding Kroton.

The Gonds attack the machine's power line. The Doc is worried – he asks for chemicals from Vana.

The Krotons notice the Gond's attack – and Jamie slips away. Doc warns Gonds of dangers of attacking power line. The tunnel caves in on the Doctor.

EPISODE FOUR

The Krotons manage to stabilize blow-up reaction. The Doc is dug out of the tunnel.

The Krotons can only hold-off the blow up temporarily. Jamie manages to slip away.

The Doc and Zoe realise that Jamie will be splatted by the machine. As Jamie is about to leave, they shout a warning and he looks back. The corrosive jet misses him …

A Kroton comes out of the Machine and demands surrender of Doc and Zoe.

Jamie hides in the machine.

The Gonds surrender Doc and Zoe. Selris passes them the

vital phial and is killed. In the machine the Krotons explain why they need their mind power. The Doc slips Jamie the phial. Jamie pours it in the tank and the Krotons dissolve.

Doc Jamie and Zoe leave ship. Doc and Zoe send the machine - the Kroton ship - into space, just before it blows up.

CHAPTER SEVEN
FRAUDULENT HONEY
1968-1969

At about the same time that Bob was commissioned to write 'The Krotons' for *Doctor Who*, he also became heavily involved in a new ATV soap opera, *Market in Honey Lane*, which had been created by Louis Marks and launched in 1967. Marks would go on to become a close friend of Bob's from around this point in time.

Market in Honey Lane was almost prescient in its format: a cockney drama set in and around an East End London street market. Being an ATV show, it was recorded at Elstree studios in London, which is now, somewhat ironically, home to the cockney street market soap opera *EastEnders*, with which it shares an awful number of similarities.

TV Times introduced the new soap opera by saying: 'You can learn more by standing here for five minutes than travelling round the world. It's all here: bustle, colour, backchat, character and humanity.' *Market in Honey Lane* was initially quite popular amongst viewers, and at one time the series looked set to give its main rival, *Coronation Street,* a run for its money.

The previous year, Bob had written the series' fourth episode, 'Snap', which was shown on ATV on Monday 24 April 1967. *TV World*'s listing for the episode cryptically stated: "'I might be old-fashioned but that seems very funny behaviour to me. Very funny in a young fellow that's asked a girl to marry him.'"[112]

The series came back for a second season in 1968, and during the early weeks of this, Bob supplied Marks with a storyline for another episode, which Marks then fleshed out into a full script. The episode, 'The Matchmakers', was shown by ATV on Thursday 1 February 1968 ('Written by Louis Marks, based on an idea by Robert Holmes').[113]

The episode revolves around the character Lisa, a stripper played by Marla Landi. The magazine *TV World* had this to say in its weekly listing: "'Immoral? What harm's she doing? Taking her clothes off to entertain a lot of sex-starved provincial businessmen? No, I think she's performing a social service.'" The same issue of the magazine also reported how Landi had been asked by the production team to visit a strip club as part of the preparation for the role.

---

112 *TV World*, w/c 22 April.1967.
113 *Market in Honey Lane*: 'The Matchmakers' no longer exists in the television archives.

'Though I don't actually strip in the programme, the producer thought it would be good for me to see some real strippers. I dressed very casually, the club was packed with businessmen but I didn't feel awkward because I was there as part of my job. It was my first visit to a strip club and actually, I was disappointed. Perhaps a woman can't judge, but none of the girls seemed to be very professional. But I met them afterwards and they were very nice.'[114]

Just a few weeks later, an episode written by Bob, entitled 'The Organisers', was shown on Thursday 22 February 1968 by ATV. *TV World* had only this to say about it: "'All I'm saying is it's bad for business to have a hulking great convict in The Lane. I mean someone's got to tell Jacko.'"[115]

Changes were afoot in the various ITV regions during 1968. A number of contracts had been won, lost or renegotiated in the regions, and separate weekend broadcasting licences were abolished (apart from in the London area). The biggest loser in all this was ABC, as ATV won control of the Midlands area for the entire week, and Granada did likewise for the North of England. However, ATV lost the London weekend franchise to a new company, London Weekend Television (LWT). ABC and Rediffusion combined to become a new company, Thames Television, which then supplied London's ITV programmes during the week.[116]

Thames Television began broadcasting on Monday 30 July 1968, and one of its first productions was an action series called *Frontier*, which was set in Northern India in the 1880s and followed the exploits of a battalion of the British Army stationed in the Indian countryside. It was produced by Michael Chapman, who had previously been producer of *Undermind*, which Bob had written for in 1965.

Bob wrote the *Frontier* episode 'Mutiny', which was screened by Thames on Wednesday 4 September 1968.[117] 'Mutiny' begins when a number of Indian troops refuse to throw a travelling holy man, Bahadoor Uzzah, out of the camp on the instructions of their commanding officer. The Indian troops are arrested on a charge of refusing to follow a direct order, but escape overnight, deserting their regiment, and taking their weapons with them. The following day, a number of other Indian soldiers also desert the barracks. The British officers are concerned that the missing troops might join forces with a nearby tribe of bandits, who are the catalysts behind a local uprising the regiment is trying to quell. The barracks is readied for an imminent attack by the newly-

---

114 *TV World*, w/c 27 January 1968.
115 *TV World*, w/c 17 February 1968.
116 Other ITV changes in this time saw the North of England region split into two, with Granada keeping one of the areas, and Yorkshire Television (YTV) being formed to service the other, both now operating seven days a week. TWW lost its franchise for Wales and West England, with a new company, Harlech Television (HTV), taking over this region for seven days a week.
117 *Frontier*: 'Mutiny' no longer exists in the Thames Television archives.

armed bandit force.

A hugely popular series of the 1960s was ITC's *The Saint*, featuring a young Roger Moore as the hero, Simon Templar. *The Saint* had begun life as a series of novels by author Leslie Charteris, most of which were turned into television episodes during the series' initial run between 1962 and 1965. The series had proved to be a hit in America, where it was syndicated despite being made in black and white, and in 1966 ITC produced a run of new episodes, this time in colour. As the backlog of original novels had been used up by now, new writers were brought in to create brand new stories for the character; and although Charteris had it written into his contract that he could request any script changes he saw fit, ITC and ATV ensured that they were not obliged to take heed of any of his suggestions. Bob scripted one episode for the final 1968/69 season of the show, 'The Scales of Justice', which was shown on ATV on Sunday 1 December 1968.

'The Scales of Justice' begins with five members of the company board of Combined Holdings all being murdered, each one being sent a card with 'The Scales of Justice' written on it before they are killed. Simon Templar is called in when board member Gilbert Kirby fears he is the next to be killed. The perpetrator is discovered to be another member of the board with a grudge against the company, which bought out his father's business some years earlier.

Leslie Charteris doggedly undertook his consultancy role on the television series of *The Saint*, offering his opinions on the scripts and storylines that were sent to him as part of the contractual obligation that underpinned its production. These were generally ignored by the production team, but Charteris sent them in regardless. On Wednesday 17 April 1968, Charteris fired off a missive after reading Bob's storyline for 'The Scales of Justice'. 'Only television executives, their ancestral generation of B-picture producers and pulp magazine editors, and the infantile public they are supposedly catering to, could believe in a paranoiac who dedicates himself to murdering an entire board of directors, or some seven or eight people, because his father "died of overwork and a broken heart" and his "inheritance vanished". My personal incredulity goes still further, and refuses to accept the assumption that a tiny needle passing through the neighbourhood of the heart would cause all the symptoms of "a plain simple coronary" with "no sign of … anything suspicious." Anyway, not until I see a confirmation signed by a qualified pathologist. Until then, I would rank it with the good old mysterious Oriental poison that kills instantly without leaving a trace. If you are reduced to considering outlines like "The Scales of Justice" by Robert Holmes, you have my sympathy. Today's available writers must be a miserably witless lot.'

When it came to Robert Holmes, it appears that Leslie Charteris was not what you might call a fan.

When he got to read the full script of the episode, Charteris was moved to fire off another irate memo to the series' production team on Wednesday 25 April 1968: 'This supposedly final script ("The Scales of Justice") reached me yesterday. Since my immediate comments on the outline were only mailed to you on April 17th, there is an inescapable assumption that the script must have been authorised without waiting one moment for any observations I might have had to make on the outline – if indeed it was not already in the works when the outline was mailed to me. In any case, my comments obviously had no effect whatever. Therefore my criticisms of the 17th, of the outline, apply exactly the same to this script. I can see no point in adding any minor-detail comments, which I have no reason to imagine would have any better reception, or be any more productive.'[118]

Meanwhile, the soap opera *Market in Honey Lane* had undergone a revamp. It had been moved to a midweek early evening slot on ITV, was shown as two 30-minute episodes a week (instead of a single 60-minute episode) and was now called just *Honey Lane*. The first series in this format ran for 52 episodes between early October 1968 and March 1969. However, the revamp and rescheduling didn't prove at all popular with viewers, and when *Honey Lane* returned for a second series in July 1969, the episodes returned to their earlier hour-long format. But this wasn't enough to save the series, and it was cancelled after just 13 more episodes, which ran from July through to early October 1969.

The series kept Bob extremely busy in late 1968 and much of 1969. During this time he weighed in with 13 half-hour scripts for the first series of *Honey Lane*, and a further four hour-long scripts for the second series.[119] Bob kept hold of his final two scripts for the series, which, apart from the names of the characters, could read like any generic episode of *EastEnders* from the 1980s. They encompassed such plot elements as: intrigue about rival fruit and

---

118 Both of Charteris's letters quoted here are reprinted in the book *The Saint: A Complete History in Print, Radio, Film and Television, 1928-1992* by Burl Barer, published by McFarland & Co, 1993.
119 Full transmission details of all of Bob's *Honey Lane* episodes can be found in the appendix at the back of this book. A flavour of some of them can be found in the following listings from *TV World* magazine: 'Lisa has a visit from the police, who ask some searching questions about Danny. Meanwhile, Harry decides to go in for nylons – and comes under attack. For Mike there is a proposition from Gervase Lorrimer, and for Sam and Geoff there is modern literature of a very off-beat type.' (Episode 1.07, shown on ATV on 22 October 1968, from *TV World*, w/c 19 October 1968.) 'Billy Bush has promised to help Ann in the basement of the new Honey Lane Bazaar for her old folks works centre but can he really keep his word? Sam and Geoffrey are about to open their new health food bar, but will the competition from Vicky prove too much?' (Episode 1.17, shown on ATV on 26 November 1968, from *TV World*, w/c 23 November 1968.) The episodes continue with stories about an overdose of sleeping pills, protection gangs, adoption issues and various market-related plots. No episodes of the revamped *Honey Lane* survive in the archives of ATV.

veg market stalls, characters referred to as 'Princess', cockney rhyming slang, drinks in the local pub of an evening, flirty barmaids, dumped girlfriends, sympathetic cups of tea and characters getting unexpectedly run over by taxis. The storylines drift lazily by, as much of the screen time is spent going from conversation to conversation. Bob, with his keen ear for good dialogue, makes something of a virtue of this slow pace. As with all soap operas, the trick was to draw the audience in with the minutia and mundane details of the characters' lives. However, without any surviving record of the actors' performances, it's hard to judge if this was achieved in practice. The cancellation of the series would suggest not, but the scheduling merry-go-round can't have helped matters much either.

Yet another new series drew Bob's writing talents towards it in 1969. *The Inside Man* was a counter-intelligence drama made by the new London ITV franchise holder, London Weekend Television (LWT), and starred Frederick Jaeger as criminal psychologist Dr James Austen. Bob wrote the episode 'The Spy Vanishes', shown on ITV on Friday 14 March 1969. The story begins with Austen visiting prison to see a man called Borozhek, a Polish national convicted of spying for the Russians. Borozhek is the subject of a proposed prisoner exchange with the Russians, and Austen has to assess his mental competence. Borozhek isn't thrilled at the idea of being sent to Russia. He overpowers Austen during one of their interviews and escapes from the prison along with his cellmate, Wishart. The escape is sanctioned by members of the British secret service, but Borozhek is seemingly killed by exhaust fumes while being smuggled in the boot of a car. CIA involvement is suspected, as Borozhek still had important information about the NATO department he worked in prior to his arrest. However, it is Wishart who has been killed in Borozhek's place. The secret service realise that they, the police and the CIA are all now hunting Borozhek, who instead contacts Austen. Austen hides Borozhek in a nursing home where he runs a clinic, with his face heavily bandaged as a disguise, while he plans to get him smuggled back to Poland. They manage to dodge the secret service and the CIA, but Borozhek is ambushed by Russian agents as he's about to leave the country. He escapes them, but is killed by a CIA agent before he can flee.

Bob returned to his old stomping ground of ATV for his next writing work. Nicholas Palmer, who had previously written episodes of *Ghost Squad* and *No Hiding Place*, had become a producer at the franchise, and was now in charge of a new series entitled *Fraud Squad*, the brainchild of Ivor Jay, a television critic from the Birmingham *Evening Mail* newspaper. The series starred Patrick O'Connell as Detective Inspector Gamble, and Joanna Van Gyseghem as Detective Sergeant Vicky Hicks. Other writers who worked on the series included Jack Trevor Story, Lewis Griefer, Richard Harris and Robert Banks Stewart. *Fraud Squad* was yet another police crime drama of the sort Bob could turn out blindfolded by now, and he duly contributed the opening episode, 'Turbot on Ice', which was shown on ITV on Tuesday 20 May 1969.

'Turbot on Ice' begins with Frank Turbot, a petty thief, burgling a house belonging to Jessie Stewart. As he's making his way home, he runs into a policeman, and tries to escape, but is arrested. The police know Turbot of old, and discover £4,000 in the holdall he is carrying, along with Jessie's address. They go to question Jessie, but she denies the money is hers. The police suspect that Jessie isn't telling the truth, and hand the case over to Gamble and Hicks. Gamble suspects that Jessie has stolen the money herself, and investigates the firm she works for as a bookkeeper, G T Hollisters. But the MD of G T Hollisters, Derek, isn't very co-operative. Once Gamble has left, he calls Jessie into his office, and asks her if she has any problems she wants to discuss. Gamble goes over Derek's head and gets the permission of the company chairman to examine G T Hollisters' accounts. Derek is forced to co-operate, but tells Jessie of Gamble's suspicions, and advises her to sue Gamble for slander. Gamble goes through the books of G T Hollisters, but can't find any discrepancies. Jessie's solicitor, Yarwood, tells Gamble he's going to sue him for the allegations he made against his client. Gamble discovers that Yarwood and Jessie are in a relationship, and that Yarwood was a trustee of a fund that made regular payments to Jessie. Yarwood arrives, and although he admits that the money was paid to Jessie from the fund, denies that anything illegal has taken place. Gamble discovers that Yarwood had previously represented Turbot in various trials over the years. Turbot confesses that Yarwood set him up to steal the money from Jessie in return for a cut of the cash.

Bob wrote two further episodes for the first series of *Fraud Squad*. The first of these, 'Last Exit to Liechtenstein', was shown on Tuesday 3 June 1969, and was described by the *TV Times* thusly: 'It's the night of the Police Ball, hardly an event to set the town talking. But this year things are different – Rex Lucien decides to go to the ball. Lucien is on bail with a fraud charge hanging over his head; and Gamble is the police officer who arrested him. It's a night when anything could happen – and does!'[120] This was followed by 'Anybody Here Seen Kelly?', which was shown on Tuesday 12 August 1969. The *TV Times* listing for that week had this to say about the episode: 'When a valuable painting believed to have been destroyed in a fire turns up in Ireland, Gamble travels to Dublin to interview Ignatius Kelly, an elderly art dealer. But Kelly

---

120 *TV Times*, w/c 31 May 1969.

disappears, hunted not only by Gamble, but also by Captain MacLennan, son of the owner of the painting – and fanatical leader of a patriotic organisation known as the Greenshirts.'[121]

Bob's final writing credit of the 1960s was an episode of ATV's play anthology series *Happy Ever After*. His episode, 'The Prank', was screened on ITV on Tuesday 16 December 1969. This was produced by John Cooper, who had also previously produced *Emergency Ward 10* and *Honey Lane*.

'The Prank' begins with two laboratory workers in a clinic, Ernie and Jackson, putting up Christmas decorations and preparing for their office Christmas party. When the party begins, the drinks start flowing, and some silly party games are started. One game sees Ernie and a spirited young girl named Sarah sent up to the attic, but they find themselves locked in by Jackson. Sarah isn't impressed, accusing Ernie of engineering the situation himself, and they argue. Sarah's boyfriend Roger turns up at the party looking for her, and is told that she's in the attic with Ernie. He argues with Sarah through the locked door and then storms off. Jackson then realises that he's lost the key to the attic. Sarah and Ernie begin to suspect that they've been forgotten about, and fear that they might end up being locked in the attic for the entire Christmas holiday. Ernie tries to get out of the window, but gets stuck on the roof in the dark. Sarah joins him, and helps him get to safety. They eventually make it to the next room, but that door is locked too. Ernie and Sarah end up talking, and getting to like one another. Sarah invites Ernie over to her flat for Christmas, should they get out. Jackson finds the key at last, and apologetically lets the couple out. Ernie and Sarah walk off arm-in-arm. Although there are some comedic moments in the script, and some nice witty dialogue by Bob, the whole storyline seems a little straight-laced much of the time, almost as if Bob is trying hard to stay within a particular brief, when his instincts may have tempted him to play up the whole affair a bit more.

The decade had ended with Bob seemingly set to cement his position as one of the most prolific and highly-regarded television writers of his day. His writing credits during this time would leave many of his contemporaries wanting in comparison, but there were emerging a few signs and hints that Bob was becoming less interested in writing for just any old series that was kind enough to offer him a commission. His interest in genre television was growing, fuelled no doubt by his early successes with his recent scripts for *Doctor Who*.

121 *TV Times*, w/c 9 August 1969.

CHAPTER EIGHT
NEW FACES
1969-1970

Barely a month after completing his script for the final episode of 'The Space Pirates', on Wednesday 12 February 1969 Bob was commissioned to write yet *another* storyline for *Doctor Who*. He had quickly earned himself a reputation as a writer who could deliver very good, workable scripts to a very tight deadline, which is exactly what *Doctor Who* needed at the time. It was this, more than anything else, that made Bob the natural choice for Terrance Dicks to launch the third Doctor's adventures on screen. 'That was certainly my idea, to get Bob to write the first Jon Pertwee story,' recalls Dicks. 'Bob and I worked on that together. Because I've always thought that Bob was one of the best writers on *Doctor Who*, probably the best, always a pleasure to work with, and his scripts were always good and solid. And very extravagant – he had very little idea of budget, Bob, he would put in things that Cecile B DeMille couldn't afford to do, but I always used to cut them down, or cut them out, or whatever, which he would mutter about, but would take with fairly good grace. So he was my choice to do that first Pertwee story. Which of course was very important, as it established a new Doctor.'

'It was at the end of "The War Games" that Troughton went out,' recalled Bob, 'and they told me that the series was coming back – it was fairly late notice, because they were never sure in those days if the series *was* going to go for another year; there was this path through the BBC machinery. They told me that Troughton was definitely out, but they didn't know who the new star was going to be. And sometime about November [1968], they asked me to start thinking about the first one for the next season, which would be the one where they would introduce whoever the new Doctor was.'

Speaking at the DWAS's Panopticon IV convention in 1981, Bob also recalled, 'They just told me, "Give us the first colour *Doctor Who*". And I thought, "Does that make any difference to me?" basically. But I had a few jokes about Jon's nose, and things like that ... eyebrows which were good for communicating with various people in different areas. But I didn't find any great difficulty in things like that.'[122]

In another 1981 interview, Bob recalled: 'Terrance Dicks asked me to write the opener for that season introducing Jon Pertwee. It had therefore to be

---

122 Panopticon IV Convention, Queen Mary College, 1-2 August 1981.

an Earth story. That almost certainly meant an alien invasion story. I wanted aliens that could pass as humans (they act better) and so came up with the idea of an alien species that could animate plastic.'[123]

Not only did Bob have to write the opening story of the new series, but he had to set the scene for the new format that *Doctor Who* was to follow for the next few years. As Dicks recalls, 'One of the problems of *Doctor Who* was that it was a low-budget show. Barry Letts managed to push the budget up when he took over, but we were always hard up, because science fiction is always expensive by definition. Peter Bryant and Derrick Sherwin came up with this brilliant idea to save money, which is that you do the whole thing like *Quatermass*, you do it on Earth, and the aliens come to you. And that of course means that you can film in the streets, you can use everyday cars, the actors can wear their own clothes. It's not like building and designing an alien planet every four weeks, and you don't have spaceships and things. So it was in accordance with that policy that the Doctor was exiled to Earth at the end of "The War Games". And I never really liked this, but I didn't have the clout in those days to change it. I argued against it, but it went through regardless, because it was a financial thing. When Barry Letts joined, he didn't much like it either, but we were stuck with it, because a season had already been laid out along those lines. So that was why we had, for a season, to do stories that were set on Earth. It was decided as a policy to exile the Doctor to Earth, purely for budget and economic reasons, not for creative reasons, but the trouble with that is it's not *Doctor Who*, it's *Quatermass*! It's an imitation of *Quatermass*. And I remember I told this to Mac Hulke, whom I'd written "The War Games" with, and Mac thought for a bit, and said, "Well, you've got two stories; either alien invasion or mad scientist." And if you think about it, there's a lot in that. It was very difficult to come up with original stories in that format.'

Bob was always slightly defensive when pushed on the similarities between *Quatermass* and the new direction *Doctor Who* was to take from its seventh season, with Earthbound stories now becoming the order of the day. More specifically, he was very quick to play down any similarities that people saw between *Quatermass II* and his script for Jon Pertwee's first story: 'I don't think I saw *Quatermass II*,' he once said. 'I deliberately don't watch much television or go to the cinema in case I'm unconsciously influenced. So any resemblance is coincidental. Anyway, wasn't the monster in *Quatermass* a big glob of chewing gum sticking to the dome of St Paul's?'[124]

---

123 Robert Holmes Interview, *The Time Meddler*: Issue 3, October 1981 – Interview by John M Kahane.
124 Robert Holmes Interview, *Renegade*: Issue 1, 1984 – Interview by Matthew Wicks. In fact, it was the first *Quatermass* serial, *The Quatermass Experiment*, that climaxed with a large monster taking over Westminster Abbey, not St Paul's Cathedral. *Quatermass II* involved the fall to Earth of batches of meteorites containing elements of an alien intelligence, which when collected by possessed humans and taken to a factory, give rise to a large tentacled creature.

The resemblance to *Quatermass* might have been coincidental, but the similarity to the 1966 film *Invasion*, which was based on a storyline written by Bob, was quite uncanny! The final script for the first episode of 'Spearhead from Space' reworks portions of the earlier film, down to actual lines of dialogue.

Terrance Dicks recalls that most of the plot of 'Spearhead from Space' came directly from Bob, with very little prompting required. 'Bob and I would have hammered out this basic idea … I think it was probably Bob's idea, the alien intelligence that could animate plastic, and then the various manifestations of it, but we would have discussed it and talked about it together, and of course you had all the apparatus of establishing a new Doctor; he turns up on Earth, he gets shot down, he turns up in hospital, he escapes from the hospital. So you've got a fair bit going before you've even got into the Autons.'

Bob was also responsible for the little details that were first revealed about the Doctor's Time Lord physiology in this story. 'Bob was very inventive in that kind of way and up until then, very little had been revealed about the Doctor,' recalls Dicks, 'so I thought it was quite nice to feed things in after a while. And of course it's a good moment, when the Doctor's unconscious in hospital, and the doctor listens to both sides of his chest and says, "Good God, this man has got two hearts …" Or when they look at the X-Ray, and they say, "There must be a fault in it, there's two hearts, it can't possibly be right …" So I think that's probably what gave him the idea in the first place, the hospital situation. But the Doctor's obviously not going to have a totally human biology.'

Bob's initial storyline was commissioned under the working title 'Facsimile', and the scene breakdown was due to be delivered on Friday 21 February 1969. Bob actually delivered it on Friday 14 March 1969. This first scene breakdown (reproduced in Interlude V below) was enough to interest the production team in commissioning the story, but first there were a number of things that they wanted to change. The story was key to the long-term success of the series – never before had a new season of *Doctor Who* begun with a completely new cast, and with the new look that colour would inevitably bring, and it was important that nothing was left to chance. To that end, Bob was told to go away and revise his scene breakdown.

In Bob's second draft, the name of Liz's character was given as Liz Shaw, not Shore. When she arrived at UNIT HQ, she did so via either a railway station or a shopping arcade (Bob suggests either as an option), and not a shop. After the Brigadier and Liz leave the hospital, Dr Henderson examines the Doctor, who awakens and asks to be given a mirror. He looks into it, and is amazed and astonished at the sight of his new face. When the Autons kidnap the Doctor from his hospital room, they run into a squad of UNIT troops in the hospital reception, and the Doctor manages to escape from his kidnappers during the confusion, and flees the hospital to head back to the TARDIS.

In Episode Two, Bob details how Dr Henderson hands the TARDIS key to the Brigadier once the comatose Doctor has been returned to the hospital. When Channing activates an Auton with a meteor early in the episode, he then goes to examine a '… huge, opaque plastic coffin, to which plastic pipes are connected'. Later, when Ransome leaves the factory after his confrontation with Hibbert, Channing refers to the creature in the plastic coffin, saying that its growth isn't yet complete, as not all the globes have been recovered. A new scene is then inserted, showing the poacher out in the woods with a young boy, as they discover another glowing meteorite. After Dr Henderson decides that the Doctor is fit enough to leave the hospital, he goes to tell Munro, and the Doctor takes the opportunity to escape out of the window of his room. He makes his way to UNIT HQ on his own, telling the Brigadier that the last time they met, the Brigadier mentioned its location to him. The poacher and young boy run into a policeman as they leave the woods, and try to glean if there are any rewards on offer for finding anything unusual.

In Episode Three, Ransome eludes the Auton chasing him through the factory, and stumbles across Channing and Hibbert showing Scobie out. The pursuing Auton freezes, and Ransome is able to escape. Once Scobie has left, Channing sends the Auton to locate Ransome. The Doctor's aborted escape in the TARDIS is described in more detail, with the dematerialisation noise cutting out, and clouds of smoke pouring out of the doors as the Doctor re-emerges. The poacher is with the young boy having supper when the Auton attacks, and the boy escapes to raise the alarm at the UNIT tent in the nearby woods. Munro and a squad of troops return to assist the poacher, and the Auton is forced to retreat. They take the trunk back to the command tent. When the Doctor, Liz and the Brigadier visit Auto Plastics, they notice a locked security area, but are denied access by Channing, who tells them that it's for top secret Government work, and not even the Brigadier has clearance to go inside.

Bob's redraft of the final episode was quite dramatic, and introduced many new plot elements into the story. Autons posing as MI5 agents infiltrate UNIT HQ and hold the Doctor and Munro at gunpoint as they try to retrieve the meteorite. Munro is shot while defending the Doctor, but the Autons escape with the globe. Back at the plastics factory, Channing uses the globe to create a creature that is revealed as the true form of the Autons. The Doctor develops a portable UHF transmitter, which he uses to destroy the Autons and the creature at the story's conclusion. One sequence notably missing from this version is the one in which the Auton shop window dummies come to life and start attacking and killing bystanders – an iconic scene that was thankfully reinstated in the final script for the episode.

'Facsimile' was structured with most of the scenes set indoors or in locations that could be easily reproduced in the BBC's own studios. As already mentioned, with the advent of the third Doctor, the series was due to be made in colour for the first time, and to give the production team time to gear themselves up for this, there was a longer gap than usual between the end of production of the sixth season and the start of work on the seventh. Throughout the 1960s, *Doctor Who* was on air for 40-plus weeks of the year, with only a few weeks off for the cast and crew between production blocks. Each season usually started airing in the autumn, and would continue right through to the following summer. For the first colour season, transmission had been put back some three or four months to begin in January 1970, while the number of episodes per year was initially reduced to just 25 (but later slightly increased to 26).

Throughout all of the development on the story up to this point, there was one crucial piece of the puzzle missing – the identity of the actor who would take over from Patrick Troughton. After Bob submitted his revised storyline for 'Facsimile' in March 1969, there was a gap of nearly two months before he received the actual commission to write the four scripts for the story, presumably as the *Doctor Who* production office agonised over their decision as to who to cast as the new Doctor. Bob was finally commissioned to write the scripts on Tuesday 3 June 1969, with a target delivery date of Monday 30 June 1969. The BBC records for this production show that the script for the first episode was accepted on Friday 6 June, so Bob either wrote it incredibly quickly, or he had already begun working on it prior to the formal commission.

Jon Pertwee was unveiled in the press as the new Doctor the following day. There was then a lengthy gap of about six weeks before Bob delivered the script for the second episode on Friday 18 July. This was formally accepted by the *Doctor Who* production office on Tuesday 22 July. The script for Episode Three was delivered a few days later. That for Episode Four followed on Friday 25 July, and was accepted just a few days later, on Tuesday 29 July.

Terrance Dicks then sent Bob a note on Tuesday 29 July 1969, thanking him for delivering by hand the script of the final episode the previous week. Bob was evidently just about to take a well-earned camping holiday, as Dicks's letter notes, 'As we agreed, I'll take care of any further rewrites on the show while you're away. Hope the roads are clear and the camp sites uncrowded!'

Bob was on unfamiliar ground when it came to his characterisation of the new Doctor. 'When I wrote the first Pertwee story, "Spearhead from Space", he later recalled, 'I had no idea how he would play the part. I made his dialogue slightly more polished (or pompous) than the kind of speeches I'd written for Troughton. It seemed to work because, looking back, the essence of the Pertwee's characterisation, as it developed, was a polished style.'[125]

On another occasion, when asked if he had had any say in the look or character of the third Doctor, Bob replied, 'I didn't really have any "say" as such. They told me Pertwee had been cast, and I wrote "Spearhead from Space", so I may have had some influence on his style. But the way he dressed and so on were matters that were probably discussed in the front office.'[126]

In his essay 'A Life of Hammer and Tongs', Bob would later recall his initial encounters with Jon Pertwee: 'I wrote Patrick Troughton out of the series and Jon Pertwee in. Now Jon's a funny chap. He doesn't use fluorescent ink (to mark his lines in a script) but simply tears off the pages where he hasn't a line. After some episodes he would sit like Worzel Gummidge on a paper dump and wave his remaining pages between forefinger and thumb. "A thin episode this week," he would say.'[127]

'It was Peter Bryant who came up with the idea of Jon Pertwee,' recalled Bob some years later, 'and I only knew him as a sort of light entertainer, and singer, and cabaret actor. It seemed very interesting, and I thought "Either it'll work or it won't." And so I wrote it ... I wanted to hold back the revelation of the Doctor's new face as long as possible. These days you couldn't do that; in any case, you've only got to look at the *Radio Times*. But anyway, that was the idea. So we kept the Doctor back for quite a while. Then we got all the hospital stuff, where you don't really see him. It's a very deliberate, slow build-up. And then I think quite a long way into the episode, I had Pertwee reveal himself, this new face.'

The story also introduced the Doctor's new female companion, Liz Shaw, as played by Caroline John. Bob was given a basic character outline for Liz by Dicks before he began writing the story. 'There was about half a page of notes,' he recalled. 'They'd tell you the name of the character, and roughly how old she is, and who she's going to be played by. It was a scientific story, there was quite a lot of laboratory stuff in it, as I recall. And that was her forté. So I tried to do that. But the companion in *Doctor Who* always tends to come down to the same kind of character, because the Doctor has to be the dominant force, and she – or he sometimes – is usually there for exposition purposes, to ask what's happening, what's going on.'

When interviewed at the Panopticon IV convention in 1981, Bob offered his thoughts on the Autons themselves, and specifically the scene of them breaking out of the shop windows. 'I thought that was such a good scene,

125 Robert Holmes Interview, *Type 40*: Issue 1, 1978.
126 Robert Holmes Interview, *Renegade*: Issue 1, 1984 – Interview by Matthew Wicks.
127 From 'A Life of Hammer and Tongs' by Robert Holmes, published in *The Doctor Who File* by Peter Haining (W H Allen, 1986).

that. Yeah! You can only do so much with a shapeless piece of plastic. And obviously we had to have human models ... That's the thing about aliens, they always tend to look like people, basically, underneath it all. Because there aren't that many alien actors! So you had these people dressed as shop window dummies. We had these people as Madame Tussauds models, at one point, and they came to life. Which is the only thing you can really do with plastic if they're going to be inhabited by an actor.'[128]

'Plastic was coming in,' Bob recalled later. 'Doomwatch did a plastic story, where an aircraft came apart or something, this stuff started eating the plastic.[129] And I just got the idea that as there was a lot of plastic around, I'd invent an alien force that could inhabit plastic and use it for its own purposes. It would be invisible, and it would slide about everywhere.'

When asked if he could recall his inspiration for naming the Autons and the Nestenes, Bob said, 'Autons comes from autonomous, Nestenes ... I don't know. Nests ... something to do with a plastic, swirling mass ... A blob of instinct. But it forms Autons, who become autonomous, they're not part of the host.'

The opening scene of the story, with the meteorites landing on Earth, was something Bob wanted to depict from very start. 'I think I had in my mind that Doctor Who very rarely sees something arriving on Earth,' he later recalled, 'and [given] the fact that this was an "Earth" season, I wanted to see the actual invasion take place.'

The story was renamed 'Spearhead from Space' shortly after all the location filming had been completed. It was shown on BBC1 over four Saturdays in January 1970, giving the new Doctor – and the new colour series – a powerful start. Television reviewer Matthew Coady, writing in the Daily Mirror, said: 'Horror fantasies affect us only if they create a sense of nightmare out of something that is essentially familiar. This Doctor Who adventure wins my vote as the best in the lifetime of the series so far. What it did was to suggest an authentic sense of the uncanny.' Coady went on to praise the Autons, while dismissing prior alien threats that the Doctor had faced: '... the Zarbi and the Sensorites were readily forgettable. Others, like the Daleks, had an oddly comic air. Your friendly multiple store tailors, on the other hand, are just down the high street, and that is where they are – their sightless eyes fixed on the plate-glass window.'[130] High praise indeed!

---

128 Panopticon IV Convention, Queen Mary College, 1-2 August 1981.
129 Doomwatch's very first episode, 'The Plastic Eaters', was shown on BBC1 on Monday 9 February 1970. It couldn't therefore have been much of an influence on Bob and his initial idea to use plastic as a threat in 'Spearhead from Space', but it might have got him thinking about the idea again just in time for him to write the sequel, 'Terror of the Autons', a few months later – see next chapter.
130 Daily Mirror, 27 January 1970.

However, the story – complete with rampaging Auton shop-window dummies – did come in for some criticism, as Terrance Dicks recalls: 'It's a sure sign that the monster's good if you arouse a storm of controversy in the press and Mrs Whitehouse doesn't like it. And you get ticked off by your superiors – but not very hard, because the ratings go up. Generally speaking, the Autons were a good, scary monster. It's always a fine line about how scary you can be, and I think when Barry did join later, he was slightly more responsible about that than I was. He was always asking, "Are you going over the edge into horror?" And I think one of the principles was, you could show something scary but you could only show it very quickly; you would cut away very quickly, you wouldn't dwell on it. And things would happen very quickly so that people imagined that they saw more than they saw in some senses. I remember Ronnie Marsh, who was the then-head of the Serials Department, he hauled me in and had a long discussion about "Spearhead from Space". But he was torn, because he thought it was too scary, and so told me to watch it, but on the other hand he thought it was a bloody good show, and he really thought it was great stuff. So as I say, the reproofs were fairly mild, internally. Officially, they might want to say, "Yes indeed, it's much too frightening, and we've spoken very severely to the producer and the script editor", but any reproofs were slightly tongue-in-cheek, in my experience.'

'Spearhead from Space' was Bob's first real all-time classic *Doctor Who* story. The fact that it was made in colour – and on film – only enhances its reputation. The Autons are an inspired creation; creepy, unswerving, indefatigable, and almost the ideal monster for the series (in that they're not as expensive as Daleks or Cybermen to construct). The story also introduces us to a new Doctor, a new companion, and sets up the next five years' worth of adventures, as UNIT becomes the Doctor's Earthbound home. Bob's reputation as the writer who best knew how to write for *Doctor Who* is perhaps evident for the first time with this story.

Producer Derrick Sherwin abruptly left *Doctor Who* after work on 'Spearhead from Space' had concluded, opting to join up with his former producer Peter Bryant on the BBC's *Paul Temple* series. He was replaced by actor-turned-writer-turned-director-turned-producer Barry Letts. Letts produced the reminder of the stories that had already been commissioned by Sherwin and Dicks for the rest of the season. Once this was finished, and the programme's long-term future had been assured, he and Dicks turned their attention to the eighth season, due to begin on BBC1 in January 1971.

INTERLUDE V
DOCTOR WHO: 'FACSIMILE'
MARCH 1969

Robert Holmes's full original scene breakdown for the *Doctor Who* story that eventually became 'Spearhead from Space' is reprinted here as originally submitted, complete with his original spellings and punctuation:

FACSIMILE

EPISODE ONE

1. FILM: METEORITES HISSING THROUGH SKY.

2. RADAR TRACKING STATION.
Two technicians are tracking the arrival of the meteorites on a radar screen. We see that they are puzzled and unable to account for them.

3. FILM: WOODLAND.
A Poacher is looking up at the sky. He comes across a mysterious sphere buried in the earth. It is pulsing with light as if emitting a signal. He approaches it cautiously and is about to examine it. We hear the sound of footsteps crashing through the undergrowth. We see the Poacher look up in horror as something unseen smashes him to one side. Hold on the sphere as two oddly white and waxy hands come into shot and carry it away.

4. RADAR TRACKING STATION.
The sightings on the screen are over. Suddenly the screen flares as some tremendous force of energy registers. Then the screen goes blank and there is nothing.

5. FILM: WOODLAND.
The Tardis stands in the middle of the woods. After a moment the door opens slowly and the Doctor staggers out,

his back towards us. He closes the door and takes a few steps before collapsing face downwards on the ground.

6. RADAR TRACKING STATION.
The two technicians discuss the strange phenomenon they have seen on their radar screen and wonder what to do about it. One of them remembers a standing order that any occurrences of this kind are to be reported to an organisation called UNIT. 'What's that?', asks the other.

7. FILM: LONDON STREET.
We see Liz Shore[131] entering a shabby run-down shop.

8. UNIT H.Q.
Concealed behind the shop is a modern office and communications centre. A branch of UNIT. Brigadier Lethbridge Stewart is told that Miss Shore has arrived to see him. Liz enters and we learn that she is a Government research scientist, assigned to UNIT much against her will. She thinks this Security business is childish nonsense and it's keeping her away from important research. The Brigadier tells her that for his part he's not particularly fond of scientists but these days science and Security are often mixed up. Which is why he has commandeered her services. He explains the function of UNIT as an international Intelligence Service and tells her of the mysterious meteor swarm which is not the first of its kind. His men are searching the area but he isn't hopeful. Nothing was found on previous occasions. Liz is an expert in meteorites and it will be her task to evaluate anything found.

9. COTTAGE HOSPITAL, RECEPTION.
Two UNIT soldiers are carrying in the Doctor on a stretcher, his face covered by a blanket. Captain Monro is explaining to Doctor Henderson that his men found this man unconscious while they were searching the area. He knows nothing about the man and doesn't tell Henderson why the area was being

---

131 The character would eventually be renamed Liz Shaw.

searched. It's obvious that Monro is anxious to be rid of this embarrassment and be back at his job. Monro phones the Brigadier and tells him of his finds adding that there is no trace of any meteorites. He's found nothing else at all except for an old Police Box abandoned in the woods.

10. UNIT HQ.
The Brigadier is taking the call. We see his astonished reaction on the mention of the Police Box. Liz is puzzled. But the Brigadier doesn't explain. He tells Monro to continue the search and that he himself will be joining him shortly.

11. COTTAGE HOSPITAL. PRIVATE ROOM.
In the background the Doctor, face still out of shot, is tossing and turning on a bed, muttering to himself. At the end of the bed Dr Henderson and a nurse are examining a set of X-rays. Dr Henderson is astonished since they show signs of a completely abnormal physiology. Either the stranger is some kind of weird freak or he must have come from another world, says Dr Henderson, half jokingly. We see that this conversation is overheard by a hospital porter and we follow the porter into …

12. COTTAGE HOSPITAL. RECEPTION.
The porter goes to the public telephone and rings a Fleet St number saying he's got a story that ought to be worth money.

13. UNIT HQ.
The Brigadier is clearing up some final business before going to join Monro. He tells Liz that she is to come with him in case the search has turned up any meteorites. But it's obvious that the Brigadier is more interested in the mysterious stranger with the Police Box. He tells Liz that perhaps they are going to see a man he once knew.

14. COTTAGE HOSPITAL. RECEPTION.
It is now some time later. The Receptionist is trying to fend off a small but noisy group of Pressmen who have come down on the 'man from space story' rumour, which

looks like being a good silly season story. Monro is trying to get rid of them but his rash announcement of his position only causes more curiosity! What connection has the stranger with UNIT? The Brigadier enters with Liz and uses his authority to clear out the Pressmen. He is furious with Monro for allowing this fuss to develop.

15. COTTAGE HOSPITAL. PRIVATE ROOM.
The Brigadier enters with Liz and Monro and Dr Henderson. Eagerly the Brigadier goes to the bed and examines the face of the man who lies there. He - and we - see the man's face for the first time. It is completely different from the old Doctor Who. The Brigadier is astonished and disappointed - this man is a stranger to him. But just at this moment the Doctor opens his eyes and in a flash of consciousness looks at the Brigadier and says 'Lethbridge Stewart my dear fellow, how nice to see you again.' Astonished the Brigadier tries to question him, but the Doctor relapses almost at once into incoherence.

16. COTTAGE HOSPITAL. RECEPTION.
One of the reporters is still hanging about. He enters the phone box and appears to make a call, saying that there is something strange about the man who has been found and that UNIT is on the scene. We see that he is apparently talking to empty space, the phone still at rest on its cradle. As the reporter goes we see Lethbridge Stewart, Liz and Monro enter. Lethbridge Stewart asks Monro what he has done about the Tardis and is furious when Monro says 'nothing'. He orders an armed guard to be put on the Tardis. No-one is to be allowed to approach it. The Brigadier will arrange for its transport to H.Q. as soon as possible. Brigadier and Liz leave.

17. COTTAGE HOSPITAL. PRIVATE ROOM.
The Doctor twisting and turning on his bed.

18. RECEPTION.
Monro is asking Dr Henderson about the Doctor's condition.

The Brigadier wants him brought to London for interrogation as soon as possible. Henderson says that this is out of the question. The man may be in a highly dangerous condition and must be retained for further observation and study. Monro reluctantly accepts this and leaves. We follow Henderson into …

19. PRIVATE ROOM.
Henderson examines the Doctor who is still in a semi-comatose state. He is discussing the case with the nurse when a small group of men force their way into the room. Completely silently they shoulder Dr Henderson aside, put the Doctor on the UNIT stretcher which is still in the room and carry him away.

20. UNIT HQ.
Liz is trying to get some information out of the Brigadier. Reluctantly he tells her that in the past he came across a man known only as The Doctor who helped him at a time when the Earth was in great danger. But this definitely isn't the same man. There is no resemblance at all. 'But he seems to know you' says Liz. The conversation is interrupted by a call from a furious Dr Henderson who accuses the Brigadier of abducting his patient. The Brigadier realises that the Doctor has been kidnapped.

21. STOREROOM.
The Doctor is slumped on a chair in a circle of light, questioned by a man whose face we do not see. Who is he? Where does he come from? The Doctor makes no reply and we see that he is given an injection. After a moment he simply crashes to the floor. Baffled, his questioners leave. Hold on the Doctor lying on the floor; obviously with a tremendous effort he drags himself to his feet. He manages to smash open a small window and make his escape.

22. FILM. WOODLAND.
The Doctor runs on blindly. We hear the sound of pursuit crashing behind him. In another part of the wood a UNIT

soldier guarding the Tardis hears the sound of running footsteps towards him. He raises his rifle and issues a challenge, but the noise comes nearer. Suddenly the Doctor bursts from the wood. The panic-stricken sentry raises his riddle and fires. The Doctor falls to the ground.

EPISODE TWO

TK 1. WOODLAND.[132]
The Doctor is shot by the panicking UNIT sentry and collapses. Other UNIT soldiers appear attracted by the shots. One of them gets on the RT to UNIT HQ.

1. COTTAGE HOSPITAL RECEPTION.
The Brigadier arrives and demands to know what's been going on. He is furious when Munro[133] explains that the Doctor has been shot by the UNIT sentry. He orders Munro to put a heavy guard on the Doctor at the hospital, and then goes to the private ward to see how the Doctor is progressing.

2. PRIVATE ROOM.
The Doctor lies in a deathlike coma attended to by Dr Henderson. Henderson tells the Brigadier that the Doctor has been drugged and shot and although the wound isn't too serious he seems to have retreated into some kind of coma: pulse and heartbeat are barely noticeable. The Brigadier asks to be informed of any change and goes back to Reception.

3. COTTAGE HOSPITAL RECEPTION.
Munro tells the Brigadier that the searching troops have found nothing but a few plastic fragments. The Brigadier orders these sent to HQ for analysis. Munro says the Doctor has said nothing since they found him and all they can deduce was that he was taken to somewhere in the area.

---

132 'TK' is BBC shorthand for telecine; basically material pre-filmed and then played into the studio on film.
133 'Monro' changes his name to 'Munro' between the typed scene breakdowns of Episodes One and Two. This and the slightly different notations for things like telecine scenes indicate that Bob probably wrote the breakdown for Episode One at an earlier point than those for Episodes Two to Four.

4. PLASTICS FACTORY.

This is a small ultra-modern automated factory. We see Channing, the man who posed as a reporter at work. A man-like Auton lies immobile connected to a piece of machinery. Also connected is one of the globes that fell from the sky! The globe is pulsing and emitting light. Then as the light dies away and the globe becomes dead the Auton comes to life. It rises and walks away to stand immobile in a corner of the factory.

5. PLASTICS FACTORY OFFICE.

Ransome, an ex-employee of the firm forces his way in to see Hibbert, the Managing Director. We learn in this scene that Ransome went to America where he got advance orders worth thousands of dollars for a new doll made by the factory. On his return to England he received a letter telling him that the factory was no longer making dolls but had changed to the window dummy field. Ransome cannot understand this in view of his previous good relations with Hibbert and has come for an explanation. He reminds Hibbert that he was promised a partnership if the deal was a success. Hibbert is cold and unhelpful, saying that there has been a change of policy and that he now has a new partner. Angrily Ransome leaves. Channing and Hibbert discuss the possibility of Ransome's making trouble. They also discuss their kidnapping of the Doctor and his escape. Channing says there must be no open trouble until they are ready for it. The programme is not complete.

6. UNIT LABORATORY.

Liz is at work on the fragments found by Munro's men. She tells the Brigadier that they seem to have passed through the Earth's atmosphere like meteorites but they have the characteristics of some incredibly strong plastic. Liz asks after the Doctor and tries to find out why the Brigadier is interested in him but he is still evasive. The arrival of General Scobie is announced. The Brigadier tells Liz that Scobie is his superior and Liaison Officer with the Regular Army. Scobie enters and asks what's been happening with all these stories about meteorites and people from space. The Brigadier says it's probably only a silly season scare but UNIT is looking into it. Scobie rather pleased with himself, mentions that he's visiting this particular area today. A firm called Auto Plastics have invited him to be measured for a waxwork which will be put in a special VIP room in a famous waxworks.

7. COTTAGE HOSPITAL, PRIVATE ROOM.
The Doctor lies in his trance as though dead. Suddenly his eyes flicker open and he sits up. Dr Henderson enters the room and is astonished to see him so revived. The Doctor says that he is now perfectly well and demands to be given his clothes and be allowed to leave. Henderson makes a quick examination and finds that indeed the Doctor does seem to be recovered. He orders the Doctor's clothes to be returned and leaves to tell Munro.

8. COTTAGE HOSPITAL. RECEPTION.
Henderson enters and tells Munro of the Doctor's amazing recovery. Munro says they can't just let him go. The Doctor appears and demands to be allowed to leave: he must get back to his Police Box. Munro tells him that the Police Box has been taken to UNIT HQ in London and that's where the Doctor's going too, whether he likes it or not.

9. UNIT LABORATORY.
The Tardis is installed in a corner of the lab, much to Liz's astonishment. The Brigadier produces a key which was found clutched in the Doctor's hand. He tries to enter the Tardis but the key doesn't work for him. He tells Liz that the owner of the Police Box is on his way to them. At this point the Doctor enters with Munro, very angry. The Brigadier tries to question him about his experiences of the previous night but the Doctor says he can remember nothing except being shot by one of the Brigadier's men. He demands that the Brigadier return the key of the Tardis and allow him to leave. The Brigadier refuses. He is far from sure that the Doctor – if he is the Doctor – isn't

involved in the strange goings-on. At this point the Doctor is distracted by the fragments that Liz is examining. He is obviously knowledgeable about them and the Brigadier seizes upon this an excuse. The Doctor can help Liz with her work. Later he will be allowed to go - perhaps.

TK 2.
Scobie arrives at the plastics factory to be warmly greeted by Hibbert.

10. PLASTICS FACTORY.
Scobie shown round by a deferential Channing and Hibbert. They explain that their new plastic waxworks are far more true to life than the old kind. Scobie is shown an Auton which bears only a rough resemblance to him. Hastily Hibbert explains that this is only the first rough base. This is why they need Scobie's presence so their measuring techniques can enable them to make a complete likeness.

TK 3.
We see Ransome moving cautiously through the woods at the perimeter of the factory and cutting a factory fence with wire cutters. He makes his way to the factory buildings.

11. FACTORY OFFICE.
Hibbert and Channing are saying goodbye to Scobie, thanking him for his co-operation. They will inform him as soon as the waxwork is ready for exhibition.

12. UNIT LABORATORY.
Liz and the Doctor work together on the fragments. The Doctor is bad-tempered, Liz very curious but gets nothing out of him. Almost against his will the Doctor becomes interested in the problem. He tells Liz that the fragments are indeed of a kind unknown on Earth. He demonstrates that they have the property of holding a charge of electrical energy. In their original form the fragments would consist of a large globe. Liz is impressed but sceptical. How can the Doctor possibly know all this. The Doctor doesn't seem too sure.

13. PLASTICS FACTORY.
We see Ransome break in through a rear door. He explores the factory which is eerily silent and deserted. He finds limbs of Autons ready for assembly and completed Autons standing motionless against a wall. As he goes by, one of them turns its head to watch him pass.

14. FACTORY OFFICE.
Channing and Hibbert have just said farewell to Scobie. As soon as they are alone we see that they are aware of Ransome's presence in the factory. Channing gives the command 'Destroy him'.

15. PLASTICS FACTORY.
Immediately the Auton comes to life behind Ransome and begins to stalk him. It grabs for him but Ransome turns in time and backs away in horror. The Auton unscrews its hand to reveal the nozzle of a gun and blasts at him. Ransome dodges and the Auton raises its gun again.

EPISODE THREE

1. PLASTICS FACTORY.
Desperately avoiding the blast of the Auton's gun Ransome dashes through the door by which he entered with the Auton in pursuit.

TK 1. WOODLAND.
Ransome crashes blindly through the woods, the Auton in pursuit.

2. PLASTICS FACTORY OFFICE.
Aware that Ransome has escaped Channing recalls the Auton since it must not be seen in the open and there are UNIT soldiers in the area.

TK 2. WOODLAND.
The Auton ceases its pursuit and turns back towards the factory. Ransome continues to run full-tilt into a UNIT

soldier and begins to babble out his incredible story.

3. ARMY TENT.

Munro is receiving reports from his search parties. Nothing has been found. The Poacher enters and says that he knows the area and offers to help in the search. No doubt there would be a reward for anyone who did find anything? Brusquely Munro gets rid of him. A puzzled sentry brings in Ransome and Munro decides to send him to see the Brigadier.

4. UNIT LABORATORY.

The Doctor tells Liz that he can't make any more progress with the primitive instruments she had. Liz says they are using all the most up-to-date equipment. The Doctor says he has far more effective equipment in his Police Box. If Liz could obtain him the key he could solve their problem.

5. UNIT HQ.

The Brigadier is interrogating Ransome about his experiences at the Plastics Factory. Ransome repeats that he and Hibbert were close friends before this business trip to America. Now the factory has been automated out of all recognition and Hibbert seems a different man. Ransome blames the new partner Channing. Liz enters during this scene but is somewhat brusquely dismissed by the Brigadier. She sees the Tardis key on the Brigadier' desk and somewhat piqued decides to take it. Unseen by the Brigadier she picks it up and leaves.

6. LABORATORY.

The Doctor is working and after a moment Liz enters with the key. Eagerly he takes it from her and disappears inside the Tardis. A moment later the Brigadier enters in hot pursuit having noticed that they key has gone. He berates Liz for giving it to the Doctor - that's the last they'll see of him. Liz is baffled. Where can anyone go in a Police Box? But after a moment the Tardis door opens and the Doctor re-appears crestfallen.

7. PLASTICS FACTORY.
Channing and Hibbert discuss the fate of the recently arrived 'swarm'. One globe disintegrated on impact and even if UNIT find the fragments they will tell them nothing. But one globe, the swarm leader, is still missing and is not transmitting its homing signal.

8. POACHERS HUT.
The Poacher enters and opens a heavy old-fashioned metal trunk. Inside wrapped in rags is one of the globes. He takes it out to admire it, telling himself it would be worth a great deal to someone. The globe begins to pulse with light. Terrified, he puts it back in the trunk and closes the lid.

9. FACTORY.
Channing tells Hibbert that the missing swarm leader has transmitted its whereabouts. An Auton will fetch it as soon as it is dark.

10. UNIT LABORATORY.
Liz reproaches the Doctor for trying to trick her. He says that he couldn't resist a chance to regain his freedom but he now realises that escape in the Tardis is impossible and that it is his duty to stay and help with the mystery with which he is involved. Perhaps when it is solved he will be allowed to leave. By the Brigadier? asks Liz. No, by others more powerful says the Doctor. He says they have now learnt all the fragments can tell them and wishes they had a complete globe. The Brigadier enters and tells them that Munro has had no success. In his report Munro mentioned the Poacher who was after a reward. The Doctor says this must be followed up and tells the Brigadier to contact Munro and find the Poacher. The Doctor says they must all get down to the area.

11. POACHERS HUT.
The Poacher is at his supper when the door crashes open. A tall shadowy figure is there and the Poacher cries out

in horror when he sees its face is blank. It throws him aside and begins to search the room.

TK 3. WOODLAND.
Munro and his men are approaching the hut when they hear the Poacher's screams and the noise of destruction. They run to the hut.

12. HUT.
Munro's men enter. The Auton smashes its way through them and retreats. Their shots have no effect on it, and it gets away.

13. ARMY TENT.
The Doctor, Liz and the Brigadier are there when Munro enters with the trunk. The Doctor examines the globe cautiously and then closes the trunk saying the metal must have muffled the homing signal. The Brigadier has the trunk sent back to HQ. Meanwhile, the Doctor who has heard Ransome's story says that they should visit the Plastics Factory.

14. PLASTICS FACTORY.
Channing and Hibbert discuss the Autons failure to retrieve the globe. Channing says they must take steps to stop UNIT troubling them further.

TK 4. EXTERIOR PLASTICS FACTORY.
The Doctor Liz and the Brigadier and Munro arrive by jeep.

15. PLASTICS FACTORY.
Channing and Hibbert show them round with great politeness and say that Ransome is just an unbalanced former employee with a grudge. Baffled the Brigadier and his party are forced to leave. When they have gone Channing and Hibbert begin work on an Auton.

16. UNIT LAB.
Watched by the others the Doctor examines the globe with

an EEG machine. He points out that it emits a brainwave like a human. It houses a form of intelligence. The Brigadier recalls that Gen. Scobie paid a visit to Auto Plastics and decides to call him …

17. SCOBIE'S HALLWAY.
Scobie is none too pleased at being called to the phone and says he noticed nothing irregular at the factory. As he slams the phone down the doorbell rings. He opens the door and recoils in horror. Facing him is an Auton. An exact replica of Scobie himself.

EPISODE FOUR

1. SCOBIE'S HALLWAY.
Scobie opens the door and recoils in horror. Facing him is an Auton. An exact replica of himself. Scobie backs away as the Auton advances towards him …

2. UNIT LABORATORY.
The Doctor is still trying to convince the Brigadier that the globe of plastic is 'thinking'. It was designed to house some form of pure intelligence. A call comes from the Brigadier from Gen. Scobie. It is a direct order to discontinue his investigation of Auto Plastics. The Brigadier protests but Scobie insists. It isn't UNIT's job to molest innocent civilians. The Brigadier tells the Doctor that he will continue the investigation. Munro brings a report on Auto Plastics which bears out Ransome's story. This small doll-making firm suddenly entered the window dummy field with great success and has contracts to supply shops all over the country. Their prices are so low as to be almost uneconomic. Nevertheless they have been buying vast quantities of raw materials and expensive machinery. They have also entered the waxworks field. The Doctor says he needs a quantity of UHF transmitting equipment. The Brigadier says this will take time to install. Then meanwhile, says the Doctor, let's all go to the waxworks.

TK 1. EXTERIOR WAXWORKS.
The Doctor Liz and the Brigadier arriving at Mme Tussauds.

3. WAXWORKS VIP ROOM.
An official of the waxworks shows them round this new feature. He explains that Auto Plastics are providing the models free of charge in exchange for the 'showcase' for their products. Liz notices that the subjects chosen are a little odd. Politicians, Civil Servants, Senior Officers etc but no more frivolous figures such as pop stars and entertainers. The Brigadier remarks that there is no waxwork of Scobie. The Doctor tries to examine one of the models but is firmly prevented. And the Brigadier does not feel in a position to insist.

4. PLASTICS FACTORY.
Channing and Hibbert discuss the 'plan'. Soon it will be time to act. UNIT can do them no harm in the short term remaining. But they are still worried about the missing globe.

5. UNIT LABORATORY.
The Doctor is absorbed with his UHF equipment, trying out the effect of various frequencies on the globe. The Brigadier asks the purpose of the waxworks. The Doctor says it's obvious that he must have one of the models to check. The Brigadier says he can't confiscate one but he can steal one. Liz and the Brigadier leave to do this. The Doctor goes on working but finds he has to remove the shielding from the globe. A particular frequency causes the globe to start pulsing, and the Doctor hurriedly replaces the shield.

6. PLASTICS FACTORY.
We see Channing and Hibbert react. Now at least they know the position of the missing swarm leader.

TK 2. EXTERIOR REAR WAXWORKS.
We see Liz and the Brigadier forcing open a rear door.

133

7. INT. WAXWORKS.
We see them through the darkened waxworks to the VIP room. The Brigadier goes to pick up a model but the model reaches hands out towards him. All around them the waxworks come to life and advance menacingly. They turn and see Channing standing in the doorway. The Brigadier grabs Channing and throws him into the Autons. He and Liz make their escape.

8. UNIT LAB.
The Doctor is working alone with his UHF equipment when he hears the sound of gunshots. UNIT soldiers retreat into the laboratory firing without effect on the advancing Autons. The globe begins to emit its pulsing signal. Frantically the Doctor works on the equipment while the battle rages around him. Almost by chance he finds the right frequency and the globe explodes. The Autons too reel and collapse. The Brigadier and Liz return and the Doctor says that he has the means to attack the Autons if he can transmit the signal with sufficient power. He tells the Brigadier to raid both waxworks and factory immediately. The Brigadier says that without Scobie's co-operation his resources are limited but he will muster all the men he can. The Doctor draws Liz aside and says he needs her help.

9. PLASTICS FACTORY.
Hibbert is activating the fighting Autons in order to defend the factory. Channing arrives and says that the waxworks duplicates are out and will soon be spreading confusion. The factory Autons can deal with the Brigadier's limited forces holding them off until the arrival of the major swarm. Then it will be too late. Channing and Hibbert order stage one into operation.

TK 3. FILM MONTAGE.
Whatever we can manage of shop window Autons coming to life and attacking key points.

10. UNIT LAB.
The Brigadier is receiving a flood of messages about

dummies coming to life and attacking key points. Services and the Police seem to be taking no effective action. All are bogged down in contradictory orders. The purpose of the waxwork duplicates is now clear. The Brigadier leaves for the attack on the factory ignoring repeated messages from Scobie and the Home Secretary to immobilise UNIT. The Doctor concludes his arrangements with Liz stressing that she is to set his plan into operation at an agreed time - say 6 o'clock.

TK 4. UNIT TROOPS.
On the move led by the Brigadier and Munro. Helicopters, jeeps, etc.

11. LABORATORY.
The Doctor rechecks his calculations, sends Liz to carry out her instructions.

TK 5. EXTERIOR PLASTICS FACTORY.
A battle is raging between UNIT troops and the Autons who are using their built-in guns and seem impervious the small arms fire. The Brigadier is having some success with grenades and trying to arrange over the RT for artillery but gets no response from the army. The UNIT force seems to making some progress when Scobie arrives in a jeep with regular Army officers. Scobie tells the Brigadier that more troops are on the way and unless UNIT lay down their arms they will be forcibly disarmed. Scobie is giving the impression that the UNIT men have simply gone berserk, aided by the fact that the Autons have withdrawn from sight. The Brigadier is faced with the choice of retreating or opening fire on British troops. The Doctor arrives in a jeep. He tells the Brigadier to wait and do nothing. Then alone the Doctor enters the factory.

12. FACTORY.
The Doctor faces Channing Hibbert and the Autons. He demands to know their purpose. Channing explains that they are all part of an Alien group intelligence which exists

as pure energy though it can animate certain plastics to give itself body. The Aliens exist in vast hives which cover entire planets. Earth is to be their next colony. England will be reduced to chaos and conquered then used as a springboard to take over the world. All other life forms will perish. Since the Aliens are in fact one intelligence they are mutually telepathic. The Doctor says the plan cannot succeed and say that if the Autons surrender they will be allowed to return to their own planet. The Autons advance menacingly and on the stroke of 6 the Doctor switches on a transmitter radio in his pocket. It emits a highpitched sound and the Autons reel back and collapse.

TK 6. EXTERIOR FACTORY.
UNIT troops advance with their radio equipment transmitting the same frequency and mop up the Autons. Scobie reels and collapses face downwards. The Brigadier turns over the body and finds the face smooth and blank.

13. FACTORY.
The UNIT troops enter the factory. Concealed they find the 'real' Hibbert and Scobie together with the bodies of others copied by the Autons. All are in suspended animation but the Doctor says they will eventually recover now their Autons are destroyed.

14. UNIT LABORATORY
The Doctor explains how Liz was sent to Broadcasting House to arrange for the broadcasting of the frequency that destroyed the Aliens. The Doctor turns his attention to the Tardis and the Brigadier says that he will of course give the Doctor every help in effecting its repair and if any more little problems should crop up perhaps the Doctor would continue to help UNIT. The Doctor is reluctant but the Brigadier holds all the cards.

CHAPTER NINE
PLASTIC FANTASTIC!
1970-1971

Producer Barry Letts and script editor Terrance Dicks found they worked extremely well together from the very start. After finishing work on *Doctor Who*'s seventh season, they began making plans for the eighth, due to go into production in the latter half of 1970 and air on BBC1 from January 1971. Dicks was keen to make sure that Bob was involved quite early on. 'What I always tried to do as script editor, and what Barry and I always continued when he became producer, was rather than say to people, "Send in some story ideas for *Doctor Who*, and we'll see if we like them", instead try and get a writer in, and then discuss an idea with him, so by the time he went away and wrote the storyline or even the first script, he knew he was working on lines that generally speaking had our approval. We tried to bring the writer in, or to interact with the writer at a much earlier stage. And that we found worked rather well.'

To that end, sometime in the spring of 1970, Letts and Dicks invited Bob in for a chat about writing another *Doctor Who* story. As Dicks recalls, 'The idea to use Bob again would have emerged, first of all, from the decision to do another Auton story. Which is an obvious idea, if you've had a very successful monster. A controversial success, but a success – we got a lot of stick for being too scary, so I think we made them even more scary the second time around! And the story would have been worked out in discussion with me, and Bob and Barry. We would always spend a lot of time talking to the writer, and getting the story on the right lines before he went away and wrote his storyline. So it would all have been built up from there. You talk about the storyline, you commission the first scripts, you talk about the first scripts and ask for the rewrites, and the thing finally takes shape.'

Letts remembered Bob well. 'He was still this angular, long chap,' he recalled, 'who seemed a bit lugubrious, but I found out later that that was more of a front. He was lugubriously cheerful underneath; he was a bit of a cynic, he was a bit of a sceptic, but when you got to know him, you found he was a lovely man, and very kind-hearted. I liked the first Auton story very much, and I liked his writing, and I got on well with him when we'd been discussing the programme.'

At the end of the first Jon Pertwee season, *Doctor Who* was still in a position where its long-term future on the BBC was far from certain. 'I think for quite a long time *Doctor Who* was fighting for its life,' recalled Bob some years later. 'I don't know what the audiences were – six or seven million – and you never knew if it was going to continue for another season in those days. And then, of course, it got more and more successful. It was fairly easy then, because you knew for sure you'd be going on, so you could plan ahead. So yes, Terrance came to me and said, "Could you do another Auton story?" And I think that was the one where I really got into trouble …'

As well as the return of the Autons, the story was notable for featuring the first appearance of the Doctor's arch-enemy, the Master, a renegade Time Lord from the same planet, played by Roger Delgado. Although the Autons were all Bob's own creation, the Master was a character wholly devised by Dicks and Letts, and Bob was asked to incorporate him into his script.

Letts recalls: 'The Master as a character was handed over to Bob, and we said, "We want to introduce him," and we also wanted a sequel to the Auton story. So those two things were the main elements of the story. Bob came up with all these little *clevernesses* of the Master, things like hypnotising people. And turning people into little mannequins about six inches long, which did come back later on – I think John Nathan-Turner reintroduced it. Bob invented all that stuff, like the Master being able to disguise himself as other people, and so on. So he had a lot of influence from that point of view, but the Master was our invention.'

Bob once remarked, 'I had a tendency to write the first episode for a lot of the characters, because Terrance found I was sort of reliable, so I used to write the first story in every season. And as a result, I ended up writing a lot of first episodes for quite a lot of people. I wrote the first Pertwee, I wrote the first Master … They told me that he was going to be a Moriarty to the Doctor's Holmes, and that he was going to be a worthy character that would run … not in every story, but when he did appear, he would be called the Master, or Colonel Masters, or El Maestro, something along those lines, whenever he appeared. And he had a TARDIS of his own, and as [his debut story] was set in a circus, I used a horsebox as his TARDIS. I didn't know Roger Delgado very well, but I do know that he was highly regarded as an actor, and people have told me he was a most generous-natured man with a great sense of humour.'[134]

Bob's new story also introduced two other new characters to the series; again both devised by Letts and Dicks. The first was UNIT's Captain, Mike Yates, played by Richard Franklin, who served as the Brigadier's second-in-command. The second was the new assistant for the Doctor, Jo Grant, played

---

134 'Holmes on Holmes', *Doctor Who Magazine Winter Special*, December 1994 (culled from quotes given to Richard Marson during his 1985 interview with Bob, and Bob's 1981 Panopticon appearance – the expanded quotes are used here).

by Katy Manning. Bob didn't mind being given so many disparate elements to include in his story. 'Depending on the nature of the challenge, in some cases, when you are given a very full brief like that and you have all these things to consider, you write better, I think. Because you've got the parameters established. If they had said, "Do us a *Doctor Who*, set it anywhere, about anything ..." you wouldn't know where to start. So it focuses your mind, if you're told it's the first story, you've got this new adversary, the Master, we're going to use UNIT. And then you start working on the permutations and combinations, and you can develop a story within the parameters. So in a way it is helpful to have certain guidelines.'[135]

As a result of all these discussions, on Tuesday 3 April 1970, Bob was commissioned to write a storyline for a new *Doctor Who* story with a working title 'The Spray of Death'. It was due to be delivered on Tuesday 12 May 1970. Bob eventually handed in his storyline on Monday 8 June 1970.

This storyline was approved by Letts and Dicks, although Dicks made a few suggestions that would ultimately be incorporated by Bob into his scripts. Bob was then given his formal commission to write the scripts for 'The Spray of Death' on Friday 12 June 1970, with a delivery date of Monday 14 July 1970 for all four episodes. Somewhat true to form, Bob delivered all four scripts a week early, on Monday 7 July 1970. The story was then renamed 'Terror of the Autons' by Dicks prior to production starting on the story in September 1970.

Bob had a great deal of fun writing 'Terror of the Autons', finding new and imaginative ways of using the plastic-loving aliens; disguising them at one point as policemen, and also having plastic armchairs, dolls, daffodils and telephone cables spring into life to attack and kill various characters.

Some years later, at the DWAS's Panopticon IV convention in 1981, Bob was asked about his experiences writing the two Auton stories, and in particular about his thoughts on the controversy that followed 'Terror of the Autons' being screened. 'There was a lot of public reaction, and I learned a very valuable point about that. The Autons were never put into a physical body, they were able to inhabit plastic, so they could be in anything – a telephone wire, or ... a plastic armchair – so we never really gave them a physical shape. In that sense, they were very flexible. I could use them anywhere, I could have them popping up anywhere.

'Although,' Bob went on to admit, 'I did make a mistake with the plastic daffodils and having these little doll-like creatures creeping about and killing

---

135 Obviously Bob felt in this instance he had been given a very clear brief by Letts and Dicks. If one is looking to compare and contrast this with future events, then we must conclude that the brief he would later be given by Eric Saward and John Nathan-Turner for the programme's twentieth anniversary story was decidedly less clear and straightforward ...

people. I discovered in the course of just thinking about it, that you could kill somebody just by getting a little bit of plastic sealed over the [area of the] breathing orifices, which is only about three inches [square] in size. And that struck me as a good idea. And when I did it, of course, it horrified people, because children felt very threatened as it was done. Way out horror in alien surroundings doesn't affect the kid as much as something that could take place in its own sitting room, or kitchen. And small children were affected by that one, and I learned not to do it again.'[136]

When asked if he thought that fantastical violence, such as was typically depicted in *Doctor Who*, was less damaging that the gritty realism of cop shows such as *The Sweeney*, Bob was very clear on the matter. 'That is stuff that can be seen, and can be copied. Motorbikes, motorcars chasing people up alleyways, knives, guns, bombs … And it's all part of the stuff they can see on the news as well, and it all reemphasises the view that the world is a dangerous place. Whereas *Doctor Who* doesn't do that. *Doctor Who* is a fantasy, in the same league for children as ghost stories. Children like nothing better than to sit by Grandpa's knee and be told a scary story with the lights out, just by the firelight. So long as they're comforted by a cup of Horlicks before they go to bed, they're okay.'

Bob despatched one character in 'Terror of the Autons' by having him suffocated by a plastic armchair. 'I was taken with this idea of the plastic armchair swallowing the man (McDermott) at one point,' he later recalled. 'And I had one of those typical lines after I killed him, didn't I? I think the Master pressed his intercom and said "Miss so-and-so, can you get his cards …" Those inflatable chairs were very much in vogue at that time. Like those beanbags that were everywhere, that you could never get comfortable on. You were always lying back with your legs at awkward angles.'

'Barry also got a letter from the police,' recalled Dicks. 'There's a scene where the Doctor is apparently rescued from a riot by a police car, and the Doctor gets suspicious and reaches out and peels off the policeman's face, revealing the face of an Auton. And the police wrote and said, "This is not helping in establishing trust in your local community policeman. You're not doing us any good." So Barry must have written them a letter of apology, saying we never meant it, or whatever, but there was that too. The police weren't at all pleased.'

'We had a lot of complaints,' continues Letts. 'We had complaints from the Managing Director of Television, Huw Wheldon. I believe a question was

---

136 Panopticon IV Convention, Queen Mary College, 1-2 August 1981.

asked in Parliament. Certainly, we had lead articles in the *Daily Express* saying, "Why My Children Will Never Watch *Doctor Who* Again", and all that stuff. Bob had a taste for the horrible, for the quirkily horrible, and yes, he put all that in. It's a natural consequence of the idea that plastic can come to life, but he put all that in, and I went along with it enthusiastically. So, although he thought of it, *I* was responsible. It's the old thing, the buck stops here. The producer is the man responsible for the show, although the ideas may have been discussed in detail in the script conferences that Terrance and I had with Bob. Bob would have come up with those particular ideas, yes. But *I* was responsible.'

'I didn't realise that it would attract the kind of flak that it did,' recalled Bob some years later. 'There were cartoons about it in the *Evening Standard*, Shirley Summerskill[137] was asking questions about it in the House of Commons[138], Mrs Whitehouse said we were destroying children's confidence in the police, etcetera, etcetera. It's a kind of pleasant fear anyway, for a child, to be mildly frightened. It's not a nightmare. Where I probably did go wrong I think in that story, and I accept some of the criticism, is perhaps attacking the child within the security of its own environment, with plastic dolls and daffodils suddenly starting to become aggressive. Whereas most *Doctor Who* stuff is so blatantly fantastic and make-believe that I think they enter into the spirit of it while they're watching it, and I don't think it does any lasting damage. Especially if someone's watching with them. And certainly a small child shouldn't be allowed to watch any television of any kind alone. Because you never know what's going to be shown.'

Sylvia Clayton, writing in *The Daily Telegraph,* composed an article entitled 'What Level of Horror is Acceptable in a Tea-time Programme?', which contemplated the current production standards of *Doctor Who*. 'The present *Doctor Who* adventure makes this question pertinent by the very effectiveness of its attack on the nerves,' she wrote. 'These plastic monsters come from within the range of a child's domestic scene. There is a murderous mannequin doll with deadly fangs, a chair which inflates to suffocate the victim, a telephone flex which strangles the caller. Policemen with apparently normal faces whip off their masks to show a hideous non-face underneath. Small children of my acquaintance have found these devices terrifying in a way fantasy figures such as the Daleks and the Cybermen were not ... *Doctor Who* is placed at a time

---

137 Shirley Summerskill was a Labour MP between 1964 and 1979, and was shadow Minister for Health between 1970-74.
138 Although there is no record of Shirley Summerskill commenting on the series at the time, the debate on Mass Media Communication in the House of Lords on 3 February 1971, as recorded in Hansard, has Baroness Bacon (Labour MP 1945-1970, House of Lords 1970-1993) stating to the House, 'I think that the programmes for the tiny children are really excellent. There is a whole new series of fairytales and fairytale characters, and a tremendous amount of work must have gone into producing them. I am not so sure about some of the series for the older children, and I wonder what has happened to *Doctor Who* recently, because many children must have gone to bed and had nightmares after seeing the recent episodes.'

when the smallest children will be watching, and adult frissions will be best left to *Doomwatch*.'[139]

As a story, 'Terror of the Autons' re-treads a lot of the same ground as 'Spearhead from Space', but does so in a more distilled, refined and focused manner. The new ways that the Autons – and Bob – employ various different forms of plastic to despatch victim after victim are quite delightfully macabre, and the criticisms that the story received at the time for these excesses seem quite churlish by today's standards. When writing the story, Bob also took the opportunity of creating a thoroughly believable character when fleshing out the first appearance of the Master, taking a one-page character brief and transforming it into a fully formed villain of the highest order. Roger Delgado seems to have relished the dialogue given to him by Bob, and it would not be unfair to say that the character's first appearance here is perhaps also his best. It's clear to see that Bob was enjoying the freedom and creativity that *Doctor Who* was now giving him as a writer, and had upped his game accordingly.

---

139 *The Daily Telegraph*, 'What Level of Horror is Acceptable in a Tea-time Programme?' by Sylvia Clayton, 18 January 1971.

INTERLUDE VI
DOCTOR WHO: 'SPRAY OF DEATH'
JUNE 1970

Robert Holmes' full original storyline proposal for the *Doctor Who* story that eventually became 'Terror of the Autons' is reprinted here as originally submitted, complete with his original spellings and punctuation:

<u>SPRAY OF DEATH</u>

<u>EPISODE ONE</u>

<u>TK 1: A TRAVELLING FAIR SETTING UP</u>
'Tardis' noises and a shapeless blur shimmers on the edge of the fairground, then solidifies into a horsebox – of which there are one or two dotted around the pitch. The Master steps out. His arrival has gone unnoticed. He walks away.

<u>1. INT. MINISTRY OF RESEARCH AND DEVELOPMENT</u>
JOHN PHILLIPS and colleague walk through the Projects Hall. Colleague leaves Phillips, saying he has to deliver a report to the Director. Phillips produces his micro-dot passkey and enters secret research section. The Master is watching from the dark side of an artefact.

<u>2. INT. RADIO TELESCOPE CHAMBER</u>
Phillips checks instruments, sets his programme out.

<u>3. INT. PROJECTS HALL</u>
Colleague returning is waylaid by Master who slays him in artful fashion and hides body behind the artefact. (A bit of rocketry hardware, maybe?) Master, armed with colleague's passkey, lets himself into –

<u>4. INT. RADIO TELESCOPE CHAMBER</u>
Phillips is in some other part of the premises. The Master goes to a zinc box, slices away the lock with a device as

143

yet undiscovered by man, and lifts out the Nestene energy unit. He takes it over to the radio telescope, makes some adjustments, and switches on …

5. INT. RADIO TELESCOPE CHAMBER (2)
Phillips, reading instruments, is confounded when he realises the radio antennae are beamed towards some unprogrammed area.

6. INT. RADIO TELESCOPE CHAMBER
Power is thrumming through the link the Master has created. The pulse of the energy unit, feeble when first seen, increases to Quasar-like intensity. Phillips comes in fast, full of protests. He retreats when he sees the menace in the Master's face …

7. INT. UNIT LAB
THE DOCTOR meets JO GRANT. He learns that the energy unit has been stolen and has a few nasty words to say to LETHBRIDGE STEWART for authorising its transfer to the Ministry of R. And D. The Brigadier is unperturbed. Ministry astronomist Phillips and a colleague have also disappeared. Obviously they have removed the energy unit for some private purpose. A full-scale search is already under way and he is confident they will be found within a matter of hours.

8. INT. PROJECTS HALL
The Doctor, investigating, meets the TIME LORD who has followed the escaping Master this far before losing the trail. Establishing scene.

9. INT. RADIO TELESCOPE CHAMBER
The Doctor discovers the telescope is beamed incorrectly for its programme. He realises its setting has been deliberately altered and draws grim conclusions which he is discussing with Jo when YATES comes in to report that the colleague's body has been found.

10. INT. PROJECTS HALL
The Brigadier now becoming alarmed. The search for Phillips is intensified.

11. INT. FARREL'S OFFICE
The Master arrives, ostensibly to discuss an order he intends placing with the factory.

12. INT. UNIT LAB
The Doctor tells the Brigadier they may be facing what they have long feared – the second Nestene assault. Lethbridge Stewart is confident they can repel any landings. The Doctor says if his theory is right, the landing has already occurred: a wave of energy, Nestene life-force, call is what you will, transmitted through the radio telescope and now stored in the surviving energy unit. Given the right medium, raw plastic, the one single unit can multiply indefinitely, like any virus.

13. INT. FARREL'S OFFICE
The Master acquires mastery over Farrel, hypnotising him with a mind-dominating ray.

TK2. INT. FACTORY
Farrel is showing the Master round. He asks a few questions about the computer that controls the mix for the production line. He then sets it to a new programme. The energy unit is linked to the tanks where the resulting mixture will be cured.

14. INT. UNIT LAB
The Doctor is telling the Brigadier about the Master (and meeting some resistance) when Yates arrives with the news that Phillip's car has been found.

15. INT. FARREL'S OFFICE
McDERMOTT, Farrel's partner and production manager, comes in angrily, wanting to know why the mix has been altered. The whole of today's output will have to be scrapped.

He produces an inflatable armchair and demonstrates that it is made of opaque plastic and not the jewel-like, translucent colour that was specified. Farrel seems unsure and hesitant: he goes to fetch the Master. McDermott rings Farrel's father and asks him to come over to the factory right away. He says that Farrel seems to be breaking up.

TK 3. FAIRGROUND AREA
The fair has left. UNIT soldiers are guarding Philip's car. The Brigadier and company arrive. In the boot of the car they find the zinc container that held the Nestene energy unit. The Brigadier is about to open it when the Doctor pounces and pulls him away. It may be a trap, says the Doctor.

16. INT. FARREL'S OFFICE
Farrel introduces Colonel Masters, his new partner. McDermott is astonished but presses his complaint. The Master says it is unimportant, the moulds are already being changed. They won't be producing any more inflatable. McDermott starts on about breaking contracts as the Master pushes him into the inflatable chair. It kills him.

TK 4. FAIRGROUND AREA
The Doctor opens the zinc container by remote control. It explodes shatteringly.

EPISODE TWO

1. UNIT LAB
The Doctor and the Brigadier now face the fact that the Nestenes are backed by a powerful and ingeniously intelligent ally. ECT tactics obviously won't work this time. It is also clear, says the Doctor, that the Master will be determined and persistent in his attacks against UNIT. They, at the moment, are working blind, without a single lead. What has happened to Phillips? Where is the energy unit?

2. INT. FARREL'S OFFICE

Farrel Senior arrives and finds McDermott dead. Have they called the doctor? The Master starts slightly at this name.

3. UNIT HQ

Yates has established that Philip's car had been abandoned the previous night when a fair had pitched on the land. They trace the fair to its new pitch. The Doctor and Jo arm themselves with pictures of Philips and his car and go off to the fairground to ask questions. (UNIT types being too conspicuous for this sort of job).

TK 1. FACTORY GROUNDS

Farrel Senior is leaving, the death of McDermott having driven other matters out of his thoughts. The Master presents him with a trollish, three-eyed doll as a specimen of the new range of products. He switches the car heater to full blast before Farrel drives off.

CAR

We see the troll come menacingly 'alive' on the back seat and starts moving towards Farrel before he switches off the heater and opens the car window. The troll slumps back.

FAIRGROUND

The roustabouts setting up, as before, when the Doctor and Jo arrive. The Doctor notices the horse box. There is something about it that bothers him … he is prowling round it when one of the fairground workers challenges him.

4. INT. FARREL'S OFFICE

The Master gives Philips a batch of troll figures. They discuss briefly the failure of the trap laid for UNIT. The Master hadn't seriously expected it to succeed but one of his maxims is never to neglect the obvious. He says that UNIT - particularly the Doctor, his most subtle adversary - must be sidetracked or eliminated. It is clear that he has some scheme in mind.

5. INT. FARREL SENIOR'S HOUSE
He is discussing with his wife the disturbing events of the day. He tells her about Colonel Masters and shows her the ugly little troll.

6. INT. CARAVAN
The fairground owner is questioning the Doctor about his interest in Phillips. The Doctor can't tell him too much. The owner doesn't like snoopers.

TK2. FAIRGROUND
Jo is hanging around the caravan, waiting for a chance to help the Doctor without getting herself involved. Phillips passes. He is distributing trolls, a dozen at a time, to people running the sideshows. Jo follows him.

7. INT FARREL SENIOR'S HOUSE
Mrs. Farrel goes off to bed, leaving the troll near a radiator. It slips off the shelf and heads for Farrel, as he sits drinking a nightcap.

8. UNIT HQ
The Brigadier is getting worried. They should have had word from the Doctor and Jo before now. He tells Yates to order a car.

9. INT. CARAVAN
The owner is called away. He hasn't finished with the Doctor yet by any means. He leaves him locked in the van.

TK3. FAIRGROUND
Jo releases the Doctor, tells him she has just seen Phillips going into the horse box. They head that way.

10. INT. FARREL'S OFFICE
The Master is receiving a report from Philips who is using the sonic maser in the Master's Tardis. The Master sets the scanners by remote control and sees the Doctor and Jo crouching outside the horse box. He gives Phillips certain

orders and switches off. He tells Farrel that Phillips was no longer of value to them as the Autons, now in production, performed all necessary manual functions far more efficiently then the most completely controlled human.

TK4. FAIRGROUND
Phillips comes out of the horse box. The Doctor and Jo hurry towards him. Then the Doctor sees the object in Phillips' hand and scents danger (or maybe recognises it as a detonation capsule from the planet Kastrities); he drags Jo back. Phillips moves towards them, glazy-eyed. They run, Phillips follows. There is a chase around the fairground, ending when Jo slips and they are trapped in some hopeless corner, a cul-de-sac in the hall of mirrors maybe. Phillips advances on them.

11. INT. FARREL'S OFFICE
The Master closes the flap of his curiously ornate pocket watch. All over, he says with satisfaction.

TK5. FAIRGROUND
The Master's control lapses at the last moment. The Doctor gets through to Phillips who instinctively throws himself away from the Doctor and Jo. There is an explosion that kills him.

FAIRGROUND
The Brigadier and Yates hear the explosion as their car draws up. They run.

FAIRGROUND (OR INT. HALL OF MIRRORS)
The Doctor takes something from Philip's pocket - the key to the Master's Tardis - and hurries Jo away from the scene. The owner and roustabouts arrive, then race in pursuit.

FAIRGROUND
Jo crouches outside the horse box as the Doctor disappears inside. He is only gone a few seconds and emerges clutching a micro-circuit. But the delay allows the owner and his

mob of toughs to catch up. They are surrounded. Cries of 'Murderers' and 'Lynch 'em'.

FAIRGROUND (OR INT. HALL OF MIRRORS)
The Brigadier and Yates find Phillips. They try to discover what has happened.

FAIRGROUND (OR INT. HALL OF MIRRORS)
The Brigadier learns the police have just driven the Doctor and Jo away. He and Yates rush off to try to catch up and explain things.

CAR
A police car roaring through the night, the Doctor and Jo in the back.

CAR INT. (OR INT. CAR B.P.)[140]
The Doctor and Jo are being reasonable, explaining their complete innocence to the two pairs of solid blue shoulders in the front seats. There is no answer and the Doctor gets a bit sharp – then one of the policemen turns and we see he is an Auton.

EPISODE THREE

TK1. CAR INT
Reprise. The Doctor pushes Jo to the floor and lunges for the steering wheel. The car crashes. Jo and the Doctor get out.

COUNTRY
Jo and the Doctor pursued through woodland by police Autons, blasting with their wrist-tubes. Lethbridge-Stewart and Yates arrive, distract the Autons with pistol fire. The four of them manage to escape in the UNIT car.

1. UNIT HQ
To the Doctor's chagrin the micro-circuit he has cannibalised

---

140 BP here refers to back projection – Bob is suggesting mounting this scene in the studio.

from the Master's Tardis is completely unsuitable for his own machine.

2. INT. FARREL'S OFFICE
Farrel and the Master are about to leave to put Stage II of the invasion plan into operation. The aim is complete paralysis of southern England. The Master is piqued because he has still not managed to eliminate the Doctor.

3. UNIT HQ
The Brigadier is piqued because the whole resources of UNIT have not so far turned up a single lead as to where the Master is operating from.

TK2. SHOPPING CENTRE OR ARCADE
Golden Daffodil Men handing out sprays to housewives. The Master watching from some vantage point.

DAFFODIL COACH
The Daffodil Men file into the coach. Farrel and the Master drive off to the next town on their itinerary. The Daffodil Men remove their helmets. We see they are Autons.

4. UNIT HQ
Jo and the Doctor speculate about the trolls Phillips was handing out in the fairground. Yates goes off to try and get hold of one.

5. BRIGADIER'S OFFICE
An emissary from the Ministry asks the Brigadier to investigate an outbreak of sudden and inexplicable deaths that is causing alarm in several districts near London. The Brigadier regrets his resources are already fully extended. During this conversation, a stolid-looking telephone engineer is changing the instruments on the Brigadier's desk.

6. UNIT HQ
Yates returns with a troll. The Doctor examines it but breaks off when the Brigadier comes in and tells them

of the Ministry-man's visit. They realise the trail of death ties in with the locations visited by the fair. The Brigadier calls the Minister and gets further details. The first deaths were those of McDermott and Farrel, directors of a plastics factory.

7. INT. FARREL SENIOR'S HOUSE
The Doctor and the Brigadier call on Mrs. Farrel and question her about the night her husband died. She happens to mention her husband was upset because their son seemed to have fallen under the influence of Colonel Masters.

8. INT. FARREL'S OFFICE
The Doctor and the Brigadier arrive and realise their bird has flown.

TK3. FACTORY
They explore the silent factory, expecting trouble at any minute. Why has the Master abandoned this base and where has he gone? The Doctor finds a plastic daffodil and studies it thoughtfully. He explains to the Brigadier that any plastic utensil, providing its mixture was suitable, could provide a physical shell for Nestene life.

9. UNIT HQ
Yates and Jo have been chatting. Yates goes out. Suddenly she sees the horrid little troll slipping towards her. She screams. Yates comes in and blasts the thing to bits with his pistol.

10. UNIT HQ
The Doctor and the Brigadier arrive back. The Doctor examines the remnants of the troll. The Brigadier decides to get on to the police and ask for all trolls dolls to be collected and destroyed. He picks up the telephone. The cord winds itself around his neck, throttling him. He drops to the floor.

EPISODE FOUR

1. UNIT HQ
The Doctor returns to the Brigadier's office. He battles with the snake-like telephone cord, severs the connection, saves the Brigadier from death by strangulation.[141]

2. INT. DAFFODIL COACH
Farrel says that UNIT forces are watching the factory. Obviously it will only be a matter of time before the coach, too, is located. The leader Auton feels the Master's plan is not working. The Master has spent too much time on his petty, private feud with the Doctor rather than on his main job of helping the Nestenes. The Master blames the weather. It has been unseasonably cold. However, a hot, dry spell is now starting and everything will go according to plan. Meanwhile he says – exerting his most masterful manner – the Doctor must be dealt with.

3. UNIT HQ
The Doctor is conducting a laboratory examination of the daffodil he brought from the Farrel factory. The Brigadier comes in, accoutred for battle. The daffodil coach has been located on the Sussex downs. The Brigadier is taking his headquarters staff and intends to surround the coach under cover of darkness while the regular army bring artillery into position.

4. INT. DAFFODIL COACH
Farrel hears something. The senses of the unsleeping Autons have already informed them that men are massing a mile or so away over the downs.

---

141 When interviewed by Richard Marson in 1985, Bob reminisced about this version of the scene, rather than the as-transmitted version, which saw the Brigadier replaced by the Doctor as the victim of the Nestene telephone flex. 'I had the Brigadier, in fact, get strangled by a telephone cord,' recalled Bob. 'The Doctor came in with a knife and chopped it, and said, "I'm sorry if I've cut your connection." I think with *Doctor Who*, you can have a fairly tense scene where the Brigadier is unexpectedly choked to death, and then you can lighten it with a quick line.' This suggests that it was Terrance Dicks, and not Bob, who may have been responsible for switching the Doctor for the Brigadier as the actual victim of the Nestene telephone cord in the final scripts.

TK1. DOWNS
UNIT soldiers are forming up. The Brigadier and Yates conduct operations from a wireless vehicle.

5. UNIT HQ
In the stem of the daffodil the Doctor has discovered a tiny programme pattern. He converts it to visual symbols and projects the pattern on a screen. Out of the blurs a stylised picture of a human nose and mouth swims into focus. The Doctor is on the point of making an imaginative leap to full understanding when he is disturbed. The Master is behind him. Confrontation scene. The Master takes time off to explain about the daffodils. Each contains a tiny, vestigial trace of Nestene energy. (The amount of energy received through the radio telescope was not unlimited and had to be carefully harboured.) At a pre-programmed temperature point each of the million daffodils spread over the country became active and selected its target – the breathing orifices of any human within an eight-foot range. So many deaths at once will disrupt the country and, during the ensuing chaos, the main Nestene invasion force will make its landing. Now the Master is going to kill the Doctor. He points his cobalt laser.

6. INT. DAFFODIL COACH
Farrel, out of the Master's mesmeric range, gradually realises that somehow he's got on the wrong side.

7. UNIT HQ
Jo comes in at the wrong moment, distracting the Master as he is about to disintegrate the Doctor. The Doctor grabs the micro-circuit off his bench. Now the Master can't blast him with the cobalt-laser because, if he does, he will destroy the micro-circuit and his own Tardis will be as earthbound as the Doctor's. A swift reappraisal. The Master threatens to kill Jo if they don't do exactly as he says. He herds them out, the Doctor warily clutching the micro-circuit.

TK2. DOWNS
The sound of an approaching motor. Lethbridge-Stewart's men are ready to open fire. The Master drives past them, shielded by Jo and the Doctor.

8. INT. DAFFODIL COACH
The Master is heading for his Tardis to contact the waiting Nestene invasion force. He will signal them to land and they should arrive simultaneously with the wave of terror that the daffodils will create. Another five degrees and the daffodils will be spitting death all over the country. The temperature is already up to 60°F. Farrel drops a knife and kicks it under his seat to where the Doctor lies.

TK3. DOWNS
Yates and the Brigadier are following the coach in their wireless vehicles. They are trying to arrange a road-block up ahead.

10. INT. DAFFODIL COACH
The Doctor frees himself and Jo He unscrews an inspection plate in the floor, punctures the exhaust and funnels the fumes in the coach interior.

TK4. DOWNS
The Master sees the roadblock and swings the coach into a minor road.

11. INT. DAFFODIL COACH
The Doctor and Jo, trying to keep their swaying senses, are breathing through the inspection trap, most of the exhaust fumes swirling past them. One of the nearest Autons collapses, his plastic melting.

TK5. DOWNS
The Master abandons the coach. The Autons, their fighting efficiency seriously impaired, spill out and are engaged by UNIT troops. The Doctor and Jo avoid the fighting and reach the wireless vehicle. The Master sees the battle is

being lost and heads over the fields. Farrel pursues him but the Master kills him.

HORSE BOX
Sporadic gunfire now in the distance. The Master reaches the horse box and disappears inside.

DOWNS
An order to destroy all the daffodils has gone out on priority channels. The Autons are being mopped up – but the Master has escaped. Don't worry, says the Doctor. He won't get far.

HORSE BOX
Tardis noises from the horse box. Suddenly it grinds down, shudders and belches flames and smoke. The UNIT wireless vehicle comes up. The Master staggers out of the horse box and makes a run for it. He is chased by the Brigadier and company. Finally he falls under a fusillade of pistol fire from Yates and the Brigadier. They go to him and roll the body over. It is a faceless Auton in the Master's clothes. At the same moment, their wireless vehicle is reversed round and driven away, the Master staring back at them malevolently. They realises the Master must have kept the Auton in reserve, for just some emergency.

12. UNIT HQ
The Doctor reveals he outwitted the Master by letting him have the dud Mark I micro-circuit from his own Tardis. Now both machines are wrecked, and the Master is trapped on Earth. But they will hear from him again. He will be desperate to get the Mark II circuit that the Doctor has in his pocket.

CHAPTER TEN
MAKING A NAME WITH AUNTY
1970-1972

Away from *Doctor Who*, Bob was still working hard in the television industry. The ATV series *Fraud Squad* – for which he had written three episodes the previous year – was given a second series of 13 episodes in 1970. Bob wrote the final episode of this second season, 'The Price of a Copper', which was shown on ITV on Saturday 12 December 1970.

'The Price of Copper' saw Detective Inspector Gamble and Detective Sergeant Vicky Hicks investigating a pair of notorious racehorse owners, the Dysart brothers, who Gamble suspects have been entering an underperforming horse, Orange Borsch, into races, only for it to finish poorly, and then substituting a more thoroughbred horse in the final race, which then romps home. A photo of Orange Borsch in a newspaper first alerts Gamble to the con, as he didn't recall it having a white patch of fur on its head when he saw it pictured previously. He and Hicks try and obtain prints of the newspaper's picture, which alerts the Dysart brothers that they're under investigation. Hicks then visits the Dysarts' stables, and is told that Orange Borsch has been destroyed earlier that day, after breaking its leg in training. She suspects that she is being told lies, and calls Gamble to tell him. When she fails to meet up with Gamble later, he realises that she's been abducted by the Dysarts, and also that a fellow police officer named Kent is almost certainly working for the brothers. Gamble manoeuvres Kent into leading him to the stables where Hicks is being held. Kent confesses to Hicks that he's in debt to the Dysarts, and has been secretly working for them for years. The brothers arrive at the stable, followed by Gamble, who tries to arrest them both. There is a struggle, and Kent is shot dead, but Hicks and Gamble manage to overpower the Dysart brothers.

It would seem that the writing of this episode was far from straightforward. Bob had to undertake several rewrites of his script before the producer of *Fraud Squad*, Nicholas Palmer, accepted it for production.

However, such run-of-the-mill writing assignments were starting to become the exception, not the norm, for Bob. His success with *Doctor Who* had seen him become once more a writer of some interest to producers and commissioners at the BBC, enabling him to look further afield for work than just those opportunities offered to him by his old ITV contacts.

Early in 1970, Bob decided to have another go at pitching an idea at *The*

Wednesday Play. Of course, his new producer back at the *Doctor Who* office, Barry Letts, had no idea that he had already had a couple of unsuccessful prior encounters with the BBC's prestigious one-off play strand. 'One of the things about scriptwriting, especially in those days, ' recalled Letts some years later, 'was that there were a lot of writers about who had been scriptwriters on all sorts of shows, from *Robin Hood*, through various detective things, and they were "just" scriptwriters; they would come up with good, solid plots and a lot of action, and a lot of conflict, but with cardboard characters, writing straight down the middle. Bob didn't do that. Bob thought like a playwright. He would get an idea, but once he'd got his characters going, the plot would derive from the characters, as they do in really good writing. They weren't just cardboard characters, there to fit in with the plot. This was something Terrance and I were trying to persuade other writers to do, and they did it to a certain extent, but Bob did it beautifully. In fact, one of his *Doctor Who* stories got a very good notice. The critic said, "This man should be writing *The Wednesday Play*." This was the single play programme that was *the* prestigious vehicle for people like Dennis Potter and so on, at that time. And the producer of *The Wednesday Play* saw this notice, and actually got in touch with Bob and said, "Well, what about it – why don't you submit an idea and write us a play?"'

'I think the thing about Bob was that he never really appreciated how good he was,' recalls Terrance Dicks. 'He limited himself. He would say, "Okay, I'm just a hack scriptwriter, I take the job that comes along." And some journalist said that his latest scripts on *Doctor Who* were as good as anything you'd see on *The Wednesday Play*, and why didn't Bob write something like *The Wednesday Play*? And Bob sort of pooh-poohed the whole thing. "I'm not one of your superior cultural writers, I do *Doctor Who*, or the latest cop show, or whatever's going," he would say. He was a bit self-limiting, in a way; he didn't want to push himself beyond a certain point … Or maybe, I don't think he had as good an opinion of himself as I think he deserved, because he could have probably done better. Actually, I don't think there is a much better class of television than *Doctor Who*, but he could have done more serious things, or had a different sort of reputation if he wanted to. But he didn't; he liked doing what he did.'

Despite the cynicism he displayed to the faces of his friends in the *Doctor Who* production office, Bob did actually try to pitch a story to *The Wednesday Play* at this time, as a result of their interest in him.

During the first week of February 1970, Bob had a meeting with the script editor of *The Wednesday Play* series, Ann Scott.[142] Bob outlined to her a story that revolved around a new, experimental chemical fertilizer, which directly causes the death of a young child who is exposed to it. The wealthy owner of the fertilizer firm hushes up the incident so as not to damage the profitability of his company, or harm the sales of the fertilizer to other farmers. To this end, he buys off the few people who know about the incident, in order to keep his business going.

Ann Scott was very enthusiastic about the idea, and wrote to Bob on Friday 6 February 1970 to ask him to write a storyline treatment, along with perhaps a few actual key scenes from the play, and to provide a title (so that a contract for the storyline could be issued). Despite this being similar to the process he'd happily undertaken for his *Doctor Who* commissions up to this point, Bob felt that he wasn't really happy doing it for *The Wednesday Play*. On Monday 9 February 1970, he wrote back to Scott. His letter is very telling, showing how much of a big thing this opportunity was to him at the time, but also throwing a little light on his working methods and thoughts:

Thank you for inviting me to prepare a treatment of my play idea. I realise this is a practical suggestion but I'm not barmy about it. Although I produce outlines all the time, as a necessary part of series work, it's a stage I skip whenever I can. (It was Robert Bolt, I believe, who observed that writing is thinking and, therefore, an outline requires one to think about what one is going to think!)

However, in this case I'm afraid that by doing a treatment and including 'a few key scenes', I might perhaps vitiate whatever it is I feel about this play and which, at the moment, is still safely tucked away inside me. I hope that doesn't sound too temperamental but, faced with the chance to do my first bit of real writing for ten years, I'm approaching the task very warily.

Perhaps a more understandable objection is that I can't write a scene before I get to it, anyway. I know some writers hop about like this. They're probably the same people who turn cherry cake into something resembling Gruyere. Disgusting self-indulgence.

The solution to this, if you're agreeable, lies in how I interpret the term 'treatment'. If you commission a treatment and I produce a first draft at the end of March, is anybody going to object? Well, my agent

---

142 The timing would suggest that Matthew Coady's *Daily Mirror* piece on 'Spearhead from Space' might be the very positive review that prompted the approach to Bob from *The Wednesday Play* production team, as recalled by both Barry Letts and Terrance Dicks

would, I suppose, but I shan't tell her. As you are sufficiently interested in the idea to commission a treatment, I'm prepared to take the slight risk that I won't produce a fantastic blinder of a script.

At the moment, unfortunately, I don't have a fantastic blinder of a title to suggest for the contract. The best I can do is "Organochlorine Farm" – very derivative but it has merit, as a working title, of being self-explanatory.

Please let me know (by secret telephone message, if necessary!) if I can plod on, in my staid manner, from the opening scene through to the end.

PS. Come to think of it, how can you stop me?

Scott discussed the situation with the producer of *The Wednesday Play*, Graeme McDonald. McDonald wasn't prepared to commission Bob to write the whole play at this juncture, and wanted to see something in writing first. Scott had some sympathy for Bob's position, and wrote back to him on Tuesday 24 February 1970 to encourage him to interpret his commission for a storyline treatment in whatever way he saw fit. The commission also followed on the same day, giving Bob a target delivery date of Tuesday 31 March 1970.

Bob missed his deadline.

He wrote to Scott on Monday 13 April 1970 to explain why. 'I apologise for not having sent you my play. I seem to remember promising it for the beginning of this month. Unfortunately, my last script for Nick Palmer[143] went to three rewrites and as a result my work programme for March had to go out the window. Anyway, I've been working on the play for nearly three weeks now and it seems to be shaping up. I hope to send you the first draft next week.'

Bob eventually delivered the whole script for the play, now re-titled 'The Brilliant New Testament', on Monday 18 May 1970. Ann Scott and Graeme McDonald sat down and read the script.

They didn't like it.

No details of *why* they didn't like it are recorded in the surviving records held by the BBC, but within a few days of them receiving the play, the script was being written off as unusable. Perhaps Bob had managed to put their noses out of joint by taking it upon himself to write a whole 75-minute play when all he'd been asked and paid to do was to prepare a storyline breakdown. Or perhaps, once he'd missed his original deadline, something else had to be moved into the slot earmarked for Bob's proposed play. No matter how good

---

143 Nicholas Palmer was producer of *Fraud Squad*. The script of Bob's that went to three rewrites was the aforementioned 'The Price of a Copper', the final episode of the second series.

the finished script was, all that was needed was a scene breakdown, and this was well over six weeks late. In television terms, such a delay could lead to serious problems for a programme on a strict production timetable.

Or perhaps 'The Brilliant New Testament' just wasn't what *The Wednesday Play* needed at that moment in time.

Or perhaps Bob had delivered a stinker of a script.

Whatever the reason, Bob would have been bitterly disappointed. After all, he had spent over a month writing an entire script that was now not going to be used. And to make things worse, he was going to get paid only his treatment fee – which was roughly 3% of the fee he would have received for writing a full script.

Bob *would* have been bitterly disappointed ... but it seems no-one from *The Wednesday Play* production team officially told Bob that his script had been written off. At least, not for some months after he'd submitted it.

What *did* happen was that on Thursday 21 May 1970 Ann Scott – perhaps because she felt more than a little sympathy for Bob's situation, or perhaps because she had initially encouraged him with the concept – sent a copy of 'The Brilliant New Testament' to the script editor of *Doomwatch*, Gerry Davis, and asked him to consider it instead for a possible episode of his series ...

The first season of *Doomwatch* had begun on BBC1 in February 1970. The creative forces behind it were writer Gerry Davis and scientist Dr Kit Pedler. Pedler had begun working with Davis on *Doctor Who* during the final months of William Hartnell's tenure in the TARDIS, and the pair had earned an early success as the creators of the Cybermen, the Doctor's second-deadliest long-running foes. Pedler was intensely interested in the advances that science was making, and in particular in the moral and ethical dilemmas that new scientific discoveries presented. Davis recognised the dramatic potential in these notions, and so between them they came up with the idea of a series that explored such concepts, *Doomwatch*. *Doomwatch* followed the adventures of a (fictitious) government department headed by Dr Spencer Quist (John Paul), who, along with his colleagues, would investigate abuses of science and technology at the cutting edge of research, and scrutinise the ecological impact of big business and/or government scientific projects.

On Thursday 28 May 1970, within a week of Davis being sent by Ann Scott the script of 'The Brilliant New Testament', Bob was commissioned by *Doomwatch*'s producer, Terence Dudley, to write an episode for the show's second season. At this stage the *Doomwatch* script was untitled, but Bob was given a delivery date of Friday 12 June 1970.[144] Such an early delivery date would seem to suggest that this was a commission for a script that had already been written …

Reading between the lines, it looks likely that Bob was contacted and asked to come and have a chat with the *Doomwatch* production team at some point during the last week of May 1970, and at that meeting was unofficially told that his script for 'The Brilliant New Testament' had been dropped by *The Wednesday Play*. Official word then followed some months later, when Ann Scott wrote to him on 1 August 1970, confirming that *The Wednesday Play* production team had found his play unsuitable for their slot, but that they had passed a copy on to the *Doomwatch* production team for their consideration. At the same time, Scott also returned to Bob his original script for 'The Brilliant New Testament'.

It would appear that the *Doomwatch* team liked the general outline of Bob's play, but asked if it could be reworked into a more *Doomwatch*-y format. Instead of the story's focus being a new chemical fertilizer, they suggested that it should now revolve around an outbreak of rabies, thought to be spread by tsetse flies, albeit an incident that was still being hushed up by big-business interests. Terence Dudley then passed Bob over to the show's new script editor, Martin Worth, who worked with him to get the *Doomwatch* version of his script into shape.

Bob's preparation for writing this *Doomwatch* episode was more akin to the groundwork he did on his *Emergency Ward 10* episodes than on any of his writing for *Doctor Who*. The various background scenarios to a potential rabies outbreak and to actual tsetse fly experimentation were thoroughly researched by Anna Kaliski, the script consultant on the series. She consulted with a Dr Tom Timsely, a virologist working at the time at the University of Oxford, and then compiled a three-page report that she passed on to Bob, as well as to Davis.

The main thrust of the report was to look at ways in which tsetse flies could conceivably be genetically engineered to carry rabies (or a rabies-like virus), at how a batch of 200-300 tsetse flies could conceivably escape from laboratory conditions, and at how far these escaped flies could spread any possible infection. However, this particular line of enquiry was not picked up strongly in the final episode, possibly because the report ends with the information that tsetse flies can flourish only in warm weather, and wouldn't

---

144 At about this time, Bob would have also been working on the *Doctor Who* story 'Terror of the Autons'. To recap, he was commissioned to write the storyline for 'The Spray of Death' on Tuesday 28 April 1970, and delivered it on Monday 8 June 1970. He then wrote all four scripts, which were delivered on Tuesday 7 July 1970. See the previous chapter for full details.

survive the British winter. Nevertheless, the information still found its way into Bob's script. Details of known rabies deaths in countries around the world were also compiled, along with information on the main vectors for transmission of the disease.

Bob eventually delivered his *Doomwatch* script, now given the title 'The Inquest', on Friday 4 September 1970. At least the work he had done writing the script for 'The Brilliant New Testament' hadn't gone completely to waste, even if the fee for writing an episode of *Doomwatch* was about two-thirds of what he would have expected to have been paid for writing an edition of *The Wednesday Play*.[145]

'The Inquest' sees the *Doomwatch* series regulars Geoffrey Hardcastle, Colin Bradley and Spencer Quist become involved in investigating the background to the death of a ten-year old girl, Marion, in a small village in Ipswich. Marion has apparently died of rabies. A nearby animal research facility is conducting research into tsetse flies, and there is a rumour going around the village that the girl died as a result of a fly bite. All the experts the *Doomwatch* team have consulted concur that tsetse flies can't carry rabies, but the animal research facility is investigated nevertheless. A scientist from the Ministry of Agriculture and Fisheries appears at Marion's inquest, and explains that the only animal that could reasonably be suspected of infecting the girl would be a dog. A number of suspect stray dogs from the local kennels have been quarantined already. Colin Bradley, giving evidence, suggests that if it was confirmed that a dog was the cause of the girl's death, then the local dog population in a five-mile radius might need to be destroyed as a preventative measure in order to stop the disease from spreading. This causes considerable disquiet in the local community. The activities of the local animal research institute are debated, and it's revealed that virus research was being undertaken there, using a virus found in fruit flies that is from the same group as rabies. One of the quarantined stray dogs then develops rabies, and it seems that Marion may have come into contact with the dog at the kennel in the period before her death. The kennel owner tells how the stray was found some days before Marion visited the kennel, along with her friend, Harry, the dog-loving son of the local publican, and suggests it might have previously escaped from the animal research laboratory. The laboratory owner confesses that some dogs were released by intruders some weeks ago, and Quist and his team find the missing animals being hidden in a nearby outhouse by Harry. Harry released the dogs as he feared they were going to be destroyed, and he

---

145 No copies of Bob's unmade *The Wednesday Play* script 'The Brilliant New Testament' are known to survive, but it would seem likely that it more or less followed the same dramatic lines as 'The Inquest'.

let his friend, Marion, visit them and help him feed them. One of the dogs was showing symptoms of rabies too, and Quist sees that Harry has dog bites on his hand. The laboratory owner confesses to illegally importing the dogs from abroad, while Quist tries to get urgent medical treatment for Harry. The inquest's verdict on Marion is death by misadventure.

Bob's script for this episode is very wordy, carefully developing the twists and turns of the arguments and counter-arguments put forward during the cross-examination at the inquest itself, which takes up the majority of the screen time.

Doomwatch creators Gerry Davis and Kit Pedler fell out with producer Terence Dudley at around this time over the direction in which he was taking the series, and both left the programme during the second season. Bob later recalled that it was his script for 'The Inquest' that had brought these matters to a head. 'Gerry Davis left over a script of mine, I think. He did fall out with Terence Dudley. I remember Terence, he was always trying to write for *Doctor Who* when I was doing it. *Doomwatch* I was sympathetic to, but the ideas for *Doctor Who* weren't there.'

The upshot of all this was that Bob never did get to write for *The Wednesday Play*. This, as Barry Letts recalled some years later, was a terrible shame. 'Bob suffered, as they say – this terrible cant expression – from low self-esteem. Which was surprising, for a man who was as assertive as he was. He didn't realise how good he was. If he had, he would have written for *The Wednesday Play*, and it would have been a great success, and would have probably got a BAFTA award. He was a very good writer of drama, quite apart from having this quirky mind, which brought up all these odd little ideas.'

Duke of Hearts was a series idea that Bob came up with in November 1970. His brief pitch begins thusly: 'Wilfred Marriot is an ordinary young man to whom an extraordinary thing happens – suddenly, out of the blue, he becomes a duke. And, as the 18th Duke of Kinlochie, he inherits, along with a castle, a debt of half a million pounds in estate duty. For a chap who has never owed more than his weekly milk bill this is a shattering position to be in. How can he pay such a debt? Wilfred's closest friend and flatmate, Tony Barber, is equal to the challenge. A duke, Tony points out, is not as other men. There are a hundred different ways that a duke can make money. And one of the easiest – for an eligible young bachelor like Wilfred – must surely be to marry it. This is the starting point for *Duke of Hearts* ...' It seems Bob had quite specific ideas for the casting of this series, suggesting John Alderton for the role of Wilfred Marriot, and James Villiers for the role of Tony Barber. Bob took the idea to Andrew Osborn, Head of Series Drama at the BBC, but nothing seems to have come from this pitch.

Slightly more information survives about a series idea that Bob took to ATV at some point in the early 1970s. *Executive Bent* tells the story of large company, the Aragon Corporation, and the impending retirement of one of its senior executives, leading to a power struggle in the lower departments as various rivals seek to replace him on the company board. Dodgy deals, and a suspect new industrial herbicide, form the background to the boardroom machinations described in Bob's pitch, but the project must have failed to gain favour with the commissioners at ATV, as it was never developed any further.[146]

Bob's next writing gig was for another new BBC series. *Trial* was script edited by his old friend and colleague Louis Marks, and was created by Martin Worth, with whom Bob had just finished working on *Doomwatch*. The producer of *Trial* was Richard Beynon, who had been the script editor of the ill-fated BBC series *199 Park Lane* in 1965. With so many familiar faces around him, Bob must have found working on *Trial* quite a comfortable experience.

Trial was a 13-part BBC1 series that followed a murder trial from beginning to end. Each 50-minute episode focused on the effects the trial had on a particular individual involved in the proceedings. Other writers on it included Lewis Griefer, P J Hammond, Don Shaw and Fay Weldon. Bob was commissioned on Tuesday 29 December 1970 to write an episode entitled 'Mister X'. He was given a target delivery date of Friday 29 January 1971, and turned in his script just a few days later, on Tuesday 2 February 1971. It was accepted within weeks, with no rewrites required. 'Mister X' was transmitted on Thursday 28 October 1971, and the *Radio Times* for that week has this to say about it: 'A senior civil servant appears to know something about the events leading to the murder of Simon Royston. For the defence this evidence could help to get Harry Crawford acquitted. But what will it do for the man himself …?'[147]

It was around this time, during the summer of 1971, that Bob and Patricia moved into a new house in Lime Grove, Leighton Buzzard, which was only a few miles away from their previous home in Pitstone. They also got themselves a pet dog, a Staffordshire Bull Terrier they named Matty.

At about the same time, Bob moved agents. Sort of. Rae Ellison had looked after Bob's interests when he had joined Lom Associates in 1966, and in 1971, Ellison set up her own agency, Rae Ellison Associates. Bob moved with her, so she continued to represent him through her new agency. However, this was not

---

146 The idea could even, conceivably, have been a reworking of 'Organochlorine Farm', depending on how big a part the suspect new industrial herbicide would have played in the scheme of things, had it have gone ahead.
147 *Radio Times*, w/c 23 October 1971. The BBC don't retain a copy of this programme in their archive.

out of any particular sense of loyalty towards Ellison on Bob's part. Robert Banks Stewart recalls the rather unhappy background to this switch. 'That was all a bit odd,' he notes. 'Dina Lom, who was the wife of the actor Herbert Lom, got into tax problems, and she fled from England – she was actually Swiss. So she cleared her office – just off Regent Street – one night, and took all the files, and went to Switzerland to avoid going to prison for tax evasion. Rae Ellison, who was a little lady who had worked for her, then set up her own agency, and Bob would have gone with her.' This switch of representation was thus prompted more out of necessity than anything else, and it's possible that it might also have left Bob's own financial affairs in quite an uncertain state at the time.

Also during the summer of 1971, Bob wrote an episode entitled 'Nobody's Strawberry Fool' for the ATV series *Spyder's Web*. *Spyder's Web* was a cold war espionage drama, somewhat in the same vein as *The Avengers, The Saint* or *The Prisoner*. The series starred Patricia Cutts alongside Anthony Ainley, Roger Lloyd Pack and Veronica Carlson as a group of British secret agents. The producer was Dennis Vance, the script supervisor was Malcolm Hulke, and the director of Bob's episode was John Cooper, with whom Bob had last worked on *Happy Ever After*. Bob's episode concerned the discovery in a Swiss glacier of the body of British agent who has been missing since 1914. Back in 1914, at the start of the First World War, the agent was sent over to Switzerland to set up a spy network, and deposited the money he was sent with – a quarter of a million pounds – into a numbered Swiss bank account. The account number and bank details have never been tracked down, but the information is thought to still be on the agent's body. The *Spyder* team are tasked to recover the body, but it goes missing in transit on its way back to London. They realise they've been set up by double agents, who now have the body, smuggled away from the airport in a crate of strawberries. The team track down the missing body and unmask the double agents, who are trying to steal the money for themselves. They discover that the money was all taken in 1914 by the dead agent's wife, just after she pushed him to his death down the ravine.

Bob's script is an assured affair, merrily leading the audience – and the series' regular characters – through a number of semi-comic interludes and improbable capers, which comes over as camp as a row of bright pink glittery tents. Of the regular cast, Anthony Ainley in particular seems to be having a ball with Bob's dialogue, while Windsor Davies, John Savident and Allan Cuthbertson all shine in their various supporting roles. What is perhaps surprising is that Bob's script is enacted almost word-perfectly by the cast, without skipping or substantively altering anything. This is a sure sign that everyone involved realised they were in pretty safe hands. 'Nobody's

Strawberry Fool' was shown on ITV on Friday 31 March 1972.

In July 1971, Bob was contacted by Terence Dudley, who was still the producer of *Doomwatch*, to see if he would be interested in writing a script for the programme's third series. Unfortunately, it would seem that the letter Dudley wrote was sent to Bob's old address in Pitstone, and by the time Dudley contacted him again in August 1971 at the correct new address, most of the story slots for the new *Doomwatch* season had already been allocated to other writers. Dudley gave Bob some potential ideas to think over, but Bob evidently couldn't come up with any storylines that could involve them, as no further dialogue was had between him and the *Doomwatch* production office.[148]

In November 1971, *The Stage and Television Today* reported that Bob was 'under contract' to write for a new LWT series, *New Scotland Yard*. Unsurprisingly, given the title, this was to be a police drama that followed the activities of a branch of the CID in their quest to bring criminals to justice. It would eventually begin on television on Saturday evenings in April 1972. The series was produced by Jack Williams and script edited by Basil Dawson, who had worked on *Fraud Squad* and *Emergency Ward 10*. However, no episodes of *New Scotland Yard* were ever written by Bob, so it would appear that if this contract was ever actually drawn up, it was annulled very soon after.

Bob then moved back into what would later be defined as the telefantasy genre for his next project. *Dead of Night* was a seven-part BBC2 horror anthology series, produced by Innes Lloyd and script edited by Louis Marks.[149] Bob was commissioned on Wednesday 15 March 1972 to write a 50-minute play for the series, with the working title 'The Big One'. A target delivery date of Monday 10 April 1972 was set. Bob delivered his script on Friday 28 April 1972, which was barely seven week prior to filming beginning.[150]

While Bob was busy writing the actual script for *Dead of Night*, his agent, Rae Ellison, got into a slightly heated exchange of letters with the BBC's Head of Copyright with regards to this particular commission. The original fee offered to Bob was only slightly higher than the one he had been paid to write his episode of *Trial* the previous year. Ellison's view was that when Bob was commissioned for *Trial*, he was given a storyline brief, the programme format and the details

---

148 It was also about this time that Bob was involved in writing the *Doctor Who* story 'Carnival of Monsters', which may have limited his involvement in *Doomwatch*'s third season. He wrote the *Doctor Who* storyline in the summer of 1971, was commissioned to write the four scripts on 24 November 1971, and delivered them just before Christmas 1971. See the next chapter for full details.

149 The same production team would go on to make Nigel Kneale's play *The Stone Tape*, which was initially commissioned as a script for *Dead of Night*, but was shown in its own right as a standalone drama on BBC2 the following year.

150 Production for the play began with location filming on Monday 19 and Tuesday 20 June 1972, followed by rehearsals at the BBC's Acton rehearsal rooms between Wednesday 21 and Friday 30 June 1972. Studio recording was done in studio TC1 at BBC Television Centre on Saturday 1 and Sunday 2 July 1972.

of the characters to write for. For *Dead of Night*, on the other hand, he was being asked to come up with a completely original story from scratch which, Ellison argued, was worth a higher fee. She then coupled this with Bob's '… high reputation and long experience,' and added that they had to '… bear in mind his high ITV fees.' Another letter sent by Ellison to the BBC a few weeks later explained: 'Writers meet and the main topic of conversation is fees, and when Robert learns that other writers of not such good standing are being paid (more), naturally he expects me to obtain a similar fee.' Eventually, Louis Marks was asked his opinion on the situation, and he told his BBC bosses that he thought Bob was being underpaid in this instance. Eventually, everything was resolved to everybody's satisfaction.

Bob's episode of *Dead of Night* – the second of the series – was eventually re-titled 'Return Flight'[151] prior to broadcast. It told the story of Rolph, a recently-bereaved airline pilot (played by Peter Barkworth) who, during a routine flight, reports seeing another craft on his flight path, causing him to take evasive action. No-one else on the crew sees the other plane, and no trace of it appears on the radar screens at air traffic control. Later, while cleaning out his wife's possessions, Rolf finds an RAF brooch that was given to her by her first husband, a Lancaster Bomber pilot who died during the war, only six months after they were married. On Rolph's next flight, he hallucinates that a wartime bomber crew are onboard his plane, which then comes under enemy fire. The radio breaks down, and the plane veers off course and crashes on the site of an abandoned airfield. An airfield that Lancaster Bombers used to fly out from during the war …

The episode was shown on BBC2 on Sunday 12 November 1972 and repeated on Sunday 24 February 1974. It is one of only three episodes of the series that still survive at the BBC. Bob's brother-in-law, Ian Watson, recalls that Bob was particularly proud of this play, and considered it to be one of his finest pieces of writing. And although the play is certainly a great character piece for Peter Barkworth as Rolph, the pace is somewhat lugubrious, even for its time.

Writing in *The Stage and Television Today*, reviewer Patrick Campbell was guardedly complimentary about the production: 'When you need an intelligent, professional script for a ghost story, you are wise to turn to Robert Holmes, who has an ear for authentic dialogue and an aptitude for creating atmosphere. Not always, however, do his storylines hold water and there are times when the long bow of coincidence is stretched a little too taught so

---

151 The script gives the title as 'The Return Flight', rather than just 'Return Flight'.

that the arrow overshoots the mark. "Return Flight", the second in BBC2's series of Sunday night spookies, did ask us to accept just a little too much. Captain Rolph, flying his airliner from Hamburg to Luton, takes emergency action to avoid another aircraft on a collision course. No-one else has seen the aircraft. Hamburg's radar has not plotted it. Captain Rolph's wife has recently died. So even when the Germans are prepared to admit that a Dutch airliner was off course that day, there are still doubts in the air. Is Rolph suffering hallucinations? Not even Rolph is quite sure. To this point Robert Holmes has us with him all the way. Well served by his director, Rodney Bennett, and by some meticulous research into air and ground control procedure, he holds us on tenterhooks. But now we are taken on another flight to Hamburg. Rolph is bringing a party of German football fans to England for a European Cup tie. As he sits in the cockpit he becomes identified with the skipper of a wartime Lancaster limping home through the flak after a bombing raid. And here the bait we are asked to swallow is not enough to conceal the hook. For some unexplained reason a sudden electrical fault throws the aircraft out of control and cripples automatic pilot, radio, landing gear, homing instructions, and all. What's more, there is low cloud and near-nil visibility. As we have anticipated for too long, Rolph is now in the position of that RAF pilot of 30 years back. The rest is inevitable. Talked down by his ghostly predecessor, Rolph ends up not at Luton but at the very spot where once lay the runway of a Suffolk RAF station. Unfortunately there has been no runway there for years ...'[152]

Back in 1970, a standalone episode of the BBC1 *Drama Playhouse* series, 'Son of the Regiment', had proved to be a great success with viewers. Its producer, Anthony Coburn[153], was consequently given the chance to make a full series based on the play. This led to the series *The Regiment* beginning on BBC1 in 1972, starring housewives' favourite Christopher Cazenove as Lieutenant Richard Gaunt. Like the pilot, the series followed the fortunes of several British army officers in the First Cotswold Regiment in the early years of the 1900s, which included the events of the Boer War in India. Like the one-off play that spawned it, *The Regiment* proved to be very popular with viewers, and a second series was commissioned to screen on the BBC in 1973. This was made under the producership of Terence Dudley, who had just finished producing the final series of *Doomwatch*. Although most of the action for a given episode of *The Regiment* was recorded in the BBC's studios, there was also a larger-than-normal degree of location filming, much of which took place in Cyprus, making the programme appear very high-budget and glossy

---

152 *The Stage and Television Today*, 16 November 1972.
153 Back in 1963, Anthony Coburn had also written the very first *Doctor Who* story.

in BBC terms.

Bob contacted the series' original producer, Anthony Coburn, in May 1972 and sent him a copy of part of his script (minus the final third act) for 'Mutiny', the episode he had written for the 1968 Thames series *Frontier*, which was very similar to *The Regiment* in many respects. Coburn greatly enjoyed the script. 'Thank you for letting me read this,' he wrote back to Bob on Thursday 1 June 1972. 'Though I'm tantalised to death at not knowing how it came out. Be in touch when I've done my homework.' This ultimately led to Bob being asked to contribute two 50-minute scripts for the second series of *The Regiment*, even though Coburn had by this point been succeeded as producer by Terence Dudley.

The Regiment gave Bob an opportunity to draw on his military experience from the Second World War. The first script he was commissioned to write, under the working title 'Frontier Incident', was scheduled to be the final episode of the series. The commissioning date was Friday 7 July 1972 and the target delivery date Monday 14 August. Bob delivered his script early on Monday 24 July 1972, and the script was formally accepted for production a few weeks later.

Bob's other script for *The Regiment*, given the working title 'Return to Cheltenham', was to be the second episode of the second series. It was commissioned on Monday 24 July 1972, with a target delivery date of Monday 21 August 1972. On this occasion Bob actually delivered a few days late, on Friday 25 August 1972. This episode, retitled 'Depot'[154] before transmission, saw a new Commanding Officer posted to take charge of the regiment in Cheltenham. The script focused on the nitty-gritty of military politics and the social etiquette between the ranks, and was topped off with a light-hearted bit of slapstick fun when one of the troops has to escape from a hotel maid's bedroom via the window in case he is discovered. 'Depot' was directed by Pennant Roberts, and was shown on BBC1 on Friday 2 March 1973.

After they had accepted both of Bob's scripts, the production team of *The Regiment* then found that they needed some rewrites done on 'Frontier Incident', perhaps because of a change of mind as to how the series should be wrapped up. In October 1972, Bob was called back in to do this work, for which he was paid an additional fee.

'Frontier Incident' was ultimately retitled 'North West Frontier' for transmission. It saw the Cotswold Regiment actually in action out in India, coming to an end of their tour of duty. Local problems threaten to escalate into

---

154 Bob's script for this episode actually bears the title 'The Black Hole' rather than 'Depot'. A line in the script explains that Cheltenham is sometimes given the nickname 'The Black Hole' by army folk, 'because so many ex-India people retire to Cheltenham' – i.e. it is an ironic reference to the historical Black Hole of Calcutta.

an armed conflict, especially after the troops find a cache of rifles being smuggled inside a coffin at a local village. The army arrests those responsible, one of whom is the son of a local tribe leader. Richard Gaunt's sister is kidnapped from the army barracks in retribution, and the Commanding Officer considers arranging an exchange of prisoners. The tribe leader's son attempts to escape from the cells, killing his guard, but is shot dead as he tries to flee. Gaunt's wife goes to the nearby village to ask for Gaunt's sister's release, as the garrison prepares to move in force and attack the village. Both women are allowed to return back to the regiment, and the attack on the village is called off.

This final episode was again directed by Pennant Roberts, and was shown on BBC1 on Friday 4 May 1973.

Bob's work on *The Regiment* almost certainly led directly to his next BBC writing assignment. Since leaving *The Regiment*, Anthony Coburn had started work on a new BBC series called *Warship*. Although the idea for this was the brainchild of writer Ian Mackintosh, Coburn had championed it at the BBC, saying that he wanted to make a series '... that would do for the Navy what *Z-Cars* had done for the Police.' Bob was commissioned on Monday 16 October 1972 to write the ninth episode of the series, and given a target delivery date of Monday 30 October 1972 for his 50-minute script.

Bob's script, titled 'The Drop', was actually delivered some months later than requested, on Monday 8 January 1973, apparently with the blessing of Coburn. The episode was then moved up to fifth in the series' running order, and was shown on BBC1 on Thursday 5 July 1973. The *Radio Times*' preview said: 'Malta – and CPO Donovan has some private business to settle ... The drop is an old Navy "custom": the officer who has responsibility for victualling a ship has a lot of friends – friends who are willing to pay.'[155] However, what starts off as a relatively undramatic story concerning a CPO looking to pick up the proceeds of a scam he ran the last time he was on Malta escalates quickly as events takes on a more sinister turn. CPO Donovan is framed for the murder of the woman who was looking after his ill-gotten money on the island, and is blackmailed into stealing a classified component from the ship's stores in return for the help of a local spiv-turned-businessman, Spiro, in covering up the crime. But Donovan is caught red-handed trying to smuggle the item off the ship, and the whole affair comes to the attention of MI5, who see an opportunity to entrap Spiro's paymaster, an agent of the KGB. Donovan is persuaded to go ahead with his rendezvous, so that the local MI5 agent can attempt to capture the local KGB paymaster. Bob's script goes through a

155 *Radio Times*, w/c 30 June 1973.

number of unexpected twists and turns, and although things don't go quite as planned for either the KGB or MI5, a sort of equilibrium is reached at the episode's conclusion, as the component is retrieved by the Navy, and both the MI5 and KGB agents' covers are blown. Poor old Donavan is left facing a prison sentence, even though it turns out the woman whose murder he was being framed for is still alive and well.

One other programme that almost benefited from Bob's scripting ability during this time was *Harriet's Back in Town*, an ITV daytime soap-cum-drama made by Thames Television, which ran between 1972 and 1973. The series of half-hourly episodes was created by writer Peter Yeldham and starred William Russell and Pauline Yates as the newly-divorced couple Tom and Harriet Preston. The premise was that after nearly 20 years of marriage Tom has gone off with a younger girl, leaving his ex-wife Harriet to fend for herself in setting up a new life, a new flat and a new business. Their teenage daughter, Jane, is a trendy it-girl-about-town who still lives with her father. Bob wrote a script for one episode of the series, but for reasons unknown it never went into production. Robert Banks Stewart briefly became story editor on *Harriet's Back in Town* during the latter part of its run in 1973, but has no recollection of Bob ever being approached to write for it while he was part of the production team.

Bob's completed script initially focuses on the character of Tom, who wants to cash in on an insurance policy he and Harriet set up for their daughter some years previously. He now needs the money so that he can buy in on a new business deal with a new entrepreneur in town, Mr Ranjit. Harriet gets a mutual friend to investigate the business deal, which she thinks is a scam, and is shocked to learn that it really does look like a good opportunity. Harriet goes to meet Tom's would-be business partner, Ranjit, who is impressed with her forceful and forthright manner, and her low-cut dress, in equal measure. Harriet later agrees to sign the papers Tom needs to release the money from the fund, and he goes to see Ranjit, who then unexpectedly manages to persuade Tom that he is not a man that Tom should be doing business with after all. The episode ends with Tom feeling quite happy that he's not investing his money from the policy into Ranjit's new company, while Ranjit and Harriet look to have joined forces in business behind his back …

Bob's dialogue is quick and sharp all the way through this witty little script, while the plot takes surprising turns when least expected. It's a real shame that the episode never saw production.

Despite the small setback of the non-production of his script for *Harriet's Back in Town*, Robert Holmes was by now on top of his game as a writer much in demand.

CHAPTER ELEVEN
DISH RAGS
1971-1972

After the internal furore over the supposed excesses of 'Terror of the Autons' had died down at the BBC, Bob was asked to come up with another four-part *Doctor Who* story by Barry Letts and Terrance Dicks; one that would be made during the programme's ninth production block. On Thursday 6 May 1971, Bob was commissioned to write a storyline with the working title 'The Labyrinth', which was scheduled to be delivered by Tuesday 1 June 1971. Bob duly delivered his storyline sometime around this date.[156]

At this point in time, *Doctor Who* had shifted from its one-episode-a-week rehearsal and recording schedule, to something more akin to a two-episodes-a-fortnight pattern. What this meant was that the cast and director would have around ten days to rehearse two episodes' worth of material, which was then followed by two consecutive studio days in which the material was recorded. The advantages to this system were that the cast had more rehearsal time to hone their performances, and studio sets that would have been erected and then struck four times for a four-part story now needed to be put up and taken down only twice, minimising the risk of damage. Sometimes, sets would be needed for only one block of studio days, if all the scenes located in them could be recorded in one go, freeing up studio space for other new sets in the next studio session.

Letts was looking to take full advantage of the flexibilities that this new production method allowed him. Bob's brief on this story was quite specific in its production requirements. It was to be predominantly studio-based (similar to 'The Curse of Peladon', made a few months earlier), with perhaps an additional day or two of pre-filming on the soundstage at Ealing. Two main settings would be required, each being used for about half of the story's duration. (That's not to say that two episodes would be all in setting one, and

---

156 The official delivery date marked on BBC paperwork for this storyline was Wednesday 1 September 1971. However, Terrance Dicks clearly received it around the beginning of July. He wrote to Bob on Friday 2 July telling him he still hadn't had chance to have a meeting with Barry Letts about the storyline, but that he had concerns about the structure of the fourth episode. Dicks wrote again on Wednesday 28 July to apologise for still not scheduling the conference with Letts, due to their overlapping holidays, but assuring Bob that things would quickly start moving in September. It's probable that Bob's initial storyline was actually received on Thursday 1 July 1971 – that date was written on the commissioning paperwork as the date of receipt, but then crossed out. Bob's 'Amendments' document, which rewrites much of the final episode, was then probably written during August 1971. This revision was possibly received on Wednesday 1 September 1971, which is the received date written on the commissioning paperwork, next to the crossed-out July date.

that the other two episodes would all be in setting two: videotape editing now meant that the narrative of the story could switch between the two settings throughout the four episodes.) That way, all the material required for setting one could be rehearsed and recorded in one studio block, while all the material in setting two could be done during the second. Only the Doctor and Jo would appear in both settings, which meant that the other characters in block one would all be different from the characters in block two – which meant that actors wouldn't have to be retained across the whole production of the story, cutting costs still further.

'I remember Huw Wheldon saying about his time as editor of *Monitor*[157] that you can always save money on one thing to spend it somewhere else', noted Letts. 'He said one of the cheapest shows he did was interviewing Orson Welles, so he was able to use the money on something spectacular later on. Well, I took that on board. So I said to Terrance that if we had one show that had no filming whatsoever, then we would be able to have much, much more filming on another show, and it could be really rather fun. And so we decided that the show we would have no filming on would be "Carnival of Monsters" – although it wasn't called that at the time, of course – and we asked Bob to write it. And the whole point was that it would all be done in the studio, with very simple scenery.'

'I think they'd gone over budget and I was asked to write a cheap show that could be played out in two lots of sets', recalled Bob. 'It was quite a challenge to one's ingenuity but worked out pretty well – so well, in fact, that the actors in the ship section of the show never met the actors playing the aliens outside the machine! But I understand it failed in its main objective: Barry Letts told me later the programme turned out as costly as any other.'[158]

When Bob delivered his storyline, now retitled 'Out of the Labyrinth', the plot was constructed so that each episode could indeed be recorded just in the confines of the BBC studios. The only specific film sequences that Bob had included were short cutaway stock footage shots of a ship at sea, plus a sunset, and some model effects sequences of a sea monster. In addition, he had included a few filmed scenes of the Doctor and Jo set in a swampland, which presumably he thought might be filmed at the BBC's film studios at Ealing. The first of the two settings that Bob had chosen for his story was the interior of a 1926 passenger ship at sea, which was to be represented by just four studio sets – deck, saloon, passage and cabin. These were all to be recorded in the first studio session. The second studio session would then have been split between

---

157 *Monitor* was a popular BBC arts programme from the 1960s, on which Huw Wheldon's position of 'editor' saw him take overall artistic control.
158 Robert Holmes Interview, *The Time Meddler*: Issue 3, October 1981 – Interview by John M Kahane.

two further settings; the alien world of the Vol-Dome, and a couple of shafts inside the alien device Bob had christened the Strobe.

It was decided to make 'Out of the Labyrinth' the final story of *Doctor Who*'s ninth production block, which would be held over to be shown as part of the tenth season in 1973. Nearly three months passed (due mainly to Dicks and then Letts going on holiday) before Bob was commissioned on Wednesday 24 November 1971 to write the four scripts for the story. The only alteration to Bob's submitted storyline that Dicks requested was to keep Jo aboard the *SS Bernice* inside the Strobe – and therefore in some degree of danger – for the majority of the fourth episode.

Bob got down to writing the scripts for the first two episodes, but then realised that he had a technical problem with the storyline, which he needed to clarify before he could go any further. He wrote to Dicks on Tuesday 23 November 1971: 'This is an immediate problem but before I reach Episodes Three and Four I shall need a directive on it: I devised the story, for budget reasons, in two sections. Keeping Jo inside the machine well into Part Four means, I suspect, that I may find it necessary to use some of the first half sets. I've already decided that the TARDIS is going to materialise in the ship's hold. Apart from solving a lot of set-design problems, I think a murky hold full of crates offers more scope for action sequences. I think Jo has to be in this hold when the sailor is killed and when the Drashigs corner her in Part Four. I will try to plan things so that this is the only set required for both studio days. I presume it will be possible to pre-tape the penultimate scene (Daly in his cabin actually getting to mark off another day on the calendar) and any brief ship sequences that I might need to show on the Glo-sphere during the course of Episodes Three and Four?'

Bob cheekily finished off his letter to Dicks by attaching a clipping of a newspaper advert. 'Finally, how about this?' he asked, indicating the advert. 'A lucrative new market for the inventive fiction writer?'

FREELANCE WRITERS WANTED for magazine. Knowledge of fetishes and erotica an advantage. Send scripts of approximately 5,000 words to *Mentor*, 187 Victoria Street, SW1.

Dicks, in a letter dated Wednesday 1 December 1971, reassured Bob that his storyline and set concerns wouldn't be a problem. He also played along with Bob's suggestion for a freelance writing gig, jokingly telling him that he'd already sent a script for 'The Secret Sex Life of Dr Who' to *Mentor*!

Letts recalled that this saucy innuendo all stemmed from Bob's response when asked by Dicks to alter a section of the first episode of 'Carnival of Monsters'. 'Terrance tells a story,' said Letts, 'and I'm not quite sure if I remember it correctly, but in "Carnival of Monsters", when the Doctor and Jo Grant were locked in the cabin on the ship, she bounced up and down on the bunk and said, "Well, we're obviously going to be here for some time." And so that line had to hastily be changed! But I think that it might be an apocryphal story ...'

Bob was given a delivery date of Thursday 23 December 1971 for all four of the scripts for this story, and managed to deliver Episode One exactly on that date, with Episodes Two, Three and Four following the very next day, on Christmas Eve.[159]

Bob could now relax over Christmas 1971, and New Year!

Like most of Bob's previous *Doctor Who* stories, this one also underwent a title change before going into production. 'Out of the Labyrinth' was initially re-titled 'Peepshow' in early 1972. It was only after the story had been recorded in July 1972 that the title changed one final time, to 'Carnival of Monsters'.

Although the story was born out of an initial planning conversation between Bob, Dicks and Letts, the end result was still mainly Bob's work. 'I imagine Bob would have come up with the idea of the scope, and the enclosed environment,' recalls Dicks. 'Again, it was something original, all those scenes on the boat where they think they're going to the South China seas in the '20s on the way to Singapore, or whatever. And it's genuinely puzzling; you don't know where you are or what's going on, and then the monster bursts through. It was a good mixture of ingredients. And then, of course, you had the alien planet, with the showman, and the fact that it was all inside a miniaturised peepshow machine. So it was a good mixture of original ideas. Many, possibly most, of those would have come from Bob, with the rest of us kind of joining in and adding things and helping him work them out.'

When he was interviewed by *Doctor Who Magazine* in 1985, Bob had very clear memories of writing 'Carnival of Monsters'. 'The cast never met!' he said. 'I can't remember the reason, but I was asked to make it cheap – though I was told afterwards that it worked out quite expensive! So I decided that the way to write it was to do it in two sections: the on board ship section and the people outside the machine. Only the Doctor and Jo Grant passed in between. They shot that with the shipboard stuff done in the first session in the studio and the outside stuff done on the second recording two weeks later. It was quite a different and amusing idea to have this peepshow. My favourite bit was when

---

159 Bob probably posted in his script for the first episode, which presumably was delivered to the BBC on 23 December. He then probably hand-delivered the final three scripts on Christmas Eve, no doubt also then joining in with the festivities at the BBC bar with Dicks and Letts afterwards!

the Doctor got out of the TARDIS at the beginning and started talking to the chickens!'[160]

'I had the functionaries, who were the plebs, you know, who kept fossil fuel in their hygiene chambers,' Bob later recalled. 'And then we had the civil servant types, the anonymous grey people, who headed the thing, and were responsible. They wouldn't let you onto this planet, they were terribly bureaucratic, and yet they were planning a palace revolt. You always had to have some nefarious activity going on – you've got to give people a little frisson, haven't you? I established that when people came out of the cabinet, as when the Doctor came out, they expanded to normal size. So when the Drashigs finally came out and escaped ... I had this chap who had been playing the three-card trick with these aliens. He'd been in the Royal Artillery or something, and so he mowed these things down. That's what I wanted, this carnival touch. It was very tacky. I mean they'd been in theatrical digs all over the galaxy. That's a bit of an in-joke, I suppose. But it gives it depth.'

One element of Bob's original idea for 'Carnival of Monsters' that didn't make it to the final version was his notion of how Vorg communicated with the alien officials of Inter Minor. Speaking on stage at the 1981 Panopticon convention, Bob recalled, 'Scripts go through stages, you have one draft and then another draft. And in the first draft I had the showman, who was the guy who arrived with the box in which the monsters were held, he was speaking to these rather august aliens in Pidgin English, rather like South-Sea Pidgin English. And the producer said, "No, we can't do this because it's not in the *Doctor Who* format." They liked to think that everybody can understand everybody else throughout the universe, so then you don't get into any of these language problems.'[161]

One aspect of the story that didn't give Bob any particular language problems was the choice to make the passengers and crew of the SS *Bernice* originate in the 1920s – an era for which he had a particular passion. 'I used to write things like *The Regiment*, you know, I did two of those. It's a period that, from the late Victorian era – which was [the era of] "The Talons of Weng-Chiang" – up to about 1925, was kind of quite rich. It was the old stiff-upper-lip, and chaps were "chaps", and girls had bobbed hair and had the "flapper" look going on, and so I quite enjoyed that. I thought how nice to have this "fossilised" group, and I loved the ending when the man finally completed his book, you know – he'd been reading the same chapter for 3,000 years! That

160 Interview – Robert Holmes, *Doctor Who Magazine*: Issue 100, May 1985.
161 Panopticon IV Convention, Queen Mary College, 1-2 August 1981.

177

saves the writer a lot of trouble too; you keep using the same dialogue!'[162]

One of Bob's creations in this story was a fearsome race of creatures that he christened Drashigs. This name was something of an in-joke on Bob's part, as he knew from his past experience with the Krotons and the Nestenes that the BBC's ability to make convincing alien creatures was … limited, shall we say, by the comparatively small budgets available to the effects crews. So Bob slyly chose a name that was an anagram of Dish Rags, which is what he suspected his monsters could be made out of when they eventually appeared on screen. However, for once, Bob's expectations were to prove largely unfounded. 'Bob has this very quirky imagination,' recalled Letts. 'His scripts were always different from everybody else's; the original ideas were surprising, and the ways he worked them out were surprising; you never quite knew where they'd go. He invented some lovely ideas, like the Drashigs for example, which were one of the best monsters that we ever had. It was a combination of his idea, and the special effects and the visual effects people making the Drashigs, and me in my role as director, making sure they worked. Which they did 90% of the time.'

As far as Letts was concerned, 'Carnival of Monsters' was a little bit special for *Doctor Who* at that time. 'I think my favourite story of Bob's that I had anything to do with, or saw for that matter, was indeed "Carnival of Monsters",' he recalled. 'It's got such a variation in it, so many different things in it, different ideas, and it's such fun. Like all things one's done in the past, I was a bit disappointed in the way some of [it] worked out, but it was nothing to do with the script, it was to do with odd things with make-up, and so on, that weren't quite as they should have been, but that's life!'

When the story was being made in the summer of 1972, Bob took up an invitation from Dicks to attend one of the studio recordings. He watched with Dicks in the studio gallery on the evening of Tuesday 20 June 1972 as the scenes set on board the *SS Bernice* from the story's final two episodes were taped.[163]

'Carnival of Monsters' ably demonstrates just how much Bob had developed as a writer since his first scripts for the series a little over three years previously. Here he takes two quite separate narratives and ties them neatly together so that the events inside and outside the scope directly impact on the characters on the flipside of the action. He positively relishes the period

---

162 Bob had finished writing his scripts for 'Peepshow' / 'Carnival of Monsters' some months prior to being commissioned for his first script for *The Regiment*, but the dates were quite close together. Given that Bob, in his interview, was recalling events that had happened over a decade ago at this point, he can be forgiven for conjoining the two events.

163 Dicks introduced Bob to Keith Miller, the secretary of the *Doctor Who* Fan Club, in the BBC bar after the evening's studio recording. Miller recalled that Bob was sprouting a beard at the time, and also was copiously smoking his beloved pipe.

setting of the *SS Bernice*, and the characters it gives him the opportunity to create, while the alien world of Inter Minor is carefully crafted using the barest minimum of backstory dialogue. In Vorg and Shirna, we have the very first *bona fide* Holmesian 'double act' of the series; something that will crop up in his *Doctor Who* writing again and again over the coming years. And it's hard not to imagine that his creation of a gaudy old vaudevillian, accompanied by a pretty dolly-bird to pull in the punters, isn't some kind of sly commentary on the TARDIS crew of the day, in the form of Jon Pertwee and Katy Manning. If it is, it seems that by being hidden in plain sight in his script, it went completely unnoticed by the cast and crew. In terms of legacy, Bob casually creates, in a few strokes of character dialogue, the planet with which the Doctor's dalliance will underlie the remainder of Jon Pertwee's era as the Doctor. 'I invented Metebelis III, which was used in "Planet of the Spiders", Bob once recalled. 'Metebelis III was referred to in "Carnival of Monsters", and it was a multi-syllable name. I tend to go for those sort of things.'

INTERLUDE VII
DOCTOR WHO:
'OUT OF THE LABYRINTH'
JUNE 1971

Robert Holmes' full original storyline proposal for the *Doctor Who* story that eventually became 'Carnival of Monsters' is reprinted here as originally submitted, complete with his original spellings and punctuation:

OUT OF THE LABYRINTH

EPISODE ONE

1. TK 1: SMALL STEAMER IN PLACID SUNLIT OCEAN.

2. SHIP'S DECK.
Major Daly parts from his daughter, Claire, and Third Officer Andrews and goes into the passenger saloon. The young couple set off to walk twelve times round the deck – their pre-prandial mile.

3. SALOON.
Daly settles down with a book, yawns, starts to doze.

4. DECK.
The Tardis materialises. Jo and the Doctor emerge – the Doctor fascinated that they have landed on a planet already showing so many similarities to Earth. Jo is convinced they are on Earth. They duck behind a lifeboat as Claire and Andrews pass, overhear them discussing the West End theatre.

5. SALOON.
Daly is asleep. The Doctor and Jo enter. She picks up the discarded novel and points out the publisher's London imprint. The Doctor is puzzled but adamant. He knows the Tardis has not landed on Earth.

6. DECK.
Claire screams and points. Simultaneously there is a hideous roar. Andrews runs with her for the shelter of the saloon.

7. SALOON.
Daly, shocked, awake, is on his feet as Andrews and the girl rush in. The roar is repeated. They cower back as a scaly monster rears up beyond the saloon window. Then it vanishes back into the sea. Andrews goes off to the bridge. At this point Daly first notices the Doctor and Jo.

8. DECK.
Andrews posts a seaman with a rifle outside the saloon.

9. SALOON.
Daly questions the Doctor and receives carefully guarded answers. Andrews enters and decides Jo and the Doctor must have stowed away at Port Said. They will be kept under guard until the captain is free to deal with them.

10. TK 2: THE SUN SETTING OVER THE OCEAN.

11. PASSAGE.
The Doctor causes confusion in the ranks when he stops abruptly. He stares at an octagonal plate of bright metal let into the mahogany bulkhead. Neither Andrews nor Daly apparently understand what he's talking about. Hallucination. Clearly gone too long without food and water. Poor fellow.

12. CABIN.
Jo and the Doctor are locked in Major Daly's cabin and try to figure out their predicament. The Doctor is convinced they are not on Earth. Is he then - Jo asks - saying that Daly, Andrews and the rest are aliens? No, he's not saying that. He draws her attention to a calendar on the wall - the days of the voyage are crossed off. The pencil line stops on June 4, 1926. The name of the ship they are on

is the SS Bernice. He tells Jo about the famous mystery of the SS Bernice: its complete disappearance from the face of the earth one night in June 1926. From the face of the earth … The Doctor is beginning to get an idea. He picklocks the door and –

13. PASSAGE.
– they examine the curious, anachronistic metal plate. The Doctor says he can slide it open with the aid of a magnetic core extractor. He has one in the Tardis.

14. DECK.
The Doctor enters the Tardis and emerges with the core extractor. Jo points to a crazy thing: the sun is higher in the sky – to the west – than twenty minutes ago. Jo and the Doctor hide as Claire and Andrews pass discussing West End theatre.

15. SALOON.
In the passenger saloon Major Daly is asleep as before. He leaps up at a sudden roar. Claire rushes in, screaming, followed by a white-faced Andrews. The monster roars again and the plesiosaurus rears up outside the saloon window before sinking back into the sea. The pattern changes, however, with the Doctor dragging Jo out before Daly spots them.

16. DECK.
Jo is bewildered. It's exactly like a stuck gramophone record. She points.

17. TK 3: THE SUN SETTING OVER THE OCEAN.

18. DECK.
As they look out the sky seems to move. An enormous bare hand and arm reaches down towards them. Jo and the Doctor dive under the shelter of a lifeboat. The gigantic hand gropes towards them and they cringe back helplessly as we –

FADE OUT.

EPISODE TWO

1. DECK.
Reprise. Then the hand gropes beyond the lifeboat and
lifts the Tardis delicately, between finger and thumb,
carrying it back up into the sky and disappearing. The
Doctor and Jo emerge from hiding. They see Andrews coming
from the bridge with the seaman and hurry into the saloon.
Andrews posts the armed seaman on duty outside the saloon.

2. SALOON.
Daly spots Jo and the Doctor. He is questioning them when
Andrews enters. Andrews decides they must be stowaways.
They will be locked in a cabin until the Captain can deal
with them.

3. CABIN.
Jo and the Doctor are left alone. Jo cannot understand why
Daly & Co. keep repeating themselves without apparently
remembering they've been through the routine before.

4. VOL-DOME.
This is the equivalent of a fairground tent but like
scientific. Plumb in the centre stands the Strobe which
looks a bit like an outsize juke box – bright and garish
and with a Glo-sphere video screen as its centrepiece.
Shirna, a lovely young Lurman girloid, is standing beside
the Strobe holding a screwdriver. A panel at the back of
the Strobe opens and Vorg squeezes out. He is like P. T.
Barnum. He says he thinks he has found the cause of the
trouble and switches on area three … On the video screen
we see Andrews, Daly and Claire on the ship's deck.
(Repeat of part of Sc. 2, Ep 1) Shirna says the monster
bit came round three times in half an hour; she adds that
she is practically certain she had never seen two of the
Tellurians before. Vorg laughs at this and, taking the
screwdriver, goes back inside the Strobe.

5. PASSAGE.
Using his core extractor, the Doctor winkles open the octagonal panel. It leads into a shaft. He enters and Jo follows.

6. VOL-DOME.
Vorg lifts the Tardis out of the Strobe. It is tiny but as he sets it down it makes its Kraken awakening sound and expands to full size. Shirna falls back in fright. Vorg is a bit shaken himself but quickly reassures her. Everything in the Strobe is miniaturised but once removed from the machine objects return to normal scale. Shirna is not reassured. She doesn't think Vorg really understands the Strobe. And suppose the Drashigs got out? Utterly impossible, says Vorg. He is about to go back into the machine to make a final check. She urges him to hurry. If they're going to eat they need to put on a show before nightfall.

7. SHAFT.
Meanwhile the Doctor and Jo are working their way along a complex of tubes and supply pipes. A panel moves aside and a huge screwdriver brushes past them. They hide but from the place of concealment they see a huge eye blinking in the aperture.

8. VOL-DOME.
Shirna changes into her ticket-selling costume and Vorg starts rustling up an audience over the Vol-Dome's external tannoy. The patter is well-worn and familiar – a cultural and educational exhibition of strange life forms gathered from all the corners of the galaxy – thrill to the fearsome Drashigs – see the fascinating Tellurians, so amusingly Lurman-like in the physiology and actions …

9. SHAFT.
Jo and the Doctor come to a dead end. They must wriggle back and try to find another way out of the maze. Jo is tired. She'd settle for going back to the cabin and having

a good kip. The Doctor reminds her they've got to find a
way out into the giant's world or they'll never see the
Tardis again.

10. VOL-DOME.
Through a peephole Shirna estimates that they've now
attracted a queue of no more than a dozen Lurmans. Then
she sees three more coming. But – oh dear – these look
like trouble. Officialdom. There is a bang on the door.
Vorg opens it and admits Pletrac 4, a crusty black-clad
customs officer, and his two aides. Pletrac 4 points out
the various regulations that Vorg has contravened. The
Glo-sphere and Strobe will be confiscated and destroyed
unless Vorg files a satisfactory Plea in Mitigation. He
has until main sundown to complete and file the necessary
documentation. Pletrac 4, ignoring the old showman's
whines and protests, leaves a sheaf of forms and exits.

11. SHAFT.
The Doctor and Jo find a hatch. They struggle upwards and
suddenly see light above. Jubilantly they press on.

12. VOL-DOME.
Vorg is cursing the bureaucratic planet. What a place
to choose for a showman's convention! If they lose the
Strobe they'll be finished. Shirna says they can always
go back to busking. Suddenly the Strobe's circuit light
starts flashing. Vorg groans. It still isn't right. There's
another field short, this time in area five. They switch to
area five on the video.

13. TK 4: SWAMP.
The Doctor and Jo struggle out of a steaming geyser hole
into a monochrome world obscured by sulphurous-smelling
mist. They move forward cautiously.

14. VOL-DOME.
On the video screen we see the Doctor and Jo stumbling
across the swamp. Shirna and Vorg are appalled. Somehow

the Tellurians have escaped from area three and entered area five – the world of the Drashigs. Vorg says it will only be a matter of minutes before the Drashigs catch their scent and then nothing can save them. Jo and the Doctor vanish into the mist. Vorg swings the controls, trying to keep the video on them. Suddenly a Drashig comes swirling up from the mud. It raises its great hooter and sounds the Last Post …

15. TK 5: SWAMP.
The shattering noise stops the Doctor and Jo in their tracks. Jo is scared rigid. They decide to retreat. Then, through the mist, get a vague glimpse of a solid shape bearing down on them like a train …

FADE OUT.

EPISODE THREE

1. TK 6: SWAMP.
Reprise. The travellers take evasive action. The Drashig bores past, head down, truffling along their outward track. The Doctor and Jo realise the thing is hunting by scent and hasten their steps towards where they think the geyser is.

2. VOL-DOME.
Shirna is urging Vorg to do something to save the Tellurians.

3. TK 7: SWAMP.
The hunting call of the Drashigs can be heard on all sides now. The Doctor realises that a pack of the brutes is closing in. He backs up, holding Jo behind him, the Very pistol in his hand. A Drashig breaks out of the mist and is about to fall on them when the Doctor shoots a signal flare into its mouth. The Drashig contorts in agony and then the rest of the pack arrives. While the travellers gain another fifty yards the pack tears its wounded member to pieces.

4. VOL-DOME.
Pletrac 4 returns. Shirna tells him Vorg hasn't yet
completed his form-filling – he has been delayed by a
little technical difficulty in the Strobe. On the Glo-
sphere's video screen the Drashigs are just polishing off
the grisly bits. Pletrac 4 is fascinated despite himself.

5. TK 7: SWAMP.
Through a gap in the mist the Doctor sees the geyser-hole
that leads to the underground shaft. Jo is about spent
but he drags her towards it. Then a bunch of Drashigs
clamours over the horizon. The Doctor realises that this
time they haven't a hope. Jo realises it, too, and urges
him to leave her. The Doctor turns to face the ravening
monsters. A great hand comes out of the sky and blocks
their advance … Jo and the Doctor run to the geyser and
scramble thankfully into the comparative safety of the
underground shaft.

6. VOL-DOME.
Vorg comes out of the Strobe. Pletrac 4 tells him his Plea
in Mitigation is not acceptable. The Strobe will have to
be destroyed. Vorg begs to be allowed to put on just a
couple of shows, enough to make his travelling money.

7. SHAFT.
Jo recovers and the Doctor urges her on. They must find a
way out. He doesn't tell her the reason for urgency but
it's noticeable that he keeps looking back with obvious
anxiety.

8. VOL-DOME.
The argument between Vorg and the customs officials is
still continuing. Pletrac 4 dispatches one of his men to
fetch an engine of destruction.

9. SHAFT.
We see the first Drashig snuffling along. It picks up the
scent and gives a scream of triumph.

10. SHAFT.
Jo freezes in horror. The things are still on their trail.
The Doctor says their only chance is to break the scent.
He sees a panel up ahead.

11. VOL-DOME.
Shirna discreetly tries to draw Vorg away from Pletrac
4. She shows him area five on the video. The Drashigs
are milling around the geyser. Is there any chance that
they will find their way out? Pletrac 4 overhears. Vorg
swears it is utterly impossible for any of the zoological
specimens in the Strobe ever to escape.

12. SHAFT.
The Doctor gets the panel open with the core extractor.
The baying of the Drashigs sounds to be right on their
heels as he pulls Jo through.

13. SHAFT (2).
Jo and the Doctor stand with a metal abyss below them. In
front there is some form of mechanism – a huge stationary
cog-wheel. It seems just possible for them to leap across
to the rim of the wheel and then work their way along
the spokes to the hub. It will be then comparatively easy
to shin across the central spindle to the far side of
the shaft. By this time there is no choice anyway. The
Drashigs are already bashing dents in the solid steel
behind them. The Doctor jumps out on to the wheel and
balances there, ready to catch Jo should she slip … She
does but he catches her … Unfortunately, their combined
weight on the extreme edge of the cogwheel is enough to
start it moving. It swings downwards, gathering speed,
and they see the meshing teeth of another cog waiting to
grind them up.

14. VOL-DOME.
Pletrac 4's henchman returns and says the request for an
engine of destruction had been put through channels. Pletrac
4 – with something suspiciously like a wink – tells Vorg

it will be at least three weeks before authorisation is received. At this point the Strobe's internal alarm signal goes off. Vorg groans. Another fault in the mechanism.

15. SHAFT (2).
The Doctor has swung his weight out across the cogwheel in an effort to restore its balance. But the meshing teeth move remorselessly nearer.

16. VOL-DOME.
Vorg locates the trouble - a slipping balance wheel in the thermal compression tube. He corrects its adjustment.

17. SHAFT (2).
The cogwheel checks in the nick of time. The Doctor and Jo are able to drop down on to the central spindle and reach the far side.

18. SHAFT.
The Drashigs break an opening in the wall of the shaft.

19. VOL-DOME.
Pletrac 4 accepts Vorg's assurances that the Strobe contains no noxious effluents or other matter likely to prove a hazard to health or pollute the environment. He issues a Temporary Performance Licence, pointing out that it is on the green form and must be renewed every seven days. Vorg thanks him and at this point Shirna screams. She has seen something creeping out of the Strobe. The Doctor and Jo explode to full size. The internal shock is tremendous. They drop to the ground.

FADE OUT.

EPISODE FOUR

1. VOL-DOME.
Reprise. The Doctor and Jo fall to the ground, apparently dead. Vorg examines them and discovers they're only

unconscious, Pletrac 4 says they will have to be dealt with by the decontamination squad. The Doctor recovers in time to hear this suggestion and is highly incensed. The Doctor checks his Tardis and then examines the Strobe. He questions Vorg about it and condemns him for keeping sentient creatures locked in an aimless time-cycle.

2. SHAFT.
The Drashigs are seen again tearing and bashing their way through the Strobe's internal mechanism.

3. VOL-DOME.
Explanations over, the Doctor and Jo now understand the situation they have escaped from. The Doctor tells Pletrac 4 there is a grave danger that the Drashigs will follow them out of the Strobe. If this is allowed to happen the entire planet will be threatened. As if to emphasise his words we hear the Drashigs crashing now against the outer hull of the Strobe.

The Doctor says the Lurmans must bring up their most devastating weapons and destroy the Drashigs as they leave the Strobe. Pletrac 4 is appalled. The Lurmans have no weapons. They were renounced at the Andromeda Convention.

Vorg and Shirna argue out of earshot of the others. She knows they can disconnect the power feed and everything inside the Strobe will die within minutes. Vorg opposes this. He will never be able to get it working again. The Strobe is his only possession, his life and his career …

Shirna says if the Drashigs escape they will all be killed, anyway; the Drashigs are the most renowned and unstoppable carnivores in the galaxy. She takes the key to the power box, eluding Vorg's grip, and runs to the Doctor.

The Doctor has unscrewed a cover at the base of the Strobe and is - with increasing desperation - trying to fathom its principles and mechanism.

Shirna brings him the key and tells him what must be done to destroy the Strobe. Jo begs him to remember Major Daly, Andrews, Claire … it will be murder. Pletrac 4 is unmoved. Shirna has the solution – the Strobe must be destroyed immediately. The Doctor asks for a little more time. They must wait until the last possible moment. He continues work on the Strobe's complex wiring circuit and the Drashigs continue bashing against the hull.

Pletrac 4's nerve breaks. He wrests the key from Shirna and runs to the power box. Jo and the Doctor chase him and are tackled by Pletrac 4's henchmen. Pletrac 4 cuts the power switch … but its contacts are old and corroded. They break off leaving the power line intact.

It seems that the last chance is gone. There is no way of stopping the Drashigs. The Doctor is still working like a beaver oblivious to the danger of the Drashigs bursting out at any moment. He hopes to activate the Strobe's feedback circuit precisely on the original setting. This will have the effect of sending the aliens in the Strobe back to their own place and time.

The leading Drashig emerges and kills one of the customs men. The Doctor electrocutes it with a surplus power cable. He energises the Strobe's hull to deter the rest of the pack temporarily. But nothing holds back the Drashigs for long once they got the scent of blood.

The Doctor is now working on the Strobe knowing that one false move will be enough to electrocute him. But he makes a final connection, screws the trigger mechanism back in place, and pulls the switch.

The Strobe shudders and vibrates. Energy drains from the Glo-sphere. The video screen goes black. Suddenly the Strobe is empty. It sags and corrodes like a mechanical Dorian Gray as its support system collapses. Vorg kicks it moodily. Now what's he going to do?

Pletrac 4 hands the Doctor and Jo buff Application for Immigration forms and asks them to fill them in. There will have to be a Board of Enquiry into the whole affair.

The Doctor and Jo go to the Tardis to fetch a pen. Jo asks the Doctor where Daly and co. have gone and he says at the moment they ought to be about three hundred nautical miles from Bombay. They enter the Tardis and it vanishes.

Pletrac 4 is very upset by this irregular behaviour. Shirna and Vorg don't notice the Tardis has gone: they are too busy polishing up their old song and dance act.

4. SALOON.
Daly shuts his book and remarks that it's a good yarn. He says goodnight to his daughter and Andrews and goes below.

5. CABIN.
Daly starts to undress, notices the calendar. He yawns and takes a pencil and crosses off June 5. It's been a long day.

FADE OUT.

AMENDMENTS [164]

Episode 1 establishes that Vorg and Shirna have brought the Glo-Sphere to Odron to attend a universal congress of travelling showmen. (Really just an excuse to hold a Universe Fair!)

The Glo-Sphere is being carefully scrutinised by the Tribunal of Examiners headed by Pletrac 4. The second member of the tribunal is X10 whose older brother, X8, is President of the Odronocracy. If X8 topples, the dynamic politically forceful X10 is a certain bet to succeed him. The third member of the tribunal is a yes-man named Grig 07.

[164] After discussing his written story outline with Terrance Dicks, Bob then went away and made a few pages of alterations and amendments, which he forwarded on to Dicks a few months later – see Chapter Eleven.

Episodes 2 and 3 show a developing plot by X10 (aided by Grig 07 and unknown to Pletrac 4) to engineer the escape of the alien life-forms from the Glo-Sphere. The very fact that this could happen under the benevolent regime of X8 will be enough to start an uproar among the nervous Odrons and bring about the President's downfall.

I may establish - for the information of Vorg and Shirna - that the Odron civilisation was almost ended in 16013rec by the accidental importation of an alien bug in a cargo of Jacrac yananas. Since which ancient date the Odrons have been the most insular planet in the galaxy.

X8 is trying to raise the iron curtain and increase galactic trade, travel, culture, etc.

In Episode 3, also, Jo and the Doctor are separated while still in the Glo-Sphere. Jo gets back to the ship and this is subsequently attacked by the monsters.

Episode 4. Because of X10's tinkering, the Doctor escapes from the Glo-Sphere. He is immediately in danger of extinction because the Tribunal is protected by a piece of mechanism called the Abstractor - levelled at the Glo-Sphere and ready to suck away any noxious substances that may emerge.

Luckily for the Doctor, when Pletrac 4 pushes the button the Abstractor's firing device fails to operate. The Doctor expands, recovers consciousness and convinces everyone that he is a reasonable chap.

In the Glo-Sphere the Drashigs can be seen breaking through into the ship.

Aboard the SS Bernice the humans are completely incapable of apprehending their danger. Monsters roaming round in the bilges? They think Jo is a madwoman. The Drashigs kill a crew member.

ROBERT HOLMES: A LIFE IN WORDS

Jo is in dire peril, locked in the hold, when the Drashigs are stopped by Vorg's long arm. At this time the Doctor's main concern is to get Jo out of the machine. Using the Glo-Sphere to keep an eye on the roaming packs of Drashigs he sends her godlike instructions – 'Turn left … Through the hatch … Watch out behind you' – to guide her to the exit.

Meanwhile Pletrac 4 has whistled up a team of technicians to remedy the fault on the Abstractor.

Jo gets out of the machine but is closely pursued by the snapping Drashigs. They hammer at the exit panel.

The Chief Technician reports to Pletrac 4 that the Abstractor is irreparable. It has been sabotaged. Pletrac realises that this is the devilish work of X10 but time is too pressing to deal with him. The Drashigs will be bursting out of the machine at any moment. They have to be stopped. Vorg, unhappily, says he can cut the main power feed. Everything inside the Strobe would be dead within minutes. Jo thinks of Major Daly, Claire, Third Officer Andrews … There has to be another solution.

The Doctor is working on it. He begs for time and questions Vorg about the Strobe. But the old chap has never understood its higher principles. He acquired the machines from another showman many years ago.

The Drashigs are now massing in force round the exit. Pletrac 4 says the Doctor has five minutes to find an alternative solution.

Pressing the technicians into service the Doctor sets to work to reverse the polarity of the Strobe's feed-in coil. He explains to Jo that the feedback should reverse precisely on its original setting.

The first Drashigs break out. Pletrac 4 cuts the main power feed. Nothing happens. X10 has linked up a secondary input. He gloats over his triumph as he prepares to make good his escape. The Presidential sceptre is within his grasp.

X10 is killed by the Drashigs.

The Doctor electrocutes the leading monsters with a cable from the Tardis. The Chief Technician reports they have made all the connections as per the Doctor's diagram.

The Doctor pulls the switch. Energy drains from the Glo-Sphere. The Strobe slowly collapses as its support systems erodes.

On board the S.S. Bernice, Major Daly finally reaches the end of chapter five. He goes down to his cabin and yawns as he marks off another day on the calendar.

Pletrac 4 is collecting witnesses for the court of enquiry. He interrupts Vorg and Shirna rehearsing their song and dance act to ask where the deuce the Doctor and Jo have got to. Vorg says he last saw them heading towards the Tardis. As Pletrac 4 turns towards the Tardis it disappears …

CHAPTER TWELVE
FIELD MARSHAL HOL MES
1973

Bob's next brief from the *Doctor Who* production team was to come up with a story to open the eleventh season, due to begin on BBC1 in late 1973/early 1974. He was also once again given the task of introducing a new companion. This was as a replacement for Katy Manning's Jo Grant, who had left the show at the end of the previous run.

On Tuesday 9 January 1973, Bob was commissioned to write a storyline for a four-part adventure with the working title 'The Automata'. This was due to be delivered on Friday 26 January 1973, which Bob duly complied with, according to the BBC paperwork.

However, nearly a month later, on Monday 26 February 1973, Barry Letts wrote to the BBC's Head of Copyright, confirming that he would not now be commissioning scripts for 'The Automata' for reasons '... as explained to your secretary on the 'phone today.' Bob was then paid in full for the work he had done on his storyline thus far. To date, no copy of Bob's storyline for 'The Automata' has been located, and Terrance Dicks has no memory whatsoever of what it might have been about.

At about this time, Bob moved agents again, leaving Rae Ellison. His new agents were Kavannagh Entertainment Ltd in Piccadilly, where Jon Thurley would look after Bob's writing interests. Thurley would remain as Bob's agent for the rest of his life, setting up his own agency a few years later, and taking Bob along with him.

Thurley had in fact been involved in Bob's career since as early as 1967. 'I joined the long defunct Lom Associates in March 1967,' he recalled, 'and was introduced to Bob shortly afterward by Rae Ellison, Dina Lom's partner, and very soon took over from her as his agent. He was an extremely nice gentleman (in the best, old fashioned sense of the word), courteous and quietly spoken, and over the years we would meet from time to time for a snack lunch somewhere, in the days when Bob could smoke his pipe wherever he chose. We didn't talk much about work or the business, but chatted about mutual friends and acquaintances.'

On the same day that 'The Automata' story idea was binned by the *Doctor Who* production office, Bob was commissioned to write another storyline to replace it. The genesis of the idea came during a lunchtime meeting between

Bob, Letts and Dicks, when the topic arose of how long it had been since *Doctor Who* had done a historical story. Letts and Dicks decided it was time to do another such story, and asked Bob to come up with an idea. His new four-parter was given the working title 'The Time Fugitive', and Bob was given a date of Monday 5 March 1973, exactly one week later, to deliver his storyline.

It was completely the idea of Dicks and Letts to ask Bob to write a story with a historical setting. And it was a something that Bob wasn't particularly happy about.

'Now that was rather interesting,' he recalled some years later, 'because they said to me … "We haven't done a historical story for yonks", and I had always hated *Doctor Who* in history mode … Doing stories where the Doctor pops in just as King Alfred is burning the cakes or something, and says, "Just a moment old chap, you've not got enough bicarbonate of soda …" I always found that sort of whimsical and rather silly, twee. So I resisted bitterly this idea that I should write a historical story. And finally we compromised, and I said, "If I can do my science fiction bit, I can do you a phoney historical story," so we went back to a totally mythical figure, a baron called Irongron … It comes out of all that Danish stuff, one of those sorts of warriors.'

On another occasion, Bob dryly noted: 'I have a feeling that *Doctor Who* was originally developed by Auntie as a format for making history interesting for children; fortunately, the fantasy side soon took over.'[165]

Dicks recalls Bob's lack of enthusiasm for the setting of the story: 'The thing about that was that Bob hated the idea of doing a historical story. In this case, I think Barry and I got the idea that we wanted a story set in the past, with knights, and castles, and armour, and whatever. And an alien coming into a medieval environment, and feeding the local warlord weapons, which of course upsets the Doctor as it's interfering in time. And that was the basic idea, and Bob always hated doing that, he never really wanted to do it.'

Bob didn't know the first thing about life in the Middle Ages for a start, so Dicks suggested that he visit his local library to research the period. Dicks went on to advise Bob that the children's section in a library was usually the best place to find books that managed to cover subjects in a concise, simple manner – ideal for writers who are just looking for background information on a subject. So Bob went off and got his children's book on the Middle Ages.

Bob successfully handed in *something* to the *Doctor Who* production office on the storyline deadline day. Only this wasn't really a storyline as such. Unlike those he had previously done (and he wasn't a great fan of doing them in

165 *The Time Meddler*: Issue 3, October 1981 – Interview by John M Kahane.

the first place, finding them quite boring to sit down and write), the proposal Bob sent in this time was in the form of a military communiqué-cum-journal, addressed to 'Terran Cedicks' from a 'Hol Mes' (see Interlude VIII). 'At some stage he sent me this comic memo addressed to "Terran Cedicks", signed "Hol Mes"', recalls Dicks. 'Bob was always quite jokey about things, and that was just one of Bob's little jokes – which was why he was fun to work with.'

Despite the unorthodox proposal, this new story idea was accepted by Dicks and Letts, and on Monday 5 March 1973, Bob was commissioned to write the four scripts for this adventure.

By this point in time, Dicks had elected to ask writers for the series to try to deliver their scripts not all in one go, but instead on a weekly basis, episode by episode. So for 'The Time Fugitive', the script for Part One was due to be delivered on Monday 12 March 1973, Part Two on Monday 19 March 1973, Part Three on Monday 26 March 1973, and Part Four on Monday 2 April 1973.

The story's title was then changed to 'The Time Survivor' – later still it would be changed to 'The Time Warrior' prior to being shown on BBC1 – and according to the BBC's surviving paperwork, Bob met his delivery dates for the first two episodes. The script for Part Four was delivered early, on Monday 19 March 1973. Part Three was the last to be delivered, a week later, but still on its due delivery date.

Dicks recalls that there was a minor hitch with that third episode. 'When we did "The Time Warrior", Bob – who hadn't wanted to do a historical story, don't forget – had put in a pitched battle with knights in shining armour charging each other on the plains outside the castle. It would have cost several million pounds! So I cut that down to just a sequence of the Doctor hiding behind a wall and lobbing smoke bombs, or something like that. And Bob didn't grumble about me changing it, because he knew he deserved it. It's basically the script editor's job to make the script work, and sometimes you do it to other people, and sometimes they do it to you. But if you're overly sensitive, you shouldn't really be in television.'

All four scripts were formally accepted by the *Doctor Who* production office on Wednesday 11 April 1973.

'Bob did have this tendency towards the gruesome,' Dicks recalls. 'In "The Time Warrior", he had a line where the bad baron is threatening the wife of the good baron about what's he going to do to her husband when he catches him, and he says, "She shall crunch on his eyeballs in her soup 'ere nightfall." And I read that in the first draft and thought, "Ewwww", and put a line through it without thinking. I mean that was too much, even for me, and it would certainly have never got past Barry Letts. Bob muttered to himself, and said, "But it's a

CHAPTER TWELVE

good line", and I said, "Maybe it is a good line, but you're not having it".

'The Time Warrior' introduced three new aspects of *Doctor Who* lore. The first came in just a single line of dialogue, but it was a line that revealed the name of the Doctor's home planet – Gallifrey – for the first time ever in the series. 'That's Bob again,' recalled Dicks. 'Bob would come up with these ideas of feeding in a bit of the Doctor's background, and we would let them go through if we didn't object to them. And we didn't. It was intriguing to have more little bits of the Doctor's background leaking out. Bob invented Gallifrey, certainly, and Bob then developed the Time Lords the first time you saw them again in the series, full-frontal as it were, in "The Deadly Assassin", much later on. That was all Bob, and I liked that very much.'

The second notable feature of 'The Time Warrior' was the alien race that Bob created for it – the Sontarans, who have gone on to become one of the most popular of the Doctor's regular foes. 'They were a very popular monster, the Sontarans,' recalls Dicks. 'They're a bit like the Daleks, in that they're unremittingly nasty. Sontarans have very few good qualities, they just like killing people. There's a line by Bob that goes something like, "Sontarans seldom smile except at the death-throes of an enemy," which is their idea of a laugh! They're engagingly bad, I think. The other thing I always remember about the Sontarans is that one of the reviews at the time said, "... at the end of the episode the monster takes off his potato-shaped helmet, revealing his potato-shaped head." So we always used to call the Sontarans the "potato-heads". Not on screen of course, but privately.'

'The original conception of the Sontarans (which is still the same) is interesting,' Bob once noted. 'Contrary to popular belief, they do have other aims besides conquest. It is simply that all else, for the time being ("the time being", in their case, having already lasted many thousands of years), has been subjugated to the single task of winning their war of attrition against the Rutans, an equally dedicated superpower. To this end they have genetically re-engineered themselves. In order to sustain their immense armies they have abolished the old, inefficient system of reproduction and now have muster clonings of a million recruits at a time. Personally, I am rather fond of the Sontarans. Terrance Dicks, when I was writing for the show, always accused me of preferring the villains!'[166]

'I said they'd got only two digits – that was a mistake on my part,' Bob later said. 'I said they'd got a bifurcated hand, only two digits, which made it very difficult for the actor to pull out his pistol, or whatever. And I hadn't

166 *The Time Meddler*: Issue 3, October 1981 – Interview by John M Kahane.

foreseen that technical difficulty when I wrote it. They're a cloned race. They take in their sustenance from their ships by their probic vents. That's also their Achilles heel ... I invented them, based on a book I'd been reading; some rather heavy tome called *Clausewitz: on War*[167], or whatever it was – it was Teutonic stuff. So I visualised a race of aliens that were totally war-obsessed, and had nothing in their minds, no other concerns, it was just to win the war. So they obviously had to have a decent adversary, so I invented the Rutans, which we didn't see for several stories. And they were having this big war with the Rutans, which had raged all over the galaxy for aeons, and this is why they turned themselves into a cloned race; they hadn't always been a cloned race. And when they attach themselves to their ships to take in sustenance, which they need to do about once every two weeks, they're monitored. There's a monitor on the ships to see that they don't spend too much time attached to the vent, otherwise you get umbilical regression. If they're found to have spent too much time attached to the ship, that's it, they're killed.'

The Sontarans had very unique-looking spherical ships, the design of which was a by-product of Bob's knowledge of the limitations of the BBC's budget. 'That is one of the things that is difficult to do,' he said some years later. 'You cannot build anything you would recognise as a *Star Wars*-type spaceship in the studio or on location, so it's got to be something simple. So I made this a scout craft, basically. Linx had lost his main ship, he was being pursued by a Rutan squadron before the story started, and he gave them the slip in the vicinity of the sun, but his scoutship wasn't able to take him all the way back to his home. So he went down with the intention of finding a planet where he could muster some resources, and create a longer-range starcraft. And that was sort of the germ of the whole idea.'

Bob got to go on location for the first time since he had started writing for *Doctor Who*, to watch some of his story being filmed in early May 1973. 'In all my time with the programme I only got to a location twice,' Bob later wrote in 'A Life of Hammer and Tongs.'[168] 'The first occasion was when they were filming "The Time Warrior" somewhere near Crewe. I travelled up with Terrance Dicks, the script editor, and he's another funny chap. He ate his British Rail kippers with vinegar instead of butter, like most of us cholesterol-clogged types. He also does Yoga exercises and probably intends to live to a hundred and fifty. Actually, I have since tried kipper *a la Dicks* and am now a confirmed

---

167 *On War* by Carl von Clausewitz (published 1832 in ten volumes) is considered to be one of the most important treatises on political-military analysis and strategy ever written.
168 From 'A Life of Hammer and Tongs' by Robert Holmes, published in *The Doctor Who File* by Peter Haining (W H Allen, 1986).

vinegar man. That's all I can remember about "The Time Warrior".[169]

The final contribution to the ongoing world of *Doctor Who* that occurred in 'The Time Warrior' was the introduction of new companion Sarah Jane Smith, as portrayed by Elisabeth Sladen. Once again it had fallen to Bob to write the first story of a new regular character. 'It would just have been that we wanted him to write the opening show, and at the same time, we wanted to establish a new character,' recalls Dicks. 'The point of Sarah Jane Smith was feminism really, the fact that you had to have a stronger, more independent heroine. I always used to say the role of the female companion is to be tied to the railway tracks and scream until the Doctor comes and rescues her. There were a lot of protests around in those days about feeble, helpless woman who just screamed, so we changed it a little with Jo Grant; she would go off and do things on her own, usually disastrously. But Sarah Jane Smith was not the Doctor's assistant in any traditional sense, she was just someone who got to know him. She was a strong, independent character, and if you remember in the first story, she doesn't trust the Doctor at all. She doesn't like him, she doesn't trust him, she thinks he's the villain.'

Bob, being Bob, had some fun in his script at the expense of these pro-feminist ideals. 'It was quite funny, there was one sexist line, wasn't there?' he later recalled 'Where the Sontaran, being a cloned species, didn't consider ordinary human reproduction to be very effective. When he first saw Sarah Jane, he looked at her very carefully, and made some comment about her thoracic development or something … The development of her thorax showed that she was a female of the species. And, therefore, quite unnecessary.'

Bob also took the opportunity to have a sly sideswipe at his leading man, knowing full well that Jon Pertwee was slightly touchy on the subject of his rather prominent nose. 'One thing I had constantly with Jon Pertwee was working in references to his nose,' Bob once said, with a slight chuckle. 'In "The Time Warrior", I wrote a line where Irongron says, "Is he a longshanked knave with a mighty nose?"'

This story also featured the character of the rather eccentric Professor Rubeish; a trope of Bob's work in many ways. 'I liked nutty old professors,' Bob later commented. 'Rubeish was totally absent-minded, would wander off in the middle of a conversation or something. I like wild characters, really. Really hammy, rich characters, and *Doctor Who* is one of the few programmes where you can get away with them. If you're doing something like [police series]

169 Eating kippers during inter-city train journeys was a tradition begun by Derrick Sherwin and Terrance Dicks sometime in the mid-1960s when they both used to work on the ATV soap opera *Crossroads* prior to them joining *Doctor Who*. The *Crossroads* script team of Sherwin, Dicks and Peter Ling would leisurely discuss future potential storylines over kippers, washed down with gin and tonics, on their regular journeys from London to Birmingham.

Juliet Bravo, you can't introduce a dotty professor.'

'The Time Warrior' allowed Bob greater freedom with the characters and the dialogue than he had ever been afforded before – the furthest back in history he'd gone in his writing up to this point had been the late 19th/early 20th Century in series such as *Mutiny* and *The Regiment*, and, of course, in *Doctor Who*'s 'Carnival of Monsters'. It's almost as if he developed some new-found confidence in his writing as a result of being taken so much out of his self-imposed comfort zone with this story.

It seemed that Bob had got quite a nice, cushy number going with *Doctor Who* in the early '70s. He'd quickly become the main 'go-to' guy for the production team, usually tasked with the important introduction stories; he'd now written the first appearances of the third Doctor, Jo Grant, Captain Mike Yates, the Master, and Sarah Jane Smith. Terrance Dicks and Bob got on fantastically well together, and Bob's skills as a clever, inventive, consistent – and most importantly, reliable – writer had stood him in very good stead with the creative powers behind the series.

All was good, but, late in 1973, Letts and Dicks both decided that they wanted to leave *Doctor Who*.

INTERLUDE VIII
DOCTOR WHO:
'THE TIME FUGITIVE'
MARCH 1973

Robert Holmes' full original storyline proposal for the *Doctor Who* story that eventually became 'The Time Warrior' is reprinted here as originally submitted, complete with his original spellings and punctuation:

FOR THE ATTENTION OF TERRAN CEDICKS

In one of the last actions fought during Galactic War 9 a V-class cursitor under the command of Captain Jingo Linx was attacked by a squadron of Rutan space-fighters. After a long and gallant resistance against overwhelming odds, Captain Linx was compelled to break off the action as a result of severe damage to his ship.

The Rutan fighters continued to harass him, however, and Linx realised that he could not reach the safety of an allied planet. He therefore took evasive action among the planets of a fringe solar system. At this time the cursitor was hit by a d.a. missile and Captain Linx ordered his crew of 7 to abandon the craft. (4 survivors eventually made it home to Sontara but their epic journey in the life-capsule was somewhat overshadowed by the outbreak of Galactic War 10.)

Alone aboard the doomed cursitor, Captain Linx continued his vain struggle to bring the ship under control. The whole of the forward compartments were engulfed in flames at this point. The ship struck a planetary atmosphere and broke in half. With only one undamaged retro-motor, Captain Linx then showed supreme skill by managing to land the rear section of the cursitor on the surface of the planet.

ROBERT HOLMES: A LIFE IN WORDS

Subsequent calculation revealed that he had landed on an unknown planet, the third in its system in an outer constellation of no strategic value. Shortly after landing Linx was approached by what he termed a 'bunch of gooks'.

These were primitive hominids led by an alien named Irongron. In the best traditions of the Sontaran space service, Captain Linx adopted a friendly posture towards the members of this species and was treated with extreme deference.

Linx had noted that the primitives possessed useful digits and might be trained in simple tool-using capacities. (He had already made an assessment of the damage to the cursitor and formed an opinion that it could be made spaceworthy, given the appropriate facilities.)

Unfortunately the aliens had not progressed beyond a technology of simple base metals. Their recorded history, Linx reported, showed only some 1200 years – time cycles based on solar evolutions. However, by relaying his orders through Irongron – a creature of slightly higher intelligence than his followers – Linx was able to have the remains of the cursitor brought to the silicon structure that Irongron inhabited.

Displaying that high initiative and unswerving determination that characterises officers of the Sontaran space service, Captain Linx then set himself the immense task of repairing his craft. To accomplish this end he had to educate a workforce and, singlehanded, create an entire technology.

His work in this direction, he reported, was severely hampered by the fact that Irongron, owing allegiance to a greater territorial leader, Kingjohn, was under hostile pressure from neighbouring groups of creatures.

From time to time, therefore, Linx found it necessary to set aside his immediate tasks in order to devise weaponry with which, to use the officer's own colourful expression, Irongron could 'pow-zap the stinking little creeps'.

By adapting the frequency-modulator of the retro-motor and connecting it to the cursitor's osmic-projector, (see technical appendix attached to this citation) Captain Linx was able to create a medium-range time surveyor.

At the full extent of the surveyor's range – approximately 1,000 planetary years – he found a developing technologically based society. Although by no means adequate for his purposes, the creatures of this period showed evidence of adaptability and Linx formed the impression that they could be trained in the skills necessary to repair his craft. He immediately put in hand the process of conveying selected individuals to his workshops …

This was an arduous time for Linx, the repeated transferences having a debilitating effect even on his rugged constitution. Very soon, however, he had the preliminary rigs constructed and was able to start testing the molecular re-assembly chamber.

While never losing sight of his primary purpose, the officer found it politic to give Irongron increasing help in the struggles that persisted locally. Such was his success that Linx noted Irongron rapidly developed paranoiac symptoms, speaking of usurping Kingjohn and even becoming master of the planet.

To protect their soft pulpy flesh from injury, the aliens covered their bodies and heads with metal plates. Although his epidermis required no such protection, Captain Linx adopted this habit in order to conceal his differing physiognomy. He had found that his normal appearance distressed the aliens and interfered with productivity.

Unfortunately it was as a result of this practice that Captain Linx ultimately was to suffer his most serious setbacks. The extraction of scientists and technicians from their 20th century habitat had not gone un-noticed. As a result leading scientists were assembled in groups and placed under guard. This precaution was, of course, a great help to the officer, enabling him to effect numerous transferences in a single projection cycle.

However, during one such visitation, Captain Linx came under attack from the guards. At this time, he had discarded his head-shield, in the interests of greater visibility, and it was discovered after his departure.

By chance – Linx learned later – a Doctor belonging to the Galfrey[170] species (the self-styled Time Lords; see Glim's Notes of an Antiquary; also the War Manual, Vol. VII, Feasibility of Further Galactic Conquest) was rendering assistance to the aliens. The Doctor identified the period of manufacture of the head-shield.

Smith, a secondary terrestrial provided Captain Linx with the first intimation that he faced further difficulties. The species had evolved, it should be noted, a laborious and unpleasant method of reproduction involving primary and secondary effort. Close study revealed slight physical differences among the creatures, according to whether their role was that of a primary or a secondary. (In his log-book, incidentally, the Captain records the opinion that this method of reproduction has no military value.)

From what was discovered subsequently, it appears that the Galfrey Doctor pursued Captain Linx in a time machine called TARDIS. While the Doctor's attention was distracted, Smith gained entrance to this machine and was inadvertently conveyed across time.

The machine settled outside Irongron's fortification. Hal, a solder of some local reputation, was at this time waiting for Irongron to show himself upon the perimeter

---

170 Later changed to become the more familiar 'Gallifrey'

wall. When Irongron appeared, Hal tried to strike him with a pointed shaft projected from a simple tension-weapon called a longbow.

He succeeded in causing only slight injury to the target and was then pursued by Irongron's guards who were guided through the dense vegetation by four-legged 'hounds'. (Linx gives no explanation of the nature of the mechanisms.) The hounds tracked down Smith as well as Hal. It is presumed the Doctor was also in the vicinity at the time but was in some way able to avoid capture.

Linx identified Smith as a 20th Century creature, but not among those he himself had transported. In this way he became alert to the nearby presence of the Doctor. The realization that his plans might now be opposed by an equal intelligence in no way deterred him.

Irongron, meanwhile, had ordered Hal to be dismembered. Captain Linx, who was developing a simple robot for Irongron's use, suggested that he could be used for demonstration purposes. This was arranged and Hal, equipped with a longbow, faced the robot in single combat.

Hal managed to shoot several shafts through the robot before it came within striking distance. At this point the Doctor appeared inside the fortress and, seizing the nearest longbow, directed a shaft through the handset with which Captain Linx was controlling the robot's movements. Unfortunately, the robot then ran amok, scattering the audience, and during the ensuing confusion the Doctor, Smith and Hal succeeded in escaping.

Psychoanalytic study of the record, suggests that from this point on Captain Linx became increasingly unstable. It must not be forgotten that from the moment his ship came under attack, he had been under intense and unremitting strain. The escape of the Doctor and his companions, coupled with the destruction of the robot, caused Linx to experience

'goal transference'. The completion of the cursitor became secondary to the destruction of the Doctor.
Frequent use of unexplained terms also suggest that by this time Captain Linx was suffering the common phenomena known throughout the space service as 'going bush'.

However despite being physically unadapted to the terrain, Captain Linx played an active part in the pursuit of the fugitives. They were tracked to the 'castle' of Edward of Wessex, a leader of similar eminence to Irongron, and it appears an inconclusive battle then resulted between the two forces.

Linx realised that his adversary, the Doctor, was skilfully directing the castle's defence and that there would be no decisive outcome until the walls of the castle were penetrated. He therefore collected together the charges of explosive powder, used as a propellant in the weapons he had devised, and placed them under a weak point of the wall.

This stratagem was successful, in that the objective was achieved and Irongron's troops stormed the stronghold. Under the cover of darkness, however the enemy force had withdrawn along a tunnel. Captain Linx now urged the advisability of immediate withdrawal but Irongron was temporarily no longer in command of his forces, a period of pillage being the custom of the aliens after a triumphant assault.

Perceiving the fatuous nature of his allies, the officer then returned alone to his workshops. He was unaware that the Doctor and Smith, in the guise of 'mendicant friars' (Unexplained term; presumably some form of sanitary service) had already gained entry to the fortification.

It is apparent that during this time the Doctor had unavailingly attempted to break the narco-hypnotic condition in which Captain Linx had placed his captive workers. He was also able to examine the restructured cursitor and must have had previous encounters with members of our race because in his last meeting with the Captain he took despicable advantage of the single flaw in Sontaran anatomy. He had been able to identify the restructured cursitor as a Sontaran vessel.

Immediately on his return the officer put in hand the last phase of work on the cursitor. He was hampered however, by the physical weakness of the creatures he was supervising. He had overlooked the fact that this species requires orally absorbed protein, combined with frequent periods of dormancy, to sustain a working energy level. The creatures began to collapse and Linx now found it necessary to adopt a more forceful posture to keep them at their tasks.

These methods appeared to create an emotional response in the Doctor and he emerged from concealment to launch an attack on Captain Linx. (Note: if this is true, a study of Time Lord psychology may prove of military value.) Linx de-activated the Doctor with a hand-impactor and was then able to interrogate him.

The Time Lord attempted to justify his interference on the grounds that Linx was tampering with the natural evolution of the planet's principal sentient life form. Linx properly dismissed this argument as irrelevant to Sontaran pragmatism.

The Doctor was removed to a cell and Captain Linx continued with his work. He was now anxious to remove himself from the planet and rejoin his comrades in the glorious struggle against the vipers of Rutan. Once again he was soon interrupted – this time by the return of Irongron and his troops.

Irongron had been under attack by Edward of Wessex and other anti-Kingjohn 'barons'. His forces suffered severe losses during the retreat to his stronghold and Irongron blamed Linx for leaving him without propellant for the new weapons. Irongron's paranoia had become perceptibly worse.

With the fortification now under attack, Linx decided to create more robots to aid the defenders. He realised that if the besiegers broke in, the final phase of work on the cursitor might never be completed.

Irongron, meanwhile, had discovered the presence of Edward's ally, the Doctor. In a gesture of defiance he ordered the Time Lord to be suspended from the 'ramparts' on a 'gibbet.' This was soon accomplished but an accurately aimed shaft by Edward's champion warrior, Hal, severed the 'rope' and the Doctor dropped into the 'moat' from which he subsequently extricated himself without difficulty. (No explanation is offered of any of these terms but the general nature of the incident seems clear.)

As Edward's assaults on his stronghold were beaten back and the work on the robots neared completion, Irongron's spirits rose again. He commanded a great 'feast' to be prepared to celebrate his forthcoming victory.

Smith, the secondary who had entered the stronghold with the Doctor, was at this time apparently working with other secondaries in some remote region of the fortification where the protein requirements of the warriors were prepared. Strangely it appears that between the primaries and the secondaries of this race (except at those times when both are engaged in the reproductive task) there is a mutually recognised hostility. Smith chose the right moment to exploit this latent antagonism and the secondaries introduced some narcotic substance into the 'dishes' prepared for Irongron and his fellow primaries.

(In this connection, it is educative to read again the late General Kask's paper 'How to Divide and Conquer.')

Narcolepsy followed in the wake of the 'feast' and Smith lowered the drawbridge to allow Edward's forces to rush in on Irongron's troops. Complete disaster was averted by Captain Linx's swift action in activating his robots.

While he was thus occupied, the Doctor and Smith again entered the workshop where work on the cursitor was now all but complete. Utilising the ship's osmic-projector, which was still beamed on the 20th century, they returned all Captain Linx's captive workers to their own space-time constants.

With the robots getting the upper hand, Linx returned to the cursitor to make his final preparations for departure. He became involved in a physical clash with the Doctor. Irongron then intervened and demanded the right to kill the Time Lord.

Curiosity over the outcome delayed Linx. This is the interpretation given to his phrase 'I tarried thus awhile.' (Psycho-syndromic analysis suggests that at this stage the officer was suffering from an efficiency-damaging degree of sub-cultural assimilation.) In the event, it was Irongron who perished in the struggle which was fought with weapons Linx described as 'blades'.

By now Linx had removed his bodyplates and was again wearing the uniform of an officer in the Army Space Service. He started to ascend to the control-deck of the cursitor, knowing that at the moment of blast-out the Doctor, the remaining creatures – and indeed the entire fortification – would be atomised.

It appears that the Doctor also had cognisance of this fact because, as Linx strapped himself into blast-out position, he took Hal's longbow and loosed a shaft through the aperture in the vacuum port. Normally Linx would have been impervious to this primitive weapon but it would seem the Doctor had aimed unerringly at the Sontaran probic vent. The shaft penetrated Linx at this vital spot and he fell, mortally wounded, across the controls.

In the automatic count-down period which followed, it would seem likely that the Doctor and his companions evacuated the stronghold and were able to observe the moment of blast-out from a safe distance. It is considered that at this time Captain Linx was already dead.

On I49-541/3 the modified V-class cursitor was detected by a Sontaran space-patrol crossing Nebulae Blue I. The craft was towed in to the home port where the body of Captain Linx, transfixed by the shaft, was found on the control deck. His body was de-vitrified, with full military honours, on I49-552/3.

The account of events contained in this citation had been prepared from the entries in Captain Linx's log and from images recorded in the cursitor's memory banks. It is considered that Captain Jingo Linx showed, throughout this period, exceptional valour and devotion to the highest ideals of the Sontaran Army Space Service, above and beyond the call of duty.

It is therefore recommended that he be posthumously awarded the Galactic Hero's Cross, 2nd Class.

(Signed) Hol Mes.

CHAPTER THIRTEEN
TRAPS AND HOSPITALS
1973-1974

Bob's other writing work for the BBC was now coming thick and fast.

Spy Trap was a new secret-agent-type BBC series produced by Morris Barry, and was the brainchild of Robert Barr, who in 1959 had devised the BBC series *Spy-Catcher*. *Spy Trap* was very much in the same mould as its predecessor; a cloak-and-dagger espionage series that revolved around a mysterious government department, DI6. It starred Paul Daneman in the lead role of Commander Ryan RN, alongside Prentis Hancock, Michael Gwynn, Tom Adams and Julian Glover, who played his main field agents.

Bob was commissioned on Thursday 22 February 1973 to write a 50-minute script for the series, with a target delivery date of Friday 9 March 1973. Bob delivered his episode, 'A Perfect Victim', just a few days late, on Wednesday 14 March 1973.[171]

'A Perfect Victim' begins with the case of ex-NATO officer Martin Venner, who was sentenced to a jail term of 20 years for spying for the East German government and is currently serving his sentence at Hanley Grange Prison. Ryan assigns one of his agents, Sullivan, to spring Venner from the prison, in order to exchange him for a terminally ill British agent being held by the Russian government. Sullivan kidnaps the young daughter of one of the prison guards as part of his scheme, but then Ryan is ambushed as he returns to the hotel suite that the DI6 agents are using as a base, and is left unconscious. It appears that the CIA wants to ensure that Venner – and the information he has on the Polaris defence programme – stays behind bars. The compromised prison guard slips Venner some chewing gum laced with a drug that will bring on the symptoms of a heart attack, and later, Venner is duly rushed to hospital after chewing on it. When he recovers in hospital, Venner realises that the gum was the cause of his symptoms, and slips a stick to the nurse watching over him. When the nurse collapses, Venner sneaks out of his room. Details of Venner's escape hit the news bulletins, putting the DI6 team at a huge disadvantage. Venner heads to a café run by the widow of an old friend, and maintains that he was innocent of the spying charges he was found guilty of. The DI6 team track Venner to the café, but they are followed by a CIA assassin, who tries to

---

171 It was at about this time that Bob was also writing his scripts for the *Doctor Who* story 'The Time Warrior' – see the previous chapter for details.

ROBERT HOLMES: A LIFE IN WORDS

shoot Venner, but succeeds only in killing his old friend's widow. Ryan locates Venner and takes him back to DI6 to set up the prisoner exchange. Venner is taken to a disused airstrip, and is exchanged for the returned British agent. Just as Venner's about to board the plane bound for Russia, the CIA assassin, disguised as a fork-lift driver, shoots and kills him.[172]

The story was an almost straight reworking of Bob's own 1969 script 'The Spy Vanishes', written for the series *The Inside Man*.

Staying with the BBC, Bob's next writing project was on *Dixon of Dock Green*. This police series had been running since 1955, and at the time was about as 'traditional' as a BBC drama series could possibly get, following as it did the everyday – and usually very mundane – work of local beat bobby, George Dixon. Bob was commissioned on Wednesday 6 June 1973 to write a 50-minute script for the series, with a target delivery date of Friday 29 June 1973. Bob delivered his script, 'The Unwanted', on Thursday 5 July 1973, just a week later than planned.

'The Unwanted' tells the story of a young girl, Carol, who vanishes while out walking her dog. The dog is stolen from her by a man named Gooch, and she goes off looking for him and her pet, and gets herself lost. She stumbles across a couple of dossers, one of whom, Archie, shows her how to find her way back to her house. A police car spots them talking, and Archie is arrested. He is ultimately released, even though he has a previous conviction for murder, while Carol is reunited with her parents. Later, Archie is told by another dosser about a local villain, Gooch, who steals dogs. Archie goes to Gooch's barge and rescues Carol's dog, and swipes a bottle of gin while he's at it. Gooch follows him to an abandoned house and tries to take the dog back. A fight follows, and Gooch falls into the cellar, breaks his neck and dies. Archie takes the dog back to Carol's house, and is given some reward money for his efforts by her parents. He spends the money on a bottle of booze, and the police later find him dead of alcohol poisoning in the park.

The episode was shown on BBC1 on Saturday 26 January 1974, and is one of the many from *Dixon of Dock Green* of which the BBC no longer retains a copy.[173]

In 1970, the BBC had begun showing a drama anthology series produced by Jordan Lawrence called *Menace*, which featured one-off plays focusing on scary and unnerving situations. The series ended in 1973 but was relaunched the following year with the same production team under the new title *Dial M*

---

172 'A Perfect Victim' was recorded at BBC Pebble Mill in Birmingham on Thursday 31 May 1973, and was shown on BBC1 on Tuesday 9 October 1973. The BBC no longer retains a copy of this programme; however Bob kept a copy of his script.
173 However, some poor quality 16mm black and white film sequences from this episode do still survive in the BBC Film and Videotape Library, running to around 23 minutes.

for Murder. In August 1973, Bob was inspired to write to William 'Bill' Slater, who had just taken over from Ronnie Marsh as BBC Head of Serials, with a story idea he had for the series:

> IBM have just developed a new telephone exchange, linked to one of their computers, which does practically everything except feed the office cat. It is called the 37/50 system, costs from £200,000, and is currently being demonstrated at their Wigmore Street centre. (I mention this in case you want to buy one).
>
> I have an idea for *Dial M for Murder* in which two people are working late in a modern office block (like the East Tower[174]); they are man and girl, boss and secretary, scientist and research assistant, whatever.
>
> The office, which I think I shall call Satterdale House, is very modern, highly automated, crammed full of electronic security devices, etc (which are all controlled by the switchboard), and a gang of five hoods break into the building using a stolen Polaroid ID card. The Commissionaire is bumped off and they take control of the switchboard. Their aim is to steal the platinum (or something of high value) stored in the basement vault.
>
> At this point they become aware they are not alone in the building. Man and girl also become aware of the hoods.
>
> The story from here centres on the efforts of the villains to kill the hero and heroine and their attempts to alert the world outside of what is taking place. Cat and mouse sequences through deserted offices.
>
> There are various possibilities (bearing in mind the potential of the 37/50 system) but I don't want to develop a plot from these basics until I've cleared the general ideas with you.'[175]

Bill Slater passed Bob's proposal over to producer Jordan Lawrence. Unfortunately for Bob, Lawrence had fully commissioned the 13 episodes of *Dial M for Murder* that would make up the 1974 season, so the idea came to nothing, at least for the time being.

Solo was another idea that Bob had for a potential television series of 50-minute episodes '... based on the activities of a man who chooses to have no official existence.' His pitch document would appear to have been drafted

174 The East Tower was part of BBC Television Centre, and was for many years the home of BBC Children's Television.
175 As basic outlines go, it's very difficult not to compare Bob's idea here to the basic premise of the 1988 Bruce Willis-starring smash-hit film *Die Hard*. Bob's idea would eventually see the light of day in 1986, as the pilot for *Timeslip* – see Chapter Twenty-Three.

at some point around late 1974 or early 1975:

> At the age of 24, eight years ago, totally disgusted with his Government's politics and attitudes, Royce burnt his passport on the steps of City Hall, South Africa. Having thus declared his position, his continued existence in South Africa was impossible. Now a man without a country and outside the law, he finds that his need to eat, and his own statelessness brings him into contact with others outside the law whose morality is not his own. This conflict is that of immorality against illegality, for whilst he is prepared to break the laws of any given country he will never break the laws he has given to himself. Royce now has a tightrope to walk. By his own choice totally expendable, his means of earning a living are dictated by expediency – thus he is used by everyone, but not anyone. He will often appear to be chosen, but will in fact choose. He will often be on the run but will often be a willing target. He will often be hunted by both police and criminal but often be alien to both. People matter to him more than he matters to people. Eight years of this existence has equipped him for almost any eventuality. But, hounded out of many countries, his struggle against compromise becomes more difficult. He has helped two prisoners to escape from French prisons. He has aided the French police in the arrest of a Marseilles drug trafficker. He is wanted on both sides. He is alone. Forced to flee France, he is helped, unwittingly, by an English solicitor to enter this country. Realising the usefulness of Royce, the solicitor provides him with an identity … but an identity always at risk. The solicitor has a reputation to protect but has clients to serve, and Royce's probity will work for them both. But the solicitor does not enjoy exclusive rights on Royce's services …

Bob then created a potted history for both Royce and the solicitor, David Grainger, giving them both short biographies, detailing their education, travels and previous business affairs. He anticipated that these two would be the only recurring characters in the series, and that they would be presented with new challenges and scrapes each week. No details remain of where Bob pitched this series idea.

Bob then returned to his old stamping ground of ATV for what would prove to be his last freelance writing job for quite some while. ATV had recently revived the *Emergency Ward 10* hospital soap opera format under a new name, *General Hospital*. This was shown as a twice-weekly afternoon soap opera, and Bob wrote two 30-minute episodes that went out on ATV on Thursday 7 and Friday 8 March 1974.

The *TV Times* says of the first of these episodes, 'Dr Knight orders Det Sgt Bentley to leave Patterson alone, but Bentley has other ideas. Nurse Hardy finds a new way to speak to Harry Jackson.' The second of the episodes is summed up simply as, 'The Patterson case takes a sudden and dramatic turn ...'[176]

Neither of these episodes of *General Hospital* (respectively episodes 145 and 146 of the series) survives in the ATV television archives, and Bob didn't retain his scripts.

Even as Bob was finishing his work on writing these episodes, he was in the process of finalising an agreement to go and work for the BBC as a full-time member of staff. On *Doctor Who* ...

---

176 *TV Times*, w/c 2 March 1974.

CHAPTER FOURTEEN
EDITING SCRIPTS,
AND OTHER PASTIMES
1973-1974

Over at the *Doctor Who* production office, big changes were afoot. Producer Barry Letts, alongside script editor Terrance Dicks, had established *Doctor Who* as a popular fixture in the BBC's Saturday evening schedules. Jon Pertwee had been a great success as the Doctor, and the small team of other regulars and semi-regulars – Katy Manning, Roger Delgado, Nicholas Courtney, Richard Franklin and John Levene – had all proved popular too. But this team was now breaking up. Katy Manning had left in 1973, after a successful three-year stint as Jo Grant. Her replacement, Elisabeth Sladen, had only just begun bedding herself into the role of Sarah Jane Smith when news came through that Roger Delgado had been killed in a car crash while *en route* to a motion picture location in Turkey. Manning's departure and Delgado's death were two of the main catalysts for Jon Pertwee to decide to call it a day, precipitating another regeneration for the Doctor at the end of the programme's eleventh season, scheduled to run on BBC1 from December 1973 through to June 1974. Richard Franklin was becoming increasingly busy elsewhere, so his character, Captain Mike Yates, would also make his last appearances during the eleventh season.

The break-up of the on-screen team was mirrored in the *Doctor Who* production office. Dicks had been script editor on *Doctor Who* since 1968, and now wanted to return to freelance writing. Letts also wanted to move on from his post as producer, which he'd been occupying since late 1969. Letts agreed to stay until a new Doctor had been cast, which would give a new producer time to work alongside him and gently ease himself into the series. Dicks would therefore be the first member of the production team to leave, but not until he had overseen the commissioning of nearly all the scripts for the eleventh season. The question was – who would be brought in to replace him as script editor? There seemed to be one obvious candidate …

'What happened was that we'd all been on the show for five years by then,' recalls Dicks. 'I'd been on a bit longer, but Barry, Jon and I had all roughly been on about the same time, roughly five years. The obvious choice was for Bob to take over as script editor from me, because he was by far the best writer on the show, and he was very experienced on it by then. As I remember, we took him out to lunch with the intention of offering him the job, and Bob said, "I hear you're leaving, why don't I come and be your script editor?" And we said, "Well it's funny you should say that ..." So that just went through very smoothly, with no problems at all.'

As things turned out (and probably unknown to Dicks at the time), there very nearly *was* a problem. Bob's appointment had to go through the formal application procedure for the post, part of which was to go in front of a 'board' – BBC-speak for being grilled by the departmental manager, which was usually a formality. In *Doctor Who*'s case, it was Ronnie Marsh, the outgoing Head of Serials at the BBC, who was the man in charge, and who would have the final say-so on the appointment of the new script editor.

Bob later recalled the events of this meeting. 'Terrance told me he wanted to leave the show to devote more time to his garden gnomes. Louis Marks advised me to apply for the job. I should have laughed him to scorn. But it seemed a rather good idea at the time. Hitler probably felt the same when he sent his stormtroopers into Poland. The lust for power gripped me and a few days later I was sitting opposite Ronnie Marsh, the then Head of Serials, across an acre of polished maple. He started telling me about the guidelines he felt the programme should follow. "Two or three seasons ago," he said, "we had some clot who wrote the most dreadful script. It had faceless policemen in it and plastic armchairs that went about swallowing people. I might tell you there were questions in the House. Mrs Whitehouse said we were turning the nation's children into bed-wetters ..." The thought of all that soiled linen made me put down Ronnie's awful coffee. Could it be that he was referring to "Terror of the Autons"? "Tut, tut," I muttered, feeling the job slipping away, "How awfully irresponsible".'[177]

Now, it's hard to judge just how much of that account is actually true, and how much is just playful embellishment on Bob's part. But if his past writing misdemeanours were an obstacle he had to overcome, then overcome them he did. Bob was quickly confirmed as the successor to Dicks as *Doctor Who*'s script editor.

'On a series a script editor has to match story to writer,' Bob once explained, 'and always be available and able to offer advice and encouragement. The script editor is responsible for the overall "mix" of a season. He/she should also know the possibilities/limitations likely to affect a particular episode (e.g. filming in January: short days and probable bad weather equals minimum film exteriors, maximum interiors). He/she has also to work closely with the director and

---

177 From 'A Life of Hammer and Tongs' by Robert Holmes, published in *The Doctor Who File* by Peter Haining (W H Allen, 1986).

be ready to do an emergency Band-Aid job on the script when necessary. As at any one time one might have four stories in various stages of development between page and screen, a good memory and phlegmatic temperament are useful assets. I don't think there was any conflict between my own writing and my duties as a script-editor.'

As Bob himself admitted, *Doctor Who* wasn't always the easiest of programmes to write for: 'Oh, it is very difficult! I'm not sure about writing accurately. Unless you're doing a contemporary show there isn't much difficulty in writing accurately. It is only when you are writing about things that people know about that they can pick you up on details. *Doctor Who* viewers are very good at picking up on details if you do go wrong. I usually avoid this by writing in the future or about mythical gods. But it is very difficult for three reasons. One is that *Doctor Who* is a science fantasy. Two is that it's a serial, which in itself creates problems for the writer. Thirdly, you have to have cliff-hangers and sustain the story. You have to make sure that for people who come into the story in the second or third episodes that they can still pick it up. There is, therefore, a certain amount of repetition in the episodes, yet you have got to do it without boring those that watched from episode one. So it is a difficult programme to write for, but it is good fun.'[178]

'I had been a script editor on other programmes about three times,' Bob recalled in 1985.[179] 'I must have done probably about seven years editing in the last 25 years – I edited *Shoestring* and *Knight Errant*, and they even asked me to edit *Blake's 7* later. So I was quite used to the idea of script editing and I had written for *Doctor Who* for some time, and had developed ideas as to how I would like the show to change. Basically I thought it was over cluttered with characters – all the UNIT people – and I wanted to get it back into space because it had been stuck on Earth for such a long time. I also wanted to toughen it, try to make it more adult – to widen the audience and incorporate the mums and dads, who previously just sat their children down to watch it. I had Mary Whitehouse and Shirley Summerfield and "great" people like that raising questions in the House of Lords, when "Terror of the Autons" was done a few years previously, so I think that was indicative of the way my mind worked anyway! I don't think fantasy violence is at all damaging to children, and as I explained to Jean Rook[180] and everybody else, if they think they have a sensitive child then they don't let it watch these programmes. It's not up to television to cater for the minority of kids who might be influenced. Fantasy

178 Panopticon II Convention, Imperial College, 12-13 August 1978, as reported in TARDIS Vol 4, No 2, April 1979.
179 Interview – Robert Holmes, *Doctor Who Magazine*: Issue 100, May 1985.
180 Details of Bob's encounter with the newspaper columnist Jean Rook can be found in Chapter Twenty.

violence is far different from the gory stuff you see in *The A Team* or *The Professionals*. They have a more realistic kind of violence and are *potentially* more harmful. But the other point to remember of course was that, with this adult approach, we pushed our audience figures up … from just under seven million per week to just over 11 – which can't be bad!'

Bob started working at the BBC in the late summer of 1973, taking up residence in the *Doctor Who* production office in Threshold House, Shepherd's Bush Green. He was there nominally to 'trail' Terrance Dicks, so that he could pick up the ropes of the BBC's internal systems, and also get to grips with the day-to-day workload of script editing *Doctor Who*.

Bob recalled that there wasn't that much of a learning curve: 'The BBC has a system called "trailing" which basically means that the incomer follows the incumbent around for a few weeks. As I already knew how to read and had been a script editor before, all Terrance had to do was show me where he kept the aspirins. He went off singing merrily.'[181] Bob had no input on the commissioning at this point; all he had to do was some minor editing in order to get the final Jon Pertwee scripts into shape for recording.

He recalled his time working on these final few Jon Pertwee stories in his interview with *Doctor Who Magazine* in 1985: 'I trailed Terrance Dicks for about three shows, including one with Daleks, and I think an Ice Warrior story as well. What that really meant was that as I worked on these shows, Terrance came in twice a week, poked his head round the door and asked "How are you doing? The aspirins are in the top right hand drawer!" and cleared off again!'[182] This whole, final, Jon Pertwee season of *Doctor Who* was later awarded the 1974 *Writer's Guild of Great Britain Award for Best Children's Original Drama Script*. The award went, collectively, to the writing team of Bob, Malcolm Hulke, Terry Nation, Brian Hayles and Robert Sloman.[183]

From late 1973 through to early 1974, Barry Letts was casting around for a suitable actor to replace Jon Pertwee as the Doctor. Meanwhile, it was down to Bob to commission an opening story for this new Doctor, whoever it might be. Someone was going to be in the same position that Bob himself was in a few years earlier, when he had to write the first story for the third Doctor without knowing who was going to play the part.

Outgoing script editor Terrance Dicks had his own, very firm, idea about

---

181 From 'A Life of Hammer and Tongs' by Robert Holmes, published in *The Doctor Who File* by Peter Haining (W H Allen, 1986).

182 Interview – Robert Holmes, *Doctor Who Magazine* Issue 100, May 1985. Bob was given a joint script editor credit alongside Terrance Dicks on the camera scripts for the third studio block of 'Invasion of the Dinosaurs' (mainly material recorded for Episodes Five and Six) and for both blocks of 'Death to the Daleks'. His name doesn't appear at all on the scripts for 'The Monster of Peladon' or 'Planet of the Spiders'.

183 The awards were announced and presented at the Café Royal, London on Wednesday 12 March 1975.

who should get to write this story. 'I invented this tradition! I went round telling Bob and Barry that there was this tradition that the retiring script editor writes the next show of the new season. I thought that I'd invented the tradition, but it was perfectly true; if you look back through the archives, it's very often the case that outgoing script editors wrote the next script.[184] If you're going out into the freelance world, you want a job to tide you over, so you try and fix that for yourself if you possibly can. Of course, it's partly an old-pals-act thing in television. I mean you don't commission your friend if he's not any good, but given the choice between a good writer that you know and a good writer that you don't know, you're rather likely to go for the writer you know. There's this old, cynical saying that it's not what you know, it's who you know, and that's completely wrong, that's nonsense. But what is true is it's what you know *and* who you know. And if you've got a good reputation, and have got good contacts, then that is obviously going to stand you in good stead; that's the way life works.'

Thus Dicks was commissioned to write the first story for the incoming Doctor.

This meant that roles were now reversed, with Bob, as script editor, ruling the roost over Dicks. However, this didn't alter the working dynamic as much as one might expect. 'It's a thing that you have to learn to accept,' recalled Dicks. 'We used to argue just as much, except that Bob now had the final say instead of me, and you just have to accept that. At the end of day, when I was on *Doctor Who*, whatever the writer wanted, whatever the writer said, … the scripts were the way that Barry and I wanted them, because we were running the show. And when you're not in that position, you have to accept that you're not in that position, that somebody else is running the show. So we got by. And we were always good friends; we got by without any sort of undue rancour really.'

Both Bob and Letts had something of a quandary when it came to the introductory adventure of the fourth Doctor. They didn't yet know how old the actor chosen to play the part would be. Seasoned actors such as Richard Hearn (66 at the time), Fulton Mackay (52) and Graham Crowden (52) were seriously considered for the role, as well as younger ones such as Jim Dale (39). In view of this, they decided that the new Doctor should be accompanied not only by Sarah Jane Smith but also by a new, younger male companion, who could be called upon to perform any of the more strenuous physical activity that any scripts might offer up. Both Bob and Letts recalled that Frazer Hines

---

184 There's a good case for Dicks's argument here. *Doctor Who*'s first story editor, David Whitaker, wrote the first story ('The Rescue') commissioned by his replacement in the role, as did Dennis Spooner ('The Time Meddler') and Gerry Davis ('The Tomb of the Cybermen'). Derrick Sherwin would have also worked this little trick (with 'The Invasion'), had he not returned to script edit 'The Space Pirates', having officially left the post at the end of his work on 'The Mind Robber'.

(as Jamie McCrimmon) had performed a similar function alongside Patrick Troughton's second Doctor, and had also proved to be immensely popular with viewers. To this end, a new character, Harry Sullivan, was drawn up, and the details passed to Dicks so that he could also introduce him in his script. Dicks was to title his new story 'Robot'.

'Robot' was a fairly simplistic story, which gently eased the new Doctor into the show alongside many of the familiar trappings of the Jon Pertwee era. UNIT, the secret taskforce that investigated otherworldly events, featured prominently. However, Bob had already decided that the UNIT regulars and plotlines would be quickly phased out of the series. 'Barry Letts always said they were short of cash,' recalled Bob some years later. 'All that UNIT stuff cost an awful lot of money – all the extras, and the soldiers, and the military stuff. The first season I became script editor, I realised we had to cut all that. It cost a lot of cash to do those sorts of things, and we'd done enough of them.'

In February 1974, Letts eventually decided on Tom Baker as the replacement for Jon Pertwee. Fortunately for Dicks, Baker was cast before he had done too much work on his scripts for 'Robot', so was able to work in some of the actor's own personality traits. However, much of the new Doctor's actual character was devised by Bob. 'I don't think there was so much actual cold blooded thinking or plotting,' Bob later recalled. 'The first thing was to find the right actor to follow Jon Pertwee. Then we decided which of the Doctor's previous character traits to carry through and emphasise. Tom suggested much of the character himself, and I wrote a brief for writers, where I said he was a cross between Professor Quatermass, Sherlock Holmes and George Bernard Shaw. I said he was witty, had flashes of bad temper, kept things to himself – all these things the Doctor's done in the past, I think. Just how the character developed was really due to the actor, and Tom really followed his own nose, so to speak, in feeling what comes over best.'[185]

185 Robert Holmes Interview, *Gallifrey*: Issue 1, September 1977 – Interview by Tim Dollin.

CHAPTER FIFTEEN
BAKER'S DOZEN
1974

As part of the planning for the rest of the twelfth season of *Doctor Who*, one of Bob's early ideas was to have a running theme going throughout the stories, revolving around a space station in the far future. He decided that the first story to follow 'Robot' on screen would be a four-part adventure set aboard this space station. Christopher Langley was a writer new to *Doctor Who*, but one Bob knew from his work on the ITV soap opera *Honey Lane* back in the late 1960s. Langley had expressed an interest in pitching a *Doctor Who* story, so Bob gave him the details of his space station story-arc. Langley then submitted his proposed storyline, with the working title descriptor of simply 'Space Station', in December 1973. Bob liked Langley's idea, and so formally commissioned him to write the four scripts for this story on Thursday 24 January 1974.

While Langley was a writer new to *Doctor Who*, Terry Nation was an experienced old-hand. He had written for *Doctor Who* with a huge degree of success in its early years, inventing the iconic Daleks back in 1963. After trying and failing to launch a spin-off based around just the Daleks in the mid-'60s, he had since returned and contributed a new Dalek story to both the tenth and eleventh seasons, and had come to view it as something of an annual assignment for him. But Nation's enthusiasm for this idea wasn't shared by Bob. 'There was a party at the BBC to mark the anniversary of the show[186]', Bob recalled, 'at which Terry said to me, "I think there should be a Dalek story every season," And I said, "Do you Terry?" Then, after a while, I got a letter from his agent, saying, "I understand you've agreed that there should be a Dalek story every season." And I disliked the Daleks so intensely – I've always said they've got no conversation – that I dug my heels in and said, "I'm not going to do a Dalek story ever again – at least while I'm here." And then pressure started to come through from Terry's agent, to [Head of Drama] Shaun Sutton, to Barry Letts – all contemporaries, who'd been actors or drama students together. And so there was a lot of pressure put down on me to do one. So I said, "Unless somebody can come up with something totally different, I'm not doing a Dalek story." And then Barry Letts came up with the idea, I think,

---

186 Held at BBC TV Centre on 10 December 1973.

of doing it about the genesis of the Daleks, of having Davros, who had created the Daleks in his own image. And so we had this character in the chair, which gave the story some scope, and we could have some actual acting going on.'

Nation did initially propose writing a completely different Dalek story for the twelfth season, but his first storyline was rejected by Letts, who pointed out that it was both formulaic and uncannily similar to many of Nation's previous Dalek scripts for the series over the years. And, as Bob recalled, it was Letts who proposed to Nation that he should instead write a story about the origin of the Daleks. Letts then passed the idea over to Bob for him to develop with Nation, and Bob quickly saw the merit in this approach. Sometime in March 1974, Nation wrote a new, expansive storyline along those grounds, entitled 'Genesis of Terror', which he quickly delivered to Bob for his approval.

Bob still wasn't greatly enthused about using the Daleks again, especially after he researched the ratings for previous Dalek stories. 'I'd looked at the graphs, and when they'd brought them back in the past, they were popular in week one, because a lot of people perhaps had never seen them before, or got excited, and thought, "Oh the Daleks are back." And there was that hangover from the '60s when it was more of a soap opera. So they'd watch episode one, and then the graph went straight down for the next three weeks because the Daleks were boring and they didn't watch it.[187] And they were terrible to use. I saw a cartoon once, when they were standing at the bottom of the Waterloo steps, and they say, "Well, that's buggered our ambition of conquering the universe".'

Bob wrote to Nation on Sunday 24 March 1974, outlining his thoughts on the submitted storyline. 'I wrote these notes on your "Genesis of Terror" story and Barry pencilled the comments on the front. I can think of no better way of letting you know the office feeling than to pass on the unvarnished memos. As you will see, we love the story, but want it brought down to something the budget will stand. If none of this cuts you too deeply, perhaps you'll ring me and we can discuss possible delivery dates – I need to put a date on the commissioning docket.' After swiftly discussing the requested revisions with Nation, Bob commissioned him to write scripts for a six-part story, now entitled 'Daleks – Genesis of Terror', on Thursday 4 April, with a target delivery date of Sunday 14 July.

187 It's not completely clear what information Bob was basing this statement upon, but in general terms he wasn't far off the mark. 1974's 'Death to the Daleks' actually bucked this trend, with 8.1 million viewers for its opening episode, rising to 9.5 for its second episode, and 10.5 for its third, before slipping back to 9.5 million for the final episode. 1973's 'Planet of the Daleks', however, did follow the trend Bob described. The first episode drew 11.0 million viewers, but this figure then dropped weekly down to 8.5 million for the final episode. 1972's 'Day of the Daleks' had a more even keel, opening with ratings of 9.8 million viewers, which grew to 10.4 million for the second episode, before falling back to 9.1 million viewers for episodes three and four. If Bob had looked further back, to the '60s, then both 'The Evil of the Daleks' and 'The Chase' also saw a slow loss of audience after the opening episode.

Also during March 1974, Bob received the scripts for the first three 'Space Station' episodes from Christopher Langley. When he read them, he had deep reservations, feeling they were not close to what he was originally looking for in the story. However, he decided to await the delivery of the fourth script before passing a final judgement on the story as a whole.

During the same month, Bob contacted his old friend and writing colleague Robert Banks Stewart and invited him to come up with a proposal for a storyline for the series. Stewart had never written for *Doctor Who* before[188], but had a strong pedigree of scripting science fiction and fantasy shows, and was keen to take up Bob's invitation. After meeting up with Bob and discussing a few ideas, he elected to take his main inspiration from his native Scotland, and proposed a storyline that revolved around Bob's suggestion of utilising the mythical Loch Ness Monster. 'As a script editor I try to suggest ideas to a writer and he says "Yes" or "No", and then we discuss it,' recalled Bob. 'I called Bob Banks Stewart in on that one, because I thought he'd give it that lift, as he's a Scotsman. I can't say it was an original idea; I just thought, "Well, they've never done the Loch Ness Monster and there must be a reason behind it that we can work into *Doctor Who*." Terrance Dicks has told me they had often thought of doing a story, but they never found a way of working it effectively into a *Doctor Who* adventure.'[189]

Bob commissioned a storyline from Stewart, entitled simply 'Loch Ness', on Tuesday 12 March 1974, with a delivery date of Tuesday 26 March 1974. Bob evidently liked the story proposal when it arrived on his desk on schedule, because the following day, on Wednesday 27 March, he commissioned Stewart to write the scripts for a six-part 'Loch Ness' story, with a target delivery date of Monday 6 May 1974 for all six scripts.

Bob spent much of April 1974 getting 'Robot' ready for production, and the story began recording on location later that same month. Terry Nation delivered his script for Part One of 'Daleks – Genesis of Terror' on Monday 22 April, and Bob was more than happy with it. However, he was less than happy with Christopher Langley's final script for 'Space Station' when that arrived on Thursday 9 May. He now felt he was correct in his earlier assessment that the story just wasn't what he originally wanted or discussed with Langley.

The next day – Friday 10 May 1974 – was the first day of studio rehearsal for 'Robot', and events were closely followed by a BBC film crew, shooting material for a proposed behind-the-scenes documentary about the making of the series. This documentary was scrapped just days later (a by-product of

---

188 ... although he had been invited to write for the series back in 1963 by original story editor David Whitaker. Stewart had declined the invitation at that time.
189 Robert Holmes Interview, *Gallifrey*: Issue 1, September 1977 – Interview by Tim Dollin.

various strikes that were hitting the BBC at this time), and the 16mm colour film just sat around and gathered dust for many years, until it was deemed surplus to requirements and junked by the BBC Film Library. Luckily, this film was saved from the skip at the last minute. The sound elements were long-gone, leaving the pictures forever silent, but this surviving mute colour film shows the cast and crew of 'Robot' sat around a number of large tables pushed together in one of the BBC's Acton rehearsal rooms. At one side of the tables sit actors John Levene, Elisabeth Sladen, Ian Marter and Patricia Maynard, while across from them sit Nicholas Courtney, Tom Baker, Edward Burnham and Michael Kilgariff. At the head of the table, conducting the rehearsal, sits director Christopher Barry. At his shoulder is a watchful Robert Holmes, and next to him the jovial figure of Terrance Dicks.

Annoyingly, without the sound to the footage, the resultant discussions and conversations captured on celluloid are now lost to the mists of time. The rehearsal room itself is akin to a typical church hall, and the central tabletops around which the cast and crew are gathered are cluttered with dozens of copies of the story's script; any remaining free space is taken up by numerous ashtrays. Most of the cast smoke heartily throughout the entirety of the footage (which runs to about an hour), and judging from the facial expressions, everyone seems to be having a comparatively good and relaxed time. Holmes and Dicks sit at the back, keeping a watchful eye on proceedings, and the conversations they have are mainly with each other, looking for all the world like a couple of mischievous schoolboys tucked away at the back of a classroom, although director Barry does get Holmes to clarify points in the script from time to time. While cigarettes are the order of the day for the cast, Bob has his trademark pipe permanently clutched in his hand throughout, and when not talking to Barry or Dicks, sits puffing out smoke, a wry grin etched on his face for most of the time. Dicks, too, puffs away at his own pipe, and seems in good spirits throughout – probably a result of bring demob happy, but also perhaps because he can see that the show he has worked on for the previous six years is in good hands.

One person who's missing from this tableau is the producer. Barry Letts' time on the show was coming to a close. The question was, who was going to replace him?

At about the same time that Bob began shadowing Dicks the previous year, he was also finishing off his last freelance writing assignments, which were (as told in Chapter Thirteen) a couple of scripts for the ATV soap opera *General Hospital*. 'At the time I was writing some episodes of a carbolic soap opera called *General Hospital*,' he recalled some years later, 'and one afternoon

I pootled down to Elstree to see how things were going. In the control room I was introduced to various ATV luminaries, including one Philip Hinchcliffe. "What else are you doing?" he enquired. (In television people expect you to have at least six balls in the air instead of the normal two.) I told him I'd just been appointed as the script editor on *Doctor Who* and he gave me an appraising stare. It was the sort of look Pasteur must have directed at a new microbe.

'At the time I thought little of it, assuming that my face was doing funny things again. Some years ago, in a funny accident, I lost a few front teeth. After I had stopped laughing I went to my dentist and he made me what he termed a bridge. While my bridge is nothing like the one over the Humber, I am very pleased with this technological feat and my newish teeth are much better than the ones that vanished. On a sunny day I can send heliograph messages at ranges up to ten miles away. The one problem I do have with them is they lack sensitivity. From time to time my upper lip adheres to them and congeals in a frozen leer so that I walk about looking like Jack the Ripper surveying a home for fallen women. The trouble is, as I'm looking the other way, I never realise this has happened until dogs and small children flee from my path. Sturdier citizens approach me truculently to ask if I need a bunch of fives.

'Anyway, a few weeks later Barry Letts appeared in my office with Philip Hinchcliffe trailing him. Philip told me that at the time of our first meeting he had already agreed to produce *Doctor Who* but as his ATV contract still had several weeks to run it was not possible for him to have said anything.'[190]

'In general, I thought Philip and I made a good team,' recalled Bob on another occasion. 'And the programme was certainly very popular during our time on it. We were always in accord as to the stories we wanted. Philip's view in 1973 was that the programme was already being watched by, probably, the maximum number of younger viewers that could be attracted to it. So we set out to try and make it popular with the family audience – in a sentence, to hold back on the cardboard monsters and make the scripts wittier and more entertaining.'[191]

During April and May 1974, Tom Baker's first story, 'Robot' was fully in production. It was eventually finished in early June 1974, and this brought to a close the eleventh recording block of *Doctor Who*. When the series returned to the BBC's studios in October 1974, Hinchcliffe was fully in charge as producer – although Letts was still at close hand during the first few months, to keep an eye

---

190 From 'A Life of Hammer and Tongs' by Robert Holmes, published in *The Doctor Who File* by Peter Haining (W H Allen, 1986).
191 Robert Holmes Interview, *The Time Meddler*: Issue 3, October 1981 – Interview by John M Kahane.

on things quietly from the background.

Hinchcliffe found that he got on extremely well with his new script editor almost from day one. 'My first impression of him,' he recalls, 'was when we first sat down and started to work together, he was covered in smoke! He used to smoke his pipe a lot. I was also struck by the fact that he had quite a quiet manner, and that he was very amusing, in a very dry way. That came across from the very first meeting we had. I think we struck up a rapport pretty much straight away.

'I was full of beans. I was a young producer, it was my first big job in television. So I was immensely excited, because this was primetime television, Saturday evening, everybody knew the programme. But I also thought that I needed to be very careful, because this was a British institution, and I didn't want to muck up on this show. So I gave it a lot of thought, but it was very exciting; you knew that what you were working on was going to be right out there, in front of the public, watched by ten million people. I used to enjoy going in every day. There was a lot pressure, pretty much from day one, because some scripts didn't work out, and there were all sorts of problems. It was a very steep learning curve for me at the same time. But I had come from a background of working with scripts, so I wanted to be very involved in the scripts for the series. I realised that this was the key. So Bob and I talked and talked about the scripts, pretty much every day. He was in the office next door to me, and right from the start, I would literally be in with him all the time. And that was a formative period, because not only was he getting the scripts right for that first season, but we were forging a relationship, setting out the way we were going to work together, finding out about each other's tastes, about our ideas. I had done a lot of reading of science fiction stories, so I had ideas about what I wanted to do for the next season. But from the start, we wanted to try and bring in a slightly different style and approach to *Doctor Who*. So there was a lot of talk, there was a lot of fun, and there was a lot of laughter. There was a lot of pressure, but we had a lot of laughter.'

In May 1974, Bob was still trying to pull together the stories he needed for *Doctor Who*'s twelfth season. Robert Banks Stewart's delivery dates for 'Loch Ness' had come and gone without any of the six scripts actually appearing. And although Bob was unhappy with Christopher Langley's 'Space Station' scripts, he had decided that it would be a good idea to commission a second story set on the same space station; the thinking being that both could be made back to back utilising the same studio sets, thus saving on cost. To this end, and at the suggestion of Letts, Bob called on Gerry Davis, himself a previous story editor on *Doctor Who*, and asked him to come up with a new story involving the

Cybermen (last featured in the series in 1968) set on the same space station. A storyline, given the working title 'Revenge of the Cybermen', was requested by the end of May.

Davis's initial storyline revolved around the space station being used as an intergalactic Las Vegas-style casino, which was then attacked by the Cybermen, using their Cybermats to spread a plague amongst the gamblers. The Doctor eventually uses the casino's gold reserves to defeat the Cybermen. Bob liked some of these ideas, but asked Davis to drop the casino element, as he felt gambling wasn't really an area that *Doctor Who* should be straying into.

Although 'Space Station' and 'Revenge of the Cybermen' were planned to be made back to back, in terms of the season running order they were to be separated by two other stories. The second of these was to be Terry Nation's six-part story 'Daleks – Genesis of Terror'. The first was to be a two-part 'filler'. Bob decided to allocate the writing of this to Bob Baker and Dave Martin – a Bristol-based duo who had been nurtured by Dicks at about the same time Bob himself had begun working regularly on *Doctor Who*. Since then they, like Bob, had managed to come up with roughly one story a year for *Doctor Who*, so Bob knew he was on pretty safe ground by commissioning them.

With his thoughts still very much on cost, Bob gave Baker and Martin his requirements for the story: 'I storylined that for them. And that used the Sontarans. I said, "You can have one of my monsters, one of my favourites".'[192] Bob knew that the Sontaran costume and the prop spherical Sontaran spaceship made for 'The Time Warrior' were both still in storage at the BBC, and this would help keep the costs of this all-location story down.

'We were put in a room with Bob Holmes,' recalls Bob Baker, 'and he proceeded to tell us the whole history of the Sontarans. After about ten minutes, we just turned to him and said, "Too much information, Bob. We don't need to know the sexual habits of the Sontaran race." But he was quite willing to go on for another hour just talking about Sontarans. He had the full history in his own head, and proceeded to tell us how the Sontarans had evolved, how they came about, the wars they'd been involved in – masses of details. We just had to stop him.'

The storyline for this two-part story, titled 'The Destructors', was commissioned from Baker and Martin on Thursday 23 May 1974, with a target delivery date of Thursday 20 June 1974. BBC records indicate that it was delivered on Wednesday 12 June, but Baker recalls that he and Martin actually 'delivered' the storyline over the course of a telephone conversation with Bob

192 Panopticon IV Convention, Queen Mary College, 1-2 August 1981.

230

some days earlier, with nothing actually committed to paper. On the strength of this discussion, Bob then commissioned the opening script from them on Wednesday 5 June 1974, with a target delivery date of Monday 1 July 1974.

As well as the cost-cutting measure of using the space station setting for two stories, Bob had also come up with a way of budgeting Baker and Martin's two-part all-location Sontaran story alongside the first four-part all-studio 'Space Station' in a manner that would cost the same as a standard six-part story. 'I think it was Bob who had come up with the idea of making the Sontaran story on location,' recalls Hinchcliffe, 'because the new OB cameras that the BBC were just phasing in were very lightweight, and Barry Letts had already begun to make use of these in the series.[193] Bob had also decided in the first season to have the stories locked into a certain order; the Doctor lost the TARDIS, and then had to work his way back to finding it. And Bob also decided to try to avoid six-part stories; he was beginning to realise that six-parters just didn't work well, and that you could instead break the stories up. So he had chosen the four-part "Space Station" to be a totally studio-bound show, but using the "studio" part of the budget for a six part story. And the "film" content in the budget for that six-parter could then be used on another two-part story to be made completely on location. However, it wasn't to be shot on film, but on these new OB lightweight cameras. And so that concept was totally his.

'Then he commissioned Bob Baker and Dave Martin to write the two-part story. I think Bob gave them the bare bones of the actual story, and because they didn't have to be tied in to using a fixed number of sets in the studio, the boys were able to be a bit more filmic in the way they wrote those scripts. And that was okay for us, because we were filming the story on Dartmoor, and so we could just go round and film on the other side of a pile of rocks, and that would be another "location". So there weren't too many rewrites to be done on that story – it worked out reasonably well.'

As Hinchcliffe notes, one thing that Bob had come to really dislike on *Doctor Who* were six-part stories. Bob's only experience of writing one was his 1969 story 'The Space Pirates'. In 1971/2, the length of a season of *Doctor Who* had been set by the BBC at 26 episodes, and Letts and Dicks had taken the decision to break this down into two four-part stories and three six-part stories. Bob thought that six-part stories usually lacked pace, and sagged quite heavily during the middle episodes, and so was looking for ways to try to

---

193 Tom Baker's first story, 'Robot', was the first *Doctor Who* to have all of its location material recorded on videotape. 'The Sontaran Experiment' - as 'The Destructors' was ultimately retitled - was a logical extension of this, made completely on location on videotape.

cut down the number of them used. He would eventually settle on a season format of five four-part stories followed by a single six-part season finale, which neatly took up the 26 episode allocation. During 1974, however, he was exploring other ways to try to reduce the six-part story count.

'Well I think four-parters are much easier,' explained Bob while on stage at the 1981 Panopticon Convention. 'I think very few ideas are strong enough to run to six parts. And as a result, the fifth part is usually a marking time episode. It is three hours of television time, a six part story, which is far more than most major budget films. So a three-hour production has got to have a very good story, and a very solid plot, with a lot of movement in it to carry through. And television generally can't accommodate that kind of budget and scale. So I prefer a four-part story, even if it's compact and compressed a bit, rather than a six-parter.'[194]

On Monday 3 June 1974, Terry Nation delivered his script for the second episode of 'Daleks – Genesis of Terror', and again, Bob was more than happy with what he received.

Bob had already decided to abandon Christopher Langley's 'Space Station' scripts, and so began looking around for another writer to produce a four-part story with a space station setting – he was now effectively stuck with the latter as a result of his decision to have Gerry Davis's Cyberman story utilise the same sets. Langley's scripts were formally abandoned by the *Doctor Who* production office on Monday 17 June 1974. It was probably around this time that Bob had an initial discussion with a young, aspiring writer named Douglas Adams, with a view to him perhaps writing the script for a new space station story. Adams had recently begun a writing partnership with *Monty Python*'s Graham Chapman, and had fond memories of watching *Doctor Who* during his childhood in the 1960s. Adams came up with a *Doctor Who* storyline set on an ark in space, which he then submitted to Bob. Adams later recalled that this was 'a synopsis which was sent back rather curtly with a note saying it was a terrible mess.'[195]

By the time that Hinchcliffe arrived as the new producer of *Doctor Who* during the summer of 1974, he found that Bob had already got the stories of the twelfth season more or less mapped out; even if some of the later ones existed only in storyline form at this point in time.

---

194 Panopticon IV Convention, Queen Mary College, 1-2 August 1981.
195 Nevertheless, Adams reworked his unused *Doctor Who* 'space ark' idea into a script he and Chapman wrote for a pilot US television show for ex-Beatle Ringo Starr, which was ultimately never made. Adams then refined the idea further, which resulted in the Golgafrincham B Ark storyline in *The Hitchhikers Guide to the Galaxy*. Quite how much of his 'ark-inhabited-by-a-useless-third-of-a-planet's-population' idea was actually present in his *Doctor Who* storyline isn't clear, but most sources cite that the notion was certainly there.

'Jon Pertwee had gone,' recalled Hinchcliffe, summing up the situation he found himself in when he joined *Doctor Who*. 'Bob had commissioned scripts, but without knowing who the Doctor would be. And so Bob was singlehandedly responsible for all the season's scripts, because I hadn't been around for the commissioning. He was on his own, thinking, "What should I do?" So he fell back on the tried and tested monsters, the villains we knew as solid and would give us good viewing figures. So he, for instance, chose to do a Sontaran story, so he could use one of his own monsters. He then thought, "Let's have a Dalek story in there." And then, "Let's have the Cybermen," so he commissioned a Cyberman story too. So he just got on and did all that while the powers-that-be decided who the new Doctor would be, and who the new producer would be. So that was the background I came into when I was made producer.

'I had to get to grips with the whole production process, and I was very fortunate to have such an experienced and imaginative script editor as Bob. The shows would not have been as successful as they were with a lesser script editor, so I was very grateful that I inherited him, and also grateful that we actually got on very well together. I wouldn't say we had the same sense of humour, but we had *enough* of the same sense of humour. There was a lot of laughter in our production office, a hell of a lot of laughter. And I think we did genuinely spark each other off; we had different approaches to stories, we were imaginative in different ways, and I think the two of us together created something quite different. There was a real spark. So it was exciting working with him. I've worked with other people subsequently, and it's like getting blood out of a stone sometimes.

'He was a very gentle man, he was quite a shy man in many ways, he was certainly quite diffident, but he was quite confident in his opinions, and he knew his job, and he wouldn't back off if he really felt strongly about something; he would gently stand his ground, which was a good thing as well. He was a lovely man to work with, very talented, and I always used to look forward to going into the office and seeing him.'

Bob now needed to find another writer to fill his 'space station' brief, and preferably one with some *Doctor Who* experience. Barry Letts suggested John Lucarotti, probably because he had worked with him on the recent BBC2 show *Moonbase 3*, which Letts had produced.

At the time, Lucarotti was living in a houseboat moored just off Corsica in the Mediterranean Sea, which meant that there were no direct lines of communication between him and Bob – not even a telephone. However, Lucarotti was visiting the UK on business in May 1974, and was able to pop in to the BBC for a meeting, where Bob briefed him on what was wanted.

Lucarotti came back with some potentially good ideas, so on Wednesday 5 June 1974 Bob commissioned him to write the script for Part One of a story that was now entitled 'The Ark in Space'. The following day, Bob commissioned the remaining three script. The target delivery date for all four was Wednesday 17 July 1974. Lucarotti then returned to Corsica to start writing his story. The plan to make 'The Ark in Space' and 'The Destructors' as a *faux* six-part story was still holding fast.

And now that he was confident that the space station setting was going to work for this new story, on the same day that he commissioned Lucarotti's final three scripts for 'The Ark in Space', Bob also formally commissioned Davis to write the scripts of his Cyberman story, 'Revenge of the Cybermen', with a target delivery date of Wednesday 31 July 1974 for all four.

Lucarotti delivered his script for Part One of 'The Ark in Space' on Sunday 23 June, a few weeks earlier than expected. Bob read through it, and once again began to suspect that the story wasn't what he wanted, feeling it was once again deviating from the outline he had discussed with the writer. When he received the completed scripts for the final three episodes from Lucarotti on Friday 12 July 1974, Bob realised that his initial instincts had been correct. The scripts just weren't usable.

'I put the idea to John Lucarotti of a story about the survivors of the human race in jeopardy because of some disaster out there in space,' recalled Bob. 'John lived in a boat moored off Corsica at that time. He went back to write the script and then there was a postal strike … By the time Episode Four arrived we knew the script wasn't working and that John, through lack of contact, had drifted off course. I remember Barry Letts looking at the studio dates and saying, "We've got 18 days to get it right!"'[196]

'My storyline for that was: something had happened and the Earth was uninhabitable,' recalled Lucarotti some years later, 'so there was this Ark full of human beings sleeping until a plot of land that resembled the Kent countryside grew inside the Ark, which would automatically wake the sleepers, telling them that it was safe to go back to Earth. But there had been a malfunction. When the Doctor makes a rendezvous – he doesn't go by accident, he tells everybody that he had something to do – he goes to the Ark to help wake everybody up, but finds that there are aliens inside already, called the Delc. One race is heads without bodies; the other is bodies without heads. I never saw Bob Holmes's version, so I don't know how close that was, but my own one was the battle between the Doctor and the Delc, with the body brigade able to

---

196 Robert Holmes Interview, *The Time Meddler*: Issue 3, October 1981 – Interview by John M Kahane.

234

reproduce themselves instantly – in a flash, one becomes 50. The title of each episode was "ball"-ish. One was "Puffball", the last I remember was "Golf Ball", and ended with the Doctor driving the last of the heads off into space with a golf club. I remember Bob writing and saying, "Sorry, that's not quite 'it'", but they did pay me, and, because I lived on a boat in Corsica, it wasn't practical for me to rewrite the scripts, so Bob did it his way.'[197]

Hinchcliffe recalled how the crisis over this story was his first real baptism of fire as producer of *Doctor Who*: 'I think Bob had got one draft script of the first episode when I started as producer, and I wasn't very impressed with it. Bob explained his overall story concept to me, which I thought was a very good concept. Anyway, we were waiting some time for the rest of the scripts ... By the time the scripts arrived with us, it was by now very near to the deadline for shooting, so I think my first major strategic decision as producer was to say, "This is not good enough." Barry Letts certainly flagged up the problem, but it was down to me to go and get permission from my Head of Department, Bill Slater, for me to commission Bob to write the replacement scripts. I persuaded Bob, not to rewrite the story, but to completely write a new set of four scripts from scratch. But based on Bob's own original concept of "The Ark in Space", which he outlined to me. And luckily, Bob agreed, and got down to the job. But he had to do it very quickly'.

This whole situation was a major headache for Bob. Not only had he now written off two sets of scripts for the same story (which, because they still had to be paid for, was something heavily frowned upon at the BBC), but as he had also banked on using the same studio sets for the space station later on in the season, he was now committed to coming up with his own space station story.

'I went home and started work on a totally fresh story. "The Ark in Space" was a great opportunity for me to try and steer the programme in a different direction – really to go for a more adult audience. As to the Doctor's philosophy about "indomitable humanity", it reflected, I suppose, something of my own views. But we had long understood that Earth was the Doctor's favourite planet so it seemed that he might share my opinion!'[198]

Deciding that the glass might be half full in this instance, Bob decided that he could also use this opportunity to make an early statement of intent as to how *Doctor Who* was now going to present itself to the viewers. 'You need a certain continuity', Bob later explained, 'because in your first season, a lot of stuff is inherited, you're just pulling it together and trying to get it ready. I was in a sense lucky, except nobody saw it. What you tend to do is to try and write

197 Interview – John Lucarotti, *Doctor Who Magazine*: Issue 124, May 1987.
198 Robert Holmes Interview, *The Time Meddler*: Issue 3, October 1981 – Interview by John M Kahane.

something that will change the show, so that people like Malcolm Hulke, Brian Hayles or whoever that you're going to call in will watch it and see that the direction has changed. Because writers are terribly conservative, and they will go on writing the stuff that they wrote ten years earlier, unless they get new ideas. And that's when I wrote "The Ark in Space", which was the sort of thing I wanted *Doctor Who* to go on to be, and I thought everybody would watch it and say "Oh yes, this is what they want now". But of course they didn't, they just came back with the old things like Cybermen ...'

It was something of an unwritten rule within the BBC that script editors didn't commission themselves to write scripts for the series they worked upon, and it was a practice frowned upon by the Writers' Guild, the union that represented scriptwriters. Philip Hinchcliffe had to make arrangements for Bob to write the replacement for 'The Ark in Space' under the BBC's internal staff contribution procedure. Basically, this was in place so that if someone was asked to do something by the BBC that was outwith their normal salaried position, they would get an additional payment for doing it. Bob, at the time, was paid to script edit *Doctor Who*, but wasn't paid to write it. Hinchcliffe had to back up his request with reasons, and on the staff contribution form, he wrote, 'The scripts originally commissioned for this serial turned out to be unusable and four new scripts had to be written in a hurry. I felt that Robert Holmes was the only person who could do this job satisfactorily in the time available.'

The form is dated Tuesday 8 October 1974, but this was merely an administration exercise to tidy things up after Bob had actually begun work on writing his scripts, which retained the title that Lucarotti was commissioned under, 'The Ark in Space'. Bob had begun writing the first two episodes of his version sometime in late July 1974, and was able to send those scripts to Philip Hinchcliffe on Monday 5 August 1974.

Bob Holmes's 'The Ark in Space' took the same basic premise as John Lucarotti's story, much of which was in the brief that Lucarotti had originally been given by Bob in the first place, some months earlier. The Ark (given the name Nerva in Bob's story) contains the last remnants of mankind, forced to flee from Earth due to intense solar flares, and awaiting the day they can reawaken to return home. While they have slept, the Ark has become home to a parasitic alien race called the Wirrn, who reproduce in the same manner as some species of wasp: by injecting their eggs into a paralysed host, which is then slowly digested by the young after they hatch. Only, in the Wirrn's case, the host is a sleeping human. The Doctor arrives on the Ark, and battles to save the sleeping humans from the Wirrn.

Speaking some years later, Bob admitted he couldn't easily identify why this story was so well regarded by the regular viewers of the series: 'Perhaps it was the thought of the destiny of the human race lying in a deep freeze chamber. These were the chosen descendants and were there when the Wirrn struck. I don't think the success of the story was due to the Wirrn; I don't think they were very successful monsters. I must say it was very well designed, the actual conception of the Ark, and that helped. It's a bit of a puzzle why one story's popular and another flops.'[199]

In another interview, Bob added, 'Tom Baker had arrived and the programme was getting a lot of publicity. It had become "news" again. And then the story was a good one so I think it picked up a lot of word-of-mouth praise. It was my first shot at making the series more adult.'[200]

Although popular with most viewers, 'The Ark in Space' did draw a certain amount of criticism from some quarters about how scary the programme had now become. As far as Philip Hinchcliffe was concerned, the criticisms of his and Bob's new-broom approach to the series just weren't valid. 'I had decided, and Bob agreed, that we would try to make *Doctor Who* appeal a little bit more to adult viewers, to make it a bit grittier and stronger in the areas where it was performing more as a children's adventure story. So we wanted to take a little bit more care with the scripts, and make the characterisation psychologically a bit more plausible in places. And alongside that, I wanted to make the cliff-hangers work better, and where the key turning points in a story were frightening, or mysterious, or suspenseful, to then push those a little bit further than they had perhaps been under Terrance and Barry. And so it was a *considered* new approach to the series. And if you accept that this was the right approach for the series at this time, then you'll see that the scenes in "The Ark in Space" didn't go too far at all. But if you compared those scenes with what Barry and Terrance had been doing, in the previous few seasons, then you might have thought, "Oh, this is stepping over the mark", and that's obviously what happened with people like Mary Whitehouse. They thought there was a change occurring in the show, and they didn't agree with the way the show was moving. But I don't see it as a producer's error of judgement. It was actually a considered thing.'

In fact, Hinchcliffe reigned in some of Bob's ideas on 'The Ark in Space'. For instance, Bob had scripted a scene where the Ark's commander, Noah, having been infected by the Wirrn, was seen to transform into one of the alien insect creatures. The transformation scene was recorded, but a special effects sequence of Noah's head cracking open to reveal the Wirrn infection underneath was removed from the final version of the programme prior to

---

199 Robert Holmes Interview, *Gallifrey*: Issue 1, September 1977 – Interview by Tim Dollin.
200 Robert Holmes Interview, *Renegade*: Issue 1, 1984 – Interview by Matthew Wicks.

transmission, on Hinchcliffe's instructions.

Bob was once asked if he relied too much on elements of horror in his stories when writing for *Doctor Who*. He replied: 'People have made this point before and I don't know the answer. Maybe it is my own preference and style. But we're not talking about *Straw Dogs* or *Soldier Blue* – we're talking about fantasy treated with an element of humour. In any case, long before I joined the programme, *Doctor Who* relied on monsters for its thrills, and what are monsters if they are not intended to be horrifying?'[201]

Bob's scripts for 'The Ark in Space' play up the body horror aspects of the Wirrn's life cycle, and the concepts at play in viewers' minds were enough to earn this story a reputation as one of the scariest the series had produced up to this point in time. They're also an unashamedly assured set of scripts, which successfully cement the character of the new fourth Doctor in the eyes of any still-sceptical viewers.

At the end of 'The Ark in Space', the Doctor and his companions leave the TARDIS aboard the Nerva beacon and transmat down to Earth, where they then have a new adventure – the two-part Bob Baker and Dave Martin Sontaran story.

The whole subplot of the Doctor, Sarah and Harry being separated from the TARDIS, and a Time Lord-supplied Time Ring being their route back, was something that Bob had developed, not from a dramatic standpoint, but from an economic one. 'The Time Ring has rather a mundane explanation,' Bob later admitted. 'I felt, for a long time before taking over, that six-part stories generally dragged. The old 26-week season was divided into three six-parters and two four-parters. I sought permission to change this format to five four-parters and one of six. The BBC said okay but it had to be done on the same budget. Necessity being the mother, etc, we hit on the idea of doing two four-parters back to back – that is, keeping the same sets in the studio. "Ark" was one and it was followed into the studio by, I think, a Cyberman story, again using the Ark sets. They were, of course, transmitted several weeks apart. The rationale of all this was that the Doctor and co became separated from their TARDIS in the first story and so had to return to find it in the last story. And to get them hither and thither in the interim we invented the Time Ring. We were worrying so much about money, I don't think we even noticed that the Time Lords had dropped their policy of non-intervention!'[202]

A popular myth around 'Genesis of the Daleks' – as 'Daleks – Genesis of Terror' would eventually be renamed – was that Nation had delivered a

201 Robert Holmes Interview, *The Time Meddler*: Issue 3, October 1981 – Interview by John M Kahane.
202 Robert Holmes Interview, *The Time Meddler*: Issue 3, October 1981 – Interview by John M Kahane.

somewhat thin set of scripts to Bob, and that Bob then slaved away night and day to polish the story into one that many people believe to be one of the finest the series ever produced. This was simply not the case.

'My memory of "Genesis of the Daleks" is that Terry Nation delivered six first-draft scripts,' recalls Hinchcliffe. 'The overall structure of the story had been worked out by Terry Nation, and it worked very well. There were some very good moments in it. So the scripts he gave us were very good first-draft scripts, with good action sequences, and stuff like that in them. But there were also a number of sillinesses in Terry's scripts, which had to be taken out. And sometimes the dialogue left a bit to be desired. But he had terrific notions, Terry Nation, and he knew how to write action. So the scripts were pretty good to start with, but I think Bob did a bit of dialogue rewriting. And also by then, we would have known that Tom Baker was to be the new Doctor, so I think Bob would have tried to make changes that would reflect the character of the new Doctor. I think Bob rewrote some of the key speeches for the Doctor, and spruced up a few of the other bits of dialogue. So there was a bit of traditional script editing that went on with those scripts. I can't remember any more details, but it wasn't a set of scripts that had to be majorly rewritten or overhauled. They just had to be tweaked a bit, improved.'

Hinchcliffe contacted John Lucarotti's agent on Tuesday 20 August 1974 and returned the four Lucarotti scripts for 'The Ark in Space', and also included copies of Bob's scripts for the first two episodes of the new story, in order to demonstrate that it was indeed a *completely* new story, separate from the one that Lucarotti had written. An agreement was reached with Lucarotti and his agent that saw him receive his full fee for writing the four original scripts, but also specified that he got no credit on Bob's version of the story, or was due any repeat or overseas sales fees from the BBC. Bob finished writing his scripts for Parts Three and Four of 'The Ark in Space' sometime in late August 1974.

Gerry Davis sent Bob his script for the first episode of his story, which he had now re-titled 'Return of the Cybermen', on Tuesday 23 July 1974. Bob wrote back to him later the same day: 'I've gone through the script and discussed it with Barry and Philip. We all feel much the same way – that you have written it only for children. It's too straightforward (particularly in characterisation) and therefore rather dull. Our audience these days is 60 per cent adult and so we need a level of interest behind the "front" action. I think if you bear this in mind when working on the remaining episodes we shall all be saved a lot of trouble. *Doctor Who* has probably changed considerably since your connection with it and, these days, we find our audience is ready to accept quite sophisticated concepts. I am accepting Episode One – despite all these wounding strictures! – because I find the flaws in the script stem more from your mental approach than anything inherently wrong in the story or its structure. However, in case any heavy rewriting does eventually become necessary, I am sending a copy of this letter to Harvey[203] so that he is fully in the picture.'

Bob spent the early part of September 1974 doing a few cosmetic rewrites on Baker and Martin's two-part story, just prior to the location recording taking place. Bob wrote to the duo on Wednesday 18 September: 'I believe you already have copies of your scripts. The story will probably be screened as "The Sontaran Experiment". You will realise that it became necessary to do some further work to them to fit the action to the location. The story is being done on location amid some curious rock formations on Dartmoor. This may be within your range[204] in a fast motor car so I also enclose a copy of the shooting schedule in case you wish to visit the scene of the crime. I'm having some Cyberman trouble so I won't be able to get down there, unfortunately, but I know you would be welcome visitors. Keep in touch. Next season is sooner than you think.'

As Bob noted, he was now having 'Cyberman trouble'. During late September and October 1974, he got to work on substantially rewriting Davis's scripts. Although the story had originally been devised as an all-studio production utilising just the sets left over from 'The Ark in Space', some additional money had since become available from the programme's annual budget, allowing some location filming to be allocated to the story, which had now reverted back to the earlier title 'Revenge of the Cybermen'. Due to this extra budget, Bob reworked the scripts so that some of the action now took place away from the Nerva space station, and was set in the mines of the planet Voga, which would be achieved via location filming in the famous Wookey Hole caves.

'I know that [the director] Michael Briant was not happy with the script,' Bob recalled some years later. 'I wrote it about three times, and it seemed to get worse each time. I didn't like the idea of it anyway. Michael was trying to do his directorial things, and it didn't always square with the demands of the story. In the end, I think it was a mess.'

Hinchcliffe suspects that if Bob had had more time, then he would have probably done even more work on 'Revenge of the Cybermen'. 'I think Bob was very busy by then. I was demanding a lot of rewrites, and Bob himself was determining that there had to be a lot of rewrites to get the scripts up to quality.

203 Harvey Unna, Gerry Davis's agent at the time.
204 Both Bob Baker and Dave Martin were based in Bristol; hence their nickname of 'the Bristol Boys', by which they were known to the various incumbents of the *Doctor Who* production office over the years. However, neither of the writers was able to take Bob up on his offer of visiting the location recording for 'The Sontaran Experiment' on Dartmoor.

And so these rewrites were now stacking up. He had to do "The Ark in Space" as a totally new page-one rewrite; he had to write four brand new scripts. "Revenge of the Cybermen" was stacked up on the in-tray for Bob, waiting for him to tackle. And I don't think he quite ever had enough time to bring that up to the level that he wanted, or to the level that I wanted. I didn't really see the attraction of the Cybermen, and the story was a bit shallow, I thought, and it was very difficult to improve it. So that was one that we didn't quite crack. I think he did as much rewriting as he could do, in the time available, but he was under a lot of pressure.'

Following these challenges, Bob could turn his attention to the planned final story of the season, Robert Banks Stewart's 'Loch Ness' script. Stewart was making very slow progress with the story, and had written to Bob on Wednesday 19 June 1974 to tell him, 'I'm not hung up over the first script – I just seem to have so many damned interruptions at the moment … Next week I'm taking off for a Kent farmhouse to keep out of everybody's way and get the job done.'

Stewart submitted his script for the first episode of the story, now re-titled 'The Secret of Loch Ness', on Wednesday 18 September 1974, but because of his heavy rewriting workload on other scripts, Bob didn't have the opportunity to scrutinise it too closely at the time. It was only toward the middle of November of 1974, after Bob had finally finished all his work on the two Nerva stories, that he started chasing Stewart for the rest of his scripts. While he was waiting for these to arrive on his desk, he tentatively began thinking ahead for the following season of Doctor Who. He found that his working relationship with Philip Hinchcliffe was both easy and enjoyable, and the two of them had quickly hit on a style of working that suited them both, and that also paid dividends for the programme.

Stewart finally delivered his scripts for the second and third episodes of 'The Secret of Loch Ness' on Monday 2 December 1974, with the final three scripts then following on Monday 30 December 1974. The six-part story was due to begin filming in March 1975, so Bob planned to spend January editing the scripts to make them ready to pass to the director.

CHAPTER SIXTEEN
PYRAMID POWER
1974

At the time that Bob was mid-way through commissioning scripts for the twelfth season of *Doctor Who*, he also had one eye on the following year's set of stories. No doubt recalling how Barry Letts and Terrance Dicks had commissioned and made an additional story at the end of each production block, which was then held back and shown as part of the following season, he and Philip Hinchcliffe began making preliminary plans to commission and make an additional four-part story as part of the twelfth production block, which would be shown as part of the thirteenth season. It was scheduled to be recorded immediately after Robert Banks Stewart's six-part Loch Ness Monster story, bringing the production run to an end after 26 new episodes of *Doctor Who* had been made.

Bob discussed his ideas for this 'bonus' story with writer Lewis Griefer.

'From what I can remember, the idea of an Egyptology or mummy story was Bob's,' recalls Hinchcliffe. 'Lewis Griefer was a writer who had been around for a long time; he was of the same generation as Bob, and had contributed to a lot of series. He had worked at ATV a lot, which is where I first met him. And Lewis was somebody I liked; he had been very good to me at the start of my career. He'd also written for *The Prisoner*, and was a very good writer. So I probably suggested that we use him. Maybe he also had some specialist knowledge in the Egyptology area, I'm not sure.'

After being given some guidance on the type of story Bob was after, Griefer wrote a storyline, titled 'The Pyramids of Mars', which he delivered in late June 1974. Griefer's proposed story was set in the present day, involved the character of the Brigadier (who apparently dies during the course of adventure), and featured mummies coming to life in the British Museum as part of a scheme by aliens who look like Egyptian gods to send alien grain to Mars. The Doctor, as usual, manages to save the day.

After considering the storyline, Bob wrote to Griefer on Friday 5 July 1974 with some words of encouragement. 'I have now had time to read and digest your *Doctor Who* story. I attach a sheaf of comments that I trust will give you food for productive thought. While none of my suggestions are very radical or likely, I hope, to cause you any loss of sleep, you might find area for debate. If you do want to talk, either on the telephone or in the office, I shall be here on Monday and probably again on Tuesday. I have initiated, as they say, the paperwork commissioning a storyline from you.'

Bob then sent Griefer a substantial document outlining his thoughts on Griefer's storyline, and detailing his ideas for making the story more suitable to the style of *Doctor Who*:

Much of what follows was covered in our story discussion yesterday. Some of it I have added since. I hope it will be helpful to have it all on paper. It is of primary importance to regard this as a science fiction story. The Egyptology is colourful and macabre top dressing. But that is all.

Seth and Shebek, therefore, are simply our standard chauvinistic aliens around whom a whole lot of legends and mythology have accrued. They came to Earth in ancient times when life on their home planet, Mars, was becoming insupportable. Seth was the leader of this recce party. The Martians of this period were the remnants of a once-powerful, technologically advanced species. The ambitions of their imperialists (economically and genetically ruinous galactic wars) brought them to the verge of extinction.

When they reached Earth they found it already inhabited by an intelligent and clearly viable life-form – *homo sapiens*. A principle of their creed, bitterly wrought on the anvil of Martian history, is that it is wrong to displace any species from its hereditary environment. They decide to return to Mars and seal themselves into their great pyramids. There they will remain in a state of suspended animation until the world is rebuilt. Osiris, the far-sighted politician, sees that one day mankind will reach out towards the stars. They will outgrow their own planet and must eventually seek to cultivate and colonise others.

By that time the Earthlings – he reckons – will have become sufficiently civilised to accept his species and will help the Martians to re-establish themselves within the solar system. Enter Seth, stage left. He doesn't accept any of these views. He is of a sterner, more piratical nature. His plan, with the aid of Shebek, is to kill off the humans and take over the world. He sets to work (hence, maybe, the seven plagues of Egypt?) but Osiris & Co finally defeat him. We can assume Osiris is killed in this battle. Seth is forced to surrender. Swearing eternal vengeance, he is entombed in an export version of the Martian pyramid.

The surviving goodies now leave Earth in peace and return to Mars for their long hibernation. As far as we are concerned this is what really happened and is the story the Doctor must eventually disentangle from the Egyptian myths.

Second Point. Seth's motivation. In the present story this is obscure but as his ultimate plan appears to be to destroy the world (by rather circuitous means) it seems to come down to an elaborate way of committing suicide. As already indicated, I think his motivation must be vengeance. He has been lying around for several thousand years getting very bitter and twisted. So his intention is to get hold of a rocket ship, fill it with fissionable material, then direct it so that it will hit the Great Pyramid of Mars where his enemies are lying. (Incidentally, this also gets us out of the difficulty of trying to make scientifically plausible the notion of entirely destroying a planet with one rocket. That this would also destroy life on Earth is in any case – as I said yesterday – far from certain. My information is that such an explosion would probably turn Mars into a belt of asteroids and have little effect on the orbit of this planet.)

Third point. I have gone off the idea of dumping a load of seed grain on Mars. It opens up too many problems (ploughing, harvesting?) for us to explain in terms of present-day science. (*Doctor Who* adventures set on Earth and involving UNIT are roughly contemporary. That is we allow ourselves the leeway of four or five years scientific 'discoveries' by suggesting they take place in the near future.) I suggest that Fawzi and his colleagues are working on an ambitious 200-year project to revitalise Mars. (Exactly as Osiris predicted.) Their first step is to cover the planet with hardy green stuff. They want to get the business of photosynthesis, carbon dioxide, chlorophyll – all the life chemistry bubbling away. They plan to chisel lumps out of the polar ice caps and fly them to Mars. They hope, eventually, to give the planet a life-supporting atmosphere and an annual precipitation like Manchester. Two centuries hence humans will be living up there and growing corn. But what they are looking for at present are suitable kinds of green stuff. They have hopefully assembled a batch of the hardiest grasses, mosses and weeds found on Earth. This is the kind of project that the Doctor would be likely to take an avuncular interest in. I think it should be known as Operation Piesky or Jam Tomorrow. Astronomical study of the red patches which wax and wane on Mars suggests that plant life might have to adapt to withstand long periods of drought. Somebody – Fawzi? – might well recall how the Nile used to flood annually and the plants that then bloomed in the desert. The attempt to type and classify these plants might well lead the scientists to the museum to study old documents and hieroglyphs, decorative frescoes, etc and thus you can integrate both barrels of the story.

Finally, a few further considerations that might affect your structuring of the story …

It is well known that the Egyptians no longer allow ancient artefacts to be taken out of the country. Therefore Shebek's sarcophagus (which is opened in the teaser) must have been in Britain for a long time and for some reason never previously opened. I suggest that either a) it has only recently been discovered (maybe in the attic of a house once belonging to a Victorian archaeologist) or b) – my favourite – that it was part of a consignment of Egyptiana lost in 1882 when a cargo ship foundered. Because of the present interest in exploring undersea wrecks the barnacle-encrusted sarcophagus of Shebek has been raised from the deeps and has arrived at the museum. Hermetically sealed with pitch and containing one or two inner boxes before one comes to the meat, so to speak, there is no reason why the contents should have been affected by their long immersion.

The opening of the sarcophagus wouldn't be done in any public area of the British Museum. It would be carried out, maybe, in a back room or basement area. This is actually advantageous in production terms because it is problematical whether we would, in fact, get permission to take an OB unit into the Museum. In any case we shall have to build sets in the studio and it is clearly easier to mock up some never-seen back room than it is to recreate a section of the well-known Egyptian Room.

Eerie effects. The scorpion / the appearing and disappearing 'Eye of Horus' / the mummy that strangles people with a fold of bandage, etc. This is all lovely stuff but I think it essential that the Doctor should have a good scientific explanation ready. Is the 'scorpion', for instance, really a pre-programmed robotic device for influencing people? What is the 'Eye', its purpose, how does it work, etc?

We need, I think, some fairly hard thinking about the basic mechanics through which Seth operates. This, of course, all comes back to my comment at the beginning about putting the emphasis on a science fiction element. The only alternative, it seems, is to make it plain that these ancient Martians had developed 'psy-powers' that are beyond our comprehension (though not necessarily the Doctor's). However, even if we follow this line I think they need to be backed up by some fairly elaborate hardware.

Again, the plastic pyramids which the mummies use to set up their rocket control centre – where did they come from? If we say it's all done by telekinesis then we must be sure to show, at some point in the story, telekinetic power in action. (This will involve a CSO sequence – known as Chromakey or Channel 9.)

I have been mentally tied for some time over the problem of explaining how, if Seth & co all belonged to the same species, their physiognomy could be as diverse as depicted by the artists of ancient Egypt. Barry Letts suggests they need not all belong to the same species or, indeed, be indigenous Martians. They are the remnants of some ancient Galactic Federation who came from a distant system to our own part of the galaxy. First stop was Earth – trouble with Seth – then they moved on to set up their life-supporting pyramid on the inhospitable but just acceptable planet of Mars.

This knocks out a chunk of what I wrote on the first page but I think it satisfactorily resolves a lot of loose ends. (I was, for instance, a bit bothered that technologically advanced Martians shouldn't already know that intelligent life existed on Earth.) The explanation that they belong to several different species covers our crocodile-faced Shebek and Ibis-faced Isis. And maybe after getting here they didn't have enough gas to be able to go on to another solar system. So they were compelled to settle for Mars.

Shape. As Seth is the arch-villain of the piece I think he should put in an earlier appearance than he does at present. (Though I'm available to be convinced otherwise.) I like the final confrontation at Cheops, however, and maybe he could come into the story earlier in projected form?

In general, although I see that after Ep 1 you set the story down in the baldest form, it seems rather short on action and deaths. We need lots of tension moments and stings, as I'm sure you know, and the Doctor (or Sarah) should be facing fearsome death come every curtain. (Incidentally, please don't leave our poor old Brigadier in suspended animation. We need him for subsequent stories!) It might be that Seth / Shebek, via their scorpion, 'take charge' of Lethbridge-Stewart and thus obtain access to a stock of hydrogen bombs. He works in cahoots with their other pawn, Fawzi, so that the Mars-shot is loaded with bombs rather than grasses.

We need this kind of thing to give us mileage through Ep 3 when the Doctor finally susses the plot. Ep 4, of course, is can he prevent the catastrophe? To help tension and audience-concern there should be some likeable humans whom we have already met aboard the

Mars-rocket … maybe even the Brigadier himself? It shouldn't be too difficult to work out a feasible reason for him being aboard.

One final point. As we have now settled on Mars as the rocket's target, we have extended the time scale. The Doctor has a lot longer to sort things out than if the rocket were heading for the moon. This, inevitably, will detract from the sense of urgency necessary in Ep 4 unless we postulate some new-fangled rocket motor which can do the Earth-Mars run in X number of hours. It's the best I can suggest at the moment.

Bob obviously liked many of the ideas that Griefer had put forward, and could see the potential in the story, and so on the strength of their discussions, retroactively commissioned Griefer to write a new storyline for delivery by Saturday 20 July 1974. Bob then added a handwritten note, dated Tuesday 9th July 1974, to the paperwork:

Now agreed that Sarah should be aboard the rocket – that it is diverted by the Dr, missing Mars, & heads back to threaten Earth. Seth is defeated & the Dr utilises the 'Eye of Horus' to be taken to the rocket in order to save Sarah. The rocket explodes in deep space, the Doc and Sarah escaping in Tardis, & the 'Eye' vanishes in the explosion. Suggested that the 'Eye' – in reality a powerful technological device of great antiquity – becomes the Holy Grail of the Dr's quest though subsequent adventures.

A new story outline, incorporating many of these suggestions of Bob's, was submitted by Griefer on Tuesday 23 July 1974, and Bob was sufficiently happy with it that on the very same day he commissioned Griefer to write the script for the first episode, with a target delivery date of Monday 9 September 1974. But when Griefer eventually delivered the script on Monday 23 September 1974, it sat, unread, in Bob's in-tray for a few weeks, as Bob tussled with the dual tasks or writing the scripts for 'The Ark in Space' and rewriting the scripts for 'Revenge of the Cybermen' (see previous chapter).

Bob eventually got around to reading through Griefer's script for Part One of 'The Pyramids of Mars' in early October 1974. He wrote to Griefer on Tuesday 15 October 1974 with his thoughts:

I am sorry I've not been in touch before but life at the moment is a little hectic. I've now read Episode 1 of your script again and my feeling about it is still, I think, pretty much the same as at our last meeting.

There is no doubt in my mind that the script will work but I feel it needs tightening, perhaps simplifying, and it certainly lacks the razamatazz we look for in *Doctor Who*. Egyptology – to our audience – means stone coffins, mysterious and eerie happenings and, above all, giant mummies wrapped in decaying bandages stalking their victims through studio fog. If this is their expectation I think they are going to feel cheated when it isn't fulfilled.

Simplification first. The cold bones of the story: Beta Project is a plan to seed Mars with green stuff. HQ of the project is a huge laboratory/ engineering complex. Fawzi tipped Hennessey off about an ancient type of grain once wild in Egypt. Several old sarcophagi brought to this country 80 years ago and previously opened have been loaned to Beta Project by the British Museum. Hennessey & Co plan to search them in the hope of finding maybe just one ear of the ancient grain.

Opening Scene: Mummy clambers out and kills camp security guard.

2nd scene: Doctor, Brigadier and Sarah discussing Beta Project with Hennessey when someone rushes in with news of the guard's death … Something on these lines, at any rate, would provide a unity in both theme and location that the script lacks at present. As far as possible, without it becoming too cramped, I'd like to confine the story to the various parts of the Beta complex.

Continuing excitement: Is it possible that now the Mummies have been disturbed they need to break out occasionally for a meal? Remembering that they are really aliens, perhaps they need to kill the odd passing human to obtain an electrical charge.

Background story. As you have it, in fact. Sebek is a wicked coloniser who has been imprisoned for thousands of years by Horus. Horus, a good alien, left Earth and with his spaceship running out of fuel, placed himself and his followers in permanent suspension inside a pyramid on Mars. He is up there waiting for the time when the humans will come to him. Sebek, the undead, is ironically released from his confinement by people actually working along the paths foreseen by Horus thousands of years ago – i.e. planetary colonisation by humans. And Sebek sees that by taking control of the Beta Project he can use its rocket to destroy his arch-enemy.'

Lewis Griefer carried on working on his remaining three scripts for the story in the final months of 1974. However, while he was writing them, he was diagnosed with a potentially serious illness, which resulted in him being hospitalised and undergoing a fairly major operation. Understandably in such trying conditions, the scripts for the remaining three episodes of 'The Pyramids of Mars' became massively overdue; Griefer eventually delivered them to Bob on Friday 15 November 1974.

At the time, Bob was tied up with getting the scripts for 'The Secret of Loch Ness' together. Because of this, it took him and Hinchcliffe several weeks before they could read through Griefer's scripts. They both still thought that the scripts held the basis of a good story, but they also decided that they would ask Griefer to do a rewrite on them, once he was well on the road to recovery after his operation.

It fell to Hinchcliffe to write to Griefer's agents, informing them of the need for a rewrite, and detailing what changes he and Bob felt were needed. But at this stage, there was no real urgency for the rewrite. It had now been decided to make the story as part of the production block of Season Thirteen, which would begin in the summer of 1975, so there was plenty of time for Griefer to do the required work on his story …

CHAPTER SEVENTEEN
WHEN THE GOING GETS TOUGH
1975

'I'd inherited my first season of *Doctor Who*,' notes Philip Hinchcliffe, 'and the reason for nearly all those stories was "Safety First" from Bob; to make sure that there were well-known *Doctor Who* characters alongside the new Doctor. Once we got to know each other, Bob and I had to plan future seasons, and the way we worked was that we would have ideas as we went along, and we'd make a note of them. You don't know where ideas come from, but they'd suddenly pop up from somewhere, and you'd think, "It would be good to do a story about this ..." So what we would do, Bob and I, is that we would set some time aside, and we would actually plan the whole of the next season, perhaps as many as four, five or six whole stories. So, for instance, I would say that I would like to do one about robots. And Bob would say he wanted to do one about Egyptology and the mummies; he thought he could do something good there. So ... most of the following seasons were half and half between Bob and me putting our ideas on the table. I would come up with a concept where I'd like to do something specific; it might not be a whole story, but I'd want to get a particular gadget in, or put a specific notion into a story. So we'd come up with these concepts between us. And sometimes these concepts would be large enough and strong enough to give us the whole story. So we would come up with five, six, seven, eight or nine key ideas, story ideas, or concepts. And sometimes they would get linked to make one story, or two or three would get linked into one story. And, roughly, he'd come up with about half of them, and I'd come up with about half.

'So the ideas came from all sorts of sources, and from all sorts of experiences. But I was very strong on trying to get a grip on the feel and the setting of a story; I felt that there had been too many stories that were made where the Doctor and the cast were just trapped in places that were obviously sets built in a studio, which didn't always look very good. If you could bring a really terrific environment and setting to a story, it would just have more of a richness and a resonance to it. So Bob and I had those conversations at the beginning of every season, and we gradually whittled all these ideas down into a season of stories. And having done that, we would farm these stories out to writers. Now and again, a writer would come in to us with a good idea, but mainly the story ideas came from Bob and me, and we would then map out a whole season. Once we had done that, we would then bring writers in, and give them these specific ideas to play with, and then Bob would do the engine-room work of trying to develop the plots with them, and the characterisations, and the rest of it. I'd get involved at various points; I'd want to look at the scripts at every stage. But crafting the stories, that would be down to Bob.

'And what would then happen was that the first draft scripts would come in from the writers, and they'd either be good, or they wouldn't be good, and so there'd be a lot more of us working together then to address the problems, and gradually he'd get back to the writers. He was very much a hands-on script editor, fixing it, getting it right. But knowing, right from the beginning, what the original story concept was, that we had both discussed. Bob would always keep those things in mind, so he was a very practical script editor, who kept to the original concepts, which were the root of the stories. I think the big change that I brought to *Doctor Who* was this notion of what would it look like, what would it feel like, before we even wrote the stories. And that was fed to the writer, and Bob always kept that in mind. It wasn't a case of, "Let's write a story," and then throw the problems to the designers. I was already talking to them, often before we had the stories written and commissioned. And Bob really grasped that, and steered that process through. So we preserved the strength of the original concept, even if there was a lot of story editing and problems to be sorted out before they were finished. I think it's very important to counteract the notion that all we did was to ask a load of writers for ideas, and see which ones came in. We didn't work like that.'

Bob himself found this approach worked extremely well. 'On the whole I fed people ideas, because part of a script editor's job is to ensure you get a good mix of stories, a nice blend – you don't want three spaceship stories in a row,' he later explained. 'Philip and I used to sit around and think up ideas, and then try and get the right sort of writer who could execute them. We had a fairly positive approach, we didn't just wait for scripts to come in – I don't think on a show like that you can do that.'

So for their second full season of *Doctor Who* – which would be the programme's thirteenth – Bob and Philip Hinchcliffe initially began discussing and deciding on story ideas they would like to pursue. The only story they had in hand to begin with for this season was Lewis Griefer's 'The Pyramids of Mars', of which the first-draft scripts had only just been delivered to them at the end of 1974.[205]

205 Other story ideas had been mulled over by Hinchcliffe and Holmes during 1974. Robert Sloman – who had written extensively for the series under Barry Letts and Terrance Dicks – had expressed an interest in pitching a story, but this approach was never followed up . Former script editor Terrance Dicks had meanwhile proposed a storyline with the title 'The Haunting'. Intrigued, Bob commissioned Dicks on Friday 12 December 1974 to write a storyline for a potential six-part serial, with a target delivery date of Friday 20 December 1974 set. Dicks eventually delivered his storyline on Monday 6 January 1975, but Bob felt it wasn't suitable for the season's final six-part story slot. Bob also approached former *Doctor Who* script editor Dennis Spooner, and commissioned him on Friday 31 January 1975 to write a storyline for a four-part adventure with the working title 'Nightmare Planet'. Spooner was asked to deliver his storyline on Friday 14 February 1975, but nothing further came of this story idea.

Terry Nation had also approached the production team, unsurprisingly with a view to submitting another Dalek story for the new season, but was persuaded to try his hand instead at coming up with a story that didn't rely on his famous baddies. 'I can't remember the genesis of that,' recalls Hinchcliffe. 'I can't claim the idea was mine, because I can't remember. But certainly the notion of people walking around who really are androids – I think that was probably Terry Nation's idea. But it really appealed to me, and I immediately thought, yes, let's not cheat this, we've really got to show real androids, with bits of electric wires behind the faces. So, very early on, I conceived this one scene I wanted to do, and I asked Barry Letts, who was there as a mentor for me, "Would it be possible to show a face that had all the wiring behind?" Because [otherwise] you can't do an android story and have the audience say, "Well, that's not an actor, that's actually a robot", because people won't actually believe you. So once I knew we could do that, then I knew we could make this into a good story. But I think that the original concept came from Terry. But I don't know what Bob said to Terry. He probably said, "Yeah, we do want a story from you Terry, but we don't want the Daleks in it."'

Terry Nation was commissioned on Friday 29 November 1974 to come up with a storyline for this android tale, which he entitled 'The Enemy Within', and was asked to deliver it by Friday 6 December. The storyline actually arrived a few days later, on Wednesday 11 December 1974, and became the second story to be commissioned for the new season of *Doctor Who*.

Another idea that both Bob and Hinchcliffe had come up with between them was to depict a truly alien planet, in a story that would also incorporate elements from the classic story *The Strange Case of Dr Jekyll and Mr Hyde* and the film *Forbidden Planet*.[206] They referred to this idea, aptly, as their 'Jekyll and Hyde Planet' story. Bob had definite thoughts about the writer he'd like to offer this idea to – his old chum Louis Marks. Bob and Marks had worked together many, many times in the previous years, and alongside Robert Banks Stewart, Marks was one of Bob's oldest and closest friends in the television industry.

'I've known Louis for many years,' recalled Bob some years later. 'We'd worked together on stuff like *Honey Lane*, and *No Hiding Place*, *Deadline Midnight* ... I'd known Louis for a long time, and knew he'd written a *Doctor Who* a long time ago, which was the one about the Doctor being miniaturised,

---

206 *The Strange Case of Dr Jekyll and Mr Hyde* is a much-adapted novella, first published in 1886, by the Scottish author Robert Louis Stevenson. It tells the story of how a well-respected doctor discovers a potion that transforms him into a wild, hedonistic new person. *Forbidden Planet* was a 1956 science fiction film that explored a similar theme; of man's personality being controlled by two opposing forces, the ego and the id. It also had an 'invisible' monster, which attacked a stranded space ship ...

called "Land of the Giants" or something.[207] And so I approached him.' At this point in time, Marks was working as a producer at the BBC, commissioning single plays for the *Centre Play* television drama strand. Like Terrance Dicks for 'Robot', and Bob himself for 'The Ark in Space', Marks had to be given special permission as a BBC staff member to be commissioned to write 'Planet of Evil' outside of his normal duties, using the BBC's staff contribution procedure.[208]

By the end of 1974, the fourth Doctor had burst onto the nation's television screens with the opening episode of 'Robot', which was shown on BBC1 on Saturday 28 December. Over the next few weeks, the audience quickly warmed to this quirky new Doctor. The average viewing figures for Jon Pertwee's stories over the previous few years had hovered around the seven or eight million mark. 'Robot' had an average audience of 10.2 million, and the figure rose for the next story, Bob's own 'The Ark in Space', the second episode of which was seen by a record (for *Doctor Who* at that time) 13.4 million viewers. Hinchcliffe and Holmes were obviously doing things right.

In January 1975, senior BBC executives began to hear whispers that ITV were planning on launching a big-budget, live action Gerry Anderson science fiction series, *Space:1999*, later in the year.[209] They assumed that ITV would schedule this on Saturday evenings as opposition to *Doctor Who*, and would probably look to launch it at the start of the autumn television season, at the beginning of August 1975. Fearing that if they did this, *Space: 1999* would then have four months or so to build up an audience before *Doctor Who* returned in January 1976, the senior BBC schedulers took the decision to bring forward the start of the thirteenth season to the autumn of 1975.

The result was that *Doctor Who* would now have to stay in production after 'The Secret of Loch Ness' was completed, with three additional stories – 'The Pyramids of Mars', Louis Marks's 'Jekyll and Hyde Planet' story, and Terry Nation's android story – being recorded over the spring and summer of 1975. A three-week breather was planned for the beginning of September 1975, after which the final two stories of the new season were due to be recorded before the end of the year. For the cast and crew, it was a gruelling schedule.

For Bob in particular, it meant there would be no chance of a holiday in 1975. Instead he and Hinchcliffe found themselves having to decide on the

---

207 Marks had written the William Hartnell story 'Planet of Giants' (31 October 1964 to 14 November 1964). More recently, he had also written the Jon Pertwee story 'Day of the Daleks' (1 January 1972 to 22 January 1972).
208 Louis Marks later became producer of the classic plays strand of programmes at the BBC in the mid-1980s. Bob met up with him again when he was working on all those old plays: 'Louis's very funny. I asked him, "How's it going?", and he said "Marvellous! All the writers I'm working with are dead, they never give me any trouble ..."'
209 Gerry Anderson had produced a number of successful puppet science fiction series for ITV in the 1960s, such as *Thunderbirds*, *Stingray*, *Joe 90* and *Captain Scarlet*. Early in the 1970s, he had moved into live action for the first time, finding success with the series *UFO*.

structure and contents of the thirteenth season of *Doctor Who* far sooner than they had anticipated. They quickly decided that the 26 episodes they needed to produce should make up five four-part stories, followed by a single six-part story to conclude the season.

However, 'The Secret of Loch Ness' had been planned as a six-part story, which did not fit this pattern. Consequently in early January 1975 Bob contacted Robert Banks Stewart and requested that he rewrite his scripts to compact the story into a four-parter.

Within a few weeks, Stewart submitted the four new scripts requested. The story was retitled 'Terror of the Zygons' during production, and told how the last remnants of the Zygons, a shape-changing alien race, planned to use a creature brought with them from their own world in a plot to take over the Earth and turn it into a new home for their species. This creature, the Skarasen, had become the basis of the mythical Loch Ness monster after being glimpsed by the local inhabitants in the past.

Stewart recalls his visits to the *Doctor* Who production office with fondness: 'I can still picture that office in Shepherd's Bush. Philip Hinchcliffe would be in his producer's office, and Bob would be just visible through the doorway to the next-door office. You'd go into Bob's office, and there would be Bob, sitting with his pipe, hammering away at the typewriter, surrounded by piles of scripts, and the typewriter would be going at a fair rate of knots. He was a very good typist, which I'm sure would have come from his days as an editor on *John Bull*. I used to be a terrifically fast typist – I was a cub reporter, my job was on the line if I couldn't type. But Bob Holmes, when he was doing his rewriting, or doing outlines, he just rattled away at this little machine, you know. And there was a lot of pipe smoke around. The "blue fug" of production meetings!'

'Terror of the Zygons' saw the departure of Ian Marter's Harry Sullivan as a regular in the series. The character had only been introduced as a safeguard against an older fourth Doctor being cast, and as Tom Baker had proven more than capable of standing up to the rigours of filming, it was felt that Harry had quickly become redundant. 'Well, he was only contracted for one season,' recalled Bob, slightly defensively. 'Artists who appear regularly are contracted to do so many programmes. If we want them to continue we ask them, and they can refuse of course. We have to get these things straightened out well ahead, to get the scripts well sorted out. Ian was very good value, but he probably felt it wasn't the right sort of part for him to play on a regular basis.'[210]

Early in January 1975, Bob finally applied himself to the scripts that Lewis

210 Robert Holmes Interview, *Gallifrey*, Issue 1, September 1977 – Interview by Tim Dollin.

254

Griefer had sent in some months earlier for 'The Pyramids of Mars'. Letts, who was still very much on hand in the background, remembers how Bob came to realise that he had a problem with the story. 'When Bob first became script editor, I was with Terrance when Terrance said to him, "You know, *Doctor Who*'s different from practically every other show". He knew that Bob had been a script editor himself, so he said, "It's not so simple as being a script editor on a normal show, you'll find it's quite difficult working with the writers, and there will be quite a considerable amount of rewriting to do." And Bob was very, very confident. He said, "No, no, don't worry, I've done a lot of this in my time. I've got one writer who is really good. I've never actually worked with him, but I'm really impressed by him, I know he's going to turn in something really good." Anyway, eventually the scripts came in, and they were on old-fashioned Quarto paper, single space, no margins, filled in very smudgy, purple ink … An old portable typewriter with a purple ribbon had been used, and you could hardly read it. He delivered this bundle of Quarto stuff, the writer, and disappeared to Israel. And Bob said, "Oh! We'd better read it," and we read it, and there were a lot of good ideas there, but it just didn't work as a *Doctor Who* script. And that was "The Pyramids of Mars". But I know that in consequence of this – this bundle of Quarto stuff that Bob had been handed, and that he was really quite shaken to get – he reverted to the idea of having the writer in and working with him, the method that we'd always used before. And discussing it in detail, so he knew what he was going to get, and having it delivered episode by episode.'

This all happened in late 1974, and Bob and Philip Hinchcliffe had already discussed the first-draft scripts that Griefer had supplied to them. They had asked Griefer to go back and rewrite them, thinking they had quite a bit of time to play with before the story was due to enter production. But now that the start date of the new season had been rescheduled, things had dramatically altered.

On Thursday 30 January 1975, Hinchcliffe wrote to Griefer in Tel Aviv and asked him to send back his most up-to-date versions of the four scripts for 'The Pyramids of Mars', in whatever state they were in. But as Griefer was now committed to a teaching position with a university in Tel Aviv, he hadn't actually got very far with his rewrites. The scripts were still in their first-draft state.

As far as Hinchcliffe was concerned, there was only one solution to this problem. 'It just didn't really work, and so I prevailed upon Bob to do a total rewrite,' he explained. 'So it was what I call a page-one rewrite, it was a whole brand new script. But it turned out to be one of the best scripts that Bob wrote, actually.'

Bob now found himself in exactly the same situation as he'd been in the previous year with 'The Ark in Space'. He spent most of February and March 1975 writing four completely new scripts for 'Pyramids of Mars' (the 'The' was dropped from the story's title at this point). As part of the agreement that the *Doctor Who* production office struck with Griefer over these rewrites, the new story went out under a pseudonym, Stephen Harris, rather than under Bob's own name. Griefer also retained the rights for repeats and overseas sales of the story.

'I commissioned Lewis Griefer, I knew him from old and that he had an interest in mythology,' recalled Bob. 'He had written some science fiction before for ITV. Anyway, the scripts arrived late and again we couldn't get him to do rewrites quickly enough, not all the way from Tel Aviv, in the style we were looking for! I also got the impression that poor old Lewis had never actually got to see *Doctor Who*, because [his version of the story] was quite different from the series' pattern, and the Doctor's character was odd and everything. So I wanted the mythology and I wanted a re-run of *Curse of the Mummy's Tomb*, or one of those, so I had to rewrite it. He didn't even give me the story basis of Egyptian mythology – I got all that from a book! His story veered all over the place and wasn't anything to do with Egyptian mythology. I wanted Horus, Sutekh, etc. "Pyramids of Mars" was, I think, his original title – he was very into pyramids, the alleged magical properties in them.'[211]

'Pyramids of Mars', as written by Bob, was now set in the year 1911, and concerned an English explorer, Marcus Scarman, working in Egypt to uncover the lost tombs of the Pharaohs. Scarman locates the tomb of the god Horus, only to discover that it is instead a prison for Sutekh, the last of the alien Osirans, whom the ancient Egyptians worshipped as their gods. The control system for Sutekh's prison is located in a pyramid on Mars, and so Sutekh arranges for Scarman to take caskets filled with equipment and mummies (in reality, robot servitors of Sutekh) back to England, in order to construct a rocket that will destroy the Martian pyramid and set him free. The Doctor and Sarah arrive in 1911 in time to thwart Sutekh's plans.

Bob was always slightly cagey when it came to the subject of pseudonyms. He was once asked about the use of the name Stephen Harris on his scripts for 'Pyramids of Mars', and the answer he gave might well have equally applied to the William Hood episodes of *Knight Errant* or, years later, the *Shoestring* scripts that were written anonymously by him. 'The whole point of a pseudonym is to protect the identity of the writer,' said Bob. 'I salvaged the script and the writer was paid; this entitled him to royalties on foreign sales and it would have created chaos in the cashier's department if my name had

211 Interview – Robert Holmes, *Doctor Who Magazine* Issue 100, May 1985.

been on the script yet royalties had to go to another writer. A pseudonym was the simple answer. The storyline was based on Egyptian mythology because I wanted to remake *The Curse of the Mummy*.'[212]

Interviewed a few years after writing his scripts for 'Pyramids of Mars', but while he was still script editor of *Doctor Who*, Bob was asked about the way the TARDIS was used in general in the series. His answer, while offering an intriguing insight into a possible *Doctor Who* story-that-never-was, also illuminates his thoughts behind the plot structure of 'Pyramids of Mars' in particular: 'I don't know that we will use [the TARDIS] more often. The trouble is it's such a big set and we don't want to clutter up the studio, and spend a lot of money on a set we only use once or twice. We know fans love seeing the TARDIS, but unless it helps the advancement of the plot it's not really worth it. I have thought of doing a story set entirely in the TARDIS, involving rooms we haven't seen before. But it's very difficult and it means some alien has to get aboard, the Doctor won't be able to spot him, so it would have to be invisible. We're toying with that one. Generally, the TARDIS is used to introduce a new story, but I usually have her materialise in the surroundings. I tend to search through for scripts to find where we can use her again. In "Pyramids of Mars", for example, we had this opening scene where Sutekh infiltrated the TARDIS, and because we had this set we used it again on a later episode. The Doctor took Sarah to what he called alternative time. You see the trouble with the historical stories set on Earth is when you threaten the world with some danger in the past, people immediately say it never happened and the world didn't come to an end. So, to get over that one I invented this theory of alternative time, where the Doctor took Sarah forward to an alternative future of 1980.'

Bob also went on to address the specific date of 1980, which Sarah Jane Smith says is the year she comes from in 'Pyramids of Mars', and which had got a few fans scratching their heads in puzzlement. '*Doctor Who* has never been said to be in contemporary time. In all the UNIT stories set on Earth, it was not necessarily the Earth of the year they were transmitted. It was a short time into the future, some four or five years ahead. This gave us the chance to say "This invention has been developed", when we wanted to use a device we knew didn't exist at the time but might do in the near future. In this way, we gave ourselves a little freedom to invent devices or political situations. Even though we may not say it to the audience, we can say it to the writer and we cover ourselves in that way. We get an awful lot of letters pointing out every mistake; the audience is very quick on *Doctor Who*.'[213]

212 Robert Holmes Interview, *The Time Meddler*: Issue 3, October 1981 – Interview by John M Kahane.
213 Robert Holmes Interview, *Gallifrey*: Issue 1, September 1977 – Interview by Tim Dollin.

ROBERT HOLMES: A LIFE IN WORDS

'Pyramids of Mars' is almost the quintessentially perfect *Doctor Who* story. It requires no pre-knowledge of the series in order to watch and enjoy the story from the very first scene. Its period setting means that the BBC's production values aren't compromised at all, and the cod-Hammer horror elements all combine to make the story a real edge-of-the-seat experience. Bob's script allows Tom Baker to give perhaps his best ever performance as an alien Time Lord (and not just as 'Tom Baker writ large'), and in Sutekh we are given one of the best foes ever to grace the series. The only time that the story's troubled genesis becomes apparent is in the final episode, when the adventure just runs out of plot, but the sheer exuberance of the production carries the story home.

With Bob tied up writing 'Pyramids of Mars' in early 1975, Hinchcliffe took over some of the script editing duties on Terry Nation's four-part android story, now called simply 'The Kraals'. Hinchcliffe commissioned four scripts from Nation on Thursday 27 February 1975, with a target delivery date of Monday 14 April 1975.[214] Hinchcliffe wrote again to Nation in early March 1975, giving him some further pointers on how he should develop his story.

In May 1975, both Bob and Hinchcliffe began thinking about the final two stories of the thirteenth season. Bob, being something of fan of classic horror movies, thought it would be interesting to try a story that put a new twist on the traditional *Frankenstein* story; an idea that Hinchcliffe approved. Hinchcliffe, in turn, suggested that they might want to explore further the ideas of robotic logic and intelligence. 'Although *Doctor Who* was a family show, Bob and I talked about making it appeal more to adults,' recalls Hinchcliffe. 'There was this rather broad and loose concept where you could bring ideas in, and change them around a bit, and reference other things. Bob was doing that with the horror genre to some extent. I think we used all those sort of ideas, but we turned them in a particular way in order to do something new. The Doctor's character and the format of the show meant that you weren't copying another story; you were using elements of it, but manufacturing something completely new ... I wouldn't say it was systematic on our part, but when you look back you can see what was on our minds, and maybe where particular ideas came from. ... People might say those stories weren't truly original. I think they were, because they were original within a *Doctor Who* context. So while we might have been inspired by other films or stories, I think we translated everything into something that was new for *Doctor Who*.'

Terrance Dicks's 'The Haunting' storyline, which had been under

---

214 Hinchcliffe also asked Nation to come up with another *Doctor Who* storyline, entitled 'Return to Sukannan', which was delivered by Nation on Friday 14 February, but which was never taken any further.

consideration for a few months, was officially scrapped by the production team on Tuesday 13 May 1975 (along with another storyline, 'The Beasts of Manzic', by a writer named Robin Smyth, which presumably was an unsolicited submission). Dicks was instead asked by Bob to have a go at coming up with a story that utilised this *Frankenstein* theme, and on Thursday 1 May was commissioned to write a storyline entitled 'The Brain of Morbius', with delivery due on Monday 19 May 1975.

Dicks kept both to his brief and to his delivery date. 'I was asked to write another show', Dicks recalls, 'and I came up with this sort of variation on the *Frankenstein* myth. Which is that Morbius, who is a bit like the Master in that he's a Time Lord who's gone spectacularly bad and rebelled, has been hunted down and executed. But he has a faithful robot, who manages to preserve his brain, and somehow or other they manage to end up on this desolate planet where a lot of spaceships get wrecked, and the robot is trying to put together a body for his master, so Morbius can live again. Being rather dim, it takes odd bits from here and there, so the body that it finishes up with is a monster. So Morbius, who is very vain and handsome, finds himself trapped in the body of a monster. And Bob liked this idea.'

Bob liked the idea so much that on Friday 6 June 1975 he commissioned Dicks to write four scripts based on this outline, with a target delivery date of Wednesday 30 July.

Sometime during May 1975, Marks delivered his four scripts for his story, now titled 'Planet of Evil'. These required very little rewriting, which was just as well, as the story was due to begin filming in mid-June. 'Planet of Evil' was set on a distant world right at the edge of the known universe, where a scientific exploration team looking to unlock the secrets of the anti-matter deposits found on the planet come under attack from a creature made entirely of anti-matter. The sole expedition survivor is rescued, but as the ship leaves the planet behind, it quickly becomes apparent that one of the crew has been infected by the anti-matter, as the killings resume.

The season's final six-part story was still to be decided upon. Once again, Bob had a very definite idea for it, drawing from his love of classic horror films. 'On the whole I'd say to people, "Do you know the film *The Hands of Orlac*?"[215] and they'd say, "No", recalled Bob, when interviewed for *Doctor Who Magazine* in 1985. 'And I'd explain that it was about this pianist whose

---

215 The book *Les Mains d'Orlac* by Maurice Renard told the story of a concert pianist who loses both of his hands in an horrific accident. He is given replacement hands in an experimental transplant operation, but he discovers the donor hands came from a recently executed murderer. He begins dreaming that the hands are capable of independent movement, and that they are taking him over, leading him to become a murderer. The book was filmed three times as *The Hands of Orlac* in 1924, 1935, and 1960.

disembodied hand went around strangling people, and I suggested that if this hand was an alien hand … I gave that idea to Bob Baker and Dave Martin. When I was script editor I was always "ripping off" the classic horror films and things. In "Pyramids of Mars" it was robot mummies, and "The Brain of Morbius" was obviously *Frankenstein*; I always found that that sort of thing worked. If an audience can say "Ah yes, that's a Cowboys and Indians story" as opposed to a Zaags versus Zoombers story, they can relate to it much easier. I always tried to look for a strand that was familiar to the viewer. If you have straight SF with aliens and without parallels people can pick up on, to my mind, it doesn't work too well.'[216]

'"The Hand of Fear" – that was really Bob's idea,' recalls Hinchcliffe. 'He wanted to do the moving hand; that came from him. He said, "I've got this idea, this moving hand", and I thought, "Oh, that could be a bit frightening". So I gave Bob the caveat that this hand couldn't be used in a domestic setting. When you've got a hand crawling around someone's home, kids that are watching might think there's going to be a hand coming through under their door. We had a lot of fun laughing about what we *couldn't* do before we even commissioned that story, and talking about how frightening it would be if you put this disembodied hand into a domestic home setting. But we just couldn't do anything like that. So he went to the Bristol Boys again, Bob Baker and Dave Martin; he thought it would be a story they could handle, so he farmed it out to them.'

Bob Baker and Dave Martin, the duo who had written 'The Sontaran Experiment' for Bob the previous year, submitted an initial storyline for 'The Hand of Fear' on Thursday 29 May 1975. This was set on Earth in the 1990s and featured a remodelled version of UNIT (now called EXIT) along with an elderly Brigadier Lethbridge-Stewart. Much of the story was set in a nuclear complex, where a disembodied fossilised hand is stalking and killing scientists. The hand absorbs radiation from the nuclear reactor and transforms into a full-sized alien called an Omegan, which has arrived on Earth from a black hole. The Omegans are silicon-based life-forms, and are split into two factions; one group want to destroy mankind, the other to help it evolve. The hostile Omegans absorb the weaker faction and plan to destroy the Earth using the nuclear complex, so the Brigadier sacrifices himself to destroy the Omegan warship in orbit over Earth, defeating the invaders at the cost of his own life.

Bob and Hinchcliffe asked Baker and Martin to meet with them at the *Doctor Who* production office on Thursday 19 June 1975. At the meeting, the

216 Interview – Robert Holmes, *Doctor Who Magazine*: Issue 100, May 1985.

260

story was discussed and refined, and some ideas, such as the future setting and the death of the Brigadier, were dropped. Once the four of them were in agreement as to the direction the story would now take, Baker and Martin were commissioned on Friday 20 June 1975 to write six scripts for 'The Hand of Fear', with the first two due on Monday 7 July and the remaining four on Monday 18 August 1975.

By the end of June 1975, the six stories that would comprise the thirteenth season of *Doctor Who* had been decided upon. First would come the already-recorded 'Terror of the Zygons' and 'Pyramids of Mars', followed by 'Planet of Evil'. 'The Kraals' would be the last story of the current production block, which would then lead into a short break. 'The Brain of Morbius' and 'The Hand of Fear' would then go into the studio to conclude the season's adventures. However, when it came to the planned transmission order of the season, it was decided to swap 'Pyramids of Mars' and 'Planet of Evil' around.

By now, Hinchcliffe had been sent all four scripts of 'The Kraals' from Terry Nation, and wasn't particularly impressed with what he'd received. Nation's storyline, which revolved around an alien race planning to launch an invasion of Earth using a small number of androids to replace real people, utilised too many sets, needed too much location filming, and had a significant number of plot weaknesses. But Nation wasn't too keen on doing rewrites, so as soon as Bob finished work on writing the scripts for 'Pyramids of Mars', he was given the task of rewriting the scripts for Nation's story, which had now reverted back to its former title 'The Enemy Within'. This work would tie Bob up for most of June 1975.

On Wednesday 25 June, Dicks submitted his script for the first episode of 'The Brain of Morbius', but as the production team were still focused on getting the last of the first four stories of the season into production ('Planet of Evil' was recorded at around this time, in June and July 1975), it meant that Dicks's script sat in Bob's in-tray for quite some time.

By mid-July 1975, Bob had finished re-writing 'The Enemy Within', and had changed the story's title to 'The Android Invasion'. *Doctor Who* story titles were regularly changed prior to transmission, and Bob certainly had a taste for ones that were just a tad sensational. '*Doctor Who* stories are always intended to be vile and lurid,' he once explained. 'They hark back to the 1930s with comics like *Whizzer*, *Hotspur*, all that kind of thing – *Rogan Rides Again*. And of course, Hollywood does it, you know, *Destry Rides Again*, *3:10 to Yuma*, all this stuff. They are lurid titles. And one tends to put up what they call a working title, a provisional title, initially, because one can't think of a good title. And then that changes later on.'

As soon as he'd written them, copies of Bob's reworked scripts for 'The Android Invasion' were sent to Nation for approval. The story finally went into production in mid-July 1975, with ex-producer Barry Letts given the task of directing. This would mark the end of Letts's involvement with the series – Hinchcliffe was by now very much his own man in the role of producer.[217]

The fact that this was a modern-day Earth-based UNIT story, directed by the previous producer, gave it a tone and a feel that were more reminiscent of the Jon Pertwee era of the programme than of the more recent Tom Baker stories. 'I think that was a story that had a very unhappy mixture of components,' muses Hinchcliffe. 'I have the utmost respect for Barry Letts, and I think he was one of the best producers of *Doctor Who* – he was innovative, there were some fantastic stories under his watch. But I do think that in the way he directed "The Android Invasion" there was a clash of styles; there were Bob and I trying to move the show on a bit, and there was Barry still with the components of his regime, which was UNIT and monsters that were handled in a certain way. And so there was a lack of balance in that story overall.'

Meanwhile, Baker and Martin delivered their scripts of the first two episodes of 'The Hand of Fear' on Wednesday 9 July 1975. The next day Bob wrote back to them, saying, 'We think the episodes are very exciting and if the standard can be maintained the show is bound to be a winner.' He also included a small list of minor revisions he felt they should make to the first two scripts in order to improve them. These included bringing back the character of Harry Sullivan for the story, and changing the name of the Omegans to something that sounded different from that of Omega, who Bob had now recalled was a character that Baker and Martin had come up with for their earlier story 'The Three Doctors' in 1972/3. Other discussions between the writers and Bob led to the introduction into the story of a character called Drax, a Time Lord who was an old friend of the Doctor's from Gallifrey. Baker and Martin took all this on board, and got down to work writing the final four scripts of the story.

On Monday 4 August 1975, Terrance Dicks delivered his scripts for the final three episodes of 'The Brain of Morbius' to Bob, who initially seemed more than happy with his handiwork. All four scripts for the story were formally accepted at the end of August, which usually meant that the production team were totally happy, and that no further rewrites were required from the writer. Dicks was paid his fee for his work, and that should have been that.

'I can't remember very much about Terrance's original scripts,' Hinchcliffe

---

217 Shortly before this, Letts was commissioned to write a four-part story entitled 'The Prisoner of Time', probably intended for the following season. Although the first episode script was written, and accepted by the production team on Tuesday 15 July 1975, the story was subsequently abandoned without the other three scripts being delivered.

recalls of the events that then followed. 'I think that Bob had a very strong notion of what the potential of that story was. And I think he felt, when the scripts came in, that they just weren't living up to that potential. And I also think it was a clash of styles. Terrance is a very funny man, but his sort of humour is not the same as Bob's sort of humour. I think that we got from Terrance a version of that story that would have fitted the Barry Letts era very well. But it didn't fit our era. Saying that, I can't remember any major plot and character defects. It was that it just didn't tackle the story with enough resonance and darkness, which obviously was what Bob initially had in mind. We weren't going to accept something that really wasn't going to work, something that seemed so out of place with the rest of what we were producing. I don't think it was a question of me saying to Bob, "Please rewrite that." I think he felt himself that it hadn't worked out, so it was up to him to tackle it.'

So Bob went away with Dicks' scripts for 'The Brain of Morbius', and spent most of August 1975 rewriting all four episodes, more or less from scratch. The main change he made was the removal of the robot that rebuilds Morbius's body and the introduction of the character of Mehendri Solon to fulfil the same role. In Bob's version of the story, Morbius, a renegade Time Lord, has been found and executed by his own people for his past crimes. But before his execution, Solon managed to remove Morbius's brain and secretly keep it alive. Solon now begins building a new body for the evil Time Lord. The Doctor and Sarah then arrive on the planet Karn, where Solon has been conducting his sinister experiments.

'I wrote the four scripts,' recalls Dicks, 'and I made the mistake of then going away on holiday, so I couldn't be reached. As far as I knew, there was nothing to worry about, the scripts were approved and everything was fine. So I came back two or three weeks later, and I said to Bob, "How's it going?" and he said, "Oh, fine, fine." I said, "How are the scripts going?" "Oh, one or two little changes, nothing very much," he said, lying through his teeth, which is exactly what I would have done in his place! I said, "Well send me a set," and so he sent me a set …'

On Monday 15 September 1975, Bob wrote to Dicks, sending him copies of the BBC-typed rehearsal scripts ('complete with the usual interesting misprints,' Holmes wryly noted), which were about to be sent out to the director and cast to use in the studio rehearsals due to begin the following month. Bob didn't make any reference in the letter to the substantial changes that he had made to Dicks's text. Perhaps he was hoping that Dicks wouldn't notice?

If so, then his hopes of getting away with his substantial rewriting of the story were dashed the following week, when Dicks wrote a slightly terse letter back to him:

> Thank you for the scripts, which I've now read through. Needless to say you've done a grand job in the time available. However, I can't help feeling that the removal of the robot, the central pivot of the story, has left a more conventional story with the plot sometimes a bit thin on the ground, and you've moved a bit further towards horror than I'd care to myself.
>
> All that's debatable. What *isn't* debatable is that these scripts don't contain a line of my dialogue and just aren't written by me. So I'll have to ask you to take my name off them – if only to avoid breaking the Trades Description Act!
>
> Hope this doesn't add to your problems too much. I'll leave it to you to devise some bland pseudonym.

Dicks recalls also phoning Bob up and asking him for an explanation as to why his scripts had been so extensively rewritten. Bob could have taken the easy option of telling Dicks that, as he was away on holiday and therefore was not contactable, he'd had no choice but to rework the scripts himself.

But he didn't.

'I rang up Bob, and said, "What's going on?"' recalls Dicks. 'And Bob said, "Look, I'm sorry, but Philip went off the robot. Philip Hinchcliffe decided we couldn't do the robot".'

Perhaps Bob was trying to be diplomatic with his old friend, trying to let him down gently, as it were?

Terrance Dicks, however, still feels that Bob didn't do his story much justice with his rewrite. 'What's in the story as-transmitted,' he later mused, 'is Mehendri Solon, the greatest surgeon in the galaxy – who's been conducting abortions or something, so he's in a shady state – is the one who's doing the Morbius body. But it's nonsense! If he's the finest surgeon in the galaxy, why can't he put a decent body together? I pointed out, fairly forcibly, to Bob that this was total rubbish. So Bob, at Philip's request and insistence, had rewritten the story. And I was very annoyed about this at the time, I was very fed up, and I said to Bob, "Well, I've got a good mind to take my name off it." I said, "Look, you know you've gone too far, because you can't make changes without consulting the writer. I could stop the show," I said, "but I'm not going to do that, but I'm going to take my name off it." "Oh, don't do that," he said. "Yes, I'm taking my name off it," I said.'

Dicks's written request that Bob put the story out under a 'bland pseudonym' was therefore acted upon.

To the letter.

'Weeks and weeks later,' recalled Dicks, 'I got the *Radio Times* for the first episode, with '"The Brain of Morbius' by Robin Bland" written in it, so I fell about laughing at that. It was never a serious quarrel, because I understood Bob's position, and I got over it. When I did the novelisation some time later, I did what was virtually Bob's script. And it's a good, gothic story. If you ignore the fact that the central premise is total nonsense! But you can ignore that, and if people do notice, they don't mind.'

'The Brain of Morbius' also featured a blink-and-you'll-miss-it cameo by Bob in the final episode. As part of the Doctor's mind-dual with Morbius, a handy video screen showed a visual representation of how the battle between them was going. Whichever Time Lord was losing the battle would be seen to regress through his previous regenerations. As Morbius gained the upper hand in the contest, the Doctor's previous selves – in the form of stock BBC photographs of Jon Pertwee, Patrick Troughton and William Hartnell – were seen briefly on the screen. But as Morbius pushed the Doctor even further back, many previous, and hitherto unseen, incarnations of the Doctor were also seen on screen.

Rather than actors being used for these images, many of the production personnel working on either this story or the final six-part story of the season were pressed into service as early incarnations of the Doctor. 'The reason we had non-actors' faces was that we didn't want actors,' recalls Hinchcliffe. 'Because if we'd had used actors' faces, the actors would then have got excited, thinking we might be thinking of casting them. We wanted anonymous faces for the Doctor, ones that would *not* be recognisable faces of actors. So everybody on the production was enlisted, plus some people planning the next show, like Dougie Camfield. We just grabbed everybody we could in the production office, and had the photos taken. So there was a reason for it, it wasn't just a production in-joke.'

As far as Bob was concerned, these faces were most definitely earlier, unseen previous Doctors. 'Oh yes, I think we went back about seven. In "The Deadly Assassin" I put in that Time Lords have only 12 regenerations, so the Doctor must be using up his lives at a fair lick,' he once noted mischievously.[218]

'The contest was a mental tug-of-war,' Bob noted in another interview. 'The Doctor got dragged, at first, back through many earlier incarnations. We saw Pertwee, Troughton and Hartnell, followed by several incarnations never seen before. I think we figured out there were about nine in all, which must indicate the Doctor is coming towards the end of his natural span as

---

218 Robert Holmes Interview, *Gallifrey*: Issue 1, September 1977 – Interview by Tim Dollin.

265

a Time Lord. The Doctor then rallied, however, and quickly recovered the lost ground, and we then saw some earlier versions of Morbius. At this point, Morbius – already a bit brain-damaged, you may remember – blew a fuse. The Doctor won the contest.'[219]

Hinchcliffe, along with George Gallaccio (production unit manager), Graeme Harper (production assistant), Douglas Camfield (director), Christopher Baker (production assistant), Robert Banks Stewart (writer), Christopher Barry (director), and Bob himself all took turns to raid the BBC's costume store, assemble vaguely Doctor-ish costumes, and pose for photographs to be used in this sequence. Bob dressed himself in a white wig with a ponytail, a tricorn hat, and an embroidered jacket over a high-collared shirt to present a former Doctor with a buccaneering background. Bob kept a large copy of this photo of himself, which he had framed and placed in pride of place on the toilet wall of his house. His grandson, James, later recalled how he used to dread having to visit the loo when he visited his grandparents' house, as he found the photograph somewhat intimidating and scary …!

'The Brain of Morbius' was now the fifth story in a little over 18 months that Bob had had to rewrite, nearly all on the say-so of Hinchcliffe. He would later satirise this frequent situation, using a fictional writer as the subject of his ire, in his essay for Peter Haining's book *The Doctor Who File*:

> Philip and I worked very well together. There is no truth in the rumour that I have bought a burial plot for him.
>
> However, I do recall one night – it was a weekend, I guess – when I was hammering away at four words an hour to get a script into shape for the director who was joining us on Monday. The telephone rang and it was Philip reeking of fresh air. He'd obviously spent the day on the golf course.
>
> 'First, the good news,' he said. 'We've got Arnold Kingfisher's script in.'
>
> 'Oh great!' I cried. 'I knew good old Arnold wouldn't let us down.'
>
> 'Now for the bad news,' said Philip. 'It's bloody useless.'
>
> Philip's a funny chap. He and Torquemada would have got along like brothers.[220]

On Tuesday 2 September 1975, Baker and Martin submitted their scripts for the

---

219 Robert Holmes Interview, *The Time Meddler*: Issue 3, October 1981 – Interview by John M Kahane.

220 From 'A Life of Hammer and Tongs' by Robert Holmes, published in *The Doctor Who File* by Peter Haining (W H Allen, 1986). Tomas de Torquemada (1420-1498) was one of the prominent leaders of the Spanish Inquisition.

final four episodes of 'The Hand of Fear'. Because he'd been tied-up rewriting 'The Brain of Morbius' in recent weeks, Bob had more or less left Baker and Martin to their own devices on the story, so they'd soldiered on writing their scripts in what they thought was the direction required of them. The director allocated to 'The Hand of Fear', Douglas Camfield, had already begun pre-production work on the story, and the search for possible filming locations had been instigated, with filming due to begin in mid-October 1975. It wasn't until the middle of September, once Bob had finished his work on 'The Brain of Morbius', that he was able at last to turn his attention to the scripts for 'The Hand of Fear'. It was only then that he realised that he had still more problems.

Bob wrote to Baker and Martin on Wednesday 24 September 1975, telling them that he thought there were substantial issues with the scripts that they had delivered to him, and that he just couldn't put the story into production as things stood. After all the work he'd done in recent months, Bob evidently wasn't keen to have to do any substantial rewriting on 'The Hand of Fear' himself. He told Baker and Martin that they had to consider reworking their story and scripts under their own steam.

As a contingency plan, Bob quickly got in contact with Robert Banks Stewart. Stewart was asked to come up with an alternative storyline for a possible six-part adventure that could potentially be used to conclude the thirteenth season. He was commissioned to write six scripts with a working title 'The Seeds of Doom' on Tuesday 30 September 1975, with his target delivery date given as 'As soon as possible'.

Stewart went into overdrive, and – writing at a prodigious rate – submitted his script for the first episode of the story on Thursday 2 October 1975. The script for the second episode followed on Tuesday 7 October 1975, with the third instalment being delivered on Wednesday 8 October 1975. Both Hinchcliffe and Bob were far happier with the story and scripts of 'The Seeds of Doom' than they were with 'The Hand of Fear' as it stood, so Baker and Martin were contacted and told that 'The Hand of Fear' was being dropped from the production schedule. Douglas Camfield and his team set about putting 'The Seeds of Doom' into fast pre-production.

Bob had given Stewart some guidance on the structure for 'The Seeds of Doom'. Because of his dislike of the six-part story format, he had come up with the idea of starting 'The Seeds of Doom' with a separate two-part plot strand set in Antarctica, which then led into a follow-up four-part storyline set back in England. Hinchcliffe recalls that a lot of the elements in the story also came from Bob. 'Well, again, it was this idea of breaking a six-parter down into two stories,' he says. 'I think that the idea of the pod was Bob's, because he was quite fascinated by the idea of the way different life-forms would have evolved in the universe, and there's no real malevolence behind an alien life-form. It's just that they *are* another sort of life-form, and if they come into contact with the human race, then there will be a clash, and a conflict. He did that with "The Ark in Space", in a way. And he also did it with "The Seeds of Doom", in the notion that there was this plant that was inimical to the human race but would be perfectly okay on its own planet. But it has to survive, to sow its spore on the winds of the universe. It happens to settle on Earth, which is very convenient for us, so we can do a story about it. This is all very much a Bob Holmes notion, so I'm pretty certain that notion came from Bob, rather than Robert Banks Stewart. The idea of the Antarctic two-parter was a nice little murder mystery in two parts, and we then went onto the mad botanist storyline. I remember one bit of Bob Holmes tweaking on the scripts. Robert Banks Stewart loves little character touches, and he'd invented this little old lady in the story, Ameila Ducat, but she had to be toned down a bit. So tweaking went on, but there wasn't a major rewrite. I think that was a successful commissioning and fulfilling of the brief, basically.'

Stewart delivered his final three scripts for 'The Seeds of Doom' on Monday 20 October 1975, and these were pushed into production with minimal work required from Bob. The story revolved around two alien seed pods that had been found buried in the Antarctic ice. The first pod opens and transforms the nearest human it encounters into a deadly plant-based creature called a Krynoid. The first Krynoid is killed, but the second pod gets taken back to England, where it also hatches. The second Krynoid grows much larger, before it too is eventually destroyed.

During the final weeks of October 1975, Bob contacted Baker and Martin to discuss with them rewriting 'The Hand of Fear' as a simplified four-part adventure for inclusion in the following year's season of *Doctor Who*. With the thirteenth season now fully commissioned and made, Bob (along with Hinchcliffe) could finally relax for the first time in nearly 18 months. Bob didn't have that much to do in November and December 1975, so he and Hinchcliffe spent time reflecting on what had worked well for them so far, what hadn't, and how best to proceed for the next batch of 26 episodes of *Doctor Who*.

CHAPTER EIGHTEEN
ASSASSINS ON EVERY CORNER
1976

While Bob was busy rewriting 'The Brain of Morbius' in August 1975, he was also casting an eye over some story ideas that had been submitted on spec to the *Doctor Who* production office by a promising new young writer by the name of Chris Boucher. 'Most of the things that were sent in were not acceptable,' recalled Bob. 'I got something sent in, though, by someone called Chris Boucher once, and I thought he'd got talent, and after several interviews and about two years I got a script out of him – he then of course went on to be a good science fiction writer and I suggested he edited *Blake's 7*.'[221]

One of the stories Boucher suggested, 'The Tower of Imelo', revolved around a mad computer that was convinced it was God. The idea appealed to both Bob and Philip Hinchcliffe, and so Boucher was commissioned to develop it as a storyline under the title 'Prime Directive', on Tuesday 19 August 1975. This was the first piece of the puzzle that would eventually become *Doctor Who*'s fourteenth season.

January 1976 saw both Bob and Hinchcliffe interviewed by Phillipa Toomey of *The Times*, in an article that mainly profiled the 'new' Doctor, Tom Baker. Bob's sole reported contribution to the piece was to tell Toomey that his greatest worry was getting some scientific aspect of the show wrong. 'I dread the 13-year old pedant who knows more about physics than I do,' he is quoted as telling her.[222]

Following the screening of 'The Brain of Morbius' on BBC1 in January 1976, the *Doctor Who* production office again received a small number of complaints about how frightening the series had recently become. One such missive, which was addressed to the writer Robin Bland, also accused the story of being 'stupid'. Unsurprisingly, Bob, wearing his script editor's hat, leapt to the defence of the absent Mr Bland, and replied to the complainant personally. 'I think you may be right,' he said, 'in feeling that *Doctor Who* is becoming more frightening – we would say more exciting – but I cannot agree that our stories are stupid. In any case your feelings seem not to be generally shared, because the programme is now attracting the largest audience in its history.'

It does rather smack of slightly childish one-upmanship on Bob's part that

---

221 Interview – Robert Holmes, *Doctor Who Magazine*: Issue 100, May 1985.
222 *The Times*, 3 January 1976.

to justify the more adult approach of the series, he had to point out the rising viewing figures. But he was quite right – the viewers did seem to be voting with their feet. Or, more precisely, with their bums. On seats …

The most vociferous critic of the series at this time was Mary Whitehouse, the self-appointed guardian of the nation's morals, who was the public face of the National Viewers' and Listeners' Association – a 'clean up TV' campaign group that she had founded in November 1965. She was also not enamoured with this particular story. Two sequences in particular in 'The Brain of Morbius' were singled out for criticism by the NVLA for their portrayal of violence and horror. The first was where Solon shoots his manservant, Condo. On screen, this effect was achieved with 'blood-bags' rigged under the actor's costume, which were detonated on cue, giving the realistic effect of bullets hitting the character's abdomen, and blood then flying out of the wounds. The second saw Morbius's brain slide out of the protective tank it had been housed in, and fall with a splat onto the floor.

'I think that probably was a bit near the knuckle,' reflects Hinchcliffe about the brain sequence. 'I remember when we were making the story, that I thought that it was more squeamish than genuinely unsettling and disturbing I think, but perhaps we were a bit near the knuckle on that.' With the benefit of hindsight, though, would he have done things any other way? 'No, probably not. Actually, no. I think it was quite responsible, but if I felt there was something that genuinely would be disturbing – because there were scenes that I did edit, as producer, such as in "The Ark in Space" – either I would seek advice from the Head of my Department, or I would say, "No, I think this is too far". I had an inbuilt barometer of how far we could go, so if I put something out, as producer, then I felt at the time that that was okay. But you know when you're pushing right up against the boundary, and I think we were right up against the boundary on that one, not for that one moment, but because the whole atmosphere of the story was quite dark and oppressive really.'

But it has to be said, both Bob and Hinchcliffe were starting to give critics such as Mary Whitehouse and the NVLA a fair amount of ammunition.

The two men had more planning time for their third full season of *Doctor Who* – due to start on BBC1 in the autumn of 1976, and again set to run for 26 episodes – than they had for either of the previous two seasons. They took some time to sit down and throw ideas around between each other, exploring concepts and themes that they would like to see in the new run of stories. 'I always wanted to do a robot story,' recalls Hinchcliffe. 'Having read the Asimov robot stories, the idea of the Prime Directive, and that a robot could go wrong and therefore could be a killer, was something that I wanted do. And also I loved the idea of trying to portray a planet being used commercially, and so the idea of people mining on planets came up, and we debated if we could use models to convey that convincingly. Those were the sort of things I wanted to get across; real science fiction ideas of how people would be living, and what work would they be doing in the future. And Bob said we could do a sort of Agatha Christie sealed house mystery, so he probably brought that idea to the robot concept of mine, and then those two suddenly meshed, and we had the concept for a story. Just the basic concept.

'I think the producer is ultimately responsible for the whole programme – particularly in any long-running series – and I think if you're an imaginative producer, you want to have input into the content. Not only what the content of the stories is, but how they look, how they come across, how they're executed, the style, the vision of the show. And your script editor is your right-hand man, a quality control person, to make sure the scripts all come up to scratch. And if they fall short, he'll do enough work to bring them up to scratch. He'll also be the person who chooses the writers, in most cases, and so it's very much a partnership. But the actual nuts and bolts of fixing a script, fixing a second or third draft, that responsibility falls on the script editor's shoulders. But the producer will be saying. "I don't think this works ..." As will the script editor. He'll be saying, "I'm sorry, but this doesn't work", and he'll come up with solutions with the writer. But the actual detailed fixing of a script, the holding of the writer's hand from the word go, the encouragement, the day-to-day contact with the writer, was very much Bob.'

The idea for the opening story of the fourteenth season came directly from Hinchcliffe. 'Bob didn't like doing historical stories,' he recalls. 'The early seasons of *Doctor Who* had a lot of historical stories, and he thought it was a way of smuggling education in for the kids. They were like a rather boring history lesson, he felt. So he had an aversion to doing period stories. But he and I hit upon a means of using historical periods, which fitted with his love of the horror genre, and then we also introduced a science fiction element that would explain what was going on that was strange. We found that formula worked really well, and he'd already done it with "Pyramids of Mars", and I'd seen that it worked. Then I had this notion of doing this Italian story, and I'd been to Portmeirion some years before, where they'd filmed *The Prisoner*. I thought we could do a historical story there. I had the idea that there could be some sort of unexplained mystery element that would sow confusion into this Renaissance period, where everybody was dabbling in sorcery, and alchemy ... a lot of all that experimentation was going on. There could be a lot of wonderful characters, and also the characterisation could be bold, and brusque, and funny. I could see that we could bring a lot of qualities that had worked in other scripts into that sort of story. So that idea came from me, really, and then Bob worked it up, and turned it into what the actual story would be.'

Bob turned to Louis Marks, and asked him to write the story based on this broad idea, and between them they firmed up the outline. 'I knew that he was an Italian scholar,' Bob later recalled of Marks. 'He'd lived in France for a long time, he'd taken a degree in Medieval Italian and all that stuff. He knew all about Machiavelli, he could go on for hours if you let him.'

'I think Bob thought up this alchemist character, Hieronymous,' recalls Hinchcliffe. 'The power struggle between the two princes, I think he worked that out with Louis Marks, so between them they put the flesh and bones on the basic idea of doing a story set in Machiavelli's period. And that worked really well, that story. We had horse chases, and sword fighting, and wonderful cliff-hangers with the Doctor about to have his head chopped off.'

Marks was still a BBC producer at this point, and as with 'Planet of Evil', a special staff contribution clearance needed to be gained for him to write this story. The paperwork was processed on Tuesday 6 January 1976, with the four-part story being given the title 'Doom of Destiny'. It was later to be retitled 'The Masque of Mandragora'.

Writing a letter to the DWAS fanzine *TARDIS* in 1980, Bob explained the background to the story in response to a recent article in the 'zine that had looked at many of the influences and inspirations that Marks had drawn upon. 'The starting point for "The Masque of Mandragora" was an idea that Louis had that there might be – or at some time might have been – some basis for the "science" of astrology,' wrote Bob. 'That the stars, in fact, did have an influence on human affairs. We tried to rationalise this idea, developing it in *Doctor Who* terms, and this led us to Demnos. We also decided that, if the story was to work properly, it should be placed in an era when astrology was taken very seriously. Louis Marks, D Phil (Cantab), is not a man with a head full of turnips. Renaissance Italy is his special subject so the *raison d'être* behind the rest of the story requires no explanation. Of course, had I known at the time that Louis was plundering from all the sources revealed in your article, I'd have paid him only half a fee for the script!'[223]

One further consideration that Bob and Hinchcliffe had when planning the new season was that Elisabeth Sladen, the actress who had played Sarah Jane Smith since 1973, had decided that it was time for her to move on. It was

223 Letter from Robert Holmes, *TARDIS*: Vol 5, No 3/4 (1980).

272

agreed with Sladen that she would appear in only the first two stories of the season. The first would be Marks's 'Doom of Destiny', but a second needed to be commissioned to form her character's swansong. Bob had discussed the matter with director Douglas Camfield during the making of 'The Seeds of Doom', and Camfield had asked to be given the opportunity to pitch such a story.

Camfield presented Bob with a story outline, entitled 'The Lost Legion', for his consideration in January 1976. Camfield was something of a military history buff, and a big fan of the novel *Beau Geste*, and so his storyline revolved around a North African French Foreign Legion outpost that was the focal point of a battle between two factions of an alien race. At the story's conclusion, Camfield suggested that Sarah Jane Smith would be killed, dying in the Doctor's arms. Bob was slightly sceptical about the story's potential, but when Camfield also offered to direct it, both he and Hinchcliffe decided to give it the green light, and on Thursday 22 January 1976 commissioned Camfield to write four scripts, with a target delivery date of Monday 9 February for the first two episodes.

Also for the new season, Bob returned to the 'mad computer' storyline that he had received from Boucher in October the previous year.

'Bob said to me one day, "I've been working with this very promising young writer called Chris Boucher, but he's still got a job, and he's writing part time"', recalled Hinchcliffe. 'I was a bit sceptical; I thought, "You don't just find writers like that." But anyway Bob was very decisive about this; he really felt that Chris had got some talent, and he had been working with him for a while. Bob very strongly sold this idea of a mad computer to me, and I thought it sounded really interesting. But basically, the whole notion was a very good science fiction concept that Chris brought along, and all credit to him and to Bob; they basically worked on it by themselves, they got the whole thing up and running, and it was a really good story, I thought.

'When the scripts came in, I remember thinking, "Bob says he's a good writer – let's hope he is!" I was very impressed when the first drafts came in; they were very imaginative, and very well-written. Bearing in mind that the roll call of *Doctor Who* writers back then was usually a mixture of people who had written for other series that were more traditional types of shows; Bob Banks Stewart wrote for *Callan*, *Public Eye*, *The Avengers*, Terry Nation wrote for *The Avengers*, Bob Holmes himself wrote for *Public Eye* and *Dr Finlay's Casebook*, things like this. There were very few writers who could actually write science fiction, and were genuinely interested in science fiction. If you were lucky you got a good professional job from them, but a lot of the time that imaginative spark that was truly a science fiction idea, just wasn't really there. So you'd get a workmanlike script from these guys, but it just lacked that extra-special "something". What Bob saw in Chris, and what I saw when the script came in, was that here was a writer who genuinely was imaginative in this area, and could also write good solid plots, good scripts, good characterisation, nice sharp dialogue, and was also witty. Also, a lot of the scripts we got in were a bit plodding, and Bob often spiced them up a bit, but Chris came with a natural edge to his scripts, and so he was a real find, and Bob had encouraged him, and brought him along.'

'I'd been writing comedy, basically, mainly three-line quickies', recalled Boucher, some years later. 'My agent had watched *Doctor Who* for years. I wrote what I thought was a full episode – it turned out to be about 15 minutes' worth – as a sort of proposal, which my agent submitted to Bob and Philip. So I got a call to go in and talk to Bob. As far as I remember, Philip was there as well. So I had a very nice meeting, they were very nice to me. I was hugely impressed, and I asked for their autographs ... I've got Bob's on a BBC compliment slip somewhere. I don't honestly remember what the next stage was, but it was the case that I had this very rudimentary storyline, and Bob, presumably with Philip in the background, encouraged me to develop it. And it reached the stage where it was a "Yes, but ..." process. I would develop a bit more of it and send it in, and Bob would come back with, "Yes, that's good, but what about so-and-so ..." and I would work that bit out and send the new thing in, and he would go, "Excellent! But what about ..." And this went on for some time, until I got a decent storyline proposal worked out. Bob always said that storylining was all the work and none of the fun, and he was right. He was right when it came to so many things. And that was my first encounter with Bob Holmes, it was that first meeting.

'My initial impression of Bob was that he was schoolmaster-y, really. I'm not sure if he was wearing a tweedy jacket, but my impression is that he was. Certainly smoking a pipe, and he had that sort of scholarly feel about him. He was a nice man. If you're going to survive in this world, you have to assume that everybody is nice until they prove that they're not. In Bob's case he never did prove that he wasn't. My first impression of him was that he was a nice man, and he was.'

As a result of all these meetings with Bob, Boucher was commissioned on Tuesday 27 January 1976 to write a four-part story with the title 'The Day God Went Mad' – later to become 'The Face of Evil'. But because of Boucher's rookie writer status, the delivery dates for the four scripts were staggered. Part One's was due to be delivered on Thursday 27 February 1976, with each subsequent one then due to be delivered every two weeks after that.

At this time, Bob and Hinchcliffe were acutely aware that they had to find another actress to replace Sladen, and that they also had to come up with an actual character for the new assistant. But in the short term, as a kind of stopgap / placeholder option, they left it to the writers they were talking to about stories for the latter half of the new season to put their own companion character into the scripts that they were developing.

'I was told at the time that because there was no established companion,' recalled Boucher, 'that all the writers were going to be asked to provide themselves with a sort of companion whom the Doctor could talk to, otherwise he would be talking to himself. Which was something Tom Baker might have preferred, to do it all on his own. So I did come up with a girl. It's not like the post-*Buffy* era we have in television today … At the time, strong girls were very new. Obviously there was *The Avengers* and things like that, and that was the sort of precursor for the whole thing; the mood was changing. And there were – I hesitate to admit it these days – but there were a few of what were known at the time as "freedom fighters", and are now known as "terrorists" – but that depends on what side you're looking at. And this was the time of Leila Khalid. She was a Palestinian. Freedom fighting wasn't quite as murderous as it subsequently became. She hijacked some aeroplanes and blew them up, without anybody being in them. And she was beautiful, and she was in the press. It was a strange mood at the time, a changing mood. So a girl seemed like a good idea. A primitive girl, whom the Doctor could not only talk to, but could, as it were, actually teach. And she should also be intelligent, self-reliant, all of that. Now, how much of that came straight out of me, and how much of that Bob fed into it, I honestly don't know, but I suspect Bob fed in quite a lot of it. The character itself I wrote. The production obviously cast and dressed and gave her existence. So I tend to think of it that the creation was mine, the existence was theirs. It's a whole mixed-up process, quite difficult to define. But I know Bob had a lot to do with it, because he had a lot to do with everything.'

'She wasn't my creation totally, because Chris Boucher named her,' recalled Bob some years later. 'But we said to him we wanted Raquel Welch in the jungle, handy with a knife. But we didn't give her a name; he did. We thought it was time we had a more positive companion – somebody who could handle things on her own, rather than let the Doctor do it. A companion who would contrast with the Doctor's own more pacific nature. He is not supposed to initiate violence, except in self-defence, but Leela was the girl who would simply go out and stab someone in the back!'[224]

---

224 Interview – Robert Holmes, *Doctor Who Magazine*: Issue 100, May 1985.

And so the character of Leela was born.

'Philip and I were probably thinking about Raquel Welch. Who doesn't?' recalled Bob in an earlier interview. 'Anyway, we decided that the new companion should be a jungle type, handy with a knife and possessed of useful primitive instincts to complement the Doctor's more cerebral approach. I feel the character developed from her beginnings in "The Face of Evil".'[225]

On Monday 9 February, Camfield delivered his script for the first episode of 'The Lost Legion'. Bob had reservations about it, but he nevertheless asked Camfield to continue with the story for the time being. At about the same time, he also revisited the scripts for 'The Hand of Fear', and made copious notes on how to simplify and revise the storyline into the proposed new four-part version he had already discussed with writers Bob Baker and Dave Martin. This re-formatting removed the Brigadier, Harry Sullivan, Drax plus all the UNIT trappings from the story. As it was still yet to be decided who the new companion character was going to be, her role in the story – originally written with Sarah Jane Smith in mind – was left somewhat generic and undefined. She now also conveniently spent half the story acting out of character, under the control of the disembodied hand. Baker and Martin got back to work on their story, scripting a new four-part version of 'The Hand of Fear' to Bob's revised storyline. This was tentatively given a slot towards the end of the new season.

Also at about this time, Bob was contacted somewhat out of the blue by David Wiltshire, a dentist from Bedford, who had aspirations of writing, both for television and as a novelist. Wiltshire sent the *Doctor Who* production office a 20-page outline for a story called 'The Menday Fault', which revolved around the Doctor and Sarah arriving onboard a top-secret nuclear submarine exploring the seabed beneath the Bermuda Triangle. Bob eventually decided that the story wasn't for him.

February 1976 came and went with Camfield missing his delivery dates for submitting his scripts for the final three episodes of 'The Lost Legion', although he promised Bob and Hinchcliffe that he was working hard on the project. He was allowed some extra time to continue writing the story, but when the scripts of Parts Two and Three arrived in early April 1976, the production team eventually realised they had to abandon the idea. 'Dougie Camfield came to me once to do a Foreign Legion story,' recalled Bob, 'because he was mad about the Foreign Legion. He actually started to write a script for us, but it never gelled and never really set out so that you could say it worked in *Doctor Who* terms – it may have worked in Foreign Legion terms but not

---

225 Robert Holmes Interview, *The Time Meddler*: Issue 3, October 1981 – Interview by John M Kahane.

our medium. So I was glad that he managed to do *Beau Geste*.'[226]

If Camfield's script wasn't working out, the same couldn't be said of Boucher's. He diligently kept to his delivery dates, bringing in a script for a new episode of 'The Day God went Mad' every two weeks to go through with Bob. They discussed the work he had done so far, and agreed areas that needed tightening, altering and improving. 'Bob's guidance was that he never forced notions on you, he sort of drew them out of you,' recalled Boucher, 'and I honestly don't remember every last part of the process. I've still got my original proposal, the carbon copies of it, and if you look at it, it's just a process of attrition, really. Bob made, as it were, negative suggestions, frequently. "Yes, but do you really think …" he would say, and you'd think, "Wow, perhaps I should look at it in a different way." And so you'd look at it in a different way and rework it, and he'd look at it and say, "That's much better." It was almost schoolmasterly, now I come to think of it, and that was the process that went on between us. I know I went through more hoops on that particular script than anything else I've ever done, perfectly correctly, because it was my first script; it was a major thing for me. It was two hours; four half-hour episodes. This was big stuff for someone whose previous major television work had been an episode of *Romany Jones*.[227] *Doctor Who* was a major thing for me, and it was the most work I ever had to do. After that it got easier.'

Working with Bob in this slow but assured manner, Boucher was able to deliver his first three scripts for 'The Day God went Mad' throughout February and March 1976.

Later that same March, Louis Marks was able to send Bob his scripts for the first three episodes of 'Doom of Destiny', which required just the most minimal of editing. Marks' script for Part Four arrived on Tuesday 13 April 1976, and similarly required very little attention. The story was then retitled 'Secret of the Labyrinth', before being retitled a second time as 'The Masque of Mandragora'.

Due to Camfield's 'The Lost Legion' being scrapped, Bob also had to change the season's running order slightly, pulling forward Baker and Martin's reworked script for 'The Hand of Fear' so that it would now follow immediately after 'The Masque of Mandragora'. Sarah Jane Smith was thus reinstated as its companion character, but then a departure scene had to be hurriedly tacked

---

226 Interview – Robert Holmes, *Doctor Who Magazine*: Issue 100, May 1985. In 1982, Douglas Camfield directed a prestigious adaption of the novel *Beau Geste* for the BBC.
227 *Romany Jones* (1972-1975) was a sitcom made by London Weekend Television, originally as a vehicle for actor James Beck. After Beck's death in 1973, the series was restyled with Arthur Mullard and Queenie Watts as the new leads. Boucher wrote the episode 'Run Rabbit Run' (which starred Beck, and was shown on LWT on 22 June 1973) and storylined the episode 'The Invitations' (shown on 23 August 1974 on LWT, after Beck's death.)

on at the end of the final episode. Rather than re-engage Baker and Martin, Bob wrote this scene himself. However, Tom Baker and Elisabeth Sladen weren't happy with the dialogue, and elected to completely rewrite it to their own satisfaction during rehearsals. Bob and Hinchcliffe decided to indulge their actors on this occasion.

Instead of following 'The Hand of Fear' directly with Boucher's now-retitled 'The Face of Evil', complete with the new proto-companion Leela, Bob and Hinchcliffe decided to place between them another four-part story. They initially toyed with commissioning one by writer Basil Dawson[228]. This would have been set in Victorian London, and would have introduced a new companion in the form of an Eliza Doolittle-type cockney, whom the Doctor could then educate on his travels. But as Boucher's script was working so well, and Leela showed potential for becoming the new companion in her own right, Bob and Hinchcliffe decided instead to do a story that would feature the Doctor on his own, without a recognised companion figure by his side for the first time in the history of the series. This was partly because Tom Baker was agitating for the series dynamic to be changed to allow for the Doctor to travel without a regular companion; he had thoroughly enjoyed working with Sladen, but doubted another actress could work as well in the series as she had done. Conversely, Bob and Hinchcliffe doubted the series format would support such a move, but were willing to try an experiment; if nothing else to prove to Baker that it couldn't work in practice. Given that the Doctor would be on his own for this story, Hinchcliffe put forward the idea that it should be set on his home world of Gallifrey – a place that had been only briefly glimpsed in the series prior to this point – and that it should also see the re-introduction of the Doctor's Time Lord nemesis, the Master.[229] Because of this, it was decided that Bob should write this story – which was given the initial working title 'The Dangerous Assassin', before becoming 'The Deadly Assassin'.

'It was Philip's idea … to do "The Deadly Assassin",' recalled Bob, 'and we decided I should write it. He said it would be good to explore this place we've never been to before – the home of the Time Lords. Lis Sladen's contract was up and we decided to see if we could do a story for the Doctor without a companion, just as a test. It was also, if you discount the Master, the first [time] we struck the "received law" that every *Doctor Who* story had to have a monster. There were no monsters and "The Deadly Assassin" was very popular.

---

228 Basil Dawson's path had earlier crossed with Bob's when Dawson was script editor on *Emergency Ward 10* in 1963. They had also brushed shoulders when Dawson had written episodes of *Ghost Squad*, *The Saint* and *Fraud Squad*.
229 The Time Lords' planet had first appeared in the final episode of Patrick Troughton's final story, 'The War Games', in 1969. A short establishing scene in 'Colony in Space' (1971) was also set there, as was some of the Doctor-less action of 'The Three Doctors' (1972/3).

It aroused a lot of anger amongst the traditionalists, but that's all right.'[230]

Bob would later note that he thought the Master was in danger of being undermined as a credible character in the series. 'The trouble with the Master as a character is that he's lost too many times now. He should win a few.'

'The basic idea behind "The Deadly Assassin",' Bob noted in an earlier interview, 'was to see if we could make a workable *Doctor Who* with the Doctor on his own – no travelling companions. Philip wanted the story to be set on the Time Lords' own planet. And we both felt that sufficient time had elapsed since Roger Delgado's death for us to be able to reintroduce the Master. However, we didn't want to tie our successors to a particular actor (by this point we both knew that our time with the programme was coming to an end) and so I got the idea that he was in the terminal stage of his existence. This led me to the story – the Master was back on Gallifrey to try to steal himself a new supply of the Time Lord life essence. Finally, it has long been said in the programme that the number of regenerations open to a Time Lord is limited. I think I probably decided that 12 lives was about the right number but I can't remember; the number might have been stated in some previous programme.'[231]

Hinchcliffe recalled that Bob particularly enjoyed the job of writing the scripts for 'The Deadly Assassin'. 'Because we were going to change the Doctor's companion, we both thought it would be quite a challenge to do a story without a companion, as a sort of a transition story. Bob hated the way the Time Lords had been portrayed previously in the series. He thought they were a load of eunuchs, basically! So he wanted to try and portray the world of the Time Lords differently from what we'd already seen, with a bit more humour, and a bit more edge and bite. I was quite fascinated by the notion that the Doctor was a rebel Time Lord; he was a bit like an angel who'd been chucked out of heaven, and so I quite liked the idea of a story that would explore the relationship between the Time Lords and this rebel who had been excommunicated from Time Lord society, and was roaming the universe in his TARDIS. Somehow Bob and I then got onto the idea of the political assassination plot. But I think the whole idea of the battle with the Master in the Matrix was Bob's; this whole virtual reality thing was Bob's. It sounded a rather experimental, risky story when Bob explained it to me, but I remember saying, "Look, what the hell, go for it. Let's do something completely different. Let's do a story that's never, ever been done before, and you can go for it." So I just backed him, crossed my fingers, and hoped for the best, really! I think it

230 Interview – Robert Holmes, *Doctor Who Magazine*: Issue 100, May 1985.
231 Robert Holmes Interview, *The Time Meddler*: Issue 3, October 1981 – Interview by John M Kahane.

was an interesting story, certainly an unusual one. It was one for Bob to stretch himself, and I think he enjoyed the challenge of that.'

Bob once again had to be given special dispensation to write this story from the BBC Heads of Department. One memo, sent by Hinchcliffe to the BBC's Head of Copyright, asking for Bob to be paid a staff contribution fee, came back to the production office with Bob's name pointedly encircled with ink and the word 'Again?' written next to it. Clearly the amount of writing that Bob was being paid to do on *Doctor Who* – above and beyond his salaried role of script editor– was raising some eyebrows amongst senior figures at the BBC.

If feathers were being ruffled at the BBC, then Hinchcliffe didn't care. 'It was something I actively encouraged,' he recalls. 'I realised that it wasn't fair to continue to ask Bob to do these major rewrites just for his salary. So I did negotiate on a number of occasions that he was commissioned and paid to do scripts. After all, what was the point of commissioning somebody else, then to find the script wouldn't work out, meaning that Bob had to spend all his time re-doing it? So I actively encouraged him to do the stories I thought he would do the best job on. He didn't seek this, he wasn't pushy, at no point was he wanting to increase his own output on the show, and he was very, very professional. Script editors in those days were aware that they would be seen to be taking the bread out of the mouths of other writers if they commissioned themselves to do stories, so he was very aware of that situation. It was always me that said, "Now, I want you to do this, I want you to do that ..." and persuaded him with some arm-twisting, because he was quite tired by the end of it all.'

Bob's scripts for 'The Deadly Assassin' incorporated elements of real-life American political intrigue – most notably references to the 1963 assassination of American President John F Kennedy, and ideas and influences taken from the film *The Manchurian Candidate*[232] – alongside the notion of a fictitious three-dimensional artificial reality, housed in a computer known as the Matrix – all done nearly 25 years before the Keanu Reeves film *The Matrix* made mega-millions at the box office with the same basic premise. All of this was played out against the backdrop of a newly-constructed Time Lord society that drew its influences from the workings of scholastic and religious orthodoxy. As Hinchcliffe notes, Bob was keen to overhaul the way the Time Lords were portrayed in the series. 'I thought they were a snooty too-good-to-be-true lot,' Bob later said. 'So I decided to have a look at what might be an alternative – and more exciting – image.'[233]

David Maloney, who'd previously directed 'Genesis of the Daleks' and

232 *The Manchurian Candidate* was a successful 1959 book by Richard Condon. It told the story of an American diplomat who was brainwashed by the Russians into becoming an unwitting assassin. The book was turned into a film starring Frank Sinatra in 1962.
233 Robert Holmes Interview, *Renegade*: Issue 1, 1984 – Interview by Matthew Wicks.

'Planet of Evil' for the current production team, was asked to return for 'The Deadly Assassin'. Philip Hinchcliffe recalls that Bob offered some casting advice to Maloney for the role of the villainous Chancellor Goth. 'It was Bob who suggested Bernard Horsfall for Goth,' recalls Hinchcliffe. 'That was his idea, that casting. And I always thought that Bernard Horsfall was a sort of romantic-looking version of Bob himself! I've got this theory that people like to cast, unconsciously, people who look like themselves. You can apply this to Hollywood movies if you know what the producers look like! I've watched a lot of shows on television and seen the lead roles often are often cast in the image of the director or producer. I think there's a very unconscious and narcissistic principle at work, and I think that was at work here.'[234]

Although popular with the general public, 'The Deadly Assassin' provoked a quite vocal backlash from some elements of the emerging fan culture of the day. This generally stemmed not from any criticism of the plot, or of the script, but from the fact that the concept of the Time Lords as presented by Bob just didn't match the fans' perceptions of them as gleaned from glimpses in previous stories. The nascent *Doctor Who* Appreciation Society ran an annual season poll, where members could vote for their favourite new story of the year. 'The Deadly Assassin' came bottom of the DWAS's 1976/77 season poll.

Bob spent quite a bit of time over the next few years defending 'The Deadly Assassin' in the fan press, and one can only assume that he had been quite stung by the criticism he initially received for the story. In late 1977, he wrote the first of these defences, for the fanzine *Gallifrey*:

You ask my views about the reception given to 'The Deadly Assassin'. This story was very popular with the mass of the public; it seems to me it was disliked by members of the DWAS because it upset their concept of the Time Lords.

Let me first explain how the story developed. Philip Hinchcliffe asked me to write a story where the Doctor would be on his own, in between Sarah Jane leaving the series and Leela arriving. We decided to set it on Gallifrey and make that the reason for leaving Sarah behind.

I looked at all that was known about Gallifrey and it was very little. The only occasion when more than one Time Lord had been seen in the programme was at the end of 'The War Games' when a group of them condemned Patrick Troughton to exile on Earth for interfering

---

234 However, Bernard Horsfall had already appeared in *Doctor Who* three times prior to 'The Deadly Assassin' – and all in stories directed by David Maloney (Gulliver in 'The Mind Robber', a Time Lord in 'The War Games' and Taron in 'Planet of the Daleks'). So perhaps Maloney didn't need too much persuasion to cast Horsfall as Goth.

in the affairs of other races –

Hang on! Wasn't it usually a Time Lord who was seen despatching the Doctor on some important mission? And didn't this normally result in a bit of some distant planet being blown to smithereens? In that case wasn't is gross hypocrisy to punish Troughton by turning him into Jon Pertwee?

This new hypothesis seemed to fit better than the old belief that Time Lords were lofty-minded, cosmic Buddhists. It explained why the Doctor never went near Gallifrey; why in 'The Brain of Morbius' he flew into a rage over their interference and used the telling phrase, 'won't soil their lily-white hands'; and why Morbius himself called them 'pallid, devious worms'. It also, I thought, explained the disproportionately high number of villainous megalomaniacs emanating from Gallifrey – the Meddlesome Monk, the Master, Omega and Morbius.

I therefore decided to depict the Time Lords as an inward-looking oligarchy involved in constant political intrigue within their own version of the Palace of Westminster. This interpretation seems fully defensible in the light of the known facts.

Of course, we had often been told what splendid chaps they were, interested solely in the welfare of the Universe, but as it was usually a Time Lord who told us this anyway, it could be dismissed as a taradiddle.

Incidentally, to digress, a weakness of the serious *Who* fan is that he will take everything said in the programme as holy writ. In 'Pyramids of Mars', the Doctor, trapped in Sutekh's tomb, informed him that the controls of the TARDIS were isomorphic – that is, only he could operate them. Later in the series, when it appeared Leela had interfered with the controls, dozens of letters were received pointing out that the controls were isomorphic. But, in my view, the Doctor was clearly lying to Sutekh in order to get himself out of a tight spot.

Having settled, to my satisfaction, the function of the Time Lords, the rest of the story quickly fell into place. Obviously they had a 'dirty tricks' department they could disown if anything went wrong (*vide* the Troughton trial) and this idea, in turn, led to echoes of Watergate, the Kennedy assassination, Condon's *The Manchurian Candidate* and Rider Haggard's *She*. To my mind, *Doctor Who* is always at its best when its sources are showing.

Because I had to tell the story just through the Doctor, without a companion to carry the exposition, the script was technically innovative, with subjective and surrealist sequences that I felt widened the vocabulary of the show.

The script also had one other purpose. It brought back the Master in a transitional stage and, at the end, established that he has acquired several fresh leases of life. He is now set up ready to appear in some totally new guise should any future script editor wish to bring the character back into the series.

DWAS members, generally, were incensed by the show and used every possible twig to belabour me with. Somebody even criticised the title (and the programme's titles are deliberately lurid) on the grounds that 'Deadly' is tautological when qualifying 'Assassin'. But the Ismaili sectaries called hashashin were a bunch of dopes, after all. Trained in the lethal arts they may have been, but I'm sure they produced many inept, incompetent, unsuccessful assassins …

Somebody else (or perhaps it was the same gentleman) took me to task for carelessness in writing 'Trapped in a 50-storey building. Now you will have to search all 49 floors.' My idea was that even small kids would notice this. 'Hey Dad –' and Dad would then explain that in the UK and on Gallifrey the first storey of a building forms the ground floor as opposed to the practice in the USA where it is called the first floor. Well, maybe he would.' [235]

A few years later, in 1981, Simon M Lydiard, a fanzine editor, wrote to Bob and persuaded him to write an article about how he had envisaged the motivations and characterisations of the Time Lords as seen in 'The Deadly Assassin'. The resultant article, penned by Bob in May 1981, and entitled '"The Deadly Assassin" and Continuity', was duly published in Lydiard's fanzine *Skaro* in October 1981. It follows the same line of defence as the earlier article, but also makes some new points as well. It's reprinted here in full, with the kind permission of Lydiard.

Thank you for sending me your interesting article about 'The Deadly Assassin'. The cries of outrage that greeted this story when it was transmitted were mainly, as you say, from *Doctor Who* traditionalists.

During my time as the programme's script editor I found that DWAS members, on the whole, were so concerned with continuity

---

235 'Robert Holmes Speaks', *Gallifrey*: Issue 2, January 1978.

that very often they failed to see matters in a broader context. They were unable to see the wood for the trees, in fact. Case in point: in 'Pyramids of Mars' the Doctor tells the villain the controls of the TARDIS are isomorphic – only he can operate them. In a later story when someone else operated the controls I received dozens of letters pointing out this 'inconsistency'. Nobody seemed to have considered that the Doctor had a very good reason for lying!

When Philip Hinchcliffe asked me to develop a story set on the planet that in 'The Time Warrior' I named Gallifrey, I had first of all to decide what sort of people the Time Lords were. I noticed that over the years they had produced quite a few galactic lunatics – the Meddlesome Monk, the Master, Omega, Morbius … How did this square with the received notion that the Time Lords were a bunch of omnipotent do-gooders? Could it be that this notion had been put out by the Time Lords themselves? Heresy!

But the Doctor himself, when one thought about it, didn't seem too keen on them. Remember in 'Morbius' how he'd ranted about them not wanting to 'soil their lily-white hands'? Remember Linx saying that Sontaran Intelligence considered the Time Lords 'lacked the moral fibre to withstand a determined assault'?

Most damning of all, at the end of 'The War Games', had they not condemned the Doctor to exile for interfering in the affairs of other planets – and yet who had sent him on half these missions? They had! Obviously, either the Time Lords were all hypocrites or someone, unknown to their high command, was running a 'dirty tricks' department.

Once I took this view of the Time Lords, the bones of the story began to take shape. Other factors that influenced the story were that we were between girls so it seemed a good time to test whether or not the Doctor needed an assistant at all. Could the Doctor carry the programme on his own? (I think we proved he could but the first episode, before he became involved with other people, was very difficult to structure.) Philip also felt it was time to reintroduce the Master in a physically transitional stage. This was so that our successors, if they wished, would be free to appoint a new actor for this popular foe.

Finally, it was the first *Doctor Who* in years that I think did not feature a monster. We decided instead to go for the surrealistic sequence of Episode Three. This meant putting all our film efforts into one episode. And this meant writing the other three episodes totally for studio. David Maloney took all three difficulties in his stride, as he always does, and directed the show brilliantly.'[236]

Bob elaborated on some of these points when asked about this story during his 1985 interview for *Doctor Who Magazine*: 'People have often asked whether I based the Time Lord society on religious grounds, rather like the Vatican with Cardinals etc, but I saw it more as scholastic. I mean you have colleges of learning with Deans and all that. I decided that from what we knew of the Time Lords, we were wrong. People said they were august and remote people who were only concerned with keeping the structure of time in place. But then I looked back and discovered that they "framed" the Troughton Doctor and got him to do various things for them, and then hauled him up in front of them on trial – like the Americans persecuting McCarthy – so I decided there were two sides to them. They have one image that they project but they were something else to themselves which every now and then produced renegades like the Meddling Monk, Omega and the Master. Every so often somebody turns up who claims to be a Time Lord who is a megalomaniac, so they can't all be good, can they? Basically I set out to overturn a lot of established theory. Again by drawing on the American parallel I called the dirty tricks department the CIA.'[237]

The subject of continuity – making sure that new stories were fully consistent with past ones – was a preoccupation of organised *Doctor Who* fandom in the 1970s. Bob was once asked which were the most important elements of a *Doctor Who* story; plot, atmosphere, continuity, or characters? 'They're all important,' came the reply. 'Continuity is, of course, vital in a serial; atmosphere is something the writer can't control – it is a matter for the director; *Doctor Who*, being an action adventure show, needs to be strongly plotted with an original twist or two. This last, story construction, is the most essential, but I can never start constructing until I have the characters clear in my mind.'[238]

---

236 Although in both articles Bob makes a spirited defence of his perception of the Time Lords and how their society operated, his argument does contain a couple of fallacies. For instance, his point about the isomorphic TARDIS controls is somewhat invalidated by the fact that it quotes dialogue that he himself had written, while putting a spin onto the context that just wasn't evident in his actual script for 'Pyramids of Mars'. He was also the architect of the dialogue quotes from Morbius and Linx that he cited. Most telling of all, especially if one considers how he wrote for the second Doctor once again in his 1985 story 'The Two Doctors', is the fact that Bob was seemingly under the misapprehension that the Time Lords had directed a number of the Doctor's missions *prior* to his trial in 'The War Games'. In fact, it was only after his trial and subsequent exile to Earth that the Time Lords first began using the Doctor as an *agent provocateur*. Arguably, though, this doesn't diminish Bob's points in any way, as the hypocrisy he accuses the Time Lords of is certainly evident in some of their appearances in the third Doctor's era, as well as in early fourth Doctor stories such as 'Genesis of the Daleks'. Incidentally, his recollection of the character of the Meddling Monk might well go back to his discussions with Donald Tosh in 1965, when he first proposed writing for the series at the same time as the Monk was being unveiled to viewers.
237 Interview – Robert Holmes, *Doctor Who Magazine*: Issue 100, May 1985.
238 Robert Holmes Interview, *Type 40*: Issue 1, 1978.

Bob spent most of May and June 1976 writing his four scripts for 'The Deadly Assassin'. On Friday 7 May 1976, he also commissioned Robert Banks Stewart to write a story outline for a prospective six-part story to finish off the fourteenth season. This was entitled 'The Foe from the Future', and had come about out of discussions Bob had had with Hinchcliffe about doing a Jack the Ripper-type story. Stewart then took this notion and spun it into a tale that featured a villain from the future conducting experiments in a sleepy little village in modern-day Devon. Stewart delivered his storyline on Tuesday 1 June 1976, and both Bob and Hinchcliffe agreed that it would make a suitable story to close the season on.

Bob delivered all four of his scripts for 'The Deadly Assassin' on Thursday 17 June 1976. The following week, he called Chris Boucher in for a meeting at the *Doctor Who* production office, to discuss the opportunity of him contributing another new story for the series. By this time, Bob and Hinchcliffe had decided that Leela would continue as the Doctor's companion, at least until the end of the season.

'I was told after the scripts went in for "The Face of Evil" that they quite liked the character, the girl, Leela,' recalled Boucher, 'and they thought it might be an idea to ride her on to another adventure, to carry her forward. Basically, Bob said, "Would you like to do another one, a four-parter, straight away? Because your scripts introduced the character, and obviously you know more about her than other writers, so would you like to do another one, a four-parter?" To which I replied, "Which of my limbs do you want me to cut off in order for me to be able to do this …!"'

And so on Tuesday 22 June 1976, Boucher was commissioned to write a storyline for a four-part adventure with a working title 'Planet of the Robots', which he delivered a couple of weeks later.[239]

The basic premise of Boucher's new story was one of the ideas that Bob and Hinchcliffe had toyed with when they had their initial planning discussions for this season some months earlier. It incorporated elements from Isaac Asimov's 'Three Laws of Robotics' concepts, alongside an Agatha Christie-esque whodunit plot, all set on a mobile mine on a faraway world.

Boucher recalls these elements being given to him so that he could incorporate them into his new story: 'I remember being told something about an Agatha Christie enclosed story. The robots were also fed into the mixer. I know when I looked at it afterwards, I thought, "My God, I've ripped *Dune*[240]

---

239 It's possible that this slot in the season only came free when 'The Hand of Fear' was moved forward in the production running order. This was the only season that Bob and Philip Hinchcliffe produced that had the same transmission order as production order for its stories.
240 *Dune* was a 1954 science fiction novel by Frank Herbert, set on the dessert world of Arrakis, which is mined for its

off here in a fairly major way!" There was a submarine element in it, there were all sort of odds and ends in it. I like to think it was my idea; the scripts were mine, with some additions from Bob, I have to say.'

Boucher was commissioned to write the scripts for 'Planet of the Robots' on Tuesday 20 July 1976[241], and although the target delivery date was given as Monday 9 August for all four episodes, Boucher once again delivered them one at a time. The script for Part One was on Bob's desk on Monday 2 August, and the story was subsequently retitled 'The Robots of Death' before entering production.

Boucher recalls one significant addition that Bob made to his script for the first episode: 'In "The Robots of Death", the very first scene, the one where they're all lying about in the cabin having massages and so forth, was a much more utilitarian scene from my point of view, and there were only two or three lines in my version of the scene. As transmitted, that scene is almost entirely Bob. I like to think that might have been because the script was slightly under length, and so it was necessary to pad it out a little. But the rest of it was pretty much me. And anything Bob did didn't detract from what I'd done; he only added to it. You can't complain about that, really, can you?'

At about this point in time – the summer of 1976 – both Bob and Hinchcliffe had decided that they wanted to leave *Doctor Who* at the end of production of the season they were working on. To that end, they had drafted out between them a proposal for a prospective new science fiction series that was designed for a more adult audience than *Doctor Who*. The working title of this was *Lituvin 40*, and the proposal was put to Bill Slater, the Head of Serials at the BBC, who was initially extremely enthusiastic about it. Both Bob and Hinchcliffe hoped that *Lituvin 40* would be their next project at the BBC after *Doctor Who*.

'We did come up with a science fiction idea, which for about five minutes we thought the BBC was going to commission,' recalls Hinchcliffe. 'Bob was going to write the scripts, and I was going to produce it, but I can't remember why it never went ahead. I think I went off to do something else, and Bob got involved with something else, and we didn't really continue with it. We thought we would set ourselves the challenge to come up with a new *Quatermass*-type of programme. It wasn't actually going to resemble *Quatermass* as a concept, but we wanted to elicit the same sort of public response in the mid-1970s that *Quatermass* had managed to do in the 1950s. It was going to be a completely contemporary, adult science fiction series.

'As I remember, it began with a husband who returns home to find that his

supply of the rare spice 'melange'.
241 As this date would have coincided with Bob's aborted holiday to Italy – see subsequent paragraphs – the commission would have been handled by Philip Hinchcliffe.

wife has disappeared. The oven's on, the evening meal's half-cooked, but she's vanished into thin air. He tries to find her, and eventually tracks her down to an institution, where he learns that his wife, along with a number of other people who have also mysteriously "vanished", is being held for treatment. He learns that his wife was taking a new experimental drug, Lituvin 40, which had been prescribed to her to treat her migraine headaches. The others held in the institution are all people who have been part of the Lituvin 40 experimental drug programme. While trying to expose this, the husband keeps coming up against shadowy figures in his quest to get to the bottom of the mysterious institution. He learns that the authorities and government are complicit in the cover-up of the side effects of Lituvin 40, whatever they may be. He learns that the man who invented Lituvin 40 synthesised the drug after dreaming about the chemical formula, and could never really explain how he managed to dream up the idea. It turns out that that the chemical formula originated from outer space, and was in a coded message that was aimed at Earth, which some people were susceptible to in their sleep. We eventually learn that Lituvin 40 is an alien chemical, which is designed to re-engineer the whole human race into a new, alien life form …

'So we did come up with an idea, and Bob was going to write it, but in the end it didn't get commissioned. Not because it wasn't good, but because I think we both went on to do something else.'

At about this time, Bob also contacted Robert Banks Stewart and informally told him to begin work on scripting 'The Foe from the Future', the six-part story intended to conclude the fourteenth season. Safe in the knowledge that the season was now fully commissioned, and with Part One of 'The Masque of Mandragora' ready to start the season off on BBC1 at the end of September, and also perhaps contemplating life away from the rigours of working on *Doctor Who* in the not-too-distant future, Bob went off on a well-earned holiday in July 1976, his first since becoming script editor on *Doctor Who*.

It did not go as planned, as Bob later wrote:

'I managed only one holiday during my time as script editor. After I'd finished "The Deadly Assassin", and with the rest of the season apparently sewn up, my wife and I slipped off for a bit of Italian sunshine.

'Now this is a funny thing. We never made it.

'On the *Autobahn* somewhere north of Munich the love of my life perforated a stomach ulcer. Our hilarity knew no bounds. Ankle-deep in blood, feet slipping on pedals festooned with tripe, I turned off at the next *Ausfahrt* and fetched up in a place called Pfaffenhosen, which means Parson's Socks in English.

'I had to hang around in Parson's Socks for three weeks while my wife was being repaired in the local *Krankenhaus*. When I returned to Shepherd's Bush there was a tangible air of crisis about the place. The irredeemable scoundrel I had engaged to write the concluding six-parter in the season had left a note on my desk. He had taken a job with Thames TV and couldn't carry out the assignment.

'By that time David Maloney, the director, was practically under starter's orders. I think I wrote "The Talons of Weng-Chiang" at rather more than four words an hour ...'[242]

Bob's wife, Patricia, was indeed taken ill *en route* to their holiday destination. Patricia's brother, Ian Watson, recalls how she was hospitalised in Germany. 'She went into a hospital, and she was quite surprised that they recommended she drink a bottle of stout a day as part of her cure!' he says with a grin.

While Bob was having his unexpected extended break away from the BBC and from England, several things occurred. The first was that Philip Hinchcliffe began to have a change of heart about leaving *Doctor Who*, and was now actively considering staying on to produce the fifteenth season. The second was that Bryan Cowgill, the Controller of BBC1, had decided that the fourteenth season of *Doctor Who* should begin slightly sooner than the production team had initially been told it would, on Saturday 4 September.

The third thing was that Robert Banks Stewart had contacted Hinchcliffe to tell him that he'd just accepted a job offer from Thames Television to become script editor on a new drama series they were making, entitled *Rooms*. He was dreadfully sorry to have to let Bob and the *Doctor Who* team down, but as he'd never officially been commissioned and contracted to write the scripts for 'The Foe from the Future', then he really wasn't in any position to turn away the job offer from Thames.

'Robert Banks Stewart was originally down to do the final show of the season,' recalls Hinchcliffe. 'Bob had originally created the idea; it was a Jack the Ripper-type story. I think Bob loved all that. He had all those ideas; the only input I might have had was that I probably just said we could do a big rat! So there was a general basic notion of what the story might be. Maybe it was a Master story as well ...? And that was all discussed with Robert Banks Stewart, and so he was set to work on the storyline. And then what happened was that he said he couldn't really do the scripts, that he'd got other commitments. Suddenly he had something else to do, and so we had a hole in the schedule.'

---

242 From 'A Life of Hammer and Tongs' by Robert Holmes, published in *The Doctor Who File* by Peter Haining (W H Allen, 1986).

Bob's unexpectedly late return from his holiday coincided with this crisis (and also scuppered a radio side-project of his – see the next chapter). He was given extended leave from the BBC until Patricia's health improved sufficiently for him to return to work, which he finally did in August 1976. He then spent September working with Boucher to get the scripts for 'The Robots of Death' ready for production.

This still left the question of what to do about the final, six-part story of the season, and both Hinchcliffe and Bob realised that there was only one real solution. Bob had to write it himself.

'I said to Bob, "You know you're going to have to do this", recalls Hinchcliffe. 'I think he was creatively excited at the notion of it, but he was also very, *very* tired by that time; he'd been at the grindstone for three seasons, with a lot of writing of original stories, and a lot of rewriting of other scripts. Initially he refused. He said, "I can't. I just can't. I'm absolutely dead on my feet." He'd been off on holiday, and then his wife wasn't very well, so it was very bad timing. I put him under a lot of pressure, and really twisted his arm to do this, and I managed to prevail. I think he refused to do it to begin with, but in the end, he did agree. Once he got into it, I think he really enjoyed it, and he realised he was doing good work. But it was a tough time for him, and a tough assignment for him.'

'I'd just come back from holiday in Germany, my wife ended up in hospital, she had burst an ulcer,' recalled Bob some years later. 'We were heading for Italy, and she suddenly collapsed, and there was blood everywhere, and so I took her to hospital. And I had just finished "The Deadly Assassin" before I went; it was my only holiday – some holiday! – and I had to be away for about 16 days longer than I expected. I came home to find my writer, who was doing the end-of-season six-parter, had taken a job at Thames and wasn't available. And so I had to leap in and try to think of something.'

Hinchcliffe set in motion the now-familiar sequence of internal paperwork and requisitions needed to allow Bob to write for the series yet again under the BBC staff contribution procedure. Once more, this raised eyebrows in the BBC's Copyright Department, who queried the request. Hinchcliffe had to send them a tersely worded missive, telling them he had been given permission by his Head of Department to commission Bob to write up to two stories per season, and that this was Bob's second commission for this particular season.

Bob also recalled that the writing of this story in particular brought him into conflict with the Writers' Guild, who weren't exactly happy at the number of times he'd apparently commissioned himself to write for *Doctor Who* while he was the script editor on the show. 'There was a bit of trouble. The Screen Writers' Guild have an objection to script editors commissioning themselves, but for me it's all right, because I have a previous track record of writing for the series myself. If I wasn't a script editor, I'd probably be working as a freelance writer anyway. I wrote "The Ark in Space" as I was joining, and was "excused" for that season, but for my second, I wasn't allowed. All I could do was tinker about with other people's. But for my third, I wrote two.'[243]

Although it was a tough time for Bob, he rose magnificently to the challenge. He got down to writing the first three episodes of his new story, which he titled 'The Talons of Greel', in October 1976, with the filming dates just a few weeks away by now. The director of the story was David Maloney, who had recently handled 'The Deadly Assassin', and who, by now, had become a firm admirer of Bob's work. Although the scripts were going to be delivered late, leaving Maloney less time than normal to scout for locations and to cast the story, he trusted Bob to deliver the goods. Bob decided to use the Victorian setting that he and Hinchcliffe had initially considered as a backdrop for the debut of the new companion character (before Leela was settled on), mixed in with a few elements taken from Robert Banks Stewart's storyline for 'The Foe from the Future'.

'I had to sit down and think of a story, and then write it,' recalled Bob. 'And it was a six-parter, and I don't like six-parters. So I wrote the first four parts, and gave them to David, and he was quite happy, and I actually spent about another ten days sitting at home trying to think what I was going to do with the last two parts. I did this dog-leg thing where I went off in a totally different area, away from the music hall set-up. And I thought David did it terribly well, and it worked.'

Bob wrote the scripts for 'The Talons of Greel' throughout October 1976. His completed scripts for the first three episodes were handed over to Hinchcliffe on Monday 8 November 1976, with the one for Part Four following ten days later. Bob's original script for the first episode included a scene that was cut from the final programme, showing the Chinese magician character Chang directing the homunculus Mr Sin telepathically as he attacked the young cabbie Buller. Additionally, shortly after Bob delivered the script for the opening episode, it was discovered that it was slightly underrunning, so he then had to go back and write a few more pages of material. As originally scripted, the first episode was due to end with the coolie who was following the Doctor throwing his hatchet at the Doctor's defenceless back. To make up the necessary time, Bob had to resolve this threat and then introduce a new cliff-hanger scene, as the Doctor and Leela investigate the sewers and

---

243 Robert Holmes Interview, *Gallifrey*: Issue 1, September 1977 – Interview by Tim Dollin.

encounter the giant rat for the first time. This also required a small amount of restructuring to the opening of the second episode.

'I'm not a fan of Sherlock Holmes, although I've read all the books,' mused Bob, 'but I am a fan of that *fictitious* Victorian period, with fog, gas lamps, Hansom cabs ... music halls. We look back on it and say that's what it was like, but of course it wasn't. People were slaving in dark, satanic mills and starving in London gutters, but the popular concept of Victoriana is this, with colourful language. I think David Maloney was a wonderful director, he got it all so right. The only thing that went wrong was pointed out afterwards by Graeme McDonald, then Head of Serials, which was the rat! The special effects department made this marvellous giant rat, as long as two tables, and they worked from scale drawings and pictures – it looked marvellous. But when it came on the box it had little pink ears, was well groomed and totally unlike a sewer rat, which should have looked scurvious and scaly and greasy and bleeding here and there, with horrible yellow teeth. Instead it was a nice, cuddly sort of rat!'[244]

Two of Bob's most memorable supporting characters appeared in this story; the theatre impresario Henry Gordon Jago, and the police doctor George Litefoot. However, in Bob's initial draft of the script for the first episode, Jago was named Sachs instead. It may or may not have been a coincidence that at the time, BBC1 had a long-running hit television show called *The Good Old Days*, which recreated the atmosphere and ambience of the Victorian music hall, complete with period costume (even for the audience), and which was compered by actor Leonard Sachs, who used the same sort of dextrous verbiage and contrived conundrums that personified the character of Jago in the final version of Bob's story.

Bob recalled how Jago and Litefoot very nearly became the stars of their own spin-off BBC series after they had appeared in *Doctor Who*: 'I remember it being mentioned, but it "fell through" because I never followed the suggestion up. Remember, I was busy at the time, and setting up a series takes a lot of hard work and selling. And I'm not very good at either.'[245]

Although Hinchcliffe had made his intention to stay in charge of *Doctor Who* for another season known to his boss, Bill Slater, some weeks earlier, Slater had been pondering long and hard about *Doctor Who*'s creative future. While the creative team of Hinchcliffe and Holmes had reinvigorated the show over the previous three years, delivering consistent ratings usually in excess of

---

244 Interview – Robert Holmes, *Doctor Who Magazine*: Issue 100, May 1985. Graeme McDonald succeeded Bill Slater as Head of Serials just prior to transmission of 'The Talons of Weng-Chiang'.
245 Robert Holmes Interview, *Renegade*: Issue 1, 1984 – Interview by Matthew Wicks.

10 million viewers, Slater was also aware of the criticisms that were now being levelled at it in some quarters, in terms of its levels of horror and violence.

Mary Whitehouse, the public face of the National Viewers' and Listeners' Association, had a particular grudge against *Doctor Who*, which she felt was regularly overstepping the boundaries for a family programme, and she gained much coverage in the press for her complaints. She had recently singled out 'The Seeds of Doom' as a particular offender, complaining: 'Strangulation – by hand, by claw, by obscene vegetable matter – is the latest gimmick, sufficiently close up so they get the point. And just for a little variety show the children how to make a Molotov Cocktail.'[246]

Because of all this rather negative publicity, Bill Slater was now giving serious consideration to moving Philip Hinchcliffe away from *Doctor Who* and appointing another BBC producer, Graham Williams, in his place, despite Hinchcliffe indicating that he was keen to stay on the series for at least another year. Slater had more or less decided that this was what he was going to do, when Mary Whitehouse launched another broadside at the BBC over *Doctor Who* in early November 1976. The focus of her ire in this instance was the second and third episodes of 'The Deadly Assassin', and especially the events leading up to the traditional cliff-hanger episode endings. She complained in a letter to Hinchcliffe, which she also copied in to the BBC's Board of Governors: 'You will be aware, no doubt, that this Association has expressed its concern about *Dr Who* on a number of occasions. I write, in anger and despair, following last Saturday's episode. In anger, because, at a time when little children would be viewing, you showed violence of a quite unacceptable kind. It permeated the programme but reached a climax when the children saw one of the characters – in modern dress – in flames, and then a shocking sequence in which this character, after a viscous close up fight, got Dr Who by the throat and held him under the water until he was drowned. Shots which could only be described as sadistic.' Whitehouse then quoted the BBC's own guidelines on the portrayal of violence on television. These guidelines pointed out that young children in particular can be affected by cliff-hanger endings, and that care should be taken if characters that they identify with are shown to be in too much peril. Whitehouse then continued, 'How can you possibly therefore – apart from anything else – justify the closing shots of the last two episodes? In the one, Dr Who's foot is caught between a railway line as a train rushes towards him and the last shot is of his agonised face. In the other, the last shot was of Dr Who's apparently dead face lying still under the water.'

---

246 As recounted in the book *Whitehouse* by Michael Tracey and David Morrison (Macmillan, 1979).

Chris Boucher recalls this period quite vividly, as within a few months, Whitehouse would go on to criticise one of his stories, 'The Robots of Death', over what she considered to be its graphic depiction of strangulation. 'I thought what was going on then was horrendous,' recalls Boucher. '*Doctor Who* was under sustained attack, but so was pretty much the whole of the BBC, and television in general. It was sad. Sir Hugh Greene[247], so I'm told, had said about Mary Whitehouse, "Be polite to her, but don't let her into the building". Which everybody had interpreted as, "Ignore the woman". But there was a failure of nerve, eventually. I suppose it was part of the Thatcher thing as well, where people were not prepared to take responsibility for other people; not their economic welfare, not their education, nothing. But they were prepared to take responsibility for their moral inexactitude. Whitehouse was a self-promoting monster. I think she was one of the worst things after Thatcher to happen to this country – but I digress. I wouldn't pass the buck, because I thought that what Philip and Bob did with *Doctor Who* was excellent. Not just because I wrote for it, but because it was strong, I felt it was clever, I felt it was taking its audience seriously. And the attacks were shameful.'

This latest broadside from Whitehouse confirmed the BBC's resolve in their decision to move Hinchcliffe off *Doctor Who*. They instead made him producer of their new police series *Target*[248], while Graham Williams, who had done all the initial groundwork on that series, was installed as the new person in charge of *Doctor Who*, with a remit to tone down the violence and horror. Much of this reorganisation was done without any consultation with Hinchcliffe. Williams was introduced as the programme's new producer to (a slightly surprised) Hinchcliffe, Bob and the rest of the *Doctor Who* production team during rehearsals for 'The Robots of Death' in early November 1976.

At the same time, Slater took Bob to one side. He understood that Bob was also looking to leave *Doctor Who* at the end of the current season, but asked him to reconsider his decision, if only for a relatively short time. It was thought by Slater that with a new producer at the helm, the show needed some degree of stability in the production office. So Bob was reluctantly persuaded to stay on as script editor, at least for six months longer than he wanted to.

The successful production partnership of Hinchcliffe and Holmes was to be split up. At the time, Hinchcliffe felt that Bob was still enjoying himself on the series, but also thought that the point was rapidly approaching when he needed to cut his losses and move on as well. 'Bob certainly enjoyed his time

---

247 Sir Hugh Carleton Greene had been Director-General of the BBC between 1960 and 1969.
248 *Target* was a gritty cop show developed by producer Graham Williams for the BBC. Williams was moved off *Target* and onto *Doctor Who*, while Philip Hinchcliffe was moved in the opposite direction, in what was, in effect, a job swap.

with me, but he did work very, very hard during the three seasons we were working together, and we did have a lot of fun. I think we both felt there was a lot of creativity going on. Sometimes if you work on a long-running television series, it does become a bit of a chore, and I hope Bob never felt like that on *Doctor Who*. I think there was always a strong creative spark going on in him and in the work. He worked hard, and I'm pretty certain he enjoyed it.'

Hinchcliffe remained as producer of *Doctor Who* during the final weeks of 1976, while Williams stayed very much in the background, quietly working on his own plans for the following season. Bob then finally finished writing the final two scripts of 'The Talons of Greel' in early December 1976.

Bob was able to visit the location filming of 'The Talons of Weng-Chiang' – as his story was now re-titled – along with Hinchcliffe in late December 1976. This was the first time since 'The Time Warrior' in 1973 that Bob had managed to go and watch *Doctor Who* being filmed. As he recalled: 'This was the only other time that I visited a location. Some of the filming was in Wapping, which, the way Philip drives, is only a minute or so from Shepherd's Bush. We arrived in the gloaming and watched people from the props department spreading artificial horse dung over the road markings. Well, I assume it was artificial. If not, Philip's car must have needed a good vacuuming …

'A nice man named John Bennett was playing Weng-Chiang. While the horse muck was still being deployed, a giggle of office girls, craning out of an upper window, sent down an autograph book for Tom Baker to sign. "And can John Bennett sign it as well?" one of them called.

'John raised his almond eyes skywards. "By the soul of my sainted godfather," he said unprintably, "why have I just spent three-something hours in make-up!"

'That's all I can remember about "The Talons of Weng Chiang".'[249]

'The Talons of Weng-Chiang' is a masterpiece of a story, which hardly ever betrays the haste and urgency in which it was commissioned and written. Bob perfectly captures that 'fictional' Victorian feel that also percolates through most modern adaptations of the works of Dickens or Conan Doyle. The dialogue, the characters, the plot; these are all seamlessly interwoven to produce a tale that still gets held up as an example of *Doctor Who* at its very, very best.

The popular press also praised the serial at the time, although not without reservations. With Bob and Hinchcliffe now unashamedly making *Doctor Who* for an older audience demographic than any of their predecessors,

---

249 From 'A Life of Hammer and Tongs' by Robert Holmes, published in *The Doctor Who File* by Peter Haining (W H Allen, 1986).

Stanley Reynolds, writing in *The Times*, couldn't help but note how this was perhaps a double-edged sword for the series: 'The period charm of Victorian London is caught well enough. Also the prejudices of the time. One wondered how much of a good influence this might have on the young. But *Doctor Who* has changed. It is no longer for the young. Leela, for example, is much the sexiest space-mate the Doctor has ever had and these stories are much more complicated than in previous series. *Doctor Who*, we are told, is now aimed at the intelligent 14 year old. Personally, I find the new *Who* more interesting, but it has rather spoiled the quiet of a Saturday evening. Where the little ones used to be silent they are now full of questions, puzzlement, and I think, boredom. It is something of a shame.'[250]

In the weeks that followed the production of 'The Talons of Weng-Chiang', *Doctor Who*'s new producer, Graham Williams, informed Bob of his plan to make the next season one long, interconnected storyline. The Doctor was about to go on an epic quest to recover the six segments of the Key to Time.

---

250 *The Times*, 28 February 1977.

CHAPTER NINETEEN
BLOODY ALIENS!
1975-1977

While *Doctor Who* consumed practically all of Bob's professional time between 1974 and 1976, he did have one side project that he dabbled with during this period.

Back in December 1967, Bob had written a storyline for a proposed science fiction drama called *Schizo* (see Chapter Five for details), which it seems he touted to various television companies, without success. Then, just after he had been commissioned to write 'The Krotons' in 1968, Bob reworked the *Schizo* storyline (retitled 'Aliens in the Blood') to incorporate the second Doctor, Jamie and Zoe, only for Terrance Dicks to turn the story down, feeling it wasn't really suitable for *Doctor Who* (see Chapter Six). Now, in the mid-1970s, Bob decided to rework and rewrite his series outline, now titled *Aliens in the Blood,* one more time. For the first page of his new proposal, Bob retyped, almost word-for-word, most of his original 1967 *Schizo* series outline, which now formed the introduction. However, he then added some newly-written material to set the scene and get the ball rolling on his proposed series:

It starts with a funeral. Gordon Dexter, the only doctor on the island of Luig, fell off a cliff one foggy night.

John Cornelius arrives from London for the funeral. He is a neurosurgeon, possibly the greatest man in his field in the whole world.

After the funeral, he is talking to Dexter's housekeeper when Professor Curtis Lark arrives from New Guinea. Lark, an American psychologist and anthropologist – and a Nobel Prize winner – has abandoned medical orthodoxy for the wilder shores of psychiatry … voodoo, witchcraft, paranormal phenomena.

Why these two brilliant men should turn up for the funeral of an obscure GP would be a matter of speculation if the islanders had ever heard of them. But Luig is a remote sort of place where the last great event, still discussed, was a brief visit from Queen Victoria.

After the tragedy that marred his career, Dexter had liked it for this very remoteness, seeking peace as a humble healer of croup and measles.

Lark and Cornelius, his oldest friends from medical student days, had tried to dissuade him from opting out of life. And they had failed. From then on their three lives had taken very different courses.

Cornelius had reached the heights of his respected profession. A KBE round the corner. A pillar of the establishment. Precise, meticulous, donnish and a widower.

Lark had become a wanderer, walking the jungles of the world, occasionally appearing to publish an explosive thesis and attend a Christening, then vanishing again. He has 11 children, ranging from infants to young adults and all tarred with genius; he is an intensely proud father who can't stand family life.

And Dexter had ended at the wrong end of a cliff.

Lark and Cornelius, drawn to the funeral of their old friend, soon become certain that his death was not quite the simple accident that everyone is pretending.

Dexter's medical notebooks reveal a patient, professional interest in the abnormally high incidence of schizophrenia on Luig. His investigations reach back almost 20 years, from soon after his arrival on the island, and only in recent months has he begun to suspect the incredible truth.

Lark and Cornelius can't accept it, either, at first. But they check Dexter's case records. He has noticed a pattern in the ramblings of schizophrenic patients. They are like badly-tuned radios receiving signals from several different stations.

Dexter discovered that while his patients might be evolutionary failures, an unknown number of successful mutants were already at large in society.

'At large' because it soon becomes clear that the Mk II Human feels no more kinship for his ancestors than we feel for the apes.

Lark and Cornelius have their first brush with death and are made aware of the immense power of these aliens in the blood.

This makes the basis of the first episode.

Lark and Cornelius, whose talents and characters are complementary, join force to fight the invisible enemy.

The mutants are all mental prodigies – though they may take care to hide this fact – and they possess faculties of telepathy and ESP that in a less permissive society would have led to their being burnt at the stake.

Counterbalancing their great gifts, however, the mutants have lost less 'useful' qualities. They are incapable of feeling compassion, love, pity, tenderness – though, of course, they may counterfeit these emotions where required.

The mutants form a small, hostile elite working separately and together in the centres of power. Their aim is to manipulate society to create conditions favourable for their own development at the expense of their unwitting hosts.

They have developed highly advanced and 'inhuman' biological techniques for increasing their species but it is by the manipulation of society that the mutants hope to achieve the vital breakthrough.

The Mk II Human is better fitted for the conditions of life in the 20th Century than the old model. Any intensification of those conditions must, therefore, work to the advantage of the mutants. Ultimately, they seek to so degrade, depress, and fragmentise society that there can be no organised opposition.

Until then, they rely on stealth.

Until then, anything that spreads alarm and dissension, anything that increases tensions at international, national, or community level, anything that causes disruption or confusion, anything – in short – that reduces the quality of life, is to their benefit.

Lark and Cornelius, alone, understand this danger and the nature of their enemy. The series is about their battle with the mutants.

They are alone because Dexter's records are destroyed in the first episode and without these, painstakingly compiled over the years, there is no evidence the mutants exist.

From the first episode to the last, Lark and Cornelius are under constant attack. They travel the world in their fight to frustrate the mutants' plans and to root out individual mutants from the corridors of power.

They are brilliant men with vast resources of knowledge, influence, and money. But it's like fighting SMERSH, the Mafia, and the Magic Circle all at the same time.

They have their hands full.

The series has a sci-fi basis but many – perhaps a majority – of the stories will have a normal adventure plotline. The world cannot be on the brink of a cataclysm every week.

One hopes also that the series would generate interest beyond the level of the immediate action. To a new, super-race, man might seem little more than an inquisitive monkey playing about in a powder magazine. But he has established dominion over the Earth – and not merely by his unique abilities to commit rape or to contract syphilis.

He is also unique in his desire to compose symphonies or to construct radio-telescopes.

Any challenge to man's supremacy, therefore, contains deep philosophical implications which Lark and Cornelius might well dwell upon in their few spare moments.

This new version of the outline is dated Monday 10 September 1973. This was about the time that Bob was writing to Bill Slater with his ideas for *Dial M for Murder*, and just prior to his being asked to take over from Terrance Dicks as script editor of *Doctor Who*. Perhaps Bob touted this idea to the BBC as a proposal for a television series, or perhaps he just shelved any thoughts of progressing with it once the *Doctor Who* job came up. Either way, the idea remained in his files for another 18 months …

Bob saw himself primarily as a television scriptwriter, and had never really considered writing scripts for radio drama. However, radio drama had come knocking on Bob's door, in a rather unexpected manner. In the autumn of 1969, BBC Radio 4 began a series adaptation of the (still popular) television show *Dr Finlay's Casebook*. The producers wanted to make adaptations of episodes from the television run, and Bob's 1964 episode 'The Hallelujah Stakes' was one of the first 13 selected to be adapted and remade in this manner. At the time, Bob was busy working on *Honey Lane* and the *Doctor Who* story 'Spearhead from Space', and so agreed to allow Pat Dunlop (who was now script editor on the television series of *Dr Finlay's Casebook*) to adapt his original script.[251]

A few years later, in late 1972, the fourth radio series of *Dr Finlay's Casebook* featured another episode of Bob's. This time it was 'Charity, Dr Finlay'.[252] Two years later, the fifth radio series featured an adaptation of 'The True Lochiel'.[253] Series Six included an adaptation of 'The Old Indomitable'. [254] All of these scripts were adapted for radio by Pat Dunlop.

Perhaps there was some connection between these radio adventures of *Dr Finlay* and Bob's out-of-the-blue submission of an idea for a science fiction radio series to Richard Imison, the BBC's Script Editor for Radio Drama, in early 1975. After all, this was the first time Bob had gone looking for a commission to write a radio series. Bob's agent, Jon Thurley, wrote to Imison on Monday 10 February 1975, offering him Bob's idea.

And what was Bob's idea? *Aliens in the Blood*.

Imison's first reaction was to suggest that it would make a better one-off

---

251 The episode, retitled more simply as 'Hallelujah Stakes', was aired on BBC Radio 4 on Tuesday 28 April 1970.
252 This episode was aired on BBC Radio 4 on Monday 18 December 1972.
253 This episode was aired on BBC Radio 4 on Tuesday 19 February 1974.
254 This episode was aired on BBC Radio 4 on Tuesday 19 November 1974.

90-minute radio play than an ongoing radio series. It would seem that Bob disagreed with him, however.

For whatever reason, things then cooled on *Aliens in the Blood* for the next six months. (Bob was tied up in the rigours of script editing Season Thirteen of *Doctor Who*, rewriting 'Pyramids of Mars', and other such pressing matters.) But then, in August 1975, Bob was commissioned by John Dyas, a producer working in the Light Entertainment department of the BBC's radio division, to write a 30-minute pilot script for *Aliens in the Blood*. Whether Imison passed over Bob's proposal to Dyas or whether Bob contacted him directly isn't clear. But Bob was commissioned to write one script, and was offered a contract that would pay him for this, and that also set down the terms for future payment of fees should further instalments of *Aliens in the Blood* be commissioned.

Bob *seems* to have written a script for the first episode of *Aliens in the Blood*, but this was returned to him in early September 1975 by the BBC's Copyright Department. I say 'seems', as there is some confusion in the surviving paperwork (detailed below) as to whether the script was one written specifically for this commission, or one Bob had first submitted to the BBC some years previously, possibly when he was trying to interest Richard Imison in the idea. There was also then some further confusion amongst the various parties as to what terms had actually been agreed, and what payment Bob was entitled to as a member of BBC staff, albeit one from television drama writing a radio script. A suggestion was made at one point by John Dyas that Bob should be asked to prepare a number of story synopses for future episodes in order to warrant the fee paid to him up front.

Perhaps as a result of all this, Bob's agent was able to negotiate a higher fee than the BBC had initially offered for the scripts of any further episodes of *Aliens in the Blood*. This was a fee that was comparatively high for radio drama – but quite substantially less than television writers were being paid at the time.

But an internal BBC memo from Monday 22 March 1976 shows that Dyas was prepared to commit to a full series of six 30-minute episodes of *Aliens in the Blood* on the strength of what Bob had delivered so far. He did feel there was a small amount of rewriting needed on the first episode, but he hoped to have the rewritten script, plus the other five new ones, delivered to him by Bob on or around Friday 16 July 1976. Bob and Dyas met up in early April 1976, and Dyas outlined his conditions for going ahead with the commission. Bob didn't raise any objections to his requests, or to the deadline, and the two of them went their separate ways with an agreement in place.

The contracts were sent out to Bob, but Bob – or, to be more specific, Bob's agent – didn't get around to signing and returning them to the BBC's legal department until the end of May 1976. The delivery date of 16 July 1976 was still on the paperwork, however …

Meanwhile, the Head of BBC Radio Light Entertainment, Con Mahoney, had got wind of the plans for the series, and was quite surprised at the high fee that Bob had been offered. He queried the figure with the Head of Copyright, who used Bob's vast experience as a television writer as justification for the deal. And as Bob's deal was structured so that he would get 50 percent of his fee paid up front, and the balance on transmission of the series, he was now owed half of his fee on five more scripts, which the BBC paid to Jon Thurley in early June. Meanwhile, it was noted that the script for the first episode still had not been accepted by the producer.

However, Bob's delivery date came and went with nothing further being written for *Aliens in the Blood*. For Bob's part, he was busy writing the scripts for the *Doctor Who* story 'The Deadly Assassin' during May and June 1976. Once that was completed, he and Patricia planned to go away on holiday. So Bob packed his portable typewriter, planning to work on these radio scripts as he lounged about in the Mediterranean sun …

Unfortunately, as recounted in the previous chapter, Patricia was taken ill and Bob was forced to take an extended break from the BBC while she recovered, not returning to work until early August 1976. When he got back to his desk at the *Doctor Who* production office, he found a number of desperate memos from John Dyas awaiting him, chasing him for the scripts of *Aliens in the Blood*.

Bob wrote to Dyas on Friday 6 August 1976: 'I came back from "holiday" – what a holiday – but although I took my typewriter, the circumstances were such that nothing got written. And the situation I find now is that, in my absence, Bryan Cowgill, our controller, has pushed forward transmission dates for the season, effectively eliminating the two month slack period I was counting on.

'I am still working out dates and commitments and will be getting in touch with Jon Thurley early next week to let him know what, if anything, I can do. At the moment, however, it looks like I am going to have to pull out of *Aliens*. I feel particularly badly about this because it was a series I wanted very much to do (and would have finished by now had I still been a freelance), and I hate, in any case, letting you down.

'If you would like to go ahead with another writer (Jon Thurley, I believe, has someone to suggest, though you probably have your own ideas), then I would, of course, be happy to help him in any way I can with the scripting. I have had, I think, a rather good idea for Ep 3 where the mutants spread the rabies virus into the biting insect population. I've checked the science and apparently this is – just – theoretically feasible. Should you decide to go ahead with the series on this basis, I would naturally return to the BBC the money that they paid me on signing the contract. I should, however, like a credit for the idea.'

Bob was quite understandably upset that he was not going to be able to write the series that he had been planning as far back as 1967, as events had conspired against him. His suggestion for the third episode – possibly an effort to show some continued commitment to the project – was no doubt the result of him rooting through his old files, looking for some quick inspiration, and finding the research work done for him by Anna Kaliski when he was writing his *Doomwatch* episode 'The Inquest' in 1970. But crucially, Bob seems to have decided against telling Dyas exactly *what* had gone so completely and disastrously wrong with his holiday. Without this crucial information, Dyas could perhaps conclude only one thing … Robert Holmes, the *television* script writer, was backing out of a *radio* commission with casual ease, and with very little obvious display of guilt or regret.

Dyas was furious with Bob. The two of them had had no direct communication since early April 1976, and Dyas had been given no reason whatsoever to suspect that things weren't going smoothly with the project until Bob's letter arrived on his desk. The studio recording dates for *Aliens in the Blood* were already booked for early November 1976, and he now realised that none of the scripts had been written. Dyas had tried to contact Bob in recent weeks, but with Bob being out of the country, he had not been successful. Presumably he had also contacted Jon Thurley, Bob's agent, to try to get updates on the scripts, but Thurley could have done no more than reassure him that everything was going smoothly.

After receiving Bob's letter, Dyas got in direct contact with Thurley, who – as Bob had hinted in his letter – had a solution to offer up. Another writer that Thurley represented, Rene Basilico, was suggested as a replacement. Basilico had previously done a small amount of television writing, scripting five episodes of the ATV comedy series *John Browne's Body* (1969), and the *Comedy Playhouse* episode 'Uncle Tulip' (1971). He would also later adapt John Le Carré's novel *Tinker, Tailor, Soldier, Spy* for radio. Basilico's and Dyas's paths had previously crossed when Basilico had scripted an episode of *The Price of Fear*, the radio anthology series starring Vincent Price that Dyas had directed in 1973. Dyas ran the idea of commissioning Basilico past the Chief Producer of Light Entertainment, who thought the proposal had merit.

Dyas spoke to Basilico, who was certainly interested in the idea of writing the six scripts needed for the series. He agreed to work to the storylines that

Bob had already written, and that had been accepted by Dyas, but wanted it understood that he wasn't going to stick to them rigidly. He also offered to have the script for the first episode written within a week. Dyas agreed to this, and also contacted Jon Thurley, who pointed out that as all payments came to his office, then the contractual side of things would be easy to administer, as any payments he had received for Bob would now get paid to Basilico. That just left the small matter of whether or not the BBC would agree to pay Basilico the same fee as had been negotiated for Bob.

John Dyas wrote to the BBC's Head of Copyright on Thursday 19 August 1976 to set out the background to the situation, and to recommend that the BBC took up this compromise option. Along the way, he pulled no punches in his thoughts on Bob's conduct in this matter, telling of his shock on learning that no work had been done by Bob on the scripts, of the missing of the delivery deadline, and of his low opinion of the excuses Bob had put forward in mitigation.

A later memo by Dyas to the BBC's Head of Copyright clarifies what work Bob had actually done on the project to date. Dyas asserted that Bob hadn't written a first episode script specifically for the radio version of *Aliens in the Blood*; the script he had seen was something the BBC had first received two or three years earlier, which Jon Thurley had copied to him as a sample of Bob's work. Dyas stated that he had wanted Bob to completely rewrite this script to make it suitable for radio. Bob had also been asked to produce some further episode synopses, which it was decided his initial script fee would now cover.

It is very unusual to find any instances of Bob blotting his professional copybook during the course of his writing career, and if Dyas had been made aware of the full reasons why he had had to pull out of writing the scripts for *Aliens in the Blood*, then perhaps his ire might have been somewhat tempered. But his strongly-worded complaints both to his bosses and to the BBC's Head of Copyright may have caused others within the BBC to start to have doubts about Robert Holmes …

All this ties in with the paperwork that Bob kept in his own files in relation to this project. Alongside his September 1973 series outline for *Aliens in the Blood* are two further documents.

The first is an eight-page breakdown of his storyline for the first episode, with a working title 'Island Genesis'. This opens with John Cornelius attending the funeral of his old friend, Hugh Dexter, on a remote Scottish island, Luig. Reverend Donal Scoular informs him there are no boats back to the mainland that day, and invites him to stay the night at his mansion. There Cornelius meets a young girl, Gersha, who is also living at the house. She has the 'island sickness', a mental affliction that affects many of the island's inhabitants when they reach adolescence, according to Scoular. Later, Cornelius visits the spot where Dexter fell to his death, and meets up with Curtis Lark, who is also on the beach examining the scene. The two men are old friends, but haven't seen each other in years. They go to visit Mrs Kyle, Dexter's housekeeper, and Lark reveals that Dexter recently wrote to him, seeming fearful of an unspecified threat. Lark suspects there is more to Dexter's death than an unfortunate accident. A clue in the letter leads the men to Dexter's library, where they find a tape cassette hidden inside a book. They play the tape, and Dexter's voice tells them about a conspiracy involving mutants who plan to destroy mankind. He stumbled across their plans through the ramblings of his schizophrenic patients, who seemed able to pick up on them. One colony of these mutants has its home on Luig. Cornelius remembers Gersha, and recalls her mentioning a meeting that night. They go back to the church, where they find Scoular addressing about 30 islanders, telling them that he suspects Dexter's friends may have discovered their secret. He mentions a mysterious leader, who has ordered the two men to be killed. The leader turns out to be Mrs Kyle, but she is killed in the trap set for the two men, when Dexter's house explodes in a fireball. The two men escape from Luig by dinghy, with Scoular in hot pursuit. They evade Scoular, who dies out at sea.[255]

The second item of paperwork that Bob kept is another eight-page document, which gives rough storylines for his proposed second and third episodes, 'The Web' and 'Counter Attack'. (See Interlude IX, where the complete document is reproduced.[256]) Bob probably also either wrote short storylines for the final three episodes, or at the very least advised Basilico of the general direction in which he planned to take the series. However, in the event, it seems that Basilico decided to develop the story in a completely different way. The storylines suggested by Bob for 'Counter Attack' and 'The Web' went unused.

The upshot of all this was that Bob was allowed to keep his initial full

---

255 The first episode as transmitted changes the name of troubled young girl from Gersha to Flora. She is revealed to be an advanced mutant, who at the end of the first episode uses her mental powers to kill Mrs Kyle. Lark and Cornelius remain on Luig at the episode's conclusion, convinced that Mrs Kyle and Flora were the only two advanced mutants there, although they suspect that there must be about 250 lesser mutants in the population. The dinghy's escape and Scoular's death at sea are omitted.

256 The second episode as transmitted, 'Hurried Exodus', begins with Cornelius and Lark still on Luig. They ponder Flora's powers, only to discover that the girl has vanished. They eventually find her and persuade her to leave the island with them, but she changes her mind when on the boat, and uses her powers to summon other mutants to help her. Lark slips her a drug that blocks her powers, and she passes out in their cabin as the boat sails away, unhindered. The third episode, 'Unexpected Visitations', sees Cornelius and Lark return to London with Flora. As they ponder how many other mutants have left Luig in the past few decades, Cornelius takes Flora to a specialist friend of his to have her evaluated at a private hospital. Flora is taken away from the hospital by a controlled mutant, but is found by the police a few hours later. The mutant who rescued her turns out to be a Member of Parliament.

payment for the first 'script' of *Aliens in the Blood* in recognition of the fact that the storylines for the series and the characters were his copyright. But he had to return his half-payments for the subsequent five scripts to Jon Thurley, who then paid the money over to Rene Basilico. Basilico also got a new payment from the BBC for his own script of the opening episode. The series was then renamed *Aliens in the Mind,* and the writers' byline read 'Written by Rene Basilico, from an idea by Robert Holmes.'

Basilico got straight down to work, and the six scripts for the series arrived in time for the November 1976 studio recordings to take place. In something of a masterstroke, veteran actors Peter Cushing and Vincent Price were cast as Dr John Cornelius and Professor Curtis Lark. The first episode of *Aliens in the Mind* was transmitted on BBC Radio 4 just a few months later, on Sunday 2 January 1977, and was then repeated the following Wednesday. Each new episode was then transmitted on a weekly basis for the next five Sundays, with Wednesday repeats.[257]

Although not regarded as a classic radio serial at the time, *Aliens in the Mind* has since taken on something of a cult status, owing to Bob's connection with it and the legendary profiles of the two main leads. Storywise, Basilico followed Bob's plot outline for the first episode, but then took the series in his own direction, although he broadly stuck to the tone of Bob's original proposals. By the end, he had made it very much his own creation, while sticking quite closely to the template that Bob had laid down. The series doesn't really break any new ground as a science fiction drama, but is underpinned by the solid performances of Cushing and Price, who are clearly enjoying themselves throughout. The whole radio series was eventually released on CD by BBC Audio in 2006, which brought it to a whole new appreciative audience some 30 years after it was made.

257 The full Radio 4 transmission dates for the series are as follows: Episode 1, 'Island Genesis' – 2 January 1977; Episode 2, 'Hurried Exodus' – 9 January 1977; Episode 3, 'Unexpected Visitations' – 16 January 1977; Episode 4, 'Official Intercessions' – 23 January 1977; Episode 5, 'Genetic Revelations' – 30 January 1977; Episode 6, 'Final Tribulations' – 6 February 1977.

INTERLUDE IX
ALIENS IN THE MIND:
'THE WEB' & 'COUNTER ATTACK'
1976

Robert Holmes's full original, unused storyline proposals for the second and third episodes of *Aliens in the Blood*, the radio series that eventually became *Aliens in the Mind*, are reprinted here as originally submitted, complete with his original spellings and punctuation:

Following on from 'Island Genesis'

Episode 2 - 'The Web'

Curtis Lark and John Cornelius arrive at Euston tired and dishevelled after their sea-crossing and the long journey down from Scotland. They take a cab to Wimpole Street; Cornelius has insisted that Lark must stay with him while in London.

At the station, during the taxi journey, and at Cornelius's house in Wimpole Street as he introduces Lark to Mrs Bellman, his housekeeper, we re-establish in quick scenes the backgrounds of the two men and the substance of their adventure on the island.

While Lark goes to freshen up and Mrs Bellman is preparing a meal, Cornelius deals with the correspondence left for him by his secretary. The housekeeper brings in a package. Cornelius is about to open it when Lark arrives and stops him. He finds the delivery of a package at that hour of the afternoon suspicious.

Cornelius scoffs at his friend's fears. Lark reminds him of Scoular's last, threatening words and we hear them again through the roar of the surf … 'Don't think you'll

307

get away from us … Wherever you go we'll find you … We'll find you …'

While Lark holds the package flat, Cornelius uses his neuro-surgeon's skill and opens the envelope with scalpel and tweezers. Inside is a fat book – 'Cromwell: Our King of Men' – and inside that a clothes-peg spring, wires, battery, detonator and a one-pound slab of guncotton.

Cornelius finds it hard to accept that the power of the mutants can have reached out so lethally and quickly to London. Lark says they may have been spreading out from the island for generations, perhaps even centuries – there is no way of knowing how much of the world is now covered by the seditious web of the mutants.

Doing the correct thing – again against lark's advice – Cornelius calls the police. Before they arrive Lark warns him, on peril of being carted off to a funny farm, not to mention the mutants. Without Dexter's papers, destroyed in the fire, they have no evidence to support charges of a mutant threat to humanity.

The investigation is handled by Det-Superintendent King who heads the local Divisional CID. As he asks Cornelius the customary questions Lark excuses himself and slips off to the bookshop whose sticker was on the flyleaf of 'Cromwell'. We go with him.

The book was new, clearly purchased for the one purpose and, therefore, possibly bought that very day. Lark is in luck. The manager produces an assistant who remembers selling a copy of the book that morning 'to a rather common sort of man'. He was not their usual sort of patron and she thought at the time that the book hardly seemed his type of literature … She is able to provide Lark with a thumbnail description: '… short, froggy-faced, wearing a fawn raincoat with a knitted collar …'

By the time Lark arrives back at Wimpole Street, the police are taking their leave. Lark seems preoccupied. Cornelius asks the reason. Lark tells him of the girl's description, then asks him to look out of the window and describe the man lounging against a railing further down the street.

'Shortish, wearing a fawn raincoat with a knitted …'

'Exactly.'

They decide to lay a trap and set off towards the park to see if the man intends to follow them. He does at first but after a few blocks he is no longer behind them. They retrace their steps until, suddenly, a taxi roars round a corner, mounts the pavement and heads straight for them. They just manage to leap aside into a doorway. The taxi strikes a wall and the driver – their erstwhile shadow – loses control. The taxi piles into a lamp-post. They drag the unconscious driver out as a crowd gathers …

Later, at Lark's instigation, they go to the hospital where the man was taken. Cornelius, using his consultant's authority, gets them in. They find a detective guarding the injured man. He explains that the man, Joe Greening, is a known criminal and the taxi he had been driving was stolen. In the police mind, therefore, it is obvious that some caper is afoot and they are waiting in the hope that Joe's associates will try to contact him.

After getting the detective out of earshot and ignoring Cornelius's delicate sense of professional ethics, Lark puts the screw on Greening. He tells the man he is dying, that only Cornelius can perform the operation necessary to save his life. Etcetera.

Greening buckles under this pressure. He admits that he had been paid by a man named Oscar Lewis to act as the bomb-carrier. The second murder attempt in Wimpole Street, however, had been a piece of personal improvisation because he was worried at the way events were shaping.

Oscar Lewis has a toolmaker's workshop in Pond Street, Wapping, and this is where the implacable Lark makes for next. Cornelius has misgivings about this personal involvement – they are, after all, professional men – but Lark replies that he always takes attempts to blow him up as a personal matter.

It is quite late when they arrive at Pond Street but Lewis's premises – part of a ramshackle building overlooking the river – are unlocked. The workshop is silent and deserted. A single lamp still burns in the tiny office. They go in and almost literally stumble on a body. It is Oscar Lewis. He has been shot at close range.

Cornelius detects a faint flicker of life and hurries out to get his bag from the car. Lark lifts the telephone to call an ambulance but the line is dead. By the time Cornelius returns Lark has found plentiful evidence of Lewis's secondary trade as a bomb-maker – a secret stache of explosive under the floorboards.

Cornelius is treating Lewis when the ubiquitous Superintendent King enters. He is accompanied by a man they immediately recognise: a senior Cabinet Minister. King displays little surprise at finding them with the dying Lewis. Things suddenly fall into place.

As a senior policeman King had been ideally placed – able to coerce a professional bomb-maker to work for him and to ensure that the assassination attempt took place within minutes of Cornelius and Lark arriving back in London. He had learned of their visit to Greening in hospital and was able to beat them to Lewis.

He had shot Lewis, who was of no further use, and laid a trap for Cornelius to walk into. This time there would be

no mistake. They were sitting on five hundred pounds of
gelignite ...

While trussing Lark and Cornelius up, the two mutants
cannot resist revealing something of the intentions and
nature of their organisation. (i.e. To bring about the
disintegration of human society on a world-wide scale –
see format.) When they have finished, Lark and Cornelius
have a much clearer picture of what they are up against.
Unfortunately they are sitting next to a three-minute
fuse so it appears unlikely that they will have long to
brood about it. King and the Cabinet Minister leave.

But now Lewis starts to move. He has recovered slightly
after Cornelius's ministrations and has been lying doggo.
The bullet has lodged in his spine and he is partly
paralysed; he is unable to reach the fuse but he manages
to get a knife and saw through the ropes holding Lark.

Even as Lark wrenches free, however, the burning end of
the fuse fizzles out of reach beneath the floorboards. There
can be only a few seconds left. Lark lifts Cornelius
bodily, chair and all, and staggers from the building.
As he turns to go back for Lewis there is a shattering
explosion and the whole of that side of the building
collapses into the Thames ...

Episode 3 – 'Counter Attack'

'A well-known London neuro-surgeon, John Cornelius of
Wimpole Street, was reported last night to have been
missing from his home for several days. He has not been
seen since Thursday.

'A police spokesman confirmed that they knew of the
disappearance but had no reason to believe there was
anything sinister about it. Nevertheless they would
welcome further news of Mr Cornelius.

ROBERT HOLMES: A LIFE IN WORDS

'Mrs Ethel Bellman, the surgeon's housekeeper, said that when she last saw him on Thursday he had seemed worried. He had said nothing to her about going away …'

The newspaper report is a small, downpage item, inconspicuous among the more lurid news of the day, and Cornelius is pleased to see that his circumspect housekeeper has said nothing about the attempted bomb attack.

He and Lark have gone to ground in a small country inn. After the Wapping affair they have deemed it prudent to encourage the mutants to believe them dead. All the same they know this can be only a breathing space and they are holding long discussions about their next move.

King and the Cabinet Minister, Ogden, had revealed some details of the mutants' future plans. An EEC meeting to develop a concerted plan for industry is due to be held in Munich. Experts from all member-countries are attending and Ogden himself is flying out with the British delegation – twenty of the top industrial and financial brains in the country aboard the same aircraft. Lark is certain that the mutants plan to destroy the 'plane. It would be a crippling blow to the nation.

The difficulty lies in determining how they will strike. With the intense security precautions surrounding the flight the use of yet another bomb seems unlikely.

Now, in the same newspaper, they read that Britain's latest airliner, the G67, will be unveiled to fly the delegates to Munich. The new, wonder aircraft is just completing its flight trials. Captain Guy Rillington, the company's chief test pilot, will be at the controls during the show flight.

Cornelius remembers that he knows Rillington. A year or two previously he had successfully treated the pilot's wife for a brain tumour. The two men agree that there is nothing to be lost, and perhaps much to be gained, by having a talk with Rillington.

The pilot is not yet home when they reach his house. Janet Rillington invites them in. They talk, naturally enough, of her operation and how well she is feeling now, etc. And then she mentions that she had been wanting Guy to see Cornelius: he has been suffering severe headaches recently. She is not convinced that the bi-annual medical check-ups that pilots undergo are sufficiently thorough.

Captain Rillington arrives home. The men talk. Lark and Cornelius explain their suspicions. Rillington scoffs. The G67 is guarded day and night. The flight to Munich will take place under the tightest security precautions ever known in peace-time Britain. And so on.

Suddenly Lark asks permission to examine Rillington. His trained eye has detected something in the pilot's manner. He puts Rillington under hypnosis. When he brings him out of hypnosis, Rillington is disturbed and nervous – a changed man.

He speaks of visits to a hypno-therapist, Dr Broadbent, that he has forgotten. Under Rillington's hairline Cornelius finds a small, recently stitched incision of a kind he is intimately acquainted with. Due to post-hypnotic suggestion Rillington is unaware that he has undergone an operation.

Now they rush the pilot to Cornelius's Wimpole Street consulting rooms where he has the facilities to make a proper examination. The anxious Mrs Bellman is pacified and sworn to secrecy. In a midnight operation, with Rillington under a local anaesthetic, the two doctors remove a tiny radio-electrode from his brain.

It had been planted in a motor-area where, when activated by a radio signal from the ground, it would have caused immediate paralysis.

Once Rillington recovers, Lark and Cornelius find themselves at Gatwick involved in a hive of security activity. They are adamant that Ogden has to be kept in the dark about developments. The Minister arrives at the airport to check on final arrangements … a nasty moment when they almost come face to face with him.

Boffin examination of the radio-electrode reveals that it is activated by a short-range transmitter of a particular frequency. It is clear that the mutants intended to strike as the G67 left the runway and before it gained height. If Rillington was incapacitated at that moment his co-pilot could have done nothing to stop the 'plane plunging into the ground.

The security plan now is for the flight to go ahead as planned with Rillington at the controls. Radio-detector vans are in position round the airport to take cross-bearings and pinpoint the mutants' transmitter.

Lark and Cornelius are in a car with Colonel Teape, the army officer controlling the security operation. Their radio keeps them linked with the airport tower and the other security vehicles. Just before the 'plane takes off they hear – as Lark predicted – that Ogden has been called back to London. He will be travelling to Munich by a later flight.

As the G67 becomes airborne the mutants' transmitter pulses. It is in a stationary car on a verge a mile from the runway. The security forces converge on the car. There is a chase. Suddenly Lark and Cornelius find themselves in the van of the pursuit. Shots are exchanged. The mutants known something has gone wrong and are desperate to escape.

Finally they crash. Their car bounces down a hillside.

Lark and Cornelius arrive at the wreckage in time to find one mutant dead and the other unconscious. Colonel Teape wants him for questioning.

They carry him back to their car but, as they reach it, he recovers consciousness and snatches the Colonel's gun. He gives a defiant cry and shoots himself. They will learn nothing from him.

Lark and Cornelius realise they have only succeeded in winning one battle. Their secret enemies are still powerful enough to win the war.

CHAPTER TWENTY
KILLING TIME
1977

As 1976 turned into 1977, Bob found himself in the position where he had been somewhat strong-armed into staying on as script editor on *Doctor Who*, at least for another six months, while new producer Graham Williams bedded himself into the job. 'I was really on my knees by that time,' Bob recalled some years later. 'After I finished "The Talons of Weng-Chiang" they then asked me to stay on … Hinchcliffe left, but they asked me to stay on for another few months to see Graham Williams into the job.' Bob wasn't the type of person to be forced against his will into any situation he wasn't comfortable with, but on the other hand he'd certainly proven over the years that he had a natural affinity with *Doctor Who*. It was a series he innately understood, and it gave him an environment that he had flourished in, professionally, both as a freelance writer in the early 1970s, and as script editor in more recent years. His working relationship with Hinchcliffe had been one of the happiest and most successful and creative periods of his working life. So, with good grace, Bob stayed as script editor under Williams.

And yet, in January 1977, things were as unstable as they'd ever been for him. Patricia was still recovering from the illness that had cut short his holiday the previous year, and Hinchcliffe was now spending less and less time in the *Doctor Who* production office, as Williams slowly took over. By the end of January 1977, with work completed on 'The Talons of Weng-Chiang', Hinchcliffe would be gone for good, moved on to produce the new police action series *Target*.

There were also simmering tensions amongst the cast of the series, as Tom Baker was less than happy to discover that the new companion Leela, played by Louise Jameson, was going to be around for a lot longer than he had first been told. 'I think she's a very high-spirited girl,' recalled Bob of Jameson, some years later, 'and she used to play around a lot in the rehearsal rooms. Tom, who's a randy devil, took a strangely puritanical view of this, you know. And the other thing was that she came in in Boucher's story about the savages, his first one, and then she did another one, and then I did "Talons". And halfway through shooting "Talons", Hinchcliffe still hadn't plucked up the nerve to tell Tom that Louise was signed up for another season. I think he left Graham Williams to do that. I kept saying to Philip, "Have you told him yet?"

But anyway, I think Tom began to suspect it, because he thought she was only in the three stories, and from that moment rumours started to break out ...'

Another factor was that Baker disliked Leela as a character. He felt that the knife-wielding savage was too violent to be the Doctor's companion; besides which, he would still have preferred the Doctor to be travelling with no regular companion at all, as in 'The Deadly Assassin', and for that reason he resented Jameson's presence. Although the working relationship between the two actors did eventually thaw a little, the first few stories made under Williams' producership were distinctly uneasy from that perspective.

Bob found that Williams was an easy enough man to work alongside, and they soon got to know each other fairly well. But in terms of producing styles, Williams was more of a 'dove' (tending to follow the trends and expectations of his management), whereas Hinchcliffe had been more of a 'hawk' (tending to produce work that was against the grain and groundbreaking), and Bob must have felt increasingly like a fish out of water in the *Doctor Who* production office.

When Williams was initially sounded out by Bill Slater about taking over the producer's role on *Doctor Who*, he had sat down and thought long and hard about the programme, and what he could do with it. He had decided that there must be a power in the *Doctor Who* universe that was higher than that of the Doctor's own people, the Time Lords, and had come up with the notion of the Black and White Guardians – two equal but opposing forces that held the universe in balance. Occasionally, the universe would slip out of balance, and a device known as the Key to Time would need to be located and assembled in order to restore harmony. Williams' plan was that the fifteenth season should be devoted to the Doctor's quest to find and assemble this mythical Key from its six segments. Each of the six stories that would comprise the season would concern itself with the Doctor's attempts to locate and recover one of these segments.

As well as this being a complex narrative strand, which would create additional complications from a scripting perspective, it also meant that the stories would have to be made in a predetermined order, which took away the flexibility exploited in previous seasons of being able to transmit them in a different sequence.

Bob wasn't happy with Williams' idea, either from a storytelling point of view, or from a practical production point of view. But he felt it was incumbent upon him to support his new producer, so he went along with it, albeit not terribly enthusiastically. Unlike for previous seasons, Bob didn't have any back-up scripts to hand and had to start work afresh on assembling six new stories.

Bob made a few phone calls to people he knew he could rely on. Terrance Dicks was the first person to be contacted, and he proposed a storyline set on a distant planet ruled by vampires. The Doctor and Leela arrive on the planet in search of the first segment of the Key to Time and get embroiled in a revolt by the oppressed underclass against their vampire overlords. The idea appealed to Holmes, and so Dicks was commissioned to write a four-part story under the working title 'The Vampire Mutation', which would kick off the Key to Time season.

The 'Bristol boys', Bob Baker and Dave Martin, had submitted an idea for a potential story with the working title 'Invisible Invader'. This didn't involve the Key to Time, but Bob felt the gimmick could probably be worked into it somehow, and they too were commissioned, on Friday 14 January 1977, to write the four scripts.

Bob still had one eye on the exit door, however. On Wednesday 19 January 1977, Louis Marks commissioned him to write a pilot script for a proposed new BBC series with the working title *Northcliffe*, of which Marks was to be the producer. The delivery date for Bob's pilot script was given as Thursday 30 June 1977. Bob had committed to stay on with *Doctor Who* for six more months, but was determined to continue no longer. *Northcliffe* was to be his next project – and that was that!

In the meantime, the BBC had decided to devote an edition of its arts magazine programme *The Lively Arts* to *Doctor Who*, and had despatched film crews to cover the studio rehearsals and production of 'The Talons of Weng-Chiang', which was being recorded during January and February 1977. As part of the documentary, its production team decided they also wanted to film a *Doctor Who* script conference. So on Thursday 27 January 1977, a film crew turned up at the *Doctor Who* production office. Bob had called in Dicks to play the part of 'writer-who-is-going-to-be-grilled', while he and Williams ruled the roost over him. Dicks had actually delivered his completed script for Part One of 'The Vampire Mutation' to Bob the previous day.

Let's set the scene. The office is small, drab and grey; the only items breaking the monotony of the painted walls are a few indistinct photos pinned to a notice board. Dicks is holding court on one side of a well-worn, script-filled desk, resplendent in one of his best turtle-neck sweaters, with a snug blazer worn on top. Next to him are several piles of yellowed scripts stacked upon on a small shelf, an ashtray perched precariously atop one of the piles. On the other side of the desk sits a rather embarrassed-looking Williams, next to the rather severe and serious figure of Robert Holmes. Both men are wearing baggy brown suits with wide lapels, atop of shirts with improbably large collars, rounded off with sombre ties the size of ironing boards. Williams puffs nervously on a cigarette, while Holmes and Dicks punctuate their conversation with airborne prods of their trusty pipes. Another overfull ashtray sits on the desk between them, alongside yet another pile of scripts. Dicks opens the conversation:

Terrance Dicks: What I've been worrying about is possibly the feeling that we've had the Doctor taking over too much in the result … in the revolt against the nobles, and acting as too much of a political figure, which I don't think is in his nature. Because, I don't think the Doctor … I mean, the Doctor knows that he isn't stopping, and he'd very much be concerned that people should solve their own problems.

Graham Williams: Ermm …

Robert Holmes: Let me take this point. It's not that he's taking over …

Graham Williams: No!

Robert Holmes: … this planet, he's going to do what he's come for, which is to steal this lump of mercury or whatever it is, and zoom off!

Graham Williams: Yeah …

Terrance Dicks: Yes, but he is going to be concerned that the people that are left behind are going to be able to cope, you know, he doesn't want the baddies to get in control again.

Graham Williams: Yeah, sure, sure. Which is what you're going to write for us!

Terrance Dicks: Well, hopefully, yes …

This was what viewers of *The Lively Arts* saw and heard, but things weren't quite as they seemed. Keen to get some behind-the-scenes insight into the production of *Doctor Who*, the documentary-makers wanted to film a script conference with some kind of controversy. But there simply wasn't one to be had! Dicks recalls what went on behind the scenes of the behind-the-scenes documentary: 'It was totally fake. They said they wanted to film a script conference, but they wanted to have something happening; they didn't want us sitting there, agreeing with each other. So they asked us to have an argument. So we tried to flog up an argument, but it is extremely fake, and extremely unconvincing. It's an extremely embarrassing piece of film in my view!'

The conversation that Dicks, Williams and Bob were having that day was, by and large, a genuine discussion about Dicks' scripts for 'The Vampire Mutation'. The whole conversation was filmed, and edited down to just a small section in which it looked like the three men were debating a controversial plot point from the script. The whole conversation was slightly more illuminating, and was transcribed by the makers of *The Lively Arts* when preparing to edit their programme together. It actually went as follows:

Terrance Dicks: Yeah. Yeah. For all the viewers though, you know, for kids. Kids are very conservative, the smaller ones, it's really got to be strapped, strapped to the …

Graham Williams: They can't remember it next week anyway, so why …

Terrance Dicks: Absolutely. Um, er – yeah. What I've been worrying about is possibly the feeling that we've had the Doctor taking over too much in the result … in the revolt against the nobles, and acting as too much of a political figure, which I don't think is in his nature. Because, I don't think the Doctor … I mean, the Doctor knows that he isn't stopping, and he'd very much be concerned that people should solve their own problems. It's not in his nature to want to be elected king or whatnot.

Graham Williams: Yeah, but then you had, what? How long ago did you debunk the Time Lords as being non-involved in …?

Terrance Dicks: That was last year, yes.

Robert Holmes: 'The Deadly Assassin'. Well, the Doctor is involved. He doesn't just wander through the universe.

Terrance Dicks: No.

Robert Holmes: So he does get involved in – if it's a political situation, then it's political by the nature of the situation, and not because of the Doctor's politics.

Terrance Dicks: Yeah, yeah.

Graham Williams: So okay, the Doctor doesn't want to be king, as you say. Or Prime Minister.

Robert Holmes: Let me take this point. It's not that he's taking over …

Graham Williams: No!

Robert Holmes: … this planet, he's going to do what he's come for, which is to steal this lump of mercury or whatever it is, and zoom off!

Terrance Dicks: Yeah … I think one – you know, should be aware that he would always be, um – he will be concerned that people like Ivo, Kalmar, are eventually going to have to solve their own problems, without him. Because when he leaves, you see, I mean when he – when he clears off in the TARDIS, at the end of the thing, it's going to be absolute chaos on this planet, really, isn't it? I mean the …

Robert Holmes: It's not going to be chaos. He's going to restore the balance, surely?

Terrance Dicks: Yeah, but you know, the situation that's left is going to be chaotic.

Robert Holmes: He's come into an unnatural situation, by virtue of that lump arriving. And that's distorted what would be a natural ecology. And he's now put that right. In fact what he's doing is letting nature take its course. Isn't it?

Terrance Dicks: But the course of nature is going to be revolution and violence and all sorts of things …

Robert Holmes: That is the course of nature …

Terrance Dicks: Yes, but he is going to be concerned that the people that are left behind are going to be able to cope, you know, he doesn't want the baddies to get in control again. So he must – he mustn't take over too much, you know, I mean although – I'm just saying that this is a problem, Bob, you know, that one's got to allow the … the characters who are part of the story and who are going … who are going to go on living after the TARDIS has left, that they have got to have a sort of sufficient strength so that we can feel that they can cope.

Graham Williams: Yeah, sure, sure. Which is what you're going to write for us!

Terrance Dicks: Well, hopefully, yes … I'm just not sort of with this kind of premise at all. I mean because everything he does, wherever he goes he's – he's going to interfere with people's lives. You know he doesn't … he doesn't leave them with … to live happily ever after. Does he?

Robert Holmes: No, no, no. Quite

Terrance Dicks: He always stirs it wherever he goes.

Robert Holmes: He often in fact stirs up a peaceful situation, you know.

Terrance Dicks: By the fact that he's a catalyst. He arrives …

Graham Williams: Yeah, this is very much in his nature.

Robert Holmes: So I mean I don't really see what you're worried about.

Terrance Dicks: Uh … it just strikes me that there was this possibility that, um, he could grow to be such a figure, you know what I mean, as he has this way of taking over, doesn't he? I mean as soon as anybody, um …

Robert Holmes: He has a way of preserving himself.

Terrance Dicks: Yeah, yeah, yeah. Absolutely. Not getting himself killed, which is always his first thing. But it's very much in his nature to take charge of things, isn't it, to take over and say no, no, no, you've been doing it all wrong; what you've actually got to do is this, you know.

Robert Holmes: Because he's the only individual on that planet in that situation.

Terrance Dicks: But you see here – here we have quite an effective resistance movement which has been going before the Doctor ever arrived.

Robert Holmes: Very unsuccessfully.

Terrance Dicks: No, reasonably successful. Not very unsuccessful. Well, they've got … they've got …

Robert Holmes: They've managed to hide.

Terrance Dicks: Yeah, well they've stayed alive … which …

Graham Williams: I think the story's slightly different anyway, because I mean the Doctor is coming here because of our umbrella theme, really. He's coming here to do a job.

Robert Holmes: He's not there by accident.

Terrance Dicks: Yeah. He's arrived there to take something and we're going to have that sort of problem throughout the season because wherever he goes and he takes away something which is a powerful source on a particular planet … Yeah, he's always going to affect … um, and I don't think we can start worrying on sort of story one of the season about something we're going to be facing all the way through. I mean we're just going to have to accept …

Graham Williams: And when we first talked about this – the idea of the Key – and it might be the power source, supposing it was the power source of the spaceship and he had to take that away, well he wouldn't take it away without leaving something in its place. You know, he would have that concern. Otherwise the spaceship just blows up, fades away, whatever.

Terrance Dicks: Maybe this is why I've noticed it, because, um, the whole business of the Key and the continuing theme is a new element, you know, which I have had to deal with …

Robert Holmes: It's just occurred to me … We had exactly this point in 'Planet of Evil', where he stopped, um … I can't remember the character he played … from removing the anti-matter. And then put him wise to the fact that he can choose, um, the sort of power of the planetary movement.

Terrance Dicks: Yes. It was rather nice the way you did that, actually, because very casually at the last moment, don't you remember, 'You're not going to use anti-matter, you're going to use the rotation of the planets.'

Graham Williams: Right.

Robert Holmes: This … mad, lunatic scheme when he came up with this idea, that we could do a 26-week season in effect. Um … I said well this … for the first it's an opportunity where in one section at least, you know, the Doctor can be seen to lose. I mean that kind of omnipotence can finally be smashed, and even sort of go away. But we'd put him behind on handicap and he's got to make it by the end of the season.

Graham Williams: Yeah. As long as he loses in the right way. Um, for the best of reasons.

Terrance Dicks: The right way of losing. You mean altruistically …

Graham Williams: No. The fact that it's out of his control anyway. That when we're thinking of him losing is out of his control anyway. And to make it inside his control would be to make it artificial and give him extra powers that he doesn't normally possess.

Terrance Dicks: I mean that sort of thing you could do is that he could win by some piece of total ruthlessness.

Robert Holmes: I mean we did have the idea that he would, um, say the source of power was held by the goodies in fact, and, um … the Doctor had to take that away. The goodies are so good they say, well take it away. We had the baddies … win on this planet, but it actually means the baddies won't win all over. So that in fact he doesn't actually mind.

So there wasn't really any one controversial element to the conversation that the three men were having, which is why the team from *The Lively Arts* had to edit the film in the manner that it eventually appeared in the finished programme, making it look as though there was.

If only they'd waited a few days ...

The BBC's new Head of Serials, Graeme McDonald, had learned in early February 1977 that the *Doctor Who* production team were planning to do a vampire story that would air on BBC1 in the autumn of 1977. What he knew, and they didn't, was that the BBC was also planning to make a big-budget adaptation of Bram Stoker's novel *Dracula*, which was due to be broadcast around the same time, in the autumn of 1977. Fearing that the BBC audience might think that *Doctor Who* was in some way spoofing the serious drama of *Dracula*, McDonald ordered that 'The Vampire Mutation' be abandoned.

'Bob had asked me to do another story,' recalls Dicks, 'and I had come up with the idea of vampires. I'm very fond of vampires, I like a good vampire. I'd sold the idea and the storyline, and Bob commissioned the scripts. I'd written the first script; possibly the first two scripts. Then Bob phoned up in a state of great agitation, and said, "How's it going?" And I said, "All right." He then said, "Stop, stop immediately", and so I said, "What's up?" He said, "We've had a memo from 'on high'. The BBC is doing a big, serious classic-serial-type authentic adaptation of Bram Stoker's *Dracula*, and the people 'on-high' have said, 'No vampires on *Doctor Who*, because the audience would think you're making fun of us, or would detract from it.'" So we'd suddenly got this show that was half-way there, practically, and they stopped it. And so I went in to see Bob for a crisis meeting, and said, "What are we going to do?" and Bob said, "I've always wanted to do a show set on a lighthouse."'[258]

'The Vampire Mutation' was scheduled as the first story of the 1977/78 season to go into production, and also the first story to be screened. While Dicks was given the opportunity to go away and come up with another story to open the season, the production slot allocated to 'The Vampire Mutation' was given over to Baker and Martin's story, 'Invisible Invader'. Because the possibility of making the season in transmission order had now been removed from them, Williams reluctantly decided that it was best if they dropped the Key to Time umbrella idea, for the time being at least, and concentrated on just getting six standalone stories commissioned and made. Bob wasn't at all disappointed with this decision. He quickly told Baker and Martin not to bother trying to shoehorn the Key to Time idea into their scripts, and the

---

258 Terrance Dicks' script for the first episode of 'The Vampire Mutation' sat in a filing cabinet in the *Doctor Who* production office for several years after the story was abandoned in 1977. It was unearthed in 1980 by newly arrived *Doctor Who* script editor Christopher H Bidmead, who had just taken over the job and found that his predecessor, Douglas Adams, hadn't actually left any storylines or scripts in hand for him to work on. Desperate for ideas, Bidmead read the script for 'The Vampire Mutation' Part One, and then called Dicks and asked him to come in to discuss the story being commissioned once again. This time there were no edicts from 'on high' to scupper things, and the story, now re-titled 'State of Decay' and with the Key to Time elements excised, was made as part of the programme's eighteenth season.

duo worked extremely fast on writing the story, delivering all four scripts on Tuesday 8 February 1977. The story was retitled 'The Invisible Enemy' and was rushed into production as the first to made for the new season, with the studio recordings scheduled for mid-March.

Doctor Who was still attracting criticism from certain vocal organisations about the levels of horror and violence depicted in the series. In the week after the second episode of 'The Robots of Death' was shown on BBC1, in early February 1977, the BBC received a request from a national tabloid newspaper, the *Daily Express*, for one of its high-profile columnists, Jean Rook, to interview a representative about the direction the show was taking. Mindful of the recent mauling from the National Viewers' and Listeners' Association, the BBC decided to grant this request. As Hinchcliffe had now vacated the producer's hot seat, and Williams hadn't actually produced anything yet, it fell to Bob to meet up with Rook and defend the way that *Doctor Who* was being made. One of the BBC's prop stores was used as the backdrop to the interview, and Bob duly posed for some suitable photographs to accompany the article, stood next to the TARDIS police box prop, surrounded by Daleks, an Exxilon and a Voc Robot.

The subsequent article, written by Rook, was published in the Friday 11 February 1977 edition of the *Daily Express*. It appeared under the rather pejorative banner headline: 'Who do you think you are, scaring my innocent child?' Rook wrote: 'What has gone wrong with the innocent teatime thrill of watching *Doctor Who*? Aged three, my son used to watch *Doctor Who* at mother's knee. At four, he squinted from behind my back. Five, he was under the armchair. Now he is pushing six. And when, last Saturday, he told me three times before noon that he didn't want to watch *Doctor Who* at 6.20 pm I accepted that psychologically, he'd come upon something slimy and monstrous …

'I blame myself for not noticing the extremely nasty turn this cult, 14-million-viewer TV programme has taken since, I gauge, last year's Sutekh episode. In which, your scalp may stir to remember, *Doctor Who*'s girl was stalked through a snapping, crackling autumn wood by two 7ft, grey-bandaged Egyptian mummies. Twin Frankensteins who would have put the wind of heaven up Peter Cushing.

'Where I have gone wrong – and the time switch to a later 6.20 should have warned me – is in not realising that *Doctor Who* is no longer suitable for children. And that it has grown out of a rubber monster show into a full, scaly, unknown horror programme. Compared with it, an old Hammer movie wouldn't crack toffee.'

Jean Rook then introduced Bob into her narrative, in none-too-flattering terms … 'Mr Holmes is tall, grey-haired, and bloodless, in a cape-shaped fawn mac. He looks like Sherlock Holmes playing Dracula. He reads Poe, Arlen and Bradbury in bed.'

Bob then manfully attempted to defend the series to Ms Rook. 'Of course it's no longer a children's programme,' he told her. 'Parents would be terribly irresponsible to leave a six-year-old to watch it alone. It's geared to the intelligent 14-year-old, and I wouldn't let any child under ten see it. If a little one really enjoys peeping at it from behind the sofa, until Dad says "It's all right now – it's all over," that's fine. A certain amount of fear is healthy under strict parental supervision. Even then I'd advise half an hour to play with Dad and forget it before a child goes to bed. That's why we switched the time-slot from 5.15 to after 6.00, when most young kids are in the bath. When it started as a true children's programme the monsters were rubber and specific and you saw them almost at once. What horrifies far more is the occasional flash of monster – bits and pieces of one. People are more frightened by what *might* come round the corner or in at the window … They're strictly fantasy deaths … we're not in the business to harm children.'

Predictably, Ms Rook had to get the final word on the matter: 'Watching this Saturday's episode, I accept that *Doctor Who* is nerve-wrenching, spine-gripping, and now totally grown up. I find I have 40-year-old friends who can't watch it. It's a great TV achievement. But I wonder if this inflated, ex-children's programme is overstretching itself to 15ft rats. And worshipping its own, uninhibited cult.'

Although it would appear that Bob gave a robust account of himself in the interview, in private, he felt that he hadn't been fully prepared for the type of questions that Ms Rook had fired at him, and that he had been hung out to dry a little by his BBC bosses by setting the interview up. Chris Boucher recalls how Bob was unsettled by the article, and the unnecessary publicity it brought both him and the series. 'I get the feeling that Bob was slightly ambushed on that one,' Boucher recalls. 'I don't think he quite expected the horrendous Jean Rook would attack in quite that way. She really was the "Glenda Slagg" of her day.'[259] Later in 1977, Bob penned a short article for the *Doctor Who* fanzine *Gallifrey*, mainly about his script for 'The Deadly Assassin'. At the end of his piece, he says: 'Despite what Jean Rook wrote about me in the *Express*, I have always regarded *Doctor Who* as, first and foremost, an educational programme!'[260]

Back behind his desk in the *Doctor Who* production office in February

---

259 'Glenda Slagg' is a fictitious columnist in the satirical magazine *Private Eye*, who parodies the heavy-handed writing style of opinionated female newspaper columnists. Jean Rook was an early inspiration for the character.
260 'Robert Holmes Speaks', *Gallifrey*: Issue 2, January 1978.

1977, Bob was working with Dicks to formulate a replacement story for 'The Vampire Mutation'. Bob's off-the-cuff notion of using a lighthouse for the setting was not one that Dicks was particularly happy about. He didn't know the first thing about lighthouses for a start. And so Bob, with a great splash of irony and just a little hint of *schadenfreude*, suggested to Dicks that he go and visit his local library so that he could research lighthouses. Bob went on to advise Dicks that the children's section was usually the best place to find books that managed to cover subjects in a concise, simple manner – ideal for writers who are just looking for background information on a subject! Four years after sending Bob off to the children's section himself, it was now Dicks' turn to go and dust off his library membership card …

'This was an example of the script editor coming up with the idea, which he sometimes does,' recalls Dicks. 'I said, "I don't know anything about lighthouses." Bob said "Go out and get a *Boy's Book of Lighthouses* and find out." I always used to say that this was Bob's revenge for "The Time Warrior". I'd dragged him kicking and screaming into the 13th Century, and he dragged me kicking and screaming onto a lighthouse. So I went out and bought several books on lighthouses and studied up on them. The obvious idea of a lighthouse is it's isolated and people are stuck on it and can't get off. So you have people stuck on a lighthouse with a monster, which knocks them off one by one. It's like the old Agatha Christie thing, *Ten Little Indians*, and so that's what we did.'

It's possible that when Dicks pointed out to Bob that he thought this was some kind of revenge for 'The Time Warrior', he was also reminded of an alien race that Bob had named in that script. 'In "The Time Warrior", Bob had established that the Sontarans were conducting an endless war with the Rutans,' notes Dicks. 'But we didn't know anything about the Rutans, other than they were always fighting the Sontarans. So my monster was a kind of giant electric jellyfish that came out of the sea, and it could electrocute people, and it could also take on their shapes. It was a shape-shifter, and it could impersonate the people it had killed. And I suddenly thought, "Why not call it a Rutan?", because it gives a nice little piece of continuity. And also the Sontarans are very squat, and defined, and definite, and it's rather nice that their main enemy is rather loose, and floppy, and blobby, and sort of all over the place. So I already had the jellyfish monster, but I decided it was going to be a Rutan, which was just a nice little bit of continuity for the fans.'

Dicks came up with a storyline called 'Rocks of Doom', which Bob liked, and so he was then commissioned to write four scripts for delivery by Wednesday 30 March 1977. Dicks kept to his deadline. Bob now had two stories lined up for the fifteenth season.

Sometime in early April 1977, it would seem that Williams had one last attempt at trying to persuade Bob to stay on as *Doctor Who*'s script editor beyond the summer. When Bob told him that this just wasn't going to happen, Williams had to start recruiting a replacement. Someone else who was looking for a script editor at the BBC was David Maloney. Maloney had directed Bob's two previous *Doctor Who* stories, 'The Deadly Assassin' and 'The Talons of Weng Chiang', and was a great admirer of his talents. Moreover, he had just been made producer of a new BBC science fiction series called *Blake's 7*, which was the brainchild of writer Terry Nation, the man who had invented the Daleks for *Doctor Who*. Maloney needed a good script editor to work with Nation on *Blake's 7*, and so he asked Bob to consider taking on the post.

But Bob was keen to return to freelance writing, and didn't want to jump straight into another script editing job after nearly four years at the helm of *Doctor Who*. He was also committed to scripting the pilot episode of Louis Marks' *Northcliffe* series, which he hoped would prove to be a great success and keep him in work for some time to come. So Bob instead recommended Chris Boucher, the writer he had nurtured over the previous 12 months on *Doctor Who*, and Boucher was duly approached by Maloney and took the job.

Boucher thinks there might have been another motive behind Bob turning down the *Blake's 7* script editing job: 'David Maloney asked him, and I know the job was offered initially to Bob. He was approached, and asked if he wanted to do it. He didn't. I seem to remember it was because he didn't want to work with Terry Nation anymore. He suggested me to David instead. I imagine the conversation went along the lines of David asking, "If you don't want to do it, have you any idea who might be any good ...?" and Bob suggested me. I remember turning up to meet David Maloney in my suit; possibly the last time I ever wore a suit. I was desperate for the job. And I got the job. But it was Bob that suggested me.'

This perhaps wasn't the shrewdest tactical move on Bob's part. If anything, he probably should have been grooming Boucher as his replacement on *Doctor Who*. Instead, as the summer rapidly approached, he realised that he had no natural successor (unlike Dicks, who had groomed Bob himself for the job in 1973). The only obvious candidate with recent hands-on writing experience with the series, Boucher, was now shortly going to be tied up on *Blake's 7*.

In his final throw of the dice as script editor of *Doctor Who*, Bob called Boucher with the offer of another story commission.

'I wanted to do a ghost story,' recalls Boucher. 'Given the chance, you get the opportunity in science fiction series, in those sort of shows, to do a particular sort of story that you've always wanted to do. You can do your spy drama, your

Western … they are wonderful storytelling devices. I'd always wanted to do a ghost story. I liked ghost stories, and I think I must have taken it to Bob. Or perhaps Bob asked me if I'd got any ideas; I don't remember the details.'

And so, on Monday 2 May 1977, Bob commissioned his final *Doctor Who* story as script editor. 'Image of the Fendahl' was the title of Boucher's new story, with a target delivery date of Tuesday 31 May.

At around this time, Bob gave an interview to the *Doctor Who* fanzine *Gallifrey*. It gave him an opportunity to look back on his tenure with the series and discuss *Doctor Who* in general. One question that he was asked was how long he thought *Doctor Who* could continue for. 'It's been going on for 13 years,' he said. 'I don't see why it shouldn't go on for another 13 and longer. It's getting bigger audiences now than it's ever had. It's got this marvellous ingredient that some genius thought of, that it doesn't depend on the individual actor. If Tom wishes to leave, *Doctor Who* doesn't die because of that. Another actor takes the part – and in a sense it's quite a unique show. I don't think there is any reason to stop. We've improved over the years, and the technical development in television has enabled us to do more effects. I'm sure there are plenty more coming up; the people in the electronics department are always working on these things, producing new noises and effects. So we should be getting bigger and better.'

Bob also pondered on which type of story he preferred – Earthbound ones, or those set in outer space. 'The difficulty with space stories is that you have to conceive the entire cosmos. You have to think of every detail to the design of a chair to a space fountain pen. It's very expensive, and we try to do it the best we can on the budget we have. I think *2001: A Space Odyssey* was a great example of a space story. On the other hand, because an Earth story is immediately recognisable, it's not so much of a challenge to a writer; but of course, some writers find the challenge of doing a space story a bit too difficult.

'As a script editor, I'm really interested in the dramatic context of the story and the imagination the writer uses on it. I was very impressed by Chris Boucher's ideas for "The Face of Evil" and I thought it was very imaginative on the part of the writer.

'But back to this business of doing an alien type story, we are a bit lumbered, because we use film and we always have to look around for an alien landscape – and there aren't that many in Britain! I'd like to work in the Sahara or somewhere, but we tend to finish up working in a quarry. We can get away with it because we can dress it up with stuff called Jablite, which is basically polystyrene rocks, or with exotic foliage if it's a jungle. The "Planet of Evil" forest was done in the studio, though.'

Finally, he was asked why he thought the series was so popular. 'Escapism?

It's funny, quirky, it has that strange sense of British humour and the Doctor's always cracking jokes, he gets up to wild escapades and comes out on top. It's got that wild escapism. The great thing about *Doctor Who* is that it is the only show on television that has created its own myth. I think if it stopped tomorrow, 50 years from now people would say, "Do you remember *Doctor Who*?" The character has become a fictional myth on the level of folklore.'[261]

In early May 1977, Graeme McDonald appointed former BBC producer Anthony Read to succeed Bob as *Doctor Who*'s script editor. Read had taken some persuading to return to the Corporation after leaving about five years previously to become a freelance writer, but it was mainly the draw of working on *Doctor Who* that persuaded him to take the job. Read started in the middle of May, and began trailing Bob just as Boucher began delivering his scripts for 'Image of the Fendahl'.

'Robert Holmes had been around on the programme for a while, and I knew of him, obviously,' recalls Read. 'But he joined the BBC after I left, because it was five years or more since I had gone away. Although I had been writing the occasional thing for different people, I hadn't come into contact with Bob before. I'd never met him before, but he was a good guy, I was very pleased to get to know him, he was very professional. In fact we had a connection, I discovered – he had been a newspaper reporter, I think for the *Daily Mail* – or it could have been the *Express* – and he had been the local guy in my hometown, Walsall, and had worked in an office literally just around the corner from where my parents had a pub, on the main street. The paper had an office on Station Street, Walsall, and I lived in a pub on Park Street, Walsall, which was just round the corner. And we'd never come into contact then either. But he was a good guy. He was a nice, steady, thoughtful chap, a good writer, a good constructor of stories. I always remember him sitting there, puffing on his pipe, and looking very steady, and very unflappable. Which is a good thing to be, particularly on a programme like *Doctor Who*. You need someone who is unflappable.'

One of the first things that Bob made sure he acquainted Read with was a little tradition that *Doctor Who* had with its script editors. Specifically, that the incoming script editor's first commission was always a story written by the soon-to-be-freelance outgoing script editor …

At this point in his professional life, Bob was not a fan of the British tax system. Although he was on a BBC staff contract as script editor of *Doctor Who*, he was still being paid residuals on episodes of programmes he'd written many

261 Robert Holmes Interview, *Gallifrey*: Issue 1, September 1977 – Interview by Tim Dollin.

years earlier that had been repeated, or sold abroad, or had been novelised (see Chapter Twenty-Eight). Not to mention the additional staff contribution payments that he had got from the BBC for writing the occasional *Doctor Who* story since he had begun his script editing job. Although his BBC salary was taxed at source through the PAYE system, he also had to compile and submit his own personal tax return every 12 months, all so that the Inland Revenue could then lay claim to more chunks of his hard-earned income. He was, to concisely sum up the situation, pretty pissed off with the taxman.

Bob decided to vent his spleen in his next *Doctor Who* commission. The resultant story, 'The Sun Makers', is a none-too-subtle attack on the British tax system. 'The story sprang from an article I'd read speculating about the possibility one day of creating artificial suns,' recalled Bob. 'I got the basis of the idea from a non-fiction book, *The Iron Sun*[262], which dealt with the possibility of mankind one day being able to create suns.' He then went on to admit, 'It was also intended as a rather broad satire on the UK tax system ...'[263]

'Well, I think I'm not a serious writer,' Bob said some years later. 'I like to get some fun out of what I'm writing. If I'm sitting at my typewriter and something makes me laugh then I think, "Well, I'll try that," and I use it. Usually, I think they accept it. I wrote a thing called "The Sun Makers", which was a skit on the Inland Revenue system, with a Gatherer and a Collector, and in that I had some reference to income tax forms, like Corridor P45, liquidation and things like that. And then there was the planet that the Collector originally came from, once it was revealed that he wasn't human and he himself went into liquidation and plopped down into this commode thing. I said he came from the planet Userers (as in people who use you) but Graham Williams was adamant that we couldn't have a planet called Userers, which both I and the director, Pennant Roberts, didn't agree with.'[264]

When asked if he had deliberately disposed of the Collector at the story's conclusion in such a way as to leave open the possibility of him returning at a later date, Bob seemed quite taken aback at the idea. 'Well, I shouldn't think so. I've never thought about it. I suppose if I were asked to write another story about him, I could find something to bring him back through the plug hole.'[265]

Bob also dropped a small element of subtext into 'The Sun Makers', telling how the population of Pluto was kept docile by the use a drug fed into the

---

262 *The Iron Sun: Crossing the Universe Through Black Holes* by Adrian Berry, published by Jonathan Cape, 1977.
263 Robert Holmes Interview, *The Time Meddler*: Issue 3, October 1981 – Interview by John M Kahane; combined with a quote from the Robert Holmes Interview, *Type 40*: Issue 1, 1978.
264 Interview – Robert Holmes, *Doctor Who Magazine*: Issue 100, May 1985. The Collector's planet of origin was eventually named Usurius.
265 Robert Holmes Interview, *Type 40*: Issue 1, 1978.

air that they breathed – a population that were quite literally drugged into compliance. 'That was partly the idea,' recalled Bob. 'But I always try to avoid plonking the moral a bit too heavily. Aside from the fact that it usually spoils the story, who am I to lecture people?'[266]

Bob worked fast on this set of scripts. He was commissioned to write the story on Saturday 30 April 1977, and delivered all four scripts between Friday 13 and Friday 20 May 1977.[267]

Just before Bob left the *Doctor Who* production office in the summer of 1977, writer Douglas Adams came a-knocking on his door once again. Since pitching his 'Space Ark' idea back in 1974, Adams had submitted another unsuccessful proposal, this one for a story entitled 'Doctor Who and the Krikkitmen', in which the Doctor and Sarah Jane Smith had to reassemble a structure called the Wicket Gate in order to defeat an army of cricket-playing robots hell-bent on universal destruction. More recently he had completed writing the script for the first episode of his science fiction comedy series *The Hitchhikers Guide to the Galaxy* for BBC Radio 4.[268] Bob had encouraged Adams with his writing, and had told him to let him know when he actually had something to show him. Adams now did so, in the form of this science fiction radio comedy script. Bob then informed Adams that he was moving on from *Doctor Who*, but introduced him to Anthony Read, and left the two of them to discuss possible future storylines for the series. Bob later recalled: 'Douglas Adams … sent in *The Hitchhiker's Guide to the Galaxy* in manuscript form and I'd thought he'd got talent, but before anything emerged out of that collaboration, I'd left the show.'[269]

In terms of Bob's day-to-day involvement with *Doctor Who* in the spring of 1977, there was just the small matter of getting the scripts for 'Image of the Fendahl' ready for production, and he increasingly left it to Read to liaise with writer Chris Boucher. Although the story was eventually transmitted with Bob's name as the sole script editor on the end credits, much of the BBC paperwork for it lists both Bob and Read as dual script editors.

Boucher recalls that the experience of writing this story and working alongside Read and Williams was dramatically different from that of working with Bob and Hinchcliffe. Especially when – against his better judgement – he accepted an invitation to attend a cast read-through of the scripts, only

266 Robert Holmes Interview, *Renegade*: Issue 1, 1984 – Interview by Matthew Wicks.
267 'The Sun Makers' as transmitted doesn't have a script editor credit. However, the camera scripts have both Bob and Anthony Read listed as script editor, with Read's name under Bob's.
268 Adams would later rework this storyline into his *Hitchhiker's* universe, when it became the basis of his third *Hitchhiker's* novel, *Life, the Universe and Everything* (1982). See Charles Norton's *Now of the Big Screen: The Unofficial and Unauthorised Guide to Doctor Who at the Movies* (Telos Publishing, 2013) for further details on 'Doctor Who and the Krikkitmen'.
269 Interview – Robert Holmes, *Doctor Who Magazine* Issue 100, May 1985.

to witness Tom Baker continually complaining about their quality. 'It was a horrendous experience as far as I was concerned,' recalls Boucher. 'I was by now working on *Blake's 7*, and I went back to my office and I kicked a very large dent into a filing cabinet, and I conceived the notion that I would like to see Tom Baker die in a cellar full of rats. That said, because it was a horrendous memory, I may have blanked Bob out of it. He may have been there. I don't know. That's odd, isn't it? Memory's a very strange thing. I think the reason we like stories is because they are pre-edited memories. I think we edit our memories in the same sort of way, and I may have edited Bob out of that incident. That was the only bad part of the experience. I actually liked the production, I actually enjoyed watching it, but then I always like listening to my dialogue. I thought it was a perfectly decent piece, but everything changed when Graham Williams took over *Doctor Who*. He was a very nice guy, but he had what I now think are called "issues". And, well, the whole situation changed. I'm sure that was the reason that Bob decided not to go on with the series any further.'

Bob departed the script editor post on *Doctor Who* in June 1977, leaving Read in charge of commissioning the rest of the season. He did though slip him the phone numbers of Bob Baker and Dave Martin. 'At that time, we were discussing "Underworld", but it hadn't been written,' Bob later recalled.[270] Read commissioned 'Underworld', a four-part story, within weeks of Bob leaving the BBC. He then sounded Bob out about potentially writing the final six-part story of the season, when a script from another writer, David Weir, fell through at the last minute. Bob declined, although he did eventually agree that his creations, the Sontarans, could be dusted off and given another outing in the story that was eventually used. This was 'The Invasion of Time', scripted by Read and Williams themselves under the pseudonym David Agnew. Bob advised Williams to structure this six-part story as, essentially, a four-parter followed by a two-parter, similar to the way that 'The Seeds of Doom' and 'The Talons of Weng-Chiang' had been done.

Bob was slightly peeved at the manner in which Leela was shunted out of the series in 'The Invasion of Time'. 'I don't like the way they decided to write her out. I would have had her laying down her life to save the Doctor,' he remarked some years later. 'I think they made a mistake with her falling in love and getting married – I feel that was fairly stupid!'[271]

270 Robert Holmes Interview, *The Time Meddler*: Issue 3, October 1981 – Interview by John M Kahane.
271 Interview – Robert Holmes, *Doctor Who Magazine*: Issue 100, May 1985.

CHAPTER TWENTY-ONE
PAPERS, PILOTS,
AND PANDEMICS
1977-1978

After nearly four years of being a member of BBC staff, Bob left the ranks of the salaried in June 1977, to focus on the pilot script for Louis Marks' *Northcliffe* project.

Northcliffe was to be a dramatisation of the life and career of the British newspaper and publishing magnate Alfred Harmsworth, the 1st Viscount Northcliffe (1865-1922). Harmsworth began his career as a freelance journalist and went on to found a popular newspaper, *Answers* (original title: *Answers to Correspondents*), along with successful periodicals such as *Comic Cuts* and *Forget-Me-Nots*. From the strength of these early titles, he built his periodical publishing empire, Amalgamated Press, which would become the largest in the world, until it was purchased in 1959 by the *Mirror* group and renamed Fleetway Publications. Harmsworth's pioneering success was built on the early days of what would become the modern tabloid press. He bought his first newspaper, the *Evening News*, in 1894 and quickly turned its fortunes around. In 1896, he launched the *Daily Mail*, and in 1903 the *Daily Mirror*. In 1905 he bought the *Sunday Observer*, and in 1908 he bought *The Times*. In a little over a decade he'd built himself a formidable media empire.

Alfred Harmsworth was essentially the Rupert Murdoch of his day, not only with his publishing empire, but also with his links to those in political office. He became baronet of Elmwood in 1904 before being elevated to the peerage with the title of Baron Northcliffe, of the Isle of Thanet, in 1905. In 1918 he became Viscount Northcliffe of St Peter's.

He began offering prizes through his newspapers, which brought him even more notoriety. In 1904, he offered 100 guineas to the first person who could swim across the English Channel from Dover to Calais, and two years later, offered £1,000 to the first person who could do the same journey by aeroplane.

His influence over the British people, through the editorial policy of his newspapers, was something of a first for the country. In the run-up to the First World War, the *Daily Mail* adopted a very strong anti-German policy, which caused a rival newspaper, the *Star*, to later declare, 'Next to the Kaiser, Lord Northcliffe has done more than any living man to bring about the war'. Later, in 1915, during the early part of the War, his newspapers were critical of the government's handling of the so-called shell crisis[272], which initially led to accusations that Northcliffe had now become pro-German, but which ultimately led to the collapse of the government of Prime Minister Herbert Asquith.

Northcliffe's influence on anti-German propaganda during the war led to him being specifically targeted by the German military. A German warship was dispatched with orders to shell his country house in Elmwood, Kent, in a deliberate attempt to assassinate him. The subsequent attack killed the wife of his gardener, but Northcliffe himself escaped unharmed. In 1918, Northcliffe joined the cabinet of David Lloyd George's government, and took charge of Britain's overseas propaganda campaign, but resigned from this position on Armistice Day later that year. In the general election that December, he refused to back Lloyd George, who nevertheless remained in power with the help of another coalition government. Northcliffe's health began to decline in the years after the War, and he died in 1922, leaving in his will the sum of three months' salary for each of his 6,000 employees, a remarkable final act of generosity.

It's not hard to see why Bob was drawn to such a project. Obviously, his early days working in newspapers and journalism would have given him some insight into Northcliffe's world, and there are elements of Northcliffe's life that chimed with his earlier 1965 series proposal *Time Over Again* (see Chapter Five). The period of Northcliffe's life either side of the turn of the century was one that also resonated with Bob; he'd previously depicted that period in his scripts for *The Regiment*, and more recently in 'The Talons of Weng-Chiang' for *Doctor Who*. So this really was something of a pet project for Bob.

In late 1977, Bob told a *Doctor Who* fanzine: 'At present I am working on a dramatisation for the BBC of the life of Lord Northcliffe, the first press baron and the originator of the newspapers as we know them today. My only problem is to shake off the feeling that things are moving too slowly and maybe I should have the Martians land and launch an attack on Fleet Street ...'[273]

Bob's commissioning brief for writing the 50-minute pilot script included the note that he was to fully research the subject and prepare a treatment for the whole project before starting work on the script itself. Although the first script was to be a pilot for a proposed series, it was initially commissioned as a standalone project under the BBC's *Playhouse* strand. This changed in March 1977, when it became a series in its own right, called simply *Northcliffe*, and Bob was issued with a new commission, still with the delivery date of Thursday

---

272 The shell crisis was the media's name for a reported shortage of artillery shells on the British front lines during World War I. The perception that the Liberal government of the day was inadequate in its handling of the matter led to its collapse and the subsequent rise to power of the new Minister for Munitions, David Lloyd George.
273 'Robert Holmes Speaks', *Gallifrey*: Issue 2, January 1978.

30 June 1977. The projected series run was set for 13 episodes. Producer Louis Marks also made provision for the BBC to buy the rights to a 1972 book called *The House of Northcliffe* by Paul Ferris, which was to form the basis of much of the details covered in the series.

However, no matter how much Bob loved the idea of *Northcliffe*, there was the small matter of the contract, which was handled, as usual, by his agent, Jon Thurley. Although he was nominally writing a one-off play for *Playhouse*, Bob was actually being asked to devise and write the pilot script for a whole 13-episode BBC series (for which Bob may or may not have been asked to write some or all of the subsequent episodes). Although this was a peculiar state of affairs, Thurley considered that the BBC were not offering Bob anything like the amount of money that he felt they should. 'It will come as no surprise to you,' he wrote to the BBC's Head of Copyright in early May 1977, 'to know that I have a couple of points on the contract. First, the fee: I am getting over twice this fee for commissioned series episodes from commercial companies, let alone for episodes where there is an "original concept" as there is in this proposed serial.'

What was worse, as far as Thurley was concerned, was that the BBC were only committing to one pilot script. He felt they should be committing to all 13 episodes from Bob. 'If, for any reason, [the producers] elected not to go ahead with the entire project, I think it would be extremely difficult to make a sale elsewhere,' he pointed out in his letter.

A fee that was suitable to both parties was agreed without much further fuss in early June, with half the amount payable up-front and the balance when the script for the first episode had been submitted to and accepted by the BBC. Marks gave an undertaking that Bob would be commissioned to write the subsequent episodes of *Northcliffe* on a similar fee-per-episode basis, but also agreed that he would get an additional 'format fee' payment for, essentially, devising the series, plus an on-screen credit on every episode saying as much. It was recognised that other writers might possibly need to be brought in on subsequent episodes, if Bob was unable to write all the scripts for whatever reason, but any such episodes would still have Bob's credit on them as the series devisor.

With everything agreed at last, Bob got down to work on writing the pilot script in the summer of 1977, and delivered it to Marks on Monday 19 September. By this time the series had been renamed, given the slightly more anodyne title of *The Chief*, with Bob's script for the first episode carrying the individual episode title 'Family Business …'

Bob's script for *The Chief* opens with Alfred Harmsworth at the age of

23, as he gears up to launch the first issue of his first periodical, *Answers to Correspondents*, as a direct rival to the already established and popular *Tit-Bits*. Bob's knowledge, garnered from his publishing background, comes to the fore, as matters such as sub-editing and print runs get debated by the central characters, along with a selection of tried-and-trusted marketing methods to get the British public to buy and then keep buying the magazine. *Answers ...* launches, but isn't the overnight success Harmsworth hopes for, and he gets sucked into an escalating circulation war with the publisher of *Tit-Bits*. But just as his title finally starts to break even, and sales steadily rise, Harmsworth's father is taken ill. The script finishes as Alfred returns to his parents' home, as he (and the audience) wait to discover just how serious his father's condition is ...

Bob even manages to sneak a small *Doctor Who*-ish in-joke into his script. When Harmsworth's parents visit their new house for the first time, Harmsworth Snr observes the nearby cemetery, and muses, 'Ah. A temporal reminder, my dear. We shall abide here in a state of grace.'

After many months of silence, on Friday 3 March 1978 the BBC finally notified Jon Thurley that they had accepted Bob's pilot script, and Bob was paid the second half of his fee.

The series, however, failed to materialise, and the pilot episode didn't even get put into production by the BBC. The reasons why this happened, however, are now lost in the mists of time. Marks instead became producer on *The Lost Boys* – a series about the life of J M Barrie, the creator of Peter Pan – which was shown by the BBC in October 1978, while Bob busied himself with other projects. *Northcliffe / The Chief*, however, was a project that was very dear to Bob's heart, and the fact it never got made was surely one of his few professional regrets.[274]

This was not to be the only disappointment for Bob during this time. In 1977, another of his long-term projects finally appeared to be taking off. *On the Run* was an idea for a comedy series that Bob had been toying with for some time, and he'd actually written several drafts of an opening episode, entitled 'The Great Escape', over the previous months. The first episode begins inside an unnamed prison, where two cellmates, Roland and Gordon (although these names sometime altered between the various drafts), yearn to be able to escape from their cell and sample the simple delights of everyday mundane life – fish and chips, pubs, football matches, and the carnal joys of the opposite sex. Bob cemented his ideas for this first episode, and produced a 30-minute script that was basically a two-hander between the two prisoners, who then

---

274 Bob would have spent December 1977 and January 1978 writing the scripts for the *Doctor Who* story 'The Ribos Operation', and so wasn't exactly twiddling his thumbs while all this was going on – see Chapter Twenty-Two.

manage to smuggle themselves out of jail in laundry baskets at the episode's conclusion.

The success of the BBC's prison-based sitcom *Porridge*, starring Ronnie Barker and Richard Beckinsale, may well have inspired Bob's notion for the series, and it also probably inspired LWT to take a punt on making *On the Run*. They commissioned a pilot episode, for which Bob supplied the script. Actors Bob Hoskins and James Cossins were cast in the roles of Roland and Gordon. At the time, Hoskins had appeared in various minor roles on television, but was not yet the high-profile star that he would become with his appearances in *Pennies from Heaven* and *The Long Good Friday* later in the decade. James Cossins was probably best known for his role as Mr Walt in the 'The Hotel Inspectors' episode of the BBC comedy series *Fawlty Towers*.

'That was going to be a great comedy series,' recalls Robert Banks Stewart. 'They made the pilot at LWT. It starred Bob Hoskins and James Cossins as the two guys in prison. I went to the recording of the pilot. We all had drinks in the bar afterwards, overlooking the Thames. It must have been about 1977. I can remember Bob being rather happy, having just created this comedy series. They made the pilot, and we all thought it was really very funny. But for some reason or another it never became a series, though it was actually very good. I remember his wife, Pat, came to that recording, and many other friends of Bob's were in the audience – it was filmed before an audience just like any other light entertainment comedy of the time. I remember him being so thrilled when it looked like LWT were going to do it. In the evening, after they did the recording, we all stood around, Bob Hoskins, James Cossins, and Bob, having a drink in that bar at LWT, overlooking the Thames.'

LWT no longer have a copy of the pilot recording of *On the Run*, and all that now exists are Bob's scripts, along with some photos of Hoskins and Cossins in costume on the set. And these photos look as if they could have come from any episode of *Porridge*, so similar is the setting. The witty banter that Bob had scripted for Roland and George was easily on a par with anything that Fletcher and Godber had uttered between them in the BBC series. And perhaps this was the undoing of the project – the pilot episode unfortunately looked and sounded like a direct copy of *Porridge*.

The irony is that, once Roland and George had escaped from prison at the conclusion of the pilot, each subsequent weekly episode would have taken them into different comedy scrapes and situations. The similarities to *Porridge* would have soon dissipated.

'Bob wrote a very funny and extremely black comedy that was piloted,' recalled Jon Thurley. 'During the course of their picaresque adventures [the two escaped convicts] meet an apocalyptic tramp who lights a cigarette and accidentally immolates himself, and a black prostitute who throws them off her pitch under Waterloo arches. Michael Grade[275] reluctantly concluded that the series was probably too rich for the audience of the time, and LWT did not make [it].'[276]

'I recall LWT passing – it was very non-politically-correct, and very funny!' Thurley recalled some years later. 'I suspect I must have discussed it with either Michael Grade or Humphrey Barclay[277] – though whether either will have more recall than I have after all these years is a moot point.'

Bob had written – or at least, had started writing – a number of other scripts for the series. What was probably due to be the second episode, 'The Petrified Forest', has Roland and Gordon hiding out in a wood, scavenging for nuts and berries to eat, but on the lookout for something meatier to tuck in to. The episode ends with Roland encountering a man improbably dressed in a gorilla suit, and the two escaped lags run away in fear. Another proposed instalment, 'The Hero', was devised by Bob only as a scene breakdown, and saw Roland and Gordon hiding out for a few days in a hospital, posing as patients. They are forced to flee at the sound of approaching police sirens, but unknown to them both, it's only a police escort for a fresh kidney being rushed to the hospital for a transplant operation.

Also in 1977, Bob tried his hand for the first time at writing a book, when he was commissioned to novelise his 1974 *Doctor Who* story 'The Time Warrior' for Target Books' ongoing range. However, he struggled with the particular discipline required to do this, and after writing a few pages, he passed the project over to his old chum, Terrance Dicks, to complete (see Chapter Twenty-Eight for more details).

Green City 9 was a series idea of Bob's that looks to have been written by him sometime in the late 1970s. His startling point was to consider the new urban landscapes that were springing up at that time; new towns such as Milton Keynes were something of a talking point. Bob's pitch for the series included some interesting ideas: 'Whether a new town succeeds depends very largely on the relatively small number of people charged with transforming paper into reality. And the series is about these people. They are image-builders, fixers and dealers. They will have a financial or legal background and will be used to thinking in cricket scores of millions. They know their way around the City and they probably also know by heart the flight times to Tokyo. It pays

---

275 At this time, Michael Grade was LWT's Director of Programmes.
276 Private correspondence with Colin Brockhurst dated 26 June 1992.
277 LWT's Head of Comedy in 1977.

them, too, to know the preferences of any particular Saudi Prince.'

However, once again, the idea came to nothing.

Bob's old friend, writer Roger Marshall, recalls that although Bob had many, many genuinely good and interesting project ideas, he always seemed to stumble at the final hurdle when it came to developing them: 'I suppose, in retrospect, I think he spent too much of his life tinkering around with lesser writers' work rather than getting on with his own. Some of his best ideas were stillborn. He had a very black comedy idea about the inhabitants of a nuclear fallout shelter after the bomb had dropped. I didn't read it, but everyone begged him to soft pedal it a bit – i.e. to make it commercial. He wouldn't, so it wasn't made. I think that was typical of him.'[278]

In what was something of a departure for Bob, his next assignment was writing a 16-minute script for a BBC1 schools magazine programme, *Scene*. The script had a working title '1999', but was retitled 'The Future' by Bob. He was commissioned to write this in late February 1978, and delivered his completed script to *Scene* producer David Taft on Tuesday 21 March 1978.

This particular edition of *Scene* actually featured two mini-dramas called 'Visions of Future', both written by Bob, and both depicting different possibilities of what life in the year 2000 might be like. The first was quite positive, and in some respects extremely prophetic, showing how people might shop at superstores via computer, carry mobile phones and have video phones at home, and how recycling was a big element of everyday life. Some of the other ideas in this segment were rather less on-the-money, predicting 'hypno courses' for learning languages via headphones, and a society where everyone wears pastel-coloured judo suits. The second mini-drama was rather more bleak, showing a Britain with meat shortages and food rationing, with no pet dogs (they'd all been killed off as a result of a rabies outbreak a few years earlier), widespread power cuts (as oil would have run out by now), no cars (for the same reason), the reintroduction of a type of National Service – although instead of serving in the army abroad, recruits would have to work in Britain's mines – and the rise of a fascistic youth movement known as the 'Defense Corps'. The whole edition of the programme ran for about 20 minutes, with the extra running time being made up of some *vox-pops* of teenagers giving their own ideas of what life in the future would be like, plus a song, titled 'The Future', performed by singer Caroline Noh. This edition of *Scene* was shown on BBC1 on Thursday 12 October 1978.

Chris Boucher, now well into his stride as script editor on *Blake's 7*'s, hadn't forgotten about Bob. The first season of *Blake's 7* – a kind of space opera take

---

278 Private correspondence with Colin Brockhurst dated 23 June 1992.

on *Robin Hood*, in which the good guys led by Blake are outlaws and the bad guys are the authority figures of the Federation – had been entirely scripted by its creator, Terry Nation. But Nation wanted to have less of an involvement with the second season (he would ultimately contribute just three of the 13 scripts), so it fell to Boucher to find other writers. One of his first ports of call was Bob.

However, there were those at the BBC who weren't that keen to see Bob being commissioned to work on the series, despite him being a candidate for the script editor's job the previous year.

'After Bob had left *Doctor Who*, David Maloney and I wanted to commission him for *Blake's 7*,' recalls Boucher. 'And this makes me slightly angry, I have to say. We used to submit our list of writers and proposals to Ronnie Marsh (BBC Head of Series), who used to look at them. And Ronnie said, "Are you sure you want Bob Holmes?" And we said, "Yes". And he said, "The *Doctor Who* people say he's burned out." I couldn't believe what I was hearing! People whom I didn't hugely respect were dissing somebody I did hugely respect. Anyway, we put Ronnie right. But it was something that shouldn't have been said about someone like Bob, who was talented. It shouldn't be said about anyone, really. In a small world, like the BBC was, I suspect that cost Bob work. But not with us.'

Boucher suspects that Bob's refusal to take up the script editing duties on *Blake's 7* the previous year may also have led to this false notion being put about amongst the senior managers at the BBC. 'There was that sort of feeling that if you don't want to take this job, then there must be something wrong with you. You've thrown back in our faces the opportunity to work on this show, and therefore you must be in some way suspect. I don't know how it came about, but I do remember that very clearly, and I do remember both David and I being quite angry about that.'

Joining the *Blake's 7* writing team in early 1978, Bob was originally slated to script the second season's third episode, which at Boucher's request would have revolved around the computer character Orac, but this storyline was never pursued. By Tuesday 28 February 1978, Boucher had re-jigged the season's running order, and Bob was now scheduled to write the fourth episode, which would have set up Blake's attempt to locate and attack the Federation's computer control centre on Earth.

Did Boucher find the role-reversal odd, in that it was now he who was commissioning scripts from Bob? 'No, it seemed exactly the same. It wasn't a problem for me, and I don't think it was a problem for him. I don't think he ever indicated that it was a problem. I liked Bob, and I assumed he liked me, but then that's the Cocker Spaniel in me; I assume everyone likes me. I was very fond of him, and it was no problem. It felt exactly the same as it always had; he was an easy bloke to work with, and I like to think that I was an easy bloke to work with – but that kind of depended upon the other person involved! It was just the same, it felt the same, it was a pleasant experience for me, and I trust it was a pleasant experience for him.'

Bob was eventually commissioned on Friday 7 April 1978 to write a 50-minute episode of *Blake's 7*, under the working title 'Killer'. By this time his storyline brief had changed again, and now revolved around the characters of Avon and Vila, considered by Bob to be the two most interesting characters in the series. The script, at the time, was scheduled to be the fifth episode of the second season. It opens with Avon and Vila sneaking into the Federation Q-Base on the planet Fosferon, looking to make off with a crystal component that they need to decrypt new Federation security codes. Meanwhile, on Blake's spaceship, the *Liberator*, the computer Zen detects a 700 year-old Earth vessel on approach to the planet, and the telepath Cally senses something malignant on board. Blake anonymously warns the station about the ship, against the wishes of Jenna, who thinks this is tantamount to helping the enemy. Meanwhile, Avon meets up with Tynus, a former associate of his, whom he threatens to blackmail unless he helps steal the crystal they need. Tynus arranges for a diversion that allows Avon to slip past the base's security, but secretly plans a double-bluff that could see Avon being captured. Meanwhile, despite Blake's warnings, the derelict ship is taken onto the base. Blake teleports down to warn the crew in person. But he is too late, as a swift-acting alien virus starts killing everyone in the base. Blake, Avon and Vila manage to escape unharmed, having gained the valuable crystal.

The script for this episode demonstrates one of Bob's key strengths as a writer; namely the development of two separate storyline strands (Avon and Vila's quest for the crystal, and Blake's suspicions about the derelict ship) that then neatly come together in the final third of the story.

Bob delivered his script for 'Killer' on Tuesday 9 May 1978, and Boucher had to do some minor tweaking to it over the next few weeks to prune back the number of characters (other than the regular cast) featured in the scenes to be filmed on location. By June 1978, Boucher had moved 'Killer' further down the season's running order, to take the seventh slot on transmission. This necessitated him making some more minor alterations to the script in order to remove the character of Gan, who was killed off in the fifth episode. 'Killer' was shown on BBC1 on Tuesday 20 February 1979.

'I have to say, there's one story I remember about Bob and that script,' recalls Boucher. 'I probably remember it because it reflects well on me. When Bob came to do that *Blake's 7* for us, the scripts used to go to the Head of

Department, Ronnie Marsh, and he used to raise any objections that he had. And there was a line in it that involved Avon pondering the teleport sending characters into the unknown, and the question was raised, "Supposing you teleport into the nuclear furnace?" And Bob's line in the script was, "That would be tough on the gonads." Now, you couldn't say "gonads" at half-past-seven on a Tuesday night, so Ronnie said, "No, we can't have that line, it'll have to go." And so I went away and came up with the line, "Not a mistake you could learn by, really." And it fitted nicely, so the recording of the episode was done with the new line. Bob told me after the episode was shown on BBC1 that Terrance Dicks phoned him up and said, "I enjoyed your *Blake's 7*, and I particularly liked the line, 'Not a mistake you can learn by, really.' That is such a Bob Holmes line!" Bob wasn't happy! ... He said, "I couldn't believe it, that's the only line Terrance picked out of the whole script!" I did like that!'

For his part, Bob seemed to enjoy writing for the series. When asked if he found writing for *Blake's 7* harder than writing for *Doctor Who*, he responded, 'I don't think so. *Blake's 7* was maybe a little less hard, and less jokey than *Doctor Who*, but otherwise it was very much in the same genre.'[279]

Boucher then got Bob back into the *Blake's 7* production office to talk about the possibility of him writing another script for later in the second season.[280] The result was a commission for him to write a second episode, under the working title 'Doc Holliday', which would revolve around the characters of Travis and Servalan and be something of a spoof of the Western gambling genre. This was due to be the season's tenth episode, and was commissioned on Thursday 3 August 1978 with a target delivery date of Thursday 24 August 1978. Bob went away and wrote his script, now re-titled 'Gambit', which he delivered about a month late, on Monday 25 September 1978.

By this time, the episode had been pushed back slightly in the running order to become the eleventh of the second season. It opens when Blake's group arrives at Freedom City – one of the last places in the galaxy not under Federation control – in search of a cyber-surgeon named Docholli, who, it is rumoured, is one of the few people who may know the secret location of *Star One,* the Federation's control centre. As Blake, Jenna and Cally search for the surgeon, they discover he is being guarded by Travis, who has sought out the doctor for a spot of maintenance on his cybernetic arm. With the assistance of a devious casino owner named Krantor, Servalan plots to eliminate Docholli. She lays a trap for him by capturing Travis and secretly placing a bomb in his

---

279 Robert Holmes Interview, *Renegade*: Issue 1, 1984 – Interview by Matthew Wicks.
280 This would have been in the summer of 1978, just after Bob had handed in his scripts for 'The Power of Kroll' to the *Doctor Who* production office – see Chapter Twenty-Two.

cybernetic arm. Meanwhile, Avon and Vila sneak a miniaturised Orac into Freedom City, in order for them to be able to cheat in Krantor's *Big Wheel* casino and thus win huge amounts of money.

'Gambit' was screened on BBC1 on Tuesday 20 March 1979. It is a totally different kettle of fish from 'Killer' in terms of storytelling techniques, in that Bob seems happy enough to play up the various clichés of a Wild West-type saloon in a futuristic setting. Again, there are dual strands to the plot, but this time they don't interact with each other, and while Avon and Vila's excursion to the casino is witty and fun, it serves no real plot purpose other than to help fill up the running time. Although not Bob's responsibility, it doesn't help matters that the production is very cheap-looking – even for *Blake's 7* – and appears quite rough around the edges.

CHAPTER TWENTY-TWO
BRIEFLY BACK
ON FAMILIAR GROUND
1977-1978

'Certainly, one day before too long, I hope to be back working on another story for my favourite programme,' wrote Bob in late 1977, probably knowing full well that another *Doctor Who* script commission was just around the corner.[281]

The new *Doctor Who* script editor, Anthony Read, had quickly realised that Bob was one of the best *Doctor Who* scriptwriters – if not the best – there was. As soon as he and Graham Williams had put to bed the fifteenth season, it was time for them to begin to plan ahead for the sixteenth. (Williams used to state, with some degree of seriousness, that it took 53 weeks of the year to make a season of *Doctor Who*, meaning that a couple of weeks were spent madly on the overlap between the end of production on one season and the start of production of the next.)

Williams had decided to implement his postponed Key to Time-themed season for *Doctor Who*'s sixteenth year. The season's structure would again follow the traditional 'five four-part stories followed by one six-part story' blueprint that Bob had introduced with Philip Hinchcliffe. As part of the preparation for the new season, Read held a meeting with a group of writers in late 1977, to brief them all about this season-long plot device and discuss the potential story line-up for the year. He was also able to allocate stories and plotlines to them. Bob was in attendance, and was the only writer with previous experience of writing for the programme. Douglas Adams was also present, as were two other writers new to *Doctor Who*, Ted Lewis and David Fisher, who had been drafted in by Read. Bob Baker and Dave Martin were unable to attend, but were sent notes of the discussion with a view to them also contributing a script.

As a result of this meeting, Bob was informally invited to come up with the opening four-part adventure; one that would set up the concept of the season-long quest for the Key to Time but also function as a story in its own right.[282] Bob knew the framework and format that Williams was looking to impose on the season, and still wasn't completely taken with the idea, but went along with

---

281 'Robert Holmes Speaks', *Gallifrey*: Issue 2, January 1978.
282 For whatever reason, it seems there was no attempt made to resuscitate Terrance Dicks' 'The Vampire Mutation' as the opening Key to Time story.

the proposals. 'I disliked the whole Key to Time gimmick and the idea of the White Guardian and the Black Guardian,' he later said. 'It is difficult enough to come up with five or six good stories a season without having to tack on an unnecessary linking theme.'[283]

In early December 1977, Bob was invited to have a one-on-one chat with Read. Bob had by now come up with a story idea that revolved around a galactic conman, whose scam involved a precious stone that would be revealed to be the first segment of the Key to Time. Read liked the idea, and so on Friday 9 December 1977, Bob was commissioned to write four scripts based on this outline. The story was given the working title 'Galactic Conman', and Bob was set a target delivery date of Monday 9 January 1978.[284]

He was slightly late, delivering the first three scripts on Monday 30 January, and the final one a week later, on Monday 6 February 1978. It was now standard procedure for all new *Doctor Who* scripts to be sent to the BBC's Head of Serials, Graeme McDonald, as soon as they had been received by the production team, so that he could read them. McDonald had a few minor queries on some of the dialogue involving Romana's character, and concluded that Bob's script '... seems to get off to a good start.' The story was retitled 'The Ribos Operation' prior to entering production.

A new companion for the Doctor, the Time Lady Romana, had been devised by Read and Williams, and Bob also had the task of ushering her into the series in his story. 'I introduced Romana in "Ribos",' he later recalled, 'but I can't remember now whether or not she appeared in the opening scene with the White Guardian. That prologue to the season was written by "David Agnew".'[285]

The story was a particular favourite of Bob's – especially the characters. 'I liked the Graff very much,' he recalled. 'The Graff obviously has German connotations, Vynda-K. And that was the sort of thing I liked to do, but you can't do them like that all the time.'

Although Bob was more than happy with the end result, he did slightly rue the casting of Iain Cuthbertson as Garron, the 'Galactic Conman' in question. Bob's displeasure didn't stem from Cuthbertson's acting ability – far from it – but from his portrayal of Garron as a cockney. 'I wrote the conman as an Australian, I think, but they didn't tend to discuss casting with me,' he recalled.[286]

'George Spenton-Foster let Iain Cuthbertson get rather camp,' Bob would

283 Robert Holmes Interview, *Renegade*: Issue 1, 1984 – Interview by Matthew Wicks.
284 It's possible that Bob was partly inspired by his response to Terrance Dicks during the staged script conference for *The Lively Arts*: 'Whose Doctor Who' that he participated in earlier in the year. After all, his reply to Dicks was: 'It's not that he's taking over this planet, he's going to do what he's come for, which is to steal this lump of mercury or whatever it is, and zoom off!'
285 Robert Holmes Interview, *The Time Meddler*: Issue 3, October 1981 – Interview by John M Kahane.
286 Panopticon IV Convention, Queen Mary College, 1-2 August 1981.

later lament. 'I mean, it's my fault, because I tend to write lines that the actor relishes, but it should have been toned down rather more. Iain Cuthbertson got away with a lot in the part of Garron. The basic joke there, of a galactic conman trying to sell a planet, amused me, and I enjoyed doing that one. But I did think that one went over the top. George Spenton-Foster was directing, and he tends to appreciate the humour in a script. He later did a *Blake's 7* for me, "Gambit" it was called. And he let that one go a bit over the top.'

The national press were quite positive about the story. Keith Baker, writing in the *Belfast Telegraph,* noted: 'The good Doctor's new sidekick is, we are told, going to be his equal, a deferential bow towards the Bionic Woman, Wonder Woman, and Women's Lib all at once.' He drolly noted that Romana soon began doing what all the other assistants before had done, '[asking] "What are you going to do now, Doctor?" just like all her predecessors, and swanning around in a white cape like some kind of snow queen. However the glittering prose is not confined to her alone. That most ubiquitous of performers, Iain Cuthbertson, who would act in anything and does, is playing the part of some interplanetary con artist in a variety of accents, none of them his own.'[287]

Bob's opening story of the season was to be followed by one called 'The Pirate Planet' by Douglas Adams, whose persistence in trying to write for the series had finally paid off. Newcomer David Fisher was to write the third story, entitled 'The Stones of Blood', while the other newcomer, Ted Lewis, was down to write story four, 'Shield of Zarak'. Story Five was yet to be decided on by Read, while Baker and Martin had been assigned the final six-part adventure, eventually entitled 'The Armageddon Factor'. Lewis delivered his scripts for the first two episodes of 'Shield of Zarak' in mid-May 1977, but Read and Williams both found them to be unsuitable. The story was dropped from the season's line-up.

Bob and Fisher were called back in to meet with Read, and both received a commission to write a further four-part story. Fisher's, 'The Androids of Tara', was given the fourth slot in the season, replacing the scrapped 'Shield of Zarak'. Bob was asked to come up with a story for the fifth slot, and was also given the challenge of featuring the biggest monster ever seen in *Doctor Who* to date. As a result of this, he was commissioned on Friday 26 May 1978 to write four scripts for a story called 'Moon of Death'.

Bob was required to deliver all four scripts on Monday 5 June 1978, but bearing in mind that this gave him only *ten days* to carry out the work, it's not surprising that he was a little late. What *is* surprising is how narrowly he missed this deadline – he actually delivered the first two episodes just two days late, on

---

287 *Belfast Telegraph*, 16 September 1978.

Wednesday 7 June 1978, and the final two just over a week later, on Thursday 15 June 1978. The story underwent several title changes, first to 'Horror from the Swamp' and then to 'The Power of Kroll', before entering production.

While he was still in the middle of writing these scripts, Bob told one *Doctor Who* fanzine that the story was '… about some Red Indians and the oil company that wants to shift them off their reservation. It won't seem a bit like that, though, because it is set in an alien civilisation'.[288]

Apart from Romana, 'The Power of Kroll' was a story with an exclusively male cast of characters. Bob was asked at the time if he was against using female characters in *Doctor Who*. 'I suppose it's basically true,' he replied. 'Women don't usually have major roles in action-adventure shows. They are always hanging around the saloon in Westerns, but they are rarely in evidence when the time comes for the shoot out. Then again it's more difficult to show a woman coming to a sticky end (convention's against it) and as characters in *Doctor Who* are always coming to sticky ends, my feeling is that female characters, generally speaking, have less value.'[289]

Once again, producer Graham Williams sent copies of the four scripts to his Head of Department, Graeme McDonald, for his thoughts. McDonald got back to Williams on Monday 7 August 1978 with his comments: 'Quite an exciting serial, though I hope it won't be one of those that masks its monster weaknesses in night sequences. One structural point worries me: the first three episodes all end with the same threat (the Kroll emerges etc.) Surely there should be more development?' However, he did veto outright a scene that Bob had written in the script of the first episode, where a character flicks some fluid from a phial at another character. McDonald thought that such an action was too easy for children to imitate. Read did a quick rewrite of the scene prior to recording.

Bob would later state that 'The Power of Kroll' was his least favourite *Doctor Who* story. '"The Power of Kroll" was one that I didn't think worked,' he recalled. 'Tony Read said to me, "I don't want any humour, and I want the biggest monster the Doctor's ever encountered". And I thought, "Oh-oh! We're in trouble now." Then we had Norman Stewart having a sort of first try as a director, and it gave him terrible problems. I think he was an old mate of Graeme McDonald's, and he got offered this story. Basically, Norman had been with the Corporation for a long time, and had gone to Graham McDonald and said, "I'd like to be a director now; I think I've won my spurs as a production manager." And Graeme said, "Well, if you think you can do it, I advise you to

---

288 Robert Holmes Interview, *Type 40*: Issue 1, 1978.
289 Robert Holmes Interview, *Type 40*: Issue 1, 1978.

resign and become a freelance director." And he did and it didn't work.'[290]

Shortly after completing his work on the scripts for 'The Power of Kroll', Bob attended his first ever *Doctor Who* convention. The DWAS had held their first ever event – indeed the first ever *Doctor Who* convention anywhere – the previous year, and now followed this up with a two-day convention, Panopticon II, over the weekend of 12-13 August 1978, at Imperial College in London. Bob took part in a panel discussion about script editing the series, alongside Terrance Dicks, Anthony Read, and Graham Williams.

Read had by now decided to move on as script editor after only 18 months in the role. The next *Doctor Who* story into production, 'The Armageddon Factor' written by Baker and Martin, was to be his last. His replacement was to be Douglas Adams, an appointment made mainly on the strength of his scripts for the 'The Pirate Planet'. Unlike Bob, or Dicks, Read didn't invoke the 'resigning script editor gets commissioned by his successor' tradition.

In an interview given shortly after completing his scripts for 'The Power of Kroll', Bob was asked about his future with *Doctor Who*. He said at the time: 'Whether I write for it again depends on: a) if Douglas Adams, the new editor, asks me; b) if I can think of a story; and c) if I have time to write it. I have had a long run, however, and I feel the programme would benefit from an infusion of fresh writers.'[291]

In fact, Bob would have to wait some years until he was next invited back to work on *Doctor Who*. One possible reason for this was that he had by now become perhaps a little complacent with regard to his abilities and the demands of the series. In the same 1978 interview, he was also asked how much of his submitted scripts got changed by the incumbent *Doctor Who* production team. 'Hardly any,' was his reply. 'The production team know what they're about and don't make changes unless they have good reasons. However, as a former script editor on the programme, I am able to anticipate most of the production problems that may arise and allow for these in my scripts. So happily my stuff doesn't get altered much.'[292]

Dicks speculates that Bob might just have become too much of a 'high maintenance' writer for the makers of *Doctor Who* at a time when behind-the-scenes pressures and soaring inflation costs made producing the series

290 Norman Stewart had worked as a production assistant at the BBC on *Doctor Who* as far back as the first Dalek story in 1963, and had more recently performed the same role on 'The Invisible Enemy' in early 1977. He resigned from the BBC to become a freelance director later in 1977, returning to *Doctor Who* almost straight away to direct 'Underworld' (which Bob probably didn't know about, as he'd left the show by then). The following year, Stewart was given 'The Power of Kroll' to direct, as well as two episodes of the BBC Scotland paranormal series *The Ωmega Factor*. He then left directing almost as quickly as he'd begun, and returned to the BBC as a production manager, working on series such as *Tenko* and *Bergerac*.
291 Robert Holmes Interview, *Type 40*: Issue 1, 1978.
292 Robert Holmes Interview, *Type 40*: Issue 1, 1978.

a trying task. 'It may have been because people found Bob difficult to work with, because he was not easy-going and acquiescent,' notes Dicks, 'and he would grumble and make a fuss, and occasionally lose his temper. Like a lot of talented people, he was occasionally hard to handle, and that may have had some effect on him not being asked to write for the series again. But I don't know that for a fact – I'm theorising.'

Perhaps the truth of the matter is something much more mundane, such as simple logistics. Williams had elected to have the Daleks return to the series for the first time since 'Genesis of the Daleks' in 1975, and that meant having to commission a script written by Terry Nation. David Fisher had written two well-received stories the year before, and so was asked to write two more this time around. Recently-departed script editor Read was given a four-part story to write. Long-time series regular Bob Baker, newly solo after splitting from his writing partner Dave Martin, was also given a story to write. And Adams had pencilled himself in to supply the final six-part story. Perhaps there just wasn't room in the schedule this year for a Robert Holmes script? As a result, Season Seventeen became the first season of *Doctor Who* in nearly a decade that didn't feature any input from Bob.[293]

When work on Season Seventeen concluded, both Williams and Adams left *Doctor Who*. A new production team in the shape of producer John Nathan-Turner and script editor Christopher H Bidmead was installed by the BBC. Nathan-Turner had been production unit manager on the series for the three years that Williams had been producer, and certainly knew Bob. 'I had enormous respect for Robert Holmes,' he once wrote. 'I knew him socially for many years before our paths crossed on *Doctor Who*. Threshold/Union House in the early '70s was a wonderful place to work, with a constant cross-pollination of ideas, individuals and aspirations.'[294]

But Nathan-Turner had his own ideas about the series, and had decided that *Doctor Who* needed an influx of writers that were 'new blood'. After initial commissions had been given (more out of desperation than choice) to two 'old guard' writers, Terrance Dicks and David Fisher, he decreed that he would in future give preference to writers new to the series. His new script editor had no choice but to follow this edict. Suddenly, Bob was *persona non grata* at the *Doctor Who* production office.

---

293 Okay, Bob hadn't actually written a story for Season Nine as it went out on television, but only because 'Carnival of Monsters' was made that year and then held over to be shown as part as Season Ten. The point remains that Bob had been at the heart of *Doctor Who* since Patrick Troughton's final year in the TARDIS, and had now suddenly become an outsider in the space of just over 12 months.
294 Private correspondence with Colin Brockhurst dated 14 July 1992.

CHAPTER TWENTY-THREE
FREELANCE NIGHTMARE
1979-1985

If Bob thought that he'd been unlucky in the 18 months since he'd stopped being *Doctor Who*'s script editor – in terms of getting his other projects onto the screen – then 1979 was to prove to be another frustrating year.

Early in the year, Chris Boucher once again got in contact with Bob, with a view to getting him to write a script for the third season of *Blake's 7*, which was now in production. Bob was commissioned on Thursday 12 April 1979 to write an episode entitled 'Sweetly Dreaming, Slowly Dying', with a target delivery date of Thursday 14 June 1979. According to the BBC paperwork, Bob delivered this script on Friday 31 August 1979, and it was formally accepted on Monday 24 September 1979. Bob was paid the first half of the fee for this script when it was first commissioned, and the second half on Wednesday 10 October 1979, which would indicate a script was indeed fully written by Bob. However, by Wednesday 14 November 1979, this was one of three third season scripts that were written off (the other two being by Jon Fletcher and Allan Prior respectively), and the episode was never put into production.

However, Boucher has no recollection of 'Sweetly Dreaming, Slowly Dying' at all. 'It's a great title! But I think that's probably all there was. It looks like we may have commissioned Bob, in which case there will have been an initial payment – but as to why there was no script that I can recall, I have no idea. By that season we had adopted the normal approach to series drama, and over-commissioned as a matter of routine. This involved an upfront fee and then a second completion payment if the writer did his/her best to meet any problems thrown up by the first draft. After that it was a question of whether there were remaining problems and, if there were, whether I as the script editor could solve them. If a substantial rewrite is done (by me in the case of *Blake's 7*) and the script is then used, the writer has the option of taking their name off the episode, but all residuals remain the property of the writer. I don't remember the three scripts we didn't use that year (although I do recall John Fletcher – a good writer, but couldn't get his head round the rudimentary science involved in science fiction or the crude framework that was *Blake's 7*). But obviously it turned out the scripts still couldn't work without major effort from me, so they were paid for but not used. It's not unusual, and any freelance writer has experienced it. I'm sure that you will look at other episodes in that third season and think (and probably say) even at his worst, Bob would have written a better script than that! But you have to define better and, to use one of the current political clichés, "That is a question of context ..." But no script was ever in the line-up for a series unless there was a rehearsal script completed. I have to tell you I don't think any of those three got that far.'

If Bob *did* write a script, then neither the BBC nor Bob kept a copy, and no other details about this lost *Blake's 7* story are known.

Robert Banks Stewart returns to the narrative of Bob's life again at this point. Stewart had gone to work at Thames Television in 1976, leaving his *Doctor Who* story 'The Foe from the Future' unfinished. He had become script editor on a series called *Rooms*, then fulfilled the same role on the first series of *Armchair Thriller*. *Armchair Thriller* had been shown on the ITV network in 1978, and was generally considered a minor success. After *Armchair Thriller* had finished, Stewart then went on to devise a children's drama serial for Thames, called *Jukes of Piccadilly*. This ran for six 30-minute episodes, and revolved around the comic exploits of Brinsley Jukes (played by Nigel Hawthorn), the owner of an exclusive tea emporium, who has a passion for private investigations. 'I was story editor at that time on *Armchair Thriller*, and at the same time I wrote the opening couple of episodes of *Jukes of Piccadilly*,' confirms Stewart. 'Originally I wanted it to be an adult series, but then it became what you might call a "kidult" series, pertaining not to children exactly, but to early evening viewing. Now what happened was, at the same time as I was finishing off on *Armchair Thriller*, I was invited to go back to work at the BBC. And Bob, being a colleague on many things I'd done, was ideally placed to carry on with *Jukes of Piccadilly*. I had no doubt about letting him write the rest of the series.'

The opening two-part story of *Jukes of Piccadilly*, 'The Corcelli Medallion', was written by Stewart, but he then asked Bob to write the second and third two-part stories. Bob's scripts were written in early 1979, and the series was recorded in May of that year.

Bob's first story, 'The Case of the Arabian Kidnap', saw Jukes being asked to investigate the kidnapping of Princess Ayallah by her uncle, Sheik Achmed. This was followed by the final two-part story, 'Dulverton Green', which saw Jukes attending a family wedding while at the same time investigating the escape from prison of the bride's father, Geoffrey Martindale, the cat-burglar suspected of stealing the famous Dulverton Green jewel.

Jukes of Piccadilly was shown weekly on ITV in February and March 1980, with Bob's first episode of 'The Case of the Arabian Kidnap' screening on Monday 25 February 1980, and with his subsequent episodes following on a weekly basis.

At around the time that Bob was writing these episodes of *Jukes of Piccadilly*, *Armchair Thriller* was renewed for a second season by Thames Television, and this new season was also scheduled to air in 1980. Stewart wasn't able to return as script editor (as he was about to go and work for the BBC as a producer), so he put Bob's name forward as a suitable replacement. A new producer, Brenda Ennis, was also appointed. Bob enjoyed his time working with Ennis, but later rued his recent run of working with first-time producers. 'I had in succession when I was a script editor, Philip Hinchcliffe, who'd never produced before, and came from ATV working on *General Hospital*; then I had Graham Williams, who had been the script editor on *Softly, Softly*; and then I went to Thames to do *Armchair Thriller*, and I had a lady called Brenda Ennis, who'd never been a producer before. She had been assistant producer on *Edward and Mrs Simpson*, but she'd never actually produced. So I had about five or six years with first-timers.'

The first series of *Armchair Thriller* in 1978 was made up of 26 half-hour episodes, consisting of five unrelated stories of either four or six episodes in length. In production terms, it was about the same length as a typical season of *Doctor Who*. Bob took over in 1979 as script editor for the second season of 26 episodes, and set about assembling the scripts that would make up this run of stories. 'Bob had become quite a regular on telly, and well-known to other producers,' recalls Stewart. 'So I think that was always inevitable, that he would follow me on *Armchair Thriller*. *Armchair Thriller* was based on a series of book adaptations; it wasn't created by any individual writer. The three or four stories that I was editor of, they were all based on books.'

Bob's work on the series would take up most of the rest of 1979.

The first (six-part) story of the second season was 'The Victim', written by Michael Ashe, who had also worked on *No Hiding Place* and *Emergency Ward 10* among others. It told the story of Vincent Craig, a wealthy electronics business executive whose 14-year old daughter, Sue, is kidnapped and held for ransom. Against the advice of the police, Craig uses his own resources and equipment to try to trap the kidnappers when they call him up with their ransom demands. But his investigations initially take him in the wrong direction, and in the meantime his daughter begins to form a bond with her kidnappers. He eventually discovers where she is being held, but does she now want to be rescued ...?

The second (four-part) story, 'Dying Day', was written by John Bowen, who had written extensively for the first series of *Armchair Thriller*. This instalment is perhaps most notable for its impressive cast, which included Ian McKellen, Anton Philips, Patrick Malahide, Michael Troughton and Prentis

Hancock. The story revolves around Antony Skipling (McKellen), who while on a train journey meets a mysterious man who plays him a selection of audio tapes he has made of obscure nature noises. The man leaves a tape behind, and when Skipling later plays it, he overhears voices discussing his own impending murder. The police think he's mad, especially as the tape, when replayed, now has the crucial conversation missing. As the date of his intended death approaches, Skipling goes in search of answers, and seemingly stumbles across a plot by his ex-wife and a mysterious recluse ...

The third (four-part) story, 'Fear of God', was an adaptation by Troy Kennedy Martin of the book *The Fear of God*[295], written by Derry Quinn. The story opens when journalist Paul Marriot sees a young girl fall to her death from the room above his flat. His investigations link her to a fanatical religious sect, but when he submits a story linking the girl's death to the sect, his editor heavily censors the article on the instructions of the Ministry of Defence. Marriot discovers the sect is in possession of sound weapon technology with which it intends to brainwash the youth of Britain and recruit them to the cult. But Marriot has now become a threat to the cult ...

The fourth (six-part) story, 'The Circe Complex', was another book adaptation, this time of the novel of the same name by Desmond Cory.[296] It was adapted by David Hopkins, who had previously written for *Dr Finlay's Casebook* and *The Adventures of Black Beauty*.[297] The story concerns Val Foreman, a young woman who is a serial seducer, and who is seemingly irresistible to men. Her husband is currently serving a prison sentence after being found guilty of stealing half a million pounds in jewels, which have never been found. She persuades her new lover, a psychiatrist, to help spring her husband out of prison so they can find out where he has hidden the heist. She enlists a young burglar to help, and the plot attracts the attention of the police. But the psychiatrist, burglar, and investigating police officer all fall for her charms, and she manipulates them all to further her scheme to locate the stashed jewels.

The final (six-part) story of the season was 'The Chelsea Murders', an adaptation of the novel of the same name by Lionel Davidson.[298] This time the adaptation was written by Jonathan Hales, who had previously had some television writing credits on *Armchair Theatre* and *Manhunt* and who would

295 Published by Magnum Books, 1978.
296 Published by Doubleday, 1975.
297 Although the television credits for this story read 'Dramatised by David Hopkins from the novel by Desmond Cory', with Bob listed as the series script editor, the rehearsal scripts for all six episodes have 'by Desmond Cory, Dramatised by Robert Holmes' printed on them.
298 Published by Arrow Books, 1978.

ROBERT HOLMES: A LIFE IN WORDS

go on to write episodes of *Dallas* and *The Adventures of Young Indiana Jones*, plus contribute towards the screenplays for films such as *The Scorpion King* and *Star Wars: Episode II – Attack of the Clones*. The story opens with the murders of four people in Chelsea in the space of a few weeks, while a fifth victim survives and tells the police her attacker was a character from a film made by three art students. More murders occur, each accompanied by a cryptic message quoting from a famous piece of literary fiction. A journalist investigating the crimes begins to stumble upon the truth ...

Although the initial plan was to show the 26 episodes of this second season of *Armchair Thriller* in early 1980, something went a bit awry higher up in the ITV chain of command. The various ITV networks did indeed begin screening it, twice-weekly, in January 1980, beginning with the story 'The Victim', but this was then followed by a four-part story called 'Dead Man's Kit', which had been made by Southern Television, and which neither Bob nor the rest of the Thames Television *Armchair Thriller* production team had any hand or involvement in. 'Dead Man's Kit' still went out under the *Armchair Thriller* series umbrella title, however, complete with the generic series opening titles, but was made totally on 16mm film – the Thames Television episodes were made totally on videotape – and had different closing titles, and so consequently has a different look and feel to it than the other Thames-produced material.

'Dying Day' and 'Fear of God' were then screened by ITV, but these episodes were followed by another interloper, once again made by Southern Television without the involvement of Bob or the Thames Television production team. This was a four-part story entitled 'High Tide', again made on 16mm film rather than videotape. 'The Circe Complex' then aired on ITV in April 1980, bringing the second season of *Armchair Thriller* to a premature close, with 'The Chelsea Murders' left unscreened.

Most of this second season was then repeated on ITV in late 1981, and it was only when these repeats concluded that 'The Chelsea Murders' was finally screened for the first time – but not in its original six-episode form. The story had been subsequently edited into a single two-hour programme, which was shown on ITV on Wednesday 30 December 1981.[299]

Just as Bob's work on *Armchair Thriller* was coming to an end, the chance of writing for a new BBC drama series came his way. Bill Slater, formerly the

---

299 The two-hour abridged version of 'The Chelsea Murders' as shown on ITV no longer survives in the Thames archives. The six-part version does survive, but only the final episode is complete. The other five episodes all lack sound effects, incidental music, and spoken recaps at the start of the episodes. All the Thames Television-produced episodes from the first and second series of *Armchair Thriller* (including 'The Chelsea Murders') have been released as a DVD boxset by Network. The two Southern Television stories have been independently released on DVD by Simply Home Entertainment.

BBC's Head of Serials, decided in late 1979 to initiate a drama series of his own. Going by the title *Won't you go Home, Bill Bailiff?*, the series was to be set in the sometimes seedy world of a bailiff by the name of (yes, you guessed it) Bill. It was later retitled to the equally bizarre *Unknown by the Name of Smith*.

Peter Draper[300] wrote two full scripts for what would probably have been the first two episodes of the series and was set to write two more, with Bob also down to write two; as were Peter Tinniswood and Johnny Byrne.[301] Slater was confident that the ten scripts he'd set in motion would all work extremely well, and he had high hopes for the series, which he was now looking to pass over to a full-time producer who would nurture it onto the screen and also look to commission further episodes.

Both of Bob's script commissions for *Unknown by the Name of Smith* came on Monday 24 September 1979, directly from Slater. The first 50-minute script was given the title 'To Make a Killing', and the storyline was quoted on the commissioning form as follows: 'Bill turns up in a plush flat overlooking the route to be taken by a visiting Arab Colonel. He finds the tenants gone, but an unexpected guest in residence who is there to assassinate the Colonel. Neither Bill nor the would-be assassin understand the other's intentions.' The target date for Bob to deliver this script was Monday 15 October 1979.

The second 50-minute script commissioned from Bob was titled 'Not Made of Stone', and had a target delivery date of Thursday 15 November 1979. The storyline on this brief read: 'Temperamental sculptor at loggerheads with wife, bankrupts himself to spite her. Bill brings about reconciliation, but as he leaves the house he hears a crash of crockery because husband and wife were born to fight and really thoroughly enjoy it. This however is a victory for Bill.' This is then followed with the note: 'NB: Mr Holmes might substitute this story for another,' indicating that this plotline may have been more of a placeholder than anything else.

Bob was issued with his contracts for the two scripts, and was paid the first half-fee for them. But the series seems to have stalled within a few months of him being brought in to write for it, and no second half-fees appear to have been paid to him, which would indicate that he never actually wrote either of the scripts.

It was at around this time that Bob, Patricia, Nicholas and Laurian moved

---

300 Draper had a good, solid background in television scriptwriting going back to the 1960s, and at the time this series was mooted had recently written several episodes of the BBC's *Poldark*.
301 Tinniswood was known for his comedy writing, contributing scripts to *I Didn't Know You Cared* (BBC, 1975-76), *Never Say Die* (Yorkshire Television, 1970) and *The Frost Report* (BBC, 1966-67). At the time, Johnny Byrne was best known for being script editor and writer on the Gerry Anderson series *Space: 1999*, but he'd go on to write extensively for *All Creatures Great and Small*, as well as for *Doctor Who*.

into a new house – a large, picturesque thatched cottage in the small village of Akeley in Buckingham. It was a quiet enough place for Bob to hide himself away in his study with his typewriter, and work on scripts and stories with no interruptions, but was also close enough to London for him to be able to get to meetings there within an hour. It was an idyllic place, and Bob and Patricia would both stay at this cottage for the rest of their lives.

Robert Banks Stewart had by now finally left Thames and gone to work at the BBC as a producer. He had initially been lined up to succeed Philip Hinchcliffe on *Target*'s third season, which was due to go into production in late 1978. However, during discussions with his Head of Department, Graeme McDonald, he learned that *Target* was considered a disposable property by BBC management, who were actively looking for a series to replace it in the schedules. Stewart then suggested doing a series about a private detective, an idea that was ultimately commissioned instead of a third season of *Target*. That series became *Shoestring*, which featured Trevor Eve as the titular Eddie Shoestring, a computer expert recovering from a nervous breakdown, who forges a new career as a private detective with his own radio show.[302]

The first season of *Shoestring* went into production in autumn 1978, with Stewart as producer and Bob Baker as script editor. It was a huge success when it aired in the autumn of 1979, after which Baker was subsequently persuaded to leave the BBC to become Head of Scripts at HTV, the Bristol-based ITV channel. This left Stewart searching for a new script editor for the second season. He had no hesitation in turning to Bob, who had just finished his stint as script editor on the second season of *Armchair Thriller*. And so in late 1979, Bob returned to the BBC as script editor on *Shoestring*, just over two years after he had left as script editor on *Doctor Who*.

Bob found he had his work cut out on the series; a number of the scripts that had been commissioned for the second season just weren't working out, and had to be heavily rewritten. It was time for 'William Hood' to come out of retirement …

'Well, Bob used the name William Hood when he was with Granada, working on *Knight Errant*,' recalled Stewart. 'When that name was used, it meant that he had rewritten the entire episode. The original author probably said something like "I don't want my name on it". And so there was a fictional writer called William Hood. William Hood worked with me some 20-odd years later on *Shoestring*, when Bob was my story editor!

302 Richard Harris, who was also named as co-creator of *Shoestring* on screen, helped Stewart devise the characters and settings, and also wrote a pilot script for the series, which the BBC didn't like. Stewart wrote a new opening episode, and Harris had no further input in the series after that point.

'We'd tell the author we were unhappy with a script. We'd probably let the writer have a go at doing a rewrite, but if the writer couldn't do it, we'd have no alternative but to get it rewritten ourselves. We were very careful; we never, ever denied the original writer the royalties, because that is not fair. To say "Sorry, your script doesn't work", that was a justification for the writer to do a rewrite, but if *that* didn't work, one was a bit desperate. William Hood was Bob when he did really profound rewrites – rewriting from the start if necessary. There were a number of writers, I won't mention their names, but they kind of screwed up, they couldn't catch the "spirit" of *Shoestring*. So William Hood was Robert.'

'There were loads of scripts hanging around when I left,' recalled out-going script editor Bob Baker. 'We had a proper pile. There was a bookcase, and it had scripts all along it; it was supposed to go Episode One, Two, Three, Four, and so on, through to Ten, or whichever was the last episode of the season. But in fact at the end of it was a big stack. These were all the "maybes", so there were all those scripts to work on. And so Bob Banks Stewart would say to Bob Holmes, "Okay – have a go at that one. It's crap, what can you do with it?"'

The two second-season *Shoestring* episodes credited as being written by William Hood were 'Mocking Bird' and 'The Farmer Had a Wife'.[303]

'Mocking Bird' revolves around a Bristol-based mugger who seems obsessed with Shoestring, and continually taunts him by ringing him up after each crime to berate him for his inability to catch him. Bob's script was greatly influenced by the events of the real-life late-'70s manhunt for the Yorkshire Ripper, when an audiotape made by 'Wearside Jack', claiming to be the Ripper and mocking the efforts made by the authorities to catch him, was sent to the police in June 1979.[304] In Shoestring's case, the mugger turns out to be an ex-policeman employed by Radio West as a night-time security guard, who's jealous of Shoestring's position at the station.

'The original idea for "Mocking Bird" was, I seem to recall, discussed with me and Bob Holmes by the original writer,' says Stewart. 'In fact, it was written originally by a successful, regular writer of *Coronation Street*, but alas he bombed. A really awful script, as I recall. Do you know, I can't remember his name, but he did get the repeat royalties! I believe the *Coronation Street* writer had the idea of the Radio West security guy who also did hospital

---

303 A third *Shoestring* episode from the second season, 'Room with a View', was credited to Robert Bennett. 'William Hood was Bob Holmes, doing quite a grand job, and a guy called Robert Bennett was me,' recalls Robert Banks Stewart. 'And we used to get enquiries about both William Hood and Robert Bennett. I actually got an enquiry once from another producer saying, "Who is this writer, Robert Bennett?" I can't remember how I handled it!'
304 It wasn't until Peter Sutcliffe was arrested and convicted of the Ripper murders in 1981 that it was discovered that the voice on the 'Wearside Jack' tape wasn't actually the Ripper's. In 2005, John Humble was convicted of perverting the course of justice by making and sending the tape to the police.

radio, and thus had ideas that he was better than Eddie Shoestring.' The idea that Shoestring would receive telephone messages from the mugger, which were recorded and replayed, was Bob's. 'I do believe that the taunting tapes of the Ripper might have been the reason for the final story as it appeared in *Shoestring*,' Stewart confirms. The finished script of this episode is extremely good, belying the production problems it had, and takes Shoestring on the sort of emotional journey that most long running series shy away from putting their lead character through.

'The Farmer Had a Wife' sees Eddie take on the case of one David Mortimer, a farmer who has antagonised many of his village locals in the years since he moved into the area. Mortimer's wife suddenly vanishes, and Mortimer is suspected of killing her and hiding the body. The police fail to find the missing woman, and village gossip over her disappearance reaches fever pitch. The deeper Shoestring investigates, the more he discovers that Mortimer has been keeping information from him, and it begins to look like the village gossip could perhaps be true. But Shoestring eventually locates the errant wife, who has left her husband to be close to the illegitimate child that she was forced to give up for adoption many years earlier. She refuses to go back to her husband, and while Shoestring tells his radio audience about his success with the case, Mortimer commits suicide with a pistol at his farm. It's a very bleak episode indeed.

Stewart recalls that Bob slipped easily back into his role of a BBC script editor. 'Bob was a script editor who very much enjoyed meeting a writer at 12 o'clock,' he recalled, 'and to then have a good solid hour to discuss the story and the approach, and then it was off to lunch in a particular Italian restaurant on Shepherd's Bush Green. I can't remember the name of the restaurant, but he was so well known there, the waitresses used to say, "Hello Mr Holmes," whenever he walked in. It was his favourite place to lunch. He always used to pick up the tab, because he was the script editor, and put it on expenses. My memory was that he was never reckless with that. I don't remember ever having lunch with him, in that Italian restaurant, where we had anything other than the standard lunchtime menu, and yes we probably did in those days have a bottle of wine, but it wasn't your expensive wine, it was just your everyday glass of wine. But Bob loved to have lunch, he was very fond of lunch. But I wouldn't like to paint it as a "heavy" lunch. He liked to end a creative discussion with a social discussion, you know.

'He was habitually there, but I don't mean anything to do with drinking! Although Bob did also like the odd glass of port. I always associate port with Bob; he liked a drink, but he did not overdo it.'

Bob's joy of lunching is also recalled fondly by Terrance Dicks: 'I remember once we took him out to lunch in the BBC restaurant. It was to discuss a story or whatever, and people in those days didn't used to eat puddings, it was considered rather low to have puddings, and when they came round with the dessert menu, people would say, "No, just coffees". And when they got round to Bob, he said "Baked jam roll and custard". And I thought, "Good for you!" That was very like Bob; if he wanted baked jam roll and custard, he didn't care if it was trendy or not. That sums him up, in a way.'

'I was a great admirer of Bob's skill as a story editor and rewriter, especially on *Doctor Who*,' Stewart continues. 'I think in some ways Bob was very much part of my success at the time of me being at Thames when I came up with *Jukes of Piccadilly*, and he wrote for that. Then he became story editor of the second season of *Armchair Thriller* just as I left for the BBC, so it seems that our careers were quite entwined as such. I suppose you could say that he was one of my favourite writers. Now people would suggest that we would all commission each other, and there was some truth in that … but I don't think I would have ever commissioned a friend just because he was a friend; I'd never do that. Bob was obviously one of the best writers. And you know, he did have a quite intellectual approach to both being a story editor and the things that he wrote. Certainly we know that from *Doctor Who*. I certainly don't think there was a finer story editor than Bob Holmes. I don't think that Terrance Dicks would disagree. Well, he might! Ha-ha!'

However, as Stewart recalls, Bob fell ill while working on the second season of *Shoestring*, during the summer of 1980: 'Graeme McDonald came to me and said, "I hear you've got problems with Bob." … Somewhere during the middle of that second season of *Shoestring*, I don't think he was very well. I don't remember what the problem was, but he was certainly very tired, and I think it was the beginning of his health problems. And Bob used to come up to London every day, all that way from his place in Buckinghamshire, which was a daily slog I thought he could do without. That is the reason why Chris Boucher came in as the script editor towards the end of the second season.'

At the time, Boucher had just finished script editing the third season of *Blake's 7* (which, as far as he was concerned, was meant to be the last season of that show). Boucher was given no explanation for Bob's sudden departure from *Shoestring*, only that he was taking over. 'He bailed: why, I can't remember – if I ever knew,' recalls Boucher. 'I stood in. Variation was: "Do you need work? Do you want to do this?" "Yes" in both cases.'

This was the second time in a few short years that a member of senior BBC management had felt the need to question a producer about employing Bob. Was the fallout from the *Aliens in the Mind* radio debacle still causing problems? Or that from Mary Whitehouse's complaints about *Doctor Who* during Philip Hinchcliffe's final season as producer? In hindsight, Boucher certainly thinks that someone at the BBC felt they had a problem with Bob.

'I have some personal experience of people covering their arses, even Bob,' Boucher recalls, 'and it occurs to me that, as was said back in the day, what goes around comes around. (There must be a prize for getting three clichés into one sentence – I must try harder – I could do with a prize!) I have no idea who he had upset and how he prompted the previous "burn out" accusation. It certainly has the smack of arse-covering or score-settling. But then one man's "burn out" is another man's "I'm mad as hell and I'm not putting up with this." I know Bob wasn't burned out, but for all I know, he may have been mad as hell.'

It's possible that Bob also suffered from some sort of writer's block at around this time, which may have had a bearing on his health. 'When he was living in Akeley,' recalls Ian Watson, his brother-in-law, 'he told me he had problems trying to think of new ideas for whatever it was he was writing. He used to sit up into the small hours, and tear up telephone directories and all sorts of things like that, looking for inspiration.'

However, Bob and the BBC were soon to be reunited. And any health problems that Bob may have had at this point were presumably resolved, and were soon put behind him.

In 1980, the BBC producer Ron Craddock[305] was given the job of looking for a suitable novel that could be adapted into a television drama. Craddock narrowed his selection down to just two books, but couldn't decide between them, and so gave them both to his secretary to read. After she had finished reading them, she reported back to Craddock with her preference. The book she chose was *Child of Vodyanoi* by David Wiltshire, which had been first published by Robert Hale Ltd in 1978. David Wiltshire was the dentist-cum-writer who had pitched an idea for *Doctor Who* while Bob was script editor on the series a few years previously. The BBC purchased the rights to adapt his novel for television, and Craddock began putting together the production team for the series. Douglas Camfield was chosen as director, and Bob was approached about turning the novel's prose into a set of scripts.

Wiltshire's novel tells the tale of the occupants of an isolated Scottish island, Inverdee, who come under attack from 'something' that appears to be not human. The small local police force is ill-equipped to deal with the situation, but a storm severs all communications with the mainland and prevents a ferry full of reinforcements from crossing to the island. The main

305 Producer of such programmes as *Angels*, *Z Cars* and *Penmarric* for the BBC in the 1970s.

character in the book is the island's dentist (no real surprise, given Wiltshire's background), Ian Dunlop, who discovers the remains of the first victim and assists the police as much as he can as more victims are found. As a blizzard descends on the island, a squadron of elite soldiers flies in, and reveals that the killer is in fact the occupant of an experimental Russian submarine, which escaped from a collision with a British submarine that was shadowing it. The nature of the technology the Russians were using meant that the pilot had to be literally wired into the cockpit of his craft, the *Vodyanoi*, which was controlled by an implant in the man's brain. After the accident, the Russian submarine came ashore on the island, and the pilot, now no more than a brainless, primal creature, is killing everyone he comes across. Dunlop goes with the army to hunt the pilot, but they then reveal themselves to be Russian soldiers on a mission to recover the sub and prevent the chemical warheads it was carrying from causing an international incident. They leave with the craft, and Dunlop is left alone in the snowy wastes of the island, where he encounters the *Vodyanoi* pilot for one final confrontation …

The novel is something of a modern masterpiece, and Wiltshire manages successfully to pull the reader into the isolated community of Inverdee in a few short chapters; detailing its history, prejudices and customs along with the everyday hustle and bustle of island life. When the murders begin, the sense of isolation becomes almost a physical character in the story, and Wiltshire manages to keep the reader guessing as to the real identity of the killer until very late in the narrative, throwing in lots of clues and red herrings in equal measure. There is a modicum of visceral horror, and some typical '70s gratuitous sex, but the main triumph of the text is the way it cranks up the suspense, really pulling the reader into the situation on the printed page.

Thematically, the novel has many similarities to many of Bob's Earthbound *Doctor Who* stories, and the remote Scottish island setting is also reminiscent of that of the opening episode of *Aliens in the Mind*. Despite the problems Camfield had in delivering his 'The Lost Legion' script for *Doctor Who* in 1976, he and Bob obviously thrived, creatively, in each other's company, and it's not inconceivable that Camfield was the person to suggest Bob's name to Craddock as someone who could do justice to Wiltshire's novel.

Turning someone else's novel into a set of television scripts was a new challenge for Bob (although he'd overseen others do it when working as script editor on *Armchair Thriller*). He successfully managed to deconstruct all the successful elements of the novel, and then wove them into a four-part serial that managed to stay very faithful to the original text. The title became *The Nightmare Man* for the BBC production, and several character names were also changed (Ian Dunlop in the book becomes Michael Gaffakin on television, Fiona Montworth becomes Fiona Patterson, etc). Some elements are elaborated upon (Colonel Howard's involvement in the plot is made more conspicuous early on), some strands are ignored altogether (such as the sub-plot with Fiona's ex-husband), and the small amount of sex in the novel is excised completely (although it is hinted at at times). The point-of-view shots of the killer stalking its victims are all handled well (Bob described them in great depth in his script), although the final denouement, when it arrives on screen, manages to be slightly underwhelming. Although the book handles rather well the revelation that the protagonist is basically a man in a funny suit, the same scene on screen is just a tad disappointing.

Bob also altered the story's ending. In the book, the Russian soldiers depart from Inverdee with the *Vodyanoi* craft, leaving Dunlop alone in a forest in deep snow at night, where he comes face to face with the craft's pilot. In his version, Bob relocates the final sequence to the island's golf course (which is also where the whole story first begins), but it is now without the oppressive snow of the novel, and is shot in broad daylight, somewhat diminishing its power. In the televised version, it is Colonel Howard who confronts the killer, and the Russian troops subsequently escape with the craft *and* the body of its pilot. The relocation of the final scenes gives the story a sort of symmetry, and director Douglas Camfield handles the military action with a great deal of aplomb, but it does all feel a bit of an anti-climax, unlike the book's conclusion.

David Wiltshire wasn't impressed with this change to his narrative. 'The only real objection I had,' he recalled some years later, 'was that the televised version finished on the golf course. The *Vodyanoi* pilot got shot and that was the end of it. I had it set at night, in a forest, with a one-on-one situation which I thought was a lot spookier! I don't know why they didn't do it like that. Apart from that, I was very pleased with the standard of everything in the production.'[306]

Bob spent much of the latter half of 1980 writing the four 30-minute scripts of *The Nightmare Man*. Filming then began in early January 1981, with a strong cast assembled by Camfield, including James Warwick, Celia Imrie and Maurice Roëves. The series was subsequently shown on Friday evenings on BBC1 from 1 May 1981 for four weeks. It garnered favourable reviews from the critics and public alike, with more than one commentator remarking that it was the most frightening thing they'd seen on television for some years.

Bob and Patricia became grandparents at about this time, when Laurian had a son, who was named Bobby in her father's honour. A year later, she had a daughter, Lucy, and Bob used to love entertaining the two children, hiding sweets around the cottage for them to find.

Chris Boucher, now back on *Blake's 7* script editing duty after the series was re-commissioned by the BBC for a fourth season, contacted Bob in October 1980 to see if he would be interested in writing for it again. Clearly there was no ill-feeling between them over the rejection of Bob's script for 'Sweetly Dreaming, Slowly Dying' the previous year.

Bob set to work on writing his script, which focused on the characters of Dayna and Tarrant and was initially entitled 'A Land Fit For Helots'. At this stage, it was anticipated that the character of Cally, as played by Jan Chappell, would be returning to the series, along with the rest of the regular cast from the third season, and so she was included in the early drafts of Bob's script. When Chappell decided not to continue with the series, a new female character, Soolin, was created by the production team, and many of Cally's lines in Bob's script were instead given to her. Conversely, the production team were not expecting Jacqueline Pearce to return to the series as Servalan, and so Bob's script saw the introduction of a new female villain for the show, Sleer. Quite late in the day, Pearce agreed to return after all, and so Sleer then became an alter-ego for Servalan herself.

Bob's script was one of the first to be commissioned for the fourth season, when its format had yet to be fully decided. The new ship that replaced the *Liberator* (destroyed at the end of the previous season) was named *Nighthawk* in Bob's first draft (it was eventually re-named *Scorpio*), while the outlaws' new home was called Eagle Base (later changed to Xenon Base). 'A Land Fit For Helots' was planned to be the season's fourth episode, and Bob delivered his script in early 1981. The episode was then recorded during May.

The episode begins with the crew of the *Scorpio* discovering that the Federation is expanding once again at an alarming rate. They have recently captured the planet Helotrix, and so Avon decides to go there to find out how the Federation are doing it so quickly and successfully. He sends Dayna and Tarrant down to the planet to gather information, and they soon come across resistance group led by a man named Hunda. They discover that the Federation is using a new fast-acting pacification drug, Pylene-50, to subdue the population, and that this programme is being led by a new security commissioner named Sleer. With Hunda's help, Tarrant and Dayna make contact with Leitz, a Federation officer who has been leaking information to the resistance. Leitz reveals where the drug is being produced, and also tells them of a possible antidote. Tarrant decides to put a stop to its production, despite Avon's orders not to get involved. However, Leitz is not a traitor to the Federation after all, but is instead acting under Sleer's orders to set up an ambush for the rebels. When the trap is sprung, Tarrant and Dayna finally catch a glimpse of the mysterious Commissioner Sleer, who is revealed to be their old foe, Servalan.

This episode, being a vehicle for the terminally dull duo of Dayna and Tarrant, could potentially have been a real dud for the series. But Bob livens it up no end by instead focusing much of the screen time on the occupying Federation forces, turning them into mock-colonials with the same prejudices and attitudes that were probably commonplace in the British Army of the late 19th Century. So much so, that whole sections of dialogue could almost have been lifted from one of Bob's earlier scripts for *The Regiment* or *Frontier*.

The idea of a population kept docile by a drug introduced by the authorities was an idea Bob had used before, in his *Doctor Who* story 'The Sun Makers'. When this was later pointed out to him, he said, 'I hadn't realised the stories had the same theme in that sense. But I've always thought that "something in the water" could be used by an authoritarian regime to pacify its population.'[307]

The story was retitled 'Traitor' prior to transmission, and eventually became the third (not fourth) episode of the fourth season of *Blake's 7*, screening on BBC1 on Monday 12 October 1981.[308] Although it's a very standard, run-of-the-mill *Blake's 7* episode, which finally completes the rebooting of the series begun in the first episode of this season, the banter between the Federation forces makes it stand out more than the subject matter does.

At about the time that work on this episode was being wrapped up, Bob was then asked by Boucher to write another script for the series. This was planned to be the eleventh episode of the fourth season, and this time the story was to revolve around Avon and Vila. The resultant episode, 'Orbit', is widely regarded to be one of the best of the entire four-year run of *Blake's 7*.

Egrorian, a scientist on the run from the Federation, summons Avon and the crew of the *Scorpio* to the hostile planet Malodar, with an offer Avon seemingly can't refuse. Avon shuttles down from *Scorpio* with Vila, and meets the scientist and his assistant Pinder. They are given a demonstration of Egrorian's ultimate weapon – the Tachyon Funnel – which can destroy anything in the universe by harnessing the power of super-dense stellar matter. All Egrorian wants in exchange for the device is the super-computer Orac. Avon reluctantly considers the deal, and agrees to swap Orac for the weapon. Servalan, however, is secretly orchestrating the whole scenario. When Avon and Vila take the shuttle back

---

307 Robert Holmes Interview, *Renegade*: Issue 1, 1984 – Interview by Matthew Wicks.
308 'Traitor' was repeated on BBC1 on Saturday 8 June 1983.

to *Scorpio* after completing the exchange, Egrorian discovers that the traded Orac he has been given is actually a fake. However, Egrorian has rigged the shuttle to crash before reaching full orbit, and Avon is faced with the prospect of jettisoning his new weapon – as well as Vila – in order to cut enough weight from the payload and reach escape velocity.

Bob's script for 'Orbit' is perhaps *Blake's 7*'s finest hour, and encapsulates the characters of Avon and Vila seemingly without effort. The interplay between the pair had always been a cornerstone of the series throughout its run, and in this episode, their relationship with each other is thrown into sharp relief. For most of the story, the audience is lulled into a false sense of security due to the witty dialogue, and the standout performance of guest star John Savidant – along with those of Paul Darrow and Michael Keating, who are on excellent form as Avon and Vila – until the final few minutes, when the situation suddenly becomes dangerously real for our heroes. 'Orbit' was screened on BBC1 on Monday 7 December 1981.[309]

Bob Baker was now well into his stride over at HTV. Among the programme ideas he developed was a fantastical children's series he had devised (along with Peter Graham Scott) called *Into the Labyrinth*, for which he also wrote a number of episodes. The basic concept of the series revolved around two timeless, feuding magicians battling over a mystical source of power called the Nidus. Rothgo (played by Ron Moody) was the 'good' magician, while Belor (played by Pamela Salem) was his evil nemesis. In the opening episode, Rothgo enlists three children (played by Simon Beale, Lisa Turner and Simon Henderson) to help him track down the Nidus, which Belor has hidden in various points throughout history. Each week would see the heroes arrive in another setting and attempt to find the Nidus, only to be thwarted in the last minutes by Belor.[310] The first series of *Into the Labyrinth* ran to seven episodes, and was shown in May and June 1981 on ITV. It proved popular enough with ITV bosses that a second series of seven episodes was commissioned before the first season had even aired. This second season was then scheduled for screening later in 1981, and included an episode written by Bob entitled 'The Case of the Silver Half-Hunter'.

'I hadn't seen Bob since the last *Doctor Who* that Dave and I had done when he was script editor,' recalls Baker, 'and I don't actually recall whether I got in touch with him or he got in touch with me. I think he got in touch with me. Anyway, we contacted each other, and I was delighted, because I really rated

---

309 'Orbit was repeated on BBC1 on Saturday 6 August 1983.
310 The idea shares more than a few similarities with *Doctor Who*'s own Key to Time season, for which Bob Baker had co-written the final six-part story, 'The Armageddon Factor'.

Bob's work. At HTV, I was in a very good position. I could just say, "Come on down, I'll buy you lunch." So he came down to Bristol, on a first class ticket, which we paid for – which he loved, of course. So he came to see me, and we went through a couple of story ideas. And the first one was "The Case of the Silver Half-Hunter". Bob had such knowledge of "Victoriana" – it was his bag, it was his passion, all the facets of it, which came out in that story – and I was delighted. The other thing, of course, was that once he had written the script, there was hardly any rewriting to do. As a former script editor, he'd already done it himself. And if there were any little tiny bits that needed altering, you'd just tell him and he'd do it, and do more than that, because being an editor, he knew what he had got to do. I was very pleased to have him on the show, and the resulting episode was terrific. It was the play on words, here and there, that he used – he just had a kind of joy with the English language, which made it funny, which was good. He had Ron Moody playing the dual role of Rothgo and the private detective who might have been Sherlock Holmes, but who wasn't. It all rolls along very, very well, and I was delighted with it.'

Bob's script for 'The Case of the Silver Half-Hunter' was delivered in May 1981. In the sewers deep under the streets of Victorian London, the children encounter a deerstalker-wearing, pipe-smoking sleuth, T J Shadrach, who has had his appearance altered by Belor so that he now looks like Rothgo. Both Rothgo and Belor seek out the next segment of the Nidus, which is disguised as part of the collection of royal jewels in the Tower of London. At the episode's conclusion, Belor narrowly beats Rothgo to the Nidus segment, and also makes off with the four Nidus pieces that the children have already collected over the previous episodes.

Bob packed his script full of cockney banter, with references to Sherlock Holmes and Jack the Ripper, all served up with dollops of cod Victoriana, as he indulged himself once again in one of his favourite historical periods. However, one lengthy sequence that would have involved a complicated CSO set-up, in which the children shrink themselves down in size in order to escape a flood in the sewers by sailing away on a paper boat, before being forced to return to full size when menaced by a 'giant' rat, was dropped from the script before recording, presumably because it was too complicated and/ or expensive to realise in the time available.[311] Bob had written the episode so that it could be realised as efficiently as possible in a television studio, but his ambitions were still more than HTV could manage to produce. Prior to transmission, the episode was retitled simply 'Shadrach'. It was screened in

---

311 The Victorian period, sewer setting and 'giant' rat all recall elements of Bob's *Doctor Who* story 'The Talons of Weng-Chiang'.

most ITV regions on Monday 7 September 1981.

Into the Labyrinth was re-commissioned for a third series, to be screened in 1982, although Ron Moody wasn't available to return as Rothgo. Instead, a new 'good' sorcerer was introduced by the name of Lazlo (played by Chris Harris). Pamela Salem returned as Belor, as did Simon Beal as Phil, now the only juvenile companion involved in Lazlo's quest. Bob was again asked to write an instalment, and came up with the episode 'Dr Jekyll and Mrs Hyde'.

This episode, as the title suggests, played with the ideas behind the classic novel *The Strange Case of Dr Jekyll and Mr Hyde* by Robert Louis Stevenson. 'He loved the classics, he just absolutely knew all the classic stories,' recalls Bob Baker. 'And films, as it happens; he was a bag of knowledge about most things in terms of film. Especially Victorian stuff. Again, this episode was right up his street – a reworking of a classic tale that he could have a bit of fun with. Which I think he did, remarkably well. It was always fun to have Bob around on the series, even if I didn't need to do much work on his scripts.'

This episode is again set in the Victorian era, as Lazlo takes on the persona of Dr Jekyll, whilst Belor, in the form of Mrs Hyde, plans to take control of London's criminal underworld. Both are seeking the new McGuffin introduced to the series to replace the Nidus, the Scarabeus. Predictably, at the episode's conclusion, Belor sends the Scarabeus off into 'Delta time' just as Lazlo thinks he's got his hands on it, so Lazlo and Phil go off once more in pursuit of the mysterious artefact. But by now, the whole series was getting extremely formulaic, and the tiny budget it had once 'enjoyed' had now seemingly shrunk to minuscule proportions. Additionally, the whole tone of the series was now unashamedly pitched at a very juvenile level, which made it difficult for ITV to sell to a mainstream audience.

'Dr Jekyll and Mrs Hyde' was meant to be screened in most ITV regions on Wednesday 4 August 1982, but was dropped at the last minute for reasons unknown, and the episode 'Eye of the Sun', written by Peter Graham-Scott, was brought forward by a week and shown in its place. 'Dr Jekyll and Mrs Hyde' was finally screened a week later, on Wednesday 11 August 1982.

Given that his work since leaving *Doctor Who* had been mainly on fantastical, science fiction-type programmes such as *The Nightmare Man*, *Blake's 7* and *Into the Labyrinth*, it's perhaps unsurprising that as the 1980s dawned, Bob decided to come up with his own original science fiction idea, which he hoped would be of some interest to the various television executives of the day. He drew on the 1976 proposal to the BBC that he and Philip Hinchcliffe had devised together, *Lituvin 40*, and reworked many of the ideas from that into *The Eskdale Experiment*, a script outline for a TV movie that he pitched to ITC in late 1981.

The story opens with two dangerous prisoners in their cell collapsing into a coma. The cause of the coma cannot be identified, and the prison sick bay is quarantined, but before they can be taken to hospital, both men die. Their corpses are placed in a temporary morgue, where they begin to swell – something is growing inside the two bodies. Later that night, the daughter of a prison guard reports seeing a giant beetle at large in the grounds of the officer's quarters. In the morning, both bodies have vanished from the morgue. The prison doctor, Michael Bailey, learns that both men had volunteered to be guinea pigs in a drug trial two years earlier. The trial was conducted by a man named Eskdale, working for a company called Hutcheon Pharmaceuticals. Not far from the prison, a policeman is killed by something unseen in the fog, and his body is found the next day, drained of all fluids. Michael tries to locate Eskdale, but learns that he left Hutcheon Pharmaceuticals just after the trial began, two years previously. He goes to Eskdale's cottage, and finds the place has been trashed. He meets the professor's old research assistant, Sue, who tells him that Eskdale also tested the drugs on himself. Michael also learns that Eskdale had a passion for astronomy, and once claimed to have heard a signal from the stars. He recalls that a team of American scientists once coded the human DNA formula and sent the signal containing it out into space. Could an alien intelligence have done something similar? Has Eskdale received the code for some alien DNA, and then synthesised it and injected into his subjects and himself? Michael deduces that the giant beetle seen in the prison grounds might well have been one of these aliens, metamorphosed from the body of one of the dead prisoners. Concerned for the isolated prison, he calls the governor, and tells him that they might come under attack, but the line goes dead. Eskdale's cottage is attacked by one of the alien beetles, and Michael and Sue barely escape with their lives. They head back to the prison, which is then left isolated as all communications to the outside world are cut. An armed party venture out to repair the telephone system, but are picked off by the beetles. The beetles then attack the prison, killing many of the occupants, and taking the prison guard's daughter away with them. Michael theorises that she will be used as live food for the beetles' newborn grubs. Michael and Sue track the beetles to their lair in a nearby abandoned mineshaft. They rescue the girl, but are trapped underground by the beetles. Michael manages to ignite a pocket of methane gas in the mine, which causes a rock fall that kills all the beetles. The three bedraggled survivors make their way out of the mineshaft, as the sun rises over the moor.

The project was under some degree of serious consideration from ITC, as producer Cecil Clarke tried to raise funding for a number of 'movies made for television' in America, one of which was to be *The Eskdale Experiment*. However, the screenplay wasn't one of those selected for development by the American backers, so Clarke returned Bob's story breakdown to him on Thursday 1 July 1982.

After *Blake's 7* had finished in 1981, Chris Boucher had stayed on with the BBC and moved to work on the popular Saturday evening police drama series *Juliet Bravo*, where he had become script editor on the third season. Unsurprisingly, given his past loyalty to Bob, he quickly commissioned him to write an episode, 'A Breach of the Peace', which was screened on BBC1 on Saturday 2 October 1982.

'A Breach of the Peace' begins with the release from prison of the itinerant gypsy traveller Tom Tulley (Alan Lake), who's been serving a five-year manslaughter sentence for the death of his rival, Billy Driscoll, during a bare-knuckle prize fight. Billy's father, Jack Driscoll (Bernard Horsfall), once a noted prize-fighter himself, is looking for revenge. Tulley, meanwhile, suspects in turn that it was Jack who 'grassed him up' to the police after the fatal fight, and blames him for the time he's spent behind bars. During his stay in prison, Tulley's wife fell ill and died, which compounds the ill-feeling he has for Jack. As other travelling members of the Tulley family begin arriving in the area, Inspector Jean Darbley seeks to avert the feud between the two families escalating into violence. She discovers along the way that Jack wasn't the person who informed the police about Tulley. Tulley himself, although not wanting to back down, also wants to ensure that the terms of his parole aren't breached, as he has vowed never to return to prison. Into this tense story, Bob injects a lighter side-plot revolving around a local CB radio enthusiast who uses illegal AM broadcasting equipment, and an ex-pub landlord with a cowboy fixation, who turns out to have been the bookmaker at the illegal prize-fight between Tulley and Billy Driscoll some five years earlier. The episode ends with a tense standoff between Tom Tulley and Jack Driscoll, which sees both men walk away from the situation without a punch being thrown, but with both of them still having their pride intact. One section in the episode sees Inspector Darbley talking to an ex-policeman-turned-undertaker, and it's hard not to suspect that Bob drew on some of his real-life experiences from his time in the police force when writing this scene.

By now, *Shoestring* had finished after just two seasons on BBC1, its star, Trevor Eve, having decided that he didn't want to become too strongly associated with the role. The BBC asked Robert Banks Stewart to come up with another series to replace it in the schedules. Stewart's solution to this was to devise *Bergerac*, a series set on the island of Jersey. The lead character, Jim Bergerac (as played by John Nettles), is a police detective who when the series begins is overcoming a serious drinking problem and recovering from a badly broken leg. Stewart again produced the series; John Kershaw was his script editor on the first season, and Dennis Spooner on the second.

Stewart contacted Bob about contributing to *Bergerac*, and together they wrote the script for the second season's fourth episode, 'Prime Target', during the latter half of 1982. Initially it was meant to be written by Bob alone, but Stewart had to finish it off as Bob fell ill once again while writing it. 'He was ill, and there were problems with the story and the script,' recalls Stewart. 'I don't think it was a problem with the writing – I mean, Bob was never less than good. I think it might even have been a story we concocted together, and somehow it didn't work out, or wasn't going to work out, and the director was highly critical of lots of the script in its original form. I must have had no alternative but to rewrite it myself. Then I think it was the old story, that as I'd rewritten so much of it, I could hardly let Bob be responsible for the script on his own. I don't think Bob had a problem with me doing that. Looking back, Bob and I never had any difference of opinion on anything. I don't remember ever having a difference of opinion with him at all.'

'Prime Target', as written by both Stewart and Holmes, was screened on BBC1 on Saturday 30 January 1983. The episode begins with Bergerac travelling to France to help the French police when the body of an unidentified Jersey resident is found on a remote farm, having been shot in the head. The victim turns out to be Jack Moberley, a private eye who was spying on an eccentric lawyer, Lionel Carteret, on behalf of the rest of his family. They were concerned about the relationship Lionel had struck up with a Countess, whose mansion-cum-hotel was due to be repossessed by a local casino due to her late husband's gambling debts with them. Bergerac tries to discover who killed Moberley; the Countess, Lionel, a member of the Carteret family, or the owner of the casino, all of whom have motives. Lionel announces that he and the Countess are to marry, but the murder weapon is then found by the French police in the Countesses's bureau at her house. Bergerac heads back to France, where he discovers that it was actually the casino owner who was behind the murder.

The storyline for the episode gets very convoluted at times, which is probably the result of the two creative forces who wrote it being not entirely in tandem with each other. With a first-rate cast, the end result is watchable, but lacks the polish one would expect from the series – and not least the polish one would expect from the likes of both Bob and Stewart.

After a year spent working as script editor on *Juliet Bravo*, Chris Boucher then replaced Dennis Spooner as script editor for the third season of *Bergerac*, and in 1983 he commissioned Bob to write the episode 'A Cry in the Night'. This time, Bob completed the script on his own, and the episode was shown on BBC1 on Saturday 14 January 1984.

'A Cry in the Night' sees Bergerac investigate the drowning of a local middle-aged playboy, Rupert Galliers, who falls overboard during a party held on a yacht owned by former rock star drummer Boy Buckley. Galliers' wife, Emerald, also falls from the yacht at the same time, but she is found at sea, alive but in a coma. Bergerac discovers that the party on the yacht was a somewhat debauched affair, and that a local art gallery owner who was in attendance, Stephen Crane, had supplied cocaine to the other guests. All the witness statements seem to indicate that both the Galliers fell overboard by accident, but Bergerac's instincts tell him otherwise. Bergerac eventually discovers that Buckley was getting amorous with Emerald at the party, which led to Buckley's girlfriend leaving the yacht. She was rowed ashore in a dinghy by Galliers, and they too ended up having sex. When Galliers returned to the yacht, he and Buckley argued and fought, which resulted in Galliers falling overboard. Emerald then became hysterical, causing Buckley to hit her and knock her overboard as well. Bergerac gets a confession from Buckley, who is then arrested for a double murder, as Emerald later dies in hospital.

This bleak story is very well handled by the production team, and it's quite brave for a series as mainstream as *Bergerac* to get into the nitty-gritty of cocaine abuse and swingers' parties in such a manner. The subjects of racial prejudice and homophobia are given an airing too, displayed in the attitudes that the various characters have towards Stephen Crane's black boyfriend – issues that early-'80s television often ducked. However, some restraint is also evident on the part of the production team – a scene scripted by Bob late in the episode, in which Stephen Crane commits suicide rather than wait for Bergerac to uncover the evidence of his drug dealing, is absent from the final transmitted programme, which now just has Crane awaiting his inevitable arrest.

Back over at Thames Television at about this time, Brenda Ennis – who had been the producer of the second series of *Armchair Thriller* a few years earlier, alongside Bob as script editor – was given the producership of a new daytime soap opera, which was due to screen on the whole ITV network. *Miracles Take Longer* was the rather opaque name of the series, which was actually set in the mundane everyday world of the offices of a Citizen's Advice Bureau. Ennis was almost certainly the reason why Bob got involved with writing scripts for the series.

Five years earlier, Bob would almost certainly have passed up an invitation to write scripts for such a comparatively lowly show, but regular work was now starting to be hard to come by for him, despite his standing amongst television writers. His fee for writing an episode of *Miracles Take Longer* was about a third of what he was paid for a 25-minute *Doctor Who* script at about the same time (of which, see next chapter). He wrote five scripts for *Miracles Take Longer* during the latter half of 1983, all of which were completed and delivered prior to November of that year.

The series began its twice-weekly screenings by ITV in January 1984, in its allocated afternoon slot. Bob's five episodes were all screened during the following month, and all focused on the minutia of daily life in the fictional Bureau, with a variety of eccentric vagrants, pregnant schoolgirls, drunks and timewasters taking up the time of the various staff volunteers. The series made almost no impact on viewers, and plans for a lengthy run on ITV were soon scuppered. *Miracles Take Longer* disappeared from the television schedules after a few short months, almost as quietly as it had arrived.

Bob's 1973 idea for an edition of *Dial M for Murder* (see Chapter Thirteen), which involved a computerised office building, was exhumed at some point in 1984, and ended up on the desk of producer Colin Callender at Yorkshire Television. At the time, Yorkshire Television were looking to make a 30-minute science fiction anthology series to sell into the US television market. They decided that Bob's idea would make an ideal pilot for this potential series, which was simply entitled *Timeslip*.[312] A writer by the name of Jim Hawkins was drafted in to write the actual script, although it was based on Bob's initial idea. The episode was titled simply 'The Block'.

The plot of 'The Block' revolves around a couple working late at night in a futuristic computer-controlled office block, who disable the various security systems in the building so that they can indulge in a bit of extra-curricular sex in the office's executive suite. The computer systems then refuse to recognise them, and the couple are almost killed by the security software, but a failsafe cuts in at the last moment. The whole story is watched by a mysterious 'hacker' (played by John Taylor from the pop group *Duran Duran*) on a computer screen. The hacker appeared only at the start and end of the programme, and was set to be a linking character who would be utilised in any future stories, with similar 'top and tail' scenes. This *Timeslip* pilot wasn't particularly well received in the US, or by the ITV network as a whole for that matter. It sat on the shelf for nearly a year, and didn't get screened until Saturday 28 December 1985, where it was dumped in a late-night graveyard slot.

Also in 1985, Chris Boucher once again commissioned a *Bergerac* script

---

312 This had nothing at all to do with the ITV science fiction children's series of the same name from the early 1970s.

from Bob. This was 'Winner Takes All', which was made the same year as part of *Bergerac*'s fourth season. 'I find *Bergerac* so heavily-laden with characters,' complained Bob at the time. 'There's the ex-father-in-law Charlie Hungerford, there's the wife, there's Bergerac's colleague, there's the secretary, there's Diamante Lil who runs a pub or something. You have to give them all a line or two, so it gets complicated.' In the event, the episode wasn't shown as part of *Bergerac*'s fourth season. Instead, it debuted on BBC1 as the second episode of the fifth season, on Saturday 10 January 1987.

'Winner Takes All' tells the story of a reclusive and bad-tempered software designer, Jarvis McLeod, who begins to receive death-threats via his computer system at the same time as Jersey is playing host to a computer conference that is being organised by Charlie Hungerford. When McLeod's wife, Monica, finds their pet dog dying, having eaten poisoned meat, all the signs begin to point towards McLeod's former partner and business rival, John Logan, as the culprit. Logan has arrived on the island for Hungerford's computer conference, where he has also begun dating Bergerac's ex-wife. She is able to provide Logan with an alibi when an intruder breaks through McLeod's security fence and tampers with the brakes of his car. As the campaign escalates, McLeod narrowly escapes death after a booby-trap bomb explodes on stage at a conference session he was meant to be addressing, killing the man who stepped in to replace him at the last minute. When Bergerac learns that Monica is as good as both Jarvis and Logan at designing computer games, he realises that she is behind the scheme, and narrowly averts McLeod falling victim to a second booby-trap device.

The script for this episode is extremely tightly constructed, as all good whodunits should be, and Bob keeps the audience guessing right until the final dénouement as to just who is behind the plot.

As mentioned, the episode was held back for Bergerac's fifth season, which meant that there was an unusually long gap of almost 18 months between Bob writing it, and it being shown on BBC1. Because of this, Bob never got to see his work transmitted.

CHAPTER TWENTY-FOUR
TIME, GENTLEMEN!
1982

Bob spent the years between 1978 and 1982 without any direct involvement in *Doctor Who*. But he kept an eye on the series whenever it was on television, watching with interest, and at times with a degree of incredulity, at the direction it was taking.

When interviewed in 1985 about his time away from the series, Bob was quite conciliatory about his break from the show. 'After I finished being script editor I was up to my eyeballs in *Doctor Who* and I wanted a break from it, which I had for a few years,' he told *Doctor Who Magazine*, in a manner that suggested the decision was more his than anyone else's.[313]

In the summer of 1980, just after the end of the 1979/80 season of *Doctor Who*, Bob wrote a letter to the *Doctor Who* Appreciation Society (DWAS) fanzine, *TARDIS*. In it, he took a quite scathing dig at the way the series was now being made: 'It is now some years since I have seen a copy of *TARDIS*, and I am most impressed by the improvement in the magazine – these days it's a very professional-looking publication. Ironic, though, that as the magazine improves, the programme it supports is doing the opposite! I suppose that comment could be construed as biting the hand that once fed me … But anyway, I'm sure that all of us who love the programme are hoping that it will recover its sense of direction in the coming season.'[314]

About a year afterwards, Bob entered into an occasional correspondence with *Doctor Who* fanzine editor Simon M Lydiard. Lydiard asked Bob if he had any plans to contribute to the series again in the future. Bob replied in a letter dated 19 May 1981, saying: 'You ask whether I intend to write for *Doctor Who* again. Well, I had a long run with the programme and enjoyed every moment – even when it was hurting! I left because I felt I'd played all the shots in my locker. I thought the programme needed new writers and ideas. Change is a healthy and necessary thing in a long-running programme. But it means, of course, that old buffers like me find it difficult to adjust our ideas. I don't feel my style of story would be acceptable in *Doctor Who* as it is today.'

Later in 1981, Bob was again asked about his thoughts on modern *Doctor Who*. 'I don't watch *Doctor Who* much these days because I find myself mentally

---

313 Interview – Robert Holmes, *Doctor Who Magazine*: Issue 100, May 1985.
314 *TARDIS*: Vol 5, No 3/4 (1980).

editing it as I watch and that prevents me enjoying it. So I can't comment on the present shape of the series,' he diplomatically replied.[315]

Bob accepted an invitation from the DWAS to attend their annual Panopticon convention over the weekend of 1-2 August 1981. This was his second and final appearance at a *Doctor Who* event. He received a warm reception when he arrived on stage, and was asked if he would be interested in writing for the series once more. His reply this time was slightly less diplomatic: 'It's not up to me to make plans; it's up to the current producers and script editors to decide if they are going to invite me to write again.' When pushed on this point, Bob added, 'I think the way the series is going at the moment, it's going in a different direction to the way I used to write for it. Although I'd be happy to have another shot, I think the series does need new writers, it does need an injection of fresh blood, and I'm very happy for those writers to come along.'[316]

Also in attendance at the convention that weekend was John Nathan-Turner, who had worked as production unit manager on *Doctor Who* during Bob's final six months as script editor in 1977, and had since taken over from Graham Williams as producer from the 1980/81 series. If Bob was making a slightly public declaration of come-and-get-me to the new producer in the hope of an invitation to pitch a new story idea for the series, then it fell on deaf ears.

During his on-stage interview, which lasted only about 10 minutes, Bob was also asked what his favourite *Doctor Who* stories were of the ones he had written. 'I enjoyed "The Sun Makers" very much,' he replied, 'and "The Talons of Weng-Chiang". And I think "Carnival of Monsters" – which I understand is going to be repeated – is quite inventive. I enjoyed that one too. I like comic dialogue, I like a certain amount of humour in *Doctor Who*, and I think all those three stories in their different ways, had quite a lot of it. "The Sun Makers" was satirical about the tax system. And "The Talons of Weng-Chiang" was Victorian, which is an era I love anyway. And the other one was just a crazy idea that I think worked very well.' He was then asked which of his stories he liked least. 'Well, nothing is ever as you quite expect it,' Bob replied after a moment's thought. 'You intend something to be perfect, and it never is. So quite a lot of them failed in my terms, but I think it would be wrong of me to sit here and say, "Oh, I didn't like that".'

As Bob hinted to the audience at Panopticon, there was to be a brief reminder of some of his earlier *Doctor Who* glories towards the end of 1981. As a way of preparing the audience – who had now had seven years of Tom Baker as the Doctor – for the arrival of Doctor number five in the shape of Peter Davison, the

---

315 Robert Holmes Interview, *The Time Meddler*: Issue 3, October 1981 – Interview by John M Kahane.
316 Panopticon IV Convention, Queen Mary College, 1-2 August 1981.

BBC had decided to give everyone a timely reminder that other actors had played the role rather successfully in the past. A repeat season of old *Doctor Who* stories, shown under the umbrella title *The Five Faces of Doctor Who*, was screened on BBC2 in November and December 1981. Two of Bob's old stories – 'The Krotons' and 'Carnival of Monsters' – were shown as part of this repeat season.[317]

All of a sudden, it was getting very difficult to ignore both Robert Holmes and the contributions he had made to *Doctor Who* in the past. Amongst the fans, there was a small but definite groundswell of opinion that he should be asked to write again for the series.

In the middle of July 1982, producer John Nathan-Turner was given the go-ahead by the BBC's Head of Serials to make a 90-minute special story to celebrate the programme's twentieth anniversary in 1983. This special was to go into production in early 1983 for screening in November, and was not to be part of the programme's regular season of stories. The task of finding a writer for it fell to *Doctor Who*'s incumbent script editor, Eric Saward.

When Nathan-Turner had taken over as producer of *Doctor Who* in 1980, he had almost immediately sought to inject new writing blood into the series, jettisoning nearly all the established writers still contributing to the programme up to that point. His diktat to his first script editor, Christopher H Bidmead, was to commission new writers, rather than rely on the 'old guard'. Eric Saward had also followed this philosophy since he had taken on the script editor's job in 1981, but as he had learned more and more about the show's history, he'd slowly become aware of the many great stories it had produced in the 1960s and 1970s. And as far as Saward could see, most of the really, really good ones seemed to have been written by a chap called Robert Holmes.

'I knew his name and I began to watch the old tapes,' Saward later recalled, 'and I discovered the Hinchcliffe period. Bob was not only script editor, he'd written some of it. I then saw "The Talons of Weng-Chiang"', which I thought was absolutely wonderful! It was everything I thought *Doctor Who* should be: it was funny, it was exciting, it was cracking entertainment – a great adventure. When I watched these very old stories, the better ones invariably had his name attached to them. And it got to a stage where, when he was script editing it, I could almost judge how much work he had put in. It was so much better.'[318]

Saward was keen to try and talk to Bob, to see if he was interested in writing for the series again, but he also knew that Nathan-Turner wouldn't be particularly happy about such a move; not because of any personal animosity

---

317 'Carnival of Monsters' was selected for repeat by its producer/director Barry Letts, who at this time was executive producer on *Doctor Who*. One proviso he asked for was that the final episode should be slightly edited to remove a scene where the bald cap worn by the actor Peter Halliday (playing Pletrac) was clearly visible.
318 Interview – Eric Saward, *DWB*: Issue 57, August 1988.

towards the man, but because the producer was so committed to his strategy of employing new writers. However, the need to find a writer to come up with a story to celebrate *Doctor Who*'s twentieth anniversary seemed a perfect excuse for Saward to contact Bob. After all, Saward reasoned, Nathan-Turner couldn't possibly object to commissioning a story from an experienced *Doctor Who* stalwart in such exceptional circumstances.

'John had got the go ahead to do the 90-minute twentieth anniversary thing,' recalled Saward, 'and I suggested that we approach Robert Holmes. Robert had worked with Troughton, Pertwee, Tom Baker … He had worked with them, knew them and written for them. Bob to me seemed an absolutely splendid choice. John was very reluctant. John is frightened, I have always thought, of experienced people. He can't manipulate them as easily and as readily as you can someone who needs the work, who will shut their mouth and get on with it. That makes a very boring working partner. Someone like Bob Holmes comes through the door and tells you what *he* thinks, which is smashing. "This is what *I* want," he says, and then you discuss that, and you tell him what you want. You throw it into the melting pot.'[319]

So Saward made contact with Bob, and invited him to come into the BBC for a chat with Nathan-Turner and himself on Friday 30 July 1982, after which Saward took him to lunch.

The idea was to discuss the *Doctor Who* anniversary special, and to see if Bob was interested in writing the script for it. This would be the first time that Bob had had any direct involvement with *Doctor Who* since he wrote 'The Power of Kroll' in 1978.

It was not the best of meetings.

'I remember when Bob walked into the office,' recalled Saward. 'He came in – a big man, tall, ex-policeman many years ago – and he still had that presence. I think he looked at John and me and thought, "Crikey, a couple of real jerks here!" He was wrong [in that] he shouldn't have made it so obvious; but he was right in that we were being silly about what we wanted.'[320]

'I did have, initially, a reticence to consider Bob as a writer,' recalled Nathan-Turner some years later. 'His involvement in *Doctor Who* had been of a specific direction, instigated in no small way by Bob himself, and I wanted to have time for our team to focus its objectives. "The Five Doctors", in our view, required a writer steeped in the *Who* mythos – QED.'[321]

However, as Saward recalled, Bob's demeanour at that first meeting

---

319 'The Revelations of a Script Editor', Eric Saward, *Starburst*: Issue 97, September 1986.
320 Interview – Eric Saward, *DWB*: Issue 57, August 1988.
321 Private correspondence with Colin Brockhurst.

between the three of them saw things start off very much on the wrong foot, as the producer and script editor both found themselves put on edge by his attitude towards them. 'He was grouchy, he was difficult, he was a little bit arrogant,' recalls Saward, 'but he had so much experience of working on the show, so I sort of understood it ... He could have been a little more relaxed. But that very soon passed, and we got on quite well, even at the first meeting. But he was very resistant to what he was being asked to do, and all we wanted initially was an outline that could incorporate all the things we were asking, and he thought it was a foolish idea, a nonsense idea, and I fear he was right.

'John wanted the Cybermen, the Master and all the other bits and pieces that came into it, and Bob said, "Forget it. The Cybermen are stupid, they don't work very well, and I like creating original characters." John hated this because he hated being challenged. Still we asked Bob to continue and we said we'd commission him to do it, but he wasn't certain he could make the story work. John was then furious Bob had the audacity to say he wasn't happy in this honest and outspoken way.'[322]

At this time, the incumbent Doctor in the TARDIS was the fifth incarnation, as played by Peter Davison. The natural idea for the anniversary special was to come up with a plot that would allow for the actors who had played the previous Doctors to return for just this single story. A similar thing had been done for the programme's tenth anniversary, when 'The Three Doctors' saw Patrick Troughton and William Hartnell join forces with the then-incumbent Doctor, Jon Pertwee, for a celebratory romp. Both Nathan-Turner and Saward agreed that the bringing together of the previous incarnations of the Doctor, alongside his current self, should form the basis of the special's storyline.

Nathan-Turner had already made discreet enquiries over the previous few months with Patrick Troughton, Jon Pertwee and Tom Baker about the potential for them to return, and had received positive assurances from all three that they would be happy to take part in such a project. The original Doctor, William Hartnell, had sadly passed away in April 1975, so the story would need to come up with a way to circumvent this issue. The idea of recasting the Doctor was already under consideration by Nathan-Turner, and he had recently made enquiries about the past BBC fees received by actors Geoffrey Bayldon[323] and Richard Hurndall[324], both of whom bore some resemblance to Hartnell.

---

322 Interview – Eric Saward, *DWB*: Issue 57, August 1988.
323 Geoffrey Bayldon had played Catweazle in the television series of the same name between 1970-71, and had recently played the Crowman alongside Jon Pertwee in *Worzel Gummidge*. Both performances were reminiscent of William Hartnell's first Doctor.
324 Richard Hurndall had appeared in a 1981 episode of *Blake's 7* ('Assassin'), playing a character who was uncannily visually similar to the first Doctor. Hurndall would eventually be cast as the first Doctor in the twentieth anniversary story.

During their lunchtime meeting, Bob must have listened to Saward's summation of these various factors and considerations with at least a certain degree of enthusiasm, because on the following Monday, 2 August 1982, the BBC Copyright Department, on Saward's instruction, issued a formal commission for Bob to write a story outline for the anniversary story, to be delivered by Monday 23 August. Bob wasn't keen on writing such outlines, and hadn't been required to produce one for *Doctor Who* since he wrote 'The Time Warrior' in 1973. The fee for this work was agreed over the next few days between Bob's agent, Jon Thurley, and the BBC. At this point, the story was given the working title 'The Six Doctors', which was almost certainly a reference to Bob's plot solution to get around the fact that there would be no William Hartnell in the story.

Nathan-Turner wrote to Hartnell's widow, Heather, on Friday 3 September 1982, to inform her of his plans for the anniversary special, and to assure her that it would be respectful to the memory of her late husband. His letter contained a hint of the plans that Holmes and Saward had at that point hatched between them in relation to the first Doctor. 'I intend to use some excerpts from Bill's era,' he told her, 'and in addition I intend to re-cast the first Doctor. I intend to get an actor to play the part who looks very like Bill, although it will be made obvious at the beginning of the special that this Doctor is an imposter, and one of the problems the other Doctors have to face is to unmask the imposter.'

However, Saward must have had reservations about Bob's ability to come up with a workable storyline for the special, because at around this point he decided to put in place a contingency plan, just in case things didn't work out. Saward contacted another writer with a long-running connection to the series, Terrance Dicks, who at this point was working as the script editor on the BBC's Sunday afternoon classic serials. Saward was aware that Dicks' pedigree on the programme was as accomplished as Bob's, and so asked him to consider developing his own idea for an anniversary story in parallel to the one that Bob was preparing.

Dicks takes up the story: 'Well, what happened was that I was at a *Doctor Who* convention in America, in New Orleans, and I had been at this very, very long party that had ended at three or four in the morning, and then at about six or seven in the morning, New Orleans time, the phone rang and a voice said, "Is that Terrance?" And I said, "Errrr … yes," and the voice said, "This is Eric …" And I thought, "Eric who? I don't know anyone called Eric." So I said, "Eric who?" And he said, "You remember, Eric Saward, script editor of *Doctor Who*. We'd like to ask you to write the anniversary special," so I said,

"Okay, fine, I'll be in the office on Monday, I'll come and see you," and put the phone down and went back to sleep. Eric and I were, at that time, working in the same building, in Threshold House on Shepherd's Bush Green; I was working with Barry Letts on the classic serials, and Eric was script editing *Doctor Who* for John Nathan-Turner. He was on the floor below me. So I went down to see him, and said, "I'll be very happy to have a go at it, and what sort of thing do you have in mind?" They didn't really have anything in mind, only they wanted an anniversary story and all the Doctors had got to be in it. Eric looked a bit shifty and said, "Well as a matter of fact, Bob Holmes is writing the storyline. What we thought we'd do is get you to write a storyline, and Bob Holmes to write a storyline, and then we'd see which one we liked the best." And I was not pleased at this. I said, "See here, Eric, this is no way to treat a writer like Bob Holmes. Come to think of it, it's no way to treat a writer like me, either. Make your mind up. If you want to go with Bob, fine, you couldn't do better, he's a super writer. If Bob doesn't want to do it, or you don't want Bob to do it, I'd be very happy to do it, but it's one or the other." I then stomped off back to the classic serials.'

Bob would spend the next few weeks grappling with various ideas for the story, hitting on a succession of possible solutions to the logistical problem of getting the previous Doctors together, before rejecting them one by one.[325] All proved fruitless, and the deadline for the storyline passed without Bob delivering anything to the *Doctor Who* production office. On the following day, Tuesday 24 August 1982, Bob rang Saward to apologise for his lateness. However, he assured the script editor that he at last had a storyline that was taking shape. Saward fixed a new date of Wednesday 1 September 1982 for them to have a meeting to discuss the story at the *Doctor Who* production office, which would also be attended by Nathan-Turner. Saward also requested that Bob prepare a scene breakdown of his storyline, and that he be sent a copy, to be with him no later than Tuesday 31 August 1982, '... so John and I can digest what you have done.'

However, Saward must have had an inkling at this point that all wasn't going smoothly with Bob, because he also wrote to Dicks later that same day: 'I spoke to Bob Holmes today, who at the moment, is still struggling with his storyline. He's asked for a little more time and will now not be delivering until 1 September. I'm sorry to mess you around like this, but hope you are able to wait for our final decision until the end of next week.'

---

325 According to an interview with Eric Saward and unofficial script consultant Ian Levine in the fanzine *DWB* (issue 106, 1992), one of Bob's early ideas for the twentieth anniversary story involved the reappearance of Sutekh from 'Pyramids of Mars', which Bob had written under the pen name Stephen Harris. No paperwork has ever surfaced to corroborate this assertion, however.

'They asked me to come back and do the "five Doctors" thing,' recalled Bob of this period, a few years later, 'and that's when the talks began, and they realised that I wasn't really the arrogant monster they thought I was. They were afraid, I think, that I would come in and be very autocratic, and say, "This isn't the way we used to do it", and stuff like that.'

It's not entirely clear if Bob ever put anything specific on paper for Saward and Nathan-Turner to mull over prior to their meeting on 1 September. What does still survive is an undated discussion document, written by Bob, which outlines his thoughts on a number of story ideas for the anniversary special. This may well be the very document that he prepared in advance of that 1 September meeting, but as it's undated, then it could also have been written a few weeks later (see Interlude X).

Saward recalls that the meeting on Wednesday 1 September did not go too well. Bob wasn't keen on all the 'shopping list' elements that were being continually added to the story by Nathan-Turner and Saward, but did agree to go away and begin writing the script, to see if he could successfully weave them all together. Saward wasn't sure that Bob would succeed, however, and wrote to Dicks again the following day, updating him on developments, and keeping him on standby. 'It seems nothing is simple in life. Bob has decided that he wants to try and write the first 20 minutes of the script, although he still has huge reservations about whether he can make it work. He plans to deliver in two weeks' time, and if everybody is happy we shall go ahead with it.'

However, Bob's enthusiasm for the special now seemed to be dramatically waning. Almost a week later, on Thursday 9 September, he wrote a whimsical letter to Saward, encouraging the script editor to look elsewhere for a writer. 'I have a garbled scribble on the back of my cheque book,' wrote Bob, 'which I interpret as follows: There is a chap called Andrew Ryssick[326] who is said to be a "v. gd. yng. wrtr." And who, apparently, has had some bad breaks recently … Point of all this is that he told my source he has a very good idea for *Doctor Who*, and went on to say that "unfortunately, the idea calls for the presence of all the Doctors!" For obvious reasons, I don't want to know what he has in mind, but I thought you might. After all, it is just possible that he has an absolute cracker of an idea that will prove far more suitable than our own laborious contrivance.' Bob concluded his letter with a promise to have written something that he could show Saward in a week or so.

Despite having no script to work to, the *Doctor Who* production office had already begun engaging actors to appear in the anniversary story, which was

---

326 Bob was probably referring to award-winning playwright, radio writer and journalist Andrew Rissick, who would have been 28 years old and just starting out on his career in 1983.

by now scheduled to be recorded between late February and early April 1983. On Thursday 30 September, the regular cast of Peter Davison, Janet Fielding (Tegan) and Mark Strickson (Turlough) were all contracted to appear, as were Patrick Troughton and Anthony Ainley (the Master). A few days later, Nicholas Courtney (the Brigadier) was also confirmed for the story, as was Jon Pertwee. Tom Baker, on the other hand, wanted to see a script before he would commit to the project.

So did Bob ever actually begin work on writing his script for the twentieth anniversary story? According to Saward, he did. 'Bob went off and wrote 14 or 15 pages of the script, and I read them and to be honest they weren't very good. I don't know what had gone wrong. I mean, they were funny, but it was ploddy and it was as if his heart was not really in it.'[327]

Bob once gave an interesting insight into how he perceived the characters of the first four Doctors. 'Hartnell was forgetful and irascible,' he noted. 'Troughton was eccentric. Pertwee was urbane and charming. I thought Tom very cleverly incorporated elements of all three previous Doctors into his characterisation. For me, he was the definitive Doctor, but I believe he lingered longer in the role than he should have done.'[328]

Bob met up with Saward again on Wednesday 13 October, and this time they both agreed that it was probably for the best if he were to withdraw from the project. So Bob was paid in full for his work to date, and that was the end of his involvement. Saward was not too disheartened, however, as he realised that not all the problems with Bob's storyline were of his own making, and he was still determined to use him on the series. 'I knew he could have done it if he really, really put his mind to it,' recalls Saward. 'But I think he felt at the time that we were making a lot of fuss that he didn't really like and didn't want. And he was a man who liked to go away and do his own thing, and because he was so good at what he did, it was often quite rewarding to see what he came back with. But at that time, it was a special, celebrating 20 years of *Doctor Who*, and we wanted specific things that he wasn't prepared to do.'

Although Bob and Saward both later said that this was an amicable parting of the ways, Dicks recalls that that there was perhaps slightly more to it than that: 'After a bit, Eric phoned me up and wearily said that Bob had had a huge row with John Nathan-Turner, and had stomped off the project, and so would I come down to talk to him? Bob withdrew in a huff; as I say, he could be difficult, and I don't think he ever got on particularly well with John Nathan-Turner, or with Eric very much. He didn't get on with them as well as he got

---

327 Interview – Eric Saward, *DWB*: Issue 57, August 1988.
328 Robert Holmes Interview, *The Time Meddler*: Issue 3, October 1981 – Interview by John M Kahane.

on with me and Barry, certainly. He would have obviously liked to have done the special, but I think they messed him about one bit too much, and so he blew his top and left.'

The upshot of all this was that Dicks was eventually commissioned by Saward to write the special. Dicks actually embraced the challenge of juggling all the components required in the story by the production team – although he probably could have done without having to rewrite the script to accommodate the late withdrawal of Tom Baker!

But Saward was unfazed by Bob's decision to withdraw from the project. Now he had got to know Bob, he was determined that *Doctor Who* would benefit from his writing talents once more …

INTERLUDE X
DOCTOR WHO: 'THE SIX DOCTORS'
SEPTEMBER 1982

Robert Holmes's full original storyline proposal for the unmade 90-minute special *Doctor Who* story 'The Six Doctors' is reprinted here as originally submitted, complete with his original spellings and punctuation. This is more of a discussion document than a story outline as such, but mainly revolves around one plotline:

<u>THE SIX DOCTORS</u>

The main problem we face is to find a satisfactory and plausible explanation for all the Doctors, plus companions, appearing at the same point in the space-time continuum. I feel that this - dramatically - is what our audience will expect. However, the clash of mighty egos has been mentioned and it is possible for them to appear in the same story without appearing together.

The purpose of this discussion document is to survey the various options open to us.

1) The planet Maladoom. Doctor Will and companion striding across a misty landscape. They've obviously just arrived as he is pointing out various botanical features and making deductions about the nature of the planet.

We pull back to see that the Doctor is being watched on video. Voices of unseen watchers comment admiringly - 'Really remarkably lifelike,' etc. (Eventually, about an hour from now, we shall learn that Doctor Will and Carol Ann are cyborgs, created by cyber-technology. This will explain why the Doctor is not quite as we remember Hartnell.)

Tardis. The Doctor helpless at the controls. Tells Tegan the machine is being drawn into a time vortex. It could mean destruction. Maybe we do some clever mirror-work and show more than one police box whirling down this sudden fissure in the ordered universe.

Maladoom. The Doctor and Tegan arrive. He is now very angry. Some irresponsible idiot must be interfering with the delicately balanced polarity of time and matter. Incredibly dangerous lunacy that could create chaos. Must put a stop to it.

Now, one by one, the other Doctors arrive with their companions. All have approximately the same reactions – although Doctor Tom may speculate that some other race has discovered the power previously known only to Time Lords. But, anyway, all go off to put a stop to it.

The Doctor and Tegan are heading across rough terrain towards a pulsing light that seems to be coming from inside a distant craggy hill. In the shadow of a low cliff they see, apparently inset into the rockface, a rectangular panel of some shiny black substance. As they examine this curiously, concealed jets puff out vapour. They collapse unconscious. Then the panel begins to open.

One by one the other Doctors are inveigled into other automated traps.

Cryogenic chamber. The Doctors and companions lie unconscious. The Master comes in for a gloat. At last he has all the time entities that comprise the total Doctor at his mercy. If he turns the freezer down a few more degrees he will achieve his final triumph over his oldest adversary. So why doesn't he? Probably because he daren't, at this stage, upset his allies, the Cybermen.

Doctor Pat is carried off to the operating theatre. The Cybermen prepare for surgery. An injection revives the patient for preliminary tests. The Cybermen intend to find the organic mechanism that separates Time Lords from other species. When they find it they will separate it and implant it into their familiar cybernetic machinery, thus turning themselves into Cyberlords.

This aspect of the plot is brought out in conversation between the Master, Doctor Pat and the top Cyberman.

As the operation begins the Doctor goes into terminal collapse. Resuscitation procedures fail. The patient is pronounced extinct. The Cybermen aren't too concerned; they expect to lose a few doctors before discovering the vital organ. That is why, with the Master's help, they have drawn all the manifestations of the Doctor's form from their various time-loops.

Doctor Pat is returned to the cryogenic chamber where he recovers from his self willed cataleptic state. Fighting against the numbing cold, he disconnects the freezer panels. As the temperature rises the Doctors slowly begin to stir.

In the operating theatre the Cybermen are reviewing their techniques before investing in another patient.

In the cryogenic chamber total bafflement at finding themselves all together. An impossible situation which they resolve by deciding they are trapped in a temporal paradox created by the Master.

The Cybermen come to collect Doctor Jon. Docs and companions take them by surprise and effect an escape.

Film. Trial by ordeal. Cybermen hunting Doctors who are all intent now on their original objective – restoring the time-space continuum to its natural order before permanent damage is done to the universe. And to this end they are heading for the shining hill.

Doctor Will – the fake cyborg – tries to lead them into an ambush. But at the last moment he is spotted as a phoney. He bounces down a cliff and all his springs fall out. Carol Ann, too, is shown to be a cyborg. This is tough on

Frazer because he was getting to like her.

They struggle on and finally reach the shining hill. Its core is a mass of technology linked to the Master's TARDIS, the effect of which is to raise its power a thousand fold. Projected through the space-time continuum this enormous force has created a time vacuum into which all Time Travellers (principally our Doctors) were inevitably drawn.

The trouble is that it is now feeding upon itself, like a nuclear reactor running out of control, and in a very short while the whole of this part of the universe will implode into a black hole. Unless they can slow the whirligig down and stabilise matters.

We've all been through this one before. The Master will, of course, turn up to provide some last-moment impediment. But, in the end, the Doctors get the machinery into phase before it goes critical. As it slows they, together with their appropriate companions, disappear back into their own sectors of time – the relative dimensions effect.

The Doctor and Tegan are alone at the end.

The sharp-eyed reader will ask what happened to the Cybermen. Well, we won't have that many to start with. Some will be blown up when the Doctors escape because, before departing, they sabotage the operating theatre. Others will be disposed of variously – buried under rock falls, sunk in swamps, pushed off cliffs and so on – during the film chase.

2) The other option. Much the same general shape of story but we open with the present Doctor and stay with him until the operating theatre scene.

The effect of the Cybermen tampering with his metabolism, however, is that he starts to regress through his various phases – i.e. turns first into Doctor Tom, then into Doctor Jon and so on.

While doing this, of course, he is also escaping, combating the Cybermen and trying to reach the shining hill. When he reaches his doctor Will incarnation he knows he is on his last legs. If he doesn't make it before his time runs out, he will finally be dead.

(This, too, offers a possible explanation as to why he doesn't exactly resemble the real Hartnell.)

The attraction of this shape is that it would allow us to have all the doctors in the story without having them meet up. Its difficulty is finding a convincing reason for Tegan also to slip back through the companion incarnations. Maybe mental projection? In each of his forms he would see the companion he had at the time.

3) We might use the TARDIS as a kind of tuning fork. We postulate that within its structure lie the echoes or 'vibes' of all who have ever been aboard. Given the right technology, therefore, it is possible to recreate any or all of the former Doctors and hold them in corporeal form as long as the energy supply lasts.

The present Doctor – perhaps finding himself out of action – might be compelled to activate this 'memory function' in order to seek help from his predecessors.

This could be a battle of wits between the Doctors and the exhausted old computer that has been drifting for twenty million years. But I see no Cybermen in it.[329]

<hr>

329 The various elements that Holmes was asked to incorporate into his story at this point were therefore as follows. A replacement first Doctor, the second, third and fourth Doctors as played by Patrick Troughton, Jon Pertwee and Tom Baker, and the current Doctor, Peter Davison. Named companions were Susan (as played by Carole Ann Ford) alongside the first Doctor, Jamie (as played by Frazer Hines) with the second and Tegan (as played by Janet Fielding) with the fifth. No mention is made in the proposal of the other current regular companion, Turlough (Mark Strickson), but this was probably an oversight by Holmes rather than an indication that the character wasn't due to appear in the special. The companions that were to be partnered with the third and fourth Doctors were not mentioned by name by Holmes, but John Nathan-Turner was certainly trying to track down Katy Manning (Jo Grant) – who was now resident in Australia – in August 1982. Elisabeth Sladen (Sarah Jane Smith) was at this point almost certainly in Nathan-Turner's thoughts to accompany the fourth Doctor, but wasn't actually signed up to appear in the special until December 1982, by which time Holmes had left the project. The villains of the piece were to be the Master (as played semi-regularly in the series since 1981 by Anthony Ainley) and the Cybermen, who had recently reappeared in the 1982 story 'Earthshock', an adventure written by the current script editor, Eric Saward.

CHAPTER TWENTY-FIVE
CAVING IN ...
1983-1984

As soon as production had finished on the 'The Five Doctors' special, Eric Saward set to work on commissioning scripts for *Doctor Who*'s next season – the twenty-first – and almost immediately offered Bob the chance to have a go at writing a straightforward, traditional four-part story. 'After he'd turned down the offer of writing the special I did approach him later', recalls Saward. 'John Nathan-Turner was very resistant to bringing him back in the first place, which was a problem for me, which is why I was disappointed all the more that he hadn't been able to deliver the goods. But I managed to persuade John that I wanted Bob to work on the show, as I still felt he had a lot to offer. As it turned out, he did.'

This time, there was only a single prerequisite specified by Saward to Bob about his prospective new story. Peter Davison had decided to leave the series after three years playing the Doctor, and so Bob's story had to feature the Doctor regenerating into his sixth incarnation at its conclusion. Bob agreed to this, and so on Friday 6 May 1983, Saward commissioned him to write an outline for a potential four-part adventure with a working title 'Chain Reaction', with a delivery date of Monday 23 May 1983.

The storyline Bob submitted saw the Doctor and his new companion, Peri, get involved in a complex power struggle between a shadowy figure named Sharaz Jek, who controlled the Spectrox mines on Androzani Minor, and the President of the nearby planet Androzani Major. Spectrox, once refined, has the rare ability to halt the body's natural aging process, and as such has become the most precious commodity in the galaxy. Peri comes into contact with a lethal dosage of raw Spectrox, and the Doctor has to battle to save her life while trying to extricate them both from the affairs of others.

Bob's written storyline for 'Chain Reaction' was very similar to the finished television production, which was eventually re-titled 'The Caves of Androzani', but differed from it in one key respect. Originally, the Doctor was to have regenerated due to a combination of exhaustion and wounds inflicted on him by the gunrunner, Stotz, earlier in the story. This was changed by Saward so that, in the transmitted version, the Doctor contracted the same Spectrox poisoning that afflicted Peri.

Getting back into the routine of writing a traditional *Doctor Who* story obviously suited Bob, and his relationship with Saward soon became less prickly, to the point where the two men struck up a close friendship. 'We enjoyed working together, I can safely say that,' recalls Saward. 'He had had three-and-a-half years of script editing *Doctor Who*, and I think it had worn him out. And I think coming back to it, he was a little concerned – I think that was partly why he was a little bolshie when we first met. I think he did enjoy it. I hope he did, because I wanted him to, and I wanted to go on using him. But we certainly enjoyed working together.'

On the strength of his storyline, Bob was commissioned to write the four full scripts for 'The Caves of Androzani' on Thursday 28 July 1983, and given a target date of Tuesday 30 August to deliver them all. As things turned out, he delivered the scripts for the first two episodes in late September 1983, and the final two scripts the following month, although the delay was seemingly approved by Saward.

Saward recalls receiving Bob's scripts. 'It was a delight. It came in an episode at a time. In fact, Bob used to bring each one in, because that's when we'd started "lunching", which was always a great joy. Bob was always fun to talk to, especially with a bottle of wine between us. He used to bring me an episode, and I'd read it, and then we'd trot across to the local wine bar, and talk about it, and also talk in general. It was a very easy way to work. Because at the time we were having so many problems with scripts in general; we used a lot of inexperienced writers. It was a policy of John's to encourage new writers, to give them television experience, but when someone like Bob came along, it was just a case of receiving the scripts and sending them off to the printers. It was lovely; a real treat! I enjoyed reading "The Caves of Androzani" for the first time. I thought it was a little melodramatic – the main character, Sharaz Jek, I thought was a little over the top. But it was a great yarn, it dragged you in, it pulled you along, and it was exciting.'

Saward was blissfully happy that he didn't have to do any substantial editing on Bob's scripts. In fact, the work required by him was quite minimal. 'I did virtually nothing,' he later recalled. 'I wrote one scene, and that was only because Bob wasn't able to do it himself, and that was the one about that stupid bit of celery the Doctor wore. We wanted an explanation, and I wrote the thing about its restorative powers and so on, and it's ironic because that was quoted by one reviewer as being wonderfully classic Bob Holmes lines! I can prove I wrote it too because if you go into the next room you'll see a typewriter called a Praxis 33, and that's where the word "Praxis" came from; I was sitting there thinking "What on Earth can I call this? ... I'll call it Praxis!"'.[330]

---

330 Interview – Eric Saward, *DWB*: Issue 57, August 1988.

'When they found out I wasn't in the bath chair just yet they asked me to write a four-parter for Peter Davison,' Bob told *Doctor Who Magazine* some years later. 'They asked, in fact, if I would like to write the death of the Doctor, and I said yes, firstly because I'd not written for Peter Davison and secondly because everyone knows this is the last story and so you have that kind of in-built drama. I was teasing the audience quite a bit really – I killed the Doctor off, apparently, at the end of the first episode – although you only had to look at the *Radio Times* [to see Davison's name in the cast list for the next episode] to see he was all right! I think that was an added "plus" as far as I was concerned, and an inducement for writing it.'

In terms of production methods, Bob was surprised to discover that not much had changed on *Doctor Who* in the five years he'd been away from it. 'They don't seem to have changed much,' he noted. 'Same rehearsal time, same film allocation, same studio time, etc. But every year some technical advance is made, of course, and it seems to me that there is now more expertise available and that more people are experienced in, say, things like setting up and shooting CSO sequences.' In terms of his inspiration for the story, Bob added, 'The basis of the story was big business – particularly as we see it today in the form of multinational companies – and armaments dealing.' Bob also conceded that the tone of the story was quite different from some of the more whimsical tales he'd penned in the past. '"The Caves of Androzani" very much falls into a more serious sort of category of script than do some of my other pieces for *Doctor Who*. The Doctor has a few jokes, but on the whole it's a fairly serious story. If you look at my stuff, I quite often kill practically everyone except the Doctor and his companions. Certainly I never thought of Jek as anything but a one-off character. But we don't know for sure that he died in the fire, do we? Salateen might have carried him out. I paced the script in a slightly different way, allowing much more room for story development, and I hope it's going to work. But then I have never found *Doctor Who* an easy show to write for.' He also noted that his decision to set the tale mainly in underground caves was not just led by story considerations, but by production considerations too: 'The practical reason, though, for using caves, is that they are comparatively simple to set up in a studio, and they can be doubled up: i.e. slightly changed and shot from a different angle so that they appear much larger than they really are. You can't do this so easily with a "straight wall" set.'[331]

The fact that the story featured an incarnation of the Doctor he'd not written for before didn't seem to faze Bob at all. Saward offers the opinion

---

331 Robert Holmes Interview, *Mondas*: Season 21 Special, 1984 – Interview by John Nicholas.

393

that Bob would perhaps write for a 'generic' Doctor, whose character was only partly driven by the actor portraying him: 'I think when he was writing for someone like Tom Baker, he was writing a character that was much more like Tom – richer, fruitier, stronger. I think Bob picked up on that in his Tom Baker stories. But on other occasions, I think he wrote for a generic Doctor. In a way, in "The Caves of Androzani", the Doctor could have been played by any of the actors who had portrayed him.'

Bob, speaking at the time he wrote 'The Caves of Androzani', echoed these sentiments. He handled the fifth Doctor, he said, '… in very much the same way as his predecessors. After all, the Doctor is always the same character. His body changes, his manners and idiosyncrasies alter, but at the bottom he remains the same person.'[332]

'The Caves of Androzani' was an unqualified success, winning plaudits from fans and general viewers alike. And while some of that success was undoubtedly down to the fine performances by the cast, and the excellent direction by series newcomer Graeme Harper, the starting point was the solid scripts that Bob had written. Saward, while acknowledging that the story was a success, stops short of giving all the credit to Bob, however. 'I don't want to undercut Bob at all,' he once told an interviewer, 'but I think you're reading far too much into that story. For Bob, it was very much a routine story. It was a good, above-average script … I was so delighted it had worked well considering the minor hiccup we'd had at our first meeting, and it was a delight to work with someone like that.'[333]

As far as Saward was concerned, Bob had quickly re-established himself as a safe and trusted pair of hands to have on tap, at a time when he was finding it increasingly difficult to find new writers who could cope with the demands of *Doctor Who*. 'He was consistently the best storyteller,' recalled Saward. 'Also he was a very good writer. Stylish in a way that might have been considered very old fashioned, but he turned a lovely phrase, and it was a pleasure to read his scripts. He was very good – he was the best we had. I know it's only an opinion, but to work with, he was the best, and he produced the best material.'

Bob was about to get another commission for the series.

It was around this time that Bob bumped into his old friend Terrance Dicks in the BBC bar, and had a chat with him about his new lease of life in the world of *Doctor Who*. 'I remember talking to Bob in the BBC bar quite some time after I had left as *Doctor Who* script editor,' Dicks recalls. 'It must have been at a change-over time for the Doctor, and he'd been asked to do a story

---

332 Robert Holmes Interview, *Mondas*: Season 21 Special, 1984 – Interview by John Nicholas.
333 Interview – Eric Saward, *DWB*: Issue 57, August 1988.

for the next season, but he wasn't absolutely certain who the Doctor was going to be. And I said, "Isn't that tough?" And he said, "No, not really, the Doctor's always the Doctor." And that, of course, is perfectly true.'

After production had finished on 'The Caves of Androzani' in early 1984, Saward asked Bob to come up with another story, which was then slated to feature in the first full season of Colin Baker's sixth Doctor, due to screen on BBC1 from January 1985. In preparation for this, Bob attended the studio recording for Baker's first story, 'The Twin Dilemma', which had gone into production straight after his own 'The Caves of Androzani'. However, this time, Nathan-Turner decided once again to give Bob a 'shopping list' of elements to include in his new story. Bob was asked to incorporate the return of the second Doctor and his companion Jamie McCrimmon (as played by Patrick Troughton and Frazer Hines) for a single story; plus the return of the Sontarans, and also an exotic overseas location – the American city of New Orleans.

Saward wasn't sure that this was such a good idea. 'Because "The Caves of Androzani" had worked so well, I thought it was best to leave Bob alone as much as possible,' he recalled. 'Unfortunately, John Nathan-Turner, the producer, had decided he wanted to film abroad again. We didn't have a story – there was no real logic to it. I don't want to slag John off for the sake of it, but at the time it seemed really rather ridiculous. A number of places were suggested as a possible location, including New Orleans, and at one stage he wanted to do it in Venice, in August …! He obviously hadn't been to Venice in August, because there would probably have been about ten million people there, and so that was quickly discarded. This was slightly a fad that John had; he wanted to take the show somewhere "else". He thought taking it abroad was an answer, but it wasn't. And Bob viewed it, again, as another irritation.'

Doctor Who had, at this time, undergone a slight alteration in format for the first time in its 21 year history. It had just returned to its traditional weekly Saturday evening teatime slot after three years of a twice-weekly midweek BBC1 transmission schedule, but the episode length had been increased from 25 minutes to 45 minutes. Saward recalls that this change didn't faze Bob in the slightest. 'As the professional writer he was, he was told to write to 45 minutes, and he would do 45 minutes. It was a challenge, it was a change, but Bob just accepted it, and was quite happy.' However, Saward recalls that Bob was less happy with having the second Doctor and Jamie imposed upon his story. 'He didn't like it,' said Saward. 'Neither did he like the idea of setting the story in America, especially when there wasn't enough money to make the programme properly.'[334]

Bob called his new story 'The Kraalon Inheritance', and Saward was happy to let him write the first episode straight off, without having to submit a scene breakdown first – Bob's preferred way of working. In terms of plot mechanics, Bob elected to return to elements of his unused anniversary special storyline for 'The Six Doctors', replacing the Cybermen with the Sontarans but still having their motive being the quest for the biological mechanism that sets Time Lords apart from the rest of the population of the universe, by giving them mastery of time travel. Needing to find a replacement for the Master as the Sontarans' ally in the new story, Bob came up with a new race of aliens; the Kraalons, a race of intergalactic gourmands who would be drawn to New Orleans by its culinary reputation.

Another strand of inspiration for the story came from Bob's time in the *Doctor Who* production office nearly a decade earlier. As Bob recalled in an interview with *Doctor Who Magazine* in 1985, when he was script editor he had '... suggested to one writer a story about aliens who visit Earth at odd times to cull the population because they rather like human meat – but now I've done that with the "The Two Doctors" story.'[335]

'Apparently Patrick Troughton and Frazer Hines so enjoyed "The Five Doctors" they asked if they could come back and do another one,' said Bob in the same interview. 'We were moving to the 45-minute time slot and this was going to be the season "biggie" – and Eric Saward wanted someone with experience of writing what is virtually an old six-parter and asked if I'd mind writing it. Then they said "Can we have Sontarans?" I don't really like bringing back old monsters but I don't think the Sontarans were really well used in their last appearances so I was glad to redress the balance.'

The story was to be three 45-minute episodes in length, and Bob was commissioned on Monday 13 February 1984 to write the script for Part One, with a target delivery date of Monday 5 March 1984. He hit this delivery date, so Saward then commissioned him on Friday 9 March 1984 to write the scripts for Parts Two and Three.

At the same time, Nathan-Turner was hard at work setting up the deal that would allow the *Doctor Who* production team to film the story on location in New Orleans itself. Key to this was getting some additional funding from BBC Enterprises, who at the time were reaping huge financial benefits from the sale of *Doctor Who* (although mainly the back catalogue of Tom Baker's stories) to PBS stations in America. However, in April 1984, just as Bob was working hard to complete the writing of his story, it started to become obvious

335 Interview – Robert Holmes, *Doctor Who Magazine*: Issue 100, May 1985.

396

that the additional funding wouldn't be forthcoming. Nathan-Turner then tried, unsuccessfully, to persuade the senior management of the BBC Drama Department to allocate extra funds for the filming. At the same time, he was still telling Bob (via Saward) to continue writing the scripts with New Orleans as the definite filming location.

However, with no extra funding for filming in America forthcoming, Nathan-Turner now began contingency planning. He was adamant that the story was still to be filmed outside the United Kingdom, and had balanced the books in such a way that the production team could at least consider potential alternative locations in and around Europe. After briefly considering, and then rejecting, Venice as a possible location, Seville in Spain was selected as a suitable replacement for New Orleans. So in early May 1984, Bob was asked to rewrite his scripts for 'The Kraalon Inheritance' with Seville rather than New Orleans as the main setting.

Saward recalls that both he and Bob were less than impressed with this turn of events: 'One minute we're in New Orleans, the next minute we're in Venice, and then we're in Spain. Bob thought it was really rather pointless. Which, as it turned out, it was. It could have been shot anywhere.'

This request for a rewrite due to the change of location affected the contractual agreement that Bob (via Jon Thurley) and the BBC had both signed off on for this story. Because of his past experience with the series, Bob's deal to write the scripts for 'The Kraalon Inheritance' had been structured so that he got the full fee for the script for Part One on being commissioned on Monday 13 February 1984. He then would be paid half of his fees for Parts Two and Three when he had written the script for Part One and it was accepted by the production team. The BBC then had a window of two months to notify Bob if any rewrites needed doing to the script for Part One, without having to pay him any additional fee. However, because of the problems with the filming location changing, this payment of half-fees for Parts Two and Three wasn't honoured straight away when Bob's script for Part One was delivered on 5 March 1984.

Bob carried on writing the scripts for the other two episodes, because, after all, his script for Part One had been accepted by the production office, and no-one had told him anything different when it came to the location. It wasn't until Thursday 3 May 1984 that Nathan-Turner elected to tell the Head of BBC Copyright that they needed to re-brief Bob about the change of location, and a further two weeks elapsed before Bob was told exactly what was going on, and where exactly the new location was.

As Bob had by now written the full scripts for the second and third episodes, and these had technically been accepted under the terms of his contract, *and* the two-month window for notifying him of any rewrites had expired, this all meant that he had to be contracted again from scratch to rewrite his scripts. Any resentment that Bob might have felt about this situation was surely smoothed over by the fact that on Wednesday 23 May 1984, he was paid in full for his original scripts for Parts Two and Three, and in full again for his revised script for Part One. The following week, he was paid in full for his revised scripts for Parts Two and Three. So he was effectively paid twice his full fee for writing the story.

The rewrites Bob was requested to make were, on the face of it, substantial. 'Bob had written the original story already set in St Louis,'[336] recalled Saward, 'and there were quite serious changes to be made because, in spite of what John thought, you can't simply transfer a story from an English-speaking country to a Spanish-speaking country, particularly when you have verbal jokes and plays on words and so on. It was quite a major rethink. Anyway, Bob went away after discussions and reworked the material to be set in Spain. It changed in some respects, not massively; the plot remained but a lot of the lines were altered. Bob by this stage, I think, was getting really fed up and tired, and the story ultimately suffered because of all this messing about.'[337]

Bob recalled these problems during his interview for *Doctor Who Magazine* the following year. 'I had written the script to be set in New Orleans not Seville. That's why I created the Androgums – I couldn't think of any reason why aliens should visit New Orleans and I recalled it was a jazz place, but not even I could envisage a race of aliens obsessed with jazz, and then I remembered it is the culinary centre of America, with lots of restaurants, so I invented the Androgums, who are obsessed with food. [Their name is] an anagram of gourmand. So they went to New Orleans for the food. They stayed however when it shifted to Seville because I couldn't think of anything else.'[338]

'That story was basically a plea for animal rights and vegetarianism,' Bob also later recalled. 'I had this vegetarian theme running through it. I was trying to point out how filthy it is to eat all this meat, although I'm not a vegetarian. The things we do to animals ...'

Bob retitled the story 'The Androgum Inheritance', but within a month of him delivering his revised scripts, the title was changed once again, this time to the rather more bland 'The Two Doctors'.

Prior to the cast departing for Spain, a read-through of the scripts was

---

336 Saward is almost certainly not referring to the city of St Louis in Missouri here, but to the district around the St Louis Cathedral in New Orleans.
337 Interview – Eric Saward, *DWB*: Issue 58, September 1988.
338 Interview – Robert Holmes, *Doctor Who Magazine*: Issue 100, May 1985.

held at BBC Threshold House on Tuesday 31 July 1984. Saward wrote to Bob to inform him: '… I will not be there to look after your side of things so for God's sake come.' Bob did indeed attend, and what he witnessed left a lasting impression on him. He recalled his experience when writing his essay for the book *The Doctor Who File*, edited by Peter Haining. He also recalled it in a separate, earlier interview: 'I'm doing a piece for Peter Haining; he's got another book coming out,' Bob told journalist Richard Marson in late 1985. 'He's asked me to do a piece, and he wants me to mention "The Two Doctors". And I remember on "The Two Doctors" last year, it was a very, very hot day, and we were sitting in a room like this, all doing the read. And there's a line where Colin Baker's mesmerizing Frazer Hines. And I remember it with some apprehension. When he started, he said, "See this pretty thing, Jamie. See how it moves, backwards and forwards, forwards and backwards …" And of course, Jacquie Pearce just fell about, and everybody else started laughing. They all collapsed, and I looked along them, and I thought, "Oh my God …!" The first Doctor I had to work with was Pat Troughton, and he was an incorrigible kind of mickey-taker. Any double entendre in the script, and he would find it, as would Frazer. I'm going to mention this in the thing, I'll start with that and then go back, to launch my reminiscences. Writers don't, basically, have any, because you don't go anywhere except behind a typewriter. But I shall write something for him, and then I'm going to come back to the rehearsal room, where Colin Baker is at it again. And he's saying, "I'll just take a scout round the back …" And everybody laughs.'

The director assigned to 'The Two Doctors' was Peter Moffat, who'd worked on several *Doctor Who* stories over the previous few years. However, Saward felt that Moffat wasn't particularly sympathetic to Bob's script. 'I remember the designer talking about putting hand grenades on Shockeye's shoulders! When Bob and I spoke about what he should look like, he was going to be in a simple butcher's smock with a simple meat cleaver, and when I asked Peter Moffat why have the ridiculous hand grenades, he actually said, "Oh, to make it look more silly." I pointed out that the whole point of Shockeye was that he was a master chef, brilliant at what he does, and what was really called for was a very simple, straightforward butcher's smock. It was as though they were trying to fight the intention of the script! Shockeye was a fascinating creature, and although they cast him well, they messed up the presentation.'[339]

Bob would later echo Saward's reservations about Moffat's direction of the story. 'I think the cast was very good on that. I just didn't think Peter got them

---

339 Interview – Eric Saward (and Ian Levine), *DWB*: Issue 106, October 1992.

399

into a proper *Doctor Who* mood,' he noted. In particular, Bob was unimpressed with Moffat's handling of the scene that saw the ex-actor character Oscar Botcherby stabbed to death by Shockeye. 'Well I don't think they did that very well. It should have been very moving. That, again, is down to the way they directed it. It should have been a moving scene, I thought. There's no good killing off somebody who isn't important. I mean, if you get to like a character, and then you kill him, the impact is much more important than if you kill off some anonymous person who's just walked in.'

However, once again, both Saward and Nathan-Turner were suitably impressed with Bob's finished scripts for 'The Two Doctors', and just a month after production had completed on the story, they asked him if he'd like to write another for the following year's season – *Doctor Who*'s twenty-third – which was due to air on BBC1 from January 1986. This was to be Colin Baker's second full season as the Doctor, and again Bob was asked to write its only three-part story. Nathan-Turner had decided that another overseas location trip would be attempted on the strength of the perceived success of 'The Two Doctors', but a firm location had yet to be identified and decided upon. Bob was also asked to incorporate another one of his old villains – the Autons – into the new story, alongside both the Master (who had recently been reintroduced into the series by Nathan-Turner, and was now portrayed by Anthony Ainley), *and* the Brigadier (as played by Nicholas Courtney). Nathan-Turner later recalled that he had also asked for the Rani (a recently-introduced villainess, as portrayed by Kate O'Mara) to be incorporated into Bob's story. Yet again, Bob was being given a 'shopping list' of ingredients.

The commissioning paperwork for the first episode's script was raised on Friday 26 October 1984, under the working title 'Yellow Fever and How To Cure It'.[340] This time, there wasn't a target delivery date given (the commissioning form simply noted that it was wanted 'ASAP'), and it seems quite likely that the commission was not officially passed on to Bob at this point. Unofficially, he would have been told to start planning the story, but a note on the paperwork, written by Saward and dated Wednesday 14 November 1984, stated: '... after much discussion about locations, etc, John Nathan-Turner agrees to wait until these are decided before commissioning Holmes – at Holmes' request.' Obviously, after the New Orleans / Seville switch that had happened during production of 'The Two Doctors', Bob didn't want to be put in the position of having to do rewrites should the location for the new story be changed at the last minute.

---

340 This was abbreviated to just 'Yellow Fever' in some later production documents.

Nathan-Turner (along with his partner, Gary Downie, who sometimes worked on *Doctor Who* as a production manager) flew out to Singapore on Thursday 18 October 1984 to spend a week ostensibly scouting for locations to use for filming Bob's story. They took a BBC-issue video camera with them to record footage of potential locations, and brought the tapes back to the BBC on their return. However, Saward recalls that their home video wasn't the greatest of successes. 'Bob Holmes and I sat in a viewing room and we watched the thing,' he recalls, 'which was about 40 minutes long, and afterwards we just shrugged and thought, "Well, what is the point of all this?" They had literally just driven around in a taxi and shot from the window. As anyone knows, you can only do location [reconnaissance] work on foot.'[341]

In early 1985, Bob was interviewed by Gary Russell for *Doctor Who Magazine*, for a feature that then appeared in the publication's hundredth edition. He was asked if he was still interested in writing new stories for *Doctor Who*. His reply was alarmingly prophetic in nearly every respect: 'Well, first let me say I see no reason why I couldn't carry on writing one script a year if I satisfy them. So hopefully I'll carry on! It's not so difficult trying to think up one story per year as it is six! I wouldn't go back to being a *Doctor Who* script editor. I understand they want me to write a story next year but they haven't decided whether or not it's going to be filmed in Singapore – I hope they decide soon because I'm due to start work on *Bergerac* afterwards and if I'm not careful I won't have enough time! With any luck though, I shall carry on writing for *Doctor Who* until its deathbed!'[342]

'It never really got to the planning stage,' recalled Saward of the Singapore story some years later. 'We looked at a bit of footage that had been shot in Singapore. Again, Bob was very resistant to it all, because it got in the way of storytelling. It was appendages that we didn't really need – we couldn't afford to film abroad. I was certainly getting very irritated, but John wanted this, and he was the producer; if he could get it out of his budget, then he was entitled to do it. There was no purpose … If you had a story that required location filming somewhere abroad, then fine. That's how it usually works. But to say "We want to go to Singapore," and then not have a reason for it … So you have to then try and fit it in, and it doesn't work. And it didn't work.'

Nathan-Turner later said that the story '… would have involved Peri hankering for a trip home to the United States and begin with her seeing the Statue of Liberty through the TARDIS screen. Then she discovers it's a

341 Interview – Eric Saward (and Ian Levine), *DWB*: Issue 106, October 1992.
342 Interview – Robert Holmes, *Doctor Who Magazine*: Issue 100, May 1985. The *Bergerac* commission he mentions here was almost certainly for his episode 'Winner Takes All', which was made in 1985 but wasn't screened until 1987 (see Chapter Twenty-Three).

replica in an ornamental garden.'[343] He later recalled still further details. 'The Singapore story never existed, other than a video of some stunningly different locations – Indian, colonial, hi-tech, shanty, Chinese, period/modern – and a request from myself to Bob to consider a story featuring the Autons, the Master, the Rani, the street theatre (like the Noh theatre) in which the Rani appeared (white face and all) and a desire that the story opened with Peri's wish to visit the US. The scanner would reveal the three-dimensional Statue of Liberty, and on exiting from the TARDIS, they would discover they were in the ornamental gardens (name forgotten) where artefacts of the world were displayed in Singapore! This is an oversimplified version of a major discussion but it puts the gem of the idea in perspective.'[344]

So Singapore was the location of choice, but the final decision to set the story there wasn't taken until Friday 15 February 1985. It was only at that point that Bob was given the official commission to write the first episode, with a delivery date of Monday 1 April 1985 for the script. Bob was also paid his full fee up-front for writing this one episode.

Behind the scenes, however, events were conspiring against *Doctor Who*'s next season...

---

343 Interview – John Nathan-Turner, *Doctor Who Magazine*: Issue 164, September 1990.
344 Private correspondence with Colin Brockhurst, dated 14 July 1992.

CHAPTER TWENTY-SIX
THE FINAL ACT
1985-1986

As 1984 turned into 1985, Eric Saward was by now becoming more and more reliant on Bob as a scriptwriter on *Doctor Who*. There were other writers on the series, of course, but Bob was the only one that Saward would return to season after season with a firm story commission. And although Bob was writing only one story per year, it was one story per year that Saward knew he didn't have to fret over. He knew that Bob was a strict professional, was able to get on with the job with little or no fuss, and required minimal editing and rewriting when he delivered his scripts to an agreed timescale. Bob was low maintenance, basically. At the same time, Saward was also keen to try to insulate Bob as much as possible from the reportedly tempestuous behaviour of *Doctor Who*'s producer John Nathan-Turner, who had by now fallen out with several other writers and directors on the series. 'He was protected from him as much as he could be,' recalls Saward. 'You must bear in mind that Bob also needed the money. Let's not forget he was a professional writer and there weren't that many other offers. Fans forget that people write *Doctor Who* to earn a living.'[345]

Sadly, Saward was right when he said that Bob needed the money he earned from *Doctor Who*. His network of contacts in the television industry had shrunk considerably in the past few years. His only writing work outside of *Doctor Who* since 1981 had come via Robert Banks Stewart, Chris Boucher or Brenda Ennis. And in the 18 months since he'd written his scripts for 'The Caves of Androzani' in late 1983, he hadn't written for any other series at all. So even as Saward was becoming increasingly reliant on Bob, Bob in turn found that he was becoming increasingly reliant on *Doctor Who* for work.

Even though Bob's writing contacts had shrunk in number over the years, he still had a few friends in high places at the BBC. And in the middle of February 1985, he was told by one such friend[346] that *Doctor Who* was to be imminently cancelled by the senior BBC management; specifically by the Controller of BBC1, Michael Grade, aided and abetted by the Head of Series and Serials, Jonathan Powell. Their plan was that after the final episode of

---

345 Interview – Eric Saward, *DWB*: Issue 58, September 1988.
346 Bob's source has never been identified, but has been rumoured to be a secretary working on the BBC's sixth floor at the time.

Doctor Who's twenty-second season was aired on 30 March 1985 (a little over six weeks away), the show would be swept into the television archives for good. The twenty-third season – and Bob's story 'Yellow Fever and How To Cure It' – was just not going to be made.

Bob phoned Saward early on Thursday 21 February 1985 to tell him what he'd heard and to find out if Saward had also heard any corroborating whispers. Saward hadn't, but Bob assured him of the provenance of his source. Saward then got straight on the phone to John Nathan-Turner, who was just about to fly over to America for a weekend-long *Doctor Who* convention, and the two of them discussed what Bob had reported. Nathan-Turner hadn't heard of any rumours of a cancellation either, and to be fair to him, he also had a very good network of contacts within the BBC. He dismissed the story as unfounded gossip, leaving Saward slightly mollified, and flew out to America the following day.

Nathan-Turner then returned, slightly jetlagged, on the morning of Monday 25 February 1985. On arriving at the *Doctor Who* production office, he was summoned into a meeting with Jonathan Powell, who told him that his show was being axed. Nathan-Turner was genuinely shocked at this news, and he returned to the production office to inform Saward that Bob had been correct. At this point, the twenty-third season was due to start production in just a little over six weeks; a number of scripts had already been commissioned and written, and the directors and crews that had been booked to make them had to be contacted and stood down. Nathan-Turner and Saward were left in limbo.

The BBC, deluged with letters of complaint from fans and viewers, were under intense pressure from the tabloid media over the decision, and both Michael Grade and Jonathan Powell were taken to task by their bosses over their handling of the cancellation. The whole mess was finally resolved a few days later, on Friday 1 March 1985, when Bill Cotton, the Managing Director of BBC Television, issued a statement saying that *Doctor Who* would return after all in 1986, but would begin in the autumn rather than in the usual January slot, effectively giving the programme an 18-month hiatus. He also stated that the series would return to its traditional 25-minute episode format.

With no real guidance being given to the *Doctor Who* production team by the senior BBC management, the only concrete information that Saward and Nathan-Turner had was the latter instruction to return to a 25-minute format, and that production would now probably need to start in the autumn of 1985 if they were to have a 26-episode series ready to go on air for autumn 1986. The format had switched to 13 x 45-minute episodes only a year previously, and as far as Saward and Nathan-Turner were concerned, given the time they had before the delayed twenty-third season was due to go into production, the best option they now had was to get all the scripts that they had originally lined up for the season written or re-written as 25-minute episodes. All of the stories that had been commissioned apart from Bob's had been of two x 45-minute length, so these would now become four x 25-minute stories. Bob's 'Yellow Fever and How To Cure It' would become six x 25-minute episodes. Both Nathan-Turner and Saward now started working towards this revised plan.

Bob was re-briefed about his story on Wednesday 20 March 1985, and told about the new episode format. Because there would be a slight increase in screen time (which totalled about 15 minutes over the whole length of the story), his fee for two 25-minute episodes was slightly higher than for one 45-minute episode. He had already been paid in full for writing the first 45-minute episode (even though he hadn't as yet actually written a word of it), so he would be due additional payments when he delivered the new Parts One and Two. One change to the story was that Bob was now asked to remove the Master. Singapore and the Autons, however, were still to be included.

Although this new deal was agreed in principle, Bob still didn't begin work on writing his scripts. Instead, he took up an offer from W H Allen, the publishers of the *Doctor Who* range of Target paperbacks, to novelise his own scripts for 'The Two Doctors'. The resultant book would be released later that same year as the range's hundredth novel (see Chapter Twenty-Eight for more details).

Bob was scheduled to appear at his third *Doctor Who* convention on Saturday 6 April 1985[347], but he cancelled his appearance shortly before the event, citing ill health as his reason. With hindsight, it's hard not to suspect that this may have been an indication that Bob was beginning to suffer a general decline in his health, perhaps more than he himself realised at the time.

In late May 1985, Jonathan Powell informed Nathan-Turner that the twenty-third season of *Doctor Who* would now comprise only 14 episodes, not the expected 26. The curtailed new season would now go into production during the spring of 1986, and not autumn 1985, as anticipated. This reduced episode count completely scuppered the plans Nathan-Turner and Saward had to utilise the stories that had already been commissioned for the season. One, two, or possibly three of these planned stories would now need to be dropped at least. Perhaps in light of this situation, Bob (via Jon Thurley) informed the production team in early June that he was now withdrawing from his commission to write 'Yellow Fever and How To Cure It', and so the

---

347 *DWASocial 5*, organised by the DWAS at the Novotel, London on 6 April 1985.

story was officially cancelled for good.

This still left Bob with his full fee for writing the first episode of this story, which had already been paid to him. This overpayment probably didn't concern him too greatly, but as not a single word had been committed to paper, he had to agree that it was a slightly unfair situation. It was decided his fee for 'Yellow Fever and How To Cure It' would be offset against his next BBC commission. Eric Saward was determined that this would be for yet another *Doctor Who* story, as he and Nathan-Turner began planning for the all-new twenty-third season.

Saward's idea was now to use *Doctor Who*'s real-life problems as a basis for the fictional drama. Nathan-Turner agreed to this, and so preparations for a new 14-week season began afresh. All previously-commissioned scripts were now scrapped. The Doctor was about to go on trial …

Saward got Bob on board with this new approach almost straight away, and they talked over the script editor's ideas. Saward came up with the overall shape and structure of the new season – with a little bit of help from Bob – which would now begin with the Doctor being captured and put on trial by his own people, the Time Lords. The first four-part story would now be written by Bob, and would form the basis for the Time Lords' evidence against the Doctor. Saward nominated Philip Martin (who had written 'Vengeance on Varos' for the show the previous year, as well as the highly regarded BBC1 crime drama *Gangsters*) to write the second four-part story. After this, it was then decided to have two two-part stories, both set in the same location, and then Bob was scheduled to write the final two-part story that would wrap everything up. Two writers new to *Doctor Who*, David Halliwell and Jack Trevor Story, were each asked to contribute one of the two-part stories to the season. Story's invitation to write for the series came partly from a recommendation Bob had made to Saward. Story had written for *No Hiding Place*, *Public Eye*, *Market in Honey Lane* and *Fraud Squad*, and had crossed paths with Bob many times since.

On Tuesday 9 July 1985, Saward met with Bob, Martin, Halliwell and Story at BBC Threshold House, so that they all could discuss the structure of the upcoming season.

A few weeks later, on Thursday 29 August 1985, Bob travelled to the Queensway offices of the magazine publishers Marvel UK, to be interviewed by *Doctor Who Magazine*'s Richard Marson. Marson was writing most of the content of the magazine's Winter Special that year, which was to be devoted to the Jon Pertwee era of the programme, and so he had asked Bob for an interview in order to get some interesting background material for his articles. 'I had tried to get him to agree to an interview before – I still have the reticent reply to my first request,' recalls Marson. However, Bob agreed to Marson's second request, and arrived in high spirits. 'I remember him as friendly, shrewd, slightly reticent, and reeking of pipe smoke,' recalls Marson. 'He was smartly dressed, with a jacket and tie. There was no sign of him being ill, or out of sorts.'

The interview that Marson conducted with Bob that day wasn't printed in full in the Winter Special, although some additional quotes from it popped up in other features in *Doctor Who Magazine* in the coming months.[348] Bob was able to tell Marson a little of the plans for the upcoming *Doctor Who* season as they stood at that point: 'I'm doing the first four parts, Philip Martin's doing the second four parts. It's intended that David Halliwell and Jack Trevor Story are going to do two parts each. And then I'm going to do the last two parts, and wind up the whole strand. And for the last three, we've got to use the same sets. I suspect we shall find the difficulty in linking them, somehow. But I'll wait and see what happens – I'll wait and see what the other guys have written beforehand.' Bob also told a little of how the season-long plot would be structured: 'We're on Gallifrey, and it starts as a trial, which they've done before. But Eric says no-one will remember that, so it won't be referred to. And the trial goes through the 14 episodes. I suspect that I might end up writing the last four, in fact ... These two guys, David Halliwell and Jack Trevor Story, have never done a *Doctor Who* before, and the first two two-parters are all part of the same story. But in case one or other of them fails, they've only given them a little strand, you see. Now if David Halliwell and Jack Trevor Storey fall down, I might find myself doing the final four, or six, episodes. Eric Saward was looking for people with rather lunatic minds this time around, to try and give it a different feel. It needs a different look. I mean, I quite agree actually with Michael Grade, when he said it was getting whimsical and old-fashioned.'

Bob revealed that he first suspected that *Doctor Who*'s days were numbered when it was moved from its Saturday teatime slot back in 1982. 'That's usually a sign of anything dying,' he told Marson, knowingly. 'It's moribund, it means the audiences are falling. But taking it away from its traditional Saturday afternoon slot was a bad move. I remember when *Emergency Ward 10* died, they started moving it about the timeslots, and making it an hour-long show.'

During the interview, Bob let it slip that should *Doctor Who* be cancelled once more at the conclusion of the new season, he wouldn't particularly mourn its passing. Instead, he saw it mainly as an opportunity for himself. 'I don't mind, really. I've got an idea that I've been quietly developing ... I've

---

348 I'm indebted to Richard Marson for letting me have access to his tape-recording of this interview for use in the preparation and writing of this book.

got this little format ready to bung in the moment I hear it's been cancelled. I might not even send it to the BBC, I might send it to Central. It would be nice to have a long-running series wouldn't it?' When Marson asked if Bob thought his potential new series had the capacity to last 22 years, as *Doctor Who* had done at that point, Bob laughed: 'I was planning on ten years actually! That'll see me out!'[349]

After all this pre-planning with Saward, Bob was officially commissioned on Monday 2 September 1985 to write the first four scripts of the season, under the working title 'Wasteland', although this later changed to 'The Robots of Ravolox'. His target delivery date for all four scripts was given as Monday 14 October. At this point, Bob was also paid his full fee for writing the script for Part One only.

Bob went ahead and wrote scripts for just the first and second episodes, and although these start out in a fashion quite familiar to anyone who's ever watched the final story as transmitted, they soon develop in a very different way.

In these scripts, the Doctor is taken out of time by the Time Lords to be put on trial. As part of the evidence against him, his prosecutor, the Valeyard, relays one of the Doctor's previous adventures to the court. It shows the Doctor and Peri landing on the desolate planet Ravolox, which the Doctor has never heard of before. Exploring, the Doctor discovers an underground tunnel complex, and leaves Peri behind to wait for him as he explores. Peri is captured by a group of savages and taken back to their camp. (This is all basically the same as in the televised version, although the characters Glitz and Dibber are absent from the narrative.) The Doctor discovers an underground settlement of around one thousand humans, controlled by a being referred to as 'the Immortal'. 'The Immortal' is Drathro, whom Bob describes as '... a tall figure in a black cloak, imposing, with a chain-mail helmet in crusader style.' The Doctor is captured by Balazar, who then takes him to Merdeen, a senior Water Guard on the base. Meanwhile, at the savages' village, Peri she is told by the tribe's leader, Katryca, that she will be married off – to Sour Smell (who has his own hut), Broken Tooth, Jack Fart-by-Night and Duke Atholl. She bribes one of her captors, Little Smith, with a ring and a bracelet, and he lets her escape from her cell. The Doctor is meanwhile taken to the underground base's inner 'castle', and finally meets Drathro, who is revealed to be a powerful L3 robot (and lives alone – he has no human assistants, unlike in the televised version). Drathro explains to the Doctor that the base's black light system is

349 No details are known of what this science fiction format might have been. It's possible Bob might have been referring to his aborted 1982 science fiction story idea *The Eskdale Experiment*, although this would have needed a lot of expanding to turn into a long-running series.

408

close to failure. His original mission was to look after some 'sleepers' from Alpha Centauri, who are also hidden in the complex, but his relief ships are now overdue by two hundred years. Drathro serves a meal for himself and the Doctor. While they eat, a terrible scream rings out, but Drathro claims he hears nothing. The Doctor then later observes Drathro removing the food he's swallowed, still undigested, from a small hatch in his body. Drathro decides to keep the Doctor on as a work unit, but then orders Merdeen to 'cull' Balazar in order to make room for him, as the base can only support exactly one thousand workers. Instead of killing Balazar, Merdeen forces him to flee above ground, telling him about the others he's helped escape in the past, and of the tales of the Tribe of the Free on the planet's surface. Peri flees back to the underground tunnels, chased by Little Smith and the rest of the Tribe. Drathro checks on the state of the sleepers, and finds that their life signs are weak or non-existent. This gives the Doctor the opportunity to escape from Drathro's castle. He heads for the surface and meets up with Balazar on the way. Drathro goes to a cell from where the screaming is emanating, and releases Jethro, another L3 robot who was once identical to Drathro, but was damaged by the fireball that originally consumed Ravolox. The second episode ends as Jethro turns to Drathro to reveal '... most of his head and half a shoulder has been melted into a shapeless ingot of metal.'

Bob delivered his two scripts to Saward, but Saward felt that they didn't entirely work, and so asked him to rewrite them. The main alteration they made to the story was the introduction of the semi-criminal, semi-comic double act of Glitz and Dibber, who now arrive on Ravolox from Alpha Centauri at the same time as the Doctor and Peri materialise in the TARDIS. They are looking to steal some unspecified secrets from the L3 robots, but are captured by the Tribe of the Free in the first episode; and when Peri too is caught, she is held prisoner in the same cell as them. All three of them escape at the climax of the second episode, and head for the underground tunnels. Meanwhile Drathro now revives – rather than releases – the damaged Jethro.

Bob then wrote his script for the third episode of the story. In it, Drathro explains to Jethro that he has revived him, despite Jethro being terminally damaged, as one of the hibernating sleepers has recently died, and Drathro now needs assistance. Peri, Glitz, and Dibber meet up with the Doctor and Balazar, and the Doctor takes them back into the underground shelter, sealing the door behind them, thwarting the pursuing tribesmen. Katryca works out how to use the guns the Tribe earlier took from Glitz and Dibber, and with them, they prepare for an attack on Drathro's base. The Doctor's group meet with Merdeen, and they all head for Drathro's inner sanctum. Drathro orders Grell, Merdeen's deputy, to hunt them all down and then kill them. The Doctor's party run into Jethro, who captures Peri. The Doctor gives himself up, and Jethro grabs him by the throat. But before he can kill the Doctor, Katryca and the Tribe arrive, and attack Jethro …

After this episode was written, Eric Saward and Bob reviewed the story so far, and between them decided that the scripts needed slightly reworking again. The whole subplot with Jethro was removed. Drathro was instead given two human servants, Humker and Tandrell, and also another robot drone, known as an L1. Additionally, more sequences switching back to the Doctor's trial on Gallifrey were requested by Saward, and the planet Ravolox became Ravalox instead.

Bob began writing the four scripts for the story once more, almost from scratch, this time under the working title 'The Mysterious Planet'. He finally delivered four completed scripts to Saward on Wednesday 15 January 1986. This now triggered a payment to Bob of half of his full fee for each of the scripts of the final three episodes, but now the money already paid to him for 'Yellow Fever and How To Cure It' was deducted. A few days later, Bob's scripts were officially accepted by the *Doctor Who* production office, and he was paid the remaining half-fees for the final three scripts.

'This is how silly it can get,' recalls Saward of this time. 'When Bob was writing the first four episodes of "The Trial of a Time Lord", he had acquired a huge amount of coloured paper, and so after he'd been to the office and we'd had a chat, he said grandly, "What colour paper would you like me to write the first episode on?" I thought, "What does he mean?" He told me about the coloured paper, so I said I wanted it on pink. It was the first thing that came into my mind. And the script duly came in, typed out on pink paper. And this freaked John out, because he thought we were having an in-joke at his expense. Which I suppose we were! "So, Episode Two," Bob said, "what colour do you want it?" I said "I'm tired of pink," and I suggested two other colours, and so it came in, in alternate coloured pages. This freaked John out even more. By the time we had got to Episode Four, we had got up to five colours, all alternate pages, and John thought it was this great conspiracy, which it just wasn't. It was just us having a bit of fun amongst ourselves. It was a silly event of no significance. But Bob was like that; he was quite happy to join in, and enjoy it.'

Multi-coloured scripts aside, Saward was having huge problems, as both Halliwell and Story had struggled to come up with any workable ideas for their respective two-part stories. So instead, Saward turned to one of his script editor predecessors on the series, Christopher H Bidmead, and asked him to write a four-part story that would cover episodes nine to 12 of the season.

Meanwhile, Saward's working relationship with Nathan-Turner, which had become increasingly uneasy for at least the previous 12 months, was now slowly deteriorating to the point where something was going to have to give. Undeterred by these problems, Saward went ahead and commissioned Bob on Tuesday 4 February 1986 to write the final two-part story of the season, under the working title 'Time Inc'. A target delivery date of Friday 28 February 1986 was given to Bob for both scripts.

Martin had by now delivered to Saward his first three scripts for the season's second four-part story, given the working title of 'Mindwarp'. Saward sent these three scripts, along with all four of Bob's for 'The Mysterious Planet', to Jonathan Powell, the Head of Series and Serials, for his thoughts.

Saward picked up the tale in a later interview: 'Let me tell you how the procedure for commissioning a script works in Series and Serials: A script is commissioned by the production office; that was John and me. We both sign the commissioning form, which then goes upstairs to the Head of Department, who approves the commission. The script is then delivered by the author, and the producer and script editor read it and ask for rewrites if necessary. The finished script is typed up by the script typists, printed, and a copy (i.e. the final version of the script) is then sent back upstairs to Jonathan Powell. His job is to read everything, not just *Doctor Who*, but everything that is produced. The above procedure was followed with every script for *Doctor Who*. Before we were cancelled we never had any comment from Jonathan Powell concerning scripts. Not one word of doubt or consideration, nothing at all. Bob Holmes wrote the first four episodes, which given the pressures were okay on paper, but Jonathan Powell didn't like them. The scripts had disappeared for weeks and we thought they had been accepted. The director had even joined. Then we got this memo saying, "Didn't like this, or that, thought this was too silly …" and all the rest of it.'[350]

Powell's memo, dated Monday 24 February 1986, was scathing in its tone. While Powell found the scripts of the first three episodes of Philip Martin's story to be most agreeable, he was fiercely outspoken in his criticism of Bob's scripts for 'The Mysterious Planet':

I've now read and considered these first two stories and my reaction is basically quite straightforward. Put simply I think that the Philip Martin story has, on the evidence of Episodes 5-7, got a lot going for it with a good narrative, involving characters and a sufficiently strong connection with the trial to make this device work. However I do

ROBERT HOLMES: A LIFE IN WORDS

feel that with the Robert Holmes story you have quite a substantial problem to which I suggest you address yourself as a matter of great urgency. I'll now do my best to outline 1) my overall objections 2) suggestions as to lines along which you might think of considering these scripts.

<u>Dr Who – Episodes 1-4</u>
<u>Overall Problems</u>

1. One of my main objections to the story is the '<u>tone</u>'. The writer is asking the viewers to believe that the Doctor is on trial for his life and existence. Yet the story comes across as very lightweight and slightly trivial. The Doctor's attitude and the circumstance surrounding him (traffic lights, the use of the umbrella, the half jokey use of names for the stations) all undercut the dramatic potential of the situation. Equally some of the subsidiary characters, in particular Glitz-Dibber are impossible to take seriously in any sense and this of course dilutes the credibility of the story. Philip Martin in creating Yrcanos and the Lukoser faces the same problems of unlikely characterisations – yet manages to show us characters with real dignity. All of these are instances but they indicate a fatal lack of conviction and seriousness in a story which <u>because</u> it is being used as evidence for the Doctor's trial must have some credibility. Without credibility, the entire structure of the story collapses.

2. Further to the above, one of the problems is that the central premise of the story never seems to me properly or convincingly set up. We are not aware what is at issue for this civilisation and it seems to me to [be] explained most confusingly without a clear grasp of what is meant to be the 'motor' of the story.

3. Since the story is unclear, seemingly unmotivated and with rather ill-conceived themes it is difficult to grasp the relationship of this story to the trial. It never seems to me clear what evidence this story offers to the Valeyard or indeed the viewer as to the Doctor's culpability for any particular transgression of the Time Lords' codes. The relationship between the story and the trial needs careful consideration and adjustment.

CHAPTER TWENTY-SIX

4. We are never really aware of what it is that the Doctor is on trial for.

Some specific Notes and Suggestions

1. I suggest that you open the story with the Doctor's arrival at the court situation and reveal at the beginning: 1. That he is on trial, 2. What the charges are. It would also be useful and interesting if we were reminded of what comprises a Time Lord's brief. What actually are the limits beyond which the Doctor is not allowed to transgress.

2. It might be interesting to have prosecution and defence 'counsel' and for the Doctor to begin by asking for his defence counsel to be removed, preferring to defend himself. The presence of prosecution and defence would facilitate the explanations of the situation and provide a more dramatic sense of confrontation between the Valeyard and the Doctor when he elects to defend himself.

3. I found the Doctor's insouciance towards the Valeyard particularly irritating and silly. I would recommend that you drop all this. You seem to me to need to work on the Doctor's stature and gravitas, if we, the audience, are to be gripped by the situation. Only by heightening the sense of the dramatic will you create a believable situation and thus a dramatically strong narrative.

The story itself seems to have several faults.

1. The humour is irritating and counterproductive.

2. The story is confusing and difficult to follow; also it is not clearly established and set up.

3. We are never properly aware of what is at stake.

4. There seems little real reason for the Doctor's involvement and certainly no evident explanation as to why he has to transgress the Time Lord's code on this particular instance.

5. The relationship of the story to the trial is unclear.

I would suggest the following.

1. Clarify the reasons why the Doctor goes to Ravalox in the first place.

2. Clarify where Glitz and Dibber come from; why they are there; and alter their characterisation making them into more substantial and threatening presences.

3. We must <u>understand</u> what is happening on Ravalox.

a) Peri and the Doctor should be plunged into the middle of the plot. Possibly arriving in the middle of one of Drathro's cullings.

b) Through such a device you should swiftly reveal the situation on earth – that Drathro and the Natives are involved in a power struggle born out of years of oppression by Drathro of the natives.

c) You must clarify the Subway Dwellers' affiliation to, presumably, the Native dwellers. This means using Merdeen's position properly, revealing and explaining his motives early on.

d) Merdeen could also, if revealed to be a Native loyalist shed some light on the situation of Drathro – the Robot. Perhaps he could report in secret to Native leader, acting as an informant on Drathro.

e) Crucially we need to know and establish early on in the story the nature of the power struggle between Drathro and the Natives <u>as well as</u> the potential havoc to the universe which could be caused by the Black Light / White Light explosion. At the moment this has no real dramatic value since it's revealed so late and so casually, and I have to say, so incomprehensibly.

f) The Doctor's involvement needs to be strengthened. I suggest that as soon as they discover that Ravalox is in fact Earth, Peri's emotional attachment to it should become the Doctor's motive – after much pleading from Peri, to avert any disaster which might threaten. Presumably Peri would naturally associate with the Earth natives and could persuade the Doctor to take their side in the struggle with Drathro. By involving the Doctor in such a way, it presumably would relate more easily to the trial as an example of the Doctor taking sides and interfering with the course of history – if that is a Time Lord sin. The later revelation that the Doctor, perhaps unwittingly, stumbles upon the potential end of the universe would presumably be his justification. Crucially – clarification and a proper basis for the story will indicate a more serious and believable narrative which will in its turn properly fit in with the trial of the Doctor and create a credible world for the viewer.

I am of course available should you wish to discuss this memo further.

It's worth reflecting, at this point, just how unusual this intervention by Jonathan Powell was. It had long been standard practice for the Head of Department to be sent the scripts for every story that the *Doctor Who* production team commissioned for production. These would be returned with perhaps a line or two of comment, criticism or praise, but that was usually as far as it went. Since *Doctor Who* had been cancelled, and then reprieved, the previous year, Saward and Nathan-Turner had been given no guidance or feedback on what their bosses were looking for with the series. They didn't know what they were felt to be doing right, or what they were felt to be doing wrong. With such silence deafening them, they carried on more or less as they had previously; the only concession Saward had decided upon was to try to lighten the tone of the series, to cut back on the violence, and to have more humour.

Saward now realised that he was seriously out of step with what was expected.

Powell's criticisms and observations on Bob's scripts were generally quite sound from a dramatic point of view. However, it's clear that he had no real idea of what *Doctor Who* was about, and how it could, at times, successfully subvert dramatic convention. But it was also true that in recent years, the series was more likely to misfire than it was to surprise and confound its critics. Many of the points that Powell singled out as problematic in the story, such as the humour, the larger-than-life characters of Glitz and Dibber, and the Doctor's pithy putdowns of the Valeyard, were amendments that Saward had guided and encouraged Bob to make to his first drafts. Bob was therefore guilty of nothing more than following his brief rather too well. Other plot elements that Powell criticised, such as the fuzzy motivations of Glitz, and the hazy backstory to the events on Ravalox, were all plot points that were being deliberately kept unfocused, to be returned to in later episodes – possibly those episodes still to be written by Bob.

Saward's main beef with Powell's memo was over the timing. Strong guidance was what he had needed several months earlier, when pre-planning for the season began. But 'The Mysterious Planet' was now due to begin recording in just over four weeks' time. Costumes were being made, sets were being constructed, and parts were being cast. It was just far too late to do anything other than make cosmetic alterations to Bob's scripts. 'Alterations were made, which he accepted and which went into the final programme,' notes Saward. 'But I think by that time Bob Holmes, he wasn't ill then, but he was, like me, absolutely pissed off at the whole way that it had gone.'[351]

For the first time in his professional life, Bob had been heavily criticised with regard to his writing ability. It deeply affected him. 'The man was very run down,' recalls Saward, 'and he'd suffered a major blow to his pride from Jonathan Powell asking for rewrites on the first four episodes. It may sound silly that a professional writer's pride could be so easily hurt, but in his time he had edited the best three seasons the show had ever had, and written or rewritten many of the best scripts. He knew more about what made *Doctor Who* work than almost anyone. I knew those episodes worked well, Bob knew they worked well.'[352]

'He was annoyed, he was angry,' recalled Saward some years later. 'He was very skilled and very professional in what he did, and he knew the material was working, as I did. And to be told that it wasn't up to scratch, or it wasn't original enough, was very galling. I don't know what it's like at the BBC nowadays, but in those days great, grand statements were made, but there was never any follow up as to precisely what was wrong. Which makes it even more difficult. If you look at a script and you read it, and you think, "This is fine," then what are the points that you're making? And we weren't getting any guidance. That was the most galling part, for him and for me.'

It was about this time that Bob met up with old chum Robert Banks Stewart. 'When I was doing *Bergerac*, I met him at Shepherd's Bush,' recalls Stewart. 'Bob looked awfully ill, and was terribly tired. One of the problems he was having, he told me, was he was trying to create a new series of *Doctor Who* with John Nathan-Turner. I was really terribly taken aback when I saw him. He looked stooped, and he was ashen, and looked really quite ill. They were being hagridden by Jonathan Powell, who by then had become Head of Series and Serials at the BBC. And Jonathan Powell was very dissatisfied. Bob said to me, "Oh, Jeez ... I just don't know what to do." And after all, Jonathan Powell had been a colleague. He'd been a producer like I was a producer, like Bob was

351 Interview – Eric Saward, *DWB*: Issue 58, September 1988.
352 Interview – Eric Saward, *DWB*: Issue 58, September 1988.

a story editor, and we all were very much part of that drama "team". And then Jonathan got promoted to Head of Series and Serials, and he gave Bob a very hard time. It was a big blow to Bob, I know. I have this terrible memory of him, it was the last time I saw him. He looked very unwell – I think it wasn't just his morale, I think that was just a part of it.'

The extra rewrites on 'The Mysterious Planet' were done in mid-March, mainly by Saward, while Bob began work on his scripts for 'Time Inc.' By now, he was becoming quite noticeably ill, which his wife Patricia originally attributed to nothing more sinister than a bad reaction to a particular Chinese meal. Bob had complained of feeling unwell a few weeks earlier, after eating the rich dish. But the symptoms didn't dissipate in the days and weeks that followed, and Bob got noticeably weaker and weaker. He soldiered on with his scriptwriting, and was able to hand Saward his first draft script of Part One of 'Time Inc.', which he had now renamed 'The Fantasy Factory', sometime around the end of March 1986. The episode begins with Mel already in the courtroom during the final stages of the Doctor's trial, and Sabalom Glitz later arrives on his own to give evidence. The Master appears, and confirms that the Valeyard is actually the Doctor's 'twelfth and final incarnation', and the Doctor then enters the Matrix in pursuit of him. Inside the Matrix, the Doctor finds himself in a virtual Victorian London and encounters the Duke of Clarence, who is hunting for Jack the Ripper. The Duke mistakes the Doctor for his quarry, and during a fierce scuffle, he pushes the Doctor into a wharf. The episode ends with Doctor sinking lifeless beneath the water, as the screams of the Ripper's next victim are heard from a distance …

However, Bob was becoming more and more unwell, and his illness was diagnosed as a liver problem. In early April, he was admitted to Stoke Mandeville Hospital, just days after his sixtieth birthday. Once at the hospital, he was diagnosed with Hepatitis B, which in turn had led to complications that had badly affected and impaired his liver function, leaving him jaundiced and extremely weak. Cirrhosis of the liver was then diagnosed, and although he was given the most comprehensive treatment for his condition, Bob didn't respond at all to the medication. After just a few weeks in the hospital, Bob's liver function failed completely, and he slipped into a coma. Robert Holmes, Bob to his family and friends, died peacefully in his sleep at around midday on Saturday 24 May 1986, aged just 60.

CHAPTER TWENTY-SEVEN
GOODNIGHT SWEET PRINCE

When Bob died, he left behind his wife, Patricia, and his two children; his son Nicholas and his daughter Laurian. He also left three grandchildren: Laurian's daughter Lucy and sons Bobby and James. The youngest of these, James, had been born just a few short months prior to Bob's death.

'Patricia phoned me,' recalls Chris Boucher. 'She said that Bob had just died, and she didn't know how to convey the information to his friends at the BBC, and would I, as it were, take the news in. It was because, for some reason, Bob had my home phone number and he didn't have other people's. I think that was the reason. She was obviously very upset. It was a hell of a shock. I went into the BBC the next day. Bob had just done a script for me, I think it was a *Bergerac*, that may have been the reason he had my number to hand. I went in, and I remember telling Bob Banks Stewart, who was as shocked as I'd been. Bob Banks Stewart had a lot more contacts in the television industry – I was very isolated in the department – and he told a lot of other people, and there was a shockwave that went through the place. Most of us didn't know that Bob was ill … I say most of us, I certainly didn't. But he'd been sick for quite some time, apparently. He did tell me at one stage that he had a heart condition, because I can remember Pat asking, "Did you know he'd been ill?" and I said, "Well, he had told me he'd got a heart condition," and that was when she said it was nothing to do with that, and he'd been ill for quite a while. So it was a real shock.

'I've got, strangely enough, ghostly memories of him. I think the last time I spoke to him, we met pretty much by accident in a wine bar just up from Shepherd's Bush Green, and I suppose my last memories of him are … of him not being there, of him being dead. He wasn't really an anecdotal sort of bloke. He was funny, he was kind, he was all those things. But he wasn't a man who generated personal stories. He was a decent bloke, a talented writer, and you have to presume everybody's decent until they prove they're not. The longer you spend with people, the more chance you have of discovering that they're not. I spent a fair amount of time with Bob, in professional terms, and he never disappointed me.'

Bob's funeral was held on Friday 30 May 1986 at St Edmunds Church, Maidsmorton, near his home in Akeley in Buckingham. Chris Boucher and Robert Banks Stewart were amongst those who attended the service. 'Unlike so many people, who are cremated, Bob was actually buried,' recalls Stewart. 'I don't know what the reason was … As far as I'm aware, it wasn't religious. There was a desire, perhaps on Pat's part, for him to be buried. And so he was buried in a churchyard near his village. A lot of people from all parts of television turned up to the funeral. Chris Boucher was there, and Chris and I were walking along a path in the churchyard … It was all family members, and the pallbearers, and the ceremony around the grave. But as we were walking, we were behind the family, and we saw this wonderful thing. The funeral director's top hat, and his gloves and a cane had been very neatly put on another gravestone. It was just such a photographic image, but Chris Boucher and I, we just fell about. I remember saying to Chris, "Cor, Bob Holmes would have loved that!" Then I remember going to the wake in his house.

'I was very, very sorry when Bob died, very prematurely. In some respects, I just regret that I didn't see him again after I saw him so unwell in Shepherd's Bush. It was terrible, because he was one of the best creative people in television of that time, no question about it. He was a … I won't use the word "legend", but he was known to be a guy that could be relied on to deliver when you commissioned him. Whether it was *Public Eye* or whatever, he'd give it the full whack. He was a very trustworthy writer.'

After his death, many of Bob's other friends and colleagues were also moved to pay tribute to him.

Allan Prior, who scripted a number of episodes of *Blake's 7*, wrote: 'Robert Holmes was an original. He was the only writer I ever knew who didn't like to see his own work performed by actors. He would even miss rehearsals, if he could. As his good friend, Michael Ash, once told me, "Bob would bristle at the idea. I've had the fun writing it, he'd say. It's done as far as I'm concerned. It simply doesn't belong to me anymore. Let them get on with it." How many of us could be as cool and detached as *that*? But was Bob joking? With him you could never tell, not for sure. His sardonic wit (delivered from behind the pipe he must have learned to smoke as a young wartime officer in the Black Watch) was always in evidence. He liked nothing better than to write, po-faced, an episode of *Doctor Who* that his terrified young audience would watch round-eyed from behind the family sofa. "Bob," I once said to him, "You're Bed Wetter to the Nation!" Bob inclined his head gravely to the compliment, and smiled. "Top viewing figures ever for a *Doctor Who*." Whether Bob learned to accept that life is a passing-parade of comedy in the Metropolitan police, where he served as a bobby on the beat in the comparatively innocent '50s, I don't know. He had lots of funny stories about those days. But of course, *nobody* ever asked him to write for any police series! For certain Bob learned to write comedy. He was good at it, and he should have done more of it than he did. But television inclines to put writers into pigeonholes, and Bob Holmes was known as a very good series-writer or as a reliable script editor, a professional you could rely on to deliver what looked like what he said he'd deliver, until suddenly the actors began to laugh. There was a joke buried in there somewhere, that nobody in the production office had seen. It had to be spoken to be noticed. If he'd bothered to look in, Bob would have enjoyed that. But he wouldn't have smiled. That would have spoiled the joke. Bob Holmes died last month, after a painful illness, nursed to the end by his devoted wife, Pat. I will miss him. So will we all.'[353]

Graham Williams, who had replaced Philip Hinchcliffe as producer of *Doctor Who* in late 1976, was also fulsome in his praise: 'I was, of course, very sorry indeed to hear that Robert died after what seemed like a relatively minor illness. He would have summed it up in something like "Silly old bugger. Worked too hard …" and would have sunk several gins on the strength of fond memories. It's that contradiction that I remember most about him – a purported cynicism and toughness bordering on the hard-boiled, but covering a centre that, he would have hated to have admitted, was as generous, as thoughtful and as caring as any number of folk whose good deeds and better thoughts are much more noised about. You certainly don't need me to tell you how sorely his contribution to *Doctor Who* will be missed – I'm sure neither Tony Read nor Douglas Adams will resent me saying that when I took over the show, the only thing I actually envied Philip was having Bob as his script editor for his time on the programme. He could combine the wackiest thoughts with the sternest discipline in a way that nobody else could match. For a very long time it was *his* style and ideas that dictated the way in which the stories would go and grow, and most of the current "legends" surrounding the Time Lords and their errant student have their basis in the work and ideas of Bob Holmes. I only hope that wherever he is now, the fees get paid quicker and the phone never stops ringing. I'm sure that'll be the way of it – even over there, they'll know a good thing when they see it.'[354]

Writer Roger Marshall, who had worked with Bob on programmes such as *Knight Errant Ltd*, *Public Eye* and *Emergency Ward 10*, said of his former colleague: 'Bob Holmes and I were great mates and I still miss him. His untimely death was bizarre and had the smell of dodgy hospital practice; however that's all speculation and it's all a long time ago now. Our last meeting was at a friend's flat. This friend was trying to get a group of like-minded thriller writers together to contribute to a series. Bob, who had a marvellously wry sense of humour, didn't rate its chances any higher than I did. We left together, went strolling round a few bookshops together in Kew High Street. We parted at some tube station, with the promise that "we must meet more

353 Writing in *The Writers' Newsletter*: Vol 2 No 11 July 1986.
354 *DWB*: Issue 38, September 1986.

420

often". And I never saw him again. His wife, Pat, said he was the nicest human being she ever met. Not a bad obituary. There are lots of shitty, phoney people working in television. Bob was neither. He was a gent!'[355]

Jon Thurley, his agent for much of his professional life, said of Bob: 'Personally Bob was quiet, self-effacing, very likeable, with a dry sense of humour, who never used two words where one would do. We used to meet periodically for one of the ferocious curries he liked so much at one of the many curry houses he ferreted out over the years.'[356]

Terrance Dicks wrote at the time: 'Bob Holmes was the first writer I ever script-edited. I probably learned more from him than he ever did from me. We met as a result of his digging out an old idea and sending it in to *Doctor Who*. I was allowed to develop it as a reserve and it later became "The Krotons". Derrick Sherwin, then script editor, was so impressed with it he asked Bob to write "The Space Pirates". However, it wasn't until the third of his *Who* stories that Bob really found his form. He wrote the first ever *Who* for Jon Pertwee, "Spearhead from Space", and for quite some time after that Bob and the programme never looked back. He was a lovely writer to work with, and had a great joy in the use of, and feel for, language, plus a mordant, not to say morbid sense of humour that sometimes got out of hand. Once he succeeded me as script editor, and was free of my restraining influence, the gore tended to flow unchecked and I wasn't a bit surprised. I think his great strength as a science fiction writer was the amount of untold "backstory" he created – witness the hints of the past, or is it the future, of Magnus Greel in "'The Talons of Weng-Chiang" – my all-time favourite of Bob's stories, though there's a lot to be said for "The Deadly Assassin". In fact there's a lot to be said for all of them – the programme, the fans, the community of writers are all the poorer for Bob's loss.'[357]

'He was a good writer,' mused Dicks a few years later. 'He came up with good science fiction ideas, good plots, he wrote good dialogue, he invented good characters, they were good scripts. He was occasionally airy-fairy about the limitations of the budget, but then again, we would always say to writers "Be generally aware that we are not epic, but don't limit yourself too much, because you might self-censure and cut out something we can do. If you think it's a good idea, put it in, and if we think we can't afford it, we'll cut it, or cut it down, or together we'll work out a good way of putting in something that is not as expensive." That was always an option. But he was just a good writer, and his

355 Private correspondence with Colin Brockhurst, dated 23 June 1992.
356 Private correspondence with Colin Brockhurst, dated 26 June 1992.
357 *DWB*: Issue 38, September 1986.

ideas were always interesting, and his scripts were a pleasure to read. We hadn't seen each other for a while, we hadn't been in regular contact, but I was very saddened, because he was a friend, he was somebody I liked very much.'

'I was very sad,' recalled Eric Saward. 'I'd got to know him and he was a very nice man. I missed him. We'd become friends, so I missed him as a friend. I missed him as a talented person. I needed someone like him around, and his demise at 60 is very sad.'

'He was difficult, arrogant, highly critical and rude ... but then people who care about their work often are,' Saward later wrote. 'I liked Bob Holmes very much both as a writer and as a person. He was a positive and honest man who said what he thought. As a writer I found him very easy to work with. Because he knew his trade well he would be quick to accept suggestions or criticisms that would strengthen or reinforce his stories – it's only bad writers who never want to listen to what others have to say. Socially Bob was great fun, full of life and energy, and by the evening, usually lots of wine as well. I only knew Bob for a couple of years – I wish it had been much longer.'[358]

'I can't remember how I heard about it, but I was devastated,' recalled Barry Letts. 'I was very, very sad indeed. I was very fond of Bob; we weren't friends insofar as going to each other's houses, but we'd worked together a lot over the years, and I liked him a lot, and I liked being with him, so I was very sad indeed. My overriding memory of Bob is of the sort of bloke he was, which was a man of contradictions. He was lugubrious and cheerful at the same time; he really was. He gave the impression of being rather glum, but when you talked to him, you found he was really quite cheerful underneath. In the same way, he sounded like he was cynical and sceptical, and hated the world, but once you got know him, you found he was really a kind-hearted man who would do anything for anybody, you know. So he was contradictory, but came out on the good side, very, very definitely. That's why I liked him so much, quite apart from the fact that he was a very good writer.'

'I hadn't seen a lot of him in the 1980s, but it was a very young age to die, and I was very, very sad about it,' recalled Philip Hinchcliffe. 'Bob belonged to what I consider to be the first generation of popular series writers. In the mid-'50s, especially when ITV came on the scene, there were a whole bunch of professional writers who moved into television ... They were dramatists like Ted Willis, they were journalists like Wilfred Greatorex, who wrote *The Power Game*, they were journalists like Bob, who was also a short-story writer for *John Bull*. There were dramatists like Alun Owen and all these people.

358 Private correspondence with Colin Brockhurst, dated 16 June 1992.

They fertilised television in the mid-to-late '50s and early '60s, and went on to write *Callan* and *Public Eye*, and *The Avengers*. There was a lot of work, a huge turnover of drama and series work at that time, all being written very quickly, and also being written to very specific constraints. Most of them were written within the studios, like *No Hiding Place* or *Dr Findlay's Casebook*, and these writers had to learn how to write within the dramatic unities of only a certain number of sets, only a certain number of characters, very little film / outside stuff, very little at all. These guys learnt the art of dramatic storytelling, how to do it within those limitations. And Bob was one of the top exponents of that group of writers in the first early flush of drama series writing in British television. I think his most outstanding contribution was on *Doctor Who* really. I think he found his niche and metier in the sort of freewheeling and open format that *Doctor Who* was. Because it allowed him to pursue imaginatively the kind of ideas and the slightly larger-than-life and humorous characters he liked to write best. And he was given his head in the format of *Doctor Who* in a way that you weren't if you were writing within the strict parameters of a police series, for example, or a doctors series. I think that Bob's strongest attribute as a writer was his imagination. He had a genuine imagination, and it was dark and quirky. As a man, and as a writer, he was very intelligent, and he had this wonderful sardonic sense of humour. As a professional, he was impeccable in his dealings with people, he was one of the old-school. He'd been a journalist, and before that he was a policeman, so he knew a bit about crime writing. He'd had a very good, solid apprenticeship; he knew how to construct a story, so his scripts, or any scripts that he worked on, were always extremely well-thought-out. The stories were always properly structured, as well as they could be within the genre. He wrote good characterisation; his characters were good and well-rounded, and he wrote very good dialogue. He was also very good at getting the best out of other writers. Some script editors are sort of compulsive rewriters, they can't stop themselves meddling with a script; Bob wasn't like that, he would only change things that really needed changing. But he always added another dimension to the script whenever he did that. So, he was a sensitive script editor, and he was a sensitive rewriter. But you always got quality when he did it. Those were his strengths as a writer and a script editor, I think. If you look back on the overall history of *Doctor Who*, I think he enriched it by introducing his take on science fiction, and his take on the format. I think without Bob the series would not have developed in quite the way it did over the seasons he contributed to it, either as a writer or as a script editor.'

Chris Boucher was particularly saddened by Bob's death. After all, Bob had given him his big break on *Doctor Who*, had recommended him for his first BBC staff job as script editor of *Blake's 7*, and had subsequently become a writer that he greatly enjoyed working with. 'He was an intelligent and meticulous writer, he was clever, and he was funny,' recalls Boucher. 'He wanted his stuff to be rooted in reality. I remember we talked one time about *Watership Down*; he'd attempted to read it. We were discussing books that might work on television, and books we were reading, and so forth, and he'd read two chapters of *Watership Down*, and then he'd thought "It's flaming rabbits!" and stopped reading it. I don't think "flaming" was actually the word he used! He was an intelligent writer, he wasn't in the With-One-Mighty-Bound-He-Was-Free school, or, "Oh look, here's a magic talisman, now we can get out of this situation." He didn't have much time, as far as I could see, for what I called "Tits and Swords", or what became more decorously known as *Dungeons and Dragons*. I don't think he had much time for that sort of thing. I think he described himself as preferring Sherlock Holmes to Dan Dare. He was an intelligent, literate writer. There aren't a hell of a lot of those about, you know. And there's one less now …'

It seems exceedingly churlish to hark back to television matters in the aftermath of Bob's death. But there were things left hanging in the air, which perhaps need discussing to understand Bob's legacy fully.

When he died, Bob had a couple of projects still in hand. One was his episode of *Bergerac*, 'Winner Takes All', the script of which had been completed the previous year, and which had already been passed to the programme's script editor, Chris Boucher. This needed no more than a minor polish by Boucher to get it ready for filming, which was completed in late 1985, and the episode went out on BBC1 on Saturday 10 January 1987 as part of *Bergerac*'s fifth season. It was to be Bob's last ever television writing credit.

Meanwhile *Doctor Who,* in the aftermath of Bob's death, was in a great deal of trouble. The criticisms that Jonathan Powell had levelled so late in the day at Bob's scripts for 'The Mysterious Planet' had upset Eric Saward almost as much as they had hurt and angered Bob himself while he was alive. Perhaps more so. Saward's working relationship with producer John Nathan-Turner had by now deteriorated further, and matters had reached breaking point. Saward had received from Bob his script for the first episode of 'The Fantasy Factory', but was distraught when Bob was hospitalised and the seriousness of his condition became apparent. Saward decided that enough was enough, and resigned as script editor of *Doctor Who* on Wednesday 2 April 1986. In his resignation letter to Jonathan Powell, Saward made it clear that he felt guilty about Bob's ill health, blaming himself in no small part for the increased pressure that Bob had been under working on the series. 'To keep *Doctor Who* afloat, a show that is at best viewed indifferently by management, I have put the best writer the series ever had in hospital,' wrote a distraught Saward.

'During my time on *Doctor Who* I had become friends with Robert Holmes and was greatly distressed by his illness,' explained Saward some year later. 'What with that and the show in such a mess and little or no support from the producer I felt I had had enough.'[359]

Christopher H Bidmead's proposed four-part story, which had been planned for episodes nine to 12 of the season, had by now fallen through, leaving a big hole in the narrative. Writers Pip and Jane Baker had then been drafted in by Saward, against his better judgement, to fill that hole. The season had now been given the single umbrella story title 'The Trial of a Time Lord', which would cover all 14 episodes. Bob's story, 'The Mysterious Planet', was now Parts One to Four of this story, while Philip Martin's 'Mindwarp' was now Parts Five to Eight. With Pip and Jane Baker now scripting Parts Nine to Twelve, this left just Parts Thirteen and Fourteen unfinished. Bob had been down to write both these episodes, but had completed only his first draft script of Episode Thirteen (which is what Part One of 'The Fantasy Factory' now effectively was) prior to his death.

Nathan-Turner asked Saward to put their differences aside while Bob was ill in hospital. Although no longer the script editor of the series, Saward was asked to work on Bob's submitted script for Part Thirteen in order to get it into a usable state for production. When Bob's condition worsened, Saward was then asked to write the script for the concluding Part Fourteen from scratch, albeit to the story plans already discussed and agreed between him and Bob. Saward took a metaphorical deep breath, and agreed. To do this, he substantially rewrote the final half of Bob's last script, creating the scenes set in the Matrix anew, and dispensing with the plotline involving Jack the Ripper and the Duke of Clarence. This led into a wholly new fourteenth episode, scripted by Saward, but sticking broadly to what he and Bob had previously planned.

'Bob and I had discussed the last two episodes of the "Trial",' recalled Saward. 'We had agreed, and John was told afterwards (he wasn't present at the meeting) what we had discussed, that we were going to have a negative end. Like Sherlock Holmes and Moriarty going over the falls, the Doctor and the Master would be locked in mortal combat, and we'd go out with this question mark hanging over the season. And John said "All right, go ahead and write it

---

359 Interview – Eric Saward, *DWB*: Issue 58, September 1988.

and see how it works," but it was never written because Bob became ill.

'I agreed to write the last episode [instead], but on the understanding of what we'd discussed, and [Nathan-Turner] said "Yes, fine," and I went away and did my version … pulling the threads together. To Bob's formula, I rewrote half the previous episode, which he'd already written, because I couldn't link up exactly with what he'd done. I think the first 12 minutes of Episode Thirteen is his and the rest is mine, and then I wrote the last episode and delivered it, and John said "Yes, that's all right I suppose." Then he turned around and said, "I can't stand this end, you can't have them going out like this," and it was a definite renege on what had been agreed, and I said "Well find someone else to do it." I had not signed the contract to write the thing anyway and then, I think, he got rather annoyed. It was a terrible mess, a pain in my life that I really hated, and then at the end of it all Bob Holmes died.'[360]

Saward, already in a very bad place in his professional life, was hit extremely hard by Bob's death, and this strengthened his resolve not to bow to Nathan-Turner's pressure to alter the ending of the final episode of 'The Trial of a Time Lord'. He was grimly determined not to back out of presenting what he and Bob had planned for the series' conclusion. Nathan-Turner, although conceding that he had agreed with the original plan, now doubted the wisdom of ending on a cliff-hanger, fearing that it would perhaps play into the hands of Michael Grade and Jonathan Powell and give them an excuse to cancel the series for good after the season had gone out. Nathan-Turner reasoned that if Part Fourteen of 'The Trial of a Time Lord' was going to be the last ever episode of *Doctor Who*, then it had better end with the Doctor clearly winning the day and going off to have more adventures. But he was unable to persuade Saward to agree to this, and so instead had to commission Pip and Jane Baker to come up with an alternative script for Part Fourteen, without them having any reference at all to Bob's notes and plans for the final resolution of the storyline, or to Saward's actual script for the episode. Saward also tried to withdraw the script that he had written for Part Thirteen, which utilised about of half of Bob's submitted script for 'The Fantasy Factory', and which had been completed with Robert Holmes credited as the sole writer. But it was adjudged by the BBC Copyright department that Saward's work on this script was done in his capacity as script editor, not writer, and so this version of Part Thirteen was still used by the programme (complete with Bob's credit as the sole writer).[361]

---

360 Interview – Eric Saward, *DWB*: Issue 58, September 1988.
361 All of the scenes set in the trial courtroom in the first half of the transmitted episode are those that were originally written by Bob. All the scenes at the end of the episode set in the Matrix are ones that were written by Eric Saward.

'The Trial of a Time Lord' began on BBC1 on Saturday 6 September 1986, with Bob's first episode. His opening four-part segment was shown weekly throughout the month of September. His last on-screen credit on *Doctor Who* then came on Saturday 29 November 1986, when Part Thirteen of the story was shown.

In the end, *Doctor Who* wasn't axed immediately after 'The Trial of a Time Lord', as Nathan-Turner had feared, but survived for a few years longer. In 1987, the character Sabalom Glitz, created by Bob for 'The Mysterious Planet', was brought back in the story 'Dragonfire', written by Ian Briggs, for which Bob received a small, posthumous, rights payment. The series was ultimately cancelled by the BBC in 1989. A one-off TV movie was screened in 1996, but that seemed to be the end of the Doctor's on-screen adventures. It therefore came as a big, but very pleasant, surprise to the series' army of fans when the BBC chose to revive it once more in 2005.

The first new episode of the new, 21st Century version of *Doctor Who*, starring Christopher Eccleston and Billie Piper, aptly saw the Doctor pitted against Bob's own creations, the Autons.

Once again, the name Robert Holmes appeared on the credits of an episode of *Doctor Who*. And with the series still going strong, Bob's influence can be felt even today. The Autons have again returned to menace the Doctor, as have his popular clone creations, the Sontarans. The Doctor still comes from Gallifrey, still has two hearts, and can still regenerate 12 times (perhaps …). Sarah Jane Smith and K-9 have appeared in the series, as has the Master – all characters introduced under Bob's watch – and the Doctor still pops back to Metebelis III to pick up the odd blue crystal (even if he can't now pronounce the planet's name correctly!) Yes, Bob's influence on *Doctor Who* is as strong as it ever was.

This is, of course, exactly how it should be.

CHAPTER TWENTY-EIGHT
TARGET CUTAWAY

There is no doubt that Bob loved being a writer. But no matter how much he enjoyed the job, at the end of the day, it was just a job, his source of income. And while Bob was working hard at his career as a television scriptwriter and then a script editor in the 1970s, another potential line of income opened up for him.

In early 1973, Target Books, a paperback imprint of Universal Tandem, made arrangements with the BBC to reprint three *Doctor Who* novelisations that had been initially published in the 1960s. The resulting high level of sales of these three books proved to the range's editor, Richard Henwood, that *Doctor Who* was popular enough to warrant publication of more novelisations; the only problem being that there weren't any further titles in print to re-publish.

So Target Books looked to commission their own novelisations of the television adventures of *Doctor Who*. Henwood's first port of call in mid-1973 was to the *Doctor Who* production office, where outgoing script editor Terrance Dicks offered his services to Henwood as a freelance book writer. He was asked which *Doctor Who* story he would like to have a go at novelising. 'Richard asked which one I wanted to do,' recalled Dicks some years later, 'and after some discussion I chose "Spearhead from Space" as they wanted something fairly current. "Oh, I don't like that title," said Richard. "What's it about?"' Dicks outlined the plot of the story, which revolved around an attempt to invade the Earth by the Autons. 'So it was renamed *The Auton Invasion*, the first of the new range ...' concludes Dicks. '*The Auton Invasion* was the first book of any kind I'd written, and I worked very hard on it.'[362]

It's unclear if Bob was ever offered the chance to novelise his own scripts at this stage, or if the opportunity to have Dicks novelise his story was presented to him as a *fait accompli*. Regardless, Bob seemed pretty happy with the deal that was struck, under which the royalties generated by the sales of the book would be split equally between him and Dicks.

In the months and years that followed, a number of other *Doctor Who* scriptwriters – such as Malcolm Hulke and Brian Hayles – elected to write novelisations of their own scripts for the range. 'For a time, there were a handful of us doing them,' recalled Dicks. 'But over a period of time, the others dropped away. This was mainly because the books weren't paying very much money –

---

362 From 'The Target Book' by David J Howe, published by Telos Publishing.

not in television terms anyway – and eventually, when I decided to leave *Doctor Who*, I was back in the freelance market, and this was a steady stream of work for me. The other writers found it all very hard work. Scriptwriters don't like writing books; they find it a lot harder than writing for television. And it's lonely. And the money is peanuts compared with television. A lot of them just didn't want to be bothered with the books in the early days. I used to explain to them that I did all the work and they got half the money – that was the way it was split. It wasn't until later on that the scriptwriters realised that they could do all the work and get *all* the money."

The ongoing arrangement for Dicks to novelise his scripts for the Target range suited Bob quite nicely in the mid-'70s. Especially as he was by now working as script editor on *Doctor Who* and just didn't have any spare time.

Dicks' novelisation of 'Spearhead from Space' was published in paperback by Target Books in January 1974 (along with a hardback version destined mainly for libraries, published by Universal Tandem's hardback division, Allan Wingate), and maintained the strong sales that the previous three reprint titles had garnered the previous year. In the years that followed, *Doctor Who and the Auton Invasion* was translated into Finnish, Japanese, Turkish, Dutch and Portuguese.

From this point on, the Target range never looked back, with new titles being published every few months for the next 15 years. This meant that, over time, all of Bob's *Doctor Who* television stories were eventually novelised, with Dicks writing the lion's share.[363]

There were, however, a couple of notable exceptions.

By the time that summer 1977 came around, Bob was back in the world of freelance writing, having stepped down as script editor of *Doctor Who*. Dicks contacted him, on behalf of Target Books, and asked him to consider having a go at novelising one of his own *Doctor Who* stories for the range. Bob was tempted,

---

363 *Doctor Who and the Terror of the Autons* (Terrance Dicks) published in paperback on Thursday 15 May 1975 and in hardback in February 1981. *Doctor Who and the Pyramids of Mars* (Terrance Dicks) published in paperback on Thursday 16 December 1976 and in hardback in January 1977. *Doctor Who and the Carnival of Monsters* (Terrance Dicks) published in both paperback and hardback in January 1977. *Doctor Who and the Ark in Space* (Ian Marter) published in hardback in April 1977 and in paperback in May 1977. *Doctor Who and the Deadly Assassin* (Terrance Dicks) published in both hardback and paperback on Thursday 20 October 1977. *Doctor Who and the Talons of Weng Chiang* (Terrance Dicks) published in paperback on Friday 15 November 1977, and in hardback a month later. *Doctor Who and the Ribos Operation* (Ian Marter) published in both hardback and paperback on Tuesday 11 December 1979. *Doctor Who and the Power of Kroll* (Terrance Dicks) published in both hardback and paperback on Monday 26 May 1980. *Doctor Who and the Sunmakers* (Terrance Dicks) published in both hardback and paperback on Tuesday 16 November 1982. *Doctor Who: The Caves of Androzani* (Terrance Dicks) published in hardback in November 1984, and then in paperback on Thursday 14 March 1985. *Doctor Who: The Krotons* (Terrance Dicks) published in hardback in June 1985, and in paperback on Thursday 14 November 1985. *Doctor Who: The Mysterious Planet* (Terrance Dicks) published in hardback in November 1987, and in paperback on Thursday 21 April 1988. *Doctor Who: The Ultimate Foe* (Pip and Jane Baker) published in hardback in April 1988, and in paperback on Thursday 15 September 1988. *Doctor Who: The Space Pirates* (Terrance Dicks) published by Target books in paperback only on Thursday 15 March 1990.

for the first time, to give this a try. He signed a contract to novelise his 1973 four-parter 'The Time Warrior', and so duly settled down in his study with his trusty typewriter and his original scripts, and began bashing out his book.

It should have been an easy enough task for him, given his background in writing prose and short stories for *John Bull* magazine. But he found it an almost impossible struggle. He missed his initial deadline, leading Dicks to call him up to ask if everything was all right. Bob persevered, and managed to write the first chapter, running to about ten typed pages of A4, before admitting defeat. He got back in touch with Dicks and persuaded him to take over the writing of the book. He sent Dicks the pages he'd written, and when *Doctor Who and the Time Warrior* was published in both hardback and paperback on 29 June 1978, it was with Dicks' name on the front cover as author. Not one to let good work go to waste, Dicks retained the chapter that Bob had written. It now forms the prologue of the book, and details the space battle that led to Jingo Linx being stranded on Earth in the first place.

'I started writing that one, and handed it over because I was busy!' Bob diplomatically noted some years later. 'We have this nice working relationship. I do all the hard work, and Terrance creams all the money out of it!' When asked his opinion of the book, Bob mischievously added: 'I thought *The Time Warrior* had a very good first chapter!'[364]

As mentioned previously, Bob attended the 1981 Panopticon convention, run by the *Doctor Who* Appreciation Society over the weekend of 1-2 August, where he was interviewed on stage. When asked about the possibility of him writing a full *Doctor Who* novelisation, he had this to say: 'It's a different function. If you've written the script, you're a bit tired of the story anyway, and you don't really want to go through the whole thing again, from a different angle, as a novel. And Terrance Dicks is so keen on writing my stuff, I let him do it. So we're in agreement!'

Just a few weeks later, in September 1981, Bob was questioned further on this subject in private correspondence with Simon M Lydiard, the editor of the *Doctor Who* fanzine *Skaro*. I'm indebted to Simon for allowing me to reprint, for the first time, Bob's reply to him: 'You ask if I've ever written any books and the answer, alas, is no. I should have done, because I started in the business by writing magazine short stories and serials and a logical step from there is to write novels. However, by the '50s when the general magazine market was dying, television had come along and I moved into writing for that.

'When one can pick up a commission for a TV play and get some money

364 Panopticon IV Convention, Queen Mary College, 1-2 August 1981.

in advance, writing 80-90,000 words on spec has always seemed to me a terrible gamble. However, I like your idea of writing a *Doctor Who* novel – it is certainly a thought that has never occurred to me. If it were not based on a television story I suppose one would have to get the BBC's permission as they own the copyright in the character. Perhaps one would have to wait until the programme is finally taken off the air. I never thought that day would dawn but I fear the effect of moving it from its traditional slot …'[365]

By 1985, the novelisations range was approaching its one hundredth title, and the then-editor, Nigel Robinson, had something rather special planned for that milestone. Despite the problems Bob had had in novelising 'The Time Warrior' in 1977, Robinson approached him and persuaded him to have another go at turning one of his television stories into prose. His most recently screened story, 'The Two Doctors', was to be the one chosen.

'I was Bob's editor during his writing of the novelisation of "The Two Doctors"', recalls Robinson, 'although I never met him; because during the writing of the book he was very ill. He was also very much a perfectionist. Because of this the manuscript was in fact delivered rather late (I suspect that our schedules were changed around somewhat to accommodate this situation, and to ensure that *The Two Doctors* was, appropriately, the hundredth *Doctor Who* novelisation). I do remember, however, that Bob wrote me a very nice note, expressing his gratitude at my patience. From my limited experience of him, I do remember that Bob was, as well as being a very good writer and a true professional, a bit of a gentlemen. *The Two Doctors* was published pretty much as delivered, though I had to tone down a little bit of the violence. Bob was approached to do "The Two Doctors" novelisation as part of the new policy of getting the original scriptwriters to novelise, whenever possible, their own material. I believe it was Terrance Dicks who finally persuaded Bob of the merits of writing *Doctor Who* novelisations. (Incidentally, if Bob hadn't wanted to do the book, I would have asked Terrance who, in my opinion, is the best adapter of Bob's work.)'[366]

Bob gritted his teeth, got writing and produced a book that was packed with wit, charm, humour and style, all wrapped around the good, meaty plot contained in his original television scripts. The novelisation was published in hardback in August 1985, followed by a paperback edition on Thursday 5 December 1985, and was greeted with universal acclaim from those who read it.

It seems that Bob may well have even mellowed towards the idea of

---

365 At the time, it had recently been announced that from its 1982 season *Doctor Who* would be moved from its traditional Saturday teatime slot for the first time, and would instead be shown by the BBC in a twice-weekly weekday slot.
366 Private correspondence with Colin Brockhurst, dated 27 July 1992.

writing more novels as result of his experiences with this book. 'Although not contracted, Bob and I agreed that he was to novelise the final two episodes of "The Trial of a Time Lord", recalls Robinson. 'I don't know how Bob's final script/novel would have turned out, but during a long and detailed chat on the phone, he said that the Valeyard was very definitely the Doctor's *thirteenth* incarnation (and not "somewhere between" his twelfth and final incarnations as stated in Pip and Jane's televised version); also he planned the ending as a physical battle between the Doctor and the Valeyard, with the open-ended final episode closing with them both falling to their "deaths" (*a la* Sherlock Holmes and Moriarty). Those were, at least, his ideas a few weeks before he died, though they may, of course, have changed during discussions with JNT and Eric Saward.'[367]

Sadly, Bob never got to write his second novel.

---

367 Private correspondence with Colin Brockhurst, dated 27 July 1992.

APPENDIX
ROBERT HOLMES: CREDITS

In chronological transmission order, the next few pages list all of Robert Holmes's television writing credits. '*' denotes programmes that no longer survive in the archives of the respective television companies.

Series Title	Episode Title	Transmission Date	Channel
Knight Errant '60	'The Creditor'	16.02.60 *	Granada
Knight Errant '60	'The Wall of Death'	26.04.60 *	Granada
Knight Errant '60	'Brother Cain'	10.05.60 *	Granada
Knight Errant '60	'Something in the City' (as 'William Hood')	14.06.60 *	Granada
Knight Errant '60	'The King of Kandoga'	01.07.60 *	Granada
Knight Errant Ltd	'The Jazzman' (as 'William Hood')	22.09.60 *	Granada
Knight Errant Ltd	'The Elopement' (as 'William Hood')	22.06.61 *	Granada
Harpers West One	(Episode 1.2)	03.07.61	ATV
Family Solicitor	'Man of Straw'	26.07.61 *	Granada
Family Solicitor	'Strike Action'	09.08.61 *	Granada
Deadline Midnight	'Man in a Frame'	30.09.61	ATV
Family Solicitor	'Statement of Affairs'	09.11.61 *	Granada
Emergency Ward 10	(Episode 507)	19.06.62 *	ATV
Emergency Ward 10	(Episode 508)	22.02.62 *	ATV
Emergency Ward 10	(Episode 512)	06.07.62 *	ATV
Emergency Ward 10	(Episode 515)	17.07.62 *	ATV
Emergency Ward 10	(Episode 518)	27.07.62 *	ATV
Emergency Ward 10	(Episode 521)	07.08.62 *	ATV
Emergency Ward 10	(Episode 524)	17.08.62 *	ATV

Emergency Ward 10	(Episode 527)	28.08.62 *	ATV
Emergency Ward 10	(Episode 530)	07.09.62 *	ATV
Emergency Ward 10	(Episode 533)	18.09.62 *	ATV
Emergency Ward 10	(Episode 536)	28.09.62 *	ATV
Emergency Ward 10	(Episode 539)	09.10.62 *	ATV
Emergency Ward 10	(Episode 542)	19.10.62 *	ATV
Emergency Ward 10	(Episode 543)	23.10.62 *	ATV
Ghost Squad	'The Green Shoes'	08.11.62	ITC
Emergency Ward 10	(Episode 548)	09.11.62 *	ATV
Harpers West One	(Episode 2.10)	19.11.62 *	ATV
Emergency Ward 10	(Episode 551)	20.11.62 *	ATV
Emergency Ward 10	(Episode 554)	30.11.62 *	ATV
Emergency Ward 10	(Episode 557)	11.12.62 *	ATV
Emergency Ward 10	(Episode 560)	21.12.62 *	ATV
Harpers West One	(Episode 2.14)	24.12.62 *	ATV
Emergency Ward 10	(Episode 563)	01.01.63 *	ATV
Emergency Ward 10	(Episode 566)	11.01.63 *	ATV
Emergency Ward 10	(Episode 569)	22.01.63 *	ATV
Emergency Ward 10	(Episode 572)	01.02.63 *	ATV
Emergency Ward 10	(Episode 575)	12.02.63 *	ATV
Emergency Ward 10	(Episode 578)	22.02.63 *	ATV
24 Hour Call	'Never Leave Me' (as 'William Hood')	03.03.63 *	ATV
Emergency Ward 10	(Episode 581)	05.03.63 *	ATV
Emergency Ward 10	(Episode 584)	15.03.63 *	ATV
Emergency Ward 10	(Episode 587)	26.03.63 *	ATV

Emergency Ward 10	(Episode 590)	05.04.63 *	ATV
Emergency Ward 10	(Episode 594)	12.04.63 *	ATV
Emergency Ward 10	(Episode 596)	26.04.63 *	ATV
Emergency Ward 10	(Episode 599)	07.05.63 *	ATV
Emergency Ward 10	(Episode 602)	17.05.63 *	ATV
Emergency Ward 10	(Episode 605)	28.05.63 *	ATV
Emergency Ward 10	(Episode 608)	07.06.63 *	ATV
Emergency Ward 10	(Episode 611)	18.06.63 *	ATV
Emergency Ward 10	(Episode 626)	09.08.63 *	ATV
Emergency Ward 10	(Episode 629)	20.08.63 *	ATV
Emergency Ward 10	(Episode 633)	03.09.63 *	ATV
Emergency Ward 10	(Episode 639)	24.09.63 *	ATV
Emergency Ward 10	(Episode 640)	27.09.63 *	ATV
Emergency Ward 10	(Episode 645)	15.10.63 *	ATV
Emergency Ward 10	(Episode 646)	18.10.63 *	ATV
Emergency Ward 10	(Episode 651)	05.11.63 *	ATV
Emergency Ward 10	(Episode 652)	08.11.63 *	ATV
Emergency Ward 10	(Episode 657)	26.11.63 *	ATV
Emergency Ward 10	(Episode 658)	29.11.63 *	ATV
Emergency Ward 10	(Episode 663)	17.12.63 *	ATV
Emergency Ward 10	(Episode 664)	20.12.63 *	ATV
Dr Finlay's Casebook	'The Hallelujah Stakes'	10.05.64 *	BBC1
Dr Finlay's Casebook	'The True Lochiel' (as 'Robin Baker')	24.05.64 *	BBC1
Dr Finlay's Casebook	'The Old Indomitable' (with William Woods)	31.05.64 *	BBC1
Dr Finlay's Casebook	'The Doctor Cried' (with Alan Gosling)	28.06.64 *	BBC1

Dr Finlay's Casebook	'Charity, Dr Finlay' (from a story by Arthur Swinson)	14.02.65	BBC1
Emergency Ward 10	(Episode 792 – as 'William Hood')	12.03.65 *	ATV
Public Eye	"And A Very Fine Fiddle Has He"	13.03.65 *	ABC
No Hiding Place	'Blood and Water'	15.03.65 *	Rediffusion
Emergency Ward 10	(Episode 793 – as 'William Hood')	16.03.65 *	ATV
Public Eye	'You Think It'll Be Marvellous – But it's Always a Rabbit'	27.03.65 *	ABC
Emergency Ward 10	(Episode 798 – as 'William Hood')	02.04.65 *	ATV
Emergency Ward 10	(Episode 799 – as 'William Hood')	06.04.65 *	ATV
No Hiding Place	'A Cry for Help'	21.06.65 *	Rediffusion
Undermind	'Waves of Sound'	10.07.65	ABC
Undermind	'End Signal'	17.07.65	ABC
199 Park Lane	(Episode 10 – credited with 'Additional Dialogue')	03.09.65 *	BBC1
199 Park Lane	(Episode 11 – uncredited re-write)	07.09.65 *	BBC1
199 Park Lane	(Episode 12 – uncredited re-write)	10.09.65 *	BBC1
No Hiding Place	'Run Johnny, Run'	15.12.65 *	Rediffusion
No Hiding Place	'The Night Walker'	15.06.66 *	Rediffusion
No Hiding Place	'Golden Boy'	06.07.66 *	Rediffusion
Public Eye	'It Had to Be a Mouse'	20.08.66*	ABC
Public Eye	'Twenty Pounds of Heart and Muscle'	17.09.66 *	ABC
Intrigue	'Fifty Million Taste Buds Can't Be Wrong'	19.11.66 *	ABC
Mr Rose	'The Jolly Swagman'	17.03.67	Granada
Mr Rose	'The Unquiet Ghost'	24.03.67	Granada
Market in Honey Lane	'Snap'	24.04.67	ATV
No Hiding Place	'Who Is This Mortimer?'	08.06.67 *	Rediffusion

Market in Honey Lane	'The Matchmakers' (by Louis Marks, based on an idea by Robert Holmes')	01.02.68 *	ATV
Market in Honey Lane	'The Organisers'	22.02.68 *	ATV
Public Eye	'It Must Be the Architecture – Can't Be the Climate'	23.03.68 *	ABC
Public Eye	'It's Learning About the Lies That Hurts'	30.03.68 *	ABC
Mr Rose	'The Frozen Swede'	31.05.68	Granada
Frontier	'Mutiny'	04.09.68 *	Thames
Honey Lane	(Episode 1.07)	22.10.68 *	ATV
Honey Lane	(Episode 1.08)	24.10.68 *	ATV
Honey Lane	(Episode 1.17)	26.11.68*	ATV
Honey Lane	(Episode 1.18)	28.11.68 *	ATV
The Saint	'The Scales of Justice'	01.12.68	ATV-ITC / BAMORE
Honey Lane	(Episode 1.25)	24.12.68 *	ATV
Honey Lane	(Episode 1.26)	26.12.68 *	ATV
Doctor Who	'The Krotons' Episode One	28.12.68	BBC1
Doctor Who	'The Krotons' Episode Two	04.01.69	BBC1
Doctor Who	'The Krotons' Episode Three	11.01.69	BBC1
Doctor Who	'The Krotons' Episode Four	18.01.69	BBC1
Honey Lane	(Episode 1.33)	20.01.69*	ATV
Honey Lane	(Episode 1.34)	21.01.69 *	ATV
Honey Lane	(Episode 1.41)	17.02.69 *	ATV
Honey Lane	(Episode 1.42)	18.02.69 *	ATV
Honey Lane	(Episode 1.46)	04.03.69 *	ATV
Doctor Who	'The Space Pirates' Episode One	08.03.69 *	BBC1
The Inside Man	'The Spy Vanishes'	14.03.69	LWT
Doctor Who	'The Space Pirates' Episode Two	15.03.69	BBC1

Honey Lane	(Episode 1.49)	17.03.69 *	ATV
Honey Lane	(Episode 1.50)	18.03.69 *	ATV
Doctor Who	'The Space Pirates' Episode Three	22.03.69 *	BBC1
Doctor Who	'The Space Pirates' Episode Four	29.03.69 *	BBC1
Doctor Who	'The Space Pirates' Episode Five	05.04.69 *	BBC1
Doctor Who	'The Space Pirates' Episode Six	12.04.69 *	BBC1
Fraud Squad	'Turbot on Ice'	20.05.69	ATV
Fraud Squad	'Last Exit to Liechtenstein'	03.06.69	ATV
Honey Lane	(Episode 2.02)	17.07.69 *	ATV
Fraud Squad	'Anybody Here Seen Kelly?'	12.08.69	ATV
Honey Lane	(Episode 2.06)	14.08.69 *	ATV
Honey Lane	(Episode 2.09)	04.09.69 *	ATV
Honey Lane	(Episode 2.12)	25.09.69 *	ATV
Happy Ever After	'The Prank'	16.12.69	ATV
Doctor Who	'Spearhead from Space' Episode One	03.01.70	BBC1
Doctor Who	'Spearhead from Space' Episode Two	10.01.70	BBC1
Doctor Who	'Spearhead from Space' Episode Three	17.01.70	BBC1
Doctor Who	'Spearhead from Space' Episode Four	24.01.70	BBC1
Fraud Squad	'The Price of a Copper'	12.12.70	ATV
Doctor Who	'Terror of the Autons' Episode One	02.01.71	BBC1
Doctor Who	'Terror of the Autons' Episode Two	09.01.71	BBC1
Doctor Who	'Terror of the Autons' Episode Three	16.01.71	BBC1
Doctor Who	'Terror of the Autons' Episode Four	23.01.71	BBC1
Doomwatch	'The Inquest'	01.03.71	BBC1
Trial	'Mister X'	28.10.71 *	BBC1

Spyder's Web	'Nobody's Strawberry Fool'	31.03.72	ATV
Dead of Night	'Return Flight'	12.11.72	BBC2
Doctor Who	'Carnival of Monsters' Episode One	27.01.73	BBC1
Doctor Who	'Carnival of Monsters' Episode Two	03.02.73	BBC1
Doctor Who	'Carnival of Monsters' Episode Three	10.02.73	BBC1
Doctor Who	'Carnival of Monsters' Episode Four	17.02.73	BBC1
The Regiment	'Depot'	02.03.73	BBC1
The Regiment	'North West Frontier'	04.05.73	BBC1
Warship	'The Drop'	05.07.73	BBC1
Spy Trap	'A Perfect Victim'	09.10.73 *	BBC1
Doctor Who	'The Time Warrior' Part One	15.12.73	BBC1
Doctor Who	'The Time Warrior' Part Two	22.12.73	BBC1
Doctor Who	'The Time Warrior' Part Three	29.12.73	BBC1
Doctor Who	'The Time Warrior' Part Four	05.01.74	BBC1
Dixon of Dock Green	'The Unwanted'	26.01.74 *	BBC1
General Hospital	(Episode 145)	07.03.74 *	ATV
General Hospital	(Episode 146)	08.03.74 *	ATV
Doctor Who	'The Ark In Space' Part One	25.01.75	BBC1
Doctor Who	'The Ark In Space' Part Two	01.02.75	BBC1
Doctor Who	'The Ark In Space' Part Three	08.02.75	BBC1
Doctor Who	'The Ark In Space' Part Four	15.02.75	BBC1
Doctor Who	'Pyramids of Mars' Part One (as 'Stephen Harris')	25.10.75	BBC1
Doctor Who	'Pyramids of Mars' Part Two (as 'Stephen Harris')	01.11.75	BBC1
Doctor Who	'Pyramids of Mars' Part Three (as 'Stephen Harris')	08.11.75	BBC1
Doctor Who	'Pyramids of Mars' Part Four (as 'Stephen Harris')	15.11.75	BBC1

Doctor Who	'The Brain of Morbius' Part One (as 'Robin Bland')	03.01.76	BBC1
Doctor Who	'The Brain of Morbius' Part Two (as 'Robin Bland')	10.01.76	BBC1
Doctor Who	'The Brain of Morbius' Part Three (as 'Robin Bland')	17.01.76	BBC1
Doctor Who	'The Brain of Morbius' Part Four (as 'Robin Bland')	24.01.76	BBC1
Doctor Who	'The Deadly Assassin' Part One	30.10.76	BBC1
Doctor Who	'The Deadly Assassin' Part Two	06.11.76	BBC1
Doctor Who	'The Deadly Assassin' Part Three	13.11.76	BBC1
Doctor Who	'The Deadly Assassin' Part Four	20.11.76	BBC1
Doctor Who	'The Talons of Weng Chiang' Part One	26.02.77	BBC1
Doctor Who	'The Talons of Weng Chiang' Part Two	05.03.77	BBC1
Doctor Who	'The Talons of Weng Chiang' Part Three	12.03.77	BBC1
Doctor Who	'The Talons of Weng Chiang' Part Four	19.03.77	BBC1
Doctor Who	'The Talons of Weng Chiang' Part Five	26.03.77	BBC1
Doctor Who	'The Talons of Weng Chiang' Part Six	02.04.77	BBC1
On the Run	(Untransmitted Pilot)	c1977 *	LWT
Doctor Who	'The Sun Makers' Part One	26.11.77	BBC1
Doctor Who	'The Sun Makers' Part Two	03.12.77	BBC1
Doctor Who	'The Sun Makers' Part Three	10.12.77	BBC1
Doctor Who	'The Sun Makers' Part Four	17.12.77	BBC1
Doctor Who	'The Ribos Operation' Part One	02.09.78	BBC1
Doctor Who	'The Ribos Operation' Part Two	09.09.78	BBC1
Doctor Who	'The Ribos Operation' Part Three	16.09.78	BBC1
Doctor Who	'The Ribos Operation' Part Four	23.09.78	BBC1
Scene	'The Future'	12.10.78	BBC1
Doctor Who	'The Power of Kroll' Part One	23.12.78	BBC1

Doctor Who	'The Power of Kroll' Part Two	30.12.78	BBC1
Doctor Who	'The Power of Kroll' Part Three	06.01.79	BBC1
Doctor Who	'The Power of Kroll' Part Four	13.01.79	BBC1
Blake's 7	'Killer'	20.02.79	BBC1
Blake's 7	'Gambit'	20.03.79	BBC1
Jukes of Piccadilly	'The Case of the Arabian Kidnap' Part One	25.02.80	Thames
Jukes of Piccadilly	'The Case of the Arabian Kidnap' Part Two	03.03.80	Thames
Jukes of Piccadilly	'Dulverton Green' Part One	10.03.80	Thames
Jukes of Piccadilly	'Dulverton Green' Part Two	17.03.80	Thames
Shoestring	'Mocking Bird' (as 'William Hood')	19.10.80	BBC1
Shoestring	'The Farmer Had a Wife' (as 'William Hood')	02.11.80	BBC1
The Nightmare Man	Episode One (from the novel by David Wiltshire)	01.05.81	BBC1
The Nightmare Man	Episode Two (from the novel by David Wiltshire)	08.05.81	BBC1
The Nightmare Man	Episode Three (from the novel by David Wiltshire)	15.05.81	BBC1
The Nightmare Man	Episode Four (from the novel by David Wiltshire)	22.05.81	BBC1
Into the Labyrinth	'Shadrach'	07.09.81	HTV
Blake's 7	'Traitor'	12.10.81	BBC1
Blake's 7	'Orbit'	07.12.81	BBC1
Into the Labyrinth	'Dr Jekyll and Mrs Hyde'	11.08.82	HTV
Juliet Bravo	'A Breach of the Peace'	02.10.82	BBC1
Bergerac	'Prime Target' (with Robert Banks Stewart)	30.01.83	BBC1
Bergerac	'A Cry in the Night'	14.01.84	BBC1
Miracles Take Longer	(Episode 13)	20.02.84	Thames
Miracles Take Longer	(Episode 14)	27.02.84	Thames
Miracles Take Longer	(Episode 15)	27.02.84	Thames

Miracles Take Longer	(Episode 16)	28.02.84	Thames
Miracles Take Longer	(Episode 18)	06.03.84	Thames
Doctor Who	'The Caves of Androzani' Part One	08.03.84	BBC1
Doctor Who	'The Caves of Androzani' Part Two	09.03.84	BBC1
Doctor Who	'The Caves of Androzani' Part Three	15.03.84	BBC1
Doctor Who	'The Caves of Androzani' Part Four	16.03.84	BBC1
Doctor Who	'The Two Doctors' Part One	16.02.85	BBC1
Doctor Who	'The Two Doctors' Part Two	23.02.85	BBC1
Doctor Who	'The Two Doctors' Part Three	02.03.85	BBC1
Timeslip	'The Block' (by Jim Hawkins, from a story by Robert Holmes)	28.12.85	Callendar Company for Yorkshire TV
Doctor Who	'The Trial of a Time Lord' Part One	06.09.86	BBC1
Doctor Who	'The Trial of a Time Lord' Part Two	13.09.86	BBC1
Doctor Who	'The Trial of a Time Lord' Part Three	20.09.86	BBC1
Doctor Who	'The Trial of a Time Lord' Part Four	27.09.86	BBC1
Doctor Who	'The Trial of a Time Lord' Part Thirteen	29.11.86	BBC1
Bergerac	'Winner Takes All'	10.01.87	BBC1

ABOUT THE AUTHOR

Richard Molesworth was born in 1968, and was hooked by *Doctor Who* when he first saw the Daleks menacing Jon Pertwee in 'Day of the Daleks' in 1972. He began writing for various *Doctor Who* fanzines in the mid 1980s, including *DWB*, where he first wrote articles about the BBC archive holdings. He has since contributed articles to publications such as *Doctor Who Magazine, Starburst* and *Sci-Fi Now*. In 1993, he acted as a researcher for *Thirty Years in the TARDIS*, the BBC documentary celebrating *Doctor Who*'s thirtieth anniversary, and became a member of the unofficial *Doctor Who* Restoration Team soon after. He worked with the team on various projects for BBC Worldwide/2|entertain in the following years, which included the first restoration of 'The War Machines' for its VHS release, and 'The Five Doctors: The Special Edition'. When *Doctor Who* started being released on DVD, he was responsible for a multitude of special features on many of the releases; producing audio commentaries with cast and crew, scripting on-screen production subtitles, and writing, directing and producing a number of documentary 'extra' features. He has also written *Wiped! Doctor Who's Missing Episodes* for Telos Publishing, and *Surf 'n' Turf: The Unofficial Skins Companion* for Miwk Books, and has occasionally written for the *Mail on Sunday*.

TALKBACK: THE UNOFFICIAL AND UNAUTHORISED DOCTOR WHO
INTERVIEW BOOK: VOLUME 1: THE SIXTIES edited by STEPHEN JAMES
WALKER
Interviews with cast and behind the scenes crew who worked on *Doctor Who* in the
sixties

TALKBACK: THE UNOFFICIAL AND UNAUTHORISED *DOCTOR WHO*
INTERVIEW BOOK: VOLUME 2: THE SEVENTIES edited by STEPHEN JAMES
WALKER
Interviews with cast and behind the scenes crew who worked on *Doctor Who* in the
seventies

TALKBACK: THE UNOFFICIAL AND UNAUTHORISED *DOCTOR WHO*
INTERVIEW BOOK: VOLUME 3: THE EIGHTIES edited by STEPHEN JAMES
WALKER
Interviews with cast and behind the scenes crew who worked on *Doctor Who* in the
eighties

HOWE'S TRANSCENDENTAL TOYBOX: SECOND EDITION by DAVID J
HOWE & ARNOLD T BLUMBERG
Complete guide to *Doctor Who* Merchandise 1963–2002.

HOWE'S TRANSCENDENTAL TOYBOX: UPDATE No 3: 2006-2009 by DAVID J
HOWE & ARNOLD T BLUMBERG
Complete guide to *Doctor Who* Merchandise released from 2006 to 2009. Now in full
colour.

WIPED! *DOCTOR WHO'*S MISSING EPISODES by RICHARD MOLESWORTH
The story behind the BBC's missing episodes of *Doctor Who*.

TIMELINK: THE UNOFFICIAL AND UNAUTHORISED GUIDE TO THE
CONTINUITY OF *DOCTOR WHO* VOLUME 1 by JON PREDDLE
Discussion and articles about the continuity of *Doctor Who*.

TIMELINK: THE UNOFFICIAL AND UNAUTHORISED GUIDE TO THE
CONTINUITY OF *DOCTOR WHO* VOLUME 2 by JON PREDDLE
Timeline of the continuity of *Doctor Who*.

WHOSTROLOGY: A TIME TRAVELLERS ALMANAC by MICHAEL M GILROY-
SINCLAIR. Illustrated by Deborah Taylor
Whostrology is a book of daily readings, zodiac signs and explanations, and other
Who-based astrological elements, designed to allow every *Who* fan to lead a life of
peace and ordered calm.

THE COMIC STRIP COMPANION: THE UNOFFICIAL AND UNAUTHORISED GUIDE TO *DOCTOR WHO* IN COMICS: 1964 — 1979 by PAUL SCOONES
Your comprehensive guide to *Doctor Who* in the comics.

THE TELEVISION COMPANION: THE UNOFFICIAL AND UNAUTHORISED GUIDE TO *DOCTOR WHO* 1963 — 1996 by DAVID J HOWE and STEPHEN JAMES WALKER
A two-volume guide to the classic series of *Doctor Who.*

TORCHWOOD

INSIDE THE HUB: THE UNOFFICIAL AND UNAUTHORISED GUIDE TO *TORCHWOOD* SERIES ONE by STEPHEN JAMES WALKER
Complete guide to the 2006 series of *Torchwood*, starring John Barrowman as Captain Jack Harkness.

SOMETHING IN THE DARKNESS: THE UNOFFICIAL AND UNAUTHORISED GUIDE TO *TORCHWOOD* SERIES TWO by STEPHEN JAMES WALKER
Complete guide to the 2008 series of *Torchwood*, starring John Barrowman as Captain Jack Harkness

24

A DAY IN THE LIFE: THE UNOFFICIAL AND UNAUTHORISED GUIDE TO *24* by KEITH TOPPING
Complete episode guide to the first season of the popular TV show.

TILL DEATH US DO PART

A FAMILY AT WAR: THE UNOFFICIAL AND UNAUTHORISED GUIDE TO *TILL DEATH US DO PART* by MARK WARD
Complete guide to the popular TV show.

SPACE: 1999

DESTINATION: MOONBASE ALPHA: THE UNOFFICIAL AND UNAUTHORISED GUIDE TO *SPACE: 1999* by ROBERT E WOOD
Complete guide to the popular TV show.

SAPPHIRE AND STEEL

ASSIGNED: THE UNOFFICIAL AND UNAUTHORISED GUIDE TO *SAPPHIRE AND STEEL* by RICHARD CALLAGHAN
Complete guide to the popular TV show.

THUNDERCATS

HEAR THE ROAR: THE UNOFFICIAL AND UNAUTHORISED GUIDE TO THE HIT 1980S SERIES *THUNDERCATS* by DAVID CRICHTON
Complete guide to the popular TV show.

SUPERNATURAL

HUNTED: THE UNOFFICIAL AND UNAUTHORISED GUIDE TO *SUPERNATURAL* SEASONS 1-3 by SAM FORD AND ANTONY FOGG
Complete guide to the popular TV show.

CHARMED

TRIQUETRA: THE UNOFFICIAL AND UNAUTHORISED GUIDE TO *CHARMED* SEASONS 1-7 by KEITH TOPPING
Complete guide to the popular TV show.

THE PRISONER

FALL OUT: THE UNOFFICIAL AND UNAUTHORISED GUIDE TO *THE PRISONER* by ALAN STEVENS and FIONA MOORE
Complete guide to the popular TV show.

BLAKE'S 7

LIBERATION: THE UNOFFICIAL AND UNAUTHORISED GUIDE TO *BLAKE'S 7* by ALAN STEVENS and FIONA MOORE
Complete guide to the popular TV show.

BATTLESTAR GALACTICA

BY YOUR COMMAND: THE UNOFFICIAL AND UNAUTHORISED GUIDE TO *BATTLESTAR GALACTICA* by ALAN STEVENS and FIONA MOORE
A two volume guide to the popular TV show.

A SONG FOR EUROPE

SONGS FOR EUROPE: THE UNITED KINGDOM AT THE EUROVISION SONG CONTEST by GORDON ROXBURGH
A five volume guide to the popular singing contest.

FILMS

BEAUTIFUL MONSTERS: THE UNOFFICIAL AND UNAUTHORISED GUIDE TO
THE *ALIEN* AND *PREDATOR* FILMS by DAVID McINTEE
A guide to the *Alien* and *Predator* Films.

ZOMBIEMANIA: 80 MOVIES TO DIE FOR by DR ARNOLD T BLUMBERG &
ANDREW HERSHBERGER
A guide to 80 classic zombie films, along with an extensive filmography of over 500
additional titles

SILVER SCREAM: VOLUME 1: 40 CLASSIC HORROR MOVIES by STEVEN
WARREN HILL
A guide to 40 classic horror films from 1920 to 1941.

SILVER SCREAM: VOLUME 2: 40 CLASSIC HORROR MOVIES by STEVEN
WARREN HILL
A guide to 40 classic horror films from 1941 to 1951.

TABOO BREAKERS: 18 INDEPENDENT FILMS THAT COURTED
CONTROVERSY AND CREATED A LEGEND by CALUM WADDELL
A guide to 18 films which pushed boundaries and broke taboos.

IT LIVES AGAIN! HORROR MOVIES IN THE NEW MILLENNIUM by AXELLE
CAROLYN
A guide to modern horror films. Large format, full colour throughout.

TELOS MOVIE CLASSICS: *HULK* by TONY LEE
A critique and analysis of Ang Lee's 2003 film *Hulk*.

APE-MAN: THE UNOFFICIAL AND UNAUTHORISED GUIDE TO 100 YEARS OF
TARZAN by SEAN EGAN
Guide to *Tarzan* in all the media.

STILL THE BEAST IS FEEDING: FORTY YEARS OF *ROCKY HORROR* by ROB
BAGNALL and PHIL BARDEN
History and appreciation of Richard O'Brien's *Rocky Horror Show*.

TELOS PUBLISHING
Email: orders@telos.co.uk
Web: www.telos.co.uk

To order copies of any Telos books, please visit our website where there are full details
of all titles and facilities for worldwide credit card online ordering, as well as occasional
special offers.